The Janaki Mangala of Goswami Tulsidas (Deluxe Edition)

Krishna's Mercy

Copyright © 2015 Krishna's Mercy

www.krishnasmercy.org

facebook.com/krishnasmercy

DEDICATION

To my beloved mother, who by helping to translate this work accomplished something like that of giving eyes to the blind.

INTRODUCTION

For my own pleasure meant,
Time with beloved Tulsidas spent.

Of Hindi very little I know,
Others thus helping immensely so.

Like unlocking secret with a key,
For Sita and Rama's marriage to see.

For mistakes and errors please forgive,
Through words that joyous occasion relive.

AUSPICIOUS INVOCATION
VERSE 1

गुरु गनपति गिरिजापति गौरि गिरापति।
सारद सेष सुकबि श्रुति संत सरल मति।।१।।

guru ganapati girijāpati gauri girāpati |
sārada seṣa sukabi śruti santa sarala mati ||1||

"[obeisance to]Guru, Ganesha, Shiva, Parvati, Brihaspati, Sarasvati, Shesha, Shukadeva, Vedas, and the sincere and intelligent saints." (1)

Essay - Auspicious Invocation

Goswami Tulsidas herein begins his wonderful short work called the Janaki Mangala, a poem which describes the marriage ceremony of Sita and Rama and also provides background information relating to the event. The poem goes back in time and gives accounts of what actually occurred on that wonderful day many thousands of years ago. Sita is the goddess of fortune herself, and Shri Rama is her husband, the Supreme Lord for all of mankind. The story of their marriage is so heartwarming that it is celebrated annually in pilgrimage sites such as Janakpur, where the wedding is reenacted and others attend the ceremony as if they were there on the original day. As the poet enters into the proper frame of mind, conditioning himself to describe with succinct poetry what happened during that time, he makes sure to first invoke the names of those who can help make his efforts fruitful, personalities who have helped him already in the past and who are the well-wishers of the Vaishnavas, or devotees of Vishnu.

Lord Vishnu is the same Rama but in a different form. He is the origin of creation and the maintainer as well. There are many specific Vishnu forms and they all have four arms and are opulently dressed. Vishnu is also known as Narayana, or the source of men. There are many celestial figures in the tradition known as Hinduism, but they all worship Vishnu as their chief. Of this there is no doubt, as even the highest authority figures in the spiritual sky can speak about vishnu-bhakti, or devotion to the Supreme Lord, very well. Some of the leaders like Lord Brahma, Lord Shiva and Lakshmiji are themselves founders of Vaishnava sampradayas, or disciplic successions that preach about vishnu-bhakti to those who are interested in tasting the fruit of their existence.

Lord Vishnu is taken to be the Supreme Lord and personalities like Rama and Krishna His incarnations. In the Gaudiya tradition Krishna is taken as the original and Vishnu as an expansion, but in either case there is no difference. It is not that any Vaishnava tradition ignores Vishnu or His place as the Supreme Lord. Vishnu worship is completely different from any other type of spiritual discipline, as the rewards granted by the object of service are not guaranteed, nor are they always what the worshiper wants.

What kind of worship is this if you don't even get what you're asking for? Isn't that the entire point to approaching a superior person? We approach our bosses to get paid for our work, the government to protect us, the store owner to provide goods and services that we need, and so on. The behavior of Vishnu can be likened to that of a parent. A child may ask for this thing or that, but they are not always guaranteed to get what they want. The parent will use discrimination, judging whether or not the child is worthy of the benediction and whether or not the desired object will be beneficial to them. In this sense the requests denied by the parents can turn out to be as influential and important as those granted.

Vishnu operates in the same way; hence worship of Him is not as prominent in the Vedic tradition. The demigods, those in charge of the material creation, which consists of elements of nature that are not related to the essence of individuality, the spirit soul, must grant their worshipers whatever they want. This ability is checked to the point that the presiding deities can only offer what they are capable of giving. For instance, in the past a few nefarious characters have asked Lord Brahma, the first created living entity who then populated the world with so many creatures, for immortality. The spirit soul is immortal, but its temporary residences are not. Therefore the request for immortality relates to remaining within the same form forever. This request is a little silly considering that our body already changes from infancy to youth and then to adulthood. Why not ask to get something back that we already lost instead of for remaining in the present form of body?

Lord Brahma himself doesn't eternally reside in his own form, though he stays in it for billions of years. Since he is not immortal in this sense, he cannot grant immortality to anyone else. Despite this limitation, those who propitiate the demigods are granted whatever else they can ask for. Vishnu does not follow suit, however. He is the original soul, the person who expands as the Supersoul and resides within our heart, just waiting for us to turn to Him and look for guidance in our pursuit for happiness. Vishnu has nothing to do with the material energy, though He generates it to please the desire of those who wish for separation from Him in the spiritual sky.

Once the living entities find themselves in the material realm, however, there is really no such thing as good or bad, beneficial or harmful. One living being may eat stool and roll around in dirt, while another eats filet mignon and sleeps on a mattress that has an electronically set firmness level, but in the end they are both operating under the conception that they are their body, that the body's enjoyment is what matters most. Vishnu makes no judgments in these areas; therefore He is not approached for benedictions relating to these things. Even if He is, He does not pay the requests any attention, for those who connect with Him can gain a higher taste, one that transcends the bonds of karma and reincarnation.

As bhakti is that discipline that connects with Vishnu, the writing of the Janaki Mangala was a total act of devotion, one meant to keep the mind immersed in vishnu-bhakti. Rama is the same Vishnu, so those who think of Him, look for benedictions in the form of His association, and regularly recite His names are on a path towards liberation. Such humble souls are already liberated in the sense that they are not after creature comforts or temporary happiness. Bhakti continues uninterrupted and unmotivated, so it cannot be checked. Not even death can stop the spirit soul from being devoted to Vishnu.

Tulsidas is so humble, kind, sweet and respectful that even though he is immersed in bhakti and thus not in need of any benediction from anyone besides Vishnu, he still starts off his poem by invoking the names of several exalted personalities. Instead of viewing the demigods as separate entities assigned to please those not interested in bhakti, Tulsidas takes full advantage of their position by asking them to help him in pleasing Rama. This same tact was previously followed by Shri Hanuman, who invoked the names of similar personalities just prior to entering the Ashoka grove where Sita was being held captive in Lanka. The life story of Sita and Rama is found in the Ramayana, an ancient poem written by Maharishi Valmiki, whom Tulsidas is considered an incarnation of. The marriage of Sita and Rama came first, which was then followed by Sita's rescue from the clutches of a Rakshasa king named Ravana.

Sita also used to pray to heavenly figures to ensure that her husband was always safe. Thus the tradition of proper demigod worship was passed down to Tulsidas and he understood its place. In the above invocation, he first offers obeisance to his guru, or spiritual master. We can only get so far with mental speculation. Even in material education, unless we are instructed by someone else, what can we really learn? Knowledge is acquired much more quickly by just accepting the information passed on to us from authority figures.

In the realm of spirituality, finding a bona fide spiritual master and submissively hearing from him are the only ways to find enlightenment, to learn about bhakti and its superiority over every other kind of religiosity. No matter how great a devotee becomes, how prolific their writing turns out, and how many fruits their devotion yields, the results are still due to the grace of the spiritual master. He is the person who plants the seed of bhakti in the devotee's heart, and then teaches them how to regularly water it with practices like chanting the holy names of the Lord, "Hare

Krishna Hare Krishna, Krishna Krishna, Hare Hare, Hare Rama Hare Rama, Rama Rama, Hare Hare".

"In the course of traversing the universal creation of Brahma, some fortunate soul may receive the seed of bhakti-lata, the creeper of devotional service. This is all by the grace of guru and Krishna." (Chaitanya Charitamrita, Madhya 19.151)

The debt to the guru can never properly be repaid, for how can we return the favor of finding a discipline that provides unending happiness to someone who already practices the same discipline? The guru can only be pleased by continued dedication in service, to devoting one's life to glorifying Vishnu. The guru is himself a benediction from the Supreme Lord. Those who are sincerely interested in connecting with the personal form of God are aided in their endeavor by the Supreme Lord. He is the one who sends the guru to those who are deserving of him.

Next, Tulsidas invokes the name of Lord Ganesha. In every important Vedic ritual, Ganesha is honored first. He was bestowed this benediction because of his wonderful standing borne of his pious nature, unmatched character, and devotion to his parents, Lord Shiva and Mother Parvati. Ganesha removes the obstacles from his devotees, regardless of who they are. The removal of obstacles in the path of a person with motives that are not directed in the proper area will not be so beneficial. On the other hand, when the obstacles are removed from the path of those practicing bhakti in sincerity, Ganesha's benedictions really stand out. Tulsidas never wanted anything for his own benefit from any spiritual personality; he always prayed to be able to continue his devotion to Sita and Rama. In some of his other poems Tulsidas starts by offering obeisance to Lord Ganesha and asking him to remove the obstacles from his path so that Sita and Rama can forever stay in his heart.

Next, Tulsidas offers obeisance to Lord Shiva and Mother Parvati. Followers of the Vedic tradition sometimes break out into factions, with some worshiping Vishnu and others worshiping Lord Shiva. The elevated Vaishnavas, however, though considered devotees of Vishnu, are all-inclusive. Just because Vishnu is the prime target of attention doesn't mean that others are ignored. Rather, the Vaishnava loves Lord Shiva and Mother Parvati for who they are and their devotion to Vishnu. Tulsidas is the emblem of devotion to Sita and Rama, but we see that he still has so much love for Lord Shiva and Goddess Durga, the husband and wife pair that takes tremendous delight from hearing about Lord Rama's activities. Lord Shiva and Mother Parvati help those who are materially motivated, so why wouldn't they help someone who was going to write a poem that was going to give even them tremendous delight?

Tulsidas next references Brihaspati, the lord of speech, and Sarasvati, the goddess of learning. The human brain may have so many wonderful ideas and sentiments, but when the person wants to express those thoughts something might get lost in the transmission; the communication may fail to accurately represent the true sentiments of the individual. Poetry is especially difficult to compose because it needs to be short, to the point, and yet completely inclusive of the sentiment being released. In this sense we are powerless, as the higher authorities can either make or break our communication efforts. As Tulsidas so nicely notes in the beginning of his Ramacharitamanasa poem, Mother Sarasvati rushes to where any poet is about to start writing, wanting to help them. But when she sees that their writing is not related to devotion, she gets very disappointed, as her benedictions then get wasted on mundane literature. Tulsidas knew that Sarasvati and Brihaspati would automatically help him in glorifying Sita and Rama, but out of kind respect he called out to them anyway.

Tulsidas then references Lord Shesha, Shukadeva Goswami, the Vedas, and the saints of sincerity and good intelligence. What all of these people have in common is that they are tireless glorifiers of the Supreme Lord Vishnu and devotion to Him. Ananta Shesha Naga is the celestial serpent with unlimited hoods. He serves as the resting bed for Lord Vishnu in the spiritual sky. He is the servitor God, the head glorifier. He uses his many hoods to continuously offer praise to his beloved Vishnu. In Rama-lila, Shesha comes to earth as Lakshmana and serves as Rama's number one protector. How then could he not help Tulsidas write a poem glorifying the beloved couple?

Shukadeva Goswami is Vyasadeva's son. Vyasa is the compiler of the majority of Vedic literature, which is known as the shrutis, or "that which is heard". There are the original shrutis and then the people who pass them on, discussing them in public. Shukadeva is best known for his discussion on bhakti and the position of the Supreme Lord that is found in the Bhagavata Purana, or Shrimad Bhagavatam. This work is considered the crown jewel of Vedic literature, for it is not tainted with any materialism whatsoever. The entire work is bhakti, and is thus non-different from Vishnu himself.

The saints who have a good mind and are sincere in their efforts are referenced because they live bhakti. By their very example they teach others what it means to follow the highest form of spirituality there is. Tulsidas hopes that they are pleased with him, for he has learned so much from them. The saints are the ocean of mercy, so if their compassion extends into the devotee's writing efforts, there is no chance of failure. For the Janaki Mangala, the subject matter itself would prove to be too strong a force for any possible defects to creep in. Aided by the personalities given to Vishnu worship, Tulsidas' finished product pleases the minds of countless generations of sincere followers looking to delight in the pastimes of Sita and Rama, and especially in their marriage ceremony that took place in Janaka's kingdom many thousands of years ago.

VERSE 2

हाथ जोरि करि बिनय सबहि सिर नावौं।
सिय रघुबीर बिबाहु जथामति गावौं।।2।।

hātha jori kari binaya sabahi sira nāvauṁ |
siya raghubīra bibāhu jathāmati gāvauṁ ||2||

"With my hands folded, bowing my head I pray to them as I sing about the marriage of Sita and Rama as I understand it." (2)

Essay - As I Understand It

The oldest scriptures in the world are known as the shrutis because they were originally passed down through a tradition of oral reception. Since these scriptures are replete with knowledge necessary for attaining life's goals, they are known as the Vedas. As the attainment of the ultimate aim in life represents the pinnacle of achievement, other aims are satisfied through these scriptures as well. Therefore the knowledge system that is the Vedas is not limited in scope, not narrow in its objectives or influence. Whoever partakes of the ripened fruit of transcendental wisdom, hearing it submissively, absorbing the information into their consciousness and then acting upon what they have learned, finds the happiness that every living entity is so desperately searching after. The resulting ecstasy creates an invigorated life, where the same information that was heard then gets repeated, but not necessarily verbatim. The devoted soul repeats what they have heard in their own way, how they have understood the concepts. This is done to please both the instructor, the originator of the knowledge, and the person doing the explaining.

Is there anything wrong with just repeating the information that we've heard? For instance, if in mathematics we learn that one plus one equals two, shouldn't we repeat that same formula to those we teach? What need is there to present the information in our own way? With perfect information, simple repetition of the principles is sufficient for passing on the necessary knowledge. Devotion to God, however, is a dynamic activity. The static laws of math and the simple, cutting postulates of philosophy and logic are binding to a spirit soul that is looking for real freedom, one not bound by the inhibiting forces of material nature, which work at every second to check whatever happiness we find.

How does this work exactly? Say that we're playing sports for a team that just made it to the playoff round. Previously, this team looked like they had no chance of victory, and yet somehow, in the most dramatic fashion, they achieved their stated objective. The elation is checked, however, by the fact that another series of games needs to be played afterwards. Even if the season is over and the championship won, there is still next year, a repeat of the cycle of hope, work, and the potential for bereavement coming from loss.

The same pattern applies to every single fruitive venture. The most blissful elation resulting from the birth of a child is matched by the tremendous sadness that occurs with death. In between there are the many ups and downs, such as the happiness over meeting with friends and family and the sadness over arguments resulting from impious behavior directed our way.

The spirit soul is immune to these changes. The soul is eternally blissful and knowledgeable. These properties are the cause of the very vitality of the living being, his repeated venturing into new areas of happiness. Simple renunciation from material endeavors thus cannot be the true definition of liberation, and neither can the strict adherence to religious principles. In whichever direction we fly, whether it's the denial of pleasure, the indulgence of sense pleasures, or the adherence to the strictest rules of spiritual life aimed at promising a better end in the afterlife, the soul retains its penchant to act on its desire for unfettered freedom.

The spiritualist accepting the shrutis from a self-realized person, one who previously learned the ancient art of divine love, or bhakti-yoga, safely kept with the Vedas, does not just absorb the information and then sit on it. With theoretical knowledge, or jnana, comes the practical application, or vijnana. The practical application is more important, for in many cases someone who is an expert in the field might not even be able to explain why they are so skilled. A person may possess the knowledge that goes into performing surgical operations, but the person who actually carries out the surgery properly plays a more important role, for he puts the principles into practical use.

The predominant message of the Vedas is that the spirit soul is inherently meant to be tied to the Supreme Soul, who is so respected, glorious and opulent that one name cannot suffice for Him. The term "God" just scratches the surface at addressing Him properly, for it says that He is a Supreme Being. To describe what "supreme" actually means is the business of the Vedas and their authors.

How can the Vedas have authors when the information is purported to have come from the Supreme Being Himself? This is the hidden secret known to those who assimilate the knowledge gathered into their own lives. The Vedas were originally just one Veda, which was implanted into the heart of the first created living entity, Lord Brahma. He then subsequently passed it down to his descendants, of which there are too many to count. The Veda passes on supreme wisdom through hymns and prayers addressing God. The way to glorify someone is to speak about their attributes, using comparisons to known objects to show how the glorified person is superior to them. To follow glorification in this way, the Vedas also document the Personality of Godhead's features and activities. It is through discussion and meditation on these areas that the living beings derive the most pleasure.

With attention focused on God's charita, or deeds, one assigns the Lord so many names. The activities of His personality of Lord Rama, an avatara appearing on earth during the Treta Yuga, are likely talked about the most, as they are documented in many Vedic texts, including the Ramayana and Puranas. Vedic literature includes the original Veda and any work expanding on the same truths. Since the Veda is about God, anyone who writes literature describing God and His glories, reaching the same ultimate conclusion of devotion to the Lord being the topmost engagement for man, adds to the massive collection of Vedic literature.

Lord Rama's activities were first described in the Ramayana, which was composed by Maharishi Valmiki, a contemporary of Rama's. Just hearing the Ramayana makes one familiar with Rama and His divine qualities, which include His kindness, His mastery over archery, His promise to protect those who humbly approach Him in earnest, His dedication to piety and virtue, His beautiful smile, His love for His closest associates like Sita, Lakshmana and Hanuman, and a host of other features. Indeed, God's good qualities are ananta, or unlimited. We could glorify God from the time we are born through the time we quit our body and we still wouldn't come close to sufficiently describing Him.

If we take up an endeavor that we can't finish, why even start it? Ah, this defect is actually known to be a precious gem by those who incorporate the shrutis into their every activity. Goswami Tulsidas, a celebrated Vaishnava poet, is one such knower. He originally heard the story of Rama's life from his guru, or spiritual master. At the time he was a young child, so he couldn't make much of it, but the seed of bhakti was implanted in him nonetheless. When he matured later on in life and became adept at writing poetry, he used his skill to glorify Rama, to describe the Lord's life and activities in a language suitable to the time, words that would make understanding God easier for the people of his community.

There are many accounts of Rama's life, with Valmiki's Ramayana being the most complete one. In addition, Rama appears on earth during each creation, which means that He has appeared many times in the past and will come again many times in the future. The Vedic seers of the past who were so attached to Rama have thus described His life and activities in their own unique ways. Tulsidas chose the version of Rama's story told by Lord Shiva to his wife Parvati as the foundation for his wonderful Hindi poem titled the Ramacharitamanasa, which means concentrating the mind on the activities of Rama. The Lord's acts are compared to a holy lake which the mind can swim in and feel the topmost bliss and comfort.

In the Janaki Mangala, Tulsidas sings about the marriage of Sita and Rama, which again is described very nicely in the original Ramayana. Rather than present the same information verbatim, with a word-for-word translation, Tulsidas decides to sing about it as he understands it. This is revealed in the above referenced prayer, which forms the opening invocation of his wonderful, short work. In the verse preceding this one, the poet references the famous personalities responsible for his knowledge. They include his guru, Lord Ganesha and his parents Lord Shiva and Mother Parvati, Shukadeva Goswami, the Vedas, and the gentle saints who have made understanding the highest truths of spirituality easy for the poet.

In this prayer, Tulsidas folds his hands and bows his head at these great personalities, for he is about to embark on the journey of singing about the marriage of Sita and Rama, an event which is indescribable. He is going to sing about the events as he understands them because this will bring great pleasure to both him and the people who will hear his song. This style of information transfer is preferable because it reveals and gives meaning to the dynamic nature of bhakti, how it is not a dry system of spirituality aimed at only providing benefits in the future. If we purchase a savings bond, we don't gain any benefit until the date of maturity. Religion is typically viewed in a similar way, for the impetus for the initial plunge may have even been a desire to avoid a hellish condition in the afterlife.

Following bhakti-yoga does indeed provide a glorious end, an afterlife full of delights, but since bhakti directly corresponds to the constitutional position of the living entity, its benefits are available immediately. The human being, during any stage of life, enjoys glorifying others. If this weren't the case, newspapers and internet news sites would be empty every single day. Bhakti allows glorification to be directed at the person most worthy of it. The same material nature that was previously the cause of pain and bondage becomes an inexhaustible source of tools with which to practice divine glorification. The words used in communication become purified when directed at the lotus feet of Sita and Rama. The pages used to print books, poems and songs become valuable when they contain the glories of Sita and Rama. The humble sage, who patiently absorbed the highest truths of life passed down to him by the spiritual master, becomes the ocean of mercy, the friend of the distressed, the savior for those disgusted with the material existence and its perpetually swinging pendulum of acceptance and rejection, when he dedicates his life to describing the glories of Sita and Rama in his own way.

The question may be raised as to whether or not describing the marriage of Sita and Rama in your own way can be harmful. If the information heard was not properly understood, then certainly there is the danger of contaminating others with faulty interpretations. But when there is pure love for God, no attempt made at glorifying the Lord and His associates can ever prove to be detrimental. Through His deputies, Rama controls speech and knowledge, so we are actually helpless in writing anyway. Shri Rama is the protector of the surrendered souls, including those who humbly accept the challenge of writing songs and poetry to describe Him. Though Tulsidas made sure to offer his obeisances to Brihaspati and Mother Sarasvati, the divine figures in charge of speech and learning respectively, the success of his work would come from Rama's influence, which is profusely distributed through many different channels.

The guru is himself a representative of the Lord, so if he is genuine in his devotion, his understanding will be perfect, and therefore whoever hears from him submissively will receive perfect knowledge as well. The disciple, wanting to keep the flame of bhakti well lit, becomes overwhelmed with the desire to continue to glorify God, to not let a moment go by without concentrating the mind on His lotus feet. By hearing of the wonderful marriage of Sita and Rama, the mind stays connected with God and His glorious devotees like Tulsidas who were kind enough to give us such wonderful Vedic literature, fresh and new and yet true to the ageless tradition that is bhakti.

Essay - Then Show Me

For those following Vedic teachings, the importance of the spiritual master cannot be overemphasized. There is no over-glorification of the guru, who gives us the key to the mint that is the endless delight of bhakti-yoga, or devotional service. The importance of the spiritual master is stressed repeatedly to break the living being's tendency towards searching after the Absolute Truth through their own effort, for no human being is capable of experiencing everything or even knowing how to fully process the information that they do accumulate. For the spiritualist who learns how to describe the glories of the Supreme Lord, telling the stories of God's pastimes and activities in their own way actually enhances the glory of their guru even further. Showing that what his guru had taught him was worthwhile and put to good use, Goswami Tulsidas embarked on singing of the marriage of Sita and Rama.

It should be noted that the story of the marriage of the beloved couple had already been told, several times in fact. First, there was the initial incident itself, which took place in the kingdom of Janakpur many thousands of years ago. We refer to this incident as being in the past, for that is how it is positioned with respect to the timeline of our current birth and the creation of the earth. However, just as the cycle of birth and death continues for the spirit soul, who travels from one body type to another, the creation itself goes through cycles of manifestation and annihilation. Not only this creation, but countless other universes follow the same pattern, which is instigated by the exhaling and inhaling of Maha-Vishnu, the Supreme Lord managing the creation. That same Vishnu ensures that the marriage of Sita and Rama takes place many times in many different creations. The marriage can be referred to as a future event as well, and also one which follows slightly different scripts. Moreover, sometimes the onlookers have their own incidents they remember, certain features they see and choose to focus on.

In this creation, the first accounts of the glorious marriage are given in the Ramayana, which was composed by Maharishi Valmiki in the Treta Yuga, the second time period of creation. In addition to touching on the event when telling the story of Rama's life chronologically, there is another incident, after the fact, in the Ramayana where Sita Devi, Rama's wife, describes how the marriage took place. During a fourteen year stint in the forest, Sita and Rama visited many hermitages, where great sages had taken up refuge to perform their austerities and live the simple life devoted to God. They wouldn't have to wait until the afterlife to see God, though. Their penances weren't just for some future benefit that was unknown. Rather, they would get the fruit of their existence by having God Himself in the form of a warrior prince visit them.

Bringing His wife and younger brother with Him, Rama once came upon the hermitage of Atri Rishi and his wife Anasuya. Even during that time, Sita and Rama's marriage was quite famous, especially since many suitors had wanted to have Janaka's daughter's hand in marriage. Wanting to hear the story from the coveted princess in question, Anasuya asked Sita to explain the events of that day. In this way Sita herself became a kind of spiritual master, one who described the glories of Lord Rama and His closest associates. She was at the wedding, so she could give firsthand accounts.

"I have heard, O Sita, that your hand in marriage was won by the renowned Raghava on the occasion of the self-choice ceremony [svayamvara]. O Maithili, I wish to hear that story in detail. Therefore please narrate to me the entire sequence of events as you experienced them." (Anasuya speaking to Sita, Valmiki Ramayana, Ayodhya Kand, 118.24-25)

The spiritual masters of the Vedic tradition describe the same events and the qualities of the participants in their own way, though they initially received the knowledgebase through a chain of disciplic succession. It is not that the genuine keepers of the faith make up any details or put things into their stories that aren't true. Rather, they highlight what is important to them, incorporating different aspects of their own experiences to properly describe the glory and beauty of the Supreme Lord and His lila.

When Goswami Tulsidas embarked on writing his short song called the Janaki Mangala, there were many sources of information he could have used as reference tools. Many Puranas describe Rama's life in varying levels of detail, and there are also the two major Ramayana compositions as well, the original by Valmiki and the version by Vyasadeva called the Adhyatma Ramayana. The latter was the one Tulsidas heard from his guru during his youth, so he was especially fond of it. In this version, Lord Shiva is the narrator, for he got to watch Rama's activities from above in the heavenly realm. Lord Shiva is a worshipable figure himself, but he takes the most pleasure from chanting the name of Rama and describing His activities to others, including his beloved wife Mother Parvati.

Not surprisingly, when it came time to write the auspicious invocation to his song, Tulsidas referenced both Lord Shiva and Mother Parvati, and also the other worshipable personalities who keep the faith of bhakti alive and help those who are sincere in their attempt to glorify God. The first obeisance went to the guru, who planted the seed of bhakti in the young poet. When Tulsidas first heard the story of Rama from his guru, he was still too young to really understand its import or take lessons from it that would change his behavior. Nevertheless, if that hearing had not taken place, there would have been no impetus to continue ahead in learning about divine love, the topmost engagement for the spirit soul. Without first planting the seed, we cannot get the wonderful tree that produces bountiful fruits. It's easy to get caught up in the gloriousness of the finished product and thereby forget who planted the initial seed that secured the maturation needed for the final outcome.

The saints never forget, for they are eternally indebted to their spiritual master and the devotees who helped them along the way. Since there were so many reference tools available to him, Tulsidas could have easily just done a "copy and paste" from several different scriptures and converted the words into the colloquial language he used for his songs. Following this tact would not have been harmful at all, for if the source information is perfect, then in whatever medium it is passed on through, the value of the original information will remain intact.

In the end of the invocation, which is referenced above, we see that Tulsidas bows down to his guru and the revered personalities of the Vedic tradition, praying that they are pleased with him, as he begins to sing about the marriage of Sita and Rama as he has understood it. This option is more preferable because when the disciple tells a story in his own words, in the way that he has heard the information and processed it, the output can be considered an extension of the original guru's work. As an example, if I have a company that does building construction and I build many houses and office spaces, I get credit for the work I performed during my time on earth. Once I pass on, however, my work stops. Yet, if I can teach others the art of building and how to go about successfully constructing many such edifices during their lifetimes, whatever they build after my departure from this earth goes to my credit as well. The disciples in this case are essentially extensions of the original teacher.

In bhakti, the influence of the teacher is further expanded when the disciple produces many works. If the work comes out successful, the disciple proves that what his teacher taught him wasn't just dry words that were meant to be memorized. Bhakti is divine love, which can be outputted in many different ways.

There is no one way to love God, though the seed of devotion is first planted through the hearing process and then best cultivated through the chanting of the holy names, such as those found in the maha-mantra, "Hare Krishna Hare Krishna, Krishna Krishna, Hare Hare, Hare Rama Hare Rama, Rama Rama, Hare Hare". Hearing and chanting are the beginning, as through steady connection in consciousness with God, the individual becomes enveloped in transcendental ecstasy which then guides their behavior. Loving God can then flow through different outlets, such as writing, singing, viewing pictures, talking with others, travelling to distant places of spiritual relevance, and instructing others on the baseline principles of a life devoted to transcendentalism following divine love.

By singing about the glories of Sita and Rama, Tulsidas showed that his mind was immersed in bhakti, that he was looking for more ways to glorify the person he learned about from his guru. Information of the divine passed on to the sincere student is meant to affect behavior. If the guru passed on knowledge that was only absorbed and then not acted upon, what would their efforts really do for anyone? I could just sit and listen to any subject matter then and not gain any benefit. I could even sit there and not pay attention at all, and the effect would be the same. The guru is supremely pleased by seeing that the information he has taught has really sunk in to his students, that they have found happiness through directing their behavior towards the divine path instead of the repetitive and miserable material path. If the student wasn't looking for a change in behavior, he never would have given aural reception to the guru's teachings. Therefore the change in behavior is almost compulsory, as it indicates that the bhakti spirit has taken over a person residing in a realm where the materialistic spirit is predominant. The guru proves to be an ocean of mercy that constantly replenishes the soul thirsty for the transcendental nectar that is God's association.

Religion in the vernacular sense can be taken to be a matter of faith, a rubberstamp system where you go through a few perfunctory rituals and regulations to remain in good standing with the powers that be. In more recent times, just inheriting your faith from your parents is good enough. The regulations are taken as secondary in importance, especially since material amenities are procured through personal effort rather than prayer. If I can get comfortably situated without ever attending church or praying to God, what need do I have for religion?

By writing about the subject matter as they have understood it, the bhaktas reveal the dynamic nature of real religion, which is known as sanatana-dharma in the Vedic tradition. These two terms are not sectarian, as they can be scientifically explained. Something based on science is much easier to accept than matters of faith. Sanatana means that which has no beginning and no end. Dharma means an essential characteristic, which can then be awakened and maintained through a specific set of actions. The real meaning of religion is to maintain the soul's essential characteristic of being a lover of God. Since this feature is awakened and maintained through specific activities, dharma becomes the set of guiding principles aimed at keeping one connected with God; hence the correlation between dharma and religion. As both the soul and its primary characteristic, or dharma, are eternal, real religion continues forever [sanatana].

Sanatana-dharma is nice in theory, but the behavior of the bhaktas who have sincerely heard from their spiritual master and fully absorbed the information lends credence to the concept. Describing God as you have understood Him allows for countless opportunities for the practice of dharma to continue. As love is more than just a profession of faith or allegiance, devotional practices maintain the characteristic of lover of God within the individual. The beautiful song composed by Tulsidas showed that the teaching efforts of his guru were fruitful, and that the divine personalities beseeched were benevolent to the poet. The saints operate to please the Supreme Lord after all, and if God sees that someone is desirous of describing His glories simply based on the motive of remaining connected with Him, how can that person ever fail? Mistakes are only made by those who are conditioned, looking for perfection over the forces of matter. As Shri Rama is above both the material and spiritual energies, He can ensure that His devotees never fail in their devotional efforts. The prolific writing of the praiseworthy saints is but just one example of this truth.

VERSE 3 - PREPARING FOR THE SVAYAMVARA

सुभ दिन रच्यौ स्वयंबर मंगलदायक।
सुनत श्रवन हिय बसहिं सीयरघुनायक॥3॥

subha dina racyau svayambara maṅgaladāyaka |
sunata śravana hiya basahiṁ sīyaraghunāyaka ||3||

"It is the good day of the svayamvara, which gives auspiciousness. By hearing of this Sita and Rama stay in the heart." (3)

Essay - Good Day To Be Alive

Goswami Tulsidas herein creates the setting for his poem called the Janaki Mangala, or the auspiciousness relating to Janaki, the daughter of King Janaka. She is also known as Sita Devi, for the good king found her one day while ploughing a field. She came out of the ground and then became his adopted daughter. The day of the svayamvara, or self-choice ceremony, was when Janaka would give her away to a suitable husband. Little did he know that the match would be Shri Hari Himself, the Supreme Lord roaming the earth in the guise of a warrior prince named Rama. From the opening stanza, Tulsidas also reveals the purpose for his composition.

Does there need to be a reason? Does the poet need to provide an excuse before writing? If we abstract every activity to the highest level, we'll see that the desire for pleasure is what motivates each and every one of us. Even doing something as painful as dieting or intense physical exercise is meant to provide a pleasurable benefit at some point in the future. With this particular poem, the story it was meant to describe was already well known at the time of composition. Sita and Rama are worshipable figures of the Vedic tradition, taken to be God's energy coupled with God. Depending on the exact tradition followed, Sita and Rama are the original set of God and His eternal consort or they are incarnations of the same, which means they are just as good as the original.

Because of their extraordinarily brilliant qualities, Sita and Rama's wedding story was well known in the land that Tulsidas lived in some four hundred years ago. Moreover, even during Sita and Rama's time, the Treta Yuga, which was many thousands of years ago, the sequence of events relating to their marriage was famous throughout the land. The short version of the story is that Janaka held a self-choice ceremony, but it wasn't as though Sita directly picked her husband. These ceremonies were called svayamvaras, or self-choice, because the groom wasn't determined beforehand. Many times the princess would get to choose her husband, but in Sita's case it was a little different. The ceremony still qualified as a svayamvara because the groom would be selected from a host of men vying for the beloved princess' hand in marriage.

Instead of having Sita choose directly, Janaka decided that whoever could lift an extremely heavy bow belonging to Lord Shiva handed down in his family would be Sita's husband. In this way the occasion of Sita's marriage was quite auspicious; the svayamvara itself brought auspiciousness that day to the participants and onlookers, and the winner would gain the goddess of fortune's hand in marriage.

But what does it mean exactly to be the goddess of fortune? Is this not some mythological status assigned to Sita? The wise person knows that the gifts they receive in life are not due entirely to personal effort. We can try as hard as we want to in a certain endeavor, but if someone else shows up who is better, we'll have no chance at succeeding or being the best. Moreover, so many impeding forces have to avoid us if we are to get to where we want to go. Even something as simple as driving to work in the morning requires outside intervention. Though the external forces seemingly operate randomly, we know deep down that every person has their own desires which they act upon, which means that there is consciousness behind actions.

"Another name for Lakshmi is Chanchala. She does not stay in one place for a long time. Therefore, we see that a rich man's family sometimes becomes poor after a few generations, and sometimes we see that a poor man's family becomes very rich. Lakshmi, the goddess of fortune, is Chanchala in this material world, whereas in the Vaikuntha planets she eternally lives at the lotus feet of the Lord." (Shrila Prabhupada, Krishna, The Supreme Personality of Godhead, Vol 2, Ch 34)

The good fortune that one receives comes from Lakshmi, who is the same Sita. Since Sita is always with Rama, it means that God is the most fortunate person. The goddess of fortune is known as chanchala because she doesn't stay in one place for too long, but when she is in God's company, she behaves in just the opposite way. Even if during Sita's time people didn't know her real identity, just getting her as a wife was considered a terrific blessing. Aside from being very beautiful, she was Janaka's daughter. As a king, there was no one more pious or more respected. He had mastery over mystic yoga and was therefore considered to be beyond personal desire. Strikingly enough, he had full affection for Sita, which started on the day he found her. This meant that his attachment to his daughter was not materially motivated; it didn't break his status as Videha, or bodiless.

"Since he was childless, and due to affection for me, he placed me on his lap and said, 'This is my child.' Thus he developed feelings of love and affection for me." (Sita speaking to Anasuya, Valmiki Ramayana, Ayodhya Kand, 118.30)

As those things personally relating to God are absolute, the auspiciousness from the day of Sita's svayamvara carries over to those who hear of the event. Even Anasuya, a famous female sage, asked to hear about what happened that day many years after the fact from Sita herself. While Sita and Rama were travelling through the forests on a fourteen year trip, they stopped at Anasuya's home, where she lived with her husband Atri Rishi. After exchanging some pleasant words, Anasuya asked Sita to describe her marriage ceremony. Anasuya had already heard what happened; the news had spread across the world. Nevertheless, she didn't tire of hearing about it. Taking advantage of having the main character from that famous day staying at her home, Anasuya wanted to hear the story again.

The same desire to hear was there in Tulsidas when he composed the Janaki Mangala. In the above referenced verse, he reveals that from hearing of what happened that day, Sita and Rama remain in the heart. In the beginning stages of practicing the highest form of religion, bhakti-yoga, there may be some requirement to follow rules and regulations that are passed on by the instructing or initiating spiritual master. Perhaps one forces themselves to chant mantras like, "Hare Krishna Hare Krishna, Krishna Krishna, Hare Hare, Hare Rama Hare Rama, Rama Rama, Hare Hare", and abstain from sinful activities like meat eating, gambling, intoxication and illicit sex. This is all done to train the devotee on how to forge the proper consciousness, to be able to relish a higher taste in the future.

Once immersed in God consciousness, the devotee feels intense loneliness when not able to think about God and His activities. Therefore refuge is sought in outlets like hearing and reading books, for they help to alleviate the pain of separation. In even more extreme cases, the person will try to recount the Lord's most notable pastimes within their mind. Expressing these thoughts down on paper is a great way to recreate the actual events, to bring to life the characters and their qualities. By mentally going back to that day of the auspicious svayamvara, Tulsidas wanted to bring Sita and Rama to his vision and keep them in his heart, a place where they would feel right at home.

With this motive, how could the poet fail in his endeavor? The beloved couple's marriage would be described wonderfully, with the underlying purpose being satisfied with each successive verse composed. The transcendental effect continues well past the time of composition, as the point of writing something down is to record sound vibrations that can be reproduced. This means that when we read sacred texts, we are actually hearing the sound vibrations, essentially giving audience to a great sage who practiced bhakti. Just by adopting the proper mindset and hearing of the svayamvara and what happened that day, we can keep Sita and Rama in the heart. God is already there as the Supersoul, or Paramatma, but with practice in bhakti that presence can be realized. As hearing is the most effective tool for the aspiring transcendentalist, setting aside some time for reading or listening to how Rama lifted that amazing bow and won Sita's hand in marriage proves to be auspicious in every way.

It should be noted that during Rama's time on earth, the Lord enacted many wonderful pastimes. The original accounts of these activities are given in the Ramayana of Valmiki. With so many important events in Rama's life, why would Tulsidas choose to dedicate a specific song to the Lord's wedding ceremony? For starters, who doesn't enjoy a good love story? The plotline has been played out in movies and dramas since time immemorial, and with Sita and Rama we got the original love story, one which showed how transcendental love operates. As part of a play perfectly performed on the stage of real life, the setting was such that it looked like no one was going to win Sita's hand in marriage. Many kings came to the scene, but none of them could even move the bow, let alone lift it.

When Rama stepped up, He lifted and strung the bow without a problem, breaking it in the process. Thus there could be no doubt as to who was worthy of Sita's hand in marriage. Their match was made in heaven, and it was there for everyone to see on that wonderful occasion. To this day, in the Vedic culture if a boy and a girl prove to be a perfect match in marriage, people will remember Sita and Rama. The whole aim of Rama-lila, or the divine pastimes, is to instill this type of consciousness in everyone. As nuptials are an important aspect of life that get a lot of attention, who wouldn't love to bask in the sound vibrations that describe how Sita married Rama?

The attention paid to this aspect of Rama's life was well worth it from the poet's perspective. It gave countless generations of sincere souls the chance to further discuss that day and sing about the glories of its main participants. As man is given to glorifying someone, why not direct that attention to the people most deserving of it? As Sita is the goddess of fortune, those who hear of her self-choice ceremony in the proper mood will gain the greatest fortune in life: Sita and Rama residing within their heart.

VERSE 4

देस सुहावन पावन बेद बखानिय।
भूमि तिलक सम तिरहुति त्रिभुवन जानिय।।4।।

desa suhāvana pāvana beda bakhāniya |
bhūmi tilaka sama tirahuti tribhuvana jāniya ||4||

"That country is looking so beautiful, and the Vedas have described its purity. Known in the three worlds, Tirahut [Janakpur] is the tilaka of the earth." (4)

Essay - Tilaka

For the Vaishnava, the tilaka is the sacred marking on the body representing the link to Lord Vishnu, the Supreme Personality of Godhead. More than just an enigmatic figure to be contemplated on within the mind, the person who is the reservoir of all energies has features that are identifiable through accessing authorized information passed on in a chain of disciplic succession. The highest form of worship is to concentrate on those attributes and become attracted to them. The devotee of Vishnu wears a tilaka on several parts of the body, and most prominently on the forehead, to indicate the various marks of Vishnu, to show that there is a dedication to worshiping Him, in any of His non-different forms. For Goswami Tulsidas, the sacred mark on the earth, the place where Vishnu's impression is very nicely felt, is Tirahut, or the ancient kingdom of Janakpur where Vishnu's incarnation of Rama married the beloved daughter of King Janaka, Sita Devi.

Why this land over others? Why not declare Ayodhya to be the tilaka, or even Vrindavana, where Vishnu appeared as Krishna? In the Janaki Mangala, the poet is mentally travelling back in time to when Lord Rama was about to win the hand of Sita Devi. The marriage of the Supreme Lord to His eternal consort is as anticipated for devotees as the marriage of a close friend or relative is for the average person. A wedding is a time to come together, an excuse for people who haven't seen one another in a long time to meet up. The event itself focuses on the shared love and commitment of two people.

Since the wedding already has purity built into it, the higher the character of the participants, the more important the event will be. With Sita's marriage, there was an air of uncertainty, as it was to be a self-choice ceremony, or svayamvara. No one knew going in who the groom was going to be. The reason for this was that the king giving away Sita's hand in marriage had no idea who Sita's parents were. He had found her as a child one day while ploughing a field. Based on her characteristics, the king knew that he couldn't just give her away to any man when the time for marriage arrived. After feeling helpless, like a man stuck in an ocean without a raft to get him across, he decided to hold a contest, where the person who could lift Lord Shiva's illustrious bow would win his precious adopted daughter's company for life.

"Knowing me to be one not born of any mother's womb, the king, after great thought, was unable to find a suitable husband for me." (Sita Devi speaking to Anasuya, Valmiki Ramayana, Ayodhya Kand, 118.37)

Based on Sita's spotless character, there could only be one match for her. Though at the time of writing, the poet was well aware of who would win the contest, for the pleasure of his mind he still travelled back to that fateful day and relived the events. The land that hosted the contest is known as a tilaka, or most important mark on the earth, because of Sita and Rama's presence there. Another benefit of the tilaka is that it immediately reminds others of Vishnu. Just as we can recognize a police officer by their uniform and a priest by the type of shirt they have on, a Vaishnava, a devotee of Vishnu, can be easily spotted by the tilaka mark on the head or the tulasi beads around the neck. Even if these things should be absent, the person who always chants the glories of Vishnu stands out as a Vaishnava.

What is the significance in noting the tilaka? For the person immersed in Rama-lila, just hearing the word Tirahut or Janakpur immediately brings to mind the time Rama lifted up Lord Shiva's bow and married Sita. What better image could there be for the mind to contemplate on? The sacred places on this earth are marked with the footprints of Vishnu during His several descents in avatara forms. The places of pilgrimage are those where noteworthy events relating to the Lord took place. Janakpur was certainly one of those places.

Tirahut also brings to mind King Janaka and his pious character. He was very famous throughout the world during his time, for his dedication to piety was unmatched. He was also an expert mystic, which meant that he was above the influence of the senses. For a king that is a very rare accomplishment, for the appeal of being king is that you get to enjoy heavenly delights and opulence while still on earth. The President of the United States flies around on Air Force One and can eat whatever he desires at any time of the day. He even gets to vacation in wonderful places. Kings similarly are supplied with whatever they desire at a moment's notice.

How then could a king like Janaka be above the influence of the senses, especially when his desires could be met so easily?

Let's think of it this way. Imagine being known for your control over eating. You meticulously measure the portion sizes of the food you are going to eat, and you never indulge in anything that will be bad for you. Thus you maintain a slim physique and never suffer from illness. Keeping the internal airs of the body in balance, you never put stress on yourself from eating. Surely you are not that rare, as many people aren't overweight. But what about if we said that you did this while sitting in front of a buffet cart for eight hours a day? Let's say that you worked in a place where you could eat whatever you wanted at any time of the day, at no charge. These circumstances make your controlled eating all the more impressive.

Take the example of getting to eat whatever you want and extend it out to every sensual pursuit, and you have what the average king's lifestyle is like. Yet Janaka was so dedicated to piety, so knowledgeable of dharma and how to maintain one's essential characteristic, that he was known as Videha, or bodiless. The senses had no influence on him. What's more is that he even advanced past the stage of mystic yoga and became a full-fledged devotee, someone so devoted that he is today known as one of the twelve mahajanas, or authorities on devotional service.

"Lord Brahma, Bhagavan Narada, Lord Shiva, the four Kumaras, Lord Kapila [the son of Devahuti], Svayambhuva Manu, Prahlada Maharaja, Janaka Maharaja, Grandfather Bhishma, Bali Maharaja, Shukadeva Gosvami and I myself know the real religious principle." (Yamaraja, Shrimad Bhagavatam, 6.3.20)

A mahajana is a great soul because of their qualities exhibited in dealings with others and also their ability to teach others about the right path in life. The twelve mahajanas relating to devotional service are listed in the Shrimad Bhagavatam, or Bhagavata Purana. It should be noted that not all the personalities mentioned are direct worshipers of Lord Vishnu. For instance, Prahlada Maharaja was a devotee of Vishnu, but he got to offer prayers to the Lord in His half-man/half-lion form of Narasimhadeva. Lord Shiva especially prefers to worship Vishnu as Lord Rama. Regardless of who was specifically worshiped, their interactions with Vishnu and their staunch devotion to him made them eligible to be known as authority figures, people that others can look to for guidance.

What did Janaka specifically do to be listed as one of the authorities on devotional service? For starters, his Videha position did not preclude him from picking up the baby in the ground and harboring affection for her. Janaka, though above the influence of the senses, immediately harbored parental affection for this precious little girl found in the field. As if the keepers of heaven knew what was in his mind, a voice in the sky then came upon the scene and said that this girl was Janaka's daughter in all righteousness, or dharma. Janaka needed to hear this because he never did anything outside the bounds of piety. The voice basically gave him the okay to love this girl as his daughter and take care of her.

From the events described in the Janaki Mangala, we learn that Janaka would also get a tremendous thrill upon meeting Shri Rama and His younger brother Lakshmana. Vishnu is not alone in the spiritual world. God has a family like we do. His eternal consort is Lakshmi Devi, who is Sita. His protector, His number one servitor, is Ananta Shesha Naga, who is Lakshmana. Janaka did not break his high position of being desire-less when meeting Sita, Rama and Lakshmana for the first time. Rather, his mastery over mystic yoga and his pious nature made him eligible for experiencing the transcendental bliss that comes with God's association.

That same thrill can be felt by those who hear of Sita and Rama's glorious activities. The stage for one of their most memorable interactions was the land of Tirahut, which thus made it worthy of being called a tilaka. Just as Janaka's kingdom is sacred for its rich history and the pious people who lived there, the incomparably brilliant works of the saint Tulsidas are forever sacred. He wrote the Janaki Mangala to stay connected in the mind with Sita and Rama, and we read his works so that we can gain his association. No other benefit in life can compare with the company of the saints, who are like travelling tirthas, bringing auspiciousness and good cheer wherever they go. The pages that house the words born in their minds thus also become sacred, like tilaka, for they immediately remind one of Vishnu and devotion to Him.

VERSE 5

तहँ बस नगर जनकपुर परम उजागर।
सीय लच्छि जहँ प्रगटी सब सुख सागर।।5।।

taham̐ basa nagara janakapura parama ujāgara |
sīya lacchi jaham̐ pragaṭī saba sukha sāgara ||5||

"Supremely famous is that city of Janakpur, where Sita Devi, the goddess of fortune herself appeared, making it like an ocean full of every type of happiness."
(5)

Essay - Every Kind of Happiness

"Don't think that I'm wasting your time", is the undertone to this verse from Tulsidas' Janaki Mangala. The poet is setting the scene for his song about the marriage of the most beautiful couple. Should one be unfamiliar with where these events took place, Goswami Tulsidas is ensuring that they know that the place is supremely famous nonetheless. Even if one has never followed any Vedic teaching and doesn't know who Sita Devi and Lord Rama are, hearing of their marriage ceremony and how it took place on that fateful day many thousands of years ago can still prove to bring every type of happiness to the heart, which can accept an unlimited amount of nectar, provided that it is of the transcendental variety.

Why the qualification? Why is the soul limited in accepting happiness of the material variety? If we find something pleasurable, how can we say that there is a limit to enjoying it? For instance, does a dog tire of enjoying sex life, a drunkard his beer and wine, and an obese person their fatty foods? Actually, the overindulgence in these areas is considered detrimental. The alcoholic may love getting drunk all the time, but deep down they know that something is wrong, as do others. The obese person has the most visible negative consequences to their behavior, and the dog is not viewed to be very intelligent for its lack of discrimination in conjugal affairs.

These defects point to the fact that the living beings are limited in their ability to enjoy certain things. There is a constraint put on the individual by their body type. The skeptic at this point may raise the argument that the limit is there for everything, so what is the point to even mentioning it? Ah, but there is no limit when one is swimming in a pool of spiritual nectar. What is the difference? How can we tell if something is spiritual? Isn't everything we see around us a collection of earth, water, fire, air and ether manifested in different ways and perceived of by the senses attached to the body? If everything is seen through the material medium, how can we claim anything to be spiritual?

The spiritual is detected by certain properties, the foremost of which is eternality. Every living being is limited in the duration of their outward manifestation, even the trees that live for thousands of years. Spirit is the energy behind such manifestations and their movements, and since there is always energy, we can understand that spirit is always in existence. From the Bhagavad-gita, we learn that the spiritual energy is localized within each individual, which means that there are many fragments of spirit. Those embodied fragments existed prior to their current births and they will remain in existence even after impending deaths. We can take the information from the authority of the Gita, and we can also perceive for ourselves the importance of spirit, how it ensures that the living being can eat, sleep, mate and defend only when there is the vital force within the body.

"While contemplating the objects of the senses, a person develops attachment for them, and from such attachment lust develops, and from lust anger arises." (Lord Krishna, Bhagavad-gita, 2.62)

The spiritual is tied to the fountainhead of all energy. Generally, that origin is referred to as God, but since He is also knowledgeable, eternal and blissful but on a larger scale, He can be described as the Supreme Spirit. Unlike the material energy, the spiritual energy provides lasting happiness. We can tell that we're in connection with the spiritual energy when there is a fervent desire to remain connected with God, and when all good qualities descend from there. Among the many detriments to overindulgence in the material energy is the loss of rationale, the rise of anger and frustration, and the misguided belief that more indulgence will lead to more happiness. The sober person is always more capable at treading the difficult waters of life than is the intoxicated person. Intoxication is marked by the effect it has on the behavior of the person. In this sense intoxication can also come from greed, lust, anger and other emotions that arise from the failure to satisfy the senses, despite repeated attempts at material interaction.

The spiritual interaction, however, has the opposite effect. Therefore we can realize the presence of the spiritual by the effect it has on behavior. Rather than just study examples involving others, one can take the plunge themselves, extending some faith to the words of the Vaishnavas, those who always remain connected with the divine consciousness, which is the all-pervasive aspect of the Supreme Spirit. Tulsidas says that the city of Janakpur is like an ocean full of every type of happiness because he has experienced it himself. Not that he necessarily lived there or went there regularly. Rather, just by situating the mind there, especially at the time of the svayamvara held by the famed King Janaka, one can find peace and felicity for extended periods of time. Moreover, no amount of repeated mental trips to this place will prove detrimental to the mind. On the contrary, with each successive visit, the pool of nectar becomes sweeter and sweeter, leaving the pilgrim wondering why they ever left in the first place.

Where do these delights come from? Why Janakpur and not another place? The goddess of fortune, Lakshmiji herself, appeared in that great land many thousands of years ago. In addition to being the Supreme Spirit, God is also described as the husband of the goddess of fortune by the Vedas. We may think that we are responsible for the results of our actions, but in actuality the material nature is a much stronger force, as is the influence of the countless other living entities populating the earth. Therefore any good fortune we do receive actually comes from Lakshmi. Money is considered a type of incarnation of Lakshmi, good fortune that can come and go on a whim.

Is Janakpur considered sacred because the kingdom was wealthy? Did Lakshmi appear in Janaka's land to make him a rich king, full of every type of opulence? As the wife of Lord Narayana, the Supreme Lord who is the source of all men, Lakshmi always serves her husband and tries to make Him happy. She is never divorced from this role, which means that wherever she goes she has the same objectives in mind. When one is graced with Lakshmi's presence, they are meant to use her association for Narayana's benefit and no one else's. As the Supreme Spirit is individually tied to the individual spirit, this proper use of fortune is beneficial to the individual as well.

In Janakpur, Lakshmi appeared as Sita, who was so named by Janaka, a famous king of the time. He found her one day while ploughing a field, and thus named her Sita because she came out of the ground. Her marriage ceremony marked the occasion where Janaka would reunite Lakshmi with Narayana, who had similarly appeared on earth in Ayodhya as Lord Rama, the famed prince of the Raghu dynasty. Janaka had not a hint of sin in him, so he was worthy of having Lakshmi as a daughter. Through her appearance would come Rama as a son-in-law, thus making Janaka supremely fortunate.

What about the happiness? How is Sita's association full of every type of delight? Well, to find lasting happiness, wouldn't it make sense to connect with the fountainhead of the spiritual energy, which is inexhaustible? Sita is herself part of the spiritual energy, and coupled with Rama she can give anything to anyone. But the fruit of one's existence is to taste the happiness that comes from the beloved couple's association. This means that just by having Sita live there, Janakpur became purified and the source of every type of happiness.

There was variety in activity in Janakpur during Sita's time. Not everyone was a yogi given to meditation. Janaka, though a pious king, was famous for his mastery over mystic yoga, which results in many beneficial qualities, including renunciation. The ability to be dispassionate towards the temporary changes in life is considered an opulence, a praiseworthy trait. George Washington, the first President of the United States, is honored because he voluntarily stepped down from office after serving two terms. He did so to set an example, to show that a ruler shouldn't remain in power in perpetuity. Janaka had full possession of renunciation, so much so that he was known as Videha, which means bodiless.

Was renunciation the fortune granted to him by Sita? Actually, when Janaka first found his soon-to-be daughter, he immediately became thrilled to the heart. This did not break his Videha status, for spiritual love has nothing to do with the swinging pendulum of enjoyment and renunciation that is concomitant with a material existence. Rather, in spiritual life there is only bliss. Separation and meeting both produce bliss, as do loss and gain, provided that one is connected with the divine consciousness.

The people in Janakpur had different occupations but they all loved Janaka and his eldest daughter very much. In this sense they were better than yogis, as they weren't purposefully trying for self-realization, renunciation, or enlightenment. They were happy all the time simply because of their association with the goddess of fortune. Their eyes would serve their true purpose when they would see Rama and His younger brother Lakshmana approaching for the svayamvara.

The onlookers had different emotions running through their minds at this time. The svayamvara was set up to decide Sita's nuptials because Janaka did not know anything about her family history or her qualities based on the time of her birth. He decided that whoever could lift Lord Shiva's bow, which was very auspicious, would win his daughter's hand in marriage. Seeing Rama approaching, the residents of the town gathered to observe the bow-lifting contest felt a variety of emotions. Some were happy to see such a beautiful youth accompanied by His younger brother, who appeared as almost a twin, except with a different complexion. Rama is of the shyama color, which is dark, and Lakshmana is gaura, or fair. While some were eager with anticipation from the sight of Rama and Lakshmana, others started to worry. They thought that the king had made a mistake with his promise to give away Sita through the contest, for what if Rama couldn't lift the bow? Lakshmana was the younger brother, so he wouldn't have tried to lift the bow in Rama's presence. In ancient times when the strictest rules and regulations of the Vedas were followed, it was considered a sin for a younger brother to get married before the older brother was married. As Lakshmana's only dharma in life was to please his older brother, he was never really a candidate for marrying Sita.

When the contest took place, nervousness borne of anticipation penetrated the atmosphere. Just like watching a big moment in a game where everything is on the line, many onlookers were so afraid of what might happen should someone else lift the bow or Rama be incapable of rising to the challenge. Some knew that He was going to do it, while others prayed to God to be allowed to have Sita wed Rama.

Thus we see that there was every type of enjoyment available in Janakpur, except that they were all of the spiritual variety. Moreover, that happiness extends to anyone who listens to the accounts of what happened that day. To provide even more emphasis on just how wonderful spiritual happiness is, even someone who is intimately familiar with the marriage of Sita and Rama can listen to the story over and over again and still find tremendous delight, as if the heart auto-expands to make more room for the renewed inflow of spiritual nectar. From the words of his song, Tulsidas revealed the purpose for his writing. Send the mind back to the time of Sita's marriage, which was situated in the ancient kingdom of Janakpur. As that was the place where the goddess of fortune appeared, it became an abode of auspiciousness. Just compiling the words gave Tulsidas so much pleasure, and that happiness extends to this day to anyone who is fortunate enough to connect with his writings. Every type of spiritual happiness is available to those who love Sita Devi and understand her position as Rama's beloved.

VERSE 6

जनक नाम तेहिं नगर बसै नरनायक।
सब गुन अवधि न दूसर पटतर लायक॥6॥

janaka nāma tehiṁ nagara basai naranāyaka |
saba guna avadhi na dūsara paṭatara lāyaka ||6||

"In that city lives the leader of all men, Maharaja Janaka. He has every good quality, and during that time there was no other king like him." (6)

Essay - No One Like Him

Just as the people who came from far and wide were benefitted by visiting his kingdom for the most famous marriage in history, he who is sincerely interested in finding transcendental happiness and living in a place full of good qualities will find auspiciousness by mentally travelling to that wonderful place set in a specific time in history. Written word artistically presented to the author's preferred style serves as an escape for the reader looking for one. Just as the perfect travel destination is one which matches the desires for activity and engagement of the traveller, the ideal mental home for the person looking to escape from their present surroundings full of constant ups and downs, which seemingly have no purpose, is a place full of good qualities meant to meet the soul's innermost desires. The kingdom of Janakpur was that place for a famous Vaishnava poet around four hundred years ago and it remains a mental haven for those looking for transcendental pleasure today.

Why this town specifically? Moreover, in what time period are we situating the mind? In the above referenced verse from the Janaki Mangala, Goswami Tulsidas gives us a few reasons why the place in question is so attractive. During ancient times, the Treta Yuga to be more precise, there was a famous self-choice ceremony, or svayamvara, held for the princess of Videha, Sita Devi. Since she was the daughter of King Janaka, she was also known as Janaki. People from around the world travelled to Janaka's capital city that day, hoping to witness history and see who would actually win the hand of the most beautiful woman in the world.

"My dear beautiful wife, what you have said is befitting the occasion and also indicative of the greatness of your family heritage. You are dearer to Me than My life, for you are My companion in the performance of religious duties [sadharma-charini]." (Lord Rama speaking to Sita Devi, Valmiki Ramayana, Aranya Kand, 10.21)

Why such attention given to a wedding? Beautiful people get married all the time, so why was this event such a big deal? When married under sacred Vedic principles, the wife becomes the goddess of fortune to the husband, giving him the support he needs to carry out his religious duties. Ironically enough, the lady getting married at this self-choice ceremony would one day be described as a sadharma-charini by her husband. One who follows the principles of dharma is considered on the right path towards rekindling their constitutional position. The wife's duty is to help the husband in that quest, for his success equates to hers as well. Therefore a good wife is a heavenly blessing, a person who reinforces dedication to dharma instead of breaking it.

In the verse previous to this one, Tulsidas remarked that Janakpur was sacred because the goddess of fortune herself had appeared there. Her appearance took place many years prior to the svayamvara, when the king of the land found a young baby girl in the ground. Rather than just leave her there, he took her in as his own daughter. He did not know that she was Lakshmi Devi, the wife of Lord Narayana in the spiritual sky. She had appeared on earth to act as Rama's support system. Shri Rama is the very same Narayana, except in the guise of a warrior prince. Narayana is the source of all men; hence He is God.

All living creatures have an original source. Depending on the spiritual tradition followed, that source is given a specific name or referred to as an impersonal force. The Vedas, the ancient scriptures of India, provide as much detail into this matter as can possibly be absorbed by the human brain. Imagine trying to explain traffic signals and the rules of the road to a young child. It's not possible to convey the ins and outs about insurance rates, driving tendencies, and the need for regulation in a hectic environment to someone who is immature. You can only explain to them as much information as their maturity level will allow them to accept.

Man's thinking is constrained by the concepts of time and space. We have no idea what eternal, or sanatana, means. Just try to sit down and contemplate what having no beginning and no end actually entails. Moreover, try to picture what it's like to keep travelling in space and never reach an end. These are brain teasers that cannot be solved. Well aware of this limitation, the sacred texts that emanate from the original person, who is sanatana both in the duration of His existence and the scope and breadth of His pervasiveness, provide as much detail as man can handle. Since we are fallible human beings that have a source, the name Narayana automatically becomes one way to address God.

To show others what Narayana looks like, what His qualities actually are, and how one can interact with Him, the Supreme Lord descends to earth every now and then. His closest associates come as well, for God is never bereft of His energies. His wife is the best wife in the world; which automatically means that Narayana is the most fortunate. Naturally, only the most fortunate person would always be graced with the presence of the goddess of fortune.

Based on her qualities, Sita's appearance turned the kingdom of Tirahuta, now commonly known as the areas of Janakpur and its neighboring towns, into a sacred land, a place of pilgrimage. Yet her divinity wasn't known to the world at the time. Nevertheless, throngs of people came to Tirahuta for her svayamvara. What was the reason for this? Janaka himself was a famed leader of men. When discussing ancient historical events, the Vedas refer to the kings by names which describe them to be the ruler of all men, the lord of men, the protector of earth, and so on. This shows that the kings during those times had large responsibilities that extended far beyond their local community. They had to be respected throughout the world to be considered good kings.

From the above referenced verse, we see that not only was Janaka the holder of every good quality, but there was actually no other king like him during his time. For starters, he had Sita as a daughter. The goddess of fortune chose him as a father during her time on earth. Obviously he must have been someone special. Janaka was also deferent to dharma, so much so that no one could find a flaw in him.

Though Janaka was the ocean of good qualities, he never rested on his laurels. He never thought that he had already accumulated enough pious credits. Rather, he was always worried about inviting scorn and ridicule from others, for that would tarnish the good standing of the kingdom. When it came time for Sita's marriage, the king faced the most difficult decision of his life. For starters, since she was the goddess of fortune in her qualities, Janaka did not want to give Sita away and lose her. Secondly, nothing was known about Sita's time of birth, which meant that her qualities determined by astrological signs could not be compared to any prospective matrimonial candidate's; there was no horoscope to look at. The ancient system of Vedic astrology was so perfect that simply from matching the horoscopes of the boy and girl a perfect match in marriage could be found.

"Even if a father be like Indra himself on this earth, he obtains ill treatment from the people in general, both subordinates and superiors, if he keeps his daughter unmarried." (Maharaja Janaka, Valmiki Ramayana, Ayodhya Kand, 118.35)

Janaka had legitimate reasons supporting the option of keeping Sita unmarried. Nevertheless, that wouldn't stop others from criticizing him, for a father who does not protect his daughter after he leaves the earth has failed in his obligations. The daughter is a younger dependent, so the good father finds a suitable husband to protect her in life. Ever the pious king, Janaka left the matter up to Lord Shiva, who would determine Sita's husband through the proxy of his bow. Having a famous bow that was so heavy that no one could lift it, Janaka decided to hold a contest to decide Sita's marriage. Whoever could lift Shiva's bow would win Sita as a wife.

Janaka was also famous for his mastery over mystic yoga. He had so much transcended the effects of the senses that he was known as Videha, or one who is without a body. The body is our vehicle for action, and as is true of any vehicle, the body carries some limitations. An automobile must be carefully constructed and then regularly maintained to operate properly. The car cannot just drive forever either; it needs to be filled up with gasoline every now and then. Similarly, the human body needs food, rest, clothing and shelter. With these needs come other influences that aren't so kind. The tendencies towards illicit sex, meat eating, gambling and intoxication are rooted in attachment to a body which does not represent one's true identity.

Though the soul is immune to the effects of the body, actually mitigating the negative influence of the senses is very difficult. It requires expert practice of yoga, the bona fide kind which is meant to connect the soul with the Supreme Soul, or God's expansion residing within the heart. From connection with the divine consciousness comes freedom from the effects of the senses. Janaka was above passion, and yet was totally deferent to his duties as a king. The two seem diametrically opposed to one another, as the appeal to being a king is having the ability to get whatever you want whenever you want it. Janaka did not want anything, and yet he was the perfect king, one so glorious that there was no other like him on earth.

Transcendental pleasure has nothing to do with the body, and this was proven by Janaka and his behavior. He was bodiless but he still felt delighted to have Sita as his daughter. In fact, his control over the senses made him all the more eligible to appreciate Sita's qualities and those of her soon-to-be husband. If consciousness is always in the gutter, how can it appreciate something sweet and sublime? Only when the senses are purified can the individual fully appreciate talks and discussions about Narayana and His many adventures on earth. For the mind looking for a pleasant escape, the sacred land ruled over by King Janaka is never a bad place to go. On that fateful day many thousands of years ago, the leader with so many good qualities would be rewarded for his piety by getting Narayana Himself as a son-in-law. The sequence of events too was a thing of beauty, something so wonderful that the mind can repeatedly go back to that day and continually derive renewed pleasure. Let the mind of him who is searching for God never forget King Janaka and his wonderful daughter, Sita Devi, the goddess of fortune and eternal consort of Lord Rama, the Supreme Personality of Godhead.

VERSE 7

भयउ न होइहि है न जनक सम नरवइ।
सीय सुता भइ जासु सकल मंगलमइ।।7।।

bhaya'u na ho'ihi hai na janaka sama narava' i |
sīya sutā bha'i jāsu sakala maṅgalama'i ||7||

"Never in the past was there, nor in the future will there be, a man like Janaka, who had Sita as a daughter, full of all auspiciousness." (7)

Essay - Daughter of Janaka

When writing a song describing the marriage of the sweetest woman in the world to the man most dedicated to protecting the innocent, a host of potential titles can come to mind. Yet Goswami Tulsidas specifically chose to use the name "Janaki" in the title of his song describing the daughter of Janaka's marriage to the prince of the Raghu dynasty, Lord Rama. A person with good qualities shows that their guardians had a role in their upbringing, that they were taught discipline at a young age and instilled values that would be beneficial to both them and the people with which they interacted. Sita was endowed with all good qualities, and though they were remarkable, they weren't that surprising considering who her father was. Already a king famous around the world for his chivalry, the day he found Sita was the day that would bring him the most auspiciousness.

Limited by time is the human being. There is only so much that can be accomplished in a given day, for there are so many responsibilities to take care of. During the week there is the grind of the forty hours of work during the daytime coupled with the responsibilities pertaining to home and family at night. Then on the weekend one can tend to all the chores they skipped during the busy week. In this way there is not much that can be done to introduce new activities into the routine of the average adult. Therefore the activities that one does take up become even more important. The more inclusive they are in scope, the more they take care of multiple needs, the better the benefit derived will be.

In spiritual life the task becomes even more difficult. The initial plunge into a discipline aimed at finding real happiness indicates that the life already followed is not cutting it. The individual contemplating acceptance of a spiritual discipline wants more out of their activities; they want to see tangible, lasting benefits from their work. The problem, however, is again related to time and what can be accomplished with the efforts that one does put forth. The more time you put in, the greater the rewards that are expected. At the same time, the more serious the engagement, the higher the benefit should be as well.

If I start out in spiritual life with just simple meditation, I gain the initial benefit of avoiding the hectic life I am accustomed to. At the very least, I get to sit quietly and avoid thinking of all the pressures, what I have to do tomorrow and what went wrong with the just completed day. Depending on the tradition I'm following and who my teacher is, I may also focus on God directly, realizing His transcendental features and basking in His sweet vision. These features are known through disciplic succession, with people being around during the Lord's advents, noting down their observations, and then passing that information on to successive generations. Tapping into this information is like hopping on a train that is passing through your city. Once on it, you can not only learn about God, but you can even create your own line off of it to bring the glorious news from the spiritual world to many other people.

In the Vedic tradition, the most inclusive type of meditation involves focus on the transcendental form of the Personality of Godhead, who is known as Krishna because of His sweetness. He is so attractive that one who has removed the influence of the senses can't help but remain devoted to Him. Indeed, it is only the influence of the material nature that causes any living entity to become forgetful of their constitutional position of lover of God. When afflicted by the material disease, the same loving spirit is present, but it gets directed towards areas that don't merit the attention. Moreover, the love is then qualified, almost a type of lust. The "love" only lasts for as long as there is a benefit received. As soon as that stops, the loving spirit gets directed elsewhere.

For one who is following meditation on Krishna's lotus feet, their progression is aided by reciting the holy names, like those found in the maha-mantra, "Hare Krishna Hare Krishna, Krishna Krishna, Hare Hare, Hare Rama Hare Rama, Rama Rama, Hare Hare". From constant recitation of this mantra in meditational trance, one can gradually learn more about the transcendental features of the Supreme Lord and how remaining in His company is so beneficial. The more one chants in a pure mood, the more they become attached to the process; so much so that even the most elevated transcendentalists keep the chanting routine as part of their baseline practices.

It's ironic to think that something that was first viewed as novel and separate from the activities we perform on a routine basis soon becomes so routine that it gets pushed to the backburner, though still not neglected. Why would it get secondary status? From the revival of Krishna consciousness comes the fervent desire to continually connect with the Supreme Lord, even during times outside of explicit meditation. In one sense the meditation never breaks, as the desire to stay with God is still there, but as the human being can follow a variety of engagements, the contemplative individual finds their way into other endeavors, new outlets for service.

Again, the constraints of time creep up. The devotee immersed in Krishna consciousness wants to glorify not only God, but also those exalted figures intimately associated with Him. Krishna is complete with His entourage both in the spiritual and material worlds. In this land they are roaming about playing different roles to show others what it means to be connected in yoga, and in the spiritual land they are by the Lord's side giving Him pleasure through a variety of transcendental mellows, or rasas.

Bhakti-yoga, or devotional service, is the constitutional engagement of the vibrant spirit because it directly addresses the root of all creation. Once the root is watered, the branches and leaves are fed at the same time. In this sense one only has to glorify Krishna to take care of their obligations. Nevertheless, devotees like Tulsidas try to glorify other important characters as well, people they love because of their relationship to the Supreme Lord. For the poet who authored the verse quoted above, his worshipable figure of choice is Lord Rama, who is considered an incarnation of Krishna, or Vishnu. In the Vedic tradition there is a divide between personalists and impersonalists. We can think of an impersonalist as someone who doesn't yet know about God's position as a personality, whereas a personalist is fully aware of it. Among the personalists, the worshipable figure is not uniform, though He always represents the same original Lord. Rama is the same Krishna but with a different manifestation and different activities enacted during His time on earth.

If Tulsidas worshiped Rama exclusively through bhakti, why would he author a poem called the Janaki Mangala. Once we find out that Janaki is Rama's wife and that the mangala refers to the auspiciousness of her marriage ceremony to Rama, the purpose behind the composition becomes self-evident. If you love God, you're going to love His wife. Just as Rama is non-different from Krishna and Vishnu, Sita is non-different from Shrimati Radharani and Lakshmi Devi. The Vedas describe God as the energetic and His immediate pleasure potency expansion as His energy. The two are the perfect match. We are also part of God's energy, meant to give Him pleasure, but in a conditioned state we have to first take to a yoga discipline to be able to realize that position. From realization comes action.

Shri Rama has many different names that reference His attributes, features, and position in the universe. Along the same lines, Sita also has many different names, of which Janaki is one. We can speculate as to why Tulsidas chose to use Janaki instead of Sita in the title for his poem, but we know for sure from the above referenced verse that one of the reasons was his love for King Janaka, Sita's father. Janaki as a word reveals that the person being addressed has a father named Janaka. In ancient times, that King Janaka was famous around the world. There was no other king like him in the past and there will never be one like him in the future.

What is so special about Janaka? For starters, he was wholly dedicated to piety, which isn't so commonplace among kings. A king lives by administering justice and levying taxes on the citizens. Without proper adherence to religious principles, the king will be degraded and so will his citizens. Janaka was also an elevated transcendentalist, to the point that he was above happiness and sadness. Nothing could faze his stoic demeanor.

Or so it was thought. When he found a baby girl in the ground one day while ploughing a field, his life would change forever. The same king that was already famous for his dedication to religious principles would gain supreme auspiciousness in accepting this girl as his daughter. Since she came out of the ground he named her Sita, and through her he would gain Shri Rama as a son-in-law. In this way Janaka proved himself ever worthy of God's favor, for the Supreme Lord's wife chose him as a father during her time on earth.

Through addressing Sita as Janaki, the great king is automatically praised. Shri Hanuman, Rama's most faithful servant, would often refer to Sita as Janaka-atmaja, or the daughter of Janaka, when thinking about her. Hanuman had to think about Sita a lot because it was his duty to find her after she went missing. Sita would be married to Rama in a grand ceremony held in Janaka's kingdom. This ceremony was the main subject matter of the Janaki Mangala. After being married for twelve years, Sita and Rama would sojourn through the forests. One day Sita would be taken away from Rama's side behind His back, and to try to find her, the Lord enlisted the help of a band of Vanaras living in Kishkindha. Hanuman was their most capable warrior and also the one most dedicated to Rama. He had to travel to the city of Lanka by himself and try to find Sita there. Therefore he often thought of Sita's qualities, remembering King Janaka's pious nature and family ancestry at the same time.

From the title of his poem and the verse referenced above we see that Tulsidas was able to offer high praise to Janaka while writing about Sita and Rama. The task for the devotional writer is quite difficult, as there are so many saints deserving praise, so many noble characters who are intimately tied to the Supreme Lord and His pastimes. Janaka is so exalted that he is listed as one of the twelve mahajanas, or authorities on devotional service. Though he deserves many books dedicated to his activities and character, just by saying the name Janaki once, so much praise and honor are given to him. By appearing in his family, Sita ensured that the king would be famous forever. Receiving his beloved daughter and showing her unmatched love, Janaka found the highest auspiciousness. The pleasure increased to unimaginable heights when she received Shri Rama as a husband, making Janaka arguably the most fortunate king to have ever graced this earth.

Essay - What Is Auspiciousness

What is the best for our welfare? Can there be just one thing that applies universally? If one person is puffed up by the false ego resulting from excessive material opulence and enjoyment, obviously what's good for them will be a humbling of that pride, something to remind them that they are not in control of everything. On the other hand, someone who is destitute, barely getting by each day with a few morsels of food, can really use some security, the peace of mind that comes with knowing that material amenities will be available in steady supply. Thus what is auspicious for one person is not necessarily beneficial to another. Yet one woman's company is so delightful that regardless of one's position, whether they are a powerful king or a renounced yogi, everything beneficial comes as a result of meeting her. She is the ocean of mercy, the reservoir of beauty, and with love offered to her in genuineness comes the fruit of our existence.

It should be noted that even in spiritual life, which is above the temporary pitfalls of acceptance and rejection that swing perpetually like a pendulum, there is not uniformity in desires. The materialist enjoyer is referred to as a karmi in the Vedas. This word points to fruitive work, something performed for a specific benefit. The work has reactions, which are referred to as fruits, or phala; hence the translation of karma into "fruitive work". The reactions aren't always intended, nor are they always expected, making karma a complicated business. The enjoyments of even the cherished results don't last forever, requiring repeated endeavor in fruitive activity.

The jnanis, yogis and bhaktas are above karma. A jnani is in search of jnana, or knowledge. In this sense there is some work applied, but it is only through the mind, so there are no visible fruits that result immediately. Rather, through theoretical exercise, the mental speculator hopefully can alter their behavior in such a way that the reactions to their work are always what they intend and that the enjoyments do not bind them in further misery. The yogis are similarly engaged in a higher cause. Through meditation they hope to block off the influence of the senses, to remain in trance so that the consciousness can stay pure.

For the karmis, yogis and jnanis the cherished rewards are not the same. For instance, the karmi considers success in their ventures to be auspiciousness. A tired worker desiring a nice vacation destination spot views a healthy bank balance and the ability to travel as favorable circumstances. The yogi, on the other hand, considers a sacred place that is quiet and peaceful as an auspicious blessing. The jnani lives off of mental speculation and the ability to accept higher knowledge. The intelligentsia class can be likened to the jnanis, so what they consider auspicious is high knowledge in the form of books and the ability to think rationally.

Only the bhaktas, however, are all-inclusive. They can follow any of the activities of the karmis, jnanis and yogis and find auspiciousness through maintaining a purified consciousness. For the bhaktas, the aim is love, the transcendental variety. When dovetailed with spirituality, bhakti is known as bhakti-yoga, or devotional service. Karma, jnana and meditational yoga can also be linked with spirituality, but again the conditions deemed beneficial are not uniform. For the bhakta, the only requirement is the ability to remain in divine trance, to be able to contemplate on the Supreme Lord.

How is this different from the yogis who sit in meditation? For starters, the conditions for performing meditational yoga are very difficult, so much so that the path is not recommended at all for the people of this age. These recommendations come from the Vedas and their derivative scriptures, which represent the original source of knowledge in this world. The entire world consists of various branches of Vedic culture, which started with the instructions of the Supreme Personality of Godhead that were imparted to the first created living entity, Lord Brahma. From

Brahma's teachings, the initial systems of religion were created, and as further time elapsed from the start of creation, deviation from the original principles increased, so much so that now there are too many spiritual denominations to count.

Common to any system of maintenance is a desired end-goal. Bhakti is the summit of religious practice because it has the highest end-goal that exists: constant association with God. The Supreme Lord is a personality with divine features, qualities which provide Him pleasure and also attract the sincere souls, who are miniature versions of God. Any being that is autonomous in its movement is a small version of God, but since their exercise of that freedom is limited, they are not equal to the Supreme Person. Fear not, however, as there is no need to try to equal God. The Supreme Lord is meant to be enjoyed through His association, a link which thus represents the most auspicious condition.

How can we say this with certainty? The Supreme Lord is described as having a transcendental body full of sweetness. He is the most beautiful, wise, strong, renounced, wealthy and famous. We are already attracted to famous and successful people, those who have bucked the odds and reached the tops of their respective fields. Beauty is attractive to pretty much anyone, as are strength and knowledge. In this way we see that God's attractiveness is not a sectarian assertion or something that can only be enjoyed by people born and raised in a certain place. Rather, God is attractive to every single person, including the atheists who deny His existence. In the absence of personal interaction with the Supreme Lord and His brilliant features, what the living entity will find appealing are various impersonal aspects, separated energy expansions. Only in these areas are there varieties of auspicious conditions, dualities in what people find beneficial. This, of course, is because of the lack of the Supreme Lord's personal presence.

In bhakti, the divine's features are talked about, relished, honored, and most of all, enjoyed. When we have the most attractive person's image within our minds, our activities will be driven towards maintaining the sight of that image. Thus the bhakta can be doing something as simple as eating and still enjoy full auspiciousness. For one king a long time ago, he was doing the odd job of ploughing a field, when in an instant he felt the thrill of a lifetime, a jolt of happiness that he had never felt before. This moment would forever change his life.

"One is understood to be in full knowledge whose every act is devoid of desire for sense gratification. He is said by sages to be a worker whose fruitive action is burned up by the fire of perfect knowledge." (Lord Krishna, Bhagavad-gita, 4.19)

Why was a king ploughing a field? Wasn't this an act of karma? If so, how could the happiness he found be the source of pleasure for others as well? Though outwardly engaged in fruitive work, this leader of men was actually doing his occupational duty, remaining unattached to the result. He was a fruitive worker who had burned up the reactions to his work by being fully in knowledge. In one sense, this wonderful king of ancient times could be thought of as a combination jnani/yogi. He had knowledge of dharma, or religiosity, which then guided his behavior. He also had control over his senses, which earned him the title Videha, which means "one who is bodiless".

As mentioned before, the karmis, yogis and jnanis each have respective definitions of auspiciousness, conditions whose merits may not apply across disciplines. Though he was known as an expert yogi, King Janaka was actually a bhakta, or devotee, at heart. This meant that through his pious acts, he was qualifying himself to gain full auspiciousness, which would arrive on the day he would find the precious baby girl in the ground. Of all the places to find gold in the form of another human being, Janaka found his little treasure in the ground that was being tilled for a sacrifice, or yajna.

What was so wonderful about this event? How would this help Janaka's piety? Aren't the karmis the ones enchanted by familial attachment, which is only temporary? This was no ordinary girl. Just as the Supreme Lord is the reservoir of attractiveness, His eternal consorts possess similarly brilliant features. In many ways God's companions are more glorious than He is, for they are completely devoted to Him. Having the audience of a devotee is the greatest blessing for the person wandering aimlessly through life in search of a higher taste, one that doesn't leave bitter aftereffects or vanish in an instant.

The girl Janaka found was the Supreme Lord's wife in the spiritual sky. Since God is the source of all men, He is given the name Narayana. Since He is the most fortunate entity in the world, His wife is known as Lakshmi, who is the goddess of fortune. That same Lakshmi appeared in Janaka's sacred land to bless him, to give him full auspiciousness. Janaka was the most pious king and thus fully deserved having Lakshmi's presence.

But why come as a little girl? Why didn't Lakshmi just visit Janaka's home and bless him? Bhakti is an eternal engagement; hence it is also known as bhagavata-dharma. In every other area of endeavor there is a state of maturation, where the cherished fruit is received and then enjoyed for some length of time. Bhakti is divine love, so it can never stop. The greatest blessing, the most auspicious condition, is to be able to continue one's bhakti unabated. God's presence and the association of His dearmost devotees are considered universally auspicious for this very reason. Whoever comes in contact with such divine figures and knows how to make use of that association will find an eternal engagement that brings forth tremendous delights. The hungry man looking for a meal finds temporary auspiciousness by being fed a few morsels of food, but he who has a tree on his land that produces endless fruits is blessed every day. Having Lakshmi appear as a little girl in his kingdom gave Janaka a wish-fulfilling tree to fulfill all his desires.

Though he was Videha, Janaka immediately had affection for the little girl, deciding to raise her as his own daughter. Since she was found in the ground, he named her Sita. Goswami Tulsidas, in writing his Janaki Mangala, which describes how Sita's marriage would take place later on, remarks that Janaka is the most fortunate, and that there was never a king like him, nor will there be one like him in the future. He received Sita as a daughter, which meant that it was his obligation to smother her with parental affection. Who can imagine receiving such a benediction? People pray to have Lakshmi, or fortune, all the time, but if they misuse her benedictions, they can lose everything. Thereby Lakshmi can end up harming someone as well, if they are not deserving of her association.

On the other hand, someone like Janaka was so pious that he was desirous to love God and His devotees without hesitation. What better way to allow for that love to continue than by giving him Sita as a daughter? The Supreme Lord knows all. He watches the behavior of the pious and sees whether or not they are qualified for receiving full auspiciousness. In addition to raising Sita as his most precious daughter, on the day of her marriage Janaka would receive Narayana Himself, in the guise of a warrior prince named Rama, as a son-in-law.

Though Sita is Lakshmi and thus a divine figure, Janaka's love for her never stops. He found real auspiciousness by gaining the ability to practice bhakti as a way of life. To extract his heartfelt emotions, Lakshmi came herself to play the role of his daughter. The king made the most of the opportunity by increasing his bhakti more and more, so much so that he is today considered one of the twelve authorities on devotional service. As Tulsidas states, there is no king like him, and by the same token, for the pious there is no auspiciousness like that of Sita's association. Just remembering her, her devotion to Rama, and the gloriousness of her father, the mind can find peace, comfort and happiness in any situation.

VERSE 8

नृप लखि कुँअरि सयानि बोलि गुर परिजन।
करि मत रच्यौ स्वयंबर सिव धनु धरि पन॥8॥

nṛpa lakhi kumari sayāni boli gura parijana |
kari mata racyau svayambara siva dhanu dhari pana ||8||

"Seeing that his daughter was unmarried and at an age suitable for marriage, the king spoke with his guru and relatives to see what should be done. They advised him to plan a svayamvara, so the king decided upon a contest, where whoever could lift Lord Shiva's bow would marry his daughter." (8)

Essay - Avoiding Scorn

Rather than individually strive for specific good qualities, just by following the highest system of regulation, the pinnacle of spirituality, the only discipline that is all-inclusive, as an aftereffect, an almost insignificant result will be the possession of every noteworthy attribute. Try to find goodness on your own and you will be tested to the limit by the impiety of others. Try to be kind to others and you'll find someone who is so unkind that they'll make you question your sanity. Try to be honest and you'll be tempted to lie to achieve your cherished benefit. Once the failure arrives, the dedication to holding on to the quality in question will diminish. With bhakti-yoga, or devotional service, the only aim is to remain connected in consciousness with the Supreme Personality of Godhead. As a result of the divine trance, every activity gets dovetailed with service to Him, the original creator. Since the beneficiary is pure, the actions taken up by the devotees are pure as well. Since the actions will be pure, the qualities exuded will be top notch as well, as was shown by King Janaka, who was a king like no other.

How can a king have all good qualities? Especially in ancient times, were not kings required to fight with enemies? We know that King Yudhishthira, the eldest of the five Pandava brothers, felt tremendous remorse after emerging victorious in the Bharata War. Though he was abiding by dharma, or religiosity, and thus had no sin attached to his killing, he nevertheless felt terrible that millions of soldiers had lost their lives on account of his fighting. Indeed, violence can be so grotesque that many believe that fighting of any kind is sinful, that violence should never be an option.

"According to Vedic injunctions there are six kinds of aggressors: 1) a poison giver, 2) one who sets fire to the house, 3) one who attacks with deadly weapons, 4) one who plunders riches, 5) one who occupies another's land, and 6) one who kidnaps a wife. Such aggressors are at once to be killed, and no sin is incurred by killing such aggressors." (Shrila Prabhupada, Bhagavad-gita, 1.36 Purport)

Without knowing the original Personality of Godhead, the person most of the world refers to as God, these issues will perpetually remain a mystery. No guiding principle can be considered absolute because of duality. What is considered beneficial for one person may not be so for another. With respect to violence, while refraining from aggression is considered pious by the person not wanting to hurt others, the lack of force then allows for miscreants to run rampant with their evil ways. From their violence comes the loss of innocent life, with no one around to protect those needing protection. Thus what one person considers pious all of a sudden becomes the cause of supreme distress to others. How then can we say that any one system is universally applicable?

With the Supreme Lord, His association is the highest benefit for every living being. The soul is naturally meant to offer love, as is seen through the behavior of living entities. Regardless of the level of maturity or intelligence, that attraction to love will be there. With the Supreme Lord, you get the reservoir of pleasure, the storehouse of virtuous qualities. The guiding virtue, the one principle of dharma that has no duality, is to remain connected with God. Those who are actually connected with Him through a bona fide system exhibit all good qualities, even when their behavior may hint at duality to others.

King Janaka's dilemma taxing his brain was an example of a situation where there appeared to be duality but the right choice was made regardless. Though a ruler of a country wielding tremendous power, there was not a hint of sin in Janaka, who ruled over the kingdom of Mithila many thousands of years ago. He never did anything wrong, for he followed the advice of his gurus. The kshatriya, or warrior caste, is responsible for protecting; therefore they can use force when necessary. The gurus belong to the brahmana, or priestly class. A bona fide priest is a teacher of spirituality, giving advice to those looking to remain connected with God. The kshatriyas serve the Supreme Lord by protecting the innocent members of society. Through their work coupled with detachment to the outcome, they steadily ascend the planes of consciousness. It is the consciousness that determines one's disposition; happy or sad, elated or morose, transcendentally situated or materially entangled.

The soul is meant to be free. The soul is so tiny that it cannot even be measured or noticed with blunt instruments. Its presence is felt through the visible actions of an autonomous living being. The covering is what limits the soul's exhibition of qualities. For instance, there is no reason to sleep; it is just that the body demands it. The soul never sleeps; it is constantly active. The soul's inherent properties are nicely reviewed in the Bhagavad-gita, the Song of God spoken on the Battlefield of Kurukshetra to Yudhishthira's younger brother Arjuna.

Since Janaka followed the advice of his royal priests, the resultant reactions of his work did not belong to him. Moreover, these priests were God's representatives, so the king was essentially following the divine order. Through this system life becomes much easier, as the burden of responding to life's difficult questions can be shifted to others, people who are more than willing to accept the challenge because of their wisdom.

One particular dilemma had Janaka puzzled and worried at the same time. One day he found a baby girl while ploughing a field, which was to be cultivated for a sacrifice. He was childless at the time, and the girl was so precious that Janaka took her in as his own daughter. Even when he found the girl, he was a little worried that maybe he was doing the wrong thing by harboring affection for her and wanting to take her home. As if the authorities above knew what he was thinking, a voice suddenly appeared on the scene and told Janaka that this girl was indeed his daughter in all righteousness. His concerns vanished, Janaka named the girl Sita and then handed her over to his wife Sunayana, who raised her with the affection of a mother.

Though Janaka was trained in mysticism and knew how to stay detached from the senses, he was very fond of his daughter, whom he viewed as his prized possession. Sita's qualities are what won Janaka over. She was just as pious as her father, and she was learned in the scriptures and considered unmatched in beauty. Janaka wanted to personally protect her for the rest of her life, but that did not square with dharma. When she reached an age suitable for marriage, the pressure really started to mount on the king. For one who is deferent to dharma, having an unmarried daughter who is at an age suitable for marriage is considered very bad. For starters, it is the father's duty to ensure that his daughter is protected throughout her life. Marriage exists to uphold this principle. Secondly, others follow the example of great men.

"Whatever action is performed by a great man, common men follow in his footsteps. And whatever standards he sets by exemplary acts, all the world pursues." (Lord Krishna, Bhagavad-gita, 3.21)

If Janaka did not marry Sita off, he would invite scorn and ridicule from others. No longer would he be the pious king so dedicated to righteousness. Not that he cared himself for the glory, but Janaka knew that if he didn't follow dharma, then he could not expect the citizens to either. In this way the execution of his duties as a king would be hampered by his transgression of keeping Sita unmarried.

To add further complexity to the matter, Janaka didn't know who Sita's parents were, so he couldn't match her horoscope up to any prospective candidate's. The horoscope created by a brahmana at the time of the child's birth is considered flawless, and it predicts the qualities of the child. These qualities are then paired up during the search for a prospective spouse, with an ideal match foretelling that the marriage will go off well.

So, what did the king do? The secret to Janaka's success was his love for God, which up until this point he harbored only through connection to the impersonal feature known as Brahman. When he got Sita as a daughter, that love extended to the Supreme Lord's wife. Sita was actually an incarnation of goddess Lakshmi, who is Lord Narayana's eternal consort. Narayana is the Supreme Lord, whose name means the source of all men. The very same Narayana had descended to earth at the time as the prince of the Raghu dynasty, Lord Rama. As Lakshmi and Narayana can never remain separated for long, Janaka served as an instrument to unite the divine pair, though he had no idea what role he was playing.

His connection in yoga to Brahman and his love for God's wife guided Janaka along the proper path. He did not need to explicitly try to develop the qualities of righteousness, for that route is very difficult. Sita is the very embodiment of dharma, so just having love for her is enough to not only get you tremendous fortune, but also to imbibe the divine qualities in you. Worried about facing ridicule from his family and losing Sita as a daughter, Janaka made the right decision by approaching his gurus and relatives. They advised him to hold a svayamvara, or self-choice ceremony. This way the choice wouldn't necessarily be made by Janaka. Svayamvaras were rarely held, only in those circumstances where the daughters were considered really exceptional by their fathers.

The svayamvara was a good idea, but Janaka needed to decide what kind it would be. He didn't want Sita to marry just anyone. Again, he tapped into his love for God and His associates to find the answer. Many years back, Janaka's family had received an extremely heavy bow belonging to Lord Shiva. Mahadeva is Narayana's number one devotee. Lord Shiva is himself so powerful that he destroys the entire cosmic manifestation at the appropriate time, and yet he is so humble that he prefers to just sit in quiet meditation and recite Narayana's name of Rama. Though this bow was impossible to move, Sita had one day lifted it with ease when she was a child. Therefore Janaka's beloved daughter was already connected to the bow.

"Having obtained the bow, my truthful father first invited all the princes of the world to an assembly of great rulers of men, and spoke to them as such." (Sita Devi speaking to Anasuya, Valmiki Ramayana, Ayodhya Kand, 118.41)

The decision was that the svayamvara would host a contest to lift Lord Shiva's bow. In this way the ceremony would honor Mahadeva, keep the relatives happy, follow the advice of the gurus, and at the same time make it extremely difficult to find a suitable match. Who in the world was going to lift this bow? Even if everyone from around the world came and couldn't lift it, at least Janaka would be off the hook. He would know then that no man was worthy of marrying his daughter, which was his inclination anyway.

What Janaka didn't know was that his decision borne out of tremendous love for God would bring to him the fruit of his existence. The result of penance, austerity, sacrifice and charity performed in the devotional mood is that one eventually gains the audience of the Supreme Personality of Godhead, the person to whom such kind acts are dedicated. Janaka already had one piece of the puzzle in Sita, and from the svayamvara he would get the other half, the Supreme Lord in the form of Shri Rama. The savior of fallen souls, the kindest living entity there is, the glorious husband of the goddess of fortune and the protector of the surrendered souls would arrive in Janakpur at Sita's svayamvara and effortlessly raise Mahadeva's bow; thus giving the world at the time and countless future generations a glorious occasion to sing about, study and remember constantly. As God's glory naturally extends to His immediate family and associates, the person who was responsible for that blessed event also earned high praise and an exalted position. Because of his devotion, King Janaka is known today as one of the twelve authorities on devotional service. His example is the best to follow, as there was no king like him in the past, nor will there be one like him in the future.

CHAND 1

पनु धरेउ सिव धनु रचि स्वयंबर अति रुचिर रचना बनी।
जनु प्रगटि चतुरानन देखाई चतुरता सब अपनी।।
पुनि देस देस सँदेस पठयउ भूप सुनि सुख पावहीं।
सब साजि साजि समाज राजा जनक नगरहिं आवहीं।।१।।

panu dhare'u siva dhanu raci svayambara ati rucira racanā banī |
janu pragaṭi caturānana dekhā'ī caturatā saba apanī ||
puni desa desa saṁdesa paṭhaya'u bhūpa suni sukha pāvahiṁ |
saba sāji sāji samāja rājā janaka nagarahiṁ āvahiṁ ||1||

"After the king declared the contest relating to Lord Shiva's bow, the svayamvara preparations started. The place became so beautiful that by looking at it one would think that Lord Brahma himself had created it, as if to show off every one of his abilities." (Chanda 1.1)

"Thereafter, in country after country the message of the king was sent, upon hearing which everyone became happy. Together with their caravans stocked with provisions, every community then came to King Janaka's city." (Chand 1.2)

Essay - Look What the Creator Has Done

As the creator, Lord Brahma can generate something simply by thinking of it. As we all trace our ancestry back to him, his ability in the department of creating is stupendous. Just as when we see something so amazing that we think that God Himself had created it, followers of the Vedic tradition, knowing that Brahma is charged with the task of creating by the Supreme Lord Himself, make the comparison to Brahma whenever they see something very beautiful. The grounds for a famous wedding many years back were so wonderfully decorated that it looked like Brahma was showing off, that he had gone overboard in making things look so beautiful. Even if he had, there would have been good reason for it. The princess being married at this ceremony was the goddess of fortune herself, and her father was the most pious ruler. This marriage ceremony thus deserved the most beautiful setting with unforgettably elegant surroundings.

Why not just have a small marriage? Why all the pomp? The king hosting the ceremony certainly had no attachment to royal fanfare. Known throughout the world for his expertise of meditational yoga, King Janaka lived without attachment. Dispassion is known as vairagya in Sanskrit and it is considered an opulence. A noteworthy characteristic doesn't necessarily have to revolve around the possession of a physical object or ability. Beauty, wealth and strength refer to physical possessions borne of the type of body one resides in. Renunciation is included in the opulence category because it is very difficult to acquire, and it proves to be beneficial. Typically, it takes many repeated attempts into a material endeavor before one realizes the futility of the effort. Only after recognizing how much effort it takes to find paltry happiness in so many material affairs does one even think of giving them up.

The drunkard swears to never drink again when they do something stupid or when they get so sick that they feel like they are going to die. The person overindulging in food vows to go on a diet to enhance their appearance, which will ideally improve their health at the same time. The person who has a health club membership and never goes swears that they'll never join a gym again after paying for so many months. Life is a pendulum of acceptance and rejection, with the initial impulse being acceptance. If the proper justification for avoiding the inevitably rejected activities remains unknown, acceptance will surely follow in the near future; thereby leading to a repeat of the same bitter taste.

Renunciation is also an opulence because one who possesses it can limit their interaction with things that they don't need. The senses are temporary after all, and they can be influenced by the mind. Through the efforts of the mind, the happiness we think we'll receive from a particular material object's association can actually be secured without any effort. In addition, through renunciation contact with the inhibiting forces of matter is strictly limited, which automatically creates a somewhat pleasant condition. If it is extremely hot outside and I decide to remain within the home to avoid the heat, I automatically gain some relief.

"The demoniac, taking shelter of insatiable lust, pride and false prestige, and being thus illusioned, are always sworn to unclean work, attracted by the impermanent [asat]." (Lord Krishna, Bhagavad-gita, 16.10)

Despite his world famous renunciation, Janaka was not beyond happiness or attachment. The difference was that his attachment was on the sat, or the permanent. Spirit is permanent while matter is not. Select worshipable personalities in the spiritual sky, who are intimately tied to the Supreme Lord's service, are also eternal. Harboring affection for them is never harmful. The more one is renounced from material life, the more they can relish the interaction with God and with His closest associates.

The supreme elation Janaka felt when he found a baby girl one day while ploughing a field proves this fact. The girl was the goddess of fortune, Shri Lakshmi, appearing on earth to correspond with the pastimes of her husband Narayana, who had appeared as Lord Rama. God exists, even if we may not recognize His presence. In the Vedic tradition, He is described by names which assess His position and give people a way to address Him and interact with His features. Narayana means the source of all men. Though Brahma is the creator, even he is Narayana's son. Since Brahma took birth from the stem growing from the lotus-like navel of Narayana, Brahma is often referred to as the self-create.

The source of men makes trips to the manifested realm, the place we currently occupy, every now and then to share His resplendence with others. Just as Narayana retains His spiritual features when appearing on earth, Lakshmi remains the brilliant and beautiful wife of the Lord wherever she goes. Though Janaka did not know who this baby girl was, he immediately harbored affection for her. So much for his detachment. He took her in as his daughter and raised her under religious principles, considering her his most cherished possession.

Attachment is only harmful when it leads to a fall from grace, a deviation from the righteous path. For instance, if I have such an attachment to my dog that I forgo attending school or work in order to spend time with it, obviously my affectionate feelings are getting in the way of my important obligations. If I love to eat and sleep so much that I don't pay attention to regulation, that I go so far as to eat unclean foods which carry bad karma and sleep through the important moments in life, obviously there will be negative consequences in the future.

The primary objective of the human form of body is to become God conscious. Whatever way allows us to go forward in reaching that goal should be tried, though there are authorized methods passed down since time immemorial to help keep one on the straightened path. Making up paths for self-realization is always dangerous, because the human mind is incapable of conceiving of the Supreme Lord's position and features on its own. Renunciation is a key practice because the strongest attachments are formed with those things which have no relation to the ultimate goal of God consciousness.

Janaka turned out to be clever in this regard. He used his attachment to Sita to remain even more dedicated to piety. He combined both forces - his attachment to Sita and the requirement that he remain committed to religious principles. He was a king after all, so people would follow his lead. If the love for his daughter caused him to just make up rules and regulations, to forgo the pressing responsibilities in life, then the citizens would follow suit and chaos would result.

Part of his duties as a king and father required Janaka to get Sita married when she reached the appropriate age. Not wanting to give her up and not knowing who her birth parents were, Janaka decided to hold a svayamvara, or self-choice ceremony. Sita would be wedded to whoever could lift Lord Shiva's bow. This compromise satisfied all the parties involved, including Janaka. He figured that no one could lift the heavy bow, and if that was the case then no one was worthy of his daughter's hand in marriage. If someone could lift the bow, then fate had obviously decided that they should marry Sita.

The dispassionate king could have easily held a subdued ceremony with no pomp, but it was his duty as a leader of men to host a grand event. Why would people want to attend a gathering that wasn't elegantly decorated, especially if the host had the ability to spend loads of money? Plus, this event was a ceremony involving the goddess of fortune. Lakshmi is the giver of wealth and opulence, and that gift is meant to further a purpose. Lakshmi is always with Narayana, trying to please Him in every way. This is the secret of devotional service; that by following the principles of religion aimed at pleasing God, the person offering the service finds the highest type of pleasure as well.

Lakshmi's gifts are meant to be used for her service and the service of her husband. Therefore no amount of money was too much to spend on Sita's svayamvara. No amount of decorating was overdoing it, for the beautiful things in this world are but God's gift to us, to show us what the Lord is capable of creating. The scene of the svayamvara was so beautiful that one couldn't help but think of Lord Brahma. Just as we say things like, "They broke the mold", when describing people and objects of amazing and unique beauty, Goswami Tulsidas tells us that an onlooker at the svayamvara would think that Brahma was trying to show off, that creating this world and populating it with creatures weren't enough for him. He wasn't satisfied with being the original creator that everyone knew. Rather, he would reserve his greatest talents for this wonderful event held in Janaka's kingdom.

The decorations turned out to be worth it, as Lord Rama would come and lift the bow in front of a large assembly of onlookers. As a match made in heaven, Sita and Rama would be married through Janaka's plan. The king's attachment for her earned him God as a son-in-law, all the while making him even more famous for his dedication to piety and virtue. The time spent decorating his kingdom for the svayamvara was not in vain, as the scene was so memorable that people still talk about it today. Sita and Rama's wedding was like none other, and the host of the occasion, Maharaja Janaka, was one of a kind as well.

Essay - Hitting The Road

"Did you hear the news? The famed King Janaka has announced that he is holding a svayamvara for his cherished daughter's marriage. Whoever can lift up the illustrious bow originally belonging to Mahadeva, the greatest of the gods, will win Sita as a wife. We must go immediately, as this will bode well for our family. Not only will we be linked to Janaka Maharaja, who is known throughout the three worlds for his piety and dedication to virtue, but we will win acclaim for having lifted a bow that is famous for its incomparable weight. Ready all the provisions and stock them in the carts. We haven't a moment to lose. Let us bring our entire clan to the sacred land of Janakpur, where we will vie for the beloved princess' hand. An opportunity like this shouldn't be missed."

That people from around the world would gather to one place for a particular event is not out of the ordinary. Companies hold conventions to show off their latest products, and widely anticipated annual sporting events are sometimes held in one particular city. People who are interested in the subject matter, in the topic at hand, will make the necessary arrangements to travel to these destinations, be it by automobile, train, or plane. The idea is that if the event is important enough, no amount of travel is too much. For the really important events, one needs to be there in person, to not only enjoy the scene, but to then later say that they were there. Many thousands of years ago, the vow of a famous king caught the attention of the many princes around the world. Just hearing about the king's contest made them get ready for the trip of a lifetime.

The road trip is nice because you can get away. Prison life is considered a punishment not only for the fact that you are held in a house against your will, but you also have limited engagements. Variety is the mother of enjoyment, so if you take to the opposite extreme, monotony, the mind will feel trapped, so much so that any break in the routine will feel liberating. Even for the human being living outside the confines of a prison, life can get to be quite repetitive, especially if one is mature and working at a job that they attend regularly. In the larger scheme, the material universe itself is considered by enlightened minds to be an enlarged prison, with the confines spread further apart but having the same punishing prohibition on action, which is especially effective on those who are not spiritually conscious.

The road trip is best enjoyed when it comes about unexpectedly. On a whim you decide to pack up your stuff and travel somewhere by car, not having any set plans. Reaching the intended destination is the stated purpose to the trip, but the fun comes more from having a break from the grind, getting to escape from the doldrums of your stale life if but even for a weekend. The family vacations provide this sort of opportunity as well, as visiting a foreign city allows you to escape your accustomed surroundings and experience new things.

For the important trips, you'll take items that you need, such as clothing, toiletries, and any gifts you would like to give to the people that will be hosting you at your final destination. The spirit of renunciation is more prominent in males, so they can get away with travelling with very little, just carrying the bare essentials. Not only are the females mindful of what they need for their own beautification, but they will consider what should be given to the people being visited as well. Even if you are going to visit just one person, they may have friends and family members around them. The mindful wife will remind the husband to pack gifts for those people, even if the husband is annoyed at having to bring extra luggage. If you're travelling by plane, you will have to check-in the extra bags, which means that your items will not always be by your side. When not in your sight, there is the increased risk of the items getting lost. In addition, you'll always have to carry those items around during transit.

The extra burden is worth it if you really want to please the people you are visiting. Also, if you're travelling with a lot of people, the heavier load is inevitable. With one event in particular many thousands of years back, families from around the world were preparing for a terrific road trip. These weren't just ordinary families either. Picture every head of state congregating in one meeting place. A head of state travels with pomp wherever they go. Just as the President of the United States has the Secret Service and other entourage following him in his trips, the kings of ancient times would bring their royal families with them to important meetings. The family included not only wives and children, but also servants, priests, and important members of the community.

The news of this event was so appreciated that everyone in the notified communities wanted to go. The caravans for each royal family were filled with provisions; everything needed for daily maintenance in the foreign land. Relatives and other important community members were part of the travelling party as well. Such preparation only takes place when the event brings delight to the heart. People flock to pilgrimage sites on important holy days of the year so they can connect with God, to have the chance to think about Him and accumulate spiritual merits. If not for the relation to the Supreme Lord, these sites would not receive the attention they get.

Though this particular event many thousands of years ago didn't openly relate to God, in the background it did. Janaka Maharaja was holding a ceremony to give away his daughter Sita in marriage. He had struggled with the decision up to this point, because he held great affection for her and he didn't know who her birth parents were. Sita was Janaka's adopted daughter; he found her as a baby when he was ploughing a field. Though a voice from the sky told him that the baby girl was his child in all righteousness, or dharma, Janaka still didn't know any of the astrological signs at the time of her birth, which meant that he couldn't get an accurate horoscope made that would be used to find a suitable husband.

Not able to use matching qualities determined from the time of birth, Janaka did one better. He had been given an amazing bow belonging to Lord Shiva. This bow was so heavy that no one could lift it. Lord Shiva is one of the famous divine figures of the Vedic tradition. While in the Puranas reserved for those in the mode of ignorance, or the lowest mode of material nature, Mahadeva is sometimes described as the Supreme Lord, he is an elevated living entity who is very powerful. His greatest strength is his firm conviction to always chant the holy name of Lord Rama, who is none other than God Himself. This bow belonging to Shiva was meant to be lifted by that same Rama. Therefore wherever there is Mahadeva, the Supreme Lord can never be too far away.

Because of the bow's origin, the contest relating to its lifting automatically had a religious significance. Add to the fact that Janaka was famous for his piety and renunciation from material attachment and you get an event that couldn't be missed. After deciding on the rules of the svayamvara, or self-choice marriage ceremony, news was sent out to country after country. Hearing of the contest made people happy, for not only would they get to witness history by seeing if someone could lift Mahadeva's bow, they would also get to see Janaka and his daughter.

What they didn't know was that Sita was the goddess of fortune, Rama's wife in the spiritual world. Shri Rama is the Supreme Lord who periodically incarnates on earth to enact pastimes. During Janaka's time He had appeared as the son of King Dasharatha of Ayodhya. Rama's family wasn't part of the clan that travelled to Janakpur because Rama and His younger brother Lakshmana at the time were escorting the sage Vishvamitra in the forests. Since he had been harassed by terrorists capable of assuming false guises, the sage wanted Rama, an expert bow warrior, to protect him for a bit, to alleviate the distresses caused by the rangers of the night. Since Rama was the eldest of four sons, Dasharatha was not going to send anyone in His place to contest for Sita's hand. When following strict Vedic regulations, it is considered a sin for a younger brother to get married before an older one does.

The guests eagerly travelling with their families and paraphernalia to Janakpur would get to see Rama nonetheless. In this way they were actually making a pilgrimage trek, one that is still followed to this day. Vishvamitra, seemingly by chance, would bring Rama and Lakshmana to Janakpur. After many princes had failed to even move Shiva's bow, Rama would step up and lift it without a problem, giving the onlookers a sight worth seeing. The beautiful Shri Rama would be reunited with Lakshmi Devi, Janaka's daughter, in front of the fortunate attendees.

Because of Janaka's position and the outstanding qualities of his daughter, when people first heard the news of the svayamvara, they were immediately pleased and decided that they had to make the journey to Janakpur. They were certainly very fortunate to be there that day, but this doesn't mean that sincere souls looking for spiritual awakening and transcendental pleasure today can't have the same benefit. Goswami Tulsidas composed his Janaki Mangala specifically so that the people of his time, and many future generations as well, could focus the mind on the marriage ceremony of Sita and Rama. Hearing of the event is as good as being there, such is the absolute nature of the Supreme Lord. Just thinking of Janaka and his immense love for his daughter that wasn't even biologically his brings so much pleasure to the heart. In one sense harboring parental affection for an adopted child indicates an even stronger love than that given to a child one is biologically linked to. It is a matter of duty to love your own children, but that duty isn't inherently there with someone else's child. Janaka found Sita and raised her as if she were his own daughter, his most prized possession. The same king that was famous for his dispassion was also appreciated for his affection.

There is no contradiction, for Janaka lived a spiritual existence,. Affection for Sita never goes in vain. Her transcendental features drew people to Janaka's kingdom that famous day many thousands of years ago. That attraction would prove fruitful for the residents of Janakpur, the attendees of the ceremony, the families involved in the marriage that would come, and the many sincere listeners who would recreate the sequence of events many times in their minds in the years to follow. The royal families from around the world hit the road to see the wedding of a lifetime, and what they took away from that event was the vision of Sita and Rama, the sight for sore eyes, the union of God and His pleasure potency. In all the worlds, one cannot find a better vision than this.

VERSE 9

रूप सील बय बंस बिरुद बल दल भले।
मनहुँ पुरंदर निकर उतरि अवनिहिं चले।।9।।

rūpa sīla baya bansa biruda bala dala bhale |
manahuṁ purandara nikara utari avanihiṁ cale ||9||

"The princes and their armies were beautiful, chivalrous, and of good age, family and birth, looking as if Indra had descended to earth and was marching towards Janakpur." (9)

Essay - Only The Best

With an arranged marriage, the union that takes place is really between two families. The bride and groom hardly know one another beforehand, so to foretell whether or not the relationship will stand the test of time, the standings of the two families involved are assessed. If it has been proved in countless past generations that such marriages worked, that the character of the support system was properly suited to the time and circumstance, then there is an increased likelihood that the same characteristics will be passed on to the present day participants. Even if the values weren't explicitly instilled, just growing up in a pious environment can do wonders. One actually teaches more with the example they set than with the words of instruction they offer. Man, being born ignorant, is always unsure of the right move to take. To settle doubts, others are observed, for if they follow a particular route and don't get harmed by it, then there is less of a risk in following their example. One event in particular saw the noblest families from around the world ready to accept the daughter of a famous king, whose qualities were so sublime that he was respected in every land.

Why were there multiple families involved? As these events took place during the Treta Yuga, all marriages then were arranged by the parents. Not to be mistaken for an artificial way of suppressing the natural desires for romantic interaction, the marriages were arranged to stay in line with dharma. The Vedic term "dharma" can be translated to mean religion, but its root meaning is an essential characteristic. The dharma of fire is heat and light, of water wetness, of grass green color, and so on. As objects can have more than one property, that which is foremost becomes its dharma. There is also no question of something assuming a dharma or rejecting it. Dharma always stays with the object; it defines its existence.

For the living beings, their dharma is the penchant to serve. To know why this penchant exists, one must know their real identity. The soul is the identifying aspect within every life form, as the temporary coverings are just that: temporary. As shirts, pants and coats can be put on and taken off, so the gross collection of material elements can be accepted, manipulated, and then eventually discarded, with the identity of the individual remaining unchanged.

When these forms are accepted, the dharma of the individual gets covered up, sort of like putting a shade on a bright lamp. The existence of the soul never ceases, so the dharma is always there. Depending on the type of dress accepted, knowledge of that characteristic may be forgotten to varying degrees. If we have a knife and think that it should be used as a spoon or fork, obviously we will not be following the proper guidelines. The knife is very sharp for a reason. It is meant to cut things. If it is used as a utensil to place food in the mouth, there is every chance of the tongue being cut or some other accident happening which carries negative consequences.

The spirit soul trapped in a material body similarly has a constitutional purpose. Through ignorance only the living being accepts their temporary forms to be their true identity. They see the gross collection of material elements on others to represent their identities as well. Sex life is based entirely on this illusion. We see someone of the opposite sex and measure their attractiveness based on their outward features, but what we don't see is that they are a spirit soul at the core. Their collection of blood, pus and mucus will gradually morph over the years to the point that they may cease to be attractive, but their identity will not change throughout the process.

What is the harm in succumbing to this illusion? Just as the knife is meant to cut, the soul is meant to serve. That service is meant for a higher entity, one who is not illusioned by the material elements. Through these truths, we get one definition of God and His standing. God is just our word to describe Him, but He can also be referred to as the Supreme Soul, for He is spirit just like us but without a tendency towards ignorance. The human life is considered the most valuable because it carries with it the potential to develop consciousness to the point that the proper identity of the individual and the proper set of activities, namely the directing of the service mentality toward the appropriate area, can be revealed.

From this information, the ultimate mission in life becomes discernable. Dharma accepts an additional definition: a type of maintenance system having guiding principles, where regulations are instilled that help the individual understand the mission in life and achieve it. It is not that everyone will be open to immediately accepting all the truths of spiritual life passed on by the Vedas. Therefore there are scales of dharma, meant to target the varying levels of intelligence. The idea is that by following the more streamlined systems of regulation, one can gradually ascend the chain of knowledge. This ascendency continues even into the next life. Therefore, should someone never learn about the soul in this life, if they follow the prescribed regulations for their order, which is their occupational duty tied to their behavioral characteristics, they can find themselves in a better position in the next life.

The next life is simply a new demarcation of time. We could even think of each new day as a new life, for the time continuum hasn't changed with the rising of the sun in the morning; only our perspective on the timeline changes. Since time is continuous, even within one's lifetime the same spiritual advancement can be made. Illusion is the largest stumbling block towards assuming one's real dharma. Illusion's strongest force is sex life, especially the kind which is not based on religious principles. Therefore ideally from the very beginning, when children are young, the tendency towards illicit sex is checked by the parents through the marriage institution.

"I am the strength of the strong, devoid of passion and desire. I am sex life which is not contrary to religious principles, O Lord of the Bharatas [Arjuna]." (Lord Krishna, Bhagavad-gita, 7.11)

In ancient times, the pious kings were especially conscious of the need to marry off their daughters when they reached the appropriate age. If you have an abundance of unmarried women in society, illicit sex will result. From illicit sex comes an unwanted and unloved population. From lack of loving attention comes a society full of rogues who have no culture in even the basic standards of decency.

The women get exploited through this system as well, for the men can easily get sex from them and not be responsible for their welfare.

The ancient marriages weren't that complicated to arrange. You get an expert brahmana, or priest, and have them review the child's astrological signs from the exact time of their birth. The constellation of stars at any particular given moment can be either auspicious or inauspicious. Any person taking birth at one of these times can thus have their future predicted, including what type of character they will grow up to have. From the different characteristics ascertained, matches would be made. It wasn't that just any boy and girl were suitable matches for marriage. The arrangement had to be "in the cards" so to speak, astrologically compatible.

One king faced a dilemma in this area. He had a most precious daughter, who was so beautiful, kind, sweet, compassionate and virtuous that the king didn't want to let her go. The daughter essentially accepts a new family after marriage, leaving her father and his family bereft of her association. This daughter was special because the king had been childless prior to her appearance. She was considered the greatest fortune in his life, because she appeared from nowhere to give him and his family tremendous happiness.

This young girl wasn't the king's biological daughter. He had found her one day while ploughing a field. Thinking it was appropriate to protect and take care of her, the king really wanted to take her home and raise her as his daughter. As if the higher authorities read his mind, a voice in the sky appeared on the scene and told the king that this girl was indeed his daughter in all righteousness. The first issue was now resolved. The king could take the girl home and raise her as his daughter.

She proved to be a perfect fit in his family. The king's name was Janaka, and he was one in a long line of pious rulers named Janaka. This Janaka was especially devoted to dharma and was famous throughout the world for being above the influence of the senses. Though he was married and ruling over a kingdom, he was not attached to any of his duties. He met every obligation as a matter of protocol, not caring for the result one way or the other. These are the godly principles, which are even lauded by Lord Krishna in the Bhagavad-gita.

"Therefore, without being attached to the fruits of activities, one should act as a matter of duty; for by working without attachment, one attains the Supreme." (Lord Krishna, Bg. 3.19)

The daughter was named Sita because she came out of the ground, not having biological parents. When it was time for Sita's marriage, Janaka was torn inside. He felt like a wealthy man about to become poor, for the goddess of fortune was going to leave his family. Sita was really Lakshmi Devi appearing on earth to take part in the pastimes of the Supreme Lord, who had appeared as Lord Rama in the family of the Raghus. Janaka knew none of this, but he didn't need to. From her qualities he could tell that Sita was special.

In addition to the trepidation over losing Sita, Janaka faced another problem. He didn't know who Sita's parents were, nor did he know the astrological signs from the time of her birth. Therefore how could he find a suitable match for her? Yet if he kept Sita unmarried, he would invite scorn from his family members and also the community that he vowed to protect. If the king could keep his daughter unmarried, why shouldn't everyone else then follow the same example?

After consulting with his priests and family members, the king arrived on a compromise. He had been given an amazing bow belonging to Lord Shiva, the worshipable figure of the Vedic tradition charged with destroying the creation at the appropriate time. The bow was so heavy that it seemed impossible to lift. Janaka vowed that if any prince from around the world could lift it, they would get Sita's hand in marriage. Through their strength they would prove to be the fittest man capable of protecting his beloved daughter.

The announcement of the king's vow went out across every country. The news was so happily accepted that royal clans gathered their things and made the trek to Janakpur, Janaka's city where the contest was being held. In the above referenced verse from the Janaki Mangala, Goswami Tulsidas says that the procession of the armies was so amazing that it looked like Lord Indra had descended to earth and was marching towards Janakpur. Indra is the king of the heavenly planets, where the residents live longer and more materially enriched lives. Indra is also responsible for fighting against the evil elements of the world. Since the beginning of time the devoted class, the suras, and the non-devoted, the asuras, have clashed. Indra is the most powerful of the demigods; hence he is their leader. His royal army resembles no other; therefore the comparison was appropriate.

It is also said that the princes arriving were beautiful and chivalrous, or disciplined. Sita was the most beautiful woman in the world, so a beautiful prince would be a fit match. She was also Janaka's daughter, which meant that her level of piety was extremely high. Though Sita wasn't formally educated, her knowledge of the Vedas was outstanding, as she observed the Vedic rites and rituals conducted in her father's kingdom while growing up. Simply through listening to the words of her parents and the brahmanas, she acquired high knowledge.

The princes coming to Janakpur were also of a good age, family and ancestry. Lord Shiva's bow would not be easy to lift. It would take more than just brute strength to raise it. One had to have a good family background, where they were trained properly in the military arts. The bow belonged to Lord Shiva, and it was obviously heavy for a reason. A prince had to be of the proper age to try to lift the bow. Men who are of the proper age for marriage typically have the highest levels of strength they will have in their life. Even in sports, it is seen that there is a typical age when the athlete's performance is at its peak. If they are too young, they may have a lot of energy but not enough strength or dexterity. If the athlete is too old, they may no longer have the strength and coordination to compete at the highest levels. These princes arriving were of just the right age.

The princes were of a good family and came from good ancestry. It would seem like these things shouldn't have mattered, but to marry the daughter of King Janaka, one had to come from a good dynasty, for the two families would be united through the marriage. The description of the armies arriving serves as a reminder that the most respected royal families came to Janakpur for the contest, showing how much Janaka was favored and how coveted Sita's hand in marriage was. A prince coming from a good dynasty and having a link to many famous kings from the past obviously will not want to marry just any princess. The girl should come from a family equally as respected, if not more so.

The scene in Janakpur that fateful day was legendary. While many of the most respected and capable princes came to try to win Sita's hand in marriage, just as the living entities have a particular dharma, so do the Lord's closest associates. Sita is God's eternal consort, which means that she can never be with any man except the Supreme Lord. During this time on earth, the external events were manipulated in just the right way so as to allow the goddess of fortune's husband to arrive on the scene and win her hand in marriage. Lord Rama, though not part of the giant procession of armies, would arrive nonetheless, coming without any fanfare or pomp. He would come as the guest of the sage Vishvamitra, who was travelling the forests at the time, with Rama and His younger brother Lakshmana acting as his protection.

Though they didn't come to Janakpur for the purpose of participating in the contest, Janaka was so invigorated by the vision of the two brothers that he allowed Rama to make an attempt anyway. At Vishvamitra's request, Rama would step up, raise Shiva's bow, and be garlanded by Sita as the victor. His family, ancestry, beauty and chivalry were unmatched, for He is the Supreme Lord that never ceases to be the most fortunate living entity in the world. He proved His worthiness to have Sita as a wife on that day. All the famous kings and princes from around the world were there to witness the history, the marriage of Sita and Rama, which is still talked about, honored, worshiped, and remembered to this day.

VERSE 10

दानव देव निसाचर किंनर अहिगन।
सुनि धरि-धरि नृप बेष चले प्रमुदित मन॥10॥

dānava deva nisācara kinnara ahigana |
suni dhari-dhari nṛpa beṣa cale pramudita mana ||10||

"After hearing the news, Danavas, Devas, Rakshasas, Kinnaras and so many snakes are very happily arriving dressed up as kings." (10)

Esay - A Red Carpet Event

There's a hot new club in town. Everyone's talking about it, raving about the ambience, how enjoyable it is to go inside, and especially how exclusive the club is. So many people want to get in, but not every person is allowed. From the line formed behind the velvet rope the bouncer can just pick someone on a whim to let in. Dress yourself up right and you just might pass the test. Curiosity is so aroused that even people who are not interested in night clubs manage to make their way out, hoping to be allowed in. Those under the age limit show their fake identifications, hoping to fool the bouncer.

A long time ago one particular event was so famous that it attracted humans and other species as well around the world. The place, time, circumstance, people involved, and event itself were of the purest variety. As it was considered a tremendous blessing just to be able to attend, people came from far and wide, matching their outward appearance to the occasion. For their efforts they would be witness to the most splendid marriage ever seen on this earth.

Why the attention given? What was so unique about this event? Why not just attend a local wedding, one involving friends or family members living in close proximity? Why the need to travel so far? Obviously a marriage is not a rare occasion, but based on the qualities of the participants, the event's significance can increase. With this particular wedding, the groom was not known beforehand. Rather, the king holding the ceremony vowed to give away his precious daughter to whoever could lift an extremely heavy bow, which initially belonged to Lord Shiva, the greatest among the gods.

The king was famous. Known as Janaka throughout the world, even the miscreant class of men respected him. It takes a lot to gain the honor and respect of those who are themselves lacking it, but Janaka managed to reach the height of stature. Virtue is its own reward, especially when it is tied to dharma, or the occupational duties governing man's conduct. Rather than speculate on who God is and whether or not He is just a manmade concoction, the Vedas remove the doubt through authorized information. Even if one isn't prone to accepting the truths about the Personality of Godhead and His merciful spiritual form, if they just follow the prescribed guidelines given for human behavior, they can make tremendous progress. Just by following virtue, adhering to religious principles, irrespective of your own realizations others will respect you.

The reprobates, thieves, cheaters and plagues on society get the opposite treatment. Their reputations are based on their behavior which goes against dharma. Everyone must follow some philosophy, which then determines their accepted system of maintenance. Under mental speculation, the human being is walking around a dark room not knowing what anything is. He and his fellow man operating under the same mindset can only speculate about their environment and thus never reach a proper conclusion. Under the veil of darkness, there is no such thing as good or bad, pious or impious. The thief's dharma is given as much credence as the honest man's, for both are based on mental speculation and not authority.

"Even kings like Janaka and others attained the perfectional stage by performance of prescribed duties. Therefore, just for the sake of educating the people in general, you should perform your work." (Lord Krishna, Bhagavad-gita, 3.20)

Janaka was not in the dark. Following the prescribed duties assigned to the royal order, he worked whenever work was called for and stayed renounced the rest of the time. This amazing ability earned him mention in the Bhagavad-gita, the Song of God sung by Lord Krishna, who is the Supreme Personality, the leader of worshipable figures, the energy behind the movements of the creation. The mental speculators can eventually conclude that there is an energy driving the forces of nature and the actions of man, yet they fail to assign intelligence to that energy. Moreover, since they are tiny fragments of that energy as a whole, they consider everyone to be their own gods, or ishvaras.

Ironically enough, the fact stumbled upon by the mental speculators is quickly revealed to those following dharma. The individual soul is indeed ishvara, or a controller, but he is not the original or even supreme controller. God can be defined by saying that He is the supreme ishvara, Parameshvara. One who knows this understands that they can perform their prescribed duties without attachment, for Parameshvara is responsible for the results of action. Though the giant collection of energy is more powerful than we are and thereby represents a force impossible to control, we still must act. Even when sitting quietly in an empty room, the mind continues to operate. To harness that potential for action, we need some type of system of maintenance, which will properly guide our behavior and remove hesitation.

We can continue to speculate on what type of behavior to follow, but whatever is produced through the mental effort will be flawed because the ultimate conclusion is not known. On the other hand, by following dharma, which is rooted in the conclusion that God is the Supreme Lord, full of form, who is meant to be the intimate friend of every living entity, hesitancy is removed in action and auspiciousness results. Janaka, just by following dharma, one day found a beloved baby girl in the ground. Naming her Sita and raising her as his daughter, he felt like the most fortunate man in the world. What he didn't know was that the goddess of fortune herself, Lakshmi Devi, was Sita and had come as his daughter. His inclination was correct, even if he didn't know the basis for that correctness.

Others around the world knew of both Sita and Janaka. The king was hesitant to marry her off because he didn't want to lose her and also because he wasn't sure he could find a suitable match. He couldn't use a horoscope comparison because he didn't know Sita's biological parents or if she even had any. Just as the Supreme Lord is original, formless and eternal, so the same properties apply to His eternal consorts. By formless we mean without a material form that is subject to defects. It is difficult for the conditioned human being to imagine that God can appear on earth and emerge from someone's womb, for as soon as you say someone is a person it means that they are flawed. "To ere is human" after all, so to describe God as being personal seems to indicate that He is flawed.

Spiritual attributes are difficult to comprehend; therefore extensive training in a bona fide spiritual discipline is required. Those anxious to see God, to see the person they think is invisible, are advised to first try to realize the presence of the soul within their own body. Without knowing that we are spirit soul and not body, how are we going to understand what formless actually means when applied to God? We need external light to be able to see the objects around us; otherwise we are clueless as to our surroundings. If we need light to see normal objects, why wouldn't we need assistance in seeing God? Moreover, just because the lights are turned out doesn't mean that the surrounding objects disappear. In the same way, not being able to see God with our paltry vision doesn't mean that He is invisible, not able to be seen, or lacking spiritual attributes.

As she had no father and mother, Sita's marriage was difficult to arrange. Through consultation with his priests and relatives, Janaka decided to hold a svayamvara, or self-choice ceremony. When kings from around the world heard the news, they flocked to Tirahuta, Janaka's capital city. The event was so eagerly anticipated and talked about that even others outside the human species decided they would try to attend. In addition to the human form, there are millions of other possible combinations of material elements that can house a conditioned spirit soul. An ant, dog, cow, fly, bird, and beast are all equal constitutionally, but we see differences based on their outward appearances. There is not just one form of the human species either; there is variety within variety. The human species in general is considered the most auspicious form of body to accept, as it carries the highest potential for intelligence. With first class knowledge comes dedication to a first class system of maintenance. A topnotch system of regulation carries the increased odds of the most suitable end being reached, that of God's association for the rest of time.

Danavas heard the news and decided to appear on the scene. The history of the creation is provided in the Vedas, the ancient scriptures of India. First there is the Supreme Lord, who resides in the spiritual sky. He is both with spiritual attributes and without, a combination that is impossible to comprehend with a brain restricted by the limits of time and space. God's personal form is His original, and His impersonal aspect is just a feature, though to Him there is no difference. Like the difference between the sun and the sunshine, the Supreme Lord's influence is seen throughout the creation, even within the tiny atom, but He still has an original body and form.

From the Supreme Lord - known as Krishna because of His all-attractiveness and Rama because of His ability to provide transcendental pleasure - come all other living entities. In the material creation, Lord Brahma, the first living entity appearing from the lotus-like navel of Lord Vishnu - the four-armed personal expansion of the Supreme Lord - takes care of populating. From Brahma come both saints and demons alike. Since the beginning of time there has been an ongoing struggle between good and evil, those devoted to Vishnu and those opposed to Him. The devotees are known as suras and their counterparts asuras. Amongst the asuras there are so many different species, with the Danavas being one of them. Though the Danavas have an ancestry described in the Vedas, their qualities can also be found in the human species. One can act like a Danava or asura without having a known link to the original creatures of the same type.

Devas also attended Sita's svayamvara. A deva is a god, someone who is worshipable but not quite on the level of the Supreme Lord. The suras as a species are devas, and they can provide benedictions to their worshipers, for this is what they are tasked with by the Supreme Lord. In the grand scheme of things the devas and the Danavas are the same, for they are both conditioned. The devas are just further along in the evolutionary process than the Danavas, for one who is devoted to God even with impurity mixed in is closer to gaining final release from the material world, which operates under karma. Through karma comes the swinging pendulum of acceptance and rejection, which manifests in both pious and impious acts.

Nishacharas also attended. The name indicates that they are night-rangers, which means they travel through the night in false guises to attack the saintly class of men. Also known as Rakshasas, these hideous creatures have no concern for piety, decency, or the right of others to live their lives peacefully. The Rakshasas had a strong influence during the period of time when Janaka's event was being held, for their leader Ravana was extremely powerful and feared throughout the world. The person to be married to Sita had actually appeared on earth specifically to do away with Ravana.

Kinnaras, who are heavenly bird-like figures expert in singing, and serpents also attended the ceremony in Janaka's kingdom. All of these non-human figures dressed up as kings to fit the occasion. They did whatever was necessary to make it to the most famous wedding ever held. They arrived happily and with excitement, for why else would they go to so much trouble? Though they wouldn't win Sita's hand in marriage, they would get to witness Narayana's amazing feat of lifting Lord Shiva's bow.

Lord Rama, the prince of the Raghu dynasty, was Lord Vishnu Himself coming to Janakpur to reunite with Lakshmi Devi, His eternal consort. The attendees got to observe a historic event, which featured a feat of strength still talked about to this day. Their eagerness to be allowed entry was indirectly tied to spiritual life. Their association with Sita and Rama would give them something to talk about for many years to come. They could say that they were there that day when Rama lifted Lord Shiva's bow and gave Janaka the son-in-law he deserved.

VERSE 11

एक चलहिं एक बीच एक पुर पैठहिं।
एक धरहिं धनु धाय नाइ सिरु बैठहिं।।11।।

eka calahiṁ eka bīca eka pura paiṭhahiṁ |
eka dharahiṁ dhanu dhāya nā'i siru baiṭhahiṁ ||11||

"Some are moving, some are on the way, and some are entering the city. Some are grabbing the bow, offering their respects to it, and then sitting down after having failed to lift it." (11)

Essay - Next in Line

In the Vedic tradition, the image of a throng of people moving systematically, as if on a conveyor belt, in an attempt to offer respects to a particular worshipable item is not out of the ordinary. The predominant message of the spiritual tradition of India is love, the divine variety. As is obvious to the sober person, love does not flow through only one outlet. There is a variety in activity for a reason, as not every person has the same desires or inherent qualities. The spirit soul is provided a playing field that is the body, so there is also variety in the recommended auspicious activities. For instance, chanting the holy names of the Lord, "Hare Krishna Hare Krishna, Krishna Krishna, Hare Hare, Hare Rama Hare Rama, Rama

Rama, Hare Hare", is considered the most effective method of the discipline of bhakti-yoga, but this doesn't mean that one who can't chant is shut out from spiritual life. Rather, every tool and practice of bhakti is aimed at cementing a consciousness fixed on the lotus feet of the Supreme Personality of Godhead, who has a blissful form. The lines of people formed generally relate to worshiping a deity manifestation of God or offering a specific item of worship, but in one case many thousands of years ago, the assembly had the purpose of winning the hand of the goddess of fortune in marriage. Though many suitors came and kept this line moving along, they failed to win the prize of the day. Nevertheless, their participation earned them tremendous spiritual merits.

Why was there a line formed to marry a princess? Was she looking at these men and then deciding who was worthy based on appearance? Isn't that kind of shallow? The marriage ceremony was a self-choice, or svayamvara. The groom was not decided beforehand, so anyone was open to compete to have Sita Devi, Janaka's daughter, as a wife. In the time period that the event took place, most marriages were arranged by the parents, as they would match up the qualities of the participants and then from there decide if the marriage was suitable.

King Janaka faced an issue in this area. His daughter came to him as a baby lying within a field. Therefore he couldn't use the time of her birth or the ancestry of her biological parents to determine her future qualities. Moreover, he didn't want to give her up. She was his precious daughter, full of every virtue imaginable. In fact, whoever gets Sita as a daughter should be considered the most fortunate human being. Janaka knew this, as the thought of her marriage made him feel like he was losing his fortune. Sita Devi, in describing the circumstances many years later to the female sage Anasuya, herself said that Janaka felt the way that a rich person would feel if they were about to lose their entire fortune.

"After seeing that I had reached an age suitable for giving me away to a proper husband in marriage, my father became overcome with fear and anxiety, like a man who was about to become poor." (Sita Devi speaking to Anasuya, Valmiki Ramayana, Ayodhya Kand, 118.34)

That's a pretty lofty comparison to make, but Sita was correct. Janaka was a chivalrous king in charge of the welfare of the kingdom of Videha, but despite his duties he was not materially attached. He was famous for having conquered over the senses. Just as we think someone is superior in their willpower when we see that they are able to control their eating habits in the face of the many delights available from restaurants and fast food places, just imagine how much respect you garner if you are controlled in every aspect of your behavior.

Janaka didn't follow virtue, piety and dispassion to gain any acclaim. Renunciation is a virtue championed by the Vedas, which try to give mankind the tools necessary for becoming God conscious by the time death arrives. Since affixing your thoughts on God at the time of death is a rare feat, just by following the rules and regulations without knowing the meaning behind them can provide much help. For instance, if a person from the laborer class should honestly serve the three higher classes, in the next life they can take birth in circumstances more conducive to yoga.

Janaka was in the royal order, or second highest division. But he was a rajarishi, or saintly king. Though he had material delights available to him, he was a transcendentalist through and through. When he found Sita, however, his renunciation went right out the window. From his behavior that followed, he showed everyone the right way to view attachment and detachment. Caring for family members, having a large heart, and being compassionate are only detrimental when they take you off the righteous path. Though he had full affection for Sita, that did not stop Janaka from carrying out his prescribed duty of getting her married.

Oh, but his piety would be handsomely rewarded. Even when carrying out his duties as a matter of protocol, Janaka kept the higher authority figures in mind. Janaka decided that for Sita's marriage he would hold a contest to see if anyone could lift Lord Shiva's bow. Mahadeva is the expansion of the Supreme Lord in charge of the material mode of ignorance. Every type of person is granted a worshipable figure, even if they are unaware of it. Mahadeva is known as Ashutosha, which means that he is easily pleased. He is only interested in worshiping the Supreme Lord in His form of Shri Rama, so anyone who comes to him with requests for material benedictions is quickly granted whatever they want. This way Lord Shiva can go back to concentrating on Shri Rama - uttering His name and thinking about His lotus feet, which are so soft and beautiful.

"Shambhu, or Lord Shiva, is the ideal Vaishnava. He constantly meditates upon Lord Rama and chants Hare Rama, Hare Rama, Rama Rama, Hare Hare. Lord Shiva has a Vaishnava sampradaya, which is called the Vishnu Svami-sampradaya." (Shrila Prabhupada, Shrimad Bhagavatam, 3.23.1 Purport)

Little did Janaka know that his decision to insert Lord Shiva into the mix would bring him the company of Shri Rama. The news went out across the land about the contest, and since the parties involved were Janaka, his daughter Sita, and Lord Shiva, everyone was excited to come. Even members of other classes and races decided to dress up and attend the event. There was no restriction imposed, as the bow was considered impossible to lift. If anyone should miraculously raise it, then certainly it would be an indication of Providence declaring them worthy of having Sita as a wife.

In the above referenced verse from the Janaki Mangala, Goswami Tulsidas is continuing his description of the scene on the day of the svayamvara. Kings from around the world are flocking to Tirahuta, Janaka's capital city. Some parties are just starting on their journey, packed together with their royal paraphernalia and entourage. Some are travelling into the city, while others are in between the two parties.

Since there are so many people arriving, the scene looks like the world's largest conveyor belt. One after another, princes are approaching the bow, paying their respects to it, attempting to lift it, and then sitting down. There is no counting how many princes are arriving, for the line just keeps on moving, similar to the gathering that forms in front of a temple on the day of an abhisheka ceremony.

"Seeing that greatest of bows, which had the weight of a mountain, the kings offered their respects to it but then left on account of being unable to lift it." (Sita Devi speaking to Anasuya, Valmiki Ramayana, Ayodhya Kand, 118.43)

The deity is the worshipable figure that depicts the spiritual attributes of the Personality of Godhead. We should all worship God; that is not a novel concept. Every major religion espouses this belief. How that worship should take place is where the details are sometimes lacking. If we don't know what God looks like, how are we to remember Him? If we can't remember someone, how can we worship them? If we don't know where they live, what they want out of us, and how they'll react to our offerings, how is anyone supposed to ever worship them?

The Vedas provide the missing details by describing God as both formless and with form. The formless aspect is only from the perspective of the living entities. In reality, God's form is all-encompassing, so gigantic that you can't even understand it. Think of it like having to look at an astronomically large number that doesn't have any commas in it. With so many digits, trying to decipher the value of that number will be very difficult.

The deity provides clarity of vision to the conditioned eye, which requires so much external support to make perceptions. We are proud of our technological advancement and philosophical mettle, but without the aid of nature's arrangements like heat and light, none of it would be possible. Similarly, for the conditioned being, making progress through study of just the impersonal aspect of the Supreme Lord is very difficult. Even those who do make progress along this path eventually turn their minds towards the personal aspect.

Janaka was a great example of this. He was known as Videha because of his renunciation and knowledge of impersonal Brahman. Because he was desireless he became the perfect candidate to have Sita Devi as a daughter. Sita is the eternal consort of the Supreme Lord, who was roaming the earth as Rama at the time. The deities of these two figures are still worshiped to this day, showing that God has spiritual attributes that can be remembered and honored. The worshipable body, the archa-vigraha, is the proxy to accept obeisances. Man can't just take any collection of metal or brass and worship it as God, but through an authorized system, where the figure is crafted as a replica of one of the Supreme Lord's many spiritual forms, the material elements become a deity that accepts the offerings directly from the worshipers.

In a temple where the deity is worshiped, there are annual occasions where the worshipers can come and pour milk, water, honey and other preparations onto the deity as part of a bathing ceremony. God in His original form may not be there for the occasion, but through His deity He allows everyone to worship Him nonetheless. The bathing is enjoyed by the Supreme Lord and the worshipers; hence there is often a line that forms, with the participants eager to see the Lord up close and give Him a nice bath.

Unbeknownst to the pilgrims visiting Janakpur, they were offering their respects to both Lord Shiva and Sita Devi. Despite their failure to lift the bow, they got to take part in one of the most blessed events ever held on this earth. Eventually prince Rama, Lord Shiva's beloved and the Supreme Lord of the universe, arrived on the scene and easily lifted and strung the bow. Sita and Rama would come together in Janaka's kingdom, and the world would be bestowed a story to delight in for countless future generations.

The conveyor belt of princes also enhanced the glory of the victor of the contest. The throng of unsuccessful participants showed just how difficult it was to lift Lord Shiva's bow and how amazing it was for any person to even come close to moving it. The difficulty of the contest substantiated Janaka's decision, alleviating his doubts about parting with Sita. Through Rama, Janaka would gain the Supreme Lord as a son-in-law. He would get to gaze upon the embodiment of Brahman, the person behind the impersonal effulgence. The personal form is always superior, because there is no mistaking the Personality of Godhead to be something that He isn't. Even those who didn't know that Rama was God gained tremendous spiritual merits just by looking at Him.

The participants' ignorance of Sita's identity as the goddess of fortune did not harm them. Instead, their natural and spontaneous love for Sita made them enjoy her wedding ceremony even more. The long line of princes arriving in Janakpur added a wonderful decoration to the beautiful sacrifice, which was as worshipable as the Supreme Lord. Just thinking of Sita and Rama's marriage is as good as being there, which means that remembering the scene over and over again keeps the beloved couple in the heart.

VERSE 12

रंग भूमि पुर कौतुक एक निहारहिं।
ललकि सुभाहिं नयन मन फेरि न पावहिं।।12।।

raṅga bhūmi pura kautuka eka nihārahiṁ |
lalaki subhāhiṁ nayana mana pheri na pāvahiṁ ||12||

"One is looking at the arena and the city with amazement. Their mind and eyes are so attracted to that place that they cannot even blink." (12)

Essay - A Captivating Scene

Goswami Tulsidas here continues his description of the scene of the svayamvara held for Janaki, the daughter of King Janaka, many thousands of years ago. The city itself was a wonderful sight, and the rangabhumi, or arena holding the event's main festivities, was also something to behold. People from far and wide arrived for this event, and they were not disappointed by what they first saw. Indeed, their reaction was one full of so much astonishment that their minds and eyes were fixed upon the main attraction. Many couldn't even bring themselves to blink, for they didn't want to deprive their eyes of the splendid vision for a second. Based on what would happen that day and who else would arrive later on, that elation was set to only increase.

If you travel from a distant place to attend an event, when you first see the arena or place where the event will take place, you will likely feel some happiness. "Ah, I have travelled so far, and look! There is the place where we are going. See how beautiful it looks. Let's hurry up and park the car so that we can get a better view." From the initial sighting the anticipation increases, and with anticipation comes an enhanced feeling of excitement when the event actually takes place.

Janaki's svayamvara wasn't a rock concert, the performance of a dramatic play, or even the forum for a grand speech. Rather, the rangabhumi in question was holding a contest, one requiring immense strength. There was a famous bow belonging to Lord Shiva that was so heavy that even heavenly figures couldn't dream of moving it. The contest was simple: lift the bow to win Janaka's daughter's hand in marriage.

Why would so many people travel to Janaka's city? Janaki was the most beloved princess, endowed with every virtuous quality. Obtaining a good wife is akin to coming in to a large fortune, but not necessarily as we'd initially imagine it. When you win the lottery or strike oil, you hope to be financially secure for the rest of your life. As woman is the energy of man, obtaining a good wife means that you will have support in your journey through life, that you will have someone to correct you when you do something wrong and lift you up when you don't feel up to performing your occupational duties.

The Vedic tradition reveals that the spirit soul is the essence of identity, and when coupled with a material covering, the aim in life becomes the forging of a permanent God consciousness. As this is not the natural inclination of a living entity who is born ignorant and required to undergo extensive education, rules, regulations and purificatory rites are instituted which span from the time of birth all the way up until death. Knowing which duties to perform and when is quite difficult; hence expert guidance from spiritual leaders is required.

In the middle stages of life, one can enter marriage to get support from a life partner, someone to live with you day in and day out. In addition, through marriage the natural urges for sex life can be acted upon in a regulated manner, thereby ensuring that society is filled with wanted children who are raised properly. From the protection of women through marriage, so many benefits come.

Janaki was no ordinary woman. She was found while as a baby in the ground that Janaka planned to plough for a religious sacrifice. He was childless at the time, and since he harbored such great affection for her, he took her in as his daughter. He didn't run the risk of taking someone else's baby because at the time of finding her, a voice in the sky came upon the scene and told Janaka that this girl belonged to him in all righteousness, or dharma.

Janaka lived by dharma, so he knew that when Sita reached an appropriate age, he had to find a husband for her. Not knowing her family ancestry and considering her tremendous virtues, Janaka decided to hold a contest and invite kings from around the world. If no one could lift Lord Shiva's bow it would be a sign from above that no man was worthy of having Sita for a wife.

Everything about Janaka was first class, including his hospitality. The excitement over the svayamvara was well worth it. The visitors travelling with their family and royal entourages were not disappointed by what they saw in Tirahuta, Janaka's capital city. People looked at the sacrificial arena in amazement, so much so that they couldn't believe what they were seeing. As if Janaka knew the event would be talked about for thousands of years into the future, he made sure not to skimp on pomp. The king who had the greatest wealth in the form of his daughter made sure not to be frugal with regards to her marriage ceremony.

What Janaka didn't initially know was that his daughter was the goddess of fortune herself, Lakshmi Devi. Think of the Supreme Lord's most confidential associate, someone who gives Him the most pleasure. That person is Lakshmi, who has many different expansions and forms in the spiritual world. To coincide with her husband's descent to earth as the hero of the Raghu dynasty, Lord Rama,

Lakshmi appeared as Sita. She specifically chose Janaka as a father because of his qualifications. He had not a hint of sin in him, and he had the purity required for offering affection to the goddess of fortune.

Janaka did not want riches, but he didn't shun them either. Whatever was needed to abide by dharma, Janaka would do. As an expert transcendentalist, he was above attraction and aversion, and yet he harbored immense affection for Sita. To prove that this love wasn't of the material variety, Sita would bring to Janaka the Supreme Lord Himself as a son-in-law. Normally attraction and aversion are considered detrimental because they are based on maya, or illusion. If I'm walking down the road on a hot day and I think I see a pool of water up ahead, I might get excited. The attraction for the water will keep me running faster towards the destination spot. When I get there, however, I see that the water was a mirage, just a bunch of heat rays rising up from the surface of the ground. In this case both the initial excitement and ending dejection were not wise, for they were based on illusion.

The material body is like a bubble, which gets created at some point and is then quickly destroyed. Even if the body remains manifest for one hundred years, in the grand scheme that is an insignificant amount of time. Though the material forms do exist, since their duration of existence is so short, they can be considered illusory. Harboring attachment to these forms is detrimental because it keeps one in the dark about their real identity as eternal spirit. Having aversion to these forms based on the same mindset is also detrimental because since these forms are temporary, what is the use in hating them?

"Even kings like Janaka and others attained the perfectional stage by performance of prescribed duties. Therefore, just for the sake of educating the people in general, you should perform your work." (Lord Krishna, Bhagavad-gita, 3.20)

Both attachment and aversion can be purified when they are used to further one's real position as servant of God. With Janaka, his initial aversion to material life kept him on the straightened path. He was Brahman realized, so he knew that the spirit soul is the essence of identity within all forms and that to act out of obligation to uphold righteousness is the right way to behave. He did what was prescribed for his order, not caring for the results of action either way.

At the same time, Janaka was not bereft of attachment. His love for Sita could not be measured, and that same love would be harbored for Shri Rama and His younger brother Lakshmana. The first time Janaka saw the two brothers, he thought that maybe they were embodiments of the Brahman he had meditated on for so long. The Lord's direct potency of yogamaya helped Janaka's transcendental attachment increase. From transcendental love Janaka was able to experience more pleasure and receive benefits not granted to anyone else. Since Janaka had Sita as a daughter and Rama as a son-in-law, we can say that there was never a king like him in the past and there will never be one like him in the future.

The svayamvara ceremony inherited that uniqueness. Those staring in wonder were feasting on the fruit of their eyes. Though the eyes are composed of material elements, when they are used to further one's God consciousness, they take on their true value. The attendees of the svayamvara got to see the city of Janakpur, which is like a tilaka, or sacred mark, on this earth. Sita Devi appeared in that great land and her marriage to Rama took place there as well. For the travellers, so many spiritual merits were accumulated just by going there. Through his piety, Janaka would attract many people to a ceremony that would benefit them immensely.

That great king's good character continues to generously benefit people today, those who are fortunate enough to mentally travel back to that famous day when Rama lifted Lord Shiva's bow and won Sita's hand in marriage. The ears are meant for hearing about God, and especially His name. At Sita's svayamvara everyone would see Sita and Rama and recite their names. Thus even the many princes who failed to lift Lord Shiva's bow got the victory of witnessing Sita and Rama married in an extravagant ceremony, one that you couldn't take your eyes off of.

VERSE 13

जनकहि एक सिहाहिं देखि सनमानत।
बाहर भीतर भीर न बनै बखानत।।13।।

janakahi eka sihāhiṁ dekhi sanamānata |
bāhara bhītara bhīra na banai bakhānata ||13||

"One party is very jealous while looking at Janaka welcoming everybody. The place was so crowded on the inside and out that one cannot describe it." (13)

Essay - General Admission

You work hard, play by the rules, administer to the needs of your close family members and are responsible with money so that you can have a comfortable establishment that is the home. The association with the spouse, relatives and children comes together when there is a nice gathering place, a dwelling you can call "home". The more inviting the establishment the more people will want to visit. The more people that come over the more satisfied you feel about the life that you work so hard to maintain. While the quality of the erected structure may draw the attention of others, what will keep them coming back is the quality of the inhabitants, the hosts who welcome the guests and provide them a pleasurable experience. One person in particular had such good qualities that when he hosted a wedding ceremony for his daughter, the number of people that came from around the world could not be counted. However long their journey was and whatever crowds they had to sift through to attend this event, the effort was worth it.

Despite your best attempt to establish a comfortable dwelling, you are not the only one living this lifestyle. Many others, especially those following religious principles, accept the grihastha ashrama, the second stage of life as delineated by the Vedas, the scriptural texts providing guidance on all aspects of life since the beginning of time. An ashrama is a spiritual institution, so even the time one spends married and raising children is meant for the cultivation of spiritual knowledge, with the consciousness ideally ascending to the platform of detachment from the rigors of daily life, which is filled with constant ups and downs.

Remaining detached is very difficult, because with each successful outcome comes a realization of just how difficult the effort was. At least for those living In America, buying a new home is not easy at all, especially if there are thirty years of mortgage payments one has to assume responsibility for upon purchase. It's one thing to enroll in school knowing that you have to attend classes for a certain number of years or accept the responsibility of a child for the first eighteen years of their life, but the mortgage on the house purchase is there for thirty years. Surely you can sell the house at any time, but if you want to continue living there, you better deliver the goods month after month for many, many years.

Knowing the difficulty in securing material possessions - especially in an advanced technological age where the simple, rural lifestyle is shunned as being outdated - it's very easy to become attached to what you do have. Moreover, if you have a system in place to provide the comforts in life going forward, if anything should happen to threaten the vitality of that system, tremendous disappointment and fear will arise. This can only happen when there is attachment, for if we don't care about something, how can we be sad when it disappears from our vision?

Adding further complexity to the mix is envy, seeing someone else in your field surpassing you. In family life, the worthiness of the home is established in part by how many guests come over and how welcome they feel. It is one thing to invite people to the home, but it is another to have them want to come over.

The householder is given a specific responsibility in the Vedas. They are to first feed the Supreme Lord through offering sumptuous food preparations, whatever can be made. If a man is wealthy and has time, he can offer elaborate preparations, and if one is not well off they can even offer something simple like a flower, fruit or some water. The Supreme Lord in His personal form of Krishna validates that such offerings are accepted, provided that the mood of the devotee is proper.

"If one offers Me with love and devotion a leaf, a flower, fruit, or water, I will accept it." (Lord Krishna, Bhagavad-gita, 9.26)

In some households, tradition calls for worship of other divine figures, those who work directly under Krishna to provide targeted benefits to their devotees. Though every ashrama is meant for reaching the final goal of full detachment from material life and complete attachment to the lotus feet of Krishna, it is unavoidable to have some fears over the potential obstructions that may arise and the loss of fortune. Therefore demigod worship has been popularly patronized since the beginning of time. The householder, if they are so inclined, can offer the remnants of Krishna's prasadam to such figures and thus maintain their family traditions.

More importantly, when prasadam is fed to guests, the Lord's mercy is distributed all around. Taking care of a guest is part of dharma, or religiosity, as is described in the Mahabharata. While many people inherently know to treat guests properly, to learn that hospitality falls in line with one's gradual progression towards a purified consciousness validates the behavior. As is the case with any endeavor, however, there is bound to be jealousy. If we see someone else who has more people coming to their house regularly, we might feel inferior. "What do they have that we don't? Why can't people come to our home instead?"

These envious feelings increase when the viewing eyes believe that their dwelling is more opulent or that they are more deserving of attention because of their standing in society. Add to the mix a royal palace, which is expected to be viewed with awe and reverence, and you can see why so many kings were jealous of Maharaja Janaka many thousands of years ago. He lived during a time when dedication to Vedic principles was very high. Though he was a ruler, Janaka was not attached to anything about material life. He went through the rules and regulations as a matter of procedure, for he had no need to purify his consciousness. This shows that even one who is above the work prescribed to those desiring fruits to their action accepts obligations to set a good example for the rest of society.

While Janaka certainly had a kingdom worth visiting, what really drew attention to his home on one particular occasion was his chivalry, knowledge of the Vedas, and general love for humanity. He also had a beautiful daughter who was considered the goddess of fortune on earth, and in reality she was the goddess of fortune from heaven, appearing on earth to take part in the real-life play that would later be called the Ramayana.

Named Sita because the king found her as a baby coming out of the earth, when Janaka's daughter reached an age appropriate for marriage, the king decided to hold a svayamvara, or self-choice ceremony, to decide her nuptials. The planning for Sita's svayamvara can't be compared to how weddings are organized today. If you don't own a large plot of land, you're limited in the number of guests you can invite. Plus, if you have to rent out a hall, the complexity of per head charges and a minimum number of guests gets thrown into the mix. With some modern weddings the host worries about either having enough people to fill the minimum seat requirement or trying to cap the number of guests so as to not go over the maximum occupancy limit reserved for the price range that they're willing to meet.

For Janaka there were no such concerns, for he was the ruler of a majestic kingdom in Tirahuta. He could accommodate as many guests as desired to come. There was no need for making elaborate arrangements in that regard, as anyone who wanted to attend was allowed. Since Janaka was known as Videha, or bodiless, and since both he and his daughter were of the topmost quality, practically all the kings from around the world attended the svayamvara. They loaded up the caravan with their royal paraphernalia and entourage and made the trek to Janaka's city.

In the above referenced verse from the Janaki Mangala, Goswami Tulsidas is continuing his description of the scene on the day the kings arrived. Though a self-choice ceremony, the occasion of Sita's marriage was more a contest. In the central arena, or marked earth [rangabhumi], was a very heavy bow initially belonging to Lord Shiva. Whoever could lift the bow would win Sita's hand in marriage. The bow was so heavy and there were so many arriving princes that from afar the line looked like a conveyor belt forming. One person was arriving, another was stepping up to the bow, another was trying to lift it, and another was going back to sit down after having failed to even move it.

While this was going on, King Janaka was welcoming the many guests. There was a huge crowd both on the inside and outside of the city. Some arriving kings couldn't help but look at Janaka with envy. How can they be blamed for this? If you have an opulent kingdom filled with every material amenity, you will naturally want others to visit it and be welcomed. The President of the United States throws elaborate State Dinners for this very purpose. Yet Janaka wasn't even trying to host any one person in particular. He was just holding a marriage ceremony for his daughter and then so many people showed up. Because of the attention he got, the other kings felt defeated by Janaka, which actually wasn't a bad thing.

Why is this? For starters, the fact that Janaka welcomed everyone added to his stature as a pious king. In addition, if you look around you, there are so many people that are candidates for receiving high blessings and honors. The fact that the honor of hosting the most widely attended wedding in history was bestowed upon Janaka meant that he was worthy of it. The source of his worthiness would prove to be an invaluable educational tool for others. Janaka's real wealth was his love for Sita, who is God's wife in the spiritual world. Janaka's love was pure too; he wanted nothing from his daughter, though Sita can turn even the poorest man into a millionaire in a second.

Janaka received spiritual wealth from being able to love Sita with parental affection. She was the goddess of fortune to him through her association, which would subsequently bring Lord Rama's company as well. Rama is the Supreme Lord Himself, who is eternally linked to Sita in the spiritual world. Not surprisingly, Rama would arrive on the scene and lift the bow without a problem. He would give the massive general admission crowd their money's worth. For even the jealous kings the event was worth attending, for they got to see Sita wed Rama, an event which is still talked about to this day. Janaka, by remaining pious and hosting a number of guests too large to count, took part in the largest prasadam distribution known to man. He distributed spiritual food for the eyes, which then turned into mental images that the onlookers would never forget.

VERSE 14

गान निसान कोलाहल कौतुक जहँ तहँ।
सीय-बिबाह उछाह जाइ कहि का पहँ।।14।।

gāna nisāna kolāhala kautuka jahaṁ tahaṁ |
sīya-bibāha uchāha jā'i kahi kā pahaṁ ||14||

"Wherever you go there are the ecstatic sounds of singing and drums beating. The excitement for Sita's marriage is so great that what words are there to explain it?" (14)

Essay - Raising the Roof

The dancing portion of a marriage reception is pretty much a staple, regardless of the culture of the participants. Festivities aim to create a festive mood, and with a festive mood you get singing and dancing. "Let loose and have fun; lose yourself to the music. Celebrate good times with your friends and family; use the excuse of the marriage to have fun and let your guard down." One wedding in particular, which took place a long time ago, had such a festive mood that the singing, dancing and drum beating took place well before the actual ceremony. Before even a groom was known, the marriage event for the daughter of King Janaka garnered so much anticipation that no words can properly describe it. The excitement was all around, and the result would validate the feelings.

How could the result top the anticipation? It seems like the excitement was partly due to the fact that the groom wasn't known beforehand. As a famous svayamvara ceremony, the bride in question got to choose who her husband would be. Of course nowadays that is the standard protocol, but in ancient times only the most beloved princesses would get this opportunity. Yet this svayamvara was even more unique in that the groom was to be decided through a contest that would measure dexterity, strength, and overall ability.

What was the contest? The host of this grand affair, King Janaka, had a long time back received a bow belonging to Lord Shiva. Think of a heavenly figure who grants his devotees pretty much whatever they want relating to material life and you get the surface view of Mahadeva, a most wonderful worshipable personality. Though it only takes a little to please him, there is no end to the opulence that Lord Shiva will provide you.

Yet if you go beyond the surface functions that Mahadeva provides, you'll see an extremely powerful heavenly figure who lives a renounced life. Though he is married to the beautiful Parvati Devi, the gatekeeper of the material universe, Lord Shiva has complete control over his senses. Though he can give the world to anyone, he himself doesn't require much. Just a little silence, peace and quiet, and a place to constantly repeat the holy name of Rama are all that Mahadeva needs.

True wealth in life does not relate to collection of material elements, which we never have full claim to anyway. We are born with nothing and we die with nothing. Everything in between is our allotment in life determined by the actions we take up. The consciousness of the individual determines their future destination, and the superconsciousness [that connected to God] travels with the individual from life to life. The latter consciousness is best solidified through recitation of the holy names, such as those found in the maha-mantra, "Hare Krishna Hare Krishna, Krishna Krishna, Hare Hare, Hare Rama Hare Rama, Rama Rama, Hare Hare".

Just as Lord Shiva attracts the Supreme Lord's presence through the recitation of the holy name of Rama, Mahadeva's amazing bow would attract Lord Rama Himself to Janaka's kingdom. Lord Rama, the worshipable deity of Lord Shiva, was roaming the earth at the time starring in the real-life play known as the Ramayana. Unlike ordinary stories which grow tired and stale after hearing only a few times, dipping into the sweet nectar of the holy lake of Rama's acts provides boundless joy with each successive visit. It is such a sweet lake that Lord Shiva himself likes to swim in it by discussing Rama's pastimes with his wife Parvati.

One of the major acts of that play involved the svayamvara ceremony in Janaka's kingdom. The pious king decided that his daughter should have only the best husband. The perfect match would come through Lord Shiva's bow, which would decide who was worthy of marrying Sita. The bow was so heavy that no one could lift it. Janaka decided, therefore, that by holding a contest, either someone would be deemed capable of marrying Sita or Sita would be judged too exalted to have any husband.

Not surprisingly, news of the contest stirred much attention. Not only princes from around the world, but their families as well, all packed into caravans and made the journey to Janaka's city. There were so many attendees and people trying to lift the bow that from afar the movement of the pilgrims looked like a giant conveyor belt. One by one, the princes tried to lift the bow, only to be defeated, having to sit down and watch other people then give a try.

In the background there was the sound of singing and drums beating. While normally this may seem annoying, for a grand occasion such as this the background noise just added to the festive atmosphere. Singing is a foundational aspect of Vedic culture, for the sound vibrations released in a loving mood in praise of the Supreme Lord and His attributes purify the heart. Try to express your thoughts through conversation and you might feel a little funny discussing such intimate feelings. Try to write them down on paper, and again you'll feel a little strange being so frank. Then there is the issue of brevity as well, as the more words you need to express a thought, the less potent the message will be.

Poems are useful in this regard, as one can express their emotions succinctly and in a way that can be remembered easily. Take that same poetry and turn it into a song and you have a wonderful way to share your thoughts with others, including the object of your emotional outpouring. As the spirit soul is meant to be a lover of God, if the living entity can regularly sing the glories of the Supreme Lord, whose spiritual attributes are immeasurable in their greatness, you get an eternal engagement that brings felicity to both the singer and the recipient. Those within audible range are also benefitted, as the songs can stay within the consciousness, sparking attraction to the Supreme Lord.

The drums added a nice rhythm to the songs. In this way not everyone had to be directly involved in the singing. Some people were singing the songs, while others were beating the drums to add to the effect. Then the many others were simply listening, as their excitement knew no bounds. Goswami Tulsidas, in the above referenced verse from his Janaki Mangala, says that the excitement at the event was so great that words really have no use in this context. What can words do to describe a scene that is indescribable?

Nevertheless, the Janaki Mangala is itself a song, meant to purify the heart of the poet and those who listen to it with rapt attention. The words of the song are so powerful that even when translated to another language they still bring the vision of the most wonderful marriage to ever take place on this earth. That excitement would turn into tremendous joy when Shri Rama, as a youth accompanying the sage Vishvamitra, would arrive on the scene. With only the sage and His younger brother Lakshmana there representing Him, Rama would step up and lift Mahadeva's bow with ease. This pleased the saintly members of the crowd and crushed the pride of those who were inimical to God.

Janaka's decision to use Lord Shiva as the deciding factor would bring Shri Rama into his family. In one sense we can consider Lord Shiva the head minister presiding over the marriage, as his bow represented his presence at the ceremony. He brought Sita and Rama together, and for this he is still honored to this day. Just as he takes great delight in talking about Sita and Rama, so others can revel in the anticipation and the glorious outcome of that wonderful day.

The question may be asked that if the excitement on the day of the wedding was so high that words cannot explain, what is the point in even talking about it? This raises the classic issue of neti neti, which means "not this, not that." In trying to explain Brahman, the all-pervasive energy of the Supreme Lord which can be noticed by the trained eye, Vedic literature states that this Supreme Truth is "not this and not that". This means that, figuratively speaking, you can go around with something like a price gun or label maker and mark every object you see as "not God."

This should make sense after all. The sun is all-pervading and unbiased in its diffusion of energy. The sun is a source of life in one sense, as we could not survive without it. Yet even something as grand and powerful as the sun is not the Supreme Absolute Truth. This is because the sun is composed of a material element: fire. Earth, water, fire, air and ether represent material substances which are not permanent in their existence. Anything which has to be created cannot be God, because with creation comes destruction. The Supreme Absolute Truth is beyond duality.

The inability to find God fully within this world does not prevent glorification of Him. Rather, neti neti is really a benefit for those who know the true dharma of the soul, that of lover of God. The ultimate characteristic of something forms its dharma, a feature which cannot be divorced from the object. Whether we are sleeping, dreaming, awake, in a dog's body or in a human form, our dharma is to love God. The fact that the Supreme Absolute Truth cannot be accurately described enables our dharma to continue to act. From the feature of lover of God comes a natural occupational duty: bhagavata-dharma, or devotional service.

Devotion to God in its purest form operates unconditionally, without interruption and without motivation. What better way to allow love to continue without stoppage than to say that God can never be properly described? Spend the rest of your lifetime trying to enumerate the Supreme Lord's features - describe how He is both formless and full of form, how He possesses mutually contradictory attributes, how He is unborn and yet can appear from the womb of Mother Kausalya - and you will never finish.

Neti neti is an invaluable blessing. The fact that the excitement was indescribable at Sita's wedding gives us another example of the inexhaustible nature of the Supreme Lord's glories. To this day we have never seen a wedding like Sita and Rama's and we never will. Fear not, however, as that sacred event can be attended within the mind by the devotee who is willing to attempt to glorify the divine couple every day for the rest of their time on earth. That devotion tied to the purified consciousness continues well into the next life, making devotional service a discipline so wonderful that words cannot describe it.

VISHVAMITRA APPROACHING DASHARATHA
VERSE 15

गाधि सुवन तेहि अवसर अवध सिधायउ।
नृपति कीन्ह सनमान भवन लै आयउ।।15।।

gādhi suvana tehi avasara avadha sidhāya'u |
nṛpati kīnha sanamāna bhavana lai āya'u ||15||

"Meanwhile, the son of Gadhi [Vishvamitra] went to Ayodhya. King Dasharatha said, 'Please bring him here to the palace', and welcomed him." (15)

Essay - All the Pieces Fall to His Wish

As with a marriage there is the merging of two families, the wonderfully auspicious event of Sita's nuptials joined two kings renowned for their ability to protect and abide by the righteous path. Thus far in his poem called the Janaki Mangala Goswami Tulsidas has set the scene in the kingdom of Tirahuta, where the leader Janaka is preparing for a svayamvara for his daughter Sita. But with every marriage there is the counterpart, though in the case of Sita's wedding the winner of her hand was not known to everyone. The person who would emerge victorious in the contest to lift Lord Shiva's bow was from the land of Ayodhya, and His journey towards the event in Mithila was not the same as any other attendee's. Vishvamitra Muni, the son of Gadhi, would be the instrument to bring Lord Rama to the svayamvara, and King Dasharatha's pious nature would sanction that move, though indirectly.

Sita Devi is the goddess of fortune; she is married to Lord Narayana, or God. Fortune is a gift from higher authorities; we cannot just create it on our own. Even the wealthy moguls who strike it big in business do so as the result of the consuming public's interest in their product or service. With investments that hit it big, there are the actions of others that cause the rise in price of the commodity.

Therefore fortune is really out of our control, though we have the tendency to think otherwise.

As Lakshmi Devi, Sita controls the fortune of the entire world. Her husband is the most fortunate living entity because He is loved and adored by Lakshmi, who showers Him with affection nonstop. Sita's association in marriage was considered a similarly fortunate blessing. Thus many royal families from around the world came to Janaka's kingdom to try to earn her company. Janaka was attractive because of his piety and Sita her beauty and family link to Janaka. The great king could think of no other way to decide her marriage than to hold a self-choice ceremony, where prospective grooms would try to lift a heavy bow initially belonging to Lord Shiva.

The future winner of the contest resided in Ayodhya, and He was not made aware of Janaka's vow because He happened to not be home when the announcement was made. The venerable Vishvamitra Muni was residing peacefully in the forest when a band of night-rangers, ghoulish creatures given to changing shapes at will, started to harass him. A brahmana is a priest, so they have no association with violence, money, or competition. They essentially have no reason to have strife with any other person. These night-rangers knew the power and sway that the priestly class hold in society. They were also keen on eating human flesh, so who better to attack than defenseless mendicants residing in a forest?

Vishvamitra Muni went to Ayodhya because it is the king's duty to protect the innocent, especially the brahmanas. King Dasharatha had jurisdiction over the forests where Vishvamitra was staying. When the sage reached Ayodhya, the king welcomed him and brought him into the palace. The proper etiquette for receiving a guest is to invite them into the home, give them a nice place to sit, and then offer food and drink for consumption. Vishvamitra was the most exalted guest, so even a royal leader like Dasharatha considered it a tremendous blessing to welcome him. Vishvamitra could only bring good fortune, for he would either give his blessings to the king and his citizens or provide needful instruction on how to improve the living situation.

What no one knew at the time was that through his desire to have protection in the forests, Vishvamitra was setting the wheels in motion for Rama to marry Sita. Dasharatha, though attached to his eldest son Rama, had to part with Him at the request of the sage. For a chivalrous king, his word is everything. Dasharatha promised to give Vishvamitra whatever he wanted, for a respected brahmana should never be denied anything. What could they want anyway? Brahmanas have no desire for wealth, money, women, or property. Dasharatha never thought that Vishvamitra would want to take Rama away from him, for the eldest son was still just a young boy. Dasharatha told the sage that he had many other fighters in his royal entourage capable of protecting him, but Vishvamitra knew Rama's special grace, His ability to fight off even the most powerful flesh-eaters ranging the night.

Accompanying Rama was His younger brother Lakshmana. After he was satisfactorily protected by Rama and Lakshmana, the sage took them to Janaka's kingdom at the same time the svayamvara was taking place. Therefore if it weren't for Vishvamitra's request and Dasharatha's acquiescence, the marriage may never have taken place. For the Supreme Lord, all the pieces fall to His wish. Every action takes place in such a way that so many other items are taken care of simultaneously.

Rama would lift the bow easily and thus win Sita's hand in marriage. The event would bring together Dasharatha and Janaka, kings who were wise enough to follow the advice of their brahmana counselors. It was the royal priestly order that advised Janaka to hold a svayamvara, and it was Vishvamitra who requested that Rama be allowed to attempt to lift the bow. Lakshmana was not a candidate because he was younger than Rama. Plus, he would never show up his brother like that. The fraternal affection shared between Rama and Lakshmana cannot be described. Several years later, when Dasharatha decided to install Rama as the new king, the Lord immediately went to Lakshmana and told him that the honor belonged to him as well, for the Lord did everything for Lakshmana's benefit. The feelings were mutual, and Lakshmana never for a second wanted to take away the glory of his beloved brother. He delighted more in seeing Rama happy and successful than in gaining any fame for himself.

"O Lakshmana, do you rule this earth with Me. You are like My second self, so this glorious opportunity has been presented to you as well. O Saumitra, do you enjoy all the pleasures you desire and the fruits of the regal life. My life and this kingdom I covet for your sake alone." (Lord Rama speaking to Lakshmana, Valmiki Ramayana, Ayodhya Kanda, 4.43-44)

From following the advice of the priestly class devoted to the Supreme Personality of Godhead, so many auspicious conditions arrive automatically. The priest in the form of a spiritual master may not always reveal their real intentions or discuss the full benefit that will come from following a particular recommendation, but the faith extended by the recipient proves to be invaluable nonetheless. Who would have thought that by agreeing to Vishvamitra's request, Dasharatha would get the goddess of fortune as a daughter-in-law? Who would have thought that the families in Ayodhya and Tirahuta would be joined simply through Dasharatha's reluctant acceptance of the son of Gadhi's request?

From following the recommendations of the spiritual masters of the Vedic tradition the benefits are there for everyone to enjoy. While the royal order has dissipated in modern times and been replaced by a democratic system that relies on relative morality, the opportunity to abide by dharma is still present. The only benefit to be found in the less auspicious conditions of today is that the pathway towards meeting God and His wife has been made easier. There is only one recommendation for every single soul living in the Kali Yuga: chant the holy names. Recite sacred formulas like, "Hare Krishna Hare Krishna, Krishna Krishna, Hare Hare, Hare Rama Hare Rama, Rama Rama, Hare Hare", as often as possible, keeping the mind attentive on the sound vibrations produced. Refrain from the most harmful sinful activities like meat eating, gambling, intoxication and illicit sex at the same time to speed up the progression towards a pure consciousness.

We may be reluctant to abandon our previous attachments, but extending faith to the recommendations of the Vaishnava acharyas, who lead by example, has safety built into it. Dasharatha didn't want to let go of his son, but in the end he would glorify the Raghu dynasty by giving in. For a famous king like Dasharatha, a predominant fear was to somehow sully the good name of the family, which had produced a long line of pious rulers starting with Maharaja Ikshvaku, the founder of the family line. Denying the request of a venerable sage like Vishvamitra would have brought scorn to Dasharatha and his family, and it would have not helped his standing that many sages would continue to be killed in the forest without protection.

Janaka as well could have forbidden Rama from participating in the contest, for the Lord was rather young at the time. Many of the onlookers in Tirahuta were afraid that the Lord wasn't going to be able to lift Lord Shiva's bow. In their minds they cursed King Janaka for having made the oath, which he could now not go back on. But staying pious, following the proper course, proved to be the right choice in the end. Similarly, regularly reciting the holy name - the sound vibration that best represents God and attacks the contaminated consciousness grown weary through the swinging pendulum of acceptance and rejection - causes the thick cloud of nescience enveloping the otherwise pure consciousness of the essence of identity, the spirit soul, to eventually dissipate.

The holy name also reminds us of Sita and Rama, how they were brought together through so many events that didn't seem to be related. In one sense, even the vile Rakshasas deserve some credit for the marriage. Had they not harassed Vishvamitra, the sage may never have gone to Ayodhya to ask for Rama. If he had not been with Rama and Lakshmana in the forests near Tirahuta, perhaps Rama would never have attempted to lift Lord Shiva's bow. This broad perspective of appreciating so many actions, even those of miscreants not interested in the final outcome, is acquired through constant connection with the holy name, which brings all the good qualities that a person could ask for. From following the chanting recommendation, from investing full faith in the words of the Vaishnava whose only business in life is to glorify God and get others to be devoted to Him, all the right pieces in life fall into place. The most auspicious condition of being able to remember blessed events like Sita's svayamvara will be accepted as well. Goswami

Tulsidas, by composing his Janaki Mangala, allowed for countless future generations to find that auspiciousness, to remember the divine couple and love them without inhibition.

VERSE 16

पूजि पहुनई कीन्ह पाइ प्रिय पाहुन।
कहेउ भूप मोहि सरिस सुकृत किए काहु न।।16।।

pūji pahuna'ī kīnha pā'i priya pāhuna |
kahe'u bhūpa mohi sarisa sukṛta ki'e kāhu na ||16||

"Welcoming his dear guest and worshiping his feet, the king said, 'Because you have visited I don't think anyone is as fortunate as I am.'" (16)

Essay - Little Did He Know

Little did King Dasharatha know that the initial words of praise he offered to his revered guest would come back to bite him, for what was first considered a great fortune would turn out to be a painful jab to the heart of this decent ruler, who for all his righteousness was completely attached to his eldest son. Not to fear though, as there would be a silver lining to the dark cloud of separation. Auspiciousness would arrive due to the desires of the worshiped guest. The youthful son and His younger brother would escort the venerable sage, who had come to visit the king to get his permission for their company. Through the direction of the muni, the two brothers would eventually make their way to the tilaka of the earth, Tirahuta, where a grand ceremony was taking place to determine the marriage of the daughter of King Janaka, Sita Devi. Dasharatha's eldest son, whose separation causes so much pain, brought immense delight to the kingdom of Videha, for He would prove to be the only man worthy of being married to the goddess of fortune, Shri Janaki.

It is not that only the criminals, miscreants and evildoers cause pain. The saints and their worshipable figure do so as well; such is the duality of the world that we currently occupy. A criminal causes pain to the person they steal from, and the philanderer to their lawfully wedded spouse. The liar inflicts hurt upon those they cheat. The impious ruler cloaks the citizens in a shroud of ignorance, to the point that they can no longer even make out what is the right course of action and what isn't. Piety and virtue are marked as such for achieving future benefits that continue into the afterlife. The proper set of regulations necessary for achieving a favorable outcome can be considered a system of piety, or dharma. Anything which goes against these regulations, and which thereby jeopardizes the successful outcome, gets tagged as sin.

The miscreant causes pain to others and themselves because they live off of sin. Through ignorance of the purpose to the regulations and the objectives they are trying to reach, or through blatant defiance of the proper path, the impious accept the wrong set of activities. If you build a house the wrong way, the deserved painful reaction will occur eventually. Just because you don't see the reaction right away doesn't mean that it will not arrive. Many thousands of years ago, a band of night-rangers [nishacharas] raided the peaceful and serene forests of Dandaka, terrorizing the innocent sages who had taken refuge of the calm confines. Since the sages were helpless and nonviolent and the night-rangers powerful and capable of changing shapes at will, there was really no contest in the battle.

"We have been greatly harassed in Dandaka-aranya by the Rakshasas wearing different shapes at will. Therefore do You protect us, O Rama." (Sages speaking to Lord Rama, Valmiki Ramayana, Aranya Kand, 10.10)

Why would anyone attack innocent sages? Obviously, to do so one has to be completely ignorant of righteousness. That ignorance causes an enhanced sense of fear. The root cause of the ignorance is the attachment to the temporary body, a form which is destined for destruction. Knowledge of impending death coupled with ignorance of the eternal existence of the spirit soul results in the foolish taking sense gratification to be the ultimate objective in life. Dharma in its original sense has nothing to do with temporary ups and downs relating to a body that is not tied to the essence of individuality, the spirit soul. Dharma as a guiding system is instituted to create the proper path, where detachment from the temporary steadily increases.

The ignorant mind has no knowledge of dharma. The level of stupidity can get so high that sometimes the people that are abiding by dharma are seen as enemies. If I don't have any scruples, if my belief is that my identity was created at the time of birth and will dissipate at the time of death, I will obviously want to cram as much enjoyment as possible into the short duration of existence that I have. Rules be damned, for what does it matter if someone else is happy? How is their happiness going to do anything for me? Rather, let me just enjoy as much as possible and squelch any competition.

The nishacharas were so ignorant that they didn't stop at competing with others who were interested in sense gratification. The sages in the forest were religious, and through their spiritual practices they could teach others about the proper aim in life, how to live according to dharma and how to remain detached from the senses. The light of knowledge is the greatest threat to those who live under the veil of darkness. For the ignorant the best option is to root out the competition, for in the arena of ideas there is no competition. How can an uneducated young child argue high points of philosophy with an older person who has experienced what life has to offer and who knows about impending death?

In the realm of spirituality, the nishacharas, or those atheists blinded by mental darkness, are like the uneducated children and the saints given to dharma the educated class. The difference with the night-rangers was that they were mature in bodily development, so they could use brute force to defeat their competition. So vile were these creatures that they would eat the flesh of the sages after killing them. Not understanding how karma works and how negative reactions are due to arrive in the future in the proper season, the night-rangers thought they were safe.

The famous ascetic Vishvamitra was being harassed by these ghoulish creatures, and instead of using his spiritual strength to counterattack their effect, he went to the king of the land, Maharaja Dasharatha, to get personal protection. A brahmana, or priest of the Vedic tradition, can cast spells against enemies, but by so doing they lose some of their spiritual merits, which are difficult to accumulate. The kshatriya, or warrior caste, is in charge of providing protection to all members of society, especially the brahmanas.

Vishvamitra didn't come to Ayodhya to get Dasharatha's personal protection. The sage knew that the king's eldest son, though still young at the time, was more than capable of defeating the Rakshasas. That famous son, named Rama, would many years later defeat 14,000 of the most capable night-rangers all by Himself. In the final confrontation of that battle, Rama informed the opposing group's leader, Khara, that the gruesome reactions to his horrible work of killing sages was coming to him in the form of death. That death would be instigated by the arrows flying from Rama's bow.

"Just as a tree starts to blossom during the proper season, so the doer of sinful deeds inevitably reaps the horrible fruit of their actions at the appropriate time." (Lord Rama speaking to Khara, Valmiki Ramayana, Aranya Kand, 29.8)

At the time of Vishvamitra's visit a much younger Rama was still capable of providing protection to the sage. King Dasharatha, not knowing the purpose for the visit, got up and welcomed the sage, worshiping his feet and declaring that the visit had made him the most fortunate. A pious king like Dasharatha had already proved his high character by getting such a wonderful son like Rama, who was loved and adored by everyone in the community. Rama's younger brother Lakshmana once remarked that even Rama's enemies couldn't find anything bad to say about Him, for they knew that Rama never held grudges or punished anyone without just cause.

"I have not seen any person in this world, be they an enemy or one punished for heinous sins, speak ill of Rama, even in His absence." (Lakshmana speaking to Kausalya, Valmiki Ramayana, Ayodhya Kand, 21.5)

Vishvamitra was famous at the time for his dedication to austerity, and his visit to Ayodhya meant that some of his auspiciousness would be shared with the royal family. In an ideal system, the warrior class provides protection under the expert guidance of the brahmanas. Think of how a politician takes advice on strategy from his campaign advisors. A military man is more focused on showing dexterity on the battlefield, so he is not expected to be supremely knowledgeable on things like dispassion, the meaning of life, and how to act properly in the many different situations that arise.

The brahmanas are completely dedicated to their craft of knowledge gathering, not spending time in fruitive ventures. They don't earn money to maintain a living, they don't fight against enemies, nor do they offer menial service to others. Even if they are relegated to these activities, they do them with detachment, maintaining their focus on the primary aim of dharma, that of connecting with the soul of all living beings. That supreme energy is all-pervading and in its original form is a person, a supreme one at that.

Since they know this all-pervading spirit, which is called Brahman, the brahmanas are enlightened. They can give so much good advice to any person fortunate and humble enough to accept it. Dasharatha exhibited the proper attitude when receiving Vishvamitra, and he didn't exaggerate when he stated that he had become blessed with auspicious merits, or sukriti, through the association. What the king didn't know was that Vishvamitra had come to take away his beloved son Rama.

The king did not want to part with Rama, but his deference to dharma took precedence over his attachment. Rather than break protocol and go against the words of the brahmanas, Dasharatha eventually relented and allowed Rama to accompany Vishvamitra. With Lakshmana following Him, Shri Rama would defend the sage's fire sacrifices, which were for the benefit of society as a whole. Just as a priest gives an auspicious prayer for the benefit of a community, the sacrifices of the brahmanas are to satisfy both the source of Brahman and its many different sparks.

Dasharatha's son was no ordinary prince. He was the very original Personality of Godhead, the source of Brahman. Lord Rama had come to earth to enact wonderful pastimes, to give pleasure to the likes of Dasharatha and Vishvamitra. Each exalted figure had their specific association they desired, so Rama played different roles to provide that satisfaction. In this way the night-rangers served as a wonderful contrast, showing what the demoniac tendencies are and how they are opposed to the divine inclinations followed by the saintly class, which can extend even beyond the brahmanas.

Though when Rama left Ayodhya His father felt sad, the move would earn the king the goddess of fortune as a daughter-in-law. After accompanying Vishvamitra for a while, Rama and Lakshmana made their way to the kingdom of Videha, where a contest was being held to determine the husband for King Janaka's daughter Sita. Once again, the same Vishvamitra would visit a kingdom and be well worshiped, but instead of taking Rama away, this time he would bring the Lord's presence to a kingdom. At Vishvamitra's behest, Rama would lift the extremely heavy bow of Lord Shiva's and win Sita's hand in marriage.

The son of Gadhi, the venerable Vishvamitra, in his heart carries love for the Supreme Lord in His form as Lord Rama. From that quality the muni beams with transcendental knowledge and auspiciousness. Whoever he visits becomes blessed by his association. King Dasharatha showed the proper attitude in welcoming his exalted guest, and from that treatment auspiciousness would come his way as well. Rama and His three younger brothers would be married in Janakpur, and the newlyweds would all return home to Ayodhya. Thus the royal family expanded with the most beautiful princesses arriving, headed by Janaka's eldest daughter Sita. To this day people still sing of Sita and Rama's marriage, and they also remember the events that led up to it. The blessed rajarshi, Maharaja Dasharatha, received the auspiciousness due him by following dharma and kindly welcoming the worshipable Vishvamitra. Those who honor and respect the same transcendental family and regularly remember their activities will never be without light in this world otherwise ruled by darkness.

CHAND 2

काहूँ न कीन्हेउ सुकृत सुनि मुनि मुदित नृपहि बखानहीं।
महिपाल मुनि को मिलन सुख महिपाल मुनि मन जानहीं।।
अनुराग भाग सोहाग सील सरूप बहु भूषन भरीं।
हिय हरषि सुतन्ह समेत रानीं आइ रिषि पायन्ह परीं।।2।।

kāhūṁ na kīnhe'u sukṛta suni muni mudita nṛpahi bakhānahīṁ |
mahipāla muni ko milana sukha mahipāla muni mana jānahīṁ ||
anurāga bhāga sohāga sīla sarūpa bahu bhūṣana bharīṁ |
hiya haraṣi sutanha sameta rānīṁ ā'i riṣi pāyanha parīṁ ||2||

"Hearing the king say, 'No one is as fortunate as I am,' Vishvamitra became very happy and praised the king. The happiness felt from that meeting is known only to the minds of the king and the muni." (Chand 2.1)

"Possessing love, fortune, good luck, humility, beauty and wearing so many ornaments, with happiness in their hearts the queens, along with their sons, all came and offered their obeisances to the feet of the rishi." (Chand 2.2)

Essay - A Very Joyous Meeting

Based on the path you follow in life, you consider yourself to be righteously situated. Not that you're the best or that you're above everyone else, but you are familiar with the meaning of life and how to go about fulfilling it. Whether others like you or not is of no concern, for you are firmly convinced of the need for following the righteous path, which for you means observing sacrifice and austerity. On one occasion you happen to visit someone else who you respect very much. Though they are in a different occupation, you understand that they are well situated in the mind, that they have earned the respect that others offer to them. You have a certain request going into this meeting, so you're not sure how you will be greeted.

To your amazement, the person you respect so much honors you immediately upon your arrival. He first pays you the highest honor outwardly with his behavior, and then his words of praise supersede the previous gesture's kindness. He says that by your visiting him he has become the most fortunate person in the world, that the amount of his spiritual merits cannot be measured. Obviously this will warm your heart, for who doesn't appreciate sincere praise? Especially when it comes from someone you respect so much, there is no measuring the delight you feel from kind words. Correspondingly, the person you are visiting feels the same happiness, for they do not make up false words of flattery to push a specific objective. They are famous for their honesty, so their praise heaped upon you not only brings happiness to your mind, but it validates the decision you have made in life to sacrifice your efforts towards the highest cause.

Take this hypothetical situation and apply it to a real life meeting held many thousands of years ago and you can begin to imagine the happiness felt by the two parties. One side was Vishvamitra Muni, the famous son of Gadhi. He had a checkered past, which included life as a king and quarrels with another saint named Vashishtha. Ironically enough, the person Vishvamitra visited on this occasion had Vashishtha as a priest. King Dasharatha of Ayodhya was famous for having maintained the good standing of the Ikshvaku family, who were a dynasty of kings dating back to the beginning of creation. Dasharatha knew of Vishvamitra's glory, of how he had undergone severe penances to take on the role of an ascetic. Dasharatha cared not for the ascetic's past life as a king nor for his quarrels with Vashishtha.

When visited by Vishvamitra, Dasharatha knew how to act. In Vedic culture there are divisions of work and spiritual institutions in society. The work is determined by the qualities of the individual. Just as in a business some people are better leaders than others, in society some men are better suited to provide protection, which involves fending off enemies. The strongest and most capable fighters will survive in conflict, so those who can protect the best make ideal leaders of government.

The potential issue of having a "meathead" running the government is alleviated by the presence of the brahmanas, or priestly class. The powerful kshatriya, or warrior, can follow the proper course of action by listening to the advice of the priestly class, who knows not only about religious life but also of how to earn success in different material ventures. When the proper aim in life is known, every action becomes spiritual. The behavior at large can be tailored towards meeting the end-goal, which means that such trivial things as ruling over a government and fighting in a war can become spiritual activities for the person who knows the self.

This technique of incorporation shouldn't be that difficult to imagine. Think of a professional athlete. In whichever sport they participate, there is a particular training regimen, where they condition the body to perform at optimal levels on the day of competition. The game itself may only involve dexterity with respect to the rules and objects used, but the training is separate from this. If I am a tennis player, what do sit-ups have to do with performing well on the court? Sit-ups are on exercise to increase strength in the abdominal region of the body. Therefore the exercise is separate from the act of playing tennis against an opponent. If the sit-ups are targeted towards increasing the strength of the abdominal region to perhaps help with serving and lunging for tennis balls, the act becomes part of the routine of the successful professional tennis player. With the higher aim in mind, the scope of activity becomes all-inclusive, for even sleep helps to optimize performance.

The Vedic system of varnashrama-dharma is the most inclusive because the dharma identified is the highest. Dharma is the essential characteristic of something, and when it applies to a system of regulation, it is the set of procedures aimed at bringing that essential characteristic to the forefront and maintaining it. The identification with the spirit soul is the most inclusive, for it brings fraternal affection for all species, not just human beings. The individual spirit soul also exists well beyond the existence of the current bodily form.

The soul's inherent characteristic is to serve the Supreme Soul, or God. Just realizing the presence of the soul and its qualities is difficult enough, therefore dharma is instituted society-wide. Each person follows activities that correspond to their body type so that gradually they can stop identifying with their form and start identifying with the soul. Under the proper procedures, every activity followed in life aims towards realizing the presence of the soul and allowing its dharma, its propensity to serve, to be directed in the proper area.

Vishvamitra and Dasharatha were in different occupations, but they were still both following the highest dharma, which is known as bhagavata. While under varnashrama-dharma one person may be situated as a ruler and another as a priest, under bhagavata-dharma one is directly engaged in devotion to the Supreme Lord. Therefore it doesn't matter what type of engagement they are taking up. As a mere formality one devotee follows administration as a way of life while another serves as a priest, but the connection to the divine consciousness is there in both cases, creating a situation of equality. If both parties understand their identities as spirit souls, part and parcel of God, there is no question of a difference.

When two people following bhagavata-dharma meet, their joy swells. This was the case with Vishvamitra and Dasharatha. The king welcomed the sage and openly declared that because of the sage's visit, he had become the most fortunate person in the world. "No one is more fortunate than I am." What a nice thing to say, no? Wouldn't it make you feel good if you heard that, especially if it came from someone who had a strict vow to tell the truth?

It's not surprising therefore that Vishvamitra praised the king right back when hearing this. To the outsider, or even to the person who was there that day, the happiness in both parties could be noticed. Nevertheless, only the minds of the two individuals could understand just how great that joy was. Rare it is to find someone who fully appreciates your work and understands why you do what you do. Better still when the person you meet is himself a pious character who has dedicated their life to serving God.

"What significance does this meeting have? You had two people who were really happy upon meeting each other, but what's the big deal? Doesn't this happen all the time?" The meeting is noted in the Janaki Mangala written by Goswami Tulsidas. The poem focuses on the marriage ceremony for Sita Devi, who is Lord Rama's eternal consort. Rama was Dasharatha's eldest son, whom Vishvamitra had actually come to Ayodhya to borrow for a while. Though these events took place a long time ago, Lord Rama and Sita exist eternally, for they are the Supreme Lord and His pleasure potency.

God should always be worshiped, remembered, and served, but that service is suppressed when we don't know much about Him. Instinctively we understand that there is a higher power who created everything, who can predict the outcome to every single event and who can grant us whatever we want. At the same time, knowing that God is great doesn't do much for us in terms of altering behavior. If great people are around, shouldn't we want to associate with them? Otherwise, what is the use of their greatness? Perhaps their influence can extend to us in a positive manner, allowing us to find some sort of temporary happiness, but real greatness extends through both the personal and impersonal.

God's impersonal influence is felt through the amazing material nature, which has things like the sun, the earth and the weather that can't be predicted. We can utilize these resources for our sustenance, but even the animals have the same opportunity. The Vedas reveal some of God's features, especially His bliss-evoking attributes. In His original feature, God is Bhagavan, who is so attractive that He is addressed as Krishna. Lord Krishna, who has a body that is eternal, knowledgeable and blissful, expands into other spiritual forms that accept the mood of worship of the interested parties. Shri Rama is not different from Krishna, except that He plays the role of a warrior prince who is so attractive and chivalrous that the pious can't help but be drawn to Him.

As wonderful as Rama is, His wife Sita might be even more glorious. She is also beautiful, with her visible features able to enchant Rama. Those who love Rama will love anyone who makes Him happy. Since no one makes Rama happier than Sita, the devotees automatically have the highest affection for her, taking an interest in her devotional activities as well.

The stories relating to the Supreme Lord and His associates are so attractive that the saintly class never tires of hearing them. In their spare time they will even compose songs about the events so that they can be remembered even more. Take a notable and preferred incident from your life. If you want to remember it, you can probably write down accounts of the incident into a book, but how many times are you going to read this? If you synthesize the key elements into a song, however, you can remember the event every single day. Others can memorize the song and honor the event in that way too.

The Supreme Lord's activities are the most attractive. Therefore the saints regularly dip in the holy lake that represents His acts. The Janaki Mangala is another one of those lakes, with the saint Tulsidas focusing on a specific pastime: Rama's marriage to Sita in the city of Janakpur. The meeting of Vishvamitra and Dasharatha was related to the marriage because without Rama leaving Ayodhya to protect Vishvamitra in the forest, He never would have come to Janakpur to attempt to lift the bow of Lord Shiva. The contest's winner would marry Sita, so Rama had to be the one to lift the bow.

Everything relating to that event is worth remembering, including the fateful meeting between the sage and the king in Ayodhya. Just contemplate upon their happiness, how their minds were filled with joy. Associating with positive people who derive happiness from spiritual life is supremely beneficial. Their examples validate for us the proper path in life, that of always chanting the holy names, "Hare Krishna Hare Krishna, Krishna Krishna, Hare Hare, Hare Rama Hare Rama, Rama Rama, Hare Hare". The happiness felt by Vishvamitra and Dasharatha can also be shared with others, allowing the recipients to honor the role they played in bringing the divine couple together.

Essay - Joyful Respect

How should you welcome a guest? What if they're an important member of the family who you haven't seen in a while? How do you properly pay respect to someone who is most deserving of it? In the Vedic tradition, such issues are handled through a simple gesture, which is easy enough to follow, but may not be presented wholeheartedly. When the practice is adopted by those with the proper attitude in their hearts, with eagerness for the task, and who also have every good virtue and quality, the worthiness of the recipient is further augmented, as is the joyousness of the situation.

Vishvamitra Muni was full of good qualities, as he was dedicated to serving the Supreme Lord through following the occupational duties assigned to him. It's one thing to possess extraordinary qualities, but it's another to use them on a daily basis even if you don't feel up to the task. The brahmana class is considered very fortunate because they have the knowledge capacity to take to righteous activities. Without guidance, the human species is really no different than the animals. In many respects, the ignorant human being lives a life of difficulty which even the animals don't face.

In higher circles of society, the ideal value system handed down to young children relates to the idea that they should become educated and thus earn a good living in adulthood. From that steady income, food, clothing and shelter will not be a problem. Getting that education is neither easy nor inexpensive. In addition to the twelve years of schooling, there is the specialized training given in college and beyond. This is all done to ensure that the young adult can manage on their own and not have a problem staying married and supporting their family.

Yet it is seen in the animal community that the same essentials can be procured without any education or training. Some animals are so amazing that they can walk and look for food immediately after exiting the womb of their mother. The human infant can hardly do anything at the time of birth except cry, but many animals have God-given abilities made specifically for their body type that surpass the young human being's abilities. The animals work too, to get their food and stay under shelter, but they don't have to work nearly as hard as the adult human being does. We essentially go to school to learn how to work to eat, but the same goal can be achieved by owning some land and producing food. Harvest the crops once a year, take care of some cows, and you're pretty much set for a comfortable existence.

The intelligence of the human species is meant to fulfill a higher purpose, something with which the brahmanas are familiar. They know that there is an all-pervading energy known as Brahman, which is the spark of life. From Brahman realization comes the understanding that spirit is the essence of identity and that it exists beyond the current form, which is ever-changing. There is birth and death and everything that happens in between, but the spirit spark of Brahman is there to stay. The Supreme Lord states in the Bhagavad-gita that He impregnates the total material energy, known as the mahat-tattva, which is also part of Brahman, and thus generates the many life forms.

"The total material substance, called Brahman, is the source of birth, and it is that Brahman that I impregnate, making possible the births of all living beings, O son of Bharata." (Lord Krishna, Bhagavad-gita, 14.3)

The source of birth is an injection of spiritual energy, which then remains localized within each individual. From the higher knowledge acquired one can follow the right set of activities, which will lead to full enlightenment. From enlightenment comes confidence and continued determination in the auspicious path, which brings the highest gain. Because the brahmanas know all of these things they are given respect in society.

Vishvamitra lived like a brahmana, though he wasn't necessarily born as one. Though he could have stayed on the path of fruitive activity and not trod the difficult road of an ascetic, he chose to stay true to his calling. Without people taking the risk to become a priest to teach others with their example, who would be there to guide society? Therefore simply through his occupation and his dedication to remaining true to it the sage was worthy of so much praise.

On the other side, a king lives a very opulent lifestyle, as that is the reward for providing protection to the innocent. When there was a meeting between Vishvamitra and the pious King Dasharatha, the two parties were coming from opposite ends of the spectrum of material life. Vishvamitra called the minimalist surroundings of the forest his home, while Dasharatha lived in an elegant palace in Ayodhya. Nevertheless, when the meeting took place, it was Vishvamitra who was greeted with attention and honor, as if he were royalty.

The king declared that he had the most auspicious merits for having received a visit from Vishvamitra, and the sage in turn felt very pleased. When a guest comes to the house, it is standard etiquette to ask how they are doing, to give them a nice seat and offer them something to eat and drink. When the guest is worshipable, someone who gives sublime wisdom to others, a person who makes the sacrifice to both understand God and spread His glories to others, the need for paying honor is increased.

In Vishvamitra's case, he received honor from those who were themselves endowed with every good quality. In the above referenced verse from the Janaki Mangala, it is said that after King Dasharatha honored Vishvamitra, his queens and their sons came and did the same. The queens were full of love, fortune and good luck. Wearing the most beautiful ornaments they arrived in front of the sage with hearts full of happiness. Rather than give Vishvamitra a hug or say "hello" from afar, they came up to him and bowed to his feet. They brought their sons with them, young men who would one day take charge of the kingdom. From an early age the boys were taught how to respect their elders and members of the priestly class.

The virtue of the queens is important to mention because the more honorable and respectable someone is, the more likely it is that others will follow their example. A similar fact is brought up in the Bhagavad-gita, where it is stated that whatever a great man does, others will follow. King Janaka, whom King Dasharatha would meet shortly after at a marriage ceremony, is mentioned in the Gita to show that even a king who has no duties to perform takes to working so that others can know the proper course in life. We accept obligations so that we can meet a specific end, but for someone who knows the eternality of the spirit soul and how it is transcendental to the shifts in matter, there is no work to perform.

"One who is, however, taking pleasure in the self, who is illumined in the self, who rejoices in and is satisfied with the self only, fully satiated—for him there is no duty." (Lord Krishna, Bg. 3.17)

Despite their high knowledge, such worshipable personalities, which include the Supreme Lord Himself, accept obligations externally to teach others the need to behave piously. Lord Rama, the same speaker of the Gita, the Supreme Lord in the guise of a warrior prince, was one of the sons that came and honored Vishvamitra. Rama was Dasharatha's eldest son and He was, ironically enough, the reason for Vishvamitra's visit. Since the queens were the most respectable and beautiful in every way, by their paying honor to Vishvamitra, the example was set for all people on how to treat those deserving of worship.

It is also said that the queens and their sons arrived with happiness in their hearts. This means that they didn't honor Vishvamitra just as a formality. They were naturally so happy to see the sage, for he always brings good news. Even if the bona fide spiritual leader should criticize errant behavior, the result is good, for the correction serves to fulfill a higher purpose. Since the end result is good, the original presence and criticism turn out to be auspicious. In addition, if the priestly class is satisfied and honored, then they will kindly bestow heaps of good counsel, ensuring that everyone can live life happily.

The king's avowed dedication to honor the brahmanas would be tested on this occasion by the request coming from Vishvamitra. The muni wouldn't criticize the king, for what could Dasharatha ever do wrong? The Supreme Lord had appeared in his family for a reason, for the result of many past pious deeds, treading the righteous path with firm faith and determination, brings the audience of the Supreme Lord. It is said that in his previous life King Dasharatha regularly performed the Satyanarayana Puja, which is a worship typically performed by householders desirous of a fruitive result. Unlike the worship of divine personalities charged with providing welfare of the material variety, worship of Shri Satyanarayana keeps one in touch with the Personality of Godhead, even though the initial motive may not be pure. Pure devotion is marked by the absence of a desire for material rewards, knowledge, or perfections in mysticism. In pure devotion, the only desire is to be able to connect with God and continue that devotion into the future.

The reason pure devotion trumps all other kinds of worship is that the person who adopts it in earnest is considered to have already performed every other kind of sacrifice. Dasharatha proved this point to be valid, for he received Rama as a son after having performed pious deeds in his previous life. Since he had already followed the other methods of religion, the king was free to love his beloved son without impediment. There is no higher benefit in life than to be able to release the natural loving spirit within the heart without interruption and without motivation. As the only person who can accept the full release of spiritual love is the Supreme Lord, the ability to love Him, to show Him prema, is the highest benefit in life. This is what Dasharatha received by gaining Rama as a son.

Despite the fact that he had no dharma to tend to besides loving Rama, Dasharatha still agreed to let Vishvamitra take Rama as an escort in the forest. Though Rama was a young boy, Vishvamitra knew that the Lord's fighting abilities were brilliant, that He could protect the saints in the forest who were being attacked by the night-rangers of the time. By allowing Rama to go, Dasharatha proved that the praise he offered to the rishi was not just empty words. It is one thing to say that you trust someone, but it is another to accept their requests that you may not like. The queens and their sons loved Vishvamitra, and that love would be tested when Dasharatha's two sons, Rama and Lakshmana, would leave with the sage to travel through the forest. The trust invested in Vishvamitra would pay off, as the decision would bring back the goddess of fortune to Ayodhya. The decision to extend faith to Vishvamitra would also give countless future generations the opportunity to sing of the marriage of Sita and Rama and remember the divine couple and honor them daily in thoughts, words and deeds.

VERSE 17

कौसिक दीन्ह असीस सकल प्रमुदित भई।
सींचीं मनहुँ सुधा रस कलप लता नई।।17।।

kausika dīnhi asīsa sakala pramudita bha'ī |
sīñcīṁ manahuṁ sudhā rasa kalapa latā na'īṁ ||17||

"Vishvamitra gave them his blessing and they all became happy, like a new kalpa creeper being watered with pure nectar." (17)

Essay - Showering Nectar

Picture a new creeper in the ground that is just waiting to be watered. There is so much potential, as from a tiny little seed a giant tree bearing many fruits can emerge. A tree that produces fruits is considered pious, for it does more than just provide oxygen to the world. Just from the fruits freely provided by a pious tree one can survive. While it seems like an austerity measure to live only off of fruits, if one is destitute and has no other source of provisions, the tree that is nature's property is there to give protection, both from the scorching hot rays of the sun and the pangs of hunger.

If you water the creeper with what it really needs, such as pure water, the growth spurt will be amazing. Indeed, the tender's primary objective is to make conditions such that the growth will take place in the most wonderful way, blessing the eyes with a vision to remind the individual of the miracle of life, how a living being can flourish when properly taken care of. The proper care offered to the creeper is an act of love, and the reward for that love is the freedom of growth, the ability for the tree to shine in all its glory.

The cow behaves in a similar manner. Allow it to run free, enjoy time with its children, and know that it won't be harmed and you'll get heaps of milk. From the trees producing fruits and the cows giving milk, what need is there to beg from any corporation or government agency for life's necessities? There is no love involved in these exchanges, as the agreement with the business is made under the expectation of remuneration. The government entity is impersonal, not caring whether or not the offered aid helps you reach a better position.

With the careful protection offered to the living entities that are completely helpless, the resulting fruits give both sustenance and a respect for life. This is naturally known to the living entity, for otherwise pets would never come into the home. With a cat or dog, there is much work required for maintenance, but the companionship resulting from that care is considered so blessed that the work is deemed worth it. With the valuable human form of body, the offering of love and respect to one particular entity brings such a pure nectar in return that the potential for bliss bursts out. This was seen with a famous meeting many thousands of years ago which Goswami Tulsidas has so nicely described in his Janaki Mangala.

Who was involved in this meeting? A famous king named Dasharatha was ruling over Ayodhya when he was visited by Kaushika, the son of Gadhi named Vishvamitra. The king already had a royal priest named Vashishtha and other members of the brahmana, or priestly, class around him all the time, but he was still excited at the prospect of meeting Vishvamitra.

The king was wealthy and his primary occupational duty was to provide protection to the citizens. What benefit then could be gained by meeting someone who was at the time living in the forests? Only a recluse chooses to abandon civilization and go meditate somewhere all by themselves. Vishvamitra had no money, and he wasn't asking for any type of material reward from Dasharatha. What could be the purpose of his visit and why would Dasharatha be thrilled upon the sight of him?

In ancient Vedic culture, which is based on the teachings handed down by the Supreme Lord at the beginning of time, the priestly class takes to an austere lifestyle on purpose. Not just to punish themselves, the lack of material attachment allows for enlightenment to accelerate more rapidly. Think of trying to study while you're intoxicated and you can begin to understand the effect material attachment has on the ability to focus on the bigger picture. In the feverish pursuit to acquire possessions and security in family life, what gets lost is the knowledge of impending death. We know that we will grow old and die some day; if we are lucky. Sometimes people don't even make it to old age. The end is guaranteed, so rather than just ignore it, the wise tact is to figure out why it happens and what can be done to find the most beneficial future afterwards.

Thankfully the mind is not left on its own in this regard. It doesn't have to sit in a room and try to figure out the differences between matter and spirit, why there is birth and death, and what happens to the individual while their body continually changes. This information is already presented by the Supreme Lord in His Vedic literature, the most widely read work of which is the Bhagavad-gita, which is spoken by God Himself in His original form of Krishna.

The truths of the Vedas need not be accepted solely on blind faith. Surely this method can help in the beginning, provided that the principles accepted are valid. The teachings are meant to affect behavior, to change the course of action so that the proper end can be reached. Therefore the more important aspect is to practice the principles, which concomitantly bring about a higher understanding. The principles create the conditions necessary for attaining enlightenment, for they remove the distractions and foster an environment where the truths can be both accepted and understood, so much so that the faithful follower soon is wise enough to teach others the same principles.

This was the case with Vishvamitra. He was living in the forest to dedicate his life to serving God, but this didn't mean that he had abandoned contact with the world. He knew that faithfully following his religious obligations would allow him to better serve humanity. His visit to Ayodhya was an example of this, and

Dasharatha, as a pious king, was also aware of Vishvamitra's high standing. Immediately upon seeing the sage, the king arose and offered his respects. He openly declared that he was the most fortunate person in the world for having the muni's vision. The king's queens and their sons soon entered the room and lovingly offered their respects to Vishvamitra's feet.

In the above referenced verse from the Janaki Mangala, Goswami Tulsidas makes a nice comparison to describe what happened next. Vishvamitra gave them all his blessing, and they in turn became very happy. Their reaction indicated that they knew his blessing meant something, for Vishvamitra was not a pretend guru or a spiritualist in name only. From his blessing could come the knowledge and auspiciousness necessary for carrying out one's prescribed duties in life. One who follows their prescribed duties, keeping devotion in mind, reaches the highest end. It doesn't matter whether one is a priest, administrator, businessman, or laborer, if they follow the duties of their order and listen to the kind words of advice from those who know the real religious principles, they can put a stop to birth and death within this very lifetime.

The blessing given by Vishvamitra and the resulting response from the queens and children was compared to a new creeper being nourished with pure nectar. The kalpa creeper is a sort of heavenly plant that can grow into a tree that provides whatever one desires. If it is nourished with pure nectar, it will grow more rapidly. This is the case with any living entity, for if we put the best ingredients into our body, we will remain fit and strong. A living being provided pure love receives the most important nourishment.

The blessing of Vishvamitra was considered pure nectar because the sage was in good standing with the Supreme Lord. Tulsidas pays Vishvamitra the highest compliment through this comparison. For the queens, their children being blessed by the muni meant that their worries could be alleviated for but a brief moment. The good parent never stops worrying about their child, no matter how old they get. In the case of Dasharatha and his queens, the concern was over the welfare of the children and whether or not they would grow up to be pious. A child that matures to the point that they can eat and sleep comfortably hasn't really done much in life, for even the animals are given provisions by nature. The aim of human life is to follow dharma, which is the only way to reach the highest end.

Someone who lived by dharma blessed children who would grow up to be protectors of dharma; such was the beauty of the interaction. Vishvamitra's real intention in visiting Ayodhya was to borrow one of Dasharatha's sons, Rama. This young child, though Dasharatha's favorite, would have to protect Vishvamitra from the attacking Rakshasas in the forest, terrorist-like figures who were recently being a tremendous nuisance on the peaceful sages looking to practice their asceticism.

Rama was none other than the Supreme Lord, which made the interaction with Vishvamitra even more amazing. There is no way to measure God's love for the brahmana class that follows their prescribed duties. If not for the priests practicing the principles of dharma, who would guide society? Even in modern times where it is difficult to find a bona fide brahmana, the presence of a few pious leaders can provide tremendous benefit to at least some people, who can then pass on the same teachings to future generations.

Lord Rama was the same Supreme Lord who first instituted dharma, yet He was paying His respects to Vishvamitra. The love offered by the muni to Dasharatha's children allowed them to grow up to be wonderful wish-fulfilling trees who would grant the desires of the sweet devotees around the world. The ability to have Dasharatha's two sons, Rama and Lakshmana, escort him in the forest allowed Vishvamitra to taste the sweet nectar of God's vision as well. So his original blessing actually turned out to be a blessing for him in the end.

This incident underscores the importance of having contact with someone who is practicing the principles of religion in earnest. In the present age, the prescribed divisions of society may be nonexistent, but dharma is still there. It has been streamlined to the point that all that is required is the chanting of the holy names, "Hare Krishna Hare Krishna, Krishna Krishna, Hare Hare, Hare Rama Hare Rama, Rama Rama, Hare Hare". One who recites this mantra with faith, love and a feeling of helplessness becomes the teacher for mankind. The recitation of the holy name under conditions where sinful behavior is eliminated brings all good qualities, including perfect knowledge.

Anyone who is fortunate enough to meet a person practicing devotion becomes blessed as well, for the person lovingly chanting the holy names is not stingy in revealing the secret to their success. Anyone who is sincerely interested in hearing about God and devotion to Him will be given the nectar for their ears by the devotee already following bhakti. The queens and their sons eagerly and happily paid their respects to the muni and he in return gave them his blessing. Such an exchange wasn't required because of the nature of Dasharatha's four sons [they were all expansions of Godhead], but the flow of love could not be stopped. The fountainhead of matter and spirit has respect and honor for the priestly class, so the merits in receiving the dust from the lotus feet of the sages are shown through the Lord's personal behavior.

VERSE 18

रामहि भाइन्ह सहित जबहिं मुनि जोहेउ।
नैन नीर तन पुलक रूप मन मोहेउ।।18।।

rāmahi bhā'inha sahita jabahiṁ muni johe'u |
naina nīra tana pulaka rūpa mana mohe'u ||18||

"When the muni looked at Rama with His brothers, his eyes welled up with tears, his body became thrilled with excitement, and his mind became so enchanted by the beauty." (18)

Essay - Love At First Sight

A painting's beauty is measured by the reaction it incites in those who look at it. This makes sense after all, for if someone tells us that something is beautiful and we don't feel anything positive when looking at it, that opinion is meaningless to us. The more natural the emotion and the more quickly it arrives, the greater the quality of goodness in the target object. Love at first sight is indicated by the emotion that emerges at the first glance. For a sage a long time ago his devotion to the Supreme Lord was revealed by the reactions he felt throughout his body upon first sight of that worshipable object in the form of a small child accompanied by His three younger brothers. The signs of devotion and the worthiness of worship of that honorable figure were both shown during that one incident.

What are some of the emotions that a beautiful object elicits? Excitement is surely one of them. "Look at what I'm seeing. I can't take my eyes off of this. I don't want to ever not be able to see this again." In modern times a person's excitement over an image can be seen through their buying of a painting or storing of a photograph on their computer or handheld electronic device. Along with excitement, there could be the enchantment of the mind. In Sanskrit mohana can refer to the ability to enchant someone through attractiveness, and the more enchanting the object is, the greater their beauty. The ability to captivate the mind belongs only to those truly special works of art.

A stream of joyful tears from the eyes is the most intense response from contact with a beautiful object. Something pure, sweet and loveable elicits this reaction, and it comes only in the rarest of occasions. Perhaps an innocent child has done something sweet for you or your paramour has done something so nice that you can't imagine why they would bestow such a reward upon you. People cry at weddings when the exchange of emotion is pure, for seeing someone transcend the bounds imposed by material nature is lovely.

With Vishvamitra Muni, his tears came from just looking at a youth accompanied by His three younger brothers. A muni is a sort of philosopher, for it is said that one can't be considered a muni unless they disagree with another muni. This explains why there are so many analysts on television giving so many different opinions. If everyone agreed with one another then there would be no need to have so many analysts. Often times it is in the best interest of the analyst to disagree with the assertions made by the other members of the panel. At least this way they'll stand out.

"The sthita-dhi-muni is always in Krishna consciousness, for he has exhausted all his business of creative speculation. He has surpassed the stage of mental speculations and has come to the conclusion that Lord Shri Krishna, or Vasudeva, is everything." (Shrila Prabhupada, Bhagavad-gita, 2.56 Purport)

Another kind of muni is a devoted soul, a high thinker who has wisely chosen in favor of bhakti-yoga, or devotional service, as a way of life. This was the case with Vishvamitra. One time he went to visit the king of Ayodhya, Maharaja Dasharatha, to ask a favor. Before the muni could even make his request, Dasharatha and his queens honored Vishvamitra very nicely. The queens brought with them their sons, of which there were four. Vishvamitra had come to ask for the eldest son, Lord Rama, to accompany him in the forest.

The kings during this time period, the Treta Yuga, were fighting men. They held on to their position as head of state because they were best at fighting off enemies. The sons were trained to follow in the father's footsteps, so it was known to Vishvamitra that Rama was an expert bow warrior. Though in the form of a small child, Rama was the most capable fighter in the world. Since it was the duty of the kshatriya, or warrior class, to protect the sages living in the forest, Vishvamitra didn't think it awkward to come and request Rama's protection.

The muni had already humbly begged for the same person's protection throughout his life. Rama was the Supreme Lord, the origin of creation, appearing on earth to enact pastimes and grant His darshana to the sincere souls who would revel in having it. From his reaction upon first seeing Rama, we see that Vishvamitra was one of those worthy souls. He didn't take God to be an enemy or an imaginary figure. On the contrary, the muni dedicated his life and soul to understanding God and giving sound advice to others on how to reach the same realization through following their prescribed duties.

In the religion of love, one can gauge their progress by measuring the emotions that result from their devotional practices. Just as a beautiful painting elicits certain responses in the viewer, the devotee regularly chanting the holy names, "Hare Krishna Hare Krishna, Krishna Krishna, Hare Hare, Hare Rama Hare Rama, Rama Rama, Hare Hare", and viewing the deity eventually reaches a stage where they feel transcendental ecstasy just by hearing a name of God once. What then to speak of remembering the Lord's pastimes, of which there are too many to count? It is said that though there are hundreds of thousands of activities of Rama described in the Vedas, Lord Shiva, the greatest of the gods, only takes Rama's name as his life and soul, chanting it all the time.

"Shri Rama's name is greater than Brahman, and it grants boons to even those who are capable of giving boons. Lord Shiva knowingly selected it out of the one hundred crore verses describing Rama's acts." (Dohavali, 31)

The holy name is the embodiment of the supreme person it represents. Through love for the holy name, love for Godhead takes place automatically. Vishvamitra's high standing in bhakti was shown by the reaction he had upon seeing Rama and His brothers. Tears welled up in his eyes, a thrill of excitement went through his body, and his mind became enchanted by Rama's beauty. In the Vedas, the god of love, Kama, who is the equivalent of a cupid, is known as Madana. The Supreme Lord is so beautiful that He is known as Madana-mohana, or the enchanter of cupid. God's spiritual form attracts even the liberated souls, captivating their minds and directing them towards transcendental love.

This attraction is beneficial because there is no illusion in the Supreme Lord's vigraha, or body. That form is full of knowledge and bliss, and it remains in existence eternally. Even though Rama would change His form during His time on earth, from boyhood to youth to adulthood, since He is the Supreme Lord, His transcendental form that so captivated Vishvamitra still exists and can be contemplated upon by the mind. Should the devotee be fortunate enough, they will get to see that enchanting vision up close some day in the future.

Rama's brothers - Bharata, Lakshmana and Shatrughna - are just as beautiful. They are plenary portions of the Supreme Lord Narayana, the source of men. Vishvamitra was so happy to be where he was, and he couldn't believe that these young boys were offering him obeisances. Such is the kind nature of the beneficiary of worship that He shows honor and respect to those who honor Him. After this meeting, Vishvamitra would ask to have Rama accompany him, and the father Dasharatha reluctantly would agree, for he was attached to Rama as well. Lakshmana went with them, and the time they spent in the forest would eventually result in Rama's marriage to the daughter of King Janaka, Sita Devi.

The incident of Vishvamitra's visit shows us what influence Rama has on people who have a pure heart. The aim of religious practice is to remove the distractions and intoxicating influence of material nature so that the sweet vision of the Supreme Lord can be relished. If we watch a movie while distracted in mind, will we enjoy the most important aspects? Can we concentrate on a conversation with our friends if our mind is distracted? Can we study for an important exam if we are intoxicated?

In a similar manner, if the mind is stuck in a feverish pursuit for a material gain or the alleviation of a specific distress, the very mention of religion, the need to worship God or even the vision of the Supreme Lord Himself will not be appreciated. Therefore to complement the assertive bhakti practices, the devotees avoid the four pillars of sinful life: meat eating, gambling, intoxication and illicit sex. These activities work best at clouding the vision of the individual, causing them to mistake illusion for reality. A rope can be mistaken for a snake only when there is an improper vision. Similarly, the Supreme Lord's form can be taken to be the image of a mundane personality only when the consciousness is not purified.

Vishvamitra, through his dedicated practice of austerity and sacrifice, had no such illusion. He thus exhibited all the signs of transcendental ecstasy when meeting Rama, who is known to have that effect on people. The description of the meeting provided by Goswami Tulsidas in his Janaki Mangala is so heartwarming that one can't help but feel some of the same excitement. Just as Rama and His brothers are beautiful, so are the devotees who delight in the association of those four wonderful sons of the king.

VERSE 19

परसि कमल कर सीस हरषि हियँ लावहिं।
प्रेम पयोधि मगन मुनि पार न पावहिं।।19।।

parasi kamala kara sīsa haraṣi hiyaṁ lāvahiṁ |
prema payodhi magana muni pāra na pāvahiṁ ||19||

"Touching His lotus-like hand, blessing Him on the head, and happily bringing the Lord towards his heart, the muni felt like he was taking a dip in an ocean of love and unable to cross over to the other side." (19)

Essay - An Ocean of Love

The lotus flower is the symbol of purity. It remains in the clean water, sprouts open upon the sight of the splendorous sun and then closes back up at nighttime, as if to indicate that the absence of light is the time to rest, to gather oneself before the next day arrives. The swans float amidst the lotus flowers, while the crows hang around rubbish. This dichotomy has been referenced by those with knowledge of the Absolute Truth since time immemorial. The above referenced verse, which describes the lotus-like hands of the hero of the Raghu dynasty, whose contact was so heartwarming to those who are above such passionate feelings that it created an ocean of nectar that one could not cross over, gives yet another example of the comparison to the wonderful lotus.

An expert swimmer can cross over a body of water, as often that is the intended purpose when getting into the water. You prepare yourself for the swim, keeping in mind where you want to go and how to pace yourself so that you don't get tired. Sometimes, though, the water is meant for relaxation and not swimming. In the winter months, one of the worst feelings comes from getting up in the morning to get ready for school or work and then seeing someone else still enjoying the warmth of their blanket. The outside environment is cold, while underneath the covers is warm and inviting. "Why should I get up? Can't I just stay like this the whole day?"

For a sage a long time ago, the ocean of transcendental nectar created through a simple and innocent embrace flooded him with comforting emotions, a transcendental type of drowning. This muni was residing in the pristine surroundings of the forest, where there were minimal distractions. What kind of work did he have that required being shut off from society? Not to be mistaken with a hermit who hates the world or a hobbit who shuns everything around him out of spite, the sages seeking refuge in the wilderness did so to advance spiritually, for that is the main objective of human life.

The first tool necessary for working towards that goal is tapasya, or austerity. This shouldn't be that difficult to understand, as control and regulation are required for success in practically every endeavor. The human being especially should pay attention to tapasya because they have the intelligence to understand its effectiveness. The lower animal species don't know anything about dieting, controlling appetites, regulating behavior, or achieving a higher end through a regulated set of activities intelligently crafted. The concept of "animal instincts" is used as a reference tool for a reason. The animal just follows its hunches and does whatever it feels like doing.

The human being has the ability to think rationally, to develop scientific experiments with relation to behavior. For instance, if I follow a particular routine day after day - which can involve waking up at the same time and eating the same foods spread out across the same intervals - should any change occur to that routine, I can note down the results as part of an experiment. "What if I wake up half an hour earlier tomorrow? I'll do everything else the same, so let me see what effect that has on my energy levels." A simple thing like shifting the time of waking up in the morning can be used to find a better condition, adjusting the routine so that the worker can perform at optimal levels.

In the Vedic tradition, much of the guesswork has been removed. Tapasya is a trusted system whose effectiveness is rooted in the control of the senses. A gosvami is considered a master of the senses, so they are eligible for making disciples and spreading the glories of bhakti-yoga, or devotional service, to a wider audience. A master is one who can turn something on and off at any time. I may say that I am in control of my senses, but if I have vices like drinking and smoking that I can't control, my senses actually own me instead of the other way around.

The senses can be owned through tapasya, which is practiced for meeting the highest goal of realizing God. There is no other purpose to the human form of body. Intelligence exists for a reason. Through intelligence a person can reach their desired end more quickly. A desired end brings a desired result, which is bitter or sweet depending on the intended taste. For the thief intelligence is the ability to successfully take someone else's property without them knowing. For a politician intelligence is the ability to win an election despite having governed poorly. A wise product engineer can develop a product to the specifications of the company, so as to appeal to a mass market of consumers and successfully carry out the desired functions.

Consciousness is absent in matter, so intelligence used to fulfill goals that deal with interaction with matter are all on the same inferior level. It looks like there is variety in taste, but in the end the same rewards are available to the animals who don't have nearly the same intelligence as the human beings. Real intelligence uses information and knowledge to achieve the highest end of association with God. That goal was fulfilled for Vishvamitra, who had previously used his knowledge of the Vedas and belief in the words of the acharyas to follow tapasya under the proper guidelines.

Since the forests were conducive to austerity, they were known as tapo-vanas. There was one slight problem for Vishvamitra though. The forest was free of distractions such as material allurements, but there was a purposeful distraction surfacing. More than just a distraction, this was a dangerous element which threatened the muni's existence. We're talking about the forest here, so perhaps the allusion is to lions? Bears? Tigers? No. Even these ferocious animals left Vishvamitra and the other brahmanas alone.

The sages weren't doing anything to anyone. Their aim was to have as little material interaction as possible. Sobriety and a renewed commitment to sacrifice, or yajna, follow tapasya. A brahmana can be an expert at performing formal sacrifices, which are meant to please Yajneshvara, which is another name for God. In the Vedas the Supreme Lord has thousands of identified names which each remind the infinitesimally small spiritual sparks occupying different bodies in the material world of the Lord's position with respect to their own standing. For example, the living being is the controller of the actions of their body. Since they are rulers in a sense, they are known as ishvara. If I know that I am a controller, one way to teach me about God is to describe Him as being the Supreme Controller, or Parameshvara.

The yajna is a central practice of followers of the Vedas, and just to let the worshipers know the real position of the person being honored, the real enjoyer of sacrifice, God is given the name Yajneshvara, or the lord of sacrifice. The yajna is very powerful when carried out in the proper mood. Through God's satisfaction, the living being's consciousness becomes purified and he is better equipped to cope with life and also teach others how to make advancement in spiritual life. The latter aspect is what bothered a specific set of bandits, who had the opposite intent. The thief is so immersed in their sinful ways that they take their own values to be virtuous. This tendency also introduces one of the defects in a system of democracy. Democracy prevents a single leader from going off the deep end and tyrannically ruling over the innocent people, but it also establishes relative morality. You and I may know that stealing someone else's property is wrong, but should a majority vote in Congress say otherwise, the practice suddenly becomes virtuous.

The ghoulish creatures concentrated on the island of Lanka during Vishvamitra's time decided that their acts of killing innocent creatures and eating them were pious. So infested by sinful behavior was their city that no amount of wine, women, or animal flesh was enough to satisfy the appetite. The Rakshasas in Lanka would regularly harass the sages of the tapo-vanas, disrupting their sacrifices. They would wear false guises and then pounce on the unsuspecting munis just as their yajnas were about to bear fruit.

Vishvamitra approached the king of Ayodhya, Maharaja Dasharatha, for protection in this area. Dasharatha had four young sons, the eldest of whom was the Supreme Lord appearing in a seemingly human form. Upon first meeting Dasharatha, Vishvamitra was greeted by the boys, and he was especially enchanted by the eldest Rama. In the above referenced verse, the muni is embracing the children after they offered him their respects.

"How can that female swan who is accustomed to sporting with the king of swans amidst lotus flowers ever cast her eyes on a water-crow that stays amidst bunches of grass?" (Sita Devi speaking to Ravana, Valmiki Ramayana, Aranya Kand, 56.20)

Rama's hand is likened to a lotus flower, a comparison made quite often in Vedic literature. The Supreme Lord's features are all pure, so the lotus flower is one of the best representations of His purity. Sita Devi, Rama's future wife, would one day compare being with Rama to living amidst lotus flowers. She would also compare the Rakshasas to crows who hung around garbage all the time. The lotus flower is beautiful and its association inviting.

Vishvamitra received young Rama's hand, embraced the Lord to his chest, and then felt so much happiness that he lost himself. This meeting was the real fruit of his yajna, the reward for his tapasya. This proves without a doubt the purpose behind austerity, the reason to observe fasting days and keep the senses in check. Gosvamis master their senses for a reason. If I starve the senses of things that are harmful, when something beautiful does come along, it is appreciated all the more.

Vishvamitra appreciated Rama's presence and delighted in the Lord's association, as any person should do. The holy name is our way to embrace God today, for simply by chanting, "Hare Krishna Hare Krishna, Krishna Krishna, Hare Hare, Hare Rama Hare Rama, Rama Rama, Hare Hare", the sweet association of the jewel of the Raghu dynasty, who has lotus-like hands and eyes, can be enjoyed. To relish that taste, to really understand how the holy name and the person it addresses are one and the same, austerity in the form of abstention from illicit sex, gambling, intoxication and meat eating is required.

How did Vishvamitra get out of that ocean? Lost in a sea of happiness, did he give up his dedication to piety, to teaching others about spiritual life? Eventually he was able to break out of the trance, but he used the opportunity of his visit to ask for Rama's protection in the forest. Through his request, Dasharatha would be troubled, but the world would be granted the gift of the image of Rama and His younger brother Lakshmana honorably escorting a worshipable muni through the forests and protecting him from the vile creatures given towards rooting out piety from society. Dasharatha granted the favor to Vishvamitra, and the sage favored countless future generations by desiring to be in Rama's association. If we should be so lucky to stay around the lotus-like Lord Rama we too will swim in an ocean of transcendental nectar.

VERSE 20

मधुर मनोहर मूरति सादर चाहहिं।
बार बार दसरथके सुकृत सराहहिं।।20।।

madhura manohara mūrati sādara cāhahiṁ |
bāra bāra dasarathake sukṛta sarāhahiṁ ||20||

"Seeing that sweet and beautiful form, the muni wants to keep worshiping it. Again and again, the muni praises the great spiritual merits of King Dasharatha."
(20)

Essay - Basking in Sweetness

In bhakti-yoga the purpose of every recommended activity is to foster Krishna consciousness, pure thoughts within the mind. The behavior we adopt, those things we pay attention to, imprint our consciousness with items for further contemplation. If our time is spent mired in filth, debauchery, and images that shouldn't be seen, the consciousness will continue to contemplate upon them long after the original contact. The same principle can be turned in our favor should we change the nature of the associated objects. This is the purpose of divine love, the highest discipline man can follow. Regardless of whether we're after spiritual merits or material rewards, gazing at the sweet and lovely form of the Supreme Personality of Godhead clears all misgivings, doubts, needless desires and erroneous thoughts.

What is an erroneous thought? Think of a conclusion that you reached that was based on ignorance. For the child this is quite commonplace, as they just don't know any better. In adulthood we are also quite commonly mistaken, thinking that someone is evil when they are really not or guessing that one way to do something is correct when it later turns out to be wrong. To ere is human after all, and the living being's propensity is to commit mistakes. The mistakes are rooted in illusion, taking something to be that which it is not. Therefore the material energy is known as maya, which is filled with objects considered to be one thing that are really something else.

The mistakes start from the time of birth, where the living being identifies with the body type accepted. Never mind the fact that you had no say in choosing the womb you would emerge from or the type of features you would assume, somehow that dwelling is equated with identity. The accepted form will constantly change through the passage of time. The infant child has a completely different body from the adult, yet the bewildered individual occupying that changing dwelling always takes identity from the body.

This misidentification indicates both illusion and mistake. From the root mistake other erroneous conclusions are reached. The family bonds are taken as absolute and the land where one was born becomes worshipable. Again, the birthplace could have been anywhere; you had no control over that. You may hate one area of land today because you consider it foreign, but you easily could have grown up there and learned to speak the language, immersing yourself in the "foreign" culture.

The doubts are dispelled through following a bona fide discipline of spirituality. In material education, there is some knowledge acquired, but the guiding conclusion is still erroneous. The fact that material nature, which doesn't represent our identity, should be exploited through effort and work shows a misidentification with the body that perpetually leads to trouble. The animals don't require education, for they instinctively know to look for food, erect shelter, mate with other members of their species, and sleep when rest is required. The human can similarly live a simple life involving these behaviors without needing any education whatsoever.

Real education teaches the individual that they are spirit and not matter. That spirit's existence is evidenced through the autonomous actions of the residence it occupies. Death thus represents the exit of the spirit from its dwelling; not the end of life itself. Rather, life in a localized area can only exist when spirit is present. The fetus within the womb only develops when there is spirit inside. Abortion is only an option when there is a life; otherwise the fetus would never develop and cause the unwanted "burden" to the mother deciding to kill her child.

Education in spirituality is meant to alter behavior, to affix upon the consciousness images and sounds that are sweet, or madhura. There is nothing sweeter than the transcendental form of the Supreme Personality of Godhead. One way to distinguish between God and the living entities is to know that the Lord is never subject to illusion. He does not commit mistakes because His knowledge is never incorrect or incomplete. By the same token, objects of illusion are relative, so even the material nature we have so much trouble dealing with is spiritualized when in contact with the Lord.

In bhakti-yoga, which teaches all of these relevant truths and imparts the proper principles within the worshiper through dedicated activity, one of the central practices is deity worship. The material elements that are mistaken for our enjoyment or identity get manipulated in such a way so as to represent the transcendental features of the Personality of Godhead, which are described in the shastras, or scriptures. The deity is not a mentally concocted idol that a foolish person all of a sudden decides to worship. The fact that someone would want to worship a fake idol reveals at least that the soul's natural propensity is to serve. Dharma as a system is built around the principle characteristic of the living entity. Despite one's current status, high or low, in a position of power or servitude, service will be the catalyst to behavior. Tyrannical regimes have flourished throughout the course of human history precisely because they exploit this penchant within their citizens.

The deity is the proper beneficiary of the worshiping propensity in man. The deity is not created on a whim; rather it is crafted from the detailed descriptions found in the scriptures. The features of the Personality of Godhead are real, with their genuineness revealed through the results that come from authorized worship. And what are the results we're looking for? The above referenced verse from the Janaki Mangala provides a few hints. The same deity that is worshiped in so many temples appeared in His own form on this earth many thousands of years ago to delight the hearts of the devotees and instill terror in the miscreants who were dedicated to thwarting the peaceful acts of the pious.

The muni Vishvamitra was visiting the city of Ayodhya, ruled at the time by King Dasharatha. Vishvamitra needed some protection while residing in the forest, as the night-rangers were assuming shapes at will and harassing the sages. Dasharatha offered the sage the utmost respect and then brought his queens and sons to give the same hospitable welcome. Dasharatha's oldest son, Lord Rama, was the one who caught the muni's eye. Rama is the very same Personality of Godhead contemplated upon by yogis and philosophers since the beginning of time.

In this specific form, God took on the role of an expert bow-warrior, committed to protecting the innocent.

When Vishvamitra first saw Rama, he was mesmerized. Though only a young child, Shri Rama's form was so beautiful, sweet in every way. That sweetness is what the living entity is looking for. In devotional service there are different transcendental mellows, or tastes through association. Even outside bhakti these tastes are seen to varying degrees. For instance, the relationship with a friend carries a different enjoyment than the relationship with a dependent child. The conjugal affair is of a different nature than the relationship of reverence established with respected personalities. Despite the differences, love can be present within all of these exchanges.

Madhurya is the highest transcendental mellow. Though it is usually taken to mean conjugal interaction, the root meaning of the word is sweetness or loveliness. In madhurya-rasa, or shringara-rasa, the Lord is appreciated for His transcendental sweetness. If we taste something very sweet that is intoxicating at the same time, the tendency is to continue to relish that taste and repeatedly indulge in it.

When intaking transcendental sweetness, the reservoir of enjoyment cannot be filled up. This was shown through Vishvamitra's reaction. Rama's form is compared to a murti, which is like a deity, and Vishvamitra's attitude was to continually worship that form. He did not want anything else. Just from worshiping the deity and appreciating the sweetness of the transcendental features, the requisite consciousness can be acquired. It is for this reason that the temple exists. Outwardly there is the regular worship that occurs, but the underlying purpose is the desire to keep God's features within the mind, to maintain that sweetness in association even when separated from the deity.

Vishvamitra was so pleased in the heart that he again and again thought of how fortunate the king was. Dasharatha must have accumulated so many spiritual merits, or sukriti, to have such a son. Ironically enough, Vishvamitra came to borrow that son, to temporarily separate Him from His father. Dasharatha would not like this proposal, but since the king's vow was to defer to the priestly class, he could not deny Vishvamitra. Thanks to that genuineness of purpose, that selfless act of sacrificing the association of the person he loved the most, the king would allow for Rama to eventually make it to the kingdom of Tirahuta, where a notable contest was taking place to determine the husband of an unmarried, beautiful princess.

Just as the murti is worshipable and brings the sweetness the individual spirit soul is looking for, the scene of Vishvamitra lovingly gazing upon the beautiful form of Rama brings so many spiritual merits to the devotee. The purpose of the poet's Janaki Mangala is to create as many such images within the mind of the listener. The poet himself got to relive the scene over and over again by singing his verses. When high concepts are put into poetry and song, they are easier to remember. Just from singing a few words and thinking about them, so much constructive thought can be triggered within the mind. The vision of young Shri Rama triggered boundless sweetness within the mind of the muni, whose thoughts were already pure. On that wonderful day in Dasharatha's kingdom, the sage showed us the purpose of the murti, and why worship of it is a central aspect of bhakti-yoga.

VERSE 21

राउ कहेउ कर जोर सुबचन सुहावन।
भयउ कृतारथ आजु देखि पद पावन।।21।।

rā'u kahe'u kara jora subacana suhāvana |
bhaya'u kṛtāratha āju dekhi pada pāvana ||21||

"With folded hands the king said the following words which were auspicious and good to hear: 'Seeing your pure lotus feet today I am very much obliged to you.'" (21)

Essay - Succeeding in Work

The pious king tirelessly works to maintain the standard of law and order, to ensure that his subjects are properly taken care of and that the rules and regulations of the administrative class are not violated. Yet it is a little difficult to know when that work is successful, whether or not the effort expended has been appreciated or made a significant impact. With the blessing of the sight of the pure lotus feet of the servant of the Supreme Personality of Godhead, however, the past work proves fruitful, and the king becomes obliged to the kind person who provides the affirmation.

Who doesn't want to make a difference? Who doesn't want to matter? A word of caution in this regard, though, for the worst tyrants in the world made an impact on history. Going on a killing spree, causing mass starvation, and bringing otherwise capable people to utter destitution make a tremendous impact on society, but not for the better. The common unstated purpose to the desire to make a difference is to positively affect someone else's life, to show that your work has meaning.

The Vedas, the ancient scriptures of India, are so intricate that they reveal the root cause of this desire. At the heart of the living being's vitality is the spirit soul, which has inherent properties, the foremost among them being the desire to serve. If you look around, you'll see that there is a common trait shared in all behavior. One person is the CEO of the company while another is a worker, but both of them are offering service. The boss is seemingly independent, not having to answer to anyone, but unless there are customers to buy the product or service, the title becomes meaningless. Hence the company head, who is the face of the organization and thus equivalent to the business, serves the customers. The worker serves the company and the customers serve their own interests by purchasing relevant products.

In the animal species the tendency towards service is also present. Motherly affection is seen just as much in the cow as it is in the human being. The cow brings forth heaps of milk when its child starts to cry, just as the Supreme Lord, who is also the Supersoul, rushes to the scene when His devotees cry out His names in a mood of love and affection. Hearing the chant of, "Hare Krishna Hare Krishna, Krishna Krishna, Hare Hare, Hare Rama Hare Rama, Rama Rama, Hare Hare", the Supreme Person takes it as a signal for help, that one of His innumerable children is requesting His loving association.

The work the spirit soul takes up when in a particular form of body can end up either successful or unsuccessful. This binary view isn't as limiting as it seems, for work can be repeated or directed to other areas. The larger the scope of the work, the more people it affects, the more important it is to see a successful outcome. Next to the authorities governing the material elements at large, the ruler of the state has the most responsibilities. His actions affect a large number of people. Therefore, for his work to be successful, kritartha, he needs someone who can see the bigger goal and assess whether or not that is being satisfied with the actions undertaken.

How do we find someone who has this proper vision? The fact that spirit exists within all species is not known to many. In fact, the external features of the species make just the opposite realization commonplace. I see that a dog and a cat have different behaviors and outward features, so I think that they are inherently different. At the same time, I know that there is variety within the human species, but in the end everyone has the desire to serve, to make a difference.

"That knowledge by which one undivided spiritual nature is seen in all existences, undivided in the divided, is knowledge in the mode of goodness." (Lord Krishna, Bhagavad-gita, 18.20)

The wise seer studies Vedic philosophy under the guidance of a bona fide spiritual master and quickly realizes that spirit is present within all forms of life, from the tiny ant all the way up to the large elephant. As spirit is the catalyst to action, it can be thought of as a singular, large energy pervading all of space.

Perceiving the presence of spirit and its equal influence within the species is one thing, but actually knowing what is good for spirit is another.

With spirit comes the penchant for service. Those who can take their desire to make a difference and direct it towards pleasing the one person who can accept the most service thereby attain the greatest profit for themselves. The ruler's duty is thus quite clear: allow for everyone in society to reach that stage of spiritual evolution, where their service is offered to God. How to fulfill this obligation is a little tricky, as not everyone will immediately be open to accepting the ultimate mission in life as genuine. Some will be too distracted to contemplate the truths of spirituality.

Just because a perfect success rate is not practical doesn't mean that the king should abandon the pursuit. Rather, the work assigned to the king is very important and should be carried out as a matter of obligation, with not too much concern placed on success or failure. Think of a school system with the different grades. The first grader can't understand algebra and the laws of physics, but this doesn't mean that their time in school is wasted. Through performing the work prescribed to their grade-level, they can gradually advance to the higher stages of knowledge.

The head of state ensures that the conditions in society are conducive towards the realization of the self, which then leads to service to the Superself, or the Supreme Lord. Though the king is supposed to be detached while carrying out his obligations, it is still nice to know whether or not progress is being made. If there are some errors, the advisors to the king, the brahmanas, can come on the scene to rectify the situation. A brahmana is a priest who understands the all-pervasiveness of spirit. If he gives a blessing to a king, saying that their work is being done properly, the king feels most obliged, for he knows that his effort is not going to waste.

One king a long time ago got that very blessing, which indicated the success of his work, when he was visited by one of the most famous sages in history. King Dasharatha of Ayodhya one day had the honor to greet Vishvamitra, who was living in the forest as a hermit. The brahmanas of the time chose the pristine wilderness as their home because it had conditions better suited for sacrifice and penance, two key aspects to any genuine discipline of spirituality. The brahmanas would teach others about their relevant occupational duties, and since the kings had the most influence through their work, they required the counsel from the brahmanas the most.

Vishvamitra visited Dasharatha and was duly honored by both the king and his family. The muni in turn gave his blessings back to them, which made Dasharatha supremely happy. Vishvamitra was a servant of the Supreme Lord, so to see his feet, to take the dust coming from those feet and place it on the head, is the greatest blessing one can ask for. That association results in purity in thought, humility in demeanor, and the chance to receive knowledge on how to make future work profitable.

The supreme profit for the living entity is to be immersed in God consciousness. Through a properly situated consciousness, even routine work becomes a kind of yoga, or divine trance. King Dasharatha was a fighter who administered the kingdom of Ayodhya, yet he was a yogi as well, as the Supreme Lord had appeared in his family as his eldest son. It was this son, named Rama, that Vishvamitra came to borrow, for he needed protection in the forest from the attacking night-rangers, who had suddenly increased in influence.

Dasharatha knew that Vishvamitra's association made all his work successful, so he couldn't go against the request, though he was reluctant to. Because of that faith in the spiritual guide, the entire world would be benefitted. Lord Rama, Bhagavan who carefully arranged this beautiful sequence of events, would travel through the forests with Vishvamitra and Lakshmana, the Lord's younger brother. The trio would inadvertently make their way to the kingdom of Videha, where a grand contest with a bow was being held. If not for Dasharatha's acquiescence, Rama may never have made it to that contest, where King Janaka's beloved daughter Sita was awaiting. Through the help of the combination of Vishvamitra and Dasharatha, the marriage of a lifetime took place.

Question: Does the opposite condition of not meeting a devotee mean that your work is unsuccessful?

If through the prosecution of his work Dasharatha hadn't met Vishvamitra, it would have indicated that the king was not worth visiting at the time. The bona fide brahmana is the spiritual master of society, but he doesn't disseminate the confidential information of the Vedas to just anyone. If something is very important to you, why would you discuss it with people who won't understand that importance? Will you trust a young child with an expensive vase that could break easily? Will you hand over your family fortune to a money manager who doesn't understand the value of hard work and money?

The distribution of transcendental knowledge occurs through the proper qualification of both parties, the sender and the receiver. Vishvamitra felt that Dasharatha was worthy of his association, and the king made sure to abide by dharma, or virtue, so that the priestly class would be pleased with him. The servant of the Lord and the sincere recipient of transcendental knowledge make the perfect combination. Through their interactions others can learn so much as well. In the case of Vishvamitra's visit, the love shared between the involved parties and their affection for Shri Rama set the best example for countless future generations to follow. The rules and regulations may shift based on time and circumstance, but the primary dharma of the soul to love God never goes away. Bring it to the forefront of your consciousness by hearing always about the Lord and humbly accepting the sincere words of instruction kindly offered by the devotees, whose lotus feet act as boats offering safe passage across the ocean of material suffering.

VERSE 22

तुम्ह प्रभु पूरन काम चारि फलदायक।
तेहिं तें बूझत काजु डरौं मुनिनायक।।22।।

tumha prabhu pūrana kāma cāri phaladāyaka |
tehiṁ teṁ būjhata kāju ḍarauṁ munināyaka ||22||

"' O Prabhu, you fulfill all desires and give the four fruits of existence. Understanding that, I am fearful of what I could possibly give to you.'" (22)

Essay - The Ingredients For Success

The pious king knew that the exalted guest kindly received at his home came to ask for something. He wasn't a resident of Ayodhya, so his visit had a purpose. For the king, there wasn't much to give in comparison to what the sage could bestow. From proper wisdom comes the attainment of life's ultimate goal, which automatically incorporates the four primary rewards that are delineated by the Vedas. The ancient scriptures of India identify the four primary rewards and go about describing how they can be achieved, and the lessons imparted are not bound by sectarian designations or specific time and circumstance. In the same way, the counsel and association of the saintly class is not restricted to any group. Just hearing about these saints many years later can provide so many benefits.

Why was this guest so exalted? How could he fulfill all desires? The plants in the garden produce fruits that can be consumed. The same goes for the farm in general, which produces the food that sustains life. In one sense, you could consider the plant to be a wish-fulfilling tree which grants our desires in life. Whatever it is we may want, it can't be achieved unless there is vibrancy in life. The vital force within the body is maintained by food; therefore the plants serve as the sustenance, the source of the boons that life can grant us.

If someone were to give us land and the ability to grow crops, that reward would be greater than anything else offered. Someone may give us money or good fortune that is temporary in its manifestation, but the resulting benefits will be targeted. Getting the source of all enjoyment is more important, because from that source there are endless possibilities for rewards. Another way to think of it is to compare a prepared food dish to the actual raw ingredients. The dish can be enjoyed by those who have a taste for it, while the ingredients can be used to prepare many other dishes. Hence the possession of the ingredients is more valuable.

In the playing field of the material world, there are endless avenues for activity, with some leading to better conditions and others leading to worse ones. The Vedas declare that the human form of body is the most auspicious because of the potential it brings for achieving the four fruits in life: dharma, artha, kama and moksha. Dharma is religiosity, which immediately signals a departure from the animal species. Following regulative principles is only possible in a civilized society. From abiding by religious principles you get artha, or economic development. Without a profitable end to your ventures, what will you have to show for your work? Economic development affords the opportunity for kama, or sense gratification. And finally, after a life filled with enjoyment of the three rewards, there is the ideal boon of moksha, or salvation. Follow religious principles, profit in your work, enjoy the rewards, and then never repeat the same cycle again.

The brahmanas, or priests, can grant these four rewards through their association. Not to be confused with magic genies who suddenly arrive on the scene and give you what you want, the saints provide instruction so that mankind can follow the proper set of activities that will bring those rewards through work. Dharma, artha, kama and moksha apply to every single human being, regardless of religious persuasion or interest in spiritual life. Indeed, by following the guidelines laid down by the brahmanas, one doesn't even need to know what the four rewards are or why they are worth attaining.

The spirit soul is the actor and the material bodies the playing field. The material elements as a whole can be considered the field as well, and with proper knowledge one will know how to succeed on that field. As the brahmanas provide this knowledge through their instruction, the value of their association can never be properly estimated. Whatever reward it is you want, whatever fruit you would like to enjoy from the tree of life, the Vedas provide the answer. Though the highest reward is to voluntarily escape from the playing field and find the constitutional engagement of loving service to God, the enjoyments derived from a material existence are not denied the follower of the Vedas.

Maharaja Dasharatha had only desires for divine association. His eldest son was an incarnation of the original person, the Supreme Personality of Godhead. Therefore the king was already living in the spiritual world, basking in the sweet vision of Shri Rama day after day. From that love for Godhead sprung natural affection for those who represent the Lord's interests on earth, the brahmanas. Already taking care of and respecting many priests in his own kingdom, Dasharatha one day had the good fortune of being visited by Vishvamitra Muni.

After properly receiving his guest and getting his blessing, the king prepared for what the muni might ask. In the above referenced verse from the Janaki Mangala, the king offers the highest praise to Vishvamitra. The muni is addressed here as Prabhu, which means "lord", and is praised for being able to grant any desire, including the four fruits of existence. One who attains dharma, artha, kama and moksha in a single lifetime is considered extremely fortunate, as the rewards don't cohabitate very well with each other. Too much religiosity dampens the urge for sense gratification, and too much economic success makes following religious principles more difficult. In addition, if I am addicted to sense gratification, how will I get release from the cycle of birth and death? Moksha is specifically hinged on desire, what the consciousness is focused on at the time of death.

The association of the brahmanas thus becomes very important. They can put the proper guidelines into place, where the four rewards can cohabitate without a problem. Almost thinking out loud, Dasharatha here remarks how he feels that he can't give the muni a proper gift. If someone gives you the four fruits of existence, what could you possibly give them In return? Ah, but Dasharatha did have something that any person would desire: God's personal association. Vishvamitra had come to ask for this, the king's most valuable possession.

What would you do in the same situation? Someone comes by your home to borrow the services of your son, who happens to be an expert bow warrior, though still of a young age. This son is your most cherished object; his vision every day makes your life worth living. You had gone many years without having children, and you fretted over whether or not the family line would continue. Only after having completed an important yajna, or sacrifice, did not only one, but four beautiful sons come your way. Now someone who doesn't live in your community wants to take your eldest son? Why would you agree?

The reason for Dasharatha's eventual acquiescence is revealed in the above referenced statement. As the brahmanas provide the most valuable information in life, their requests cannot be denied. Indeed, it was the brahmana class who had urged Dasharatha to perform the sacrifice that brought Shri Rama to his family. The ways of the Lord are so mysterious and perfect at the same time. Though God is never influenced by external action, He arranges events in such a way so that it looks like a specific behavior leads to His presence. It was a fact that Rama had desired to appear as Dasharatha's son a while back and that the advice of the brahmanas was given to increase the value of their association, to show how much respect they deserve.

Lord Rama and His younger brother Lakshmana would be the reward for Vishvamitra's graceful presence. Of course the exchange was not an even one, for the four fruits of existence cannot compare to the presence of Rama and Lakshmana. The two beautiful youths are splendid in their appearance, dedicated in their vow to protect, and most sincere in their efforts. Just being able to say the names of the two brothers is a boon that brings many auspicious merits. Vishvamitra didn't ask for Rama's protection as a means of getting even. He was having difficulty living peacefully in the forests, as the night-rangers had harassed many innocent sages. The brahmanas unable to carry out their religious duties, their protector, brahmanya-devaya, Shri Rama, would go to the forests and weed out the toxic influence of the ghoulish enemies of the saintly class.

By following the regulations advised by the brahmanas, the four fruits of existence can come to us, but this path is very difficult. On the other hand, through following the recommendation of pure devotion to the Supreme Lord, the four rewards become insignificant. Dasharatha felt like his life was taken away whenever he was separated from Rama, which shows just how cherished God's association is. As the holy name is the best way to connect with that sweetheart who roamed the forests as a young child protecting Vishvamitra, the most recommended practice for spiritual upliftment is the chanting of the holy names, "Hare Krishna Hare Krishna, Krishna Krishna, Hare Hare, Hare Rama Hare Rama, Rama Rama, Hare Hare". The acharyas of the Vedic tradition have done so much for us that we really have no way of repaying them. Through dedication in bhakti-yoga, or devotional service, we honor their efforts and hopefully please them. The benedictions offered by the saints are meant to culminate in spontaneous devotion to God, so if we take up the processes of bhakti right away, their past tireless efforts will prove to be fruitful for us.

Essay - What To Give

Just imagine being the wealthiest person in the world, capable of going into any area and taking property because of your ability. Then picture coming up to someone else and telling them that you can't give them anything valuable. Your statement isn't one based on sentiment and it is not rooted in a deficiency in ability. Rather, the person you're speaking to is the one who can give you anything that you really desire, anything important to you. Though they outwardly have nothing, their wealth is more valuable than anything else, so it is impossible to repay them when they are kind enough to bestow benedictions upon you. Such a scene was present in the city of Ayodhya many thousands of years ago, but the acknowledged wealthy party in this scenario, the king Dasharatha, was able to provide the exalted sage Vishvamitra something invaluable. That gift is the most cherished item for every single person, and the fact that Dasharatha would voluntarily part with it for a moment only enhances his wonderful stature.

Who is Maharaja Dasharatha? The ancient kings of the world were concentrated in the area today known as India. Not that their influence was confined locally; they were addressed by such names as Mahipati and Bhupati, which mean "lord of earth". The names weren't assigned out of sentiment either. The kings had control over the entire earth, through either personal supervision or the influence of their many proxies. There were other kingdoms headed by other leaders, but the main king would have a recognized supremacy.

"The Blessed Lord said: I instructed this imperishable science of yoga to the sun-god, Vivasvan, and Vivasvan instructed it to Manu, the father of mankind, and Manu in turn instructed it to Ikshvaku." (Bhagavad-gita, 4.1)

With that firm authority came great responsibility. King Dasharatha and those rulers appearing before him in the family upheld virtue. Maharaja Ikshvaku set the standard for good governance, having heard the truths of the Bhagavad-gita from his father Manu. Manu heard it from Vivasvan, who heard it from Shri Krishna, the original speaker of the Gita. The Bhagavad-gita is a song containing the essence of Vedic teachings, the true meaning of life and the ultimate philosophy to guide mankind's behavior.

How can we make qualitative comparisons between philosophies? How do we determine if one philosophy is better than another? The more the philosophy tackles the root issue of life, especially with respect to identity, the more valuable it will be. For instance, if we read a book on how to succeed in business, it will only benefit us if we identify with businessmen. The same goes for cookbooks, marriage counseling, and instruction on how to be a good life partner.

Sometimes even philosophies that seem larger in scope get mistaken to be guiding philosophies on life. The Constitution of the United States of America is a nice example in this regard. A document formed off of compromise and aimed to rebuke the perceived harsh treatment from the past government, the Constitution serves as the foundation of the American government. Some revere the Constitution and its principles so much that they refer to the document as their "Bible", which is a stunning admission. For something other than the original Bible to be considered the guiding philosophy on life indicates that the Bible is either misunderstood or deficient in its ability to guide behavior.

Religion in the true definition is not based merely on sentiment. It is a science which has laws that cannot be denied. Just as it would be silly to say that we believe or don't believe in the law of gravity, to deny the existence of spirit and its position transcendental to the material nature can only be a sign of ignorance. Documents like the Constitution negate behavior that is considered harmful from governing bodies, championing the concept of freedom and its benefit to society. At the same time, tyranny, oppression and those acts of government which are shunned by the founders of the United States are the very result of freedom. Without an exercise of freedom, we cannot get any outcome in behavior. Therefore freedom itself cannot be the answer to life's problems.

The Bhagavad-gita addresses all of these issues, as it puts forth the ultimate philosophy on life, the primary guiding principle. It is said that the Vedas, the system of spirituality instituted by Shri Krishna, are the root of the tree of material existence. This means that every philosophy, existing past, present or future, is derived from the Vedas. Lord Krishna is the head of Vedic philosophy, and since He is the Supreme Personality of Godhead, His original system of religion is meant for connecting the living entities with their most preferred destination. Thus every rule presented by Vedic philosophy, including the recommendations given to kings, is intended to carry the living entity further along towards the ideal destination of the Supreme Lord's company.

A king like Dasharatha knew the governing principles, how to guide human behavior properly. Freedom is wonderful, but if it is misused you get chaos and misery. A document only limiting the actions of government will not provide man the guidance that he so desperately wants. History is filled with tyrannical regimes who killed millions of people to meet the demands of their brutal leaders. This could only occur because of the soul's inclination to serve. Even with full freedom, with no restrictions on action, the living being will have a desire to offer some service.

Vedic philosophy does not overlook the service issue. Rather, the tendency towards service is completely embraced, with every member of society given an object of service that matches their body's inherent qualities. The pious ruler implements these matches to keep safe what is known as the varnashrama-dharma system. Because of their fidelity to the Vedas and the nature of the work they had to perform, the pious kings like Dasharatha were in possession of so much wealth. They distributed charity, but only to the brahmanas, the priestly class of men who were voluntarily living by austerity.

One such austere brahmana was Vishvamitra, who visited King Dasharatha's palace one time. The king could give away in charity pretty much anything valuable to a brahmana, even if they didn't specifically ask. All special occasions were marked by the donation of such things as gold, cows and jewelry to brahmanas, who thus didn't have a hard time surviving despite not specifically working for a living. The priests engaged in sacrifice, penance, austerity, learning the Vedas, teaching the Vedas, and giving instruction to society and its leaders. Since they were so busy providing valuable instruction, they didn't have time to earn a living through fruitive activity.

King Dasharatha was so pleased to have Vishvamitra visit him and bless his family that he offered the above referenced sincere words of praise. The sage could grant any desire, including the four fruits of a human existence: religiosity, economic development, sense gratification and ultimate salvation. As this combination of rewards is difficult to come by, one is considered very fortunate to get all of them. If Vishvamitra, who had no possessions, could provide this to the king, what could Dasharatha possibly give in return? This imbalance instilled some trepidation in the king, for perhaps the brahmana would ask for something that he couldn't give. If that were the case, it would be a shameful stain on the Ikshvaku line that Dasharatha belonged to. The king must always give the bona fide brahmanas whatever they want, for why else do they rule the earth? If the most intelligent and munificent members of society are not pleased and protected, how can the king say that he is doing a good job?

Fortunately for the king, Vishvamitra would ask for something that he could give. Nevertheless, the request tore at the heart of the pious ruler. Vishvamitra wanted protection while living in the forests. Some night-rangers were causing a disturbance, and rather than exhaust his spiritual merits by casting curses on them, Vishvamitra thought it would be better to have expert fighters guarding him for a while.

Did the sage ask for the most experienced fighter in Ayodhya? Did he ask Dasharatha for his most capable man who had proven his fighting ability in the past? Oddly enough, Vishvamitra asked for the king's eldest son Rama to be his escort. This was strange because Rama was still a young boy, who barely had signs of maturity on His face. We know this from the accounts of one of the attacking night-rangers.

"At the time, there were not yet visible any signs of manhood on the boy's beautiful face, which was dark-blue in complexion and had an all-auspicious gaze. Rama had a gold chain round His neck, a small tuft of hair on His head, wore only one piece of clothing, and held a bow in His hands." (Maricha speaking to Ravana, Valmiki Ramayana, Aranya Kand, 38.14)

Rama was Dasharatha's most prized possession, his favorite person in the world. The king would have to agree to the sage's request though, so Rama went with Vishvamitra, with Rama's younger brother Lakshmana following along. Lakshmana would never do anything without Rama, so strong was the love he had for his elder brother. While in the forest, Vishvamitra would get attacked by a night-ranger named Maricha during a time of sacrifice. Though Rama was so young, Vishvamitra's intuition would prove correct, as Dasharatha's eldest son would unhesitatingly string His bow and pierce Maricha with an arrow. The blow was so fierce that the night-ranger was thrown many miles away into an ocean.

Shri Rama was none other than the Supreme Lord, appearing on earth to enact pastimes and rid the world of the influence of Maricha's clan, which was concentrated on the island of Lanka at the time. Dasharatha sacrificed his most beloved son, and for that kindness his stature as the most wonderful king would increase even more. Through Vishvamitra, Rama and Lakshmana would make it to the famous bow sacrifice held in the kingdom of Videha. There Rama would win the hand of Sita Devi, King Janaka's daughter, in marriage. Thus it can be said that Dasharatha's love for the brahmanas acted as a catalyst for the eventual meeting of the divine couple, Sita and Rama, the savior of the fallen souls.

VERSE 23

कौसिक सुनि नृप बचन सराहेउ राजहि।
धर्म कथा कहि कहेउ गयउ जेहि काजहि॥23॥

kausika suni nṛpa bacana sarāhe'u rājahi |
dharma kathā kahi kahe'u gaya'u jehi kājahi ||23||

"Hearing the words of the king, Vishvamitra complimented him in return. The sage then discussed dharma and his reason for coming there." (23)

Essay - Dharma-katha

While it's nice to have peers to share your experiences with, it is more beneficial to be in the company of authority figures who are capable of assertively identifying and revealing the real religious principles, remaining unafraid to discuss them with whoever is worthy. Our friendships are formed for our own immediate satisfaction, as it is beneficial to have people around whom we consider to be equals. Just being able to share experiences with others, to let them know what you are feeling and not have them judge you in return, is such a contributing factor towards mental health that people who lack this association often have to resort to approaching trained professionals to hear their problems. Dharma-katha, or discussion on religious topics, is a primary benefit coming from the brahmana community, and in this interaction the relationship is one between teacher and student. Hearing about dharma is so powerful that even a famous king like Dasharatha stood by quietly and listened attentively while such words came from Vishvamitra, an exalted sage who visited his community.

What would a king have to gain from listening to a person with a long beard who lived in the woods? Can a homeless person give us advice on how to live our lives, which are dependent on technological advancements and involve the constant pressure of having to meet the monthly bills? What would they know about raising a family, tending to matters at work, or maintaining a sound financial footing? The brahmanas of ancient times weren't poor without cause. They voluntarily accepted a meager lifestyle so that they would have a wealth of knowledge. From distractions in activity, through the feverish pursuit to best our fellow man in competition, a loss of rational thought results.

The first thing to go is proper identification. The country of origin, religious tradition, bank balance, skin color, gender, and so many other factors get used for identification, when in reality such attributes are transient. The bank balance can change quickly, as can the country of residence. Our physical abilities gradually diminish over time, yet we still remain vibrant living beings. Therefore identification must come from something besides the body or external attributes.

A brahmana earns their distinction by knowing Brahman, which is pure spirit. Strip away external appearances and conditions and you're left with a vibrant energy, a spark of life if you will. Since that spark pervades nature, it can be thought of as a singular collective energy. The Vedas give a name to that force: Brahman. The living beings are all part of Brahman, which means that their identity comes from pure spirit and not external conditions.

Hearing about Brahman is easy, but actually realizing it is a totally different matter. To maintain the proper identification, to not get sidetracked by illusion, the Vedic literature institutes dharma, which can be thought of as religiosity or religious law codes. Dharma actually means an essential characteristic, so when it is used in place of religiosity, the guiding principles are meant to maintain the essential characteristic of Brahman within the living being.

Dharma is flawless, so even the person not willing to accept any philosophy at all can progress in knowledge through following the guiding principles. Not everyone you meet will be up for philosophical discussion. They will sometimes be guided by emotion, the problem of the day. The worldwide news media exploits this tendency. Television news especially caters to emotion rather than intellect. The latest murders, shootings, rapes and statements from politicians are presented as important events, but if you looked at the entire picture from a mathematical point of view, these incidents are trivial. For instance, yesterday the majority of the world lived peacefully, didn't die, and didn't have anything horrible happen to them. Yet if only one tragedy occurred, it becomes the most talked about event due to the influence of news providers and their consumers.

Following dharma maintains sobriety of thought within the living being. Each personality type is provided their own religious principles to follow, with the idea being that eventually, maybe even in a future life, full enlightenment will be reached. The brahmanas are already at this stage, and their occupational duties call for teaching others about virtue and how to follow the proper principles. A wise king like Dasharatha was already a devoted soul, so he didn't need a lecture on dharma. He was a wealthy king, but this didn't mean that he somehow took his identity from his wealth or his standing in society. Rather, he viewed everything within the framework of his purpose, what role he had to play in upholding dharma for the good of everyone else.

Vishvamitra, a forest-dwelling brahmana, once visited the good king. Dasharatha received him nicely and offered him kind words of praise. The sage complimented the king in return and then discussed matters of duty, or dharma-katha. He also revealed the purpose of his visit. Brahmanas don't need much for their maintenance. As their aim is to behave righteously and stay connected with Brahman and its source, the Supreme Lord, they can get by with a small amount of land and basic food. In Vedic rituals held by pious kings, the brahmanas were always gifted things so that they didn't have to work for a living. Gold, jewelry and cows were regularly donated to the priestly class for their benefit.

Vishvamitra didn't need any of these things from the king, however. He required expert protection, for the terrorist-like night-rangers in the forest were disturbing his adherence to piety. These creatures would appear in the dark with false guises and then attack just at the moment that a fire sacrifice was culminating. In the Vedic tradition a religious sacrifice is known as a yajna, which is another name for God. A sacrifice didn't have to involve an animal being killed or offered up. A sacrifice generally consisted of a fire, with clarified butter offered as oblations. With a fire sacrifice, the component actions are pure and the presiding deities of creation are pleased. As Lord Krishna points out in the Bhagavad-gita, even though other figures take their portions of the sacrifice, it is the Supreme Lord who is responsible for the rewards distributed by the demigods.

"Endowed with such a faith, he seeks favors of a particular demigod and obtains his desires. But in actuality these benefits are bestowed by Me alone." (Lord Krishna, Bhagavad-gita, 7.22)

Krishna, or God, is the enjoyer of sacrifice. If one isn't worshiping Him directly, the Lord still must be present for any of the worshiped personalities to receive their share. In this way sacrifice is very important. It is the backbone of a life dedicated to dharma. In the modern age the most effective sacrifice is known as the sankirtana-yajna, where one regularly recites the holy names: "Hare Krishna Hare Krishna, Krishna Krishna, Hare Hare, Hare Rama Hare Rama, Rama Rama, Hare Hare".

To try to picture what Vishvamitra was going through, imagine sitting in meditation in your room and then getting attacked just as you started to think about God. This was basically what the sages in the forest were facing, as the night-rangers weren't just attacking but also killing them and then eating their flesh. Dasharatha had jurisdiction over that part of the forest, so Vishvamitra came to request special protection. What the king didn't know was that the sage had a special protector in mind, He who protects all the fallen souls.

Dasharatha's eldest son Rama was the same Krishna, the Supreme Lord, in the guise of a human being. Though quite young at the time, Rama was an expert bow warrior. He played the role of a fighter to give pleasure to Dasharatha's family line, the Ikshvakus, and protect the surrendered souls, the pious brahmanas, living in the forest. Dasharatha would rather die than part with Rama, but since he lived dharma, since he swore to uphold it, since he praised Vishvamitra with the sweetest words, he had no choice but to agree to the request.

From that acquiescence Rama and His younger brother Lakshmana would accompany the good sage into the forest. As a brahmana thoroughly understands Brahman and how to maintain realization of it, Vishvamitra's dharma-katha continued when he was in the company of the two boys. They would make sure to regularly tend to the sage and perform their morning and evening prayers. In return, the sage would speak to them about dharma, narrating ancient stories of historical incidents relating to God. How amazing is Lord Rama? His pastimes are so wonderful that even He likes to hear about them.

Vishvamitra would also impart on the boys confidential mantras to be used in fighting. Rama is the creator of the universe and Lakshmana His eternal servant, so they don't require any aid in fighting. Nevertheless, to add to Vishvamitra's stature, to prove just how important discussing dharma and teaching it to others is, they listened attentively, as if they were ignorant on the matter. Maintaining that veil of ignorance, the boys would enter King Janaka's kingdom on the day of a grand sacrifice, where Janaka's daughter would wed whoever could lift the extremely heavy bow given by Lord Shiva. The maintainer of dharma, Dasharatha, listened to the words of the speaker of dharma, Vishvamitra, and thus ensured that the object of dharma, Shri Rama, could lift Shiva's bow and reunite with His eternal consort, Sita Devi. In this way attention to dharma always pays, as it is beneficial for both those who follow it and those who hear about it.

Vishvamitra didn't need to provide a reason for his visit to Ayodhya, but he did so to let Dasharatha know that he wasn't just taking his son away without cause. Moreover, Dasharatha didn't need to worry about whether or not the request was appropriate, for by hearing about dharma, the king was reminded of his duty to uphold it. The most elevated brahmanas live bhagavata-dharma, or devotional service, so their cogent requests should never be denied, especially by one who is capable of meeting them. The king would benefit from his wise decision by receiving Sita as a daughter-in-law and giving countless future generations the opportunity to bask in the glory of the couple's marriage story.

VERSE 24

जबहिं मुनीस महीसहि काजु सुनायउ।

भयउ सनेह सत्य बस उतरु न आयउ ॥24॥

jabahiṁ munīsa mahīsahi kāju sunāya'u |
bhaya'u saneha satya basa utaru na āya'u ||24||

"When the lord of munis told the king the reason for his visit, the king became caught between love and truth and thus couldn't come up with a response." (24)

Essay - Rock and a Hard Place

There was a rock and a hard place, and in between was the king of Ayodhya, dumbfounded as to what to say to a stunning request, one he wasn't expecting. As the mind is capable of working tremendously fast, within an instant the stunned king remembered both his love for Rama and his dedication to the truth. As the age-old problem between what to follow, your heart or your mind, rose to the surface, the king couldn't settle upon a proper response. The lord of munis, Vishvamitra, had really stumped him with his request, but due to the all-pervading nature of the person whose association was desired, all parties involved would be satisfied in the end.

What was the dilemma facing King Dasharatha? Let's look at the truth angle first. Kings in those days, the Treta Yuga, were dedicated to piety. Their guidebook for governance of the innocent citizens was the Vedas, especially the truths pertaining to the laws of man, which were handed down by Manu. The origin of life is God, who has more defined features in the Vedic tradition. Though there are many pictures of God and different realizations of Him, the lack of detail in one spiritual tradition doesn't mean that the attributes are absent in the original person Himself. A child may not know that the sun rises and sets every day, but their lack of understanding has no influence on the operations of the sun itself.

In the same way the living entity's ignorance of spiritual matters, of the transmigration of the soul, of the source of identity being the individual spirit located within the heart, of the paltriness of rewards pertaining to material sense gratification, of the need for following law codes of spirituality to reach a better end, and of the need to ultimately think of the Supreme Personality of Godhead at the time of death, has no bearing on the effectiveness of the teachings of the Vedas. Every living being is born ignorant after all, and since the duration of life is so short, it is impossible to acquire perfect knowledge. Nevertheless, the Vedas make sure that man is not left totally in the dark. The caretakers are provided instruction on how to guide the human being from the time of birth all the way up until death. At every step there is instruction, and for every type of person there is an occupational duty.

The administrators, known as kshatriyas, are responsible for government. As the primary duty of government is to protect life and property, the kshatriyas must be skilled at fighting. An aggressor has no concern for another's life or their property, so in order to combat the aggressive forces, a more powerful fighter is required. The key to a successful government is applying justice equally. Not that one person's protection is more important than another's. Even the life of a cow is to be considered on a level equal to that of the wealthiest citizen of the state. A cow can provide some milk to be used for food, while a wealthy businessman can account for a large portion of the treasury through tax revenue, but the ruler is not supposed to see a distinction between the two. Every spirit soul is equal constitutionally, and thus every innocent being living within a particular jurisdiction is to be protected by the heads of state.

King Dasharatha upheld his dedication to the truth very well. He accepted that responsibility from his predecessors, who belonged to the line of kings started by Maharaja Ikshvaku, who was actually the son of Manu. Hence the rulers in Dasharatha's family were known as Ikshvakus. King Raghu was another famous king in the line, so the princes were sometimes addressed as Raghava. As a kshatriya is expert at fighting, he is not required to be supremely intelligent on matters of spirituality. If there is a question on how to administer justice, he consults the royal priests, who belong to the brahmana community. The deference to the brahmanas is unconditional. This means that whatever a bona fide brahmana asks for, the king obliges. This usually isn't a problem, because their requests turn out to be beneficial to everyone involved. The brahmana not only knows the duties of his own order, he is familiar with the occupational duties of every single person as well. Hence he can guide any person on the proper path in life. Think of it like a high school teacher who can teach pretty much any class perfectly.

Not surprisingly, love is what got in the way of Dasharatha's commitment to the truth. He was childless for a long time. Though in the grand scheme this doesn't matter, as the spirit soul is the essence of identity, still to uphold the family name, to keep the line of kings going, Dasharatha wanted a son. He would be granted that wish after performing a sacrifice at the insistence of brahmanas. The king would be blessed with four sons, with the eldest being his favorite. A parent usually doesn't play favorites, even if their behavior indicates otherwise. A father may be closer with one son than another but it usually doesn't mean that he loves any of his children more.

Dasharatha definitely did love Rama, the eldest son, the most. You couldn't blame him, as Rama was the Supreme Lord appearing in the guise of a human being. It is said in the stories recited during the Satyanarayana Puja that Dasharatha in his previous life was pious and regularly performed the puja. Hence through his good deeds he became qualified to have the Supreme Lord appear as his son. The benefit of this, of course, is that you get to share your love without impediment. If we worship a deity or chant the holy names, "Hare Krishna Hare Krishna, Krishna Krishna, Hare Hare, Hare Rama Hare Rama, Rama Rama, Hare Hare", we show our love through our actions, but having the same object of worship in front of you every day in the form of a child represents another level. The childhood form is the most effective at extracting the natural loving sentiments of the caregiving living entity.

The more attractive the child, the more endearing his visage and activities, the more that love will come out from others. No one is more attractive than God, so Rama thus enchanted everyone in Ayodhya. His younger brothers all loved Him, with Lakshmana especially attached to Him. It is said in the Ramayana that Lakshmana would not eat or sleep without Rama by his side. It is not uncommon for a younger sibling to latch onto an older one, but sometimes there are fights and rivalries. This was not the case with Rama and His brothers. All four thoroughly enjoyed each other's company.

Vishvamitra, who is described as the lord of munis because of his high standing and his dedication to austerity and penance, once visited Ayodhya. Dasharatha received him properly and felt ashamed in a sense. The king openly declared that Vishvamitra could fulfill any desire and easily provide the four fruits of existence: dharma, artha, kama and moksha. Religiosity, economic development, sense gratification and ultimate emancipation for the soul are the four rewards available to the individual who follows the system of religiosity passed down by the Vedas. The king was ashamed because he couldn't think of anything he could give in return to Vishvamitra. Nevertheless, the king had vowed to give the brahmanas whatever they asked for, so he was a little fearful of what Vishvamitra wanted.

As if the muni knew exactly what to say to put the king in a bind, he asked for Rama to accompany him in the forest. A band of night-rangers had been causing a major disturbance in the forest, where other brahmanas lived. Can we ever imagine such a thing? Do thieves think of robbing homeless men? These brahmanas had nothing. They barely ate anything and they lived under trees or in conditions not seen in the poorest countries today. Yet they had tremendous wealth in their dedication to God, which these night-rangers despised. One ghoulish creature in particular was having a strong influence. His name was Maricha, and Vishvamitra specifically mentioned him when talking to the king.

"Please allow Rama to protect me during those times when I am observing religious functions and trying to keep my concentration. O chief of mankind, a terrible fear has befallen me on account of this Rakshasa Maricha." (Vishvamitra speaking to Maharaja Dasharatha, Valmiki Ramayana, Aranya Kand, 38.4)

Dasharatha was in the toughest situation. For starters, why Rama? Why not any of the other royal fighters? Rama wasn't mature in terms of years. Later on, when the same Maricha would try to attack Vishvamitra with Rama by his side, the night-ranger would notice that there weren't yet any signs of manhood on Rama's face. This meant that the Lord was quite young at the time. Dasharatha was bound by love to his eldest son, so how could he let Him go? At the same time, to deny a well-meaning brahmana is the most egregious violation of piety. What would happen to his standing as a pious king? He would likely destroy the good name of the Ikshvakus.

Very, very reluctantly, Dasharatha acquiesced. Lakshmana, true to his nature, followed Rama and the muni to the forest. The same Maricha would attack, but this time Rama would teach him a lesson never to be forgotten. Without hesitation, without blinking an eye, the young Rama would string His bow and then shoot an arrow at Maricha that had such force that the demon would be thrown hundreds of miles away into an ocean. Vishvamitra knew what he was asking for; he knew that Rama was the most capable bow warrior in the world. God assigns Himself the duty to defend the religious practices of the devotees who take shelter under no one else except Him.

Externally, Dasharatha followed his mind instead of his heart, but since thinking about Rama is as good as seeing Him, the king's love for his son never dissipated. If anything, in separation the fondness grew stronger. The majority of us don't have God as our son, so the option of worshiping in separation is all we have. Through a consciousness fixed on God, even following your mind ends up keeping your heart pure. Vishvamitra's request and the king's rightful acquiescence would enhance the glory of the Raghu dynasty, and it would give countless future generations more of Rama's pastimes to remember and honor.

CHAND 3

आयउ न उतरु बसिष्ठ लखि बहु भाँति नृप समझायऊ।
कहि गाधिसुत तप तेज कछु रघुपति प्रभाउ जनायऊ॥
धीरज धरेउ सुर बचन सुनि कर जोरि कह कोसल धनी।
करुना निधान सुजान प्रभु सो उचित नहिं बिनती घनी॥3॥

āya'u na utaru basiṣṭha lakhi bahu bhāṁti nṛpa samajhāya'ū |
kahi gādhisuta tapa teja kachu raghupati prabhā'u janāya'ū ||
dhīraja dhare'u sura bacana suni kara jori kaha kosala dhanī |
karuṇā nidhāna sujāna prabhu so ucita nahiṁ binatī ghanī ||3||

"Seeing an answer not forthcoming from the king, Vashishtha tried all kinds of ways to make him understand. He said that the son of Gadhi is powerful through his great austerities and explained that Rama is also very capable.'" (Chand 3.1)

"Hearing Vashishtha's words with patience, folding his hands the protector of Koshala said: 'My lord, you are an ocean of kindness and knower of everything, thus it is not proper for me to request anything from you.'" (Chand 3.2)

Essay - Rest Assured

When in doubt, don't say anything. Stumped on a particular question, if you say the wrong thing, you might offend the person you're speaking to. Moreover, if the cameras are rolling, your incorrect answer will be remembered and repeated over and over again. One king a long time ago was dumbfounded at the request coming from an innocent sage. Having just praised the vipra for his standing and good deeds, the king couldn't now outright reject the request, as it would invalidate his previous words. At the same time, saying 'yes' would mean parting with his most beloved son. At this time a well-wishing adviser, another member of the priestly class, stepped in to offer some calming words.

We're not always so lucky. In the trickiest situations, coming up with the right thing to say is not easy. If politicians should hesitate on national television in a debate, their candidacy can end immediately. Nobody wants to be led by someone who can't speak with confidence and knowledge. The leader is in the top position for a reason. Good communication skills can mask the lack of intelligence, but at the same time someone who is knowledgeable can be perceived to be a dunce if they cannot in a short amount of time come up with the proper words to convey their thoughts.

There are so many issues to contend with in troubling situations that sometimes even if there is pressure to respond, it is better to just stay silent. After all, you can't hurt someone's feelings if you don't say anything. In fact, the Miranda warning given to people arrested in the United States starts off by saying that the detained person has the right to remain silent. The reason for this is that anything said during the time of arrest can be used against them in the court of law. If that's the case, why not stay silent throughout, not divulging any information? If you stay quiet long enough, maybe the troublesome situation will pass.

Vashishtha knew that the king of Ayodhya could not afford to hesitate for long. The son of Gadhi, Vishvamitra, had come as a matter of urgency. Night-rangers were foiling the religious practices of the ascetics living in the forest. More than just foil, these creatures would attack with force, often killing the sages and then eating their flesh. One ghoulish creature in particular was intent on harassing Vishvamitra. Named Maricha, he was a chief counselor to the king of Rakshasas in Lanka, Ravana.

"Please allow Rama to protect me during those times when I am observing religious functions and trying to keep my concentration. O chief of mankind, a terrible fear has befallen me on account of this Rakshasa Maricha." (Vishvamitra speaking to Maharaja Dasharatha, Valmiki Ramayana, Aranya Kand, 38.4)

Ironically enough, though Maricha was on the other side of justice, he later turned out to be a speaker of the glories of both Vishvamitra and the person the sage desired for personal protection. In one way through his wickedness Maricha increased the fame of the eldest son of Maharaja Dasharatha and also affirmed the king's dedication to piety. As the leader of a famous land, Dasharatha's primary desire in life was to uphold righteousness. In a world full of duality, the right course is not always discernable, so the safe bet is to follow the direction of the brahmanas.

But here now was a brahmana asking the king to lend his eldest son. There was a massive royal army that could have gone with Vishvamitra, guarding the perimeter of his ashrama. But as if to strike at the very heart of the king, to take the one possession that meant more to him than anything else, Vishvamitra asked to have Rama as an escort. Rama was not even twelve years old yet, but the sage knew that only He could protect against the attacks of Maricha.

Before future events could validate the sage's premonition, Dasharatha's royal priest stepped in to offer some sound words of advice. After Vishvamitra made his request, the king was stunned, basically speechless. Seeing that an answer was not forthcoming, Vashishtha reminded the king of the qualities of the people in question. He rightfully said that Vishvamitra was a strong ascetic, completely dedicated to austerity. In the Bhagavad-gita, the song of God, Lord Krishna states that He is the penance of the ascetic.

"I am the original fragrance of the earth, and I am the heat in fire. I am the life of all that lives, and I am the penances of all ascetics." (Lord Krishna, Bhagavad-gita, 7.9)

Krishna's statement was part of a series of remarks meant to indicate how God is the life of everything. To make this concept easier to understand to the conditioned living beings, Krishna went through some common activities and occupational positions and revealed how He is the specific identifying feature in each of them. For the ascetic to have true value, he must be dedicated to austerity. The statement, "If I could only be king for a day", indicates a desire to get whatever you want and enjoy the regal life but for even a brief period of time. The ascetic lives with just the opposite mindset. "What more is there that I can renounce today? So far I have fasted and lived in the wilderness, but surely there is something more that I can live without."

Asceticism and its powers are so great that the Vedas, the ancient scriptures of India, are filled with accounts of historical incidents where famous personalities took to asceticism and achieved a higher end. The potency of austerity for religious purposes is not limited to men either. The daughter of the mountain king was told in her youth by Narada Muni that she should marry Mahadeva, the greatest of the gods. Mahadeva, or Lord Shiva, is in charge of the material mode of ignorance, so he is the ideal worshipable figure for those who are into black magic, those desirous of material opulence to be used for nefarious purposes, and the ghosts and the goblins. Lord Shiva is himself completely renounced, yet his devotees are often very wealthy, having acquired their riches through simple offerings made to him.

The mountain king and his wife were a little taken aback by Narada's words. Lord Shiva wears a garland of skulls around his neck and has ashes smeared all over his body. He hovers around crematoriums and holds poison in his throat. What kind of husband would he make? None of this mattered to Parvati, the king's daughter. She immediately went to the forest to perform austerities, with famous seers arriving many years later to test her devotion. Parvati was even offered Lord Vishnu, the same Krishna and Rama, as a husband, but she refused, stating that she would abide by the words of her guru, Narada. Through her penance she was able to please Mahadeva and earn him as a husband. The two are to this day happily engaged in devotional service and overseeing the affairs of the material world.

Vishvamitra was not an ascetic in name only. He had previously been a king, but due to his asceticism he was now recognized as a saintly man. King Dasharatha had a vow to uphold righteousness at the direction of the priestly class, so he should not have thought that Vishvamitra's request would cause harm. Vishvamitra knew what he was doing, as he was very powerful through his austerity.

Vashishtha also reminded Dasharatha that Rama was capable, though He was very young. Dasharatha didn't know that Rama was the Supreme Lord appearing in his family to delight the residents of Ayodhya. The Lord would charm the world and countless future generations of man with His splendid deeds, which included protecting Vishvamitra from Maricha. As described by Maricha to Ravana in the Ramayana, Rama, though a young man with barely any signs of manhood on His face, without hesitation strung His bow and thwarted Maricha's attack on Vishvamitra's sacrificial fire.

"Then I, resembling a cloud and having molten-golden earrings, made my way into Vishvamitra's ashrama, for I was very proud of my strength due to the boon given to me by Lord Brahma. As soon as I entered, Rama quickly noticed me and raised His weapon. Though He saw me, Rama strung His bow without any fear." (Maricha speaking to Ravana, Valmiki Ramayana, Aranya Kand, 38.16-17)

The force of the arrow released by Rama was so strong that Maricha was thrust thousands of miles away, never daring to bother Vishvamitra again. In this way Vashishtha's words were prescient, and Dasharatha was fortunate to have him around. When we are in doubt or if we don't want to do what is right, hearing from someone else about what to do isn't always pleasant. We may even get angry with them for speaking the truth, but in the end we are benefited by their honest and wise counsel.

Dasharatha knew that Vashishtha was correct, though the king never looked at Rama as being supremely powerful. The Supreme Lord's splendor and might take a backseat to His beauty, charm and endearing qualities in the eyes of the divine lovers. The fact that He is God and offers protection from wicked characters and speaks pearls of wisdom like those found in the Bhagavad-gita is not the primary cause for the dedication to bhakti-yoga, or devotional service. Rather, in divine love the emotions can be so strong that the devotee starts worrying about the Lord's welfare and whether or not He will be able to handle different situations.

Taking Lakshmana with Him, Rama would protect Vishvamitra from the attacks of several Rakshasas. Through the good steward's leadership, Rama and Lakshmana would be led to the kingdom of Videha, where the marriage of Rama's eternal consort was being arranged. Her husband was not already decided. Whoever could lift Mahadeva's bow would win Sita's hand. Just as Parvati was meant for marrying Shiva, Shri Rama was meant to raise the bow and live happily ever after with Sita Devi, the daughter of King Janaka. Thanks to Vashishtha's good counsel, the wheels were set in motion for that wonderful marriage to take place.

Essay - Door Number Two

In the classic television game show, "Let's Make a Deal", the contestants' curiosity was piqued by first giving them a certain prize that they could have immediately. There would be no doubt as to what they could take home, but then there was another prize, which was unknown, suddenly introduced into the equation. If the contestant should be so willing, they could change their mind and trade for what was behind a curtain. It was a gamble, for if something worthless was behind the curtain they would lose the initial prize that they were previously guaranteed to have.

In a retail outlet, sometimes the same game is played by the salespeople to the customers, except the intent is to sell something that needs to be moved. What the customer actually wants is not important to the salesperson. Instead, what the salesperson wants to get rid of takes precedent. The person holding something of value will not want to part with it, but the knowledgeable customer will not be taken off track. Their intelligence is insulted by the pitch of the salesperson looking to push something else. Many thousands of years ago, a sort of similar situation occurred in the kingdom of Ayodhya. Since all the participants were pure of heart, their small exchange turned out to be celebrated for many years into the future. No wrong was committed by either party, for through their efforts their knowledge and dedication to virtue shined through for everyone to see.

The buyer in this scenario was a venerable muni named Vishvamitra. The son of the king named Gadhi, Vishvamitra was famous during his time for having converted from a warrior to a priest. Though during his initial period of austerity and penance Lord Brahma, the creator of the universe, failed to recognize him as a brahmana, Vishvamitra still reached such an exalted position that when he one day visited the king of Ayodhya, everyone stopped what they were doing and offered him the utmost hospitality.

The brahmanas are to be protected by the head of the state. The teachers in an education establishment earn a living and they provide instruction only upon payment. Why should they act otherwise? You need money to survive in a world where the majority of the population isn't self-sufficient through farming. Why should not the person accepting valuable information pay for the teacher's time? Only a miser would think that others owe them something, that they should work without compensation.

Under ideal circumstances, however, the priestly class does not charge money for what they do. They receive plenty of charity from those who are in positions to give it, but the purpose for the brahmana is to remain enlightened and on the path of dharma, or religiosity. The wise know that material dispositions change constantly, like a rollercoaster that goes up and down. The person with few material possessions and attachments weighing them down can focus more on studying the nature around them, performing sacrifices, teaching others about the difference between matter and spirit and, most importantly, worshiping God.

Your worship is more effective when you don't get sidetracked by fears over maintaining your possessions. Who can blame the person sitting in church praying to God to maintain their livelihood and ensure that food gets put on the table? As the material land is a place full of miseries, there is constant uncertainty with respect to the future. You work so hard to pay your bills and keep your family happy, but you know that one small wrinkle in the equation can cause the entire system to collapse. Thus it is not surprising that the fearful worker would look to the Almighty to save them from peril.

But when you have no possessions to maintain, your worship can be more pure. You don't need anything from God; instead you look to offer Him your time and attention. In any loving relationship the key ingredient is the quality time spent in each other's company. This relevant fact is easily forgotten through the many responsibilities that require attention each day, but the more the quality association is present, the more pleasure will be derived from the relationship.

The brahmanas on the highest platform of understanding have an intimate relationship with God, who is all-pervading. Simply by chanting His names, "Hare Krishna Hare Krishna, Krishna Krishna, Hare Hare, Hare Rama Hare Rama, Rama Rama, Hare Hare", the devoted soul can see God, remember His activities, become anxious for His personal association, and steer clear of behavior that will jeopardize that future meeting from happening. The brahmanas devoted to the Personality of Godhead, Lord Vishnu, swim in an ocean of transcendental nectar. They offer their services to society for little to no money because they don't require much to live. Their goal in life is not to be wealthy or to have material comforts provided to them. They only look for circumstances favorable for bhagavata-dharma, or the system of religiosity in devotion, connection to Bhagavan, the Supreme Lord who is endowed with every opulence.

Vishvamitra visited Ayodhya's king because his ideal circumstances were being threatened. Was Vishvamitra bugged by his wife to find a better house? Were his children asking for money? Was he worried about how to get nice food to eat? On the contrary, these worries were absent in his life. What was threatening his pious activity, however, was the influence of night-rangers. One fiend in particular, Maricha, loved to harass the brahmanas living in the forests. The sages had abandoned material life, they weren't looking to surpass anyone in stature, and they didn't have any possessions of value. Just based on this we can see how fiendish Maricha and his Rakshasa associates were.

Without a life dedicated to the mode of passion, where one pursues enjoyable fruits through hard work and competition, there is no reason to commit violence on anyone else. Hence the brahmanas live by the general principle of nonviolence. The attacks by the night-rangers presented a problem, so Vishvamitra approached the king, whose responsibility it was to protect the innocent. Dasharatha was thrilled to see the son of Gadhi, but he was a little hesitant at the same time. He knew Vishvamitra had a purpose for his visit. The king also knew that Vishvamitra could give him anything, including the four rewards of life: dharma, artha, kama and moksha. If someone can provide you anything through their counsel and association, when they should ask for something in return, the benefactor can't possibly deny the request, lest he feel like the greatest miser.

"...There is no one else in this world who has the power to resist the Rakshasas except your son Rama. O king, you are undoubtedly a great protector of the demigods, and your exploits performed during past wars are well-known throughout the three worlds. O annihilator of the enemy, even though your son is merely a boy, He is very powerful and capable of controlling the enemy. Therefore, O destroyer of foes, let your great army remain here and please allow Rama to accompany me. May there be all good fortune for you."(Vishvamitra speaking to Maharaja Dasharatha, Valmiki Ramayana, Aranya Kand, 38.8-11)

Dasharatha's concerns were validated when Vishvamitra asked for Rama to protect him. Dasharatha lived in opulence as a king, but he was not attached to material life. He lived by dharma, or virtue. He had no desire to enjoy the senses, but he acted as a good king in order to maintain the society. He did have one weakness, though. His attachment for Rama could not be broken. Lord Rama, Vishnu Himself appearing in the form of an ordinary human being with extraordinary capabilities, was Dasharatha's eldest and most favorite son. Dasharatha would sooner die than part with Rama's company.

In hindsight, Dasharatha's initial thoughts were not something he was proud of. He wanted Vishvamitra to take the entire royal army led by the king himself instead of Rama. The king knew that Rama was capable, though He was still under the age of twelve. Using that age as an excuse, Dasharatha tried to convince the knowledgeable Vishvamitra to "buy" something else, to look at another product on the shelf, all the while knowing that what Vishvamitra wanted was the most valuable item in the store that was the kingdom of Ayodhya.

Since the king remained in silence after seeing Vishvamitra's insistence, the royal priest Vashishtha stepped in and tried to make the king understand. He reminded Dasharatha that Vishvamitra was powerful through his austerity and that he knew what he was doing. He told Dasharatha that Vishvamitra's assessment of Rama being the most capable was accurate. The king needn't worry about Rama's welfare in the forest, for the Lord was expert at fighting already.

Deep down Dasharatha knew that his priest was correct. In the humblest way possible, Dasharatha responded to Vishvamitra by praising his kindness and knowledge. He said that it wasn't proper for him to try to ask him to take someone else, for the brahmana's request was one based on knowledge. Dasharatha certainly can't be blamed for trying to change the sage's mind. If you had the most beautiful prince as a son, who was so affectionate to you that you wondered what you had done to deserve such association, wouldn't you fight your hardest to try to keep that son with you all the time?

Dasharatha's eventual confidence in Vishvamitra would prove correct, as Rama would protect the sage from the attacks of the Rakshasas, including one intrusion by Maricha himself. The night-ranger was so impressed by Rama's ability to protect that he later recounted his experience to his leader Ravana in the hopes of dissuading him from perpetrating an iniquitous deed.

"I am your dear friend and ask you again to desist from this plan. If you should aggressively take Sita away by force, you and your relatives will lose your life and be taken to the abode of Yamaraja, being destroyed by Rama's arrows." (Maricha speaking to Ravana, Valmiki Ramayana, Aranya Kand, 38.33)

Vishvamitra would borrow Rama and His younger brother Lakshmana to be escorts for a brief period of time in the forest. Rama had barely any signs of manhood on His face, yet when the group was attacked, the Lord would string His bow without a problem. During Maricha's attempted attack, the force of Rama's arrow that struck the demon in return was so great that it launched the night-ranger over eight hundred miles away into the sea.

The knowledgeable brahmana knew what he was asking for and the king of Ayodhya knew what he was holding on to. Therefore neither party could be blamed for their behavior in that famous meeting in Ayodhya. Through Vishvamitra, Rama would visit the kingdom of Videha and marry Janaka's daughter Sita. Thus the son of Gadhi, through his request, would bring the goddess of fortune back to Ayodhya, which allowed the city to flourish even more.

VERSE 25

नाथ मोहि बालकन्ह सहित पुर परिजन।
राखनिहार तुम्हार अनुग्रह घर बन।।25।।

nātha mohi bālakanha sahita pura parijana |
rākhanihāra tumhāra anugraha ghara bana ||25||

"' Dear Sir, my children, relatives and citizens are protected by your blessings, either at home or in the jungle.'" (25)

Essay - The Sage's Favor

It's a tough fight. You're not sure what the outcome is going to be. You've invested so much time and effort travelling throughout the region that will be governed. You have shaken so many hands, flipped numerous pancakes, and kissed about every baby there is in each town. Despite your best efforts, you're still in danger of losing. The polls say that the race is neck and neck. What you really need to get you over the top is the endorsement of this one particular group. If they can favor you, you will get the necessary votes on election night to sweep into office. Once at the helm, you have all the power. You can do whatever you want and make a real difference in the lives of others.

Now the election is over. The group you wanted support from came through and pushed you across the finish line. Ah, but governing is a totally different story. The groups that supported you now want their favors returned. Thus you have to appoint connected people to important posts and pass legislation specifically targeted to their interests. The groups in question may be benefitted, and you may have been helped by getting elected, but the welfare of your family, children and most importantly, citizens, is not guaranteed through this practice.

Why is this the case? From a moral standpoint the interests of one particular faction shouldn't automatically take precedent over others. For instance, if one group is in favor of passing a law to help their particular business, what about the group that doesn't want the bill to pass? All citizens are equal in the eyes of the law, despite the discrepancy in incomes. Perhaps the person who pays millions of dollars in taxes feels more entitled to government protection than the person who pays no tax, but a good head of state doesn't take this difference into account. The government's duty is to provide for the general welfare by first protecting life and property, and in this respect the property of the poorest man is equally as worthy of protection as the largest estate of the multi-millionaire.

By rule, focusing attention on specific parties, repaying them for favors granted in the past, is a losing proposition. Unless everyone is benefitted by what you do, you are not a good leader. King Dasharatha of Ayodhya knew this hidden gem of the Vedic teachings a long time ago. Though he had it all and could give favors to any specific group, he knew that the blessings of one particular class would be beneficial to everyone. He thus praised Vishvamitra Muni to no end, telling the sage that the family, children and citizens under the protection of the king were actually protected by the blessings of the saintly class.

Let's say that I get favored by Vishvamitra, whose position in this case can correspond to that of a priest, or religious figure. Vishvamitra is a single person, so how is receiving his favor any different from getting the endorsement of a powerful lobbying group? The special interest organizations at least represent so many other people, but someone like Vishvamitra is a loner. He doesn't have family to support or a business to run. In one sense you could say that he is selfish. He lives in the forest alone, and worships God through austerity and sacrifice. Why should the king or any man of prominence be interested in what the sage wants?

Well, Vishvamitra's dedication to austerity is what makes him most eligible for being heard from. He doesn't have any possessions. He calls the forest his home and the holy name of the Lord his wealth. Abandoning a life of sensual pursuits, exalted sages like Vishvamitra prefer the quiet surroundings of the forest, where they can worship God fully and thus remain enlightened. From connecting with God one acquires the knowledge necessary to survive in any situation. A special interest group looks for a benefit that temporarily aids their situation, but life has much more important things than mere bodily maintenance. The form accepted at the time of birth will eventually be renounced, but the spirit soul, the vital force within, is always there. Its needs take precedent over the body's.

Someone like Vishvamitra accepts knowledge from the shrutis, or the scriptural tradition passed on through aural reception. From the shrutis one can impart wisdom to others, regardless of the target's position in life. In this way Vishvamitra's favor can mean acquiring knowledge on how to take care of children, relatives and citizens. Not everyone is in the same position or has the same desires, but through following the direction of the brahmana community, those who are by quality in the mode of goodness and dedicated to God, every person can advance spiritually, which is the real purpose of the human form of body.

The animals enjoy eating, sleeping, mating and defending, including bouts with intoxication and illicit sex. In fact, there is no such thing as marriage in the animal community. They don't operate under piety and sin because they are not intelligent enough to understand these higher concepts. Right and wrong are introduced to the human being because soberly following guidelines allows a better end to be reached. The instruction manual accompanying the new appliance allows the owner to properly assemble and operate their purchased item. The instructions are rules in a sense, lines drawn between virtue and sin. Accepting virtue brings one closer to the desired end and sin brings about negative consequences.

The brahmana knows right and wrong, good and bad, favorable and unfavorable, for any person. Thus having their favor turns out to be the greatest blessing for a king. Dasharatha was hesitant to give up the company of His son Rama, whom Vishvamitra requested as a personal bodyguard. The sage was being harassed in the forest by night-rangers, a situation similar to terrorists going after priests while they are delivering a sermon. These vile creatures would attack the sages and then eat their flesh. Vishvamitra knew that Rama was the most capable bow warrior in the world, that He could defeat anyone though He was not yet twelve years of age.

Dasharatha had fatherly affection for Rama, the eldest of his four sons. As a lesson to us all, Dasharatha showed that even attachment to family members can be renounced for a higher purpose. Vishvamitra's desires and instruction were beneficial to everyone, regardless of where they were living. If Rama were in the forest or in the royal palace, the sage's favor would protect Him nonetheless. The hidden secret was that Rama was the Supreme Personality of Godhead, Lord Krishna Himself in the guise of a warrior prince. This made parting with Rama that much more difficult for Dasharatha and Rama's protection in the forest more necessary for Vishvamitra.

The issue may be raised that if you invest so much trust in one person, if they lead you astray then so many other people will be negatively affected. This highlights one of the appealing aspects to democracy, the insulation from tyrannical rule gone wrong. If you have just one leader who messes things up, there is nothing anyone can do to stop them. In a democracy, however, major change requires majority vote, so passing legislation that goes against the wishes of the general population is more difficult, but still not impossible. There was certainly a risk in assigning so much stock to Vishvamitra, but the sage's qualities were what made him worthy of his position. He was not a spiritualist in name only. He was known for having only the welfare of the people in mind. He didn't have much, so why would he act in a way that would harm Dasharatha? Vashishtha, Ayodhya's royal priest, reminded Dasharatha of Vishvamitra's lofty standing, how he knew very well what Rama was capable of.

The sage's intuition would later prove to be correct. Lord Rama, accompanied by His younger brother Lakshmana, would protect Vishvamitra from many attacking night-rangers. By pleasing the sage, the brothers would learn mantras applicable to the standard method of warfare of the time, bow and arrow. From uttering a specific mantra Rama could make one of His arrows equal in force to modern day nuclear weapons. Aside from benefitting Dasharatha with his blessings, the world would be better off as a result of Vishvamitra's actions. The sage would bring Rama and Lakshmana to Tirahuta to attend a contest to determine the husband for King Janaka's daughter Sita. Rama, the only Lord for the surrendered souls and the only husband for the goddess of fortune, would win Sita's hand in marriage. Thus having Vishvamitra's favor continues to bring benefits to the eager souls of today looking to connect with God by hearing about His glorious deeds.

VERSE 26

दीन बचन बहु भाँति भूप मुनि सन कहे।
सौंपि राम अरु लखन पाय पंकज गहे।।26।।

dīna bacana bahu bhāṁti bhūpa muni sana kahe |
saumpi rāma aru lakhana pāya paṅkaja gahe ||26||

"The king said these words to the muni in a very humble and polite way. He presented Rama and Lakshmana to the muni and then touched his lotus feet." (26)

Essay - The Guardian

With a young child's first day of school, the moment is much more difficult to handle for the parents. Should the child start to cry immediately upon separation, through interaction with fellow students and classroom activity during the day, the separation can be forgotten rather quickly. The parents, however, are always left to worry about the child. They have raised them from the time they emerged from the womb, so to suddenly hand them over to the care of a teacher is not easy. For a particular king a long time ago, the pain was doubled by the fact that two of his four sons were leaving home. They would be under the care of an expert teacher, but they would be required to serve as his protection of all things. Because of that generosity, this king would go down in history as one of the most famous.

The Janaki Mangala, the sweet song written by Goswami Tulsidas that describes these events so nicely, presents some of the interactions between the king and the guardian of this situation. King Dasharatha did not have a son for the longest time. For a king following Vedic traditions that is a big deal. At the time of birth three debts are incurred. We owe our present circumstances to the past actions of spiritual entities. From the demigods, or devas, we get the rain necessary to maintain life. If our parents couldn't survive from eating grains, milk and fruits, we never would have developed within the womb to the point that we could take birth. If not for the rishis of the past, who safeguarded Vedic wisdom and the knowledge necessary for flourishing in life, we would live like animals, following only our sensual pursuits.

The third debt is what troubled Dasharatha. If not for our forefathers, the family that we are born into wouldn't exist. For the king of Ayodhya, his family was quite famous and well-known for their dedication to virtue. If you're born into a family of reprobates, perhaps you're not overly concerned with keeping it going. But if you take birth in the most pious family that the society relies on for its welfare, you want to make sure that the legacy continues after you depart this world.

Long without a son, Dasharatha took the advice and consent of the priestly class and performed a grand yajna, or sacrifice. The remnants of that sacrifice were handed over to the king's three queens, who simply by consuming the spiritualized food became pregnant. Four male children were soon born: Rama, Bharata, Lakshmana and Shatrughna. The four boys were naturally fond of each other, and they enjoyed growing up in the family environment in Ayodhya.

The eldest Rama was everyone's favorite. This was especially true for Dasharatha. A parent is not supposed to have a favorite, as they love their children equally. Yet the bond of affection was strongest towards Rama. The child was the leader of His brothers, and they all worshiped Him like a father. Though they all loved Rama equally, Lakshmana was the one closest to the Lord. He would not eat or sleep without Rama by his side. He would not do any of these things before the Lord would. He would never dishonor his eldest brother; not in thought, word, or deed. To use a common modern expression, Lakshmana would gladly take a bullet for Rama.

The boys were groomed to follow in their father's footsteps. The kings in those times weren't just administrative heads; they were the best fighters in the world. After all, the primary duty of government is to protect property and life. These two vital aspects are threatened by miscreants, those who don't have respect for what others have lawfully earned. A miscreant will not take well to logic and understanding. Imagine being the victim of a holdup like a carjacking and then trying to explain the issue of property rights to the culprit. "Sir, excuse me, but I bought this car with my own money. Therefore I am the owner. If you would like a car I suggest you work honestly so that you can buy one yourself."

The warrior class of men exists to deal with the thieves in society. As an aggressor has no concern for rules of propriety, the defenders must use force when necessary. In the Vedic tradition it is considered a laudable sacrifice to lay down your life on the battlefield fighting bravely. The slain warrior is immediately granted residence in heaven, so noble is their bravery. To get to heaven involves many pious deeds. One must be quite religious, without sin and following the guiding principles presented by the priestly class. Yet the same benefit of ascension to heaven can come by nobly defending the innocent and dying in battle.

Dasharatha was a world-famous fighter, a protector of dharma, or virtue. His sons were to follow in his footsteps. Yet a fighter should be mature. You wouldn't send children out to act as police officers. There is an age restriction for a reason. This made the visit by Vishvamitra all the more strange. An exalted sage living in the forest, Vishvamitra one day visited Ayodhya and was greeted hospitably by King Dasharatha and his family. The king was ready to give the world to the sage, as the administrator class operates off of the advice and consent of the priests, who are knowledgeable on all affairs.

Vishvamitra wanted to take Rama and Lakshmana with him. This wasn't necessarily to teach the two boys about the art of fighting with the bow and arrow, the standard method of warfare of the time. He didn't need to instruct them further on the Vedas or have them live with him so that they could find enlightenment. Vishvamitra was being attacked by the worst kind of villains. He knew that only Rama and Lakshmana could protect him.

In the father's eyes, the two boys were quite immature. They hadn't left home, and they were enjoying the company of the family. Dasharatha had a royal army full of capable fighters, so why wouldn't the sage want one of them? Dasharatha was ready to lend his entire army headed by himself instead of giving over Rama, his favorite son.

In the above referenced verse from the Janaki Mangala, we see the end result of the interaction between the king and the sage. In utmost humility and kindness, Dasharatha offered praise to the muni, saying that his blessings would grant any reward to any person. The king brought Rama and Lakshmana before Vishvamitra and then touched his lotus feet. Just imagine the situation. A chivalrous fighter whom the entire community honored as the chief person in the city was bowing down before a mendicant with a beard. The brahmanas may look meek, but in mind they are the strongest. Their wealth is their devotion to God, and by accepting the dust of their lotus feet one can receive the most wonderful blessings in life.

Though Rama and Lakshmana would be protecting Vishvamitra from the attacking Rakshasas, the sage was essentially their guardian. Dasharatha wasn't watching his children go away to school for the first time. Instead, he watched his two boys leave to certainly face attacks from creatures that were known for eating human beings. The anguish the king faced is unimaginable. Yet the incident once again proved his dedication to dharma. The famous ruler worked with detachment, following the guidelines prescribed to his order without concern over outcome. If he had kept his sons with him out of familial affection, then the responsibility for the outcome of the actions would belong to him. But since he followed protocol, Vishvamitra, and more specifically the person he was serving, bore the burden of the results.

Who were Vishvamitra and the other sages worshiping? Dharma comes from God. The material world is a sort of playing field which can provide different results based on the game that one plays. Dharma is the set of rules aimed at allowing the field to provide the sweetest tasting fruit of devotion to God. The playing field allows for all sorts of other activity, so following dharma is very difficult. Yet the reward is worth the effort, so the highest class of men known as the brahmanas remains on the righteous path. They worship God through their actions, and since they have sublime wisdom, they share it with others when appropriate.

Dasharatha's eldest son was actually the person who originally instituted dharma. In this sense the king and the sage both were serving God, as loving Rama is the highest dharma for any person. Bhagavata-dharma, or devotional service, is the spirit soul's constitutional engagement. Dasharatha loved Rama so much that he was willing to let Him go at the behest of the brahmanas. Vishvamitra loved Rama so much that he made sure to use his position in society to gain the Lord's association. Rama and Lakshmana would prove the sage correct by valiantly protecting him from all sorts of attacking Rakshasas. For their bravery, the fame of the Ikshvaku dynasty and its leader at the time, King Dasharatha, would increase exponentially.

Though we may not be in the royal or priestly order in this lifetime, the same sacrifice can be made by regularly chanting the holy names, "Hare Krishna Hare Krishna, Krishna Krishna, Hare Hare, Hare Rama Hare Rama, Rama Rama, Hare Hare". Recitation of the holy name through love and devotion is the only dharma for this age. It is applicable to every person, regardless of their social standing. The dark age of Kali has broken three of the four legs of dharma, leaving only one left standing. Therefore the many rules and regulations that previously formed the pillars of dharma cannot be erected. Yet just the dedication to chanting, to remembering God and glorifying Him, is enough to bring the same benefit of the Lord's association. Hearing about Rama and Lakshmana going away with Vishvamitra is as good as having witnessed it. Hearing about God in the proper mood is as good as sacrificing work efforts for His benefit. Rama and Lakshmana protected Dasharatha's good name and they supported Vishvamitra's dedication to sacrifice. In a similar manner, the Lord and His personal energies will protect the surrendered soul who takes chanting of the holy names to be their life's primary engagement.

VERSE 27

पाइ मातु पितु आयसु गुरु पायन्ह परे।
कटि निषंग पट पीत करनि सर धनु धरे।।27।।

pā'i mātu pitu āyasu guru pāyanha pare |
kaṭi niṣaṅga paṭa pīta karani sara dhanu dhare ||27||

"Getting the permission of their mother and father, they came and touched the guru's feet. They then put on yellow garments, tied a quiver around their waist, and held arrows and a bow in their hands." (27)

Essay - Respectable Boys

"Mom, do I have to go? Dad, can't I stay home? Why do I have to do this? You always make me do things I don't want to do. I'd rather stay home and play. I don't want to go to that place." That parents would compel their children to do things they don't want is not out of the ordinary. And that children would protest vehemently to doing chores and travelling to places to accept responsibility is also not uncommon. With one king in particular, however, his children were so well behaved that even when they were sent to escort an innocent sage and protect him from vile attacking creatures in the wilderness, they were respectful, honorable, and eager to the task. The description of the scene where they prepared for leaving is delightful to the heart, with each aspect infused with transcendental goodness.

Normally, if you hear about someone getting ready to go somewhere, the words of description aren't necessary. If a fighter is preparing for a large conflict, what is the big deal about them putting on their clothes or preparing mentally? The real action occurs when the conflict starts. In the scene in Ayodhya many thousands of years ago, two youths were getting ready to leave home, and they wouldn't face danger until later on. Nevertheless, the personalities in question were divine, beautiful sons of King Dasharatha. Any time the mind can remember those two youths there are countless benefits received. Every aspect of their behavior, including their dedication to one another, is remarkable.

Why were divine personalities roaming the earth as children? Why not wield tremendous power and show off your true ability? This way people could then know who you are and worship you properly. With the Supreme Lord, the more amazing His displays of affection, kindness, compassion, honor, chivalry, and dedication, the greater the chances that others will take up worship in earnest.

To use a simple example to see the principle in action, we see that many athletes and celebrities rise to the top of their profession. Yet the ones who struggled in the beginning, who defied the odds, are given more attention. If someone who is considered less likely to succeed ends up winning in the end, their victory is more appreciated; it garners more attention. The person struggling through poverty, overcoming family adversity, dealing with debilitating diseases and handicaps, and then eventually rising to the top of their profession serves as a role model for others. If they can do it, why can't anyone else?

When the Supreme Divine Being appears on this earth, He rarely displays His awesome powers immediately. Instead, He shows that even in the tiniest of forms, which normally wouldn't have success in difficult ventures, He can succeed and live up to His role as the ultimate protector of the surrendered souls. Why protect only the surrendered and not everyone else? If someone doesn't want protection, how are they going to be protected? For instance, we may have a fire extinguisher in the kitchen, but when the next fire arises, if we don't use the extinguisher how can we be protected?

If the protection is not used, it cannot be blamed for anything bad that happens. With the Supreme Lord, His energy is everywhere. The energy belongs to Him, so it is an extension of His mercy. Yet depending on how the target living entities utilize that energy, there can be either benefits or harm. Under the spell of maya, or illusion, the external energy is utilized for personal gain, for trying to become the most successful enjoyer in the absence of God's association.

From consulting Vedic wisdom it is revealed that the essence of identity is the spirit soul. One of the soul's properties is blissfulness. In the constitutional state, the bliss arises from voluntary, unmotivated and uninterrupted service to the Supreme Lord. Accepting that constitutional position is difficult for one deluded by maya. The illusory energy of the material world belongs to God, but it is described as external because it can have different uses. If one wants to live in illusion, they can. For illusion to have a detrimental effect, the Lord's internal potency cannot be used. Instead, maya turns into the temporary presiding deity, as she fosters lust, anger, greed and vice. Through her agents of wine, women, animal flesh and gambling she deludes the otherwise pure soul into searching after contaminated happiness.

For the Supreme Lord there is never a chance of association with maya. The energy belongs to Him, so when He appears on earth it acts under His direction to give the appearance of fallibility to others. The material energy provides no protection from calamity; that is why she is known as durga, or difficult to overcome. The spiritual energy is present within all of us, and it is a positive force. Yet unless we know how to utilize that energy, how to connect with it and take direction from it, maya remains the sole benefactor. You can think of maya as the horrible boss who makes you work like a dog and pays you very little. At the same time, your job is always threatened; never is there a moment of peace.

The Supreme Lord offers protection in different ways to those who sincerely desire it. In the most basic exercise, just thinking of the Lord's personal form is protection enough, as the mental image creates peace within the consciousness. The ability to develop consciousness is unique to the human being; hence the species is considered superior by the Vedas, the original scriptural tradition of India. In no other form of body is there the chance for becoming fully Krishna conscious by the end of life.

In His original form God is known as Krishna because He is all-attractive. Attractiveness is coupled with a form, or spiritual manifestation. Sometimes this form is described as nirguna or avyakta, which can mean without qualities or unmanifested. The spiritual manifestation is unknown to us; it is a concept that cannot be conceived by the mind. For instance, if Krishna were to stand before us, He might appear to be a certain height. Yet there is no height limit for the Lord. He is both larger than the largest and smaller than the smallest. In this way He is not manifested. We are graced with His visible presence in the form of the avatara every now and then to get a slight idea of His features.

In the Treta Yuga, Krishna came as Lord Rama. The servitor God, the most dedicated servant of Krishna in His unmanifested, spiritual form is Baladeva, who is also known as Lord Ananta Shesha Naga. That divine personality appeared simultaneously with Rama as His younger brother Lakshmana. Dasharatha was their father, and the two boys had two other brothers. One time the venerable Vishvamitra Muni visited Ayodhya and asked to have Rama accompany him in the forest. It was not revealed to anyone that Rama was God. Rather, everyone just had a natural attraction to Him. The Lord was so pious that He could only be Dasharatha's son. There was not a hint of sin in Him, and His three younger brothers looked up to Him like a father. Lakshmana was closest to Rama in affection, as he would always follow his elder brother around.

When Dasharatha finally allowed young Rama to go with Vishvamitra, Lakshmana was told to accompany them as well. The king was worried about his eldest son, for He was not even twelve years of age yet. There were many mature fighters that were part of the royal army, but Vishvamitra specifically told them to remain where they were. The enemy forces in the forests were a unique breed of man-eaters, capable of changing shapes at will. They were careful in their attacks, waiting until religious ceremonies were taking place. They were thus the vilest creatures who required an expert bow-warrior to be handled.

In the above referenced verse from the Janaki Mangala of Goswami Tulsidas, the actions of Rama and Lakshmana right before they left for the forest are presented. Many things would happen while protecting Vishvamitra, and indeed the main subject matter of the poem is the eventual marriage that would take place between Rama and the daughter of King Janaka, Sita Devi. Nevertheless, something as simple as Rama and Lakshmana's preparation while leaving home is presented to give the mind something wonderful to think about. This mental image provides just as much protection as Rama and Lakshmana's arrows did to Vishvamitra.

Why is this the case? We see that the two boys first got the permission of their parents and then touched the guru's feet. Rama is God and Lakshmana is practically identical to Rama. They don't need permission to do anything. With a simple exhalation, Lord Krishna's form of Vishnu creates this and many other universes. To show just how much they loved their caretakers, Rama and Lakshmana set an example of ideal children. This behavior is more heartwarming coming from children because there is innocence. An adult showing respect in this way has the ability to discriminate, so perhaps they are following protocol to receive a benefit later on. Rama and Lakshmana innocently loved their parents and would do whatever they asked. They weren't being sent off to camp or to a local playground either. They were to act as guardians for someone who was so exalted that the king himself took direction from him.

The boys did not hesitate in going. They showed respect to the people that deserved it. They next put on yellow clothes. Generally, Lord Rama wears a yellow robe and Lakshmana a blue one. When the brothers appear as Krishna and Balarama they follow the same tendency. The matching colors are also present with their appearance as Lord Chaitanya and NItyananda Prabhu. The brothers then tied their quivers around their waists. Again, they weren't preparing for playing laser-tag or a day of innocent fun. Though youths at the time, they were getting ready to battle the world's strongest fighters. Vishvamitra, as an expert teacher, would give them powerful mantras that could turn their arrows into weapons with the ability to create devastation like a nuclear weapon.

To complete the picture, they took bow-and-arrow sets in their hands. This wonderful scene of the two brothers readying for their journey with Vishvamitra cannot be contemplated enough. They say that a picture is worth a thousand words, and since Rama and Lakshmana are transcendental, just creating a mental picture through hearing has a similar, if not greater, effect. From this one scene we see how to properly respect our elders and spiritual guides. We see how dedicated to protecting the innocent the Supreme Lord is. We also see just how much Lakshmana loves Rama. Wherever the Lord goes, Lakshmana is right behind Him to act as protection. Rama doesn't require this, but then Lakshmana doesn't need anything except his brother's association in life. As Akampana, a fierce Rakshasa fighter, would later point out, Rama is like a raging fire and Lakshmana a powerful wind that extends the reach of that fire.

"Rama's younger brother, Lakshmana, has reddish eyes and a voice that resounds like a kettledrum. His strength matches that of Rama's, and his face shines like a full moon. Just as wind gives aid to a raging fire, Lakshmana has joined forces with his brother. It is that best of kings, Shriman Rama, who has brought down the Rakshasas fighting in Janasthana." (Akampana speaking to Ravana, Valmiki Ramayana, Aranya Kand, 31.16-17)

The same protection offered to Vishvamitra exists in the image of Rama and Lakshmana and also in the holy name itself. The Supreme Lord has thousands of names which describe His transcendental features, and they are best sequenced together in the maha-mantra: "Hare Krishna Hare Krishna, Krishna Krishna, Hare Hare, Hare Rama Hare Rama, Rama Rama, Hare Hare". The holy name is the transcendental fire to burn up the sinful effects of the dark age of Kali, and the spiritual master, following Lakshmana's lead, is the powerful wind to spread those flames throughout the world. With that combination, how can maya ever stand a chance against the sincere devotee?

VERSE 28

पुरबासी नृप रानिन्ह संग दिये मन।
बेगि फिरेउ करि काजु कुसल रघुनंदन।।28।।

purabāsī nṛpa rāninha saṅga diye mana |
begi phire'u kari kāju kusala raghunandana ||28||

"The king, queens and all the citizens of the city gave their minds to Rama. 'Return home quickly, doing Your work successfully, O delight of the Raghu dynasty.'" (28)

Essay - Bon Voyage

For Rama to return home, He'd have to be successful in His work. The king, queens and townspeople knew this, so they wished Him the best as He departed from their vision. The delight of the Raghu dynasty, the bright full moon to dissipate the darkness of ignorance and despair that envelops the material world, was departing with the sage Vishvamitra. This was no camping trip or pleasure vacation. Rama, though only a young child, had the most difficult responsibility put on His shoulders. But just as He had previously bore the burden of the world as the boar incarnation Varaha, Rama would dutifully accept the responsibility of protecting the sages.

One can only imagine what the people in the town were thinking. Rama was their cherished prince, the eldest son of the King of Ayodhya, Maharaja Dasharatha. Though there was variety in classes, with not every person belonging to the royal order, everyone felt as though Rama was part of their family. This occurs when there is good government and the king is respected for his implementation of justice. As Rama's younger brother Lakshmana would note several years later, Rama was so respected that even those He punished couldn't find anything bad to say about Him.

"I have not seen any person in this world, be they an enemy or one punished for heinous sins, speak ill of Rama, even in His absence." (Lakshmana speaking to Kausalya, Valmiki Ramayana, Ayodhya Kand, 21.5)

Police and other authority figures are not liked because of the power they wield. Does every student like the teacher of the classroom? Do workers not despise their bosses for their position? Rama had to deliver justice on behalf of the people, but even those He punished respected Him. As a beautiful child not yet twelve years of age, Rama was taken away from His home, bringing Lakshmana with Him. Vishvamitra insisted on this protection, though, so what could anyone say? Dasharatha was ready to send the royal army into the forest to act as protection, but the muni insisted that the only person he required was Rama.

It is interesting to note that the onlookers seeing Rama off did not curse the muni or hold any grudge against him. Vishvamitra was equally as exalted as Dasharatha, and the people understood that he was in significant danger. He was a brahmana after all, so by nature, quality and work he lived in the mode of goodness, the highest of the three modes of material nature.

"O son of Pritha, that understanding by which one knows what ought to be done and what ought not to be done, what is to be feared and what is not to be feared, what is binding and what is liberating, that understanding is established in the mode of goodness." (Lord Krishna, Bhagavad-gita, 18.30)

Goodness equates to knowledge, sort of like following the instruction manual for an appliance that you just bought. In the mode of goodness one accepts the proper guidelines to attain a beneficial end. In the mode of passion, you are driven by the desire to get a reward, so you end up expending so much effort to reach an eventual neutral position. The mode of ignorance is bereft of both knowledge and a worthy fruit to enjoy. While there may be so many varieties of activity that include combinations of the three modes of nature, thus making it difficult to decide what is good and what isn't, any behavior that gradually increases one's real knowledge can be considered part of the mode of goodness.

What is real knowledge as opposed to fake? Real knowledge pertains to the self, the essence of identity. There is a larger collection of energy pervading nature, but at the core we are individuals. We are tiny sparks of that giant energy, so we have the same properties as the sum collection and also its origin. The sun is a gigantic body of fire and heat, and its many rays are tiny samples of that body. At the same time, just because the sunshine leaves the sun doesn't mean that the sun is altered in any way.

We living entities are tiny samples of God, who is known as Brahman to those unaware of His transcendental features. The mode of goodness allows for the realization of Brahman, wherein we see ourselves and every other living entity as individual sparks of pure spirit covered by temporary manifestations of matter. The mode of goodness is better than passion and ignorance, and one who wants to realize the true destination, the proper home for the spirit soul, should follow the advice of someone living in that highest mode, a person who is Brahman realized.

Vishvamitra lived in the mode of goodness as a matter of procedure, but he had transcended all the modes of nature. He was devoted to the Supreme Personality of Godhead by occupation, so there was no question of ignorance with respect to the Lord's features, a fact evident during his visit to Ayodhya to get Rama to be his escort. A band of night-rangers, those living in the mode of ignorance, was harassing the sages living in the forest at the time. On one side you had a ghoulish creature who can change their shape at will, sort of like a terrorist who dresses up in civilian clothes to avoid attack by the military. At the last second they reveal who they are to the unsuspecting target.

The brahmanas, on the other hand, have no weapons. Fighting is reserved for those in the mode of passion, for one can only fight when they see bodily distinctions. The brahmanas know the equality of spirit, so to the best of their ability they try to avoid conflict. Dasharatha had jurisdiction over the particular areas besieged by the Rakshasas hailing from Lanka, so Vishvamitra did the right thing by approaching the king.

The sage's credentials were well known to the people, so they also indirectly prayed for his welfare by thinking of Rama. Shri Rama, the Supreme Lord in the form of a warrior prince, is never alone. His closest associates and those people He protects are intimately tied to Him. By praying that Rama would do His work successfully, it automatically meant that those who would be protected by Rama would get the full blessings of the Lord.

The strain on the mother and father was the hardest, for they lived with Rama every single day. They made the ultimate sacrifice by putting their son in the custody of a sage who was being attacked. Despite their willingness to part with Rama, they never stopped thinking about Him. In the highest form of spiritual practice known as bhakti-yoga, or devotional service, thinking is as good as doing. Hearing about the Lord is as good, if not better, than seeing Him face to face. With sight mental distractions can arise and the consciousness isn't forced to focus as much. With hearing, attention is required, and as the focused thoughts stay in the mind, there is a stronger link formed to the object in question.

Thinking of Rama in separation is the superior method of worship because the longing creates a strong attachment. The exalted yogis of the past all practiced this method of worship, and most of the time not on purpose. The Supreme Lord knows best on how others can worship Him, so He creates situations where the mood of separation can flourish. In His descent to earth as Lord Krishna, the same Rama created separation from the gopis of Vrindavana, who thought of the Lord so often that they are considered the topmost devotees by exalted spiritual masters and saints like Shrila Rupa Gosvami, Shrila Sanatana Gosvami, and their teacher, Shri Krishna Chaitanya Mahaprabhu, who is Krishna Himself.

Worship in separation is not a theoretical exercise, for the object in question must be real for the effects to manifest. To know that Rama is real is to have some interaction with Him, even if for only a brief moment. The absolute nature of Rama's names, forms, pastimes and attributes does not apply to His external energy of matter. For instance, we cannot worship a tree in separation, no matter how hard we try. Attempting to imitate the principles of bhakti-yoga practice - which are so nicely presented in sacred texts like the Shrimad Bhagavatam and Bhagavad-gita through explicit instruction and in real-life stories documented in works like the Janaki Mangala and Ramayana - on objects not personally related to God does not work. Making up gods, inventing systems of religion, and denying the Lord's existence outright are failing methods.

For those of us living in the present age, the worship in separation of the Supreme Lord can best take place through regularly reciting the holy names: "Hare Krishna Hare Krishna, Krishna Krishna, Hare Hare, Hare Rama Hare Rama, Rama Rama, Hare Hare". These names are not sectarian, nor are they powerful sound vibrations addressing a fictitious person. The strength in chanting this sacred mantra lies in the potency of the beneficiary, in His absolute ability to deliver the surrendered souls through the mind. The residents of Ayodhya felt the burn of separation from Rama's departure, but they were soothed by the memory of His activities. The very mention of His name would cause joy, bringing to life His vision at a time when He was far away.

Raghunandana, the delight of the Raghu dynasty, would indeed return home successfully. He wouldn't come back alone though. He would bring with Him a new wife, along with wives for His three younger brothers. Vishvamitra's request for Rama's company would serve many purposes. It would show that Dasharatha was a man true to his promise to protect the brahmanas. It would allow the citizens of Ayodhya to worship Rama in separation, and it would also remove the influence of the Rakshasas from the forests in question. Since the above referenced verse is from the Janaki Mangala written by Goswami Tulsidas, we know that the ultimate purpose served by Vishvamitra was to bring Rama to the sacrificial arena in Tirahuta, where the svayamvara of the daughter of King Janaka was taking place. The delight of the Raghu clan would soon delight the many onlookers by lifting Lord Shiva's enormously heavy bow and winning the goddess of fortune's hand in marriage. Thus Rama's time in the forest was extremely fruitful.

VERSE 29

ईस मनाइ असीसहिं जय जसु पावहु।
न्हात खसै जनि बार गहरु जनि लावहु।।29।।

īsa manā'i asīsahiṁ jaya jasu pāvahu |
nhāta khasai jani bāra gaharu jani lāvahu ||29||

"They pray to God to grant them blessings: 'May You garner fame and return victorious. May You not lose a single hair while bathing.'" (29)

Essay - *Suffer Not Any Pain*

The influence of yogamaya is so strong that even while in the presence of the Supreme Lord others are overcome with fear and concern over the future. In His spiritual manifestation as the eldest son of King Dasharatha, Lord Rama was so much loved and adored that the residents of the town prayed to God for His welfare as He embarked on a journey with Vishvamitra, the exalted sage residing in the forest. Rama and His younger brother Lakshmana were not yet twelve years of age according to the time elapsed from their appearance in the world, and yet they were called upon to protect Vishvamitra from hideous creatures who fought unfairly. Rama stayed true to His role as protector, and the residents, ignoring His tremendous fighting ability, prayed that He and His brother may return home safely, and especially victorious. They prayed that not a single head of hair would be lost while He would bathe.

What is the significance of this prayer? Why such a strange request made to God? The idea is that they didn't want Rama to get hurt. Losing a single hair while bathing in a lake is as trivial a loss as you'll find, but this fact was given attention because the residents of Ayodhya did not want any harm done to their beloved Rama and Lakshmana. The Lord's sweet smile, the beautiful hue of His skin, which was similar to the dark-blue raincloud or the blue lotus that springs forth upon the sight of the sun, and His overall demeanor enchanted everyone. His brother Lakshmana was like a twin, with the only difference seen in his fair skin color. Isha is a word that addresses God's position as the controller. The term Ishvara is also often used, which means the chief controller.

The prayer by the residents who watched Rama depart shows that they did not know He was God. Isn't ignorance a bad thing? If we can't identify someone properly, how can we interact with them in a meaningful way? Complete knowledge of another's standing isn't always helpful. For instance, if one of our friends or family members becomes famous or wealthy, should we then treat them differently? In these instances the more we can forget about their external stature, the better the relationship will be.

The same concept holds in the dealings with the Supreme Lord. His position as the most beautiful, renounced, wise, strong, wealthy, and famous is only worth knowing for those who originally believe that mortal men can hold this superior position. If you already believe in God, you are better off dealing with Rama under the sway of yogamaya, which is His direct energy responsible for clouding the vision of the surrendered souls. Through yogamaya, Rama's mother Kausalya thinks He is helpless. King Dasharatha holds the strongest parental affection for the Lord. Even Rama's eternal companions like Lakshmana and Sita, who both know how great Rama is and how He can defeat anyone in battle, still have concern for His welfare, not wanting Him to suffer in any way.

It is this concern that makes these personalities ideal candidates for receiving Rama's association. Why would someone want to be around enemies? If you know that someone doesn't like you, has no idea what makes you tick, and has reached erroneous conclusions about your position in life, would you enjoy spending long stretches of time with them? If, on the other hand, you had someone who cared about you so much that even if you were already taken care of they would never stop loving you, wouldn't that person's association be the most enjoyable to you?

Shri Rama was a descendant of the Raghu dynasty, which aside from having a reputation for piety was successful in its protection of the innocent. Therefore the concerned residents first asked God to make Rama successful in His mission. He was sent to protect Vishvamitra, and they knew that if He could do this His fame would increase at the same time. They didn't curse the sage for taking Him to the forest or even the Rakshasas for causing such disturbances. The evil elements of society will always be there. Appeasement, diplomacy, and psychological warfare can only do so much. In some instances, the last resort of danda, or force, is the only worthwhile option.

When it is time for stiff punishment, the deliverer of justice must not be meek. He cannot be merciful either. The warrior must come strong or not come at all. The night-rangers scouring the forests looking to destroy the fire sacrifices of the sages did not play by the rules of warfare. They would hide their hideous forms until the last minute, thus lulling the sages into a false sense of security. Shri Rama and Lakshmana would have to defend Vishvamitra from these demons, and they would have to let their arrows fly without concern for the well-being of the attackers.

The prayers offered by the residents were very sincere as well. They wanted nothing for themselves. This is the natural sentiment of the spirit soul, which exists in all living body types. Only in the human species, however, can that loving spirit be consciously directed towards a particular area. You'll see that during awards ceremonies the winners spend most of the time thanking other people that helped them. It is seen that most people prefer praising others over talking themselves up. It is said that a true hero doesn't speak much, which shows that the chivalrous and brave fight out of duty and not out of the desire to earn fame. Selflessness is a byproduct of a saintly demeanor, which is acquired through following the highest system of maintenance, known as bhagavata-dharma.

The residents of Ayodhya followed bhagavata-dharma, though they may not have known it. They did pray to God often, but not for their own benefit. They performed their regulative tasks as a matter of duty, not out of any desire for personal upliftment. What could someone who has the divine vision of Rama in front of them ever want anyway? If I am in the company of the most merciful, the person who is most beloved and kind in return, why should I worry about any other kind of reward?

"May Indra protect you on the East, may Yama protect you on the South and Varuna on the West and Kuvera on the North." (Sita Devi speaking to Lord Rama, Valmiki Ramayana, Ayodhya Kand, 16.24)

These kinds of prayers would be regularly directed towards Rama during His time on earth. Many years later, after Rama would return home, He would be summoned to the royal palace around the time that it was announced He would succeed His father on the throne. At the time, Rama had already proven His immeasurable strength and His ability to stay safe through danger. Nevertheless, right before He left home, Rama's wife Sita prayed to the different presiding deities of the material creation to protect her husband.

Many thousands of years later, the same Rama would appear in Vrindavana as Lord Krishna, the delight of Maharaja Nanda and mother Yashoda. The evil element at the time was concentrated in the neighboring town of Mathura, where the leader Kamsa was intent on killing Krishna. He once sent a powerful witch to Vrindavana to try to find baby Krishna and kill Him. Like the night-rangers in the forest harassing Vishvamitra, Putana changed her form into a beautiful woman that wouldn't look conspicuous in the holy land of Vrindavana.

Putana was able to sneak into Krishna's room and place Him on her lap. She came in with poison smeared on her breasts, so she was ready to kill the Lord by breastfeeding Him. Krishna granted her wish to temporarily act as a mother by kindly sucking milk from her breast. The problem for her, however, was that Krishna sucked the very life out of her. As she struggled to remain alive in the last moments, her original, hideous form revealed itself. The witch was so gigantic that after she was killed, her tumbling to the ground created a loud thud.

Hearing this, the cowherd women of Vrindavana came upon the scene and saw baby Krishna innocently crawling on the witch's corpse. They couldn't believe the hideous scene so they quickly picked up the young child and smothered Him with affection. Mother Yashoda then offered so many prayers to the Supreme Lord to protect her young son Krishna. She did not know that the person she was addressing, Lord Vishnu, was the very same Krishna standing in front of her. This innocent and heartfelt prayer was thoroughly enjoyed by Krishna, for there was no personal motivation on Yashoda's part.

Rama and Lakshmana would not be harmed during their time with Vishvamitra. Shri Rama's company is always beneficial, even to those He punishes. He would do away with several powerful Rakshasas, and also liberate Ahalya, the wife of the sage Gautama. But best of all, Rama would return home with a beautiful new wife named Sita. Through Vishvamitra's request for protection, Rama would coincidentally make His way to the town of Tirahuta, where a self-choice ceremony was taking place to determine the marriage arrangements for the daughter of King Janaka.

The contest in Janaka's kingdom was simple, but difficult at the same time. There was an enormously heavy bow belonging to Lord Shiva placed in the sacrificial arena. So many kings from around the world tried to lift it, but none of them could. Seeing Rama's beautiful and enchanting appearance, the onlookers in Tirahuta prayed to God to have Rama win the contest. Again, the prayer was not needed since Rama is the most powerful. Yet, just as in the case of the residents of Ayodhya, the well-wishers in Janaka's kingdom did not know that Rama was God. Through pure love they worried for His well-being and also Sita's. With a sincerity of purpose, they would gain the fruit of their eyes by seeing Rama lift the bow and marry the goddess of fortune.

The prayers offered by the residents of Ayodhya would eventually be granted. Rama would have to leave their company once more, this time for fourteen years. That was a long time of separation, but eventually He would return home triumphant and then happily take the helm as their leader. That same sweetheart holding the bow in His hands and standing on guard to protect the innocent can stay with us at all times through the chanting of His names: "Hare Krishna Hare Krishna, Krishna Krishna, Hare Hare, Hare Rama Hare Rama, Rama Rama, Hare Hare". The saints pray to always have the opportunity to recite the holy names and to make sure that as many people in the world as possible can do the same. As the prayers are offered in pure love, the Supreme Lord answers them.

VERSE 30

चलत सकल पुर लोग बियोग बिकल भए।
सानुज भरत सप्रेम राम पायन्ह नए॥30॥

calata sakala pura loga biyoga bikala bha'e |
sānuja bharata saprema rāma pāyanha na'e ||30||

"Walking along, all the townspeople are so fearful of separation that they have lost consciousness. Bharata, along with his younger brother, with love approaches Rama's feet to offer respects." (30)

Essay - Parting Is Sweet Sorrow

It is much easier to leave a place as the guest than it is to be the host and watch your guests depart. When you're leaving, you have the upcoming journey to keep your mind preoccupied. If you arrived with a band of people, that same group follows you during egress. In addition, you're the one instigating the separation, so you don't feel abandoned. The hosts, on the other hand, enjoyed having you around, so when you leave their place feels a little more empty. The residents of a sacred town a long time ago felt tremendous sadness when their most honorable family member left them, though it was only for a brief period. Their attachment to this young child was not based on ignorance of the difference between matter and spirit, for any attachment to the Supreme Spirit is worthwhile.

Normally, attachment and sadness over the separation from someone's association is not considered wise by those who know the true nature of the soul. At the time of birth the newborn child has no possessions and no attachments. Every attachment that is formed throughout the journey of life starts from a blank slate. This means that the people we are so afraid of losing were once not a major part of our lives. A new work environment may not seem inviting to us, but the place at which we currently work was once that way too. Through familiarity that comes with the repetition of days the mind loses sight of the fact that everything will be relinquished at the time of death.

How cruel it is that those things we cherish the most are destined to be removed from our vision. The body, the vehicle for action, itself will gradually diminish in abilities. The elderly person has poorer vision, hearing, and energy. Eventually, the life force is forced to exit the dwelling it was so comfortable in. The wise who study the difference between spirit and matter through instruction from a bona fide spiritual teacher are taught to transcend the dichotomy of acceptance and rejection. Don't dwell too much on the body, for it is a kind of illusion. You think matter is one thing, but it is really something different.

In addition to the influence of matter, the ways of time can trick us as well. Just because certain events take place day after day, for year after year, doesn't mean that they are guaranteed to continue in the future. For the parents of young children, a day will come when their help is no longer required. The children may even leave home to start their own families, for this is part of the parents' objectives. A mature adult is someone who can take care of themselves. If an adult is self-sufficient, what need do they have to live under the protection of the parents?

In Ayodhya a long time ago, the king's four sons were trained to be expert military men. In those times the military consisted of warriors skilled in using the bow and arrow. In addition to fighting, they were tasked with administering justice fairly. They also had to be up to the call of duty. They were never to shy away from a battle and they would always protect the most innocent members of society, the priestly class. The issue with King Dasharatha's four sons was that they were so loveable. Starting with the eldest, Lord Rama, down to the youngest, Shatrughna, the boys were a delight for everyone in the town. Though they were the king's sons, everyone accepted them to be their own children. Such practices are commonplace in small communities where everyone feels like they are neighbors and part of an extended family.

The upside to that attachment was that they got to see Rama and His brothers every day. The residents got to see the most beautiful person in the world and love Him unconditionally. Though He was learning the art of the trade from His spiritual masters, Rama was still adorable and kind. The residents, unaware of His divine nature, would pray for His welfare, not wanting even a hair on His head to fall while taking a bath. But as fate would have it, Rama's dexterity with the bow and arrow would bring Him to the forests, where the sages were being harassed.

It is one thing to feel sadness when a guest who stayed only for a short while leaves, but Rama had lived in Ayodhya for almost twelve years. That He would be called to the forest did not sit well with the citizens. Yet they knew it was His duty to keep the venerable Vishvamitra safe from the attacks of the night-rangers. Therefore they prayed primarily for Rama to be successful. Only with that condition met would they wish for Him to return home. For a kshatriya, or one in the royal order, nothing is more honorable than fighting valiantly against an enemy. Regardless of the nature of the war, whether you're fighting for the good guys or the bad, you automatically go to the heavenly planets should you lay down your life on the battlefield.

"O Partha, happy are the kshatriyas to whom such fighting opportunities come unsought, opening for them the doors of the heavenly planets." (Lord Krishna, Bhagavad-gita, 2.32)

In the Vedas, the ancient scriptures of India, it is recommended that to get spiritual merits one should perform yajnas, or sacrifices. In the typical fire sacrifice, oblations of clarified butter are poured into the fire for the enjoyment of the celestials. The spirit soul is eternal in its existence, but based on work and desire it can be placed into different bodies which have varying durations of manifestation. In the heavenly planets, the spirit soul gets placed into bodies which live for a long time and get to enjoy tremendous material opulence. To reach that realm one must be pious, adhere to the regulations of their order, and perform sacrifices regularly.

The soldier giving up his life on the battlefield is compared to the ghee poured into the fire sacrifice. The specific life is offered up for a higher cause, so there is spiritual merit accrued as a result. Therefore, for a kshatriya, nothing is more honorable than laying down your life on the battlefield. Despite knowing that Rama was capable in fighting, the citizens couldn't help but feel the pain of separation. They were so attached to Dasharatha's eldest son that they started to faint when they saw Him walking away with Vishvamitra and Lakshmana. As Rama's closest younger brother, Lakshmana refused to allow Rama to go anywhere unprotected. It was two-for-one with either brother. With Rama you always get Lakshmana, and vice versa.

From the strict textbook point of view, the attachment of the residents of Ayodhya was based on ignorance. Rama was just a child after all, and it was also His duty to protect the innocent. Why should anyone have such a strong attachment to a family member? The ways of Providence are such that people come together and separate all the time. Many thousands of years later, in the kingdom of Hastinapura the elderly aunt and uncle of King Yudhishthira would one day suddenly leave home and go to the mountains to practice austerity. The king didn't know where they were, and he was afraid that they had left on his account. The couple's one hundred sons had just died in a bloody war where Yudhishthira's side emerged victorious.

"As a player sets up and disperses his playthings according to his own sweet will, so the supreme will of the Lord brings men together and separates them." (Narada Muni speaking to King Yudhishthira, Shrimad Bhagavatam, 1.13.43)

Narada Muni would later arrive on the scene and explain to the king what had happened. In explaining the situation, the muni said that the ways of the Supreme Lord are such that people are constantly coming together and separating. The purport of the message is that the way the dice rolls is not in our control. Life is packed with unexpected ups and downs, starting with the time of birth. We had no control over when and where we took birth, though through our past actions we were able to indicate to the higher authorities what type of body we wished to receive. Nevertheless, the time of birth is determined by higher powers, as is the time of death.

Knowing the ways of Providence, the residents had no reason to overly lament. Yet since Rama was the Supreme Lord in the form of a human being, the loss of consciousness on the part of the residents was actually beneficial. There is no such thing as harmful illusion when it comes to Rama and His association. Attachment and aversion are only two extremes not worth paying attention to when there is the issue of illusion, something taken to be something that it is not. With Rama, what you see is what you get. If you are attached to Him, you are attached to something permanent, something which is linked to your true identity.

The spirit soul is eternal, and in its constitutional position it is a servant of God. This type of service is entered into voluntarily, and it provides lasting happiness. The residents of Ayodhya were not forced to love Rama. Their emotions flowed naturally, and they were so sincere that upon seeing the Lord walk away they lost consciousness. They couldn't stand the thought of not seeing Dasharatha's beloved son.

Rama's two other younger brothers felt the same way. As Rama was leaving, Bharata, along with Shatrughna, approached Rama with love and paid respects to His feet. The three younger brothers are all expansions of the Supreme Lord, so it is not surprising that they would be so close during their time on earth. The brothers all looked out for each other, and their common link was the love they felt for the eldest Rama. The citizens and the brothers would not have to wait too long, as Rama and Lakshmana would glorify their family by protecting Vishvamitra from the hideous night-rangers attacking the innocent. And as a bonus, they would return home with beautiful wives received in the kingdom of Videha. First there was sadness at Rama's leaving and then there was rejoicing upon His return with His new wife, Sita Devi, who is the goddess of fortune. The sweet sorrow of parting from the Lord thus indicated the high standing of Ayodhya and its residents. The Supreme Lord is non-different from His land, and so today the area of Ayodhya

VERSE 31

होहिं सकुल सुभ मंगल जनु कहि दीन्हेउ।
राम लखन मुनि साथ गवन तब कीन्हेउ।।31।।

hohiṁ sakula subha maṅgala janu kahi dīnhe'u |
rāma lakhana muni sātha gavana taba kīnhe'u ||31||

"By offering good tidings and wishing for all good things to happen, it was as if the people invited auspiciousness to the scene. Rama and Lakshmana then left with the sage." (31)

Essay - Inviting Auspiciousness

In the Vedic tradition, it is important to keep an eye out for signs of auspiciousness. A long time ago, while the king of Hastinapura ruled over his kingdom after victory in a very bloody war, he began to notice auspicious signs. There was no quarrel anywhere, and greed and fierce competition were not allowed entry into the city. The subsequent inauspiciousness followed the introduction of these unwanted elements in society. Once the bad omens were noticed, that the Supreme Lord had left the phenomenal plane to return to His spiritual abode was evident. As the Lord's absence represents the most inauspicious condition, King Yudhishthira knew that the immediate future wasn't so bright. Many thousands of years prior, however, the same Supreme Lord was in the process of leaving from a local town, but instead of relying on the external signs around them, the people of the town offered such nice prayers that auspiciousness personified arrived on the scene as an invited guest.

How does this work exactly? How can you create auspiciousness just by uttering a few words? Whether someone likes me or hates me, does it really matter in the end? If my boss says negative things behind my back or praises me to the hilltops, in the end all that matters is what he pays me. This is especially true if the relationship is based squarely on a business arrangement, where remuneration is expected. Isn't every relationship the same way? How then can auspicious signs be found when the conditions speak otherwise? Are not the external circumstances the harbinger of things to come?

The outside signals are paid attention to in the Vedic tradition, which is the oldest system of spirituality in existence. Spirituality is an all-encompassing field. From knowledge of the internal comes the ability to cope with the external. It doesn't work the same way when the order is reversed. I may know how to maintain a shirt and coat, but this doesn't mean that I can automatically take care of myself. On the other hand, if I feed myself regularly, go to bed on time, and properly treat illnesses, I can then figure out how to get dressed properly and wear the clothes appropriate to the situation.

"As the embodied soul continually passes, in this body, from boyhood to youth to old age, the soul similarly passes into another body at death. The self-realized soul is not bewildered by such a change." (Lord Krishna, Bhagavad-gita, 2.13)

Spirituality deals with the internal spark at the lowest level, the tiny but powerful force of spirit localized within the body. The fact that spirituality is considered separate from any other endeavor or narrow in scope shows just how much attention the external gets. The Vedas provide the first instruction that we are spirit soul, not part and parcel of the body. Our current dwelling changes constantly, from boyhood to youth to old age. However, the spirit soul's fortunes can be shaped by how this body is utilized. To be put to the best use, the body must take actions under the proper conditions. Every collection of matter has an ideal utilization. If that property is violated, the item is not put to its proper use. Think of driving your car in the snow or using a fork to eat soup.

With the duties prescribed to each member of society based on their specific order, there is a proper time and circumstance for action. When marriage arrangements take place, members of the priestly class determine an auspicious sign based on the qualities of the participants and the specific alignment of stars. If the conditions are not conducive to a future full of wedded bliss, the marriage ceremony will not be held at that time. On a larger scale, the outside conditions at any given time can portend good or bad things for the future. For a group of citizens a long time ago, their desire for future auspiciousness was so strong that they did not worry about the external circumstances. Instead, they gave everything - body, mind and soul - over to their beloved Lord Rama and His younger brother Lakshmana, who were on their way out of the town to escort a venerable rishi in his travels through the forests.

Why were the townspeople so enamored with Rama? Why not offer the same dedication to their own children? Shri Rama is the soul of all creatures, the original life force. From one have sprung many, and that one is supporting all the many at the same time. Because of His inherent qualities, every single life form is naturally attracted to Him. In the perverted version of that natural desire, the love turns to hate, but the attraction is still there. Even in apathy the attraction leads to association with the external feature of the Lord known as material nature.

With the residents of Ayodhya during the Treta Yuga, the personal presence of that original person was available. Everyone made the most of that opportunity by offering their love purely, without motive. An absence of motive means that there is no desire for personal benefit. I work at the office so that I can get paid. I go to school so that I'll get an education. I give money to the poor so that I won't feel as bad about their situation. I offer help to someone because I am afraid of the negative consequences that will come from not offering that help.

The residents of Ayodhya had no such motives or fears. They were tied in a bond of affection to the eldest son of King Dasharatha. Rama was a boy of less than twelve years of age when He had to leave the town for a short while. Vishvamitra Muni, a member of the priestly class, previously faced harassment in the forests from a Rakshasa named Maricha. That demon had fellow night-rangers with him to help in attacking the priests. Rama was a member of a royal family, so He was trained in the military arts. Vishvamitra knew that Dasharatha's eldest son could protect him. Rama took Lakshmana with Him because the younger brother could not live without Rama. Lakshmana was equally as capable a fighter, with the duo combining to have a fire and wind effect. Fire can only burn the local area, but if combined with wind, it can spread across a much greater distance. With Lakshmana by His side, Rama could extend the reach of His protection to all the saints residing in the forest.

"Rama's younger brother, Lakshmana, has reddish eyes and a voice that resounds like a kettledrum. His strength matches that of Rama's, and his face shines like a full moon. Just as wind gives aid to a raging fire, Lakshmana has joined forces with his brother. It is that best of kings, Shriman Rama, who has brought down the Rakshasas fighting in Janasthana." (Akampana speaking to Ravana, Valmiki Ramayana, Aranya Kand, 31.16-17)

Now that we have this information, the behavior of the residents seems odd. On the one side you have a mature adult approaching the king of the town for help in getting protection against the wickedest terrorists in the world. The rishi came to Ayodhya only to ask for this young boy to protect him. Meanwhile, the residents of the town viewed the same youth as helpless. Therefore when Rama was walking away, they prayed for His welfare. They asked God that Rama return successful and that He not as much have a single hair removed from His head while taking a bath. Can we imagine such purity in emotion? They prayed to God for God's welfare. It seems silly to do this, but this behavior actually represents the height of devotion. It is the embodiment of selflessness.

Goswami Tulsidas very much appreciated these sentiments. In the above referenced verse from his Janaki Mangala, we see that the poet has personified mangala, or auspiciousness, and said that through their offerings of good tidings the residents essentially invited auspiciousness to the area. Omens be damned, what they offered to Rama was better than any external sign of nature. It was during these conditions that Rama and Lakshmana walked away with Vishvamitra. The same practice has been followed ever since that time by sincere devotees. In temples where God is worshiped, the deities are awakened to the chanting of the holy names. Auspiciousness is invited to the scene by first offering prayers to Tulasi Devi, the Lord's beloved servant. Next, the spiritual master is honored, for he is the Lord's representative. With the blessings from Tulasi Devi and the guru, the proper mood of worship is created, allowing the further proceedings to have lasting effects.

Though there are different methods of religion, and even smaller sub-religions that meet targeted goals, nothing can be higher than the mood of worship shown by the residents of Ayodhya. They prayed to God for God to be safe, and the same type of prayer can be invoked by reciting the maha-mantra, "Hare Krishna Hare Krishna, Krishna Krishna, Hare Hare, Hare Rama Hare Rama, Rama Rama, Hare Hare". Not to be confused with a prayer asking for personal wealth, the elimination of distress, or the perfection of mysticism, the sacred syllables uttered in the most wonderful prayer ask God and His energy for the benediction of being able to continue in service to Him.

Yet the innocent people of Ayodhya didn't even ask for that. They just wanted Rama and Lakshmana to be okay. Of course the duo would always be in good spirits, and their vision would remain in the minds of the sweethearts protected by King Dasharatha. The boys would protect Vishvamitra well, and they would have the pleasure of escorting him to Videha, where a grand sacrifice was taking place. The auspicious conditions under which Rama and Lakshmana left were matched with the wonderful atmosphere of their return, when Sita Devi, the goddess of fortune herself, came to Ayodhya as Rama's wife.

Just as the residents did not worry about outside conditions, time or circumstance when praying for Rama's welfare, the sincere devotee does not have to pay much concern to the circumstance when reciting the holy names. The sound vibration representation of the same Shri Rama can be invoked, honored, cherished, and held on to for sustenance at any moment. Correspondingly, Shri Rama's association, including the vision of His beautiful form leaving Ayodhya with His younger brother Lakshmana, can be created at any moment, even right at this very second, should we so choose.

VERSE 32

स्यामल गौर किसोर मनोहरता निधि।

सुषमा सकल सकेलि मनहुँ बिरचे बिधि ॥32॥

syāmala gaura kisora manoharatā nidhi |
suṣamā sakala sakeli manahuṁ birace bidhi ||32||

"The two youths, one dark-skinned and one fair, are treasures of beauty. It appears that Lord Brahma has taken all the beauty in the world and placed it in them." (32)

Essay - Shyama-Gaura

As if you have found a treasure chest full of the most beautiful objects in the world, watching Lord Rama leave along with His younger brother Lakshmana brought so much joy to the eyes. Any chance to get a glimpse at these sweet boys was time well spent, as the material conditions have never been able to bring about such a benefit. The eyes are provided for a reason, and without the proper target to gaze upon the enchantment of material allures can lead us astray, in the process giving the eyes a bad name. With Dasharatha's two sons leaving with the sage Vishvamitra, however, it seemed as if all the beauty in the world had been stored in one place. That same beauty is available to the eyes of the mind to feast on through the sacred works of Goswami Tulsidas.

King Dasharatha's sons are the Supreme Lord and His support systems respectively. Why would God need support? It is the soul's dharma to serve. In general, in the perverted state the individual living being seeks out the role of lord or master, when in reality they are ideally suited to be servant. Think of a high school production of a play, where the different acts represent the timeline through life. Every conditioned being is trying to audition for the leading role of controller, the person responsible for creation, maintenance and destruction. No one wants to try out for the role of servant, though characteristically everyone is properly suited for it.

The Lord's younger brother Lakshmana, who is always His support system, has no interest in being master. He is already the leader of the disciplic succession of spiritual instruction, which teaches the many fragments of spirit their ideal condition, but he is always at the helm ready to provide service. As he can never disassociate from his dharma, he is considered the exemplary living entity, someone who is worshipable by his acts. Lakshmana is glorious and so dedicated to his service that not even Rama can stop him. Though God is the Supreme Controller capable of defying the law of gravity and controlling every outcome to events, He does not stand in the way of pure devotion that is inspired without motivation and without interruption.

In His spiritual manifestation as Lakshmana, God's primary supporter has a fair complexion. The Supreme Lord, on the other hand, is darker. In some traditions the personal form of the Supreme Lord is denied, or it is taken to be subordinate to His impersonal feature. "Just as the living entities accept bodies and then reject them, so the Supreme Lord must follow the same tact, even when He appears before our very eyes." This logic is flawed, as even the Vedas don't support it. Impersonalism defined as a scientific discipline originates in the Vedas, the oldest scriptures for mankind. Every type of religious system and every system of maintenance descends from the original word of God handed down to Lord Brahma at the beginning of creation.

Yet only in the original system is the proper understanding of God as a person revealed. That personal feature has specific attributes that follow the different personal expansions. In the Vaishnava traditions it is agreed that Lord Vishnu is the original Personality of Godhead. Though some lines of disciplic succession take Lord Krishna to be the original and others Lord Rama, in any case there is no difference because Vishnu, Krishna, and Rama are practically the same person. The Vishnu-avataras are the expansions of the original personality, so they are equal to one another. Their spiritual manifestations are varied slightly, but in their original features they possess a shyama color.

"The shyama color is not exactly blackish. Shrila Bhaktisiddhanta Sarasvati Thakura compares it to the color of the atasi flower. It is not that Lord Krishna Himself appears in a blackish color in all the Dvapara-yugas. In other Dvapara-yugas, previous to Lord Krishna's appearance, the Supreme Lord appeared in a greenish body by His own personal expansion. This is mentioned in the Vishnu Purana, Hari-vamsha and Mahabharata." (Shrila Prabhupada, Chaitanya Charitamrita, Madhya 20.337 Purport)

Shyama is dark. It can refer to dark blue or even green sometimes. The shyama color is like the tamala tree, of which very few are still left on this earth. Shyama is also like the color of the atasi flower or the raincloud that is just about to start pouring down its water. Generally, dark colored skin is not as visually appealing as fair-colored skin, but with the Supreme Lord His shyama complexion is still beautiful. For this reason He is also addressed by the name of Shyamasundara, which more specifically refers to His form as Shri Krishna.

With King Dasharatha, two of his sons were dark-skinned and two were fair. Bharata and Rama were of the darker shade and Lakshmana and Shatrughna were lighter. They were all either directly Vishnu or expansions of Him, so they were not lacking anything in beauty. In the above referenced verse from the Janaki Mangala, Goswami Tulsidas is specifically referring to the beauty of Rama and Lakshmana, who at a young age left the town of Ayodhya to escort the venerable Vishvamitra Muni through the forests. All attention was on the two youths, for who could imagine that they would leave home for such a purpose? Young children commonly go on trips, perhaps to have fun or to learn something from someone. You can throw kids into an open field without any direction and they will find a way to stay entertained.

The onlookers weren't worried about Rama and Lakshmana being bored. Rather, Vishvamitra was taking them to the forest to act as protectors. Rama was not yet twelve years of age, so how much protection could He offer? Again, we are reminded of the difference between God and the living entities. A normal twelve year old is limited in both mental and physical maturation, so their capabilities aren't as great as they will be in adulthood. With the Supreme Lord, any of His outward manifestations is equally as capable. As a young child in Vrindavana, the same Shri Rama would destroy the wicked plots of so many nefarious characters sent to the town by the neighboring King Kamsa. As a young child, Rama as Shri Krishna would lift a massive hill and hold it over His head for seven days to act as an umbrella to protect the residents of Vrindavana.

The young Rama was ready to protect Vishvamitra, for age did not hamper His ability to use the bow and arrow. Lakshmana came along because he would never leave Rama alone. Not to be mistaken for an annoying younger brother who insists on tagging along, Lakshmana's presence was cherished by Rama. The true strength of the fraternal bond of affection shared between the two is known only to them, but through outward actions and the recorded events found in the Ramayana and its derivative literatures we gain a slight understanding of it.

Rama and Lakshmana were beautiful in their appearance and also in their behavior. They didn't complain about going with Vishvamitra. They were happy to protect the priestly class, an obligation vital to their order. They were descendants of King Raghu, so they were sometimes addressed as Raghava. They were taught from birth to follow righteousness and to always respect the brahmanas, who eschew material life in favor of worshiping God and teaching others how to follow that worship through the execution of their assigned duties. Seeing the boys carrying their bows and arrows and happily following Vishvamitra, the hearts of the residents just melted. Children are the essence of innocence, so when they take up serious tasks the sincerity of purpose is revealed. There were no ulterior motives in Rama and Lakshmana. They operated out of love only.

It is difficult to accurately describe God's beauty, so the kind poet Tulsidas has here made a very nice comparison. Lord Vishnu is the origin of life and matter, but the specific faculties for creating are invested in Lord Brahma. If we see something possessing natural beauty, it is to be understood that it is the handiwork of the creator, Brahma. But with God such references to Brahma's creating ability only relate to appearance, as Rama and Lakshmana's bodies are not created. There is no difference between spirit and matter for God or His plenary expansions like

Lakshmana. Nevertheless the comparisons are made in an attempt to describe what an onlooker might think.

Tulsidas says that it looked like Brahma had taken all of the beauty in the world and placed it into Rama and Lakshmana. This is a nice form of flattery in one sense, but a true statement at the same time. Rama is the owner of matter, so His spiritual features represent the height of all opulence. As Bhagavan, He possesses beauty, wealth, strength, fame, renunciation and wisdom simultaneously and to the fullest extent. He is not lacking in anything. Lakshmana, Rama's constant companion, is the servitor-God, so he has the same features to an almost identical level.

This would not be the only time Tulsidas would use such a comparison. Similar kinds of statements are found in passages describing Rama's future wife, Sita Devi. The two youths following Vishvamitra would eventually cause that union to take place on earth, though Sita and Rama are forever together in the spiritual sky. Pretty soon thereafter, the fourth piece of the group, Shri Hanuman, would join. Rama therefore never leaves the worshiper alone. If you honor Him then you get to bask in the sweet vision of Lakshmana, Sita and Hanuman as well. With those four beauties giving pleasure to the eyes, what more could anyone ask for?

CHAND 4

बिरचे बिरंचि बनाइ बाँची रुचिरता रंचौ नहीं।
दस चारि भुवन निहारि देखि बिचारि नहिं उपमा कहीं।।
रिषि संग सोहत जात मग छबि बसत सो तुलसी हिएँ।
कियो गवन जनु दिननाथ उत्तर संग मधु माधव लिएँ।।4।।

birace birañci banā'i bāṁcī ruciratā rañcau nahīṁ |
dasa cāri bhuvana nihāri dekhi bicāri nahiṁ upamā kahīṁ ||
riṣi saṅga sohata jāta maga chabi basata so tulasī hi'eṁ |
kiyo gavana janu dinanātha uttara saṅga madhu mādhava li'eṁ ||4||

"After Brahma created them, there was no beauty left for the rest of the world. If you searched the entire fourteen bhuvanas you wouldn't find anything that could compare to their beauty." (Chand 4.1)

"Travelling along the way with the rishi they are looking so beautiful. That beautiful image lives within Tulsi's heart. When the trio was going, it looked like the sun travelling north, taking with it the spring season." (Chand 4.2)

Essay - Two Handsome Boys

There are fourteen planetary systems in each universe. With innumerable universes, we get an idea of just how unlimited the material creation is. In each sphere Lord Brahma is tasked with creation, with developing the material nature to act as the playing field for the bodies of the many living entities who make up the population. The spirit souls exist eternally, so Brahma has no powers of creation on the spiritual side. Depending on their desires, if they should so choose to leave the constitutional area of the spiritual sky, they get to roam in a land that has a temporary manifestation. For those who don't know better, Brahma is considered the master behind all the manifestations of matter. Therefore when looking at two handsome youths, sons of King Dasharatha, the only thought that could be made was that Brahma ran out of beauty. There was none left after the bodies for these two boys were made. Hence the rest of the world became bereft of splendor and beauty, a fact noted instantly by gazing upon these two handsome princes.

"There are fourteen planetary systems within the universe, and all living entities reside in those planetary systems." (Chaitanya Charitamrita, Madhya, 1.267)

The fourteen planetary systems don't all have the same environment. There are varying levels of enjoyment with the many systems, which accounts for the distinctions between heaven, earth and hell. The heavenly planets are in the upper portion. The residents there live for long durations of time in comparison to the residents of the earthly planet. Heaven brings enhanced enjoyment, but which is still temporary. The earthly planet has a mix of heavenly and hellish life, and the lower planets are reserved for the most sinful. Regardless of the residence, the occupants are part of a temporary stay, though through attachment to the matter shaped and molded by Lord Brahma forgetfulness of mortality arises.

The mention of the fourteen planetary systems in the above referenced verse from the Janaki Mangala is made to try to accurately convey just how beautiful Rama and Lakshmana were as they were departing Ayodhya for the forest with Vishvamitra Muni. Lord Rama is the Supreme Lord in the guise of a warrior prince and Lakshmana is His chief companion, the servitor-God. The Supreme Lord is the father of even Brahma, so there is no question of any of His bodies ever being created. Lord Brahma crafts the forms of the conditioned living entities based on their past karma, but the system of fairness taking into account action and reaction does not apply to God.

Lakshmana is a Vishnu-tattva expansion, so He too does not have a material body. Rama is of the darker, or shyama, color, while Lakshmana is gaura, or fair. To enhance the delight of the fortunate souls with whom they associated, Shri Rama and Lakshmana masked their divine identities. It was not known to everyone that they were God. With the Supreme Lord's personal self, the brilliant features cannot be masked fully. I may not know what gold is as a young child, but if I see it sparkling in front of me, I will still be enamored by it. I may not know what sweets and chocolates are, but if I eat them, I will still enjoy the wonderful taste.

In a similar manner, those sinless souls who are blessed with the company of Rama and Lakshmana may not know that they are the Supreme Lord and His number one servant, but through the association they enjoy the brilliant features nonetheless. Through Rama's potency of yogamaya the mind starts to wonder just where a splendid body like that could come from. The comparison to Lord Brahma and the fourteen worlds is brilliant because the hidden meaning is that Rama and Lakshmana are not of this universe. You could search through every inch of space, look at every living entity and their temporary manifestation, and still not find anyone who could compare to the beauty of the two youths.

Why is it important to mention this fact? The purpose of the Janaki Mangala is to provide transcendental enjoyment, to both the author and the listeners. The preacher gets so much enjoyment out of discussing the glories of the Supreme Lord. Since His features are inexhaustible in their endurance, the opportunities for glorification never cease. The spirit soul, the essence of identity, has inherent characteristics. Rather than try to decipher these on our own through the tedious process of elimination, we can take it on the authority of the Vedas that the soul is eternal, knowledgeable and blissful. Only something that is knowledgeable from the start can do complex math and think rationally after receiving proper training. Only something that is inherently blissful can feel happiness through association and activities that speak to its inherent tendencies.

In the same way, only something that is eternal in its existence can continue to remain vibrant through the cycle of birth and death, the constant acceptance and rejection of bodies. The spirit soul is the same in quality when it is in the pea-like body within the womb as it is when it is in the body of a fully matured adult. The best way for the soul to seek happiness is to find an engagement that meets its natural characteristics. That internal bliss is found through service, which is ideally directed at the Supreme Lord. Rama is meant to be served and the numerous sparks of spirit are meant to provide the service.

Shri Lakshmana is always in a devotional mood because he never breaks from the divine consciousness. He then passes on the wisdom necessary for accepting that mood of service with confidence to the people he teaches. The spiritual master of the Vedic tradition, the guru, is Lakshmana's representative. In the Janaki Mangala, we get an idea of how glorious Rama and Lakshmana are, and at the same time we are given an outlet for extending our service to God. We may be very rich or very poor, but in either case there is the same opportunity to serve the Supreme Lord and feel happiness.

The devotee sacrifices their time and effort in composing poetry and sharing it with others, and the consuming public lends their ears to these works, basking in the sweetness of the words and the mental pictures they paint. The image of Shri Rama and Lakshmana escorting Vishvamitra, the son of Gadhi, into the dangerous forests is a pleasure for the consciousness, which needs a vital source of happiness while residing in a land full of bewilderment furthered by constant creation and destruction.

Why was the forest dangerous? A band of night-rangers, headed by Maricha, was wreaking havoc, disrupting the sacrifices of the brahmanas, the priestly class. Think of a priest delivering a sermon in church on Sunday when a terrorist comes in and blows everything up. A similar thing was happening in the forest of Dandaka, where many ascetics had sought refuge because of the peaceful surroundings. Rama and Lakshmana were sons of King Dasharatha, so they were trained from birth to protect the innocent. Dasharatha did not want to part with Rama, but Vishvamitra insisted that only Rama could protect him. Thus the two beautiful sons left their comfortable home to reside in the austere settings of the forest. Not once did they complain nor did they fail to uphold their responsibilities. Vishvamitra, pleased with them, gave the boys mantras to be used when fighting. Rama and Lakshmana don't need any help from anyone, but so great is their respect for the priestly class that to boost the stature of figures like Vishvamitra they pretend to require help.

The devotees have limited abilities in the area of glorification, but the kind Lord pays more attention to sincerity than to the end result. What can we really create anyway? Lord Brahma is much more powerful than we are, for he is responsible for the 8,400,000 different species that appear in the fourteen worlds. Despite his abilities to create, there is no beauty available on his massive palette of qualities to create something comparable to Rama or Lakshmana.

You could search the entire fourteen worlds and not find anything like those two youths. Similarly, you can scour the whole of literature, spiritual or otherwise, and not find anything as sweet and heartwarming as the works crafted by Goswami Tulsidas, the author of the Janaki Mangala. Because he was selfish enough to want to bask in the sweet vision of Rama and Lakshmana with Vishvamitra, we are today fortunate enough to have the same mental image painted for us.

Essay - Dina-natha

From this one verse found in the Janaki Mangala, courtesy of Goswami Tulsidas we get so many lessons coupled with feelings of transcendental pleasure. The simple image of an elderly rishi travelling along the road with two new disciples can be studied over and over - with the mind contemplating on the significance of the parties involved and the righteousness they were upholding - and new delights can be found with each renewed mental effort. The comparison to the sun is most significant, as the fiery body in the sky is the giver of light. Depending on its positioning, the residents of the affected land are either optimistic about the immediate future or unhappy about the change in weather that is about to occur. The sun's influence is seen in so many areas but is especially evident in the seasons. When a new season ushers in the beginning of life again, the residents feel optimistic. In a similar manner, the sun that is Vishvamitra was taking the two months of the spring season to the residents of the forest.

In the above referenced verse the poet says that the two boys, Rama and Lakshmana, are looking very beautiful travelling with the rishi. Rama is the eldest son of King Dasharatha, a pious ruler of Ayodhya who lived on this earth many thousands of years ago during the Treta Yuga. Lord Rama is an incarnation of the Supreme Personality of Godhead, as stipulated by the Vedas and their foremost literatures like the Shrimad Bhagavatam and Ramayana. If one is hesitant to believe that God can appear on earth in human form or that Rama Himself is a historical personality and not just a mythological concoction, following the events relating to Rama documented in the sacred texts, hearing about them from those who truly understand the Supreme Personality of Godhead and His features, will dissipate the darkness of ignorance and provide a kind of enlightenment not found through any other endeavor. The results from hearing about Rama give indication enough of His divine nature. That benefit is there for one and all, irrespective of religious faith, family tradition, skin color, nationality, or the language spoken. Just as the sun distributes its heat and light to everyone, so the spiritual sun that is Bhagavan pays no attention to sectarian boundaries.

"Whenever and wherever there is a decline in religious practice, O descendant of Bharata, and a predominant rise of irreligion-at that time I descend Myself." (Lord Krishna, Bhagavad-gita, 4.7)

Why Rama would appear on earth is always a mystery not completely understood by the living beings that require an education to learn how to do anything important. In the Bhagavad-gita, the same Rama in His original form of Krishna says that whenever there is a rise of irreligion, in order to reinstitute the principles of dharma, or the occupational duty for mankind, He descends Himself to earth in His personal form. The personal form extends to Krishna's direct incarnations as well, which include Shri Rama. Therefore we can deduce that during Rama's time there was a rise in irreligion, a fact confirmed when one time King Dasharatha welcomed a notable rishi to his kingdom.

A rishi is a devoted soul, kind of like a priest, but someone who lives a certain lifestyle that maintains a certain type of consciousness. That consciousness is one focused on God. God consciousness is the ultimate objective in life, for every single person. The rishis are those who are fortunate enough, through many austerities and pious acts from previous lives, to pursue the divine consciousness as their primary objective in life. The lifestyle they follow thus aims to foster that thinking of God and keep it at active levels. Just as there are best practices when administering a database, writing code for a new application, or keeping your documents on your computer in order, there are certain ideal principles one can follow that best allow for God consciousness to remain alive.

A common principle in all of the recommendations is minimalism. Keep the attachment to material nature to a minimum, preventing the senses from getting spoiled. If I eat every time I think I'm hungry or if I sleep whenever I get the slightest hint of fatigue, I will actually do harm for myself going forward. This is because the next time I get hungry, it will be even more difficult to control myself. The same goes for sleep. If you sleep for an extended number of hours each night, you will actually be more tired throughout the day, for your body gets accustomed to the rest.

On the other side, if your senses can be trained to remain controlled, you can better stay alert and focused on your tasks. The best way to train the senses is to limit the number of objects of interaction in the immediate environment. Think of it like trying to lose weight by keeping food out of your radar. If you're on a diet, you won't do so well if you're seated at a buffet table the entire day. Similarly, if you're around material allures throughout the day, you won't stand a good chance of staying detached.

A famous sage by the name of Vishvamitra was following these principles in the serene setting of the forests. There was one problem, though, which would indicate why Shri Rama advented on earth. A band of night-rangers, Rakshasas who could change their shapes at will, rose in influence and began to harass the peaceful sages in the forest. Vishvamitra came to Ayodhya to ask for King Dasharatha's protection. The king was not part of the priestly order, but he still had occupational duties to perform that would complement the activities of the rishis. The royal order is to provide protection to the innocent, and by following that obligation with faith and detachment, the same control of the senses can result. Thus we see that although the brahmana class has the best opportunity for arousing God consciousness, the ultimate objective in life is open to anyone to attain, provided they follow the guidelines prescribed for their order.

Vishvamitra asking for help wasn't out of the ordinary, but what was strange was that he asked specifically for Dasharatha's eldest son Rama. At the time, the jewel of the Raghu dynasty was not even twelve years of age, but Vishvamitra knew that He had divine abilities, that He could easily fend off the Rakshasas. Dasharatha reluctantly agreed, and Rama took Lakshmana with Him. Lakshmana is an incarnation of Ananta Shesha Naga, the expansion of the Supreme Lord that plays the role of the servitor-God, the number one protector of Bhagavan's interests. True to his nature, Lakshmana would not allow Rama to leave home alone. He had to come along as well.

In the verses preceding this one, Tulsidas remarks that Rama and Lakshmana's beauty could not be described. They appeared as if Lord Brahma had taken all the beauty in the world and concentrated it into them. Whatever beauty the creator had left over he used for the rest of the creatures. Lord Brahma is the first created living entity. As a spirit soul he lives forever, but since he accepts a material body, he is destined for death, though for him it occurs after billions of years. Since he is in charge of creation, every living entity in the material world is related to him. The comparison to Brahma is very nice because it illustrates that Rama and Lakshmana are not of the material world; their spiritual forms are so magnificent that nothing can compare to them.

The image of Rama and Lakshmana leaving Ayodhya to escort Vishvamitra is so beautiful that Tulsidas keeps it within his heart. In that safe location, the image can be conjured up whenever the poet wants. And what comes from remembering that sweet vision? For starters, one gets to remember how Rama advented on this earth to protect the innocent. The mind is reminded of Lakshmana's unselfish dedication to Rama and how Vishvamitra was so fortunate to be wise enough to approach King Dasharatha. The mind remembers the kind residents of Ayodhya who took to the streets to bid Rama and Lakshmana farewell. So many things can be remembered just by finding that image in the heart and bringing it to life. Even the image of the poet keeping that scene in his heart is tremendously heartwarming.

The second part of the above referenced verse says that when they were leaving, it looked like the sun was taking the two months of spring towards the north. As winter dissipates, the sun's repositioning towards the north indicates the return to life of the plants. The spring season is considered auspicious because of the chance for a new beginning, as it also stirs the passions of those who are responsible for keeping life going. It was during the spring season that Rama would remember His wife Sita Devi, whom He would marry soon after travelling the forests with Vishvamitra.

"Those who know the Supreme Brahman pass away from the world during the influence of the fiery god, in the light, at an auspicious moment, during the fortnight of the moon and the six months when the sun travels in the north." (Lord Krishna, Bg. 8.24)

In the Bhagavad-gita, it is said that the mystic who knows Brahman passes away during the months that the sun is in the northern position. This departure represents a kind of liberation. Reincarnation is automatic for as long as there is not a permanent God consciousness. Mysticism, contemplating on the Supreme Absolute Truth in the impersonal form, is a way of focusing the mind on God at the time of death, but this path is fraught with difficulty. If the mystic should pass away during the six colder months of the year, that same liberation is not guaranteed. Therefore from Krishna's statements we see that the more auspicious time is when the sun travels in the north.

In the above comparison, Rama and Lakshmana represent the two months of spring and Vishvamitra the sun, or dina-natha. Dina is the day and natha is lord, so the sun is the lord of the day. Though Rama is often compared to the sun, in this circumstance Vishvamitra was acknowledged to be the superior entity, for he was the guru and Rama and Lakshmana his students. By figuratively travelling north into the forest, the sun that was Vishvamitra was taking the spring season in the form of Rama and Lakshmana with him. This meant that the occupants of the forest would be given life through the protection of the two boys. Vishvamitra would impart confidential mantras to them that would augment the power of the arrows shot from their bows. During that particular time period, all warfare took place with the bow and arrow, and Rama and Lakshmana were so powerful that their arrows could create blasts similar in strength to today's nuclear weapons.

The spiritual master is always like the sun, and with him comes the sweetness of the spring season represented by the personal association of the Supreme Lord. In addition to the external protection, Rama and Lakshmana would grant their divine vision to the residents of the forest, who would have a renewed life thanks to that association. In a similar manner, since the image of those three figures resides in the heart of Tulsidas, there is never a chance for the poet to feel the pangs of winter, for it is always spring when Vishvamitra is travelling north with Rama and Lakshmana.

VERSE 33

गिर तरु बेलि सरित सर बिपुल बिलोकहिं।
धावहिं बाल सुभाय बिहग मृग रोकहिं।।33।।

gira taru beli sarita sara bipula bilokahiṁ |
dhāvahiṁ bāla subhāya bihaga mṛga rokahiṁ ||33||

"He is looking at the many mountains, vines, rivers and ponds on the way. As part of His childish play, He is running after birds and trying to stop deer." (33)

Essay - Running Like a Child

Travelling in the forest, the young son of King Dasharatha is having a good time, as any child close to twelve years of age would want. Seeing the birds and tigers,

He is trying to catch them, and gazing at the beautiful surroundings, the origin of all life and matter is appreciating His marvelous abilities. At the same time, the boy's younger brother Lakshmana is accompanying Him, and they are guarded by Vishvamitra, the pious muni. This combination of characters makes for a delightful scene, one which can be contemplated upon again and again.

Why was Lord Rama chasing after birds and trying to stop deer? As the father of the creation, all creatures come from Him. It is not that the intelligent species who can understand God slightly through the good fortune of meeting a spiritual master are the only candidates for the Lord's mercy in the form of His personal association. Even the less intelligent deer, who run out into the road and get mesmerized by the headlights of an oncoming automobile, can delight in seeing Rama's countenance. When God chases after them, tries to stop them, or shows any attention to them at all, how could they not feel pleasure?

Animals have souls? They most certainly do. In fact, all forms of life have the same quality of spirit residing within them. The outer forms may not always have the same appearance, but the makeup of the spirit soul, the spark of life, in the individuals is not different. This shouldn't be that difficult to understand. A spirit soul resides in a body so helpless that it requires diapers and then stays within that body until it is old enough to drive a car, go to work, and produce offspring. The soul is the constant; it does not move or change in quality.

Take the same principle and apply it to every single species and you get the vision known as Brahman realization. Brahman is pure spirit. It is not affected by the changes to the external features. Just as when we might be angry one day and sad another our identity doesn't change, just because one soul is in the body of a deer and another in the enlightened human being doesn't mean that there is any distinction in the end. If you gather together every instance of spirit and put it into one collection for observational purposes, you get the concept of Brahman.

Obviously, acquiring the Brahman vision is very difficult. The principles of a bona fide religion are meant to bring about the realization of Brahman. In the Vedas, the oldest system of spirituality in existence, strict austerity and dedicated sacrifice coupled with instruction from a spiritual master at a young age sets up the necessary conditions for attaining the enlightened vision of seeing all spirit souls as equal.

Yet the vision doesn't represent the end point, as was proven by Vishvamitra Muni. On the surface Vishvamitra, the son of Gadhi, was a brahmana practicing the principles of the Vedas aimed at seeing all living beings as equal. At the same time, he knew that there was one spiritual force which was superior, which was the source of Brahman. That singular entity, the Supreme Personality of Godhead, happened to appear in the pious Raghu dynasty as the son of King Dasharatha.

Known by the name of Rama, this incarnation of the Supreme Lord was loved and adored by all the members of His family, including His three younger brothers: Bharata, Lakshmana and Shatrughna.

Four sons of King Dasharatha and his wivesIt was Rama and Lakshmana playfully travelling with Vishvamitra in the forests because the sage was being harassed by night-rangers looking to disrupt the religious practices of the ascetics avowed to following their occupational duties. While all living entities are the same constitutionally, realization of that fact and the connection with the Supreme Lord can only take place through dedication in yoga. Yoga means to link up the individual soul with the Supreme Soul, God's expansion residing within the heart. Yet not all kinds of yoga are the same, though unknowing mental speculators and unauthorized commentators may say otherwise.

Through his dedicated practice of asceticism, Vishvamitra was also a yogi, following meditation and also the route of karma, or action, with detachment. Yet his real business was bhakti-yoga, or divine love. If this were not the case, Shri Rama would never have accompanied Him in the forest. To understand why, think of who the people are with whom you currently associate. Are they friends or enemies? Do you purposefully go out of your way to hang around people who hate you? Better yet, do you cherish the association of someone who pretends that you don't even exist?

With the paths of impersonal study of Vedanta, fruitive work with the results renounced, and meditational yoga, the Supreme Lord in His blissful features, the sach-chid-ananda vigraha, is not acknowledged. Therefore, by definition how can anyone following these paths bask in Rama's company, gaining His divine vision? Not that these paths are illegitimate, for they are mentioned in shastra for a reason. It takes the conditioned soul many lifetimes just to attempt to adopt an authorized system of spirituality in earnest. Therefore those who don't take to the path of bhakti are not shut out immediately; they are given the chance to progress through other, more difficult paths.

Only in bhakti-yoga, the linking of the soul with God through acts of love, can one hear about and relish the activities of the Supreme Lord Rama travelling through the forests with Vishvamitra and Lakshmana. The impersonalist can hear the same above referenced passage from the Janaki Mangala and not get any delight from it. Using only mental speculation and knowledge limited by time, space and logic, the philosopher may think that Rama was foolish for chasing after birds and stopping deer. "Also, why did the mountains, lakes, rivers and vines need to be appreciated? These are all objects of maya, or illusion. The birds are just spirit souls, part of the Brahman energy, so why the need to pay them any attention? Shouldn't Rama have just sat back and stayed renounced?"

The Supreme Lord is always in ananda, or bliss. He derives this pleasure in whichever manner He sees fit, but at the core of any real pleasure is the exchange of emotion. In order for there to be an exchange, there must be more than one party. With the birds and deer, Shri Rama was having a good time with His parts and parcels, spirit souls who would appreciate His appearance. The animals enjoy God's personal presence, at any time and at any place. It is said that the same Shri Rama, when appearing on earth as the preacher incarnation named Chaitanya Mahaprabhu, would get even the tigers to dance along to the chanting of the holy names, "Hare Krishna Hare Krishna, Krishna Krishna, Hare Hare, Hare Rama Hare Rama, Rama Rama, Hare Hare". Shri Rama as Govinda, one who gives pleasure to the cows and to the senses, was loved and adored by all the animals in Vrindavana.

The lower species worship God in the mood of devotion called shanta-rasa, wherein they can't directly offer obeisances. This mood is known as neutrality, but it is still part of devotion because love for God is present. Shri Rama always plays the part perfectly. Younger children are more energetic and difficult to restrain when let out into the open. A young child doesn't require a television set or a video game console to be entertained. Simply by running in a field, seeing nature's creation, a young child can find endless opportunities for excitement, avoiding boredom throughout. Shri Krishna and Balarama used to go out daily with their friends to play and they had such a good time that the dear mother Yashoda had to repeatedly call them to come home and eat.

Shri Rama similarly enjoyed travelling through the forests with Lakshmana, staying under the care of Vishvamitra. Ironically enough, the guru had specifically requested Rama's company for the purposes of protection. Rama and Lakshmana were trained from childhood to be military fighters, and due to their divine natures, they were already expert at fighting at a young age. The most hideous creatures had been attacking the sages in the forests, so Vishvamitra knew that Rama and Lakshmana were the only ones capable of defeating these enemies and eliminating their influence.

As the Supreme Lord is Absolute, His fighting and His playing serve the same purpose. He fights with the enemies to protect the innocent and give them pleasure, and He plays with the deer and birds in the forest to enjoy their company. Thanks to the saints like Tulsidas who record these adventures in poetry format, any person can bask in the same sweetness by regularly hearing about the Lord's activities. Vishvamitra certainly was delighted to have Rama with him, as was the entire population of creatures who called the remote wilderness their home.

VERSE 34

सकुचहिं मुनिहि सभीत बहुरि फिरि आवहिं।
तोरि फूल फल किसलय माल बनावहिं।।34।।

sakucahiṁ munihi sabhīta bahuri phiri āvahiṁ |
tori phūla phala kisalaya māla banāvahiṁ ||34||

"They are so hesitant and very fearful when seeing the muni that they come back. Plucking flowers, fruits and leaves, they make garlands." (34)

Essay - Adult Supervision

When there is an adult around, the young child will be more mindful of the rules. The natural inclination is to run free, but the adult keeps that voice inside the child's head that says, "No. Don't do that." The child may even come close to breaking the rules but at the last minute, looking back as if to see if someone is watching, they will check themselves. Such behavior is very endearing in innocent young children, so the Supreme Lord in His form of Shri Rama and His younger brother Lakshmana made sure to mimic it, giving the guru Vishvamitra tremendous delight.

How can God be fearful? Why should He require a guru? Does not this make the spiritual master the superior entity? Through mental speculation alone we can't understand the Absolute Truth. When learning things on our own, such as a new language through immersion into a foreign culture, there must be observation of external behavior in order to pick up the necessary components. You can't just automatically start speaking a new language without having heard it from someone else first.

This principle applies to all areas of learning. The knowledge of the soul and its travels through transmigration represents the most important and difficult to acquire pieces of information. Therefore the mind, which is limited by time and space, cannot possibly alone collect all relevant information in just one lifetime. Even if we could remember every one of our experiences in this life, so many other living beings have accumulated an infinitely larger number of experiences. If the mind could expand to the size of a giant computer and store every single person's experiences, it still would have no way of knowing what to do with that information. The mind would be something like a library, which in itself has no intelligence. The library can only lend information for brief periods of time to interested readers and researchers.

The highest truths of life are easy to accept, provided one goes to the right source. The spiritual master following in a line of teachers that starts with the Supreme Lord is the only authorized source. Approaching any other teacher for spiritual information will either lead the student astray or cause them to miss out on the opportunity of feeling the pleasure that comes from the company of the reservoir of pleasure. There are different pathways towards true enlightenment, but once that superior vision is acquired, there is only one source of pleasure beyond that. The knowledge that is first acquired is that of Brahman, or pure spirit. Seeing Brahman is difficult because sight itself can be illusory. Start with your own body. You look in the mirror every day but you can't see that you're slowly dying, a process which starts from the time you were born and culminates with the exit of the soul from the body. Thus seeing deludes you into thinking that you are your body, which you are not.

Brahman realization sees the spirit soul within the body. Not only is spirit localized internally, but it also exists within every other species. Thus there is a large collection of individual fragments of spirit. The sum total is known as Brahman, and only one who is sober in mind and following the real principles of religion can understand the equality shared between the various species. The bona fide principles of spirituality involve austerity, sacrifice and dedication to study.

The chance to learn about Brahman is a boon for the human birth, affording the opportunity to acquire real knowledge. Knowing how to eat, sleep, mate and defend requires no explicit education, for the animals take care of these responsibilities without a problem. The Vedic tradition stipulates that the person wanting to know about the Absolute Truth should approach a bona fide spiritual master and render service to him.

In actuality, service starts from the very beginning of life. The mother and father are the first worshipable figures, or gurus in a sense. Knowing that there is a God is beneficial, but actually serving Him is difficult because He is considered inanimate. If I want to talk to God, where should I go? How can I see God and know that He is real? The personal interaction with the Supreme Lord is certainly possible, but it can only occur after the purification of vision. That purification takes place after one offers service to those who are worthy of it. From that dedication comes a simultaneous withdrawal from the interest of the senses.

After the parents are served, the spiritual master then takes over as the worshipable figure. He is a servant of God, so he knows how to teach his students the right way, so that through their actions in adult life they can attain the same God realization. It is not that everyone will follow the same path. There are divisions in society based on a person's natural qualities. From those divisions comes different prescribed work. For the royal order, the primary business is to take care of protection. They must protect the innocent, and especially the priestly class.

As Lord Rama, the Supreme Absolute Truth appeared on earth in the famous Raghu dynasty, which had chivalrous kings dating back to the beginning of time. As God, Rama did not require an education. He is the source of Brahman, so what need does He have to learn about the all-pervasiveness of the impersonal spiritual force? Yet to set the proper example of how one should carry out their prescribed duties, He accepted Vishvamitra as a guru, serving him perfectly.

In the above referenced verse from the Janaki Mangala, Shri Rama and His brother Lakshmana are holding back a little after having run through the forests chasing bird and deer for fun. Rama and Lakshmana were escorting Vishvamitra through the forests because the sage was being harassed at the time by wicked night-rangers who could change their shapes at will. Rama was not yet twelve years of age, so He was still very young and showed signs of youthful exuberance.

Vishvamitra was older, so Rama made sure to show the proper respect. In remembering the muni's presence, the boys drew back and returned to his side. In this way Rama shows that He is a sweetheart who loves His devotees so much. He gives them the pleasure they deserve in their specific mood of choice. Vishvamitra got to have Rama as a protector while outwardly acting as His guardian. Lakshmana was there too, showing the muni the tremendous fraternal affection the brothers felt for each other.

A child listens to people they respect. Therefore Rama coming back to the camp after having run off in fun shows that Vishvamitra was held in high esteem. The muni would give the two brothers secret mantras to be chanted during fighting. With the power of the sound vibrations, the arrows flying from their bows would then pack a punch similar to nuclear weapons. Again, Rama and Lakshmana didn't require these mantras, but they accepted them to show the value of the guru and how he can help the sincere students to carry out their prescribed duties.

It is also stated above that the brothers plucked flowers, fruits and leaves and made garlands out of them. The beautiful nature we see around us isn't meant only to further strengthen illusion. If I take nature to be the sum and substance of everything, the very cause of creation, I am obviously mistaken and will have to suffer rebirth in the future. On the other hand, if I use the same aspects of creation to serve the Lord, I am making the best use of those gifts.

"If one offers Me with love and devotion a leaf, a flower, fruit, or water, I will accept it." (Lord Krishna, Bhagavad-gita, 9.26)

In the Bhagavad-gita, the same Rama in His original form of Shri Krishna states that anyone who offers Him a leaf, a flower, fruit or some water with devotion will have their offering accepted. In the case of Rama in the forest, the leaves, flowers and fruits were taken and accepted by the Lord to be a garland worn around His neck. To this day devotees who worship the Supreme Personality of Godhead take the time to make flower garlands and offer it to the deities and the spiritual master. Flowers are nature's beauty. They are so amazing that no mind except the Supreme

Mind could ever come up with something so wonderful to look at, which has a nice fragrance at the same time.

The flowers, fruits and leaves were used for the Lord's pleasure and thus fulfilled the highest purpose. This material body of ours is intended to be sacrificed in the same manner. The tongue exists to taste the remnants of foodstuff offered to God and to chant His names, "Hare Krishna Hare Krishna, Krishna Krishna, Hare Hare, Hare Rama Hare Rama, Rama Rama, Hare Hare". The feet are meant to take us to holy places of pilgrimage and to any place where the glories of the Lord are sung. The eyes are meant to gaze upon the wonderful deity. And most importantly, the ears are meant to hear about the Supreme Lord and His pastimes, such as those so beautifully presented in the Janaki Mangala of Goswami Tulsidas.

VERSE 35

देखि बिनोद प्रमोद प्रेम कौसिक उर।
करत जाहिं घन छाँह सुमन बरषहिं सुर।।35।।

dekhi binoda pramoda prema kausika ura |
karata jāhiṃ ghana chāṃha sumana baraṣahiṃ sura ||35||

"Seeing the children playing happily Vishvamitra's heart fills up with love. Wherever they go the clouds hover above to give shade and the demigods drop flowers from the sky." (35)

Essay - Vinoda Pramoda

Seeing children play happily, as if there are no other worries in the world, brings delight to the caretakers. What more can the guardian ask for than to have their dependents naturally jubilant and playing innocently without a care? Many thousands of years ago a famous muni received two young children as an escort through the forest. Though they were in childhood forms, they were the best fighters in the world, capable of protecting anyone who surrendered to them in a mood of affection. To delight the onlookers and to show their happiness in interacting with their creation, the two young brothers joyfully played about. This vision gave the muni so much delight that his heart filled up with love.

Who were these youths? Why were they escorting a muni at such a young age? Rama and Lakshmana were sons of King Dasharatha. Rama was the eldest son and Lakshmana was His dearest friend, the closest to Him of the three younger brothers. Vishvamitra, the son of Gadhi, was residing in the forests to seek spiritual enlightenment. Sobriety of mind is a prerequisite for understanding the highest truths of life. If we are constantly distracted by where to find employment, how to make our paramours happy, or what kinds of food to eat for dinner, how will our mind be able to notice that the influence of time is guaranteed and that everything around us is temporary?

Traditionally, those seriously seeking spiritual enlightenment take to the renounced order, minimizing their interaction with nature and reducing their attachments and dependencies. In times past, the renounced order was tied to life in the forest. If you live in the forest, your biggest concern each day is how to eat. With the berries that fall off the trees and the roots found in the ground, you're forced to live off of nothing and enjoy it. Your water is taken care of by the neighboring rivers, and your shelter can be found in a cave or through erecting a thatched hut. The fires provide the heat, and the holy names of the Lord provide the delight to the mind. Just sitting quietly and regularly chanting mantras from the Vedas are enough to bring about a spiritual awakening.

The wise know that the higher authorities are in charge of distributing the rewards we see in front of us. Just because there is meat on the shelves of the grocery stores for purchase doesn't mean that an animal wasn't previously killed. Just because the produce section is always fully stocked doesn't mean that there aren't farms to produce that food. At the root of all fuel is the earth, which is sustained through the higher forces of nature. We can maybe try to shop at different stores to get the type of food we prefer, but were it not for the rain we couldn't eat at all.

The Vedic seers honor the benefactors of the living creatures on earth by regularly performing yajnas, or sacrifices. These sacrifices typically include an offering of clarified butter into a fire. The worshiped deities then take their share of the offerings and enjoy them. From being pleased they agree to provide good fortune and conditions auspicious for continuing the pursuit towards full enlightenment, which is the ideal mission of the human being.

Vishvamitra ran into some problems, though. A band of night-rangers concentrated in Lanka was harassing the ascetics during their times of sacrifice. The goons would change their shapes at will, destroy the sacrificial arenas, and then try to kill the sages. The night-rangers were Rakshasas, or man-eaters, so they wouldn't stop at just killing. Vishvamitra, a powerful brahmana, could have retaliated with curses, but that would have involved losing some of his spiritual merits. Moreover, it wasn't his duty to fight enemies. That responsibility fell on the royal order.

Bearing this in mind, it was not an extraordinary request for Vishvamitra to go to Ayodhya and ask for protection. What was strange, however, was that he asked specifically for Dasharatha's eldest son Rama. The Supreme Lord Vishnu, the leader of the gods, the person from whom the entire creation has emanated, had appeared in the Raghu dynasty to reestablish the principles of religion and give protection to the innocent. As God, Rama could not fully mask His amazing abilities. Though He was less than twelve years of age, it was known to everyone that Dasharatha's eldest son was the best fighter.

The king reluctantly agreed, and Rama took Lakshmana with Him. During the initial days of the journey in the forest, Rama and Lakshmana played the parts of young boys perfectly. They would chase after deer and birds and make garlands out of plucked flowers, leaves and fruits. If they would get a little too wild in their play, they would look back at Vishvamitra and calm down a bit. This is a wonderfully endearing behavior shown by young children. They might try to test the parents' authority, but if deep down they know that they shouldn't be doing something, they won't do it. For instance, if you tell a child not to touch a particular object, they might, in defiance, run up to that object and threaten to touch it. But right before they are about to break the restriction, they look back at the parents and realize that they are being watched. Through this behavior the children show the elders that they respect them and that they are cognizant of their authority.

Thus Rama and Lakshmana showed Vishvamitra that he was the authority figure of the situation, the guru who shouldn't be dishonored. Vishvamitra was so overjoyed by the vinoda-pramoda, or delightful play, of the children that happiness filled his heart. The cynic may raise the objection that in the Ramayana of Valmiki accounts of this incident are absent. Thus Goswami Tulsidas may be using poetic license here in his Janaki Mangala. Yet knowing the inherent characteristics of the Supreme Lord, can there be any doubting that this incident occurred? As Shri Krishna, the same Rama would regularly sneak into the homes of the neighbors and steal their butter. It is also described in the Ramayana that Lakshmana never ate or slept unless Rama had done so first. Thus it is known that the two brothers always played together as children.

The Supreme Lord loves to interact with His devotees, giving them delight through the personal attention. The deer and birds in the forest were Rama's adherents after all, so why shouldn't they get the pleasure of having Rama chase after them? Typically, the situation is reversed. Every living entity is searching after God, even if they don't know it. The atheist searches for the Lord through surrender to sense gratification, the mystic through meditation, the philosopher through study, and the worker through fruitive engagement. But the bhaktas, or devotees, are held in such high esteem by their object of service that He sometimes comes to earth and playfully chases after them.

In the above referenced verse it is also stated that wherever Rama and Lakshmana went, clouds followed them to provide shade. The demigods also showered flowers from the sky. Again, these descriptions aren't found in the original Ramayana, but we know that in many other instances similar things were seen. The celestials often shower flowers on the Lord when there is an occasion of victory. There are many references to such happenings in the Vedic literature. The clouds providing shade also isn't that surprising, as even the Mainaka mountain arose from the ocean to lend service to Shri Hanuman when he was leaping to Lanka. That incident is mentioned in the Ramayana, for the ocean was indebted to the Ikshvaku dynasty, the family in which Rama appeared. Wanting to offer some service to that dynasty, the ocean asked the mountain to rise up and give aid to Shri Rama's dearest servant, Hanuman.

"O Sita, see the golden lord of mountains [Mainaka], which is golden-peaked and which rose up, piercing the ocean, to provide rest to Hanuman." (Lord Rama speaking to Sita Devi, Valmiki Ramayana, Yuddha Kand, 123.18)

Vishvamitra's joy from seeing Rama and Lakshmana play is meant to fill every heart. The kind poet included this verse in his Janaki Mangala precisely to allow the mind to remember that incident, to focus on it and to marvel at the divine sport of the Supreme Personality of Godhead and His brother. Those two sons of the king would go on to protect Vishvamitra and enhance the fame of the Raghu dynasty. The director of the clouds would gain immeasurable spiritual merits by providing shade and the demigods to this day are still under the Lord's protection. Thus there is never any effort wasted in devotional practices, which can take place under any circumstance.

The refuge of the forest is not a viable option today. Left to live in a world full of chaos, turmoil and uncertainty, the mind still has the sanctuary of the descriptions of the Supreme Lord's pastimes found in the Vedic texts. The appreciation of those topics increases all the more through regular chanting of the holy names, "Hare Krishna Hare Krishna, Krishna Krishna, Hare Hare, Hare Rama Hare Rama, Rama Rama, Hare Hare". Let the childish play of Rama and Lakshmana delight your heart every day and fill it with love that never exhausts.

VERSE 36

बधी ताड़का राम जानि सब लायक।
बिद्या मंत्र रहस्य दिए मुनिनायक।।36।।

badhī tāṛakā rāma jāni saba lāyaka |
bidyā mantra rahasya di'e munināyaka ||36||

"Rama showed His tremendous knowledge of fighting by killing the demon Tataka. The muni then gave to Him knowledge of secret mantras to be used in fighting." (36)

Essay - Passing The Test

Sometimes we're asked to do things that we really don't want to do. The suggested acts seem to break all the rules of propriety, every standard of decency which we have instinctively followed for many years. But when the request comes from a superior, someone we respect and who we know will not lead us astray, perhaps we will go ahead despite our reluctance. In the Vedic tradition, such requests sometimes come from the spiritual master, and if they are true to their vow to remain devoted to the Supreme Personality of Godhead, the acceptance of those instructions and their prosecution with firm faith, attention and honor by the disciple will prove beneficial in every way. This system of acceptance and action is so important that the object of service Himself shows its merits through His behavior.

Case in point the incident with Lord Rama and the female Rakshasa Tataka. Rama is the person most of the world refers to as God. More than just a vague concept of someone who may or may not get angry with us depending on what we do, the Supreme Lord is the person from whom everything emanates. His "personality" is a little different than ours. He is not limited to one manifestation, nor is He bound by the influence of time and space. Intelligence is rooted in Him, for the concept of a person or living creature descends from His very existence.

Lord Rama is the Supreme Lord in the spiritual manifestation of a warrior prince, carrying with Him the bow and arrow wherever He goes to slay the wicked elements harassing the saintly class. In a world full of relative good and bad, it's difficult to say who actually deserves protection and who doesn't. For instance, the person being attacked by another person may think they are innocent, but perhaps in the past they were not so kind to a helpless creature like an ant or a cow. The person being attacked may also have ill motives to act upon in the future. The person doing the attacking may be acting as a vehicle to deliver the sinful reactions to past work.

"Just as a tree starts to blossom during the proper season, so the doer of sinful deeds inevitably reaps the horrible fruit of their actions at the appropriate time." (Lord Rama speaking to Khara, Valmiki Ramayana, Aranya Kand, 29.8)

The dualities in the phenomenal world make it a little difficult to understand God's position and even acknowledge His existence. For instance, is it wise to pray to God for help in a football game? The last second field goal attempt by the kicker will grant victory to his team, but defeat to the opposition. If he should miss, the opposition will be elated, but the kicker will have to deal with the pain of having lost the game for his team. In this scenario, is praying for an outcome one way or another something that God should have to deal with? Is He really interested in trivial things like football games?

"Whenever and wherever there is a decline in religious practice, O descendant of Bharata, and a predominant rise of irreligion - at that time I descend Myself." (Lord Krishna, Bhagavad-gita, 4.7)

The divine descents give us a slight understanding of what really interests the Lord and where He decides to intervene. It is said in the Bhagavad-gita by the same Shri Rama in His original form of Lord Krishna that whenever there is a decline in religious practice and a rise in irreligion, the Lord descends Himself. This one statement reveals that there is no difference between Rama, Krishna and any other personal incarnation of Godhead. The "myself" indicates that Krishna is personally arriving on the scene, though His outward form may be suited to the current situation in society.

How do we tell if there is a rise of irreligion? Isn't this a relative measurement? Is not religion practically nonexistent today? The key is to see how much the pious members of society are being harassed in their daily affairs. If the entire population voluntarily chooses against religious life and instead turns towards temporary material satisfaction, the personal intervention of the Lord isn't necessarily required. But when the pious elements that do exist all of a sudden can't carry out their duties because of the intentional interference of the miscreant class, then the attention of the by-default neutral Supreme Lord is caught.

In His descent as Rama, the Lord dealt with many nefarious characters harassing the innocent sages in the forests. Rama appeared in the dynasty of King Raghu, who was a famous ruler known for his piety. Therefore Rama and His three younger brothers were taught from an early age about chivalry and how to respect and honor the most honorable members of society. Vishvamitra, one of the sages facing harassment in the forest, approached King Dasharatha of Ayodhya and asked to have the king's eldest son Rama escort him through the forest. Rama was ready to carry out the request, and He took the younger brother Lakshmana with Him. The boys were still very young at the time, but Vishvamitra knew that Rama was capable of providing full protection.

Capability and implementation are two different things. You can say that you're capable of performing the job responsibilities during an interview for the position, but once you get the job you have to deliver. Otherwise you will prove to be a failure and also show that the people who hired you made a mistake. Rama's initial test came with the female demon Tataka. She was a ghoulish looking creature who had a vendetta against the saintly class. She was previously a beautiful woman but was then later cursed by Agastya Rishi through a series of events. She became a hideous looking Rakshasi that would eat whoever would come near her. She loved to harass the sages living in the forest, including Vishvamitra.

It was now time for Rama to slay her. But the Lord was hesitant. Why should He kill a woman? The chivalrous fighters of the Raghu dynasty never did anything inappropriate. Dasharatha did not want to part with Rama, but since a venerable rishi made the request, the king felt obliged to follow. Now Rama was showing how well His father had raised Him by not desiring to break the standard rules of warfare. In reality, there was no risk of sin, for Tataka had been killing and eating people. In this sense she was more a vicious animal than a woman. She lost her standing as a member of a protected class by the actions she took.

Vishvamitra tried to dispel Rama's doubt by telling Him that she needed to be killed and that doing so would not break any rules of conduct. Thus Rama twanged His bow to get the attention of the demon, who then proceeded to attack. But in the back of His mind Rama had decided that He wouldn't kill her. He would just attack her, rough her up a little bit, but then let her live. Tataka started by releasing an onslaught of crags, and Rama responded by using His arrows to protect Himself. Then Lakshmana stepped in and lopped off the hideous creature's ears. Rama too started attacking her with His arrows.

The Rakshasas are also masters of illusion, using black magic when necessary. Thus Tataka started disappearing and appearing at will, making it very difficult to attack her. Vishvamitra at this time told Rama not to wait much longer. Nighttime was about to fall, and during that period the Rakshasas become almost unbeatable. Rama should not pay any concern to her gender. He should instead shoot to kill. Following the sage's words, Rama showed His ability to fight enemies using just sound. Locating the invisible demon, He pierced her in the chest with His arrows, ending her life.

Vishvamitra was so pleased by Rama's act. The son of Gadhi could have attacked Tataka with a curse, but then he would have lost some of his accumulated spiritual merits. The brahmanas are not meant for fighting. If you have a hired security firm to protect you, why would you want to use your own effort to fend off attackers? If you did that, what need would there be for the hired security? In a similar manner, the entire society is meant to be protected by the kshatriya class. The brahmanas can take to any activity if necessary, but their primary purpose is to worship God and teach others how to carry out that same worship through their occupational duties.

Rama was hesitant to kill Tataka but He followed through because Vishvamitra, the guru, requested it. By pleasing the guru, Rama received so many valuable weapons and secret mantras to chant to invoke those weapons. Just by calling up on the celestial weapons, they would appear to Rama and help Him in fighting off enemies. Lord Indra, the chief of the demigods, watching the slaying of Tataka from above appeared on the scene afterwards and advised Vishvamitra to give to Rama the many weapons that would help Him in the future.

The irony is that Rama never needs any help from anyone. He simply exhales to create this and many other universes. When He inhales, everything comes back into Him. But just to show how important the guru is, and how respected Vishvamitra was, Rama acted like a servant. He pleased the guru by passing the test placed in front of Him, even though He was not desirous of taking that test. It is impossible to measure the merits of the blessings received from the guru. Vishvamitra was a devotee, so by pleasing him one could get only auspiciousness as a result.

The Vaishnava spiritual masters, those who follow the same devotion as Vishvamitra, advise everyone to regularly chant the holy names, "Hare Krishna Hare Krishna, Krishna Krishna, Hare Hare, Hare Rama Hare Rama, Rama Rama, Hare Hare". Always think of the Lord, become His devotee, revel in His many triumphs, and follow the direction of His servants. Even if you are reluctant to chant and don't see what the benefit in it is, just know that the gurus most enthusiastically recommend the chanting of the holy names, that they beg as many people as possible to at least say the name of Krishna or Rama one time. By obliging their request, we receive secrets that unlock the door to boundless future happiness, which includes the sight of the Supreme Lord's lotus feet day after day.

VERSE 37

मग लोगन्हके करत सुफल मन लोचन।
गए कौसिक आश्रमहिं बिप्र भय मोचन॥37॥

maga loganhake karata suphala mana locana |
ga'e kausika āśramahiṁ bipra bhaya mocana ||37||

"The people observing received auspicious fruits for their eyes and mind. Rama accompanied Vishvamitra to his ashrama, with the fears of the sages removed."
(37)

Essay - All Things To All People

There is the saying that you can't be all things to all people. This means that whatever behavior you adopt, you're not going to give everyone a favorable result. For instance, if you should decide to dedicate more time to your job, you may make the coworkers and boss happy, but at the same time you'll spend less time with your family. Perhaps the wife and kids will be upset with your decision, so you're essentially caught in the middle of competing interests. With one person, however, whatever He does satisfies the desires of all the people He affects, even if those people belong to separate communities and keep different goals in mind.

Is the person we speak of God? Isn't that too broad a generalization? God is everything, sure, but what does that really mean? Ah, the Vedas and their many branches of literature exist precisely to expand upon this concept, to give it some meaning. The above referenced verse from the Janaki Mangala, fulfilling many purposes, also sheds light on this issue. The scene at hand is the forests of India many thousands of years ago. At the time, there was no such thing as India, but we refer to the modern day country for geographical purposes. The entire land was known as Bharatavarsha, or the area ruled by King Bharata and his descendants. There were different states and provinces but everyone lived under the recognized authority of one king, though the rogue states sometimes tried to usurp control.

At the time, the island city of Lanka, which was ruled by a fiendish character by the name of Ravana, had become a state where sinful life thrived. On the complete opposite end, there were the forests that were inhabited by the animals and the ascetics given to piety. The forests were under the jurisdiction of the pious kings, and since the rogues in Lanka were against dharma as it was meant to be practiced, there were clashes. Rather than fight the kings outright, Ravana and his band of Rakshasas would head straight for the lifeblood of society, the vipras.

A vipra is a kind of high-thinker, someone who avoids material association. Think of playing video games as a child and then giving them up in favor of more important obligations when you grow older. With increased maturity comes a reassignment of priorities, realigning which things are more important in life and which things can be relegated to the category of entertainment. For the enlightened vipra, the true purpose in life is to find the Supreme Absolute Truth, that one energy which is beyond duality, and then stay immersed in thoughts of Him.

What is duality? Think of a pendulum that swings back and forth. On one side is acceptance and on the other is rejection. The living being constantly swings on this pendulum, all the way through to the time of death. One activity is accepted with anticipation and eagerness only to be rejected later on in favor of something else. The cycle of birth and death represents the largest swing of acceptance and rejection. Take on a form, have it develop, leave some byproducts, and then exit that same form.

There has to be a higher purpose to fulfill. At least this is what the vipras think. In order to even ponder this issue one must be very sober. So many other outlets are tried first, before the final approach towards learning the truth in earnest is made. "Perhaps if I try my hand at increased sense gratification, I will be happier. My current lifestyle isn't cutting it, so maybe I should get a more expensive car or take up a new hobby. Or maybe renunciation is the answer. Live a minimalist life and try to stay peaceful in mind."

The vipras of the Vedic tradition take the route of austerity and penance, but with a purpose. The Absolute Truth is known as Brahman, which is formless. It does not have a visible manifestation, but we can sort of see it through the autonomous functions of the living beings. You can't really see the wind, but you know it's there if flags are blowing or trees are shaking. Similarly, you can tell that the life force of Brahman is present when living creatures are moving around and operating on their own.

The formless Brahman is not tainted by duality, so one who can realize it is highly enlightened. The flawless properties of Brahman stay with the living being even while they are encased within a material covering. For Brahman realization to take place, association with Brahman's covering, known as maya, must be limited. Therefore traditionally the vipras would take to austerity and penance in the forest, to realize Brahman and make the most of their human birth.

The Rakshasas concentrated in Lanka not only didn't care about Brahman, but they didn't like anyone who went against the life dedicated to service to maya. To make sure that the influence of the brahmanas, the vipras who know Brahman, was limited, the Rakshasas would attack the sages in the forest. If your life is dedicated to spiritual pursuits, you're obviously not much interested in violence. You don't have a group of secret service agents around to protect you nor are you quick to pull the trigger when dealing with attacking enemies.

Vishvamitra, one of the more exalted vipras of the time, approached King Dasharatha of Ayodhya for protection from the Rakshasas. The vipras could have cast curses back on the demons, but this would have caused their accrued spiritual merits to decrease. Why have so much effort go to waste when it was already the duty of the king and his class to protect the innocent? Vishvamitra specifically asked for Dasharatha's eldest son Rama to protect him. Rama and His younger brother Lakshmana then left home and escorted the vipra for some time.

While Brahman is formless, it has a source that is full of spiritual form. Rama is that source. He is the Supreme Personality of Godhead in the manifestation of a warrior prince. His association provides the delights of choice, cherished fruits, to every single person. For the vipras in the forest, the predominant desire was to be protected from the Rakshasas. They were living in fear, so there was no peace of mind. And without peace, how can there be happiness?

"One who is not in transcendental consciousness can have neither a controlled mind nor steady intelligence, without which there is no possibility of peace. And how can there be any happiness without peace?" (Lord Krishna, Bhagavad-gita, 2.66)

As an initial test of His strength, Rama had to defeat a powerful female Rakshasa named Tataka. He did not want to slay a female, and even though Vishvamitra advised Him to do so, the Lord was still resolved upon only hurting Tataka instead of killing her. Finally, when she started using her illusory tricks, appearing on the scene and then quickly vanishing, Vishvamitra pleaded more emphatically with Rama to give up His unnecessary kindness. The Lord obliged and slayed the wicked creature who had been harassing the sages.

As a result, Rama removed the fears of the vipras, including Vishvamitra. He made good on His promise that is found in many sections of the Vedas to protect the innocent, to make sure that the demon class cannot vanquish them. At the same time, the observers in the forest received the fruit of their eyes and mind. All of the onlookers, which included vipras, forest dwellers, and householders living innocently, watched the most beautiful form of Shri Rama, who was accompanied by His equally as beautiful younger brother Lakshmana.

God's vision is more delightful when He is actively working on something for the good of the devotees. Rama was very young at the time, as was Lakshmana. When the two were fighting a very formidable enemy, the vision was something wonderful to behold. Imagine seeing two young boys able to pick up a car or run a marathon. While those feats are amazing, the sight of the two sons of Dasharatha ridding the forest of a wicked creature with just their bows and arrows was so splendid that the mind didn't want to forget it.

The fruit of the eyes is the sight of the Supreme Lord. The same goes for the mind, as the external vision creates the image that can then be remembered over and over again within the mind. The young Rama and Lakshmana walked with Vishvamitra back to his hermitage, where they would continue to protect the vipras. Eventually, the trio would make its way to Tirahuta, where a marriage contest was taking place. The winner would win Sita Devi as a wife. There too, the residents had the desire to see Sita marry the beautiful Rama, and the Lord would oblige their request.

The slain enemies of Rama got the pleasure of liberation, which is achieved by seeing the Supreme Lord at the time of death. The atheists also take temporary pleasure in Rama's external energy of maya, proving again that the Supreme Lord gives every person what they want. When the innermost desires are shifted towards the transcendental realm, the true fruit of existence is tasted and relished.

VERSE 38

मारि निसाचर निकर जग्य करवायउ।
अभय किए मुनिबृंद जगत जसु गायउ।।38।।

māri nisācara nikara jagya karavāya'u |
abhaya ki'e munibṛnda jagata jasu gāya'u ||38||

"After Rama killed so many night-rangers, the yajnas were performed. Without fear the munis of the world sing of the fame and glories of the Lord." (38)

Essay - Worship In Peace

The kind Lord Rama, the Supreme Personality of Godhead who descended to earth to protect the innocent, does good with all of His activities, including His fighting. Normally violence is not welcomed, for why would one man want to kill another? Why should there ever be fighting between rational adults, people who should know better? Life is short after all, so there shouldn't be a reason to raise hostilities. But from the above referenced verse from the Janaki Mangala, we get an idea of when violence is necessary and how when it is invoked properly it can bring the greatest benefit to man.

It is said that Lord Rama killed so many night-rangers. A nishachara is a sort of ghoulish creature that can change their shape at will. This species was especially prevalent on earth during the Treta Yuga, the second time period of creation. We know of their existence from the documented historical evidence of Vedic literature, which includes the original Vedas, Mahabharata, Puranas and Ramayana. The original Vedas are generally not read today because their content is very short and difficult to understand. The original hymns could long ago be understood by the highest class of men, whose intellect was so sharp that just by hearing information once it could be remembered fully. Reading a translation of the original Vedas today doesn't really do much for us, as there is no underlying culture to complement the songs. If a particular hymn glorifies the Supreme Lord as being exquisitely beautiful and kind to His devotees, how is someone who never worships God and who is constantly worried over temporary ups and downs going to understand the meaning?

The more detailed scriptures are thus targeted for the less intelligent. As the current age is the Kali Yuga, the dark period of quarrel and hypocrisy, every person is deemed unintelligent. The smartest people of the world today are still less fortunate than the people who lived in previous times. There is nothing wrong with connecting with the more detailed scriptures, for the same benefit of association with God is present within them. Along with the stories of the Supreme Lord's exploits, you get information of what kinds of creatures were present on earth in ages past and what their behaviors were.

The night-rangers chose to attack at night because their victims would have less chance to spot them. Think of the prowler who waits until there is no light outside to commit crimes. What were the crimes committed by the night-rangers? They weren't innocent by any means. They would attack human beings, kill them, and then eat their flesh. What was the motive for these attacks? After all, with every crime there is some type of motive. Perhaps the victims deserved what they were getting?

One would be surprised to learn that the victims were the most innocent members of society, as far as adults go anyway. Children don't know any better, so they are not taken to be serious threats by anyone. The ascetics, who were adults, living in the forests had no ties to anyone. They were renounced from worldly life so they could concentrate on their spiritual duties. They didn't have large plots of land or stockpiles of wealth in the bank. Rather, they lived in thatched huts, ate whatever berries were on the trees, and spent the rest of the time chanting the holy names of the Lord and performing formal rituals known as yajnas.

"In the beginning of creation, the Lord of all creatures sent forth generations of men and demigods, along with sacrifices for Vishnu, and blessed them by saying, 'Be thou happy by this yajna [sacrifice] because its performance will bestow upon you all desirable things.'" (Lord Krishna, Bhagavad-gita, 3.10)

It was these yajnas, or sacrifices, that the night-rangers specifically didn't like. In a formal sacrifice there is a beneficiary, and if that beneficiary is pleased, they grant rewards to the performers making the offerings. The brahmanas, the priestly class, dedicated to yajna wanted to please the Supreme Lord. They could have remained in the cities, but the forests provided limited distractions. In this sense, who were they really bothering? Yet the night-rangers were the embodiments of sin. They not only violated the laws of propriety, they thought that anyone who was pious was a threat to their way of life.

Lord Rama killed many of these night-rangers. They deserved that end because of what they were doing. Rama outwardly appeared in a family of princes that traced its ancestry back to one of the first kings on earth, Maharaja Ikshvaku. Therefore, as a matter of formality it was the Lord's obligation to provide protection to the innocent. That one man could protect against the attacks of such fierce fighters was rather amazing. At the same time, the dedication shown by Rama revealed the purpose to His personal advents and His purpose for acting.

One should only have to live in fear if they are ignorant. Fear is rooted in the loss of life, which is not a valid thing to fear because the soul lives on after the current form is destroyed. Nevertheless, it is stated by Rama Himself that for the mature adult there is no greater fear than death. You mature through youth and make it into adulthood and take care of all your responsibilities. What else do you have to do after that except die? This process is likened to the mature fruit that hangs off a tree just waiting to fall.

"Just as the ripened fruit has no other fear than falling, the man who has taken birth has no other fear than death." (Lord Rama, Valmiki Ramayana, Ayodhya Kand, 105.17)

In spiritual life, however, there should not be any fear. Real religion maintains a connection with God that persists into the afterlife. The present life is just the afterlife from a previous existence, so in this sense the future life isn't that big a deal, except for the fact that we're not exactly sure where it will be and when it will start. The brahmanas in the forests were living in fear while worshiping God because of the attacks of the night-rangers. Therefore Rama came on the scene and eliminated that fear. Hence the Lord is known as Hari, or the remover of the fears of His devotees.

In the above referenced verse it is also said that the munis of the world sang of the glories and fame of the Lord. Worship of God shouldn't be an abstract concept. To use software development terms, it must have a class definition and an object instance. Without instantiation, the idea of dedicating your life to the origin of both matter and spirit will never manifest. For that worship to bear fruit, to really take hold in one's life, knowledge of the Supreme Lord's features and activities is helpful. To this end, just looking at Rama is enough to get plenty of material to work off of. Just think of His smiling face, His lotus-like hands holding His bow and arrow, the pitambara tied around His waist, and His dedicated brother Lakshmana following Him wherever He goes. The delight of the Raghu dynasty, Raghunandana, is so sweet and charming to look at that the mind wonders why it would ever choose to contemplate upon anything else.

As if Rama's spiritual form isn't enough, there are His numerous activities. Picture Him effortlessly raising His bow and aiming His arrows at the night-rangers that are ready to pounce on the innocent sages. Picture Him kindly looking about to make sure that His devotees are no longer in fear. Picture Him never tiring of standing on guard to defend those who protect dharma, or religiosity. Hence it is no wonder that the world still sings the glories of that kind son of Dasharatha, whose name directly represents Him. Thus the most potent form of worship for the fallen souls of this age is the recitation of the holy names, "Hare Krishna Hare Krishna, Krishna Krishna, Hare Hare, Hare Rama Hare Rama, Rama Rama, Hare Hare", which brings the association of that dedicated bow-warrior, who will do anything to please His devotees.

Follow divine love, bhakti-yoga, without fear. Should impediments arise, know that not a single moment is wasted when connecting with the Supreme Lord. He promises to offer conditions for that worship to bear fruit, either in this life or in a future one. Singing of Rama's glories never gets tiring, and so poets like Goswami Tulsidas compose wonderful songs like the Janaki Mangala to please the soul and give countless future generations a chance to keep the mind fixed on the lotus feet of the controller of the universe.

Question: Why didn't other people take care of the night-rangers?

Others were certainly around at the time who could have dealt with the nishacharas attacking the sages. Even today there are many evil elements in society and we don't see the Supreme Lord descending from His spiritual abode to deal with them. The purpose of Rama's advent was special, and His personal intervention is more notable because of the many lessons it provides. Just from the one verse above we get so much knowledge about when violence is necessary and the purpose to sacrifice. Not for self-aggrandizement, the procurement of material rewards, or even the removal of distress, the real purpose of a yajna is to please the lord of sacrifice, Yajneshvara, which is another name for Rama.

Know also that from Rama's personal protection the conditions conducive for the glorification of the Supreme Lord, which is man's ideal occupation, are created. For the child, the most desired condition is placement in a playroom with many toys. For the adult male it might be the living room with the video game system and for the adult female the shopping mall. Yet if you took every living creature at their core, analyzed the properties of their souls, you'd see that the most ideal condition is one where the glories of the Supreme Lord are sung without fear and without interruption. From His dealings in the forest many thousands of years ago, we see that Rama personally offers the protection to keep that ideal situation a reality, and therefore His kindness knows no bounds.

VERSE 39

बिप्र साधु सुर काजु महामुनि मन धरि।
रामहि चले लिवाइ धनुष मख मिसु करि।।39।।

bipra sādhu sura kāju mahāmuni mana dhari |
rāmahi cale livā'i dhanuṣa makha misu kari ||39||

"Keeping in mind the work that needed to be done for the demigods, sadhus and vipras, bringing Rama with him the mahamuni proceeded ahead towards the bow sacrifice." (39)

Essay - The Integral Player

The saintly class, which includes both the celestials in the heavenly realm and the devoted souls living on earth, a long time back needed a specific job to be completed. They were being harassed by a miscreant class that was tremendously powerful, capable and willing to assert their dominance. With strength comes responsibility. Just because one entity is superior in both wisdom and physical dexterity doesn't mean that their influence should be negatively exercised. Parents are the best example in this regard. They can do whatever they want to the innocent child, especially to the newborn that just emerged from the womb. Yet with a proper mindset the good parent uses all of their mature abilities to protect the child, granting guidance and imparting wisdom. This particular miscreant class that roamed the earth many thousands of years ago lacked sobriety of mind. They thought their powers were products of their own work, so they decided to wreak havoc around the world and try to eliminate the pious class altogether. Not surprisingly, they were wrong in thinking that they could continue in this path without opposition.

"Day after day countless living entities in this world go to the kingdom of death. Still, those who remain aspire for a permanent situation here. What could be more amazing than this?" (Maharaja Yudhishthira speaking to Yamaraja, Mahabharata, Vana-parva, 313.116)

Why would someone think they can dominate everyone and never have to suffer the consequences? Well, why does someone mistake a rope for a snake? Why does someone think that they will live forever? Maharaja Yudhishthira, a famous king, when once asked by Yamaraja, the god of justice, what he thought the most amazing thing in the world was, responded that nothing could be more amazing than the fact that people think they are not going to die when they have seen everyone they know from previous times pass away. This is quite a relevant and accurate assessment by the famous Pandava king. We know that our ancestors have died. Sometimes the deaths didn't occur in old age. The news shows us that people can die at any time, but somehow we still don't apply that knowledge to our own lives. Either that or we just try to forget it as a way of avoiding despair.

It is fine to not dwell at every second on the reality of imminent death, but to act as if we are completely ignorant of it is not wise in the least. If you're working at a company that is about to shut down its doors in a week, what is the use in taking on a new project? Perhaps you can keep your mind engaged throughout that time, but in the end your hard work will go for naught. The living being similarly creates so many temporary structures during their particular stint within a body, but at the time of death the relationship to those objects vanishes. With the passage of time, everything will eventually dissipate, with the exception of the spirit soul within.

The wise take the knowledge of impending death as a wakeup call for finding the real purpose to life. Is there something beyond the temporary ups and downs? What happens to the soul after death? Where does it go? Where was the soul prior to birth? These questions and more are answered in the Vedic literatures, whose most concise and complete work is the Bhagavad-gita. Not surprisingly, the author of the Gita's verses is the Supreme Personality of Godhead, Lord Krishna. Not a mere sectarian work calling for blind worship of a particular personality, the Gita covers all aspects of philosophy and thought. In the beginning, Krishna addresses the issues of life and death and the temporary nature of the body. Only through understanding the many concepts and applying the principles in everyday practice does the final step of surrender unto God really mean something to the sincere soul.

The saintly class follows the Bhagavad-gita's principles, which are immortal. Though the specific discussion held between Krishna and Arjuna took place on a battlefield some five thousand years ago, the core concepts of Vedic culture have been around since the beginning of time. Even in the Treta Yuga, an era prior to the time of the Gita's most famous delivery, there were men on earth dedicated to worshiping God, to fulfilling the true purpose of life. They had a problem, however, with the miscreant class. The night-rangers concentrated on the island of Lanka had no clue about the meaning of life. If they ever gave a thought to impending death, they would use it as impetus for finding more sense gratification, at any cost. If the city you live in is burning down, being destroyed, will you go into store after store and loot or will you try to make sure that everyone safely evacuates? The night-rangers during this particular time were of the looter variety, trying to get whatever they could through any means possible.

They particularly enjoyed eating human flesh; hence the sages living in the forests were ripe targets. The powerful celestials residing in the heavenly planets also couldn't do much. Ravana, the leader of the night-rangers in Lanka, was so strong that the demigods were afraid of him. Impotent against Ravana's clan, the demigods decided to petition the Supreme Lord directly, to have Him appear on the scene to protect the innocent. Krishna states in the Gita that He comes to earth to protect the sadhus, or pious men, and reinstitute the principles of religion.

"In order to deliver the pious and to annihilate the miscreants, as well as to reestablish the principles of religion, I advent Myself millennium after millennium." (Lord Krishna, Bhagavad-gita, 4.8)

The dramatic real-life play that is the Ramayana chronicles the life of Lord Rama and His pastimes, which included His eventual killing of Ravana. There were many pivotal actors in the play, with Vishvamitra Muni being one of them. He was one of the sadhus being harassed in his daily religious practices. The Supreme Lord had appeared as the eldest son of the King of Ayodhya. When Rama was still under the protection of His parents, Vishvamitra petitioned the king to have the Lord accompany him in the forest, which Rama kindly did, taking His younger brother Lakshmana with Him.

To prove that He was worthy of Vishvamitra's trust, Rama slew a powerful female Rakshasa name Tataka, who had been harassing many of the saints. After this incident, both Rama and Lakshmana were given special mantras by Vishvamitra to be used in fighting against enemies. The sages and onlookers were quite pleased with Rama when he stayed with Vishvamitra at the muni's hermitage. They could once again live peacefully and follow their prescribed duties without a problem.

It would have been great for Vishvamitra to keep Rama and Lakshmana with him in his ashrama indefinitely, but there was a higher purpose to fulfill. Ravana needed to be slain, and for that to happen Rama needed an excuse to take him on in a fair fight. The Supreme Lord never has to justify His actions, but He sets a good example by the work He follows. Ravana deserved to be attacked simply off his previous acts, but Rama had not had any direct hostilities with him yet. Therefore, to attack Lanka would not have been appropriate under the circumstances.

The matrimonial bond between Sita and Rama gave birth to the trap that would do Ravana in. Sita Devi was the precious daughter of King Janaka of Mithila. To find the appropriate husband for his daughter, the king decided to hold a contest, where the person who could lift Lord Shiva's heavy bow would be the winner. Vishvamitra needed to get Rama to this contest in order for the work of the demigods and the sadhus to be complete. Keeping this in mind, the muni left his ashrama and took Rama and Lakshmana with him.

In this way Vishvamitra played an integral role in both bringing Sita and Rama together and ending Ravana's reign of terror. The surrendered souls only look to the Supreme Lord for sustenance, for they know there is nothing wrong with asking God to help them in their sincere worship. That devotion to Rama continues for life after life for the spirit soul who is not entangled in the web of karma. The impending death that was previously feared or ignored becomes a welcomed end that will signal the return to the spiritual sky, where the Supreme Lord's company is enjoyed without cessation.

Question: Why didn't the sadhus and demigods just ask Rama to go and kill Ravana directly? Why did they have to arrange His marriage to Sita first?

The Supreme Lord's acts are enjoyed by the surrendered souls. In fact, it is seen that in every person there is a desire to hear about the activities of others. The daily news websites are visited for this very reason, as are the latest news feeds posted on the now-popular social media websites. With topics relating to Krishna, the process of hearing gets purified. If I remain in contact with purity, naturally my thoughts will start to become pure as well. If I only think good thoughts, naturally my disposition will be better and I will be a more pleasant person to be around.

With Rama's many activities documented in the Ramayana, the soul desirous of hearing about others gets a trusted supply of audible nectar that can be tasted over and over again without the reservoir ever depleting. If Rama had gone directly to Lanka, we would have missed out on the wonderful protection He offered to Vishvamitra. We'd also be denied the chance to hear about how He delivered Ahalya from a curse and how He defended the innocent sages from the wicked night-rangers. Getting to know Vishvamitra too is a benefit, for the Lord is never alone. His trusted entourage is always with Him, and contact with any of the component members is just as beneficial as contact with Rama. It is for this reason that Rama is worshiped alongside Sita, Lakshmana and Shri Hanuman. Vishvamitra too, a key player in bringing Sita and Rama together in Mithila, is always with Rama in thought, word and deed.

VERSE 40

गौतम नारि उधारि पठै पति धामहि।
जनक नगर लै गयउ महामुनि रामहि।।40।।

gautama nāri udhāri paṭhai pati dhāmahi |
janaka nagara lai gaya'u mahāmuni rāmahi ||40||

"After the wife of Gautama Rishi was liberated and sent to the abode of her saintly husband, Vishvamitra continued on towards Janaka's city, taking Rama with him." (40)

Essay - Deliverance of Ahalya

Goswami Tulsidas herein briefly touches on a famous incident from the life of Lord Rama, the Supreme Personality of Godhead who roamed the earth in the guise of a warrior prince many thousands of years ago. The Janaki Mangala poem focuses on Rama's marriage to Sita Devi, the daughter of King Janaka, so many of the events that led up to that occasion are only touched on in one or two verses. The accounts of the incident with Ahalya vary, but the general story is the same. The

Ramayana of Valmiki likely provides the most details, and it gives so much insight into the glory of Rama and how Vishvamitra played an integral role in saving others and bringing Sita and Rama together.

From the variation in accounts a misconception arises that the event never really happened. You see, we're supposed to take Rama's life and pastimes for their symbolic meaning. Ahalya was a woman who was absolved of her sins by the touch of God, so from the story we are to learn that God is great and that contact with Him leads to our benefit. While this kind of lesson can be taken away from so many past incidents, the story of Ahalya is not fabricated nor is it a mythological tradition. The authors of the Vedic literature sometimes used metaphors and stories with personification, but when they did there was full disclosure. The incidents of the Ramayana are real history, and since the creation goes through cycles of manifestation and annihilation, sometimes the events don't follow the exact same sequence. Rama, as the Supreme Lord, appears in other universes as well, thus allowing for many more versions of His acts to be distributed between the members of the numerous creations.

The accounts from the original Ramayana say that the incident took place as the trio of Vishvamitra, Rama and Lakshmana entered the outskirts of the city of Mithila. Vishvamitra was a renounced brahmana, which is a sort of priest who lives in austerity. Why would someone want to live in the forest away from everyone else? Why do we need to shut people off to practice religion? The purpose to all the rules and regulations of the Vedas, the ancient scriptures of India, is to foster God consciousness at the individual level. Once that exists at full maturity, the same benefit can be gifted to others. The brahmanas are the class that has the best opportunity to reach this purified consciousness, so whatever they can do to make the goal a reality is considered worthwhile. Sort of like the message the flight attendant tells you about securing your oxygen mask first before assisting a child, when the brahmanas are true to their vows and always thinking about God, they can do tremendous good for the rest of society.

The brahmanas in the forest at the time were being harassed by night-rangers. By harassed we mean getting attacked during the times of sacrifice and then fearing for their lives. The brahmanas accumulate tremendous spiritual merits through their work, so they can cast curses in response to threats of violence. The problem with this practice is that the spiritual merits diminish with each curse thrown. It's similar to accepting a diet and exercise routine to become fitter, and then going on an eating binge that erases some of your accumulated fitness gains. The more effort you put into reaching the fit condition, the less likely you will be to overeat and erase some of your progress.

Vishvamitra did the right thing by approaching the King of Ayodhya, Maharaja Dasharatha, for help. While the brahmanas are generally nonviolent and focused on religious duties, the kshatriyas, the warriors/administrators, are charged with protecting the innocent. If violence is required in this endeavor the warriors must not be hesitant to use it. Dasharatha had no problem protecting the brahmanas. He was ready to send the entire royal army into the forest to protect the exalted muni. Ah, but Vishvamitra was doing the work of the sadhus and the celestials, who needed Dasharatha's eldest son Rama to be at certain places at certain times.

Through asking nicely, Vishvamitra was able to gain Rama's protection in the forest. If you get Rama, you get Lakshmana too. The Lord's younger brother will never leave Him alone. While it may seem like Lakshmana is the equivalent of the annoying younger brother, such a glorious personality who is full of fraternal affection and the eagerness to serve and accompany Rama only enhances the Lord's stature as the best friend of every living entity and the one person whose attributes cannot be properly measured. Thus the trio roamed the forests, with the brothers providing protection from the attacking night-rangers.

At one point during their travels, the group made its way into Mithila. At this time Rama noticed a beautiful asylum, which appeared to be vacated. Like a kind disciple, Rama nicely put the question before the knowledgeable Vishvamitra to explain what this beautiful place was. Vishvamitra, pleased to hear the inquiry, took the opportunity to narrate the story of Ahalya, the wife of Gautama Muni. A long time back Gautama was engaged in penance and austerity, living with his beautiful wife in this asylum. One day, he happened to leave the hermitage for a little bit. Whenever a brahmana starts to advance in asceticism, the celestials in the heavens can get jealous over their progress. Through austerities and penance one can attain great powers, even surpassing those of the demigods.

To knock Gautama down a peg, the celestials petitioned Indra to descend to earth and enter the hermitage. The lord of celestials took on the guise of Gautama and petitioned the sage's wife for conjugal relations. The wife hesitatingly agreed, and on the way out Indra ran into Gautama. The sage could tell what had happened, so he immediately cursed Indra to become castrated. Ahalya, for her part, was cursed to remain in that asylum alone, unseen for many, many years. Gautama then retreated to the Himalayas to continue his penance. He told his wife that she would be reunited with him when she would see the eldest son of King Dasharatha and treat Him hospitably.

When Vishvamitra finished his narration, Rama and Lakshmana followed him into the hermitage. There they saw the most beautiful woman, who could not be seen by anyone else up until that time. The brothers went to pay their respects to her feet, and she in response gave water for washing their feet. She treated the brothers hospitably and got their blessings in return. She was then able to reunite with her husband.

In other places in Vedic literature, the story is very similar, except Ahalya is instead cursed to be a stone. She gets her form revived when Rama places His foot upon the stone. After honoring Him, she gets to return to the abode of her husband. In either case, the general outline is the same, for the most beneficial end is to see Rama's lotus feet. Contact with the Supreme Lord in a mood of devotion fulfills all desires for the pious souls. Ahalya desired to keep her husband happy and to remain in his company, and thanks to Gautama's curse the wife was able to meet the Supreme Lord.

There is a famous incident relating to Lord Chaitanya Mahaprabhu which similarly reveals the benefit of contact with the Supreme Personality of Godhead. One of Mahaprabhu's associates had once offended Him. Because of that transgression, that person was not able to see the Lord anymore. Begging and begging, the person finally was able to get someone else to ask Mahaprabhu when that anger would subside. Lord Chaitanya replied that only after a million births would that person again get to see Him. Instead of being dejected over the long duration, the person was excited at the heart to hear that they would again get to see Lord Chaitanya, even if it should take many years.

In a similar manner, though Ahalya was cursed for a long time, she was guaranteed of seeing the Supreme Personality of Godhead in His most charming form as Lord Rama. Therefore the acts of Indra and the instigation of the celestials, and even the curse offered by Gautama, were all purified through the simple contact with Rama. Just as Rama's foot liberated Ahalya, the sound vibrations of the Vedic literature describing His forms, names, qualities and pastimes liberate the conditioned soul mired in a cycle of birth and death. Through contact with wonderful works like the Janaki Mangala, Ramayana and Puranas, the ears get the much needed nectar to restart spiritual life. And when those narrations aren't readily available, just chant the holy names, "Hare Krishna Hare Krishna, Krishna Krishna, Hare Hare, Hare Rama Hare Rama, Rama Rama, Hare Hare", to mentally clasp the beautiful lotus feet of the delight of the Raghu dynasty.

CHAND 5

लै गयउ रामहि गाधि सुवन बिलोकि पुर हरषे हिएँ।
सुनि राउ आगे लेन आयउ सचिव गुर भूसुर लिएँ।।
नृप गहे पाय असीस पाई मान आदर अति किएँ।
अवलोकि रामहि अनुभवत मनु ब्रह्मसुख सौगुन किएँ।।5।।

lai gaya'u rāmahi gādhi suvana biloki pura haraṣe hi'eṁ |

suni rā'u āge lena āya'u saciva gura bhūsura li'eṁ ||
nṛpa gahe pāya asīsa pā'ī māna ādara ati ki'eṁ |
avaloki rāmahi anubhavata manu brahmasukha sauguna ki'eṁ ||5||

"Taking Rama with him, the son of Gadhi became happy in the heart when he saw the city. Hearing the news of their arrival, the king, bringing his advisers, guru and priests, comes to welcome them." (Chand 5.1)
"The king went and received blessings and then paid so much honor and respect after that. When he saw Rama, he experienced a happiness one hundred times that of Brahman realization." (Chand 5.2)

Essay - A Welcoming King

The pattern of behavior exhibited by the noble characters stays consistent throughout these meetings from an ancient time. First there was the dilemma faced by King Janaka. Having found his most beautiful daughter while she was in the earth as a baby, the king had to arrange for her marriage to a suitable husband when she reached the appropriate age. The astrological charts could not be made because of the circumstances of her birth, thus the king couldn't settle upon the right way to ensure that she got the husband that she deserved. So he decided to ask his chief counselors, the brahmanas, to devise a plan to settle the situation. As this was going on, in another place King Dasharatha greeted the brahmana Vishvamitra very nicely when he came to Ayodhya to borrow Lord Rama as an escort. The king hesitatingly agreed to allow his eldest son Rama to leave, who took the younger brother Lakshmana with Him. Now the story returns to Janakpur, with the same deference to the priestly class again shown by Janaka.

Why so much attention to members of society who practice religion? Don't we see so many stories in the news today detailing the faults of priests and how they are cheating the system to get what they want? The key in determining the genuineness of a man of the cloth is to see how their recommendations affect your life. The kings of ancient times earned their high standing through sometimes exercising violence. Through force, or at least the threat of it, peace, law and order could be maintained. But there is more to life than just having food to eat and a roof over the head. The animals find the creature comforts without requiring education or university degrees. They eat without a problem, sleep when necessary, and get ample sex life whenever they desire it.

"As a boat on the water is swept away by a strong wind, even one of the senses on which the mind focuses can carry away a man's intelligence." (Lord Krishna, Bhagavad-gita, 2.67)

The human being needs more, especially due to the influence of the mind and the senses. The mind focused on just one of the senses will carry away the intelligence of even the most sober thinking individual. Therefore, in order to control the mind, to keep it in a good place, pure activities should be adopted. If I want to stay happy all the time and someone recommends that I watch the television news channels throughout the day, obviously my pleasant mental disposition will not last very long. If I want to take a long drive somewhere, carrying passengers and important cargo, drinking heavily will not be a wise preparatory step.

In a similar manner, if the human being wants to make the most out of the human form of life, seeking out basic sense gratification is not the proper path to follow. The brahmanas remove the doubt in this area through their good counsel. The king has so many responsibilities, so without advisers they wouldn't know what to do. By acting properly, by following guiding principles that lead to better conditions, righteous behavior becomes almost automatic.

Because of their value, the brahmanas were treated very nicely during the Treta Yuga by the kings. When Janaka saw that Vishvamitra, Rama and Lakshmana had arrived, he happily greeted them, taking the brahmanas of the court with him. Janaka wasn't sitting at home bored either. The compromise previously reached relating to his daughter's wedding was that a contest would be held. All the famous princes from around the world would bring their families to Janakpur to witness the contest of Lord Shiva's bow.

Whoever could lift that bow would win the daughter Sita's hand in marriage. Previously in the Janaki Mangala, which is a wonderful poem authored by Goswami Tulsidas that describes these events, it was said that the line of kings entering Janakpur for the contest was tremendous. Lord Shiva's bow was extremely heavy, so no one was getting anywhere in the contest. One after another, the princes were coming and then sitting back down as failures. While this was going on, King Janaka was welcoming so many people that other kings were jealous of how popular he was.

As would be expected, Janaka took the time to properly greet the sons of Dasharatha and their spiritual guide Vishvamitra. It is said in the above referenced verse that Vishvamitra was also very happy in the heart upon seeing Janaka's capital city. Just as everything about God is wonderful, so is everything related to His dearmost servants and companions. Sita is together with Rama always. During the performance of the real-life play known as the Ramayana, the two spend some time apart physically, but mentally and emotionally they are always together.

The Supreme Lord's energy pervades through space. He is absolute, so with Him close personal proximity and physical separation are the same. To the affected conditioned individual there is a distinction, but this is due to a poor fund of knowledge, illusion strengthened by attachment to a form that is temporary. Since God is capable of granting His association even when not personally present, chanting the holy names, "Hare Krishna Hare Krishna, Krishna Krishna, Hare Hare, Hare Rama Hare Rama, Rama Rama, Hare Hare", can bring to mind the sweetheart son of King Dasharatha who was set to marry Sita.

Sita Devi is just as glorious as Rama. The daughter of King Janaka deserved the grand ceremony and the contest to determine her nuptials. With that event so many people of the time got to witness history and receive the fruit of their eyes. The eyes are meant to look at beautiful things and derive pleasure from those visions. No woman on earth has ever been more beautiful than Sita, and no one was more qualified for marrying her than Rama. Thus the meeting of the two was a feast for the eyes. That joyousness also extended to the moments prior to the actual lifting of Shiva's bow by Rama.

The dichotomy in arrival fanfares made the above referenced situation unique. The many princes that had come to lift the bow arrived in style, for they were royal families. They packed up the caravans with royal paraphernalia and brought along so many members of their family. In King Dasharatha's case, his eldest son, the one first eligible for marriage, was away from home defending the forest-dwelling sages from attacking night-rangers. These vile creatures had harassed the brahmanas for too long, and with Rama and Lakshmana by his side, Vishvamitra and the other sadhus were safe. The sadhus could once again peacefully carry out their prescribed duties once Rama arrived on the scene. Seeing Him enter the ashrama of the great muni brought so much delight to the residents of the forest.

Vishvamitra was already in a renounced garb, and Rama and Lakshmana didn't have much with them except their weapons. Yet Janaka greeted them so nicely anyway, for Vishvamitra was famous throughout the world for his austerities and spiritual strength. Seeing Rama and Lakshmana, Janaka would be mesmerized. He was dedicated to his occupational duties, but he was not attached to the outcome of actions. It is said in the Bhagavad-gita that one has a right to carry out their prescribed duties, but they are not entitled to enjoy the fruits that result.

"You have a right to perform your prescribed duty, but you are not entitled to the fruits of action. Never consider yourself to be the cause of the results of your activities, and never be attached to not doing your duty." (Lord Krishna, Bg. 2.47)

An extension of this truth is that one should not be attached to the outcome of events, for the higher forces are responsible for distributing results in a fair and timely manner. All that you can control is the effort you put in and the attention you give to righteousness. Even if you do everything the right way, the outcome will not always be what is expected. From the proper attitude, one learns how to stay above attraction and aversion. Janaka was in this exalted position, and he was famous throughout the world for being an expert yogi. Yet seeing Rama and Lakshmana broke his neutral stance, as had also previously happened when Sita as a baby was found in the ground.

This shows that the spiritual qualities are not void. They are full of variety and can elicit positive emotional responses within the target recipients. At the same time, the beneficiaries must be worthy of that association. We can look at the same flower every day and not appreciate it if our mind is elsewhere, if we are distracted by obligations that don't really mean much. But with a sober mind, with a proper understanding of the beauty of nature and how wonderful this creation is, the flower can all of a sudden be appreciated and used to please the eyes.

Janaka's neutral disposition and high moral standing made him eligible for enjoying the transcendental sweetness of the visions of Sita, Rama and Lakshmana. Though this entering party did not have the fanfare of the other royal families, Janaka knew they were something special. At the request of the son of Gadhi, Rama would be allowed to attempt to lift the bow and thereby change the course of history. That divine couple, Sita and Rama, married in the company of Janaka, Vishvamitra, Lakshmana and so many other worshipable personalities, resides in the hearts of the sincere devotees who never want to forget them for even a second. Sita and Rama also stay in the heart of the poet Tulsidas, who sings their glories and helps to make sure others know of them too.

Essay - More Than Brahma-Sukha

There is happiness when one realizes Brahman, or the all-pervading spirit. With maya, which is not Brahman, there is perpetual misery. The resulting happiness felt only arrives in short bursts and then vanishes very quickly thereafter. The next time the same experience will not bring as much happiness, for the living being gets accustomed to sense satisfaction, in effect raising the threshold for sense pleasure. The concept of a "proper perspective" can only apply in a realm where ignorance reigns supreme. Though the happiness of association with Brahman is everlasting and different from temporary sense pleasure, the source of Brahman is the real reservoir of pleasure. For a famous king a long time ago, the thrill felt from seeing the Supreme Personality of Godhead gave him a happiness he never experienced before.

How do we know that the senses spoil us into requiring more for gratification? Think about why athletes and celebrities involve themselves in children's charities and other philanthropic ventures. If you're worried about performing well in the big game, the mental toil will have an impact on your psyche, on your overall happiness. At the same time, when you see a young child suffering from cancer, your problems don't seem to be as big. One side is worried about how to succeed in a life where living is taken for granted, while the other side is struggling for existence at a young age. Because of the influence of the senses it is easy to lose sight of the proper perspective.

In the larger scheme, even death itself isn't that big a deal. Sure we don't know what lays ahead in the future, but the uncertainty of upcoming time doesn't mean that our existence will cease. The present moment is the culmination of much past thought and struggle. Ten years ago we likely worried about the immediate future, and yet somehow we managed to make it through. Prior to our birth we had no say in the circumstances of our upcoming life, but everything worked itself out anyway.

"For the soul there is never birth nor death. Nor, having once been, does he ever cease to be. He is unborn, eternal, ever-existing, undying and primeval. He is not slain when the body is slain." (Lord Krishna, Bhagavad-gita, 2.20)

The Vedas reveal that everything in life that we know about is temporary in its manifestation. Those who are illusioned by the temporary easily lose perspective, both in the short and long term. That which is permanent, knowledgeable and blissful is the opposite of the material nature. The Vedas refer to this force as Brahman, and its realization is the main objective of the living entity gifted with a human birth. Within a human body the dichotomy between Brahman and maya can be studied. The most mature living entity can follow instruction and guidance to train the senses to cope with hardship. The marathon runner can run for long distances without any discomfort, while the person new to running finds one mile difficult to complete. The difference between the two individuals is in the training of the body.

In the larger picture, if the body is trained to rely only on limited sense interaction, the realization of Brahman can be attained. The entire breadth and scope of religion is meant for this connection with Brahman, the understanding that I am a spirit soul, part and parcel of God. Though the ultimate realization may not be disclosed immediately to the sincere spiritualist, the purpose of austerity, sacrifice, and religious practice is the knowledge of the Absolute Truth.

From that knowledge comes happiness. And why shouldn't there be happiness? If I know that I am an eternal spiritual force, will I get distracted with temporary ups and downs? The greatest fear for the mature human being is death, similar to how the ripened fruit on the tree has nothing left to do but fall. With a fear of death gone, so many other fears are eliminated. Absorbing the authorized information of the Vedas, which reveal the process of transmigration of the soul, which is better known as reincarnation, the living being understands that there is no reason to lament the loss of the temporary body. Neither is a temporary gain a cause for excessive celebration.

"He who is without attachment, who does not rejoice when he obtains good, nor lament when he obtains evil, is firmly fixed in perfect knowledge." (Lord Krishna, Bg. 2.57)

Brahman realization is meant to continue uninterrupted. You can know theoretically that you are spirit soul and not body, but practically every activity you are inclined towards from birth follows the realization of maya, which requires no effort. Thus to attain and stay on the Brahman platform is quite difficult. King Janaka a long time ago mastered the art of real yoga to keep the Brahman vision within his mind at all times. He still followed work. He did not become a robot or give up his obligations without cause. Brahman realization can occur through any type of activity, provided it is authorized and the worker keeps the proper vision within the mind.

King Janaka had a kingdom to rule over, but he carried out his responsibilities with detachment. He did the work because that was his duty, but he had no concern for the result, success or failure. Through his equipoised condition he realized Brahman. He knew what brahma-sukha, or the happiness of realizing Brahman, felt like. Nevertheless, when he saw one young man in particular, the immediate happiness he felt was like no other.

By the very nature of the reaction we can understand that the object viewed was not maya. Thus in the above referenced verse Goswami Tulsidas has affirmed Lord Rama's position as the Supreme Personality of Godhead. King Janaka saw the eldest son of King Dasharatha enter his kingdom alongside Vishvamitra and Rama's younger brother Lakshmana. As a good king, Janaka kindly welcomed the arriving party. Their entrance wasn't as pronounced as the others, but Janaka nevertheless followed protocol.

Who were the others that arrived? At the time, Janaka was holding a bow-lifting contest to determine the husband for his daughter Sita Devi. Interestingly enough, when Janaka found Sita as a baby girl one day on the field, he immediately felt tremendous affection for her. He loved her so much that he took her in as his daughter. Again, this happiness was not related to maya, for it did not distract from his religious duties. If anything, having Sita as a daughter only made Janaka more committed to the righteous path.

Seeing Rama now Janaka felt a happiness that was one hundred times that of brahma-sukha. The Personality of Godhead has this effect on the pure souls who cherish His company. Janaka didn't know that Rama was God appearing on earth in the guise of a human being to do the work of the demigods in eliminating the nefarious character Ravana, but he didn't have to. The purity of the Brahman realization made Janaka eligible for appreciating the transcendental form of the Lord.

That form is meant to provide happiness to the observer. The eyes have a purpose. Through fulfilling that purpose they provide a fruit that can be enjoyed. More than anything the eyes exist to gaze upon the sweet, charming, lovely, and beautiful vision of the Supreme Personality of Godhead, who so innocently goes about His business, caring for the welfare of His devotees at every step. It should be noted that seeing Rama is not dependent on Brahman realization. The reference to brahma-sukha made by Tulsidas is only for comparison purposes. One seeking the happiness of merging into the spiritual light of Brahman does not get the same happiness that the devotees do.

Why did Janaka ever bother with Brahman then? Why didn't he just go straight for God realization at the start? It is said in the scriptures that one who sincerely follows the devotional path, bhakti-yoga, has already performed so many religious sacrifices and penances. In this way we see that the other methods of yoga do have a purpose. The target aim of the human form of life, the fruit of the eyes, is not reached when personal interaction with Shri Rama is absent, but there are still benefits to be gained with disciplines such as jnana-yoga, karma-yoga and hatha-yoga.

If one has the good fortune to hear about bhakti, they should take to it right away, bypassing Brahman realization altogether. Know it for certain that if you have the rare chance to bask in the sweet vision of Shri Rama entering Janakpur to lift Lord Shiva's bow, you have certainly performed all the necessary rituals and regulations in a previous time. The soul's reward for pious behavior is the company of the person whom Janaka so delighted in welcoming as a guest. In a short amount of time, that same guest would formally join the king's family.

VERSE 41

देखि मनोहर मूरति मन अनुरागेउ।
बँधेउ सनेह बिदेह बिराग बिरागेउ॥41॥

dekhi manohara mūrati mana anurāge'u |
baṁdhe'u saneha bideha birāga birāge'u ||41||

"Seeing Shri Rama's enchanting form, in mind the king felt ecstatic love and affection. Bound up in love, the King of Videha renounced his renunciation." (41)

Essay - Renouncing Renunciation

The good poet uses license every now and then to get their point across. Perhaps they throw in an extra word or two for emphasis or they insert superlatives and adjectives to emphasize a specific trait or feature. In the above referenced verse from the Janaki Mangala, Goswami Tulsidas carefully uses just the right words to bring home the point that renunciation is only meant for fulfilling a higher purpose. It is not the end by itself. You give up sweets to improve your health. You give up fatty foods to lower your cholesterol, and you give up drinking to stay sober. Once that healthy condition is reached, however, your activity doesn't stop. King Janaka, who was known as Videha, renounced his world famous renunciation when the jewel of the Raghu dynasty appeared in front of him.

Why was Janaka known as Videha? "Deha" refers to the body, and the prefix "vi" says that King Janaka was without a body. What was he then, a ghost? If he's a ghost how is he going to do anything? Ghosts can haunt us and maybe serve as enchanting figures to star in motion pictures, but in reality they are not capable of much. Did a ghost rule over the kingdom of Janakpur many thousands of years ago?

A body is defined by what it can do, and also what it can inhibit. For instance, a glass container prevents the liquid inside from pouring onto the surface that the glass is resting on. In this way the container inhibits the motion of the entity within. At the same time, it provides the function of allowing liquids to be consumed easily. It has both a restrictive element and a functional purpose.

With the form of body granted the living entity residing in the material world, the inhibiting aspects may not be so easily discernible. The fact that we have to sleep every night is a notable example of an inhibition. Why can't we just stay awake perpetually? We know that everyone sleeps, but why? Also, why do we sometimes get indigestion from eating foods that we like? Shouldn't we all be allowed to eat whatever we want, whenever we want? Children can eat fatty foods and sugar-rich delights such as laddus and not feel the aftereffects. Why do the harmful consequences have to accompany maturation of the body?

The inhibitions are automatically imposed from the time of birth, but the functional purpose of the body is not easily known. For instance, with the body we can make the choice to place our hand into a fire. Picture a raging fire that has large flames that don't seem to lessen in intensity. As an adult, you wouldn't dare think of placing your hand into that intense heat, for you know what the consequences will be. But what if you are intoxicated and not thinking straight? What if you're an ignorant child and just don't know any better?

The individual residing within, the spirit soul, has a choice in how they use their body. In an arena sporting a full range of possible actions and corresponding outcomes, there is the option to choose activities which are harmful. Hence someone could easily decide to place their hand into the fire. The result will be pain. The burn can be so severe that it takes a long time to heal. The wise person will not repeat the same activity, but the ignorant, who don't know any better, might require more evidence before reaching an assertive conclusion. "Will my hand burn every time I place it into the fire? Will I get hurt from this again? I know I was in severe pain the last time, but maybe that was a fluke. Perhaps all fires don't have the same properties."

Hence the repeated action can take place, and the wise can guess what the reaction will be. Over and over again, you follow behavior that you know is not good for you, but you somehow think you'll see a different outcome. The hand in the fire is just one example out of countless others where a negative reaction comes as the result of ignorance. At the same time, the activities themselves show the range of motion of the body, how it can be a very powerful instrument. That the same body which places the hand into the fire can do complex mathematics equations and run marathons is quite amazing.

If all we see are the negative aspects of having a body, we might be tempted to renounce activity. In one sense this is not a bad option, for if we avoid something harmful we will obviously prevent the negative outcome from occurring. In the spiritual tradition of the Vedas, renunciation is referred to as vairagya, and it is an important tool that is coupled with jnana, or knowledge. Use the knowledge of the spirit soul to your advantage. Follow action that will keep you in knowledge, not wasting your time in areas where there are pain and misery awaiting you.

But where to get knowledge? Though we could figure out that the fire will burn us if we place our hand into it, it is better to learn to prevent that behavior by taking instruction from someone else. If the instructor is presenting perfect information to us, they are an authority source on that particular subject matter. We know that the teachers in school are authority figures based on the fact that we learn to read and write from their guidance. If we learn to become doctors by listening to our instructors in medical school, we know that their teachings are valid.

Similarly, the acharyas of the Vedic tradition prove their high standing and the validity of their knowledge by the effects resulting from the application of their recommended principles. Learn from the spiritual master that you are spirit soul, aham brahmasmi. You are Brahman and not maya. Brahman is spirit; it is truth. Maya is material nature; it is illusory. Only through the influence of maya can you possibly think that a fire will not burn your hand upon contact. Through maya's influence you can mistake a rope for a snake and your body for your identity. You are Brahman; learn what this means and act off of that knowledge.

The jnana acquired by learning about Brahman and the workings of reincarnation can reinforce the dedication to vairagya. If I know that I am spirit, why am I going to follow a path that will make that realization harder to keep? For instance, if I know that drinking is bad for me and that I shouldn't be intoxicated, am I going to want to hang around a bar all the time, where people are constantly consuming adult beverages? I will instead want to follow behavior that is conducive to experiencing the knowledge that I am taking in.

Renunciation helps to keep the Brahman realization, the awareness that you are spirit. Renunciation from attachment to maya is the key. If I identify only with my body, I will feel negative effects, either immediately or in the future. The person who remains attached to maya all the way up until the time of death is guaranteed of rebirth in the ocean of material suffering. On the other hand, knowledge of Brahman at the time of death indicates a desire to retain a spiritual existence in the next birth.

"And whoever, at the time of death, quits his body, remembering Me alone, at once attains My nature. Of this there is no doubt." (Lord Krishna, Bhagavad-gita, 8.5)

If renunciation is helpful, should I just cease all activity? To experience bliss, should I give up even moving my body? The key is to remain detached from the external energy, or maya. You are compelled to work in order to both set a good example and maintain the life force within the body. However, you should not work in such a way that you will become attached to the fruits of your labor or the body that performs the work.

King Janaka was exemplary in this area. He earned the title of Videha because of his realization of Brahman. Nothing could phase him because he was not under the influence of maya. Maya could not touch him. He was equal in both happiness and distress. He ruled over a kingdom, so it would be expected that the mode of passion would run through him. In the material world there are three modes governing activity. In goodness one acts in a way that they retain knowledge of Brahman, understanding the differences between spirit and matter. In ignorance one follows a path where they are only hurt in the end, not reaching a tangible goal or enjoying a cherished fruit.

In the mode of passion, hard work is applied to enjoy a fruit that is temporary in its manifestation. Thus the mode of passion leads to a neutral state, sort of like pushing a rock up the hill only to have it fall back down after you're done. During Janaka's time, the kings were expected to live in the mode of passion, for they had to provide protection to the innocent, using violence when the time and circumstance called for it. But Janaka was a pious king who followed the advice and consent of the priestly class, the brahmanas. Thus through proper instruction, he performed his work without attachment and thus remained Brahman realized.

Janaka had a body, but he was considered bodiless because it had no inhibiting influence. It did not lead him towards disaster or misery. Rather, the body was there as a formality, but the spirit inside was what guided all actions in the proper direction. Because he was famous for his renunciation, Janaka was known as Videha.

With his exalted position in renunciation established, the above referenced verse from the Janaki Mangala becomes all the more puzzling. It is said that when Janaka saw the form of Lord Rama, which was enchanting to the mind, loving attachment, or anuraga, immediately formed. The king became bound up in love, and because of that his vairagya ran away.

From this verse so carefully crafted by Tulsidas we see that jnana and vairagya are not the end. Renunciation can be renounced when there are feelings of love directed at the Supreme Lord. Shri Rama was God Himself appearing on earth in the most enchanting form of a warrior prince. Janaka was above excitement and attachment, and this position was not broken when looking at Rama. Attachment to God has no relation to attachment to anything material. Matter is inhibiting and damaging to one's future fortunes when taken to be one's identity or source of pleasure. When that same matter is seen on the form of the Personality of Godhead, it becomes spiritual in nature.

How could Janaka love Rama instantly? The question should be how could someone who was Brahman realized and pious in every way not have spontaneous attraction to the beautiful form of the Supreme Lord? Jnana and vairagya are tools to help learn how to use the body properly. The individual soul within the body is very powerful. Through the vehicle of the temporary form the spirit soul can do amazing things which don't have to be harmful. It was Janaka's body which decided to hold the grand sacrifice in Janakpur, which would determine the husband for his daughter Sita.

In the spiritual world, Sita and Rama are always together. They are the combination of God and His pleasure potency. Janaka played a hand in reuniting them during their play in the phenomenal world. His formal renunciation went away as soon as it was no longer needed. Attachment to Shri Rama's form and name never proves detrimental, and King Janaka is the authority figure in this regard. No one is more renounced than he is, and no one was quicker to abandon that renunciation when seeing the Supreme Lord. From that spontaneous affection he would soon gain Rama as a son-in-law and the world would be better off for it.

VERSE 42

प्रमुदित हृदयँ सराहत भल भवसागर।
जहँ उपजहिं अस मानिक बिधि बड़ नागर।।42।।

pramudita hṛdayaṁ sarāhata bhala bhavasāgara |
jahaṁ upajahiṁ asa mānika bidhi baṛa nāgara ||42||

"Now happy in the heart, the king compliments the good qualities of the ocean of material existence: 'The creator is very smart, for such gems like this grow here'." (42)

Essay - Gems On Earth

While superbly informative, this verse from the Janaki Mangala is also quite humorous. Through a pronounced shift in emotion that happens suddenly the audience can't help but question the reason for the change. If it occurs abruptly due to an unexpected reversal of fortune the new sentiment from the actor evokes laughter from the audience members. In this particular instance, the king had gone from staying strictly detached from a world deemed false and full of ignorance to all of a sudden praising it. A gem is something beautiful and worth having. Without connection to the Supreme Lord, the many objects floating in the ocean of material existence are temporary, a cause of misery and pain, and detrimental towards one's spiritual advancement. Once that connection is made, however, that same ocean becomes pleasurable, where the person who originally placed everything into it is praised for their cleverness.

As a pious king well versed in the philosophy of Vedanta, Janaka knew that the material creation operates off of an energy known as maya. At the root meaning of the word, maya is "that which is not". Just like the magician performing his tricks which rely on illusion, the material nature has an influence that causes us to take things to be one thing when they are really something else. The magician's assistant on the stage isn't really sawed in half and neither can a rabbit emerge from a hat from out of nowhere. In the same way, the material bodies that we take to be our identities are actually just temporary coverings that will vanish at some point in the future; they are guaranteed to vanish like a bubble coming off the water that eventually bursts.

"As the embodied soul continually passes, in this body, from boyhood to youth to old age, the soul similarly passes into another body at death. The self-realized soul is not bewildered by such a change." (Lord Krishna, Bhagavad-gita, 2.13)

The illusion is so strong that even after we see others lose their temporary forms, we still think that the same fate doesn't await us. In the off chance that we are aware of the reality of impending death, we will take every step possible to forget about it. The audience member doesn't view the television show or movie as a scripted performance, for that would take the fun out of viewing. In the same way, why should I worry about the inevitable end to my life if my desire is to enjoy right now?

Ah, but there is a purpose to knowing what maya is and why her influence exists. Taking things for what they aren't may help children to enjoy their make-believe play in the sandbox, but adults can't follow the same behavior. If they did, they couldn't care for anyone else, let alone themselves. The spirit soul is the identifying agent within every form of body, and since it has the potential for action it has a say in where it will end up in the future.

Does this mean that we chose the womb that we emerged from in the present life? The choice is made between association in the material ocean and life in the spiritual planets. Once that "yes" or "no" vote is tallied at the time of death, a suitable home is prepared for the next life. At the same time, there are millions of other creatures who are making the same choice; they also have results due to arrive based on their past actions. Thus living entities are placed into just the right circumstances to fulfill so many other rightfully planned occurrences.

King Janaka knew that maya is the cause of bondage, for it ensures that rebirth occurs at the end of life. Rebirth is guaranteed for every living entity that is not God conscious at the time of death. As only the human being has the opportunity to know what death is and how consciousness influences the future, they have the most auspicious form of body. The aim of the human form is thus quite obvious: tailor your activities in such a way that you'll always remember God. Remembering God today will help you remember Him at the end of life, which will in turn grant you an auspicious residence.

"Whatever state of being one remembers when he quits his body, that state he will attain without fail." (Lord Krishna, Bg. 8.6)

If my objective is to think about God all the time, anything that I see in front of me that will put that goal in jeopardy will be rejected. Hence it is quite common for a serious spiritualist to renounce much of material existence, choosing a life of austerity and penance instead of the fast-paced world of fruitive activity centered on sense gratification. King Janaka had larger responsibilities, so he couldn't just give up the throne and move to the forest. Nevertheless, his mental attitude was such that he might as well have been living in a thatched hut with no connections to the outside world.

The pious king showed the way, how to find transcendental enlightenment while not abruptly giving up occupational duties. Yet there is more to life than just rejecting everything in the ocean of material existence. The land where maya rules is likened to an ocean because it is very difficult to cross over. The length of the ocean is quite large, and the current flows in the direction opposite of where you want to go. If you don't believe this, ask yourself why it is so difficult to wake up in the morning? Why is it easier to quit than continue trying? Why is procrastination easier than perseverance and why are negative thoughts more commonplace than positive ones?

The conditions in maya's land are such that just endeavoring for spiritual emancipation is difficult. It is thus rarer to find someone out of that group who succeeds. With the odds stacked in maya's favor, the more you can renounce things and the more detached you can become, the better off you'll be. Ah, but there is a catch, which is so nicely pointed out in this pleasant verse from the Janaki Mangala. Maya has a boss, someone from whom she receives orders. Her influence only applies to the living entities desirous of residence in the material existence. When the Supreme Lord descends to earth or when He sends a representative who acts above the influence of maya, there is no question of suffering or receiving harmful effects on the consciousness on the part of the affected parties.

In this instance, King Janaka viewed the transcendental form of the Supreme Lord in His manifestation as the warrior prince of Ayodhya named Rama. It must be said that this wasn't the first time that Janaka broke away from his position of videha, or bodiless. When he found a baby girl in the ground many years prior while ploughing a field, he felt attachment to her right away. He wanted to take her home and raise her as his daughter, but he was a little hesitant. For starters, a transcendentalist shouldn't be overly attached to any living entity. At the same time, what if this girl belonged to someone else? A king lives off of piety, which includes respecting the property rights of others.

"Then a voice, sounding like a human being, was heard from the sky which said, 'O king, this child is rightfully your daughter.'" (Sita Devi speaking to Anasuya, Valmiki Ramayana, Ayodhya Kand, 118.31)

A voice from the sky appeared on the scene and told Janaka that the girl was his daughter in all righteousness. This hinted at the fact that the girl, to be named Sita, was not part of this world. Her form was transcendental as well. This meant that Sita's body and spirit were identical. The same held true for Shri Rama, who arrived in Janakpur with His younger brother Lakshmana and the sage Vishvamitra. Janaka at the time was holding a bow-lifting contest to determine who would marry Sita.

Janaka's reaction upon seeing Rama and Lakshmana, who was basically identical to Rama in appearance except for a lighter skin color, is quite interesting. In a material existence, a person constantly swings on the pendulum of acceptance and rejection. One day we like someone and the next day we hate them. One day we love a certain ice cream flavor and later on we think it is disgusting. If there is a slow period for sense gratification, we'll binge on a certain activity. Then when we suffer the aftereffects, we'll swear off that behavior and assure ourselves of renunciation in the future.

For the spiritualist trying to realize Brahman, or God's impersonal effulgence, the material existence is viewed as being a place of only misery. Thus Janaka, as a full renunciate in mind, did not like anything in the world. He was not attracted by anything, with the notable exception of his daughter Sita. When he saw Rama and Lakshmana, however, their beauty was so out of this world that Janaka changed his tune. The ocean of material existence that was previously miserable and hard to cross over was now warm and inviting. It deserved to be praised, for in it were found gems like Rama and Lakshmana.

Since the divine brothers were gems to the eyes, Janaka praised the creator for his handiwork. In one sense maya was still acting on Janaka, but it was of a different nature. The Supreme Lord's personal energy sometimes clouds the intelligence of the sincere souls in order to enhance the pleasure they feel through interaction. Janaka here is thinking that Rama and His brother are part of the material world, even though they aren't. The king is presuming that the creator, Lord Brahma, was responsible for crafting their bodies, even though he wasn't. The material bodies consist of combinations of the three modes of nature: goodness, passion and ignorance. Bhagavan, the Supreme Personality of Godhead, has a body which is completely in pure goodness, and His form never leaves Him. Hence He is always spiritual. The same goes for Lakshmana, as he is practically identical to the Supreme Lord, a part of Bhagavan.

This verse shows us that the transcendental touch can turn anything previously considered material into an object of spiritual value. Just by seeing Rama, Janaka changed his outlook on life, on how he viewed the objects of the world. In a similar manner, if we take ordinary things which were previously detrimental to our spiritual evolution and dovetail them with service to the same Shri Rama, the place we live in can be considered a storehouse of gems. The eyes that previously sunk into despair upon seeing another's good fortune can delight in the wondrous beauty of Rama's creation. The ears that used to get annoyed at the miserable sounds produced all around can hear the chanting of the holy names, "Hare Krishna Hare Krishna, Krishna Krishna, Hare Hare, Hare Rama Hare Rama, Rama Rama, Hare Hare", and feel God's presence. The tongue that previously tasted unpalatable foods that led to ignorance and laziness can now relish food first offered to Bhagavan. The prasadam, the Lord's mercy, spiritualizes the eating process, which then positively influences other activity.

Renunciation in the true sense of the term means to have attachment to God. From that disposition, the illusory effect of maya vanishes, leading to a condition where nothing needs to be rejected outright. Rather, the same material ocean can be used for finding delights in the form of endless opportunities to serve God. Ordinary poems and books can lead the consciousness astray and thus be considered maya, but sacred works like the Janaki Mangala and Ramayana remind us that there are gems to be found in literature which can change our outlook on life for the better.

VERSE 43

पुन्य पयोधि मातु पितु ए सिसु सुरतरु।
रूप सुधा सुख देत नयन अमरनि बरु।।43।।

pun'ya payodhi mātu pitu e sisu surataru |
rūpa sudhā sukha deta nayana amarani baru ||43||

"' Like an ocean of purity are the mother and father of these children, who are like a heavenly desire tree, who have a spotless beauty that gives the eyes so much happiness that is without end.'" (43)

Essay - Endless Happiness

The vision of Shri Ramachandra and His younger brother Lakshmana is so sweet that there is really no way to properly describe it. It is one thing to look at something beautiful and be awestruck, but it is another to try to put what you are feeling into words. Goswami Tulsidas, in singing of the famous initial meeting of Lord Rama and His beloved consort Sita Devi, touches on some of the emotions felt by the different parties, describing what they felt when they first laid their eyes upon Rama and His brother. Indeed, the eyes exist for this very purpose. The eyes can move very quickly, and depending on what is in front of them, they may inadvertently glance upon something that is unpleasant. But the act of seeing should not be shunned, for under the right circumstances the reason for existence can be revealed through a quick glance.

How does this work exactly? So one day we'll be lucky enough to see something that is out of this world, something which will force us to ask the right questions? If you look into the sky on a clear night, you'll notice the many stars in the solar system. You can't see everything that's out there, but the infinite beyond reveals a portion of itself to the person viewing it from thousands of miles away. In a second you can go from feeling important to knowing how insignificant you really are. The universe is so vast and complex, and this fact is reinforced just by looking into the night sky.

If you are fortunate enough to gaze upon the spiritual form of the Personality of Godhead, a higher realization will come to you, provided you have the proper mood. You'll wonder how anything could be so beautiful and how you lived so long without having seen it. With King Janaka, the astonishment went further. He immediately thought of the parents of the vision in question. Where did they live and what did they do to get such beautiful sons? Surely they must be full of virtue, like an ocean of purity. To be pure in thought, word and deed is very rare, for it requires a long time of practice and dedication in saintly life, administered by bona fide spiritual leaders who are themselves pure.

"Whatever state of being one remembers when he quits his body, that state he will attain without fail." (Lord Krishna, Bhagavad-gita, 8.6)

As is so nicely revealed in the Bhagavad-gita, whatever we think of at the time of death is the state that we will attain in the next life. This occurs without fail. There is no flaw to the system; what we think is what we get. Obviously the moment of death is the time of greatest panic in one's life, so there is little control over the faculties of the brain at that moment. What you will remember is what you thought about most during your time on earth. For the pious individual, a pure consciousness will be the reservoir of thought at the precise moment of exiting the body.

In the next life, the reward for that piety is birth in circumstances that are favorable for spiritual elevation. The quickest pathway towards the ultimate destination of the imperishable spiritual sky is the association of that land's leader. When that association exists through a bond of love, which involves service flowing in both directions, there is no requirement to even wait for the afterlife. The present circumstances turn into a spiritual land, a place where there is no concern over past, present, or future. There is no worry over change because the association you have is with the changeless. The only concern is over whether or not the love will be offered properly, and because of this sincerity, the object in question ensures that the conditions are always auspicious.

King Dasharatha of Ayodhya in his previous life accumulated pious merits by regularly observing the Satyanarayana-vrata. The vow relates specifically to a form of the Supreme Lord that accepts a certain kind of worship offered at regular intervals by householders and those looking to gain pious credits. The vow isn't directly related to bhakti, which is the pinnacle of religious practice. Nevertheless, pious behavior followed under authorized guidelines never fails to provide spiritual benefit. In his subsequent birth, Dasharatha would taste the fruit of his existence.

That would come through obtaining Shri Rama as a son. Rama is God Himself, who appears on earth in every Treta Yuga, or second time period of creation, as a warrior prince to annihilate the miscreants and protect the pious. No one was a better defender of religious principles than Dasharatha, who followed the example set by the ancestral line he belonged to known as the Ikshvakus. Thus Rama blessed the family further by appearing in it and granting Dasharatha a way to offer love without motivation and without interruption. Dasharatha's three wives also had gained many spiritual merits from previous lives. Queen Kausalya got Rama as a son. The bond the mother has with her son is unique. The good mother cares for her son so much that she is not concerned with what he asks for or what he wants. Mother knows best, so the son can never stop her from offering love.

Dasharatha had three other sons through his queens. They were all sweethearts in behavior and reservoirs of pleasure. Shri Rama is a direct incarnation of the Supreme Lord Vishnu, and His three younger brothers are partial incarnations of Vishnu. Thus they were really one and the same, though Rama was the leader. Every day the parents got to enjoy the company of their divine children, who were seemingly sent from heaven to delight everyone in Ayodhya.

On the particular day referenced in the quote above, King Janaka was attune to noticing qualities of parents. He was holding a bow-lifting contest to determine who would marry his daughter Sita. In the spiritual world Sita Devi is Rama's eternal consort. She is the goddess of fortune, Lakshmi, who is also an incarnation of Krishna's pleasure potency Shrimati Radharani. Janaka, while welcoming the many guests that came to his kingdom to witness the ceremony, paid attention to the attributes of the participants. In the arranged marriage system, the parents are just as important as the children. The wife is marrying into the groom's family after all, so the support system must be in place for the girl to be protected for the rest of her life.

The more pious the parents are the more likely the children will be to grow up pious. Seeing how beautiful Rama and Lakshmana were, Janaka immediately noted that the children's parents must be an ocean of purity. The boys are compared to a surataru, or heavenly desire tree. If one is still on the material platform at the time of death, if they have acted piously enough they get to enjoy many years of life on the heavenly planets. In that place, which is still part of the perishable material world, there are trees that can grant any desire immediately.

Shri Rama, or God, is often compared to a desire tree because whatever you want from Him you can get. This seems strange because don't many people not pray to God at all and still get benedictions? Ah, but what is it exactly that they receive? The absence of a desire to approach God is simultaneously a desire as well. While there is not an explicit desire to turn away from God, the implicit is just as good in this scenario. If someone doesn't want to love God, they are granted every ability to exercise that mistaken choice in an arena where the personal influence of the supreme master is absent. Hence even the spiritually disinclined get benedictions from God.

But the desire tree is best used to receive specific rewards. In the case of Rama, the reward He granted was supreme happiness, which was facilitated through His spotless form, which was as sweet as nectar. Nectar gives happiness to the person who consumes it. If it is in liquid form, it is enjoyed through drinking. With Rama and Lakshmana, the nectar came through their vision, the spiritual forms that stood before whoever was fortunate enough to see them. The eyes which drank that nectar received so much happiness that was amarani, or immortal or unending.

How can one vision give so much? Well, think about this specific occasion. Rama was in the kingdom of Janakpur, with He and His younger brother Lakshmana escorting the exalted sage Vishvamitra through the forests. The son of Gadhi had brought the two sons to Janaka's kingdom to have Rama try to lift the bow. Janaka had sent invitations out to every kingdom across the world to come to his town to participate in the contest, but Rama was not home at the time. He was the eldest son in the family, so only He could attempt to win Sita's hand. In the traditional Vedic system, it is considered a sin for a younger brother to get married before an elder one does.

Rama was away from home, but were the parents back home bereft of their beloved children's company? Were King Dasharatha and Queen Kausalya unable to see Rama when He wasn't at home? Dasharatha certainly felt the pain of separation when Rama left with Vishvamitra. The sage kindly asked for protection in the forest, and the king was ready to send his most capable fighters, his whole army if he had to. Ah, but Vishvamitra knew what he was doing. He only asked for protection as a pretense to have Rama's company. The saintly class are selfish in this regard, as they want to spend as much time with God as possible. Thankfully there is plenty of Him to go around, as any person can hold on to the Lord as their best friend by chanting, "Hare Krishna Hare Krishna, Krishna Krishna, Hare Hare, Hare Rama Hare Rama, Rama Rama, Hare Hare".

A brahmana's request should not be denied, especially by a king. Therefore Dasharatha had to agree to allow Rama to go, who in turn took Lakshmana with Him. It should be noted that Lakshmana was as beautiful as Rama, a spitting image of the jewel of the Raghu dynasty except that he had a fair complexion while Rama was dark. Sumitra, Lakshmana's mother, was not happy to see Lakshmana go either, but she knew that he couldn't live without Rama. The faithful younger brother would never leave Rama's side, for he would only eat after Rama had eaten and sleep after Rama had fallen asleep.

While Rama and Lakshmana were with Vishvamitra, their visions remained within the consciousnesses of the parents. In this way we see that God's personal form grants a nectar to the eyes that never dies. Seeing God is only the beginning, for that sight ideally results in a dedication to service that continues forever. Janaka was amazed at the purity of the children's parents, but little did he know that he was equally as qualified to see God. He already had Sita as a daughter, so there was no questioning his spiritual merits. Through his contest, the divine couple would be reunited, and that divine vision would remain in Janaka's mind eternally.

Essay - Who You Represent

Like it or not, your behavior is a reflection on your upbringing. The people who raise you are responsible for making sure that when you're an adult you follow the proper standards of conduct, that you obey the law and don't cause a nuisance to society. A parent especially understands how difficult it is to raise a child and make sure that they grow up to be properly educated and well-behaved, so when they see good traits in another child they immediately think of the role of the parents. This was the case with a famous king who cast his glance upon the transcendental form of the Supreme Personality of Godhead, Lord Rama.

What is a transcendental form? Can God have any other kind of form? God is everything, a fact which isn't too earthshattering. In mathematics there is the concept of sets and what different values they can contain. The most inclusive set is that which has the most values, the largest amount of numbers that represent the possible aggregations one can find. If we looked at the entire creation from a mathematical perspective, we'd see that there is a sum collection of space and its component objects. Obviously the measurement of that collection is unfathomable, but there is nevertheless a total amount. If we see a jar full of jellybeans, we can't be exactly sure to the number how many jellybeans there are, but there is still a specific total.

If we calculated a total for the universe, it'd be a representation of God. His universal form, or virat-rupa, is one way to think of Him, but at the same time this only represents a partial view. "How is this possible? If we include everything, is that not the limit to existence? The Absolute Truth is the entire collection of gross matter, or a form that is considered invisible to the mind. We can't see the universal form but we know that it exists. Therefore God is not a perceived reality. He must be accepted as an impersonal force that is always present in some way."

But the Vedas, the ancient scriptures of India, reveal that the Supreme Lord is both formless and with form. The distinction itself is a necessary product of illusion, pointing to a limitation in understanding. Just as we say that the sun is not out on a particular day because of the influence of the clouds, since we can't understand what a spiritual form is, we say that the macrocosmic vision of the Lord is His only feature. But to show what it means to have a transcendental form, that Absolute Truth kindly appears before our eyes every now and then. The foolish still don't understand His true nature even when looking directly at Him, but for those who are humble enough to know their limitations and accept the statements of the bona fide acharyas on faith in the beginning, the fruit of existence is revealed.

Shri Rama, the young boy who accompanied Vishvamitra Muni through the forests many thousands of years ago, showed the pious exactly what God looks like. The Lord has many spiritual forms and the fact that they appear within this material world is not extraordinary. A person who is superior and in charge of a particular energy can never be beholden to that energy's influence. The material nature, which spreads illusion that results in an identification with dull matter, has no existence on its own. Rather, it is consciousness that brings the presence of life, and the source of that consciousness is God.

In every vibrant life form, including our own body, the consciousness derived from the Supreme Lord's superconsciousness is present. We can think, feel and will because we are similar in quality to God but vastly inferior to Him in quantitative powers. We can be illusioned, but He cannot. With proper training in the system of spirituality descending from Shri Rama, illusion can dissipate, paving the way towards basking in the sweetness of God's transcendental form.

Even the exalted figures are sometimes bewildered by this apparent duality, the fact that God is everything and still capable of appearing within a smaller section. Mother Parvati once asked her dear husband Lord Shiva to describe the glories of Shri Rama and explain how Rama is actually God and not an ordinary man. Lord Shiva began his discourse by remarking that there is no difference between the personal and the impersonal features of the Supreme Personality of Godhead. There is only a perceived difference, and due to that one tends to think that Rama accepts a material form and then rejects it. The Supreme Lord is never subject to illusion nor is He ever away from us. He pervades all of space and at the same time He is not personally present within everything. His divine vision is granted to the kind souls who know how to properly utilize His energies.

When King Janaka saw Rama and Lakshmana entering his kingdom, he was enamored by their beauty. Vishvamitra brought the brothers to Janakpur to witness the bow-lifting contest that was taking place. Up to this point, Janaka was intimately familiar with Brahman, which is a theoretical understanding of spirit but one that is still not complete. To know Brahman is to know that spirit is the essence of identity and that it is transcendental to matter. Knowing Bhagavan, however, is knowing that Brahman has an origin.

Rama is Bhagavan, the Supreme Personality of Godhead appearing before the eyes of the earth's creatures in the guise of a warrior prince. In Bhagavan's original feature, He is Shri Krishna, the charming youth with a blackish complexion holding a flute in His hands and enchanting the residents of the spiritual planet of Goloka

Vrindavana. The personal expansions of Krishna are identical to Him in potency. The only difference is in the transcendental mood of devotion that they instill in their followers. Rama was especially attractive to Janaka upon first sight. The king couldn't believe what he was feeling, a sort of ecstasy that he did not think was possible. By understanding Brahman one learns to keep their emotions in check, to not be distracted by temporary highs and lows. Indeed, Janaka was holding this contest only to follow dharma. Personally he did not wish to part with his beloved daughter Sita, but dharma called for the king to marry off his daughter when she reached an appropriate age.

When Janaka, a good parent in his own right, saw Rama and Lakshmana, he immediately thought of their parents. He thought that the parents must be an ocean of purity, for the boys were like a wish-fulfilling tree whose beautiful forms granted so much unending happiness to the eyes. The children are produced by the parents, and in the Vedic culture one follows so many rules and regulations to ensure that their offspring are beautiful and virtuous. Rama was the most beautiful and Lakshmana was like His twin, so whoever produced them must have had the largest store of virtue.

Rama would uphold the good name and fame of His parents by His outward beauty and by His actions. As God, Rama does not have any parents, but to give pleasure in the mood of bhakti known as vatsalya-rasa He appears from the womb of mother Kausalya during every Treta Yuga, or second time period of creation. He accepts King Dasharatha as a father to give the pious leader an heir to the throne of Ayodhya. Dasharatha also develops a firm attachment to Rama, who becomes the king's life and soul.

Rama would give so much fame to His family line by winning the contest, being the only man capable of lifting Shiva's bow. It was almost as if Lord Shiva had coordinated the events, for he delights in hearing about Rama and discussing His pastimes with others. Goswami Tulsidas, the author of the Janaki Mangala, follows Mahadeva's example by giving the world delightful poetry to be used in remembering Sita, Rama, Lakshmana and the Lord's most faithful servant Hanuman.

King Janaka was very sweet in his observations on Rama and Lakshmana and their family, and the same sentiments could be applied to him. How pious the parents of Janaka must have been to get a son who would take care of the goddess of fortune, Sita Devi, and then invite Shri Rama Himself to the kingdom. Tulsidas sparks the same question in the reader. Where did Rama find someone so kind to describe His pastimes? Where does Rama find a dedicated brother like Lakshmana and a heroic servant like Hanuman? These questions are difficult to answer even for the Lord, for He is so pleased by the service of the devotees.

From this incident with Janaka we get a good idea on how to serve our parents, who do so much to protect us in life. The parents have a difficult job because they cannot slip in their behavior. The impressionable young child will follow the behavior of the parents more than their words. If we do acquire any good qualities, if we are fortunate enough to chant the holy names of the Lord, "Hare Krishna Hare Krishna, Krishna Krishna, Hare Hare, Hare Rama Hare Rama, Rama Rama, Hare Hare", it should be understood that our parents did a good job in raising us, even if it may seem otherwise. Somehow or other we were put into the position to connect with the holy name, which fully represents the Supreme Lord and His personal self.

To repay the service offered by the parents, one should follow the highest system of piety, which is known as bhagavata-dharma, or devotional service. Rama upheld the virtue of His parents and ancestors by following the prescribed duties of His order, the kshatriya. The kshatriyas are royal administrators, so they must exhibit bravery in combat and impartiality in the distribution of justice. In the current age of quarrel and hypocrisy, the lines have been blurred to the point that one can't figure out what their occupational duties are. Thus there is only one dharma that need be followed: devotion to God. From regularly chanting God's names, hearing about His pastimes and worshiping and honoring His servants, we give the highest service to our parents. We represent them in our behavior, so if we can show that life's mission of understanding God is reached, we prove that they are full of purity as well, for they gave the world a sincere servant of the Lord, whose association is a terrific boon.

VERSE 44

केहि सुकृती के कुँअर कहिय मुनिनायक।
गौर स्याम छबि धाम धरें धनु सायक।।44।।

kehi sukṛtī ke kumara kahiya munināyaka |
gaura syāma chabi dhāma dharem dhanu sāyaka ||44||

"' Who, O leader of munis, are the parents of pious merits who have sons like these, one fair and one dark, who are a reservoir of beauty and are holding bows and arrows?'" (44)

Essay - A Beautiful Picture

Lord Rama is dark-skinned, of the shyama complexion, while His younger brother Lakshmana is fair, or gaura. Despite the difference, they are both equally as beautiful, and together they make for an enchanting portrait, a divine vision for the eyes to feast on. They are carrying their weapons so innocently, ready to protect the elder muni, the exalted Vishvamitra. Just from their faces not a single blemish can be detected in the boys, and their beauty is so splendid that the eyes don't want to look anywhere else. In a state of amazement, the onlooker searches for answers, as so many questions immediately come to mind.

If you see something that you've never seen before, will you not ask from where it came? If you stop at a farmer's stand on the side of the road and purchase some mangoes, if the fruits taste better than anything you've ever had before, will you not seek out the cause of the distinction? "What makes these particular mangoes any better?" The same concept applies to eating out at restaurants. If you've had the best pizza in the world, you will like to know more about what went into making it. "What is the chef's secret? Pizza is just a collection of simple ingredients after all, so why should there be such a contrast from establishment to establishment?"

The journey through life is a series of questions and answers. With each new experience there are new questions, and sometimes the answers just lead to more questions. Especially if something is extraordinary and very well liked, the questions will start to mount. If you purchase a DVD set of a particular television series that you enjoy, the discs will often contain bonus content. There really should be no need for this. The customer has proved that they are willing to buy the product based only on their appreciation of the original content. They perhaps watched the television series when it first aired on network television or maybe they got into it from watching the reruns that aired during syndication. Regardless, the episodes were preferred so much that the customer felt the need to shell out money to own the DVDs.

The bonus content is there not only to entice potential buyers, but to also answer the many questions fans might have. For instance, how did the initial cast get together? Why is this show successful, while others fail? What goes into the writing, and how much leeway do the actors have in the lines that they read? How long does it take to get a show to air? What is the process of taking an idea and turning it into an episode? To answer these questions and more, the discs will contain audio commentary for many of the episodes. A writer, producer, or actor will sit and watch the episode and provide commentary as the show moves along. You get more insight into the same episodes that you saw many times previously.

What are some of the things that you can learn? For starters, if one of the female actors was pregnant during the shooting, you can start to notice some of the camera angles. "Ah, so that's why she is always pictured seated in bed or on a couch with a pillow over her. They were just trying to hide her stomach area. Oh wow, they continued this practice for several episodes. I never would have known were it not for this commentary." The intent of providing behind-the-scenes information is to give the inquisitive fan a greater appreciation of the show they like so much.

Many thousands of years ago, King Janaka was holding a well-known contest in his kingdom. The event was known to the world because the king had broadcast the news of it to everyone. He was looking for a suitable husband for his eldest daughter Sita. She was found one day when she was a baby, so the king didn't know who her biological parents were. Thus he could not use astrological signs at the time of birth to determine a suitable match in a husband, as was customary during that time. Indeed, the same horoscope comparisons are used to this day for marriages that are arranged in traditional Hindu families.

The arranged marriage seems like a sentence to torture for those who are not accustomed to it, but the fundamentals behind the tradition help to ensure a successful and lasting bond between bride and groom. The two families are joined, and they are there to support the young children who enter the marriage arrangement. If the participants are compatible based on personal characteristics, which are revealed in the constellation of stars at the precise moment of birth, then there is a good chance that the two will love each other and remain committed throughout life.

For the father, the lasting protection of his daughter is the most important matter to consider. He is her guardian, and with marriage the responsibility of protection is handed over to the new husband. King Janaka could not think of a proper way to pick Sita's husband, so he decided to hold a ceremony where all the princes from around the world would be invited. They would participate in a contest where they had to try to lift Lord Shiva's bow.

With the rules of the contest, you would think that arriving first would be to your advantage. Ah, but this was no ordinary bow. It was so heavy that likely no one would be able to lift it. If someone could, it would be a sign from above that they were meant to marry the beautiful daughter of Janaka, who was his most valuable possession. When the time came for her marriage, he felt like a rich man that was about to lose his fortune.

"After seeing that I had reached an age suitable for giving me away to a proper husband in marriage, my father became overcome with fear and anxiety, like a man who was about to become poor." (Sita Devi speaking to Anasuya, Valmiki Ramayana, Ayodhya Kand, 118.34)

Janaka was a pious king, so he was very hospitable to the many guests who arrived in his kingdom. Oddly enough, Vishvamitra Muni also came. He wasn't on the so-called guest list, but then again a brahmana didn't require an invitation for coming to Janaka's kingdom. The pious rulers during those times were known as rajarishis, or kings who are devoted souls. Janaka welcomed Vishvamitra and was thrilled to have a meeting with him. A brahmana imparts supreme wisdom that can be used to find happiness in any situation. Therefore their association is always considered a great blessing.

Janaka's interest was further sparked by Vishvamitra's companions at the time. Two young boys, splendid in their beauty, were accompanying the exalted sage. Janaka was a famous yogi known for his dispassion. Nothing could phase him. Whether it was a joyous occasion or a time for sadness, Janaka never shirked his responsibilities. He understood that the individual is Brahman, or pure spirit. Brahman has nothing to do with temporary changes to the body. We all emerge from the womb at birth and then quit the body at death. Throughout the time in between shifts may occur, but the essence of identity, the spirit soul, does not ever change.

Whatever Janaka's level of dispassion was, it ran away as soon as he saw Rama and Lakshmana, the two youthful princes escorting Vishvamitra. The attraction to them was spontaneous, and it was transcendental. This pleasure Janaka felt was like none before. He had felt the bliss of Brahmasukha, or the happiness associated with realizing Brahman. This new pleasure far surpassed that, so when Janaka finally regained control of his senses, he started to ask some questions.

For starters, who were the parents of these children? Rama and Lakshmana were like a wish-fulfilling tree, who provided happiness that would never run out. The parents who produced such children must be an ocean of purity. They must have accumulated so many pious merits to get such beautiful sons, who look so wonderful carrying their bows and arrows. Normally, if we see an armed law enforcement person, we don't think they're particularly beautiful because of their uniform. We may be comforted to know that they are on the scene, but it is understood that they are on duty. Rama and Lakshmana, though carrying weapons, provided so much pleasure just based on their natural beauty. The weapons actually became enhanced in appearance because of the transcendental nature of the two boys.

This fact is noted by great devotees many times in Vedic literature. The author of the above quoted verse is Goswami Tulsidas, and in his Gitavali he describes how when Rama was a young child He wore so many ornaments that appeared beautiful as a result of being on His body. Typically, we wear jewelry and nice clothes to enhance our appearance. Since Rama is the Supreme Lord, His transcendental body actually enhances the beauty of the ornaments and not the other way around. The same thing is said about the youthful and beautiful form of Lord Krishna, who is the same Shri Rama but in a different outward visible manifestation.

The parents of Rama and Lakshmana indeed did accumulate spiritual merits in their past lives. Of course King Janaka was not to be left out of the equation. His unsolicited affection for Shri Rama, the Supreme Lord, and Lakshmana, God's number one servant, proved that he was a possessor of tremendous virtue. He also had the goddess of fortune, Sita Devi, as his daughter, and because of his contest Sita and Rama would be reunited. Though youthful and possessing delicate features, Rama was able to lift Shiva's bow without a problem. He is God after all, so what contest is too difficult for Him? His shyama complexion is the most attractive, and with Lakshmana and his fair complexion next to Him, the Lord's beauty is enhanced even further. The more questions Janaka would ask, the more he would find out about the two boys, and the more his love for them would grow.

In a similar manner, if we daily consult the Vedic literatures and hear the purports to the many verses from the writings and verbal teachings of the exalted saints who follow in King Janaka's mood of devotion, our appreciation for God will also grow. And if one is fully anxious to continue association with the Supreme Lord at the time of death, they no longer have to suffer through reincarnation. With that reward they get to appreciate transcendental beauty even more in the subsequent lifetime in the spiritual sky.

VERSE 45

बिषय बिमुख मन मोर सेइ परमारथ।
इन्हहिं देखि भयो मगन जानि बड़ स्वारथ।।45।।

biṣaya bimukha mana mora se'i paramāratha |
inhahiṁ dekhi bhayo magana jāni baṛa svāratha ||45||

"' I had turned my mind away from sense gratification and instead did service for meeting spiritual interests. But now seeing them [Rama and Lakshmana] I knowingly want to seek out selfish interests.'" (45)

Essay - Real Self-Interest

In the Shrimad Bhagavatam, the crown-jewel of Vedic literature, there is a statement by Prahlada Maharaja relating to the self-interest of every human being. Artha refers to profit or interest, and it can be of two kinds. First there are the selfish desires, those things we want for our body as it is currently constituted. Then there are the spiritual interests, desires to be met in the afterlife, after we have exited our current body. Though typically a distinction is made between the two types of interest, Prahlada kindly notes that one's self-interest can actually be met by going towards Vishnu, the Supreme Lord. In that endeavor there is no question of a difference between the interests of the self in the present world and the assets accumulated for the afterlife.

"Persons who are strongly entrapped by the consciousness of enjoying material life, and who have therefore accepted as their leader or guru a similar blind man attached to external sense objects, cannot understand that the goal of life is to return home, back to Godhead, and engage in the service of Lord Vishnu. As blind men guided by another blind man miss the right path and fall into a ditch, materially attached men led by another materially attached man are bound by the ropes of fruitive labor, which are made of very strong cords, and they continue again and again in materialistic life, suffering the threefold miseries." (Prahlada Maharaja, Shrimad Bhagavatam, 7.5.31)

A distinction is only seen because there is a supposed difference in behavior guided by the particular state of mind. With focus on svartha, or self-interest, there is so much work to be done. If my selfish interest is to be wealthy, I will purchase some land and try to either flip it for a higher price or have tenants to pay the monthly bills. Another pathway towards wealth is owning your own business, providing a good or service to society for a fee that enables you to earn a profit. These interests are selfish, as they only relate to the present body, which is destined for destruction.

To use another example, let's say that you are in your senior year of college. You know that you will be graduating and moving on to the real world of working at the end of the year, so your focus isn't so much on school anymore. The real self-interest is in preparing yourself for graduation and then working after that, but you instead foolishly concentrate only on the right now, the present. Because of this you take your self-interest to be partying and drinking with your friends, night after night. In the short term you will feel pleasure, but the behavior isn't wise because your identity as a graduating college student will expire very shortly. Once that identity leaves, the partying you did previously will not help you going forward.

Svartha as a whole suffers from the same defect, namely the changing of identity. Therefore the Vedas put emphasis on paramartha, or supreme profit. These are the interests relating to the afterlife, where one heads after the present life completes. To acquire unselfish, spiritual merits one has to turn their back on the things presently constituting svartha. Eating, sleeping, mating and defending are activities of the animals that the human being follows as well. Nevertheless, they do not meet the higher interests of the living entity, so with proper instruction one can learn to indulge in them as little as possible.

In this way paramartha generally equates to renunciation. Give up those things which don't relate to your true identity as a spirit soul, who is beyond the temporary manifestations of matter. To meet paramartha, follow the Vedic rituals and regulations, live by austerity, don't get too attached to anything of the phenomenal world, and then be Brahman realized. Brahman is the Absolute Truth. It is pure spirit, a giant collection of energy of which we are part. Every living entity is a spark of Brahman, so they are eternal, blissful and knowledgeable by constitution, though the current collection of material elements inhibits that position from rising to a fully active state.

Though he was the ruler of Mithila, King Janaka was solely focused on paramartha. He had renounced the pursuit for selfish interests in favor of abiding by dharma. He was an adept yogi, capable of withdrawing the mind from the objects of the senses. Even though he was renounced and focused on paramartha, he still exhibited model behavior by taking care of his occupational duties. He managed his kingdom very well, and when his eldest daughter reached the proper age, he arranged for her marriage.

In the kshatriya community, it is quite common for marriages to be determined by a show of dexterity or bravery. Lord Krishna, the Supreme Personality of Godhead, married over sixteen thousand wives during His time on earth, and almost every one of them were won through a contest or a kidnap-style arrangement. A warrior must fight, just as a general must have a mission to lead. If these opportunities for action are absent, the titles don't mean anything. The kings of the past would welcome any opportunity to show their fighting prowess. From the father's side, if he could see a young man showing off his strength in battle, he would take it as a sign that his daughter would be protected by him.

Janaka held a contest for lifting an extremely heavy bow. The winner would show that they were the strongest man in the world. They would prove their ability to protect Sita Devi, the beloved daughter of the king. Though he was renounced from the world, Janaka still held high affection for his beloved daughter, whom he had found one day while ploughing a field. She was a baby at the time, and Janaka took her in and raised her as his daughter. Now it was time to give her away.

We got a hint of the true meaning of svartha when Janaka held affection for Sita upon seeing her for the first time, and in the above referenced verse from the Janaki Mangala, we are again reminded of that meaning. Lord Rama and His younger brother Lakshmana came to Janaka's city to witness the festivities. They were accompanying the exalted Vishvamitra Muni through the forests. When Janaka saw the two brothers, he couldn't believe how beautiful they were. "Who are their parents? They must be an ocean of purity. These boys are unbelievably beautiful and I can't stop looking at them."

In the above referenced verse, which is both insightful and humorous, Janaka remarks on how he had previously given up sense gratification in favor of chasing paramartha, but now he was only interested in seeking selfish-interest to a large degree by looking at these youths. Yet from the instruction of Prahlada Maharaja, we see that Janaka was actually not breaking from his previous position. Because

Shri Rama is Vishnu Himself and Lakshmana the Lord's eternal servant, harboring affection for them does fulfill paramartha. Since they appeared in a world where the general pursuit is for selfish interests, Janaka thought that appreciating their beauty and wanting to soak in the visual nectar over and over again was a selfish desire.

In the arena of bhakti, becoming selfish actually equates to happiness both in the present and future. The self-interest of the living entity is met by immersing oneself in the transcendental qualities of the Supreme Lord. One can hear about these qualities, chant mantras describing them, or witness them personally as Janaka did. Suddenly, the great king's renunciation went out the window. No more strict austerity, penance, and sacrifice for worrying about merits that may or may not arrive in the afterlife. His focused shifted to the here and now, looking at God and His younger brother while they were in front of him.

Should one be interested only in paramartha, the steps they take to secure it nevertheless purifies them and makes them eligible for witnessing the same beauty that Janaka saw. But with worship of Vishnu you don't have to wait until the afterlife to enjoy the benefits. The spirit soul is constitutionally situated to be a lover of God, so that love can be released at any moment and at any stage in life. Both selfish and unselfish merits exhaust after a certain period of time, but harboring a loving attachment for God only brings more opportunities for service in the future.

Seeing Rama and Lakshmana, Janaka developed a strong affection for them, and though he thought he had fallen back into the world of material association, he actually started his real service to God. His dispassion made him pure and his attention to dharma made him respected and worthy of spiritual merits, but it was his love for Sita that brought Rama and Lakshmana to his kingdom. It would be his love for the Supreme Lord that would make him famous throughout history, as he is still celebrated and honored to this day for his devotion.

VERSE 46

कहेउ सप्रेम पुलकि मुनि सुनि महिपालक।
ए परमारथ रूप ब्रह्ममय बालक॥46॥

kahe'u saprema pulaki muni suni mahipālaka |
e paramāratha rūpa brahmamaya bālaka ||46||

"When he heard this, the muni said with love and excitement, 'O king, these children are the appearance of your spiritual profit; they are the very Brahman.'"
(46)

Essay - Brahman's Form

Brahman is the Supreme Absolute Truth. It is beyond duality. Whatever we see in front of us has two sides. There is the visual aspect given off to the perceiver, and there is also the actual constitutional position. From afar, we can capture the sun between our two fingers squished together, but in reality the sun's size is massive. We cannot even get very close to the sun, for its heat would be too much to bear. On a hot day in the summer the heat coming from the sun causes us tremendous pain, and this is just the effect from thousands of miles away. Thus based on a visual image alone we can't get a full understanding of something. Take the same principle and apply it to every single object and you get an idea of the strong presence of duality in the world we presently inhabit. Brahman is truth. It is not two-sided; it is not favorable to one individual and unfavorable to another. Though it lacks duality, Brahman still has a tangible form, a fact realized through practice in bhakti-yoga, or devotional service.

Why would someone think that Brahman is formless? For starters, the presence of a form sort of indicates a defect. If I see someone who is tall, that attribute automatically means that they are not short. Every feature is the negation of some other feature. Someone who is right-handed is not left-handed; though it is possible to be ambidextrous, but again that eliminates the attribute of either hand being dominant. A male cannot be a female and vice versa.

Brahman is pure spirit; it is not related to the temporary forms that the spirit souls occupy during their travels through reincarnation. Learning about Brahman is rare enough, but putting that information to good use is on a completely different level. I can tell myself that I am spirit and not matter but if my actions are based on the designations formed off of outward appearances, my acknowledgment doesn't mean that much. It's sort of like saying that you're religious and then going out and killing innocent creatures, either human beings or animals. An innocent life is an innocent life, regardless of whether it's flesh tastes good or if it serves as a nuisance to others.

In the Vedic tradition, the steps required for understanding Brahman are difficult to follow. Therefore the education and training start from a very young age, where the students are sent to live with a spiritual master. Before there is a specific instruction offered on the differences between matter and spirit, the students learn to live with austerity, eating only what is necessary to maintain the body and not being puffed up by false prestige. A simple dress and shaved head help to reinforce those principles. Since the purpose of the training is to understand Brahman, the students are known as brahmacharis.

Going forward, a person who went through brahmacharya can rely on the training they received previously, as it is more difficult to understand Brahman during adulthood. For a king especially, not having attachment to outcomes is quite difficult. If it is my duty to protect the innocent people of the state and fight with the evil elements when necessary, how will dispassion help me? Should I not be passionate about carrying out my duties? Is not desire a necessary ingredient to success?

A king who is detached while simultaneously taking care of his obligations is very rare, which gives us an idea of why King Janaka is still talked about to this day. He practiced the principles of brahmacharya though he was a householder ruling over the kingdom of Mithila. He had no attachment to anything related to his body but he carried out his duties to preserve the good name of his family and to protect the citizens.

Detachment helps to further the realization of Brahman, and the purpose of knowing Brahman is to feel happiness. That pleasure of contemplating Brahman is known as brahmananda or brahmasukha. Janaka regularly felt this happiness because his consciousness never broke from Brahman. He knew that the body is a temporary vessel to be used to carry the wayward spirit soul back to its original constitutional position. Every living entity is meant to be God conscious, but through the influence of duality that awareness is missing, or at least temporarily forgotten.

Time's influence on the mind also helps to further the illusion. We may be worried about what will happen tomorrow at work, but within a few short weeks that same period of time will be forgotten. In the grand scheme of things our duration of life is nothing. The spirit soul has travelled through many bodies in the past, so there is no need to pay too much attention to the immediate future. The soul will live on, so where it ends up after death becomes vitally important, especially if that destination can be a permanent one.

Knowledge of Brahman brings the realization of God's impersonal feature, which in turn allows for release from the cycle of birth and death. But Brahman does have a form, a fact which can be accepted with certainty through training in the ultimate discipline of bhakti-yoga. In the above referenced verse from the Janaki Mangala we get an idea of what Brahman's form looks like. The same dispassionate Janaka had the great fortune of hosting a grand sacrifice to determine the husband for his unmarried daughter Sita. Many princes from around the world came to attempt to lift Lord Shiva's bow, but it was a pair of brothers that really got Janaka's attention.

They hadn't come specifically for the contest. They were escorting the exalted Vishvamitra Muni through the forests at the time. Janaka welcomed Vishvamitra as a good king should. The brahmanas, the members of the priestly class who know Brahman, are held in high esteem by the saintly kings. When he saw Rama and Lakshmana, Janaka's happiness was unimaginable. He had felt brahmasukha before, but this happiness far surpassed that. Previously he was worried about paramartha, or spiritual profit, benefits which relate to the afterlife, but now seeing Rama and Lakshmana he wanted to only focus on svartha, or worldly interests, namely in looking at them.

Vishvamitra alleviated the king's concerns by telling him that the two boys were indeed manifestations of Brahman. In this way what Janaka thought to be svartha was actually paramartha. The Supreme Lord has that effect on people when they view Him in the proper way. Brahman is but an angle of vision applied to Bhagavan, the Supreme Personality of Godhead. Just as one way we can understand the sun is to notice the sunshine, one way of understanding God is to learn about Brahman and practice the principles that help one to attain the Brahman realization.

Our level of understanding doesn't have an effect on the actual position of Bhagavan, though. He is beyond duality, so His spiritual form is not anything like the temporary forms that the jivas, or individual souls, accept and reject. Within the form of a young man Bhagavan can capture the hearts of the liberated souls. Lakshmana is practically equivalent to Bhagavan, as he is the Lord's number one servant, always by His side. Thus Janaka got the true fruit of his pious acts by seeing Rama and Lakshmana and harboring spontaneous affection for them.

A point may be raised that if Brahman has a form that is Rama and Lakshmana, why is it said that Lord Krishna and Lord Vishnu also represent Bhagavan? What about all the different avataras of Vishnu? Bhagavan has an original form, which is taken to be Lord Krishna in the Vedic tradition. Vishnu is also sometimes considered the original, though the two are identical. One personality has four hands and the other two, but for all intents and purposes they are the same. The avataras are also non-different from Bhagavan; thus to say that Rama is the source of Brahman is accurate.

Just because there are many forms doesn't mean that Bhagavan is formless or that the living entities are Bhagavan. With His spiritual forms the Supreme Lord can do things ordinary forms can't. As a young child in Vrindavana, He lifted up a massive hill and held it over His head for seven consecutive days. As a young prince in Janaka's kingdom, Rama lifted Lord Shiva's bow and easily strung it. In fact, Lord Shiva has emphatically warned against thinking that Rama has a material body, declaring the mindset to be the pathway to doom. Bhagavan can eat with His ears, talk with His hands, see with His feet, etc. He is formless in the sense that His form is not limited in its abilities, but the form still exists.

King Janaka got to bask in the sweet vision of Rama and Lakshmana, and that provided a benefit that stayed with him after the fact. Paramartha and svartha become identical when the individual is immersed in bhakti-yoga and regularly chants the holy names, "Hare Krishna Hare Krishna, Krishna Krishna, Hare Hare, Hare Rama Hare Rama, Rama Rama, Hare Hare". To the followers of bhakti, the true form of Brahman is one day revealed, and it is a sight worth waiting for.

VERSE 47

पूषन बंस बिभूषन दसरथ नंदन।
नाम राम अरु लखन सुरारि निकंदन।।47।।

pūṣana bansa bibhūṣana dasaratha nandana |
nāma rāma aru lakhana surāri nikandana ||47||

"These two are the sons of King Dasharatha, are jewels of their family line, are named Rama and Lakshmana, and are here to vanquish the enemies of the demigods." (47)

Essay - Friends of the Demigods

The enemies of the saintly class are tagged as demons in the Vedic tradition. There has been a constant clash between the forces of good and the forces of evil since time immemorial. The good want to follow the dictates of the Supreme Personality of Godhead, whereas the miscreants want to disobey every legitimate law code ever instituted. In a localized area, defiance of the established rules perhaps doesn't amount to much of a negative consequence, but in the larger scheme the influence of demonic behavior can be quite strong. The most lasting influence is the effect had on thwarting God consciousness, which is the ultimate aim for every living being.

"How can we say that any specific aim is universally ideal? Isn't everyone different? We are born into different circumstances, have different inherent characteristics, and thus develop varieties in tendencies. Therefore what is good for one person may not be for another." But when it comes to law codes, especially those instituted by the higher authorities, there is no need for attention to variety. For instance, the red light in the traffic intersection applies to all travellers on the road, not just those who feel like getting to their intended destination. One side of traffic is stopped by the red light, but the restriction is in place to prevent an accident for everyone, as the traffic crossing on the other side is provided the right of way. Once they get a red light, the other traffic that was previously stopped is allowed to continue.

The laws of God can be likened to a set of instructions meant to allow every person to direct their natural tendency in action to the proper channels. The "good" therefore at least pay deference to these laws, though they may not understand the purpose to them. As the material world operates on duality, not everyone is forced to abide by the laws guiding conduct. Just as in our smaller communities the lawbreakers are punished with sentence to jail, in the larger scheme those who violate the laws of God are punished through nature's influence. Birth itself is a punishment, as accompanying it is death. Whatever you accept in life, you must eventually renounce later on. How can such a ride ever be considered a pleasurable experience?

The conduct of the lawbreakers is another punishing aspect of birth in the material world. The person who runs the red light not only puts their own life in jeopardy, but they also cause damage and pain to those who had faith in the ability of the stoplights to prevent other traffic from entering the intersection at the wrong time. In this way the pious turn out to be innocent and victims of the misjudgments of the impious. Therefore the governing bodies must be unflinching and impartial in their administration of justice. The lawbreakers should have the fear of punishment within them, for otherwise the pious will have to live without trusting anyone.

During the Treta Yuga, the saintly class was concentrated in the forests, where they found peace and quiet. The priests who were devoted to God and understanding Him sought shelter in the holy name and austerity and penance. The devotees are referred to as suras in Sanskrit, and their counterparts are the asuras. "Ari" refers to enemies, so the worst miscreants are known as surari. The king is generally responsible for protecting the suras residing on earth, and in the heavenly realm the Supreme Lord Himself is petitioned for help to defend against the attacks of the most powerful suraris, or the asuras.

"Whenever and wherever there is a decline in religious practice, O descendant of Bharata, and a predominant rise of irreligion-at that time I descend Myself." (Lord Krishna, Bhagavad-gita, 4.7)

Whenever there is a decline in religious practice and a predominant rise of irreligion, the Supreme Personality of Godhead personally descends to earth. In the Treta Yuga, He appeared as Lord Rama, the eldest son of King Dasharatha. A partial expansion of the Supreme Lord Vishnu appeared as Rama's younger brother named Lakshmana. These two youths were jewels of the Raghu-vamsha, the dynasty of King Raghu. Because of their family relation to the famous king, both Rama and Lakshmana were often addressed as Raghava.

Aside from their divine beauty, the brothers were expert bow-warriors, capable of defending the suras from attack. Rama and Lakshmana's position with respect to this defense was explained to King Janaka, who hosted a famous ceremony one time. The king's daughter, Sita Devi, was going to marry whoever could lift the extremely heavy bow handed down to Janaka from Lord Shiva. Rama and Lakshmana weren't specifically there to take part in the contest, for they were away from home when the news went out. They were escorting Vishvamitra Muni in the forests, protecting him from the attacks of the Rakshasas, the night-rangers who were the greatest enemies of the suras on earth.

The demigods were in great distress due to the influence of the leader of the suraris, Ravana. In order for Ravana to be defeated, a human being needed to fight him. Since no ordinary human being had the prowess necessary to defeat Ravana, God Himself appeared on earth in the guise of a human. Since Rama was part of the Raghu-vamsha, He made dedication to the governing law codes His way of life. Because of this deference to dharma, Rama needed an outward excuse to take on Ravana in battle. That excuse would come through Sita.

It was not uncommon for kings to fight openly with other kings and then take the defeated king's princesses as a reward. In this sense Ravana's desire to have Sita was not out of the ordinary, but since he knew that Rama couldn't be beat, he set up a ruse whereby he was able to steal Sita in secret. This took place after Rama lifted Shiva's bow and won Sita's hand in marriage. Therefore the meeting between Vishvamitra and Janaka was very important.

In the above referenced verse from the Janaki Mangala, we get some details of that meeting. Janaka couldn't believe how beautiful Rama and Lakshmana were. They looked like they weren't from this world, and in this regard Janaka's intuition was correct. Vishvamitra informed the king that the two boys were ready to defend the suras from the attacks of the demons. If we know that a powerful figure is there to protect us from the worst kind of miscreants, we are a little comforted. Despite their powerful influence, the Rakshasas could not defeat Rama and Lakshmana, who would rid the earth of Ravana and his reign of terror.

Of course there are more than just the stated enemies of the saints to contend with. The material land is conducive to lethargy, impiety and general deviation from the righteous principles. Maintaining a high ethical standing with respect to general moral principles is difficult, and it's even more difficult to follow the righteous path aimed at fostering God consciousness, which is the ultimate aim for every spirit soul. We may have different external conditions and attributes, but deep down every living entity is a spirit soul, part and parcel of God. The religious principles espoused by the saints are meant to bring the most favorable end for every single person, regardless of what they may or may not know about God.

If you think that God is formless and just an impersonal energy named Brahman, you can follow the brahminical principles of austerity, truthfulness, mercy and cleanliness for advancement. If you think that God is just material nature meant to be enjoyed by the senses, follow the recommended sacrifices and rituals in fruitive activity to reach a higher end. If you think that God exists within the heart to be used for attaining terrific abilities, do meditational yoga and see the lasting benefits.

If you are fortunate enough to know God's true position as Bhagavan, the Supreme Personality of Godhead, regularly recite His names in a mood of love: "Hare Krishna Hare Krishna, Krishna Krishna, Hare Hare, Hare Rama Hare Rama, Rama Rama, Hare Hare". Think of Him always, remember His activities, and keep in mind His peerless vision. Just regularly hearing Vishvamitra's words describing the attributes of Rama and Lakshmana fulfills the mission of life, of connecting with God and staying by His side.

Indeed, the purpose of every ritual and regulation, of every law code instituted and protected by the suras, is to taste the sweetness of the association of the Personality of Godhead. There is variety in this interaction, as Bhagavan is Shri Krishna, the two-handed youth who holds a flute in His hands and wears a peacock feather in His hair. Krishna is the delight of the Yadu dynasty, and He too protects the suras from their enemies. He offers protection through both His physical action and His pearls of wisdom presented in the Vedic texts like the Bhagavad-gita.

Regardless of your worshipable figure of choice - Krishna, Vishnu, Rama, or the generic God - the aim of life is to connect with the Supreme Lord, knowing that His protection is flawless. That protection's existence is proven by the ability to think of Him, to rely on His names, forms and attributes to get us through difficult times, where the enemies of the devotees try to assert their influence. The weight of Lord Shiva's bow was no match for Rama, and the same went for the attacks of the night-rangers. Rama and Lakshmana saved the day many thousands of years ago, and their names continue to rescue the fallen souls today.

VERSE 48

रूप सील बय बंस राम परिपूरन।
समुझि कठिन पन आपन लाग बिसूरन।।48।।

rūpa sīla baya bansa rāma paripūrana |
samujhi kaṭhina pana āpana lāga bisūrana ||48||

"Understanding that Rama's beauty, patience, age and ancestry were completely perfect, the king remembered his own oath and thus started to lament." (48)

Essay - Don't Break The Oath

You think long and hard about a difficult decision. You don't want to mess up because the stakes are high. Rather than make an impulse move, you get advice from the people you trust. This way you gather all sorts of opinions and viewpoints that you may not have considered yourself due to the attachment you have to the particular situation. Finally, you settle upon something, a move that will hopefully satisfy your wishes and alleviate your concerns. If you are a man of honor, this decision represents your vow, something you can't break. But then later on, after the decision is made, a wildcard enters the equation. If you knew about this beforehand, you never would have made your vow. So now you are in trouble. What to do?

This was the situation faced by a famous king many thousands of years ago. He was childless when he found a beautiful baby girl in the ground one day while ploughing a field for a sacrifice. What an odd place to find a young child? How was she still alive? Who had placed her there? These things didn't matter to King Janaka once he picked her up. Though he was above the influence of the senses, he couldn't help but harbor affection for this innocent girl, wiping the dust off her face. He wanted to bring her home immediately, but he knew that he shouldn't take someone else's property. Then a voice from the sky told the king that the girl was his daughter in all righteousness, or dharma.

Dharma was important to Janaka. A king who doesn't follow dharma isn't much of a king. To be a good protector, one must be able to govern the citizens in such a way that they all stay happy, regardless of their situation. The only way to make this a reality is to follow the established law codes of scripture, which are presented nicely in the Vedas. If you go on your own whim, others will then have license to do so as well. As desires for personal satisfaction are sure to clash, the result is stiff competition. Man's actions are then guided by the motto of "win at all costs". In fact, this is the situation at present, where government leaders operate on the mentality that whoever will provide them the most votes should gain the most favor from government. Never mind that every person is equally a citizen and that the leader should be impartial. Send money to a candidate and you will get a seat at the table of power should they get elected.

Janaka's guiding principle was to defer to dharma, so he was thrilled to hear that this girl was actually his daughter. The higher powers decided he should raise her as his own daughter, that he was worthy of having her and that she would bestow good fortune upon him. The baby girl was Lakshmi Devi appearing on earth to grace the line of Videha kings with the greatest fortune of all, the appearance of the Supreme Lord in their kingdom. Janaka, of course, did not know these things. He had a spontaneous and loving attachment to his daughter.

This attachment made arranging for her marriage quite difficult. As Janaka belonged to the royal order, he typically would find a suitable match based on strength. The ability of the prince to protect his daughter would be the overriding factor in determining his eligibility for marriage. The suitable match would also be determined off personal characteristics calculated from the alignment of stars at the time of birth. The problem was that Janaka didn't know his daughter Sita's exact date of birth or who her parents were. How then was he going to find a suitable match? Comparing horoscopes using Vedic science takes the guesswork out of these arrangements.

Janaka met with his counselors, and they settled upon a compromise. The king would hold a contest. Whoever could lift Lord Shiva's bow would win Sita's hand in marriage. First come, first serve. No round robins or heats. Whoever could lift it first would win the contest. The idea was that the bow was too heavy for anyone to lift. Just as Sita had amazingly appeared from the ground, her future husband would have to appear on the scene and miraculously lift the bow.

There was another side to this contest that Janaka didn't immediately realize. If someone should attempt to lift the bow and fail, they would be automatically disqualified from marrying Sita. The focus was on finding someone who could lift the bow, which meant the elimination factor was ignored. But what if someone showed up to Janaka's city who was perfect in every way? What if their beauty was unmatched and their ancestry sparkling? What if they had tremendous patience and dedication to chivalry? What if they were quite strong and had a charming visage? Then what could the king do?

Wouldn't you know it, this is precisely the predicament that arose. Though princes from around the world came to participate in the contest, two notable warriors didn't get the invitation. They were away from home at the time, protecting the sadhus from the enemies of the demigods. A sura is known as a demigod or devotee in Sanskrit. Their enemies are the asuras, the negation of the word "sura". "How can someone be an enemy of a sadhu, a person who has no possessions and who hardly bothers anyone? A demigod is a deity in charge of a particular aspect of creation. Why should they have enemies?"

As we know, sometimes the workings of the criminal mind are impossible to figure out. There are bad guys out there, whether we like it or not. Since they do horrible things, someone needs to be there to punish them, to protect the innocent from their influence. Rama and Lakshmana, though very young, were quite able to protect a notable sadhu named Vishvamitra. He was being harassed by night-rangers who fought dirty. In conventional warfare, the participants wear identifiable uniforms and engage in conflict once the other party is ready. It seems strange, but warriors usually follow some sort of standard procedure when engaging in armed conflict.

Oh, but not these night-rangers. They would not announce their presence until the moment of attack. Should they be spotted, they could use illusion to disappear from the vision. They would take on another shape to mask their appearance as well. Rama's first test was to fight against and kill a very wicked female night-ranger named Tataka. Rama was very hesitant to kill her since she was a female. Vishvamitra had to insist a few times to Rama to fight with as much force as possible. The night-ranger would use illusion quite often to try to escape, but no one can live when the Supreme Lord decides that they shouldn't.

Rama was the Supreme Lord appearing on earth in the guise of a human being. The purpose given for His descents is to annihilate the miscreants and defend the pious, but in reality there needn't be a specific purpose. Whatever makes the Supreme Lord happy, He does. He finally killed Tataka, and Vishvamitra was pleased with Him. He then gave both Rama and Lakshmana secret mantras to be used in fighting.

The group subsequently went to Janaka's kingdom while the contest was going on. The king welcomed them hospitably, and was enamored by the vision of Rama and Lakshmana. As Rama was the elder brother, Janaka wondered if He should maybe participate in the contest. Seeing that Rama was perfect in every way, Janaka became lost in transcendental bliss. He had previously felt brahmasukha, or the pleasure of merging into the impersonal effulgence of the Lord, but this new happiness defeated that many times over.

After that initial happiness, Janaka remembered his vow. "Oh no! What if Rama tries to lift the bow and fails? Then He can't marry Sita, though He is perfect for her." In this way Janaka felt a kind of fear in devotional ecstasy. This emotion is described in more detail in Shrila Rupa Gosvami's Bhakti-rasamrita-sindhu, which is nicely translated and commented on in the book known as The Nectar of Devotion, authored by His Divine Grace A.C. Bhaktivedanta Swami Prabhupada.

In devotional service, or bhakti-yoga, there are different tastes that are available to the devotee. Sometimes fear is an enhancer of delight, as through that trepidation one thinks even more about God. Thus Janaka's worrying over the contest was on par with his happiness over first seeing Rama. There needn't be any worry, though. Lord Rama was meant to arrive in Janaka's kingdom and marry Sita. Only He would be able to lift Mahadeva's bow and thus prove to the world that Sita could only be His wife. Janaka's regret would soon disappear, as his vow would further glorify both Sita and Rama, the divine couple who bestow good fortune upon the surrendered souls.

CHAND 6

लागे बिसूरन समुझि पन मन बहुरि धीरज आनि कै।
लै चले देखावन रंगभूमि अनेक बिधि सनमानि कै।।
कौसिक सराही रुचिर रचना जनक सुनि हरषित भए।
तब राम लखन समेत मुनि कहँ सुभग सिंहासन दए।।6।।

lāge bisūrana samujhi pana mana bahuri dhīraja āni kai |
lai cale dekhāvana raṅgabhūmi aneka bidhi sanamāni kai ||
kausika sarāhī rucira racanā janaka suni haraṣita bha'e |
taba rāma lakhana sameta muni kahaṁ subhaga sinhāsana da'e ||6||

"Feeling bad over his vow after understanding what it meant, the king started to lament. Yet he kept himself very patient and went and showed his guests the svayamvara grounds, offering them all kinds of respect." (Chand 6.1)

"Hearing Vishvamitra compliment the beautiful arrangements, the king became happy. Then, he offered beautiful thrones for Rama, Lakshmana and the muni to sit on." (Chand 6.2)

Essay - Shrugging It Off

"Uh oh. I made a big mistake. What seemed like a good idea at the time is now turning out the wrong way. Everyone is watching me too, so how do I hide my feelings? I'm not just a little sad; I'm utterly dejected. How am I going to fix things so that my previous error does not result in the worst possible loss? I made my decision based on the good counsel of people I trust, and there was deliberation, because the decision would have resounding effects. It wasn't a choice made on a whim, and still somehow now it looks like it was a mistake. Oh well, what choice do I have but to continue on, to pretend like I am not affected?"

The mind can move very quickly, and so thoughts like these rushed through King Janaka's mind within a few seconds after he glanced upon the jewel of the Raghu dynasty, Lord Rama. The eldest son of King Dasharatha had a beauty that seemed unimaginable. Lord Brahma is the creator, so every visible covering on an individual is his handiwork. Sort of like the sculptor who takes their raw materials to make something beautiful, Brahma has the ability to give any person beauty, wealth, good parentage and intelligence. Yet Rama's beauty was something out of this world. His younger brother Lakshmana, who was accompanying Him at the time, had an almost identical countenance, with the lone exception his bodily complexion, which was fair while Rama's was dark.

The thought was that these two boys must have been Brahma's first creation. Then, with whatever elements he had left over he created the rest of the world and its creatures. King Janaka had previously felt brahmasukha, or the pleasure of realizing Brahman. That happiness is not tasted by everyone. In fact, it is one of the most difficult pleasures to find, as no amount of exercise or money can bring it about. Only through steadfast practice in yoga, with a mind connected to the impersonal feature of the Supreme Spirit, can one even think of tasting the transcendental association of Brahman.

Janaka tasted brahmasukha from practicing yoga while simultaneously carrying out his occupational duties as a king. This is the method of practice followed by the most elevated transcendentalists. The eligibility for tasting transcendental happiness is not dependent on gender, social status, or explicit desire for yoga. Many years later a sweet mother in the farm community of Vrindavana would follow Janaka's behavior, tending to her household chores throughout the day but remaining in yoga the whole time.

As Janaka could carry out a king's duties, which require passion in defending the innocent and detachment in distributing charity, without breaking his yoga, any temporary bout of elation or sadness surely couldn't phase him. But the vision of Rama had a profound effect on him. Rama and Lakshmana were visiting the kingdom with Vishvamitra Muni. Think of a set of bodyguards who protect a priest and you sort of get an idea of the particular role of the two brothers. They were disciples at the same time, so they treated Vishvamitra like their revered spiritual master, whose orders are never to be disobeyed. The muni derived tremendous pleasure from being protected by the brothers, who though young at the time could defeat the most powerful enemies.

At the time Janaka was holding a svayamvara for his beautiful daughter Sita Devi. The marriage hadn't been arranged yet; the groom would be chosen from the visitors. As the daughter of the most pious king deserves the most chivalrous prince for a husband, a contest would determine the winner of Sita's hand. Whoever could lift Lord Shiva's extremely heavy bow would win the company of Sita, the goddess of fortune. She would grace the triumphant prince with her beautiful vision every day, and she would bless his family with great fortune.

Janaka settled upon the contest option after consulting with his priests. He wanted only the best for his daughter, so any ordinary fellow would not do. But now seeing Rama, Janaka remembered his vow and started to lament. Why the worry? Well, what if Rama didn't win the contest? What if He failed to lift the bow? Then, by rule, Sita couldn't marry Rama. Janaka settled upon the contest because he couldn't think of a suitable husband for her. But now here He was, more perfect than anyone could imagine. We each have our own idea of what a perfect person is, but the Supreme Lord breaks all boundaries of thought. The human brain has limited abilities, which means that imagination is limited as well. No one could ever imagine Rama's beauty, which was accompanied by His terrific character. No one is more respectful than Rama, and since He had protected Vishvamitra from the attacks of vile creatures like Tataka, no one was more powerful than He. His family line was also splendid. So everything about Him was compatible with Sita.

As if dealt a blow to the stomach, Janaka couldn't get the vow out of his mind. What a mistake he had made, or so he thought. Despite the situation, he shook off the despondency and took his guests around the svayamvara grounds. Such a great king never allows anyone else to know that he's not doing well. Why would he want to bring everyone else down? He was the host after all. It is said in the above referenced verse from the Janaki Mangala that the guests were given all sorts of respect as they were shown around. To disrespect a guest means to make them feel unwelcome. If the host should burden the guests with their problems immediately upon their arrival, what sort of welcome would that be?

Janaka's worries would turn out to benefit him in the end. For starters, it would add some anticipation to the contest. When Rama would step up to the arena, all eyes would be on Him, with many praying to God for His victory. This is ironic considering that Rama is the person who would hear those prayers. Deciding to grace the Raghu dynasty with His presence, Rama was the Supreme Personality of Godhead in the guise of a human being, with His primary mission to take out the evil element concentrated on the island of Lanka at the time. Thus there was no way for Rama to fail at lifting the bow.

Janaka's vow also further enhanced the glory of Rama, and Lakshmana too. Rama is celebrated today for lifting a bow that no one else could even move, and Lakshmana is His faithful younger brother. A younger brother like that is loved and appreciated by an elder one like Rama, who has such good qualities. The king's vow increased the fame of the Raghu dynasty, which had previously set the table for Rama to appear in its family. The king and his queens who raised Rama were made proud on that day, and all the people of Ayodhya who loved and adored Rama basked in His victory as well.

If the vow had not been taken, or if it had been revoked, the grandeur of the event would have been diminished. Janaka would have been blamed for being dishonest, someone who doesn't follow through on what they say. Though he felt sad over having made a vow that had the potential to hurt him, he nevertheless stayed true to his character, giving respect to Vishvamitra, Rama and Lakshmana. Thus Janaka gives a great example on how to live life. So many decisions will be made that don't pan out or which seem like they will bring bad results. There is no such thing as peace in a land where everything is temporary. If you win the lottery and have all your expenses taken care of for the rest of your life, you still have to worry over what to do with your time. You have to make sure to protect your winnings as well.

There can never be full protection in a place where everything is destined for destruction, be it in one day or one hundred years. Therefore the concern over the outcome of events never should take precedence. The attention to dharma, or religiosity, is what proves to provide the ultimate good to the individual, as it did for Janaka. He stayed true to his vow to uphold religious principles, harboring love for the Supreme Lord all the while. That love was all that was required to have the right outcome: Rama as Sita's husband.

Essay - The Royal Treatment

The lion is the recognized king of the jungle, as it can even scare away the larger elephant. Its roar is so mighty that just upon hearing it the inferior animals run away. As the most powerful person in the jungle is a kind of ruler, many aspects of a ruler are likened to the leader of the jungle. The king is a lion in the sense that whatever he says goes. In ancient times he was the most powerful fighter, and thus he could protect his citizens from foreign attack. In Sanskrit, the king's sitting place is described as a simha-asana, or lion-seat. Today this is better known as a throne, but the reference to the lion is still there, as you will see images of lions on the corners of the throne. Many thousands of years ago, King Janaka, the lion of the kingdom of Videha, offered such nice thrones to three exalted guests, who weren't even specifically invited.

Why was it notable that they weren't given specific invitations? This wasn't an ordinary event. King Janaka was marrying off his lovely daughter Sita, who is the goddess of fortune. The marriage ceremony was a contest, where the winner would have to lift Lord Shiva's bow. First come, first serve. Whoever would first lift the bow would win, ending the contest immediately. Two guests in particular were notable figures, but since they were away from home they didn't receive the personal invitation that had gone out to all the kings of the world. Nevertheless, Janaka learned who the two were very quickly by talking to their leader. Once knowing that information, he did not fail to honor them properly.

The leader was Vishvamitra, who actually called the forest his home. He was a brahmana, or a member of the priestly class, so he wasn't in Videha for the contest. With him, however, were two handsome youths, both of age suitable for marriage. As the younger was a devoted soul who would never do anything to dishonor his beloved brother, only the elder was eligible for participating in the contest. Before he knew who they were, Janaka was enamored by them. He had never seen such beauty before. Perhaps Lord Brahma, the creator, made their bodies first and then used whatever materials he had left over to make the rest of the creation, including its beautiful natural wonders.

Janaka had previously experienced brahmasukha, the happiness of realizing the impersonal feature of the Supreme Lord known as Brahman. Yet from seeing the elder brother, Janaka felt a happiness hundreds of times greater than that. Vishvamitra then informed Janaka that these two boys were descendants of King Raghu, jewels of their line. The elder, the delight of Maharaja Dasharatha, was the leader of his four brothers. Named Rama, He was loved and adored by the younger brother Lakshmana. The two were roaming the forests with Vishvamitra to annihilate the enemies of the demigods.

A demigod is a sort of saintly character who can provide marginal benefits to a devotee. Likened to a cabinet member or administrative department head, a demigod works at the direction of the Supreme Lord, who is known as Vishnu or Krishna in the Vedic tradition. The royal order has the duty to protect the innocent people of the world and defend them against the attacks of the enemies of the demigods. The more powerful enemies can put up a good fight against the exalted heavenly figures. In those situations, Vishnu Himself arrives on the scene to offer protection, as He did in His incarnation of Lord Rama.

Once he learned more about Rama, Janaka remembered his oath. He had sworn to give away Sita to whoever could lift Lord Shiva's extremely heavy bow. But now there was a problem. He wanted Sita to marry Rama, this beautiful youth who was so strong and brave that Vishvamitra used him for protection. Lakshmana was not eligible for the contest because a younger brother didn't marry before an older one did. What if Rama couldn't lift the bow? What would Janaka do? He never wanted to lose sight of this beautiful youth, who had captured his heart already.

Janaka shook off his fear over the contest and put on a good face. He gave the trio a tour of the svayamvara grounds, which he had elaborately arranged. The entire place was beautiful, as it hosted all the kings of the world. Janaka was famous for his chivalry, and thus his daughter garnered much attention. To receive a beautiful, chaste and devoted wife is considered a great blessing not only to the groom but also to his family. A good wife can make up for all the shortcomings of the husband, and through her support the husband and his family can stay dedicated to the righteous path and meet auspiciousness at the end of life.

While giving the tour, Vishvamitra complimented Janaka on his work. This made the king feel very happy. What happened next is quite significant. In the Vedic tradition, those not personally in the presence of the Supreme Lord are given a variety of tools to use in their worship. Just because you're not in a church or temple doesn't mean that you should forget about God, who is the reservoir of pleasure. To facilitate proper worship in any area, there is the tradition of deity worship. The deity is the signature representation of the Supreme Lord in a form that is worshipable and honorable. Proper worship of the deity is as good as offering obeisances personally to the Supreme Lord.

Deity worship can be simple and it can also be quite elaborate. In the larger temples, the carved statues are offered thrones to sit on. This way the worshiper can look at God the proper way. Without a developed consciousness focused on bhakti-yoga, or devotional service, looking at God as an equal is not a good thing. If the worshipable object is on the same level as us, what good is worshiping them? We treat our friends differently than we do our elders. We make jokes with our friends and we never let them win an argument, for they are our equals after all. The offering of the throne is a nice gesture, as it shows the respect needed for understanding God in the beginning stages.

Along with the throne, there are opulent decorations and regular offerings of prepared food items, flowers, water, incense, lamps and other authorized paraphernalia. The pattern should be quite easy to recognize by now. Pretend that the deity is the actual person it depicts. In other circumstances, this sort of imitation doesn't actually affect the worshiped figure. You may worship a picture or statue of someone else, but they have no way of knowing what you are doing. There is a difference with God, however. His deity is identical to Him. It is an authorized form that accepts the obeisances of the sincere souls who approach Him in a mood of love and devotion. The conditioned living entity doesn't have the eyes to see God right away, though His presence is everywhere. The mercy of the deity accounts for that deficiency and thus allows anyone to make progress in their worship.

Janaka offered Rama, Lakshmana and Vishvamitra thrones to sit on, so in a sense he did deity worship in person. Rama and Lakshmana were junior to him, but Janaka used the pretense of hospitality to worship them properly. Vishvamitra was a member of the brahmana community, whose advice and consent can grant any benediction in life. It was through the advice of the brahmanas that Janaka initially settled upon the idea of a svayamvara, or self-choice ceremony. Now that decision was bearing fruit, with Rama and Lakshmana seated on thrones in his kingdom. Janakpur turned into a temple that day, and the deity of Rama seated on the throne would be so pleased that He would return the favor by getting up and easily lifting Shiva's bow. The jewel of the Raghu dynasty fulfilled destiny and alleviated Janaka's fears. Keeping that same husband of Janaki seated on the throne of your heart, worship Him daily and He will never leave your sight.

THE BOW CONTEST
VERSE 49

राजत राज समाज जुगल रघुकुल मनि।
मनहुँ सरद बिधु उभय नखत धरनी धर ।।49।।

rājata rāja samāja jugala raghukula mani |
manahuṁ sarada bidhu ubhaya nakhata dharanī dhara ||49||

"In that royal meeting, the two jewels of the Raghu family were looking so beautiful, like the brightest moons of the fall season amongst the stars that brighten the earth." (49)

Essay - Sharada Purnima

In the Vedic tradition the auspicious rituals observed every month go off the lunar cycle. The months and years are determined by the position of the moon, how full it is, etc. In the autumn season the full moon is especially auspicious because of its brightness. Known as the Sharada Purnima, this full moon stands out the most in the sky which is already full of so many stars. This particular moon was referenced to try to describe how two sons of King Dasharatha looked in an assembly of kings gathered to participate in a contest where the winner would receive the goddess of fortune as a wife.

The earth is more important than the objects which grow on it because the seeds of life are found within the earth. The vegetation, grass, and general plant life sustain the population, which includes the meat eaters, but without the seeds found within the earth there would be no question of life continuing. Therefore the earth is the more important object to have. In a similar manner, the stars in the sky brighten the dark night, but the sky itself is more important. The sky contains all the stars, so as soon as you have the sky, you will automatically get the stars.

"Just as within the earth are found every kind of seed and within the sky live all the stars, Tulsidas knows that Shri Rama's holy name is the reservoir of all dharma." (Dohavali, 29)

If you have the holy name of the Lord, you will automatically have dharma, or religiosity. Chant the sacred maha-mantra, "Hare Krishna Hare Krishna, Krishna Krishna, Hare Hare, Hare Rama Hare Rama, Rama Rama, Hare Hare", and don't worry so much about being religious. The holy name is all you need to find enlightenment, freedom from constant distress, and release from the painful cycle of birth and death. The holy name and a deep love and affection for it satisfy the emotional needs of the individual as well.

The secret to the holy name is that it directly represents the Supreme Personality. Wherever He stands, He is complete in Himself. In His avatara of Lord Rama, He is compared to the beautiful moon, as His glowing visage gives light to a world otherwise filled with darkness. Wherever He goes, He stands out, showing that He is not an ordinary person. The same goes for His younger brother Lakshmana, who is the servitor god, essentially on an equal level with Rama.

The brothers once made their way to the kingdom of Janakpur. They were escorting Vishvamitra Muni through the forests because he was being attacked by night-rangers of mighty strength and cunning tactics. They wouldn't attack during open conflict, nor would they only fight their own kind. They attacked renounced hermits of all people, and after attacking they would eat their flesh. Rama and Lakshmana, two sons of King Dasharatha, were called on for protection. Though they were both young at the time, due to their divine natures there was no one who could defeat them.

Keeping in that line, they entered King Janaka's land, where a sacrifice was taking place. The pious king had invited the famous princes from around the world to attempt to lift Lord Shiva's bow, which was very heavy. Rama and Lakshmana weren't specifically invited, because they weren't home at the time. Rama was the eldest son, and as He was unmarried only He was a candidate for participating in the contest. When Janaka saw Rama, he remembered his vow and started to worry. What if Rama couldn't lift the bow? He was perfect for his daughter Sita, so it would be such a shame if another man lifted the bow. Worse, if Rama failed then He would not be eligible to marry Sita.

Enchanted by their beauty, Janaka gave the brothers nice thrones to sit on. Vishvamitra was also given a throne. This assembly was quite large, as no one could count how many guests were there. Yet Goswami Tulsidas, in the verse from his Janaki Mangala quoted above, likens Rama and Lakshmana to moons from the autumn season. The rest of the kings assembled represented the other stars in the night sky of the Sharada Purnima. They may have been very bright also, but compared to Rama and Lakshmana they couldn't be noticed.

The Sharada Purnima is also quite auspicious, as it occurs at the end of the harvest season. It was during this particular full moon that Lord Krishna danced with the gopis in the pastime known as the rasa-lila. Shri Krishna is the same Rama but in His two-handed form of an attractive youth who plays on the flute and delights the residents of Vrajabhumi. The gopis are the topmost transcendentalists, for they love Krishna without motivation and without interruption. They renounce ties to family and society in favor of Krishna's protection. Their only desire is to love Him, and dancing facilitates that desire very nicely.

Since the gopis are married they can only rendezvous with Krishna at night. Of course the drawback with this is that the night is quite dark. It does help in the sense that it keeps their cover, but at the same time seeing their beloved Krishna becomes more difficult. In the full moon night in the autumn season, the light from the moon is so bright that Krishna can be seen without a problem. Therefore it is quite conducive to dancing with the Lord. Krishna is so kind that He will not deny the heartfelt requests of the sincerest devotees. Though the gopis are many in number, Krishna dances with each one individually by expanding Himself.

The brightness of the Sharada Purnima thus creates conditions auspicious for bhakti-yoga, or devotional service. We can just imagine then what the residents of Janakpur were thinking. Here were two bright moons giving light to the largest crowd on earth. They were quiet and well-behaved young boys, without any trace of haughtiness or pride. They followed the command of the spiritual master Vishvamitra, and they were not looking to defeat anyone at the time. But God's resplendence from His personal self cannot be hidden. Perhaps in the material world those divine qualities are covered from the eyes due to the feverish pursuit for material fame and opulence, but when directly in Bhagavan's presence His personal features are noticeable.

The stars brighten the earth in the night, and in the same way Rama and Lakshmana brightened the assembly in Janakpur. The many residents looking on were hopeful of Rama's triumph. They wanted Him to marry Sita very badly. Janaka's daughter was the emblem of virtue, and her beauty matched Rama's. Lakshmi Devi is also worshiped during the Sharada Purnima, for she is the goddess of fortune. Just as Rama is the same Krishna or Vishnu, Sita is the same Lakshmi appearing on earth to give delight to her husband Shri Rama.

What would happen? Would the brightness of the morning steal the splendor of the autumnal moons sitting on their thrones? Rama's brightness never dissipates and His fame would extend throughout the three worlds after He would lift and break Shiva's bow. He was not called to the assembly specifically, but through Vishvamitra's influence and King Janaka's pious nature, the Lord would fulfill the destiny set forth by the celestials and win Sita's hand in marriage. The couple is always together, but on that particular occasion the anticipation and fear over potential separation enhanced the experience for the onlookers.

What if Rama hadn't won? What if Sita had to marry someone else? King Janaka would have been vilified by the residents for his vow, for his rules would have prevented the bright moon that was Rama from joining the family. But just as Rama's name is complete, His personal self fulfills all the desires of His devotees. Just as the gopis desired Krishna's association through dance during the rasa-lila, the observers cherishing Rama and Lakshmana's personal brightness hoped for Sita to wed the eldest son of King Dasharatha. God is not known for denying requests that relate to His personal association. His triumphs are also guaranteed, but the devotees nevertheless pray for them to occur.

After Rama lifted Shiva's bow, the worship did not stop. The people fortunate enough to be there that day kept that sweet vision within their minds, and saints like Tulsidas immortalized that moment by describing it in song. As the Sharada Purnima is already a noted event every year on the Hindu calendar, the next time it occurs the scene from Janaka's court can be remembered immediately. The two bright sons of King Dasharatha would make the Raghu clan proud with their presence in Janakpur, and through their travels they would eventually rid the world of the wickedest night-ranger, the king of Lanka. Their brightness can never be defeated, and so anyone who chants the Lord's holy names, having full reliance on that chanting, will never be left out in the dark.

VERSE 50

काकपच्छ सिर सुभग सरोरुह लोचन।
गौर स्याम सत कोटि काम मद मोचन॥50॥

kākapaccha sira subhaga saroruha locana |
gaura syāma sata koṭi kāma mada mocana ||50||

"With their beautiful hair on the head and their eyes like lotuses, the beauty of Rama and Lakshmana defeats the pride of millions of cupids." (50)

Essay - Eyes Like Lotuses

Goswami Tulsidas here continues his description of Rama and Lakshmana seated in the assembly in King Janaka's court. The two brothers were innocently looking upon the festivities, but others took notice of their wonderful bodily marks and auspicious dimensions. Rama was dark-skinned and Lakshmana fair, and every one of their facial features was notable. The poet fails to find words to describe their beauty, so he resorts to comparisons to known objects. With the proper reference, doing a comparison and stating that the object in question is superior to the reference object, the listener can begin to get an idea of the wonderful qualities extolled by the poet.

To be defeated by a powerful figure is one thing, but if you took millions of the same formidable force, it would be next to impossible to achieve victory. In the Vedic tradition the god of love, Kamadeva, is known for his beauty. He has the emblem of the fish on his banner and acts as cupid wherever he goes. He takes full advantage of the spring season, which enhances the desire for conjugal love within the earth's population, who have just survived the harsh winter. Difficult it is to conquer cupid, for it takes a powerful ascetic like Lord Shiva to burn up the fire of lust from within the body.

Now just imagine if you had millions of cupids standing side by side. The combined beauty would be too much to fathom. Immeasurable would be the reservoir of kama, or desire, produced. Yet Tulsidas says that Rama and Lakshmana, while sitting in Janaka's court, not overly dressed either, would easily defeat millions of cupids in beauty. One takes their pride from their most outstanding attribute. A fighter feels self-worth from emerging victorious in combat. A police officer takes pride from their ability to defend and protect the innocent. Supreme wisdom and knowledge are what fill the exalted teacher with pride, and dexterity the athlete.

For cupid, pride comes from outstanding beauty. Therefore to find someone more beautiful equates to having your pride defeated. You are humbled in defeat, made to know that you are not supreme in your attributes. Only Bhagavan, the most fortunate, possesses the opulences of beauty, wealth, strength, fame, knowledge and renunciation to the fullest degree and at the same time. Bhagavan's name is rooted in fortune, which is the same word used here by Tulsidas. He says that Rama and Lakshmana are subhaga, or supremely fortunate. Rama is the very same Bhagavan, appearing on earth in the guise of a warrior prince. Lakshmana is His devoted younger brother and also a partial incarnation of God.

It should be noted that Bhagavan retains His fortunate standing in every circumstance. In the scene in question, neither Rama nor Lakshmana were opulently dressed. They were living in the forests as protectors to the exalted sage Vishvamitra. They belonged to the famous Raghu dynasty, but their visit to Janakpur was not an official one. Vishvamitra led them to the kingdom, where a grand sacrifice was taking place. The religious function in question was to determine the husband for King Janaka's daughter Sita.

Sita Devi is known as the goddess of fortune, so whoever has her association automatically becomes supremely fortunate. As Rama is Bhagavan, or the most fortunate, He is eternally in the company of the goddess of fortune. The sacrifice in King Janaka's kingdom was to merely reunite the divine pair, who are still together to this day. Rama was the elder brother, so only He was eligible to marry Sita, as the younger brother would not marry before the older one.

Janaka, a pious king, gave Rama and Lakshmana thrones to sit on. The king didn't know who they were at first, but Vishvamitra introduced them. He described the brothers as conquerors of the enemies of the demigods. The suras are the pious class, and they can live on earth or in the heavenly realm. Either place has the same basic feature set, except in the heavenly realm the duration of life is much longer.

Opposite to the sura is the asura, or demon. They are generally against religious principles and thus like to harass the saintly class as much as possible.

"I envy no one, nor am I partial to anyone. I am equal to all. But whoever renders service unto Me in devotion is a friend, is in Me, and I am also a friend to him." (Lord Krishna, Bhagavad-gita, 9.29)

Bhagavan is neutral by default, but if He sees that devotional activities are being thwarted, He either personally intervenes or sends one of His representatives. In the case of Vishvamitra and the suras during this particular time, Bhagavan personally descended upon the scene as Shri Rama. While in the forests with Vishvamitra, Rama, though very young, killed the wicked female night-ranger named Tataka. He and Lakshmana defended the sage so well that in return the muni gave the boys special mantras to be chanted during fighting. The sacred chants would transform the arrows shot from their bows into mini-nuclear weapons.

Janaka offered the trio special favor in his kingdom because of their splendid qualities. The king was reluctant to carry on with the ceremonies after seeing Rama. Though the Lord was shyama, or dark, in color, He was still the most beautiful person in the assembly. He was so chivalrous that He had left home at a young age to defend an elderly brahmana. The sage personally vouched for Rama and Lakshmana's chivalry by declaring them to be protectors against the enemies of the demigods. Rama also belonged to the famous Ikshvaku dynasty, so His ancestry was spotless.

In other words, Rama was the ideal match for Sita. The person Janaka thought didn't exist was now right in front of him. Ah, but too bad, for the contest was already set. The king can't go back on his vow after the fact. The rules stipulated that whoever could lift Lord Shiva's enormously heavy bow in front of the gathered assembly would immediately get Sita's hand in marriage. All Janaka could do now was hope. He gave his guests a choice viewing location with comfortable arrangements. Hopefully no one else could lift the bow and Rama wouldn't fail to deliver.

Bhagavan never fails in His mission, so there was no chance for Sita to marry anyone besides Rama. The beauty of the two brothers in the assembly set the proper mood for the onlookers. The beautiful eyes of the boys looked like the lotus flowers that float in the pond. Their beauty would crush anyone's pride, including cupid's, and yet they were just sitting there innocently, as if they had no idea what effect their presence had on others.

With that vision the pure-hearted saints and residents of Janakpur got to soak in the visual nectar. They formed an attachment to those two brothers which would last well beyond Sita and Rama's upcoming marriage. The same attachment can be formed by regularly remembering that scene and cherishing it. If the vision of the fair and dark sons of King Dasharatha should ever slip away, recite the holy names found in the maha-mantra, "Hare Krishna Hare Krishna, Krishna Krishna, Hare Hare, Hare Rama Hare Rama, Rama Rama, Hare Hare".

Janaka could have called off the contest, but sheer beauty was not enough. The credentials earned off of past accomplishments could be challenged by the other kings as well, as news of Janaka's contest had spread throughout the world. "Why should Rama and Lakshmana be granted special favors? Shouldn't they have to earn their victories like everyone else?" These were the issues at hand. The immense strength required to lift the bow and the delicate features of the two youths created a nice paradox. Kamadeva, or cupid, isn't known for being an excellent fighter. He is passion personified, so if anything he can strike at the heart of one's strength and weaken them through desires for conjugal affairs.

Bhagavan is purna, or complete, so His beauty is as full as His strength. He would remind us of this fact by stepping up to the sacrificial altar and easily lifting the extremely heavy bow that so many kings had previously failed to even move. Janaka's name and fame would be established by keeping his promise and creating a contest where Rama's standing as the strongest person in the world would be known to all. Rama deserved to have the beautiful Sita as a wife, and the pleased onlookers deserved to delight in the scene. In the same way, the pure-hearted souls of the world should get to hear the wonderful pastimes of the Supreme Lord that are described in the Vedic texts and are so nicely synthesized in the poems and songs of Goswami Tulsidas.

VERSE 51

तिलकु ललित सर भ्रुकुटी काम कमानै।
श्रवन बिभूषन रुचिर देखि मन मानै॥51॥

tilaku lalita sara bhrukuṭī kāma kamānai |
śravana bibhūṣana rucira dekhi mana mānai ||51||

"On the forehead, situated between the eyebrows, there is the beautiful tilaka which looks like an arrow from Kamadeva's bow. The earrings are so beautiful that when looking at them the mind becomes very happy." (51)

Essay - Weapon of Prema

When the warrior releases his weapon, the intent is usually to cause pain to someone else. Though the release of the weapon defeats an enemy of the innocent, and thereby does an overall good, the act itself still belongs to the category of violence. With the god of love, the weapon released from his bow causes the target to develop amorous feelings, which are enhanced by the onset of the spring season. The same type of weapon exists on the forehead of the Supreme Lord, except what is instilled is loving devotion furthered by a captivating beauty that one never wants to forget.

In the Vedic tradition the god of love, or desire, is known as Kamadeva. He is the equivalent to the commonly known cupid. It should be noted that though cupid can be called the matchmaker in love, the word kama itself is not exactly related to love. In Sanskrit prema is the closest equivalent to love, but it has a specific connotation. The affection in prema must be directed in a pure mood, where there is no expectation of reciprocation. Moreover, it must not be hinged upon some benefit to be received later on.

Kama is different in this regard. Kama can be translated to mean desire, sense gratification, or lust. Thus the conjugal affairs between members of the various species are based strictly on personal sense gratification. What satisfies us today may not do the trick in the future. Today I may crave a few slices of pizza from my favorite shop, but were I to eat that same food day after day, after a while I'd probably want something else.

Taste changes with maturation as well. In childhood perhaps we liked sugar drinks and junk food. As you get older, you have different tastes and concerns. Through the experiences accumulated in life, you get a new way of thinking, and your priorities shift as well. Dieting is introduced in adulthood because there is concern paid to the intake of food. The pleasure aspect of eating expands to incorporate the effect had on energy and the level of comfort within the stomach.

The same principle of changing tastes applies to amorous relationships. Therefore it is not surprising that there are common "break ups" and divorces. You may love someone today, but if they anger you enough, show you enough disrespect, you will want to break that relationship off. Divorce should be a rare occurrence, as the relationship was previously codified through marriage, where vows were made to honor, protect, defend, and serve until death did part you. The definition of death gets humorously broadened when the relationship can be severed many years before you actually depart this earth.

The break ups are difficult to deal with, as there are even feature length movies made about them. But despite the relationship ending, the same desire for conjugal affairs continues. The spirit of kama does not abate; it just shifts its target. Kamadeva, as the deity presiding over sense gratification, can shoot his arrows and arouse those strong feelings within people. When the lusty desires strengthen, one can go about trying to satisfy them with whatever is in close proximity. Thus Kama's influence is quite strong.

It takes a dedicated renunciate to defeat Kama. Lord Shiva, the deity in charge of the mode of ignorance, once had an encounter with Kama's shafts. Cupid tried to instill passion in Lord Shiva so that a child could be born, as this was the request of the demigods. Though a deity who can grant benedictions to others, Lord Shiva is not interested in kama or artha, which is economic development. His pleasure comes from hearing the name of Rama, so He regularly chants that name, over and over again as if his life depended on it.

From that chanting a deep meditational trance develops. If you're secured in a "happy zone", will you not be angered if someone tries to break you out of it? This is what happened with Lord Shiva when he was attacked by Kamadeva. In retaliation, Lord Shiva glanced at cupid and burned him instantly with his look. As he was only doing the bidding of the demigods, Kamadeva was granted reprieve by being allowed to take birth in the future as Pradyumna, the son of Lord Krishna. Krishna is the same Rama that Shankara Bhagavan cherishes. The Lord appeared on earth many years after Rama did, and with Pradyumna, Kamadeva's wife Rati was reunited with her husband. The story of Pradyumna's birth and his reunion with Rati is nicely described in the tenth canto of the Shrimad Bhagavatam, with a highly readable version of the entire canto presented in the book, Krishna, the Supreme Personality of Godhead, by His Divine Grace A.C. Bhaktivedanta Swami Prabhupada.

Prema is different from kama, but the comparison to Kamadeva is made by Goswami Tulsidas in the above quoted verse from the Janaki Mangala to show the effect Rama has on people. The Supreme Lord is with a form, though there is polymorphism with His avataras. The incarnations are expansions from the original personality, so they retain the same divine qualities, but their visible manifestations and functions may vary. As Rama, the Supreme Lord is in the beautiful form of a warrior prince, whose vision enchants the devoted souls.

When Kamadeva shoots his arrows, unless one is as strong as Lord Shiva in dedication to devotional service, they will be instilled with amorous feelings and ready to act upon them. Shri Rama, through His facial features, shoots similar types of arrows, but the poison these weapons carry is prema. Once infected, you cannot be cured, as you belong to God for the rest of your life. You can't help but be enchanted by His beautiful figure, His activities, and His names. The disease of prema is the best one to have because it doesn't lead you astray. Instead, it brings you the happiness you have been searching after for many lifetimes.

"Let Krishna tightly embrace this maidservant who has fallen at His lotus feet, or let Him trample Me or break My heart by never being visible to Me. He is a debauchee, after all, and can do whatever He likes, but still He alone, and no one else, is the worshipable Lord of My heart." (Lord Chaitanya quoting Shrimati Radharani, Chaitanya Charitamrita, Antya 20.47)

Even if you should forget about Rama after being shot by His arrows, you will never be totally away from Him. Prema works unconditionally, so whether Bhagavan reciprocates on the affection shown to Him is of no concern. Lord Chaitanya Mahaprabhu, the preacher incarnation of Godhead, offered a nice set of prayers once in the mood of Krishna's consort Radharani, where she stated that Krishna, her cherished Lord, could do with her what He wanted. Mahaprabhu's only desire was to continue in His service, similar to how Lord Shiva continues to mutter the sacred syllables that make up Rama's holy name.

What kinds of arrows does Rama shoot at His devotees? In the above referenced verse, Tulsidas compares the tilaka mark on the Lord's forehead to an arrow. The curved eyebrows give the appearance of a bow that has just released the tilaka arrow. Since these features are on the face of the Supreme Personality of Godhead, the effect they have is the spreading of prema. Only the devoted soul can pick up on these comparisons, as they take supreme delight in the divine vision.

Rama's earrings are beautiful as well. One who looks at them becomes so happy within the mind. Though the earrings are ornaments, their beauty is enhanced by Rama, and not the other way around. Typically we dress something nicely to increase its outward beauty. You put on a nice suit and people will notice you more than if you were to wear a sweatshirt and shorts. With Rama, when you put ornaments on His body, the ornaments become more beautiful. A similar description was given in the Shrimad Bhagavatam with respect to Lord Krishna's body.

"My dear sir, Krishna's form was most wonderful when He appeared on this planet and exhibited the potency of His internal energy. His wonderfully attractive form was present during His pastimes on this planet, and by His internal potency He exhibited His opulences, which are striking to everyone. His personal beauty was so great that there was no necessity for His wearing ornaments on His body. In fact, instead of the ornaments' beautifying Krishna, Krishna's beauty enhanced the ornaments." (Uddhava speaking to Vidura, Shrimad Bhagavatam, 3.2.12)

The arrow that was the tilaka was shot at the pure hearted onlookers in King Janaka's assembly. Kings from around the world were gathered in Janaka's city to attempt to lift Lord Shiva's bow. Whoever was first to lift it would win Sita's hand in marriage. Sita Devi was Janaka's beloved daughter, the goddess of fortune herself. Through their interest in seeing who Sita was going to marry, so many people were infused with prema. Rama, a youth at the time, stood out amidst all the other princes. Rama was there with His younger brother Lakshmana and their preceptor Vishvamitra. It was Vishvamitra who had brought them there, so he deserved some of the credit for so many people rekindling the bhakti spirit through the vision of Rama and Lakshmana.

Just by imagining Rama's tilaka and thinking of it as an arrow of prema shot from the bow of the enchanter of cupid, one can receive the same effect. If you see that your friend is sick with a cold and that his mother is tending to him nicely with hearty food preparations and a comfortable resting place, you almost wish that you were sick yourself, so that you could get the same treatment. In the same way, by hearing of the fortune of the residents of Janakpur one almost hopes to find dire circumstances so that the Supreme Lord, as He promises to do in the Bhagavad-gita, will come to the scene and protect the innocent who are being harassed.

"In order to deliver the pious and to annihilate the miscreants, as well as to reestablish the principles of religion, I advent Myself millennium after millennium." (Lord Krishna, Bhagavad-gita, 4.8)

Whether we know it or not, that helpless condition already exists, and so does the soothing presence of the delight of Maharaja Dasharatha and Queen Kausalya. The vision of Rama's tilaka is needed because without such spiritual nectar, the mind is left vulnerable to the attacks of Kamadeva and his arrows. Lord Shiva showed the way by constantly chanting the holy names, and Lord Chaitanya taught the world the proper mood in which to chant those names. Thus by chanting, "Hare Krishna Hare Krishna, Krishna Krishna, Hare Hare, Hare Rama Hare Rama, Rama Rama, Hare Hare", repeatedly and in a humble state, Rama's arrows of love will surely come to our rescue.

VERSE 52

नासा चिबुक कपोल अधर रद सुंदर।
बदन सरद बिधु निंदक सहज मनोहर।।52।।

nāsā cibuka kapola adhara rada sundara |
badana sarada bidhu nindaka sahaja manohara ||52||

"The nose, chin, forehead, lips, and teeth are beautiful. The entire body is so beautiful and enchanting that it embarrasses the full moon of the autumn season."
(52)

Essay - Embarrassing The Moon

Shri Ramachandra, the hero of Raghu's clan, is so kind and sweet that He doesn't intend to harm anyone. He walks the virtuous path, and if there are any doubts, He relies on the advice and consent of the brahmanas, who are dedicated to Him in thought, word and deed. As God Himself, Rama doesn't need to abide by any laws, but only to set a good example, to reveal His true nature of kindness and compassion, does He show the world that He is dedicated to virtue. In spite of His humble attitude and reserved demeanor, He serves to embarrass those things in life which are at the top of their respective fields.

The truly great ones don't speak much. Only when one is unsure of themselves do they talk excessively, as their words of self-praise serve to buck up their own spirits more than anything else. If you see an athlete excessively celebrate or constantly pump themselves up, it should be taken as a sign of hesitancy, an indication of self-doubt. Those who are truly confident in their abilities have no need to pound their chest.

"My dear King Jarasandha, those who are heroes do not talk much. Rather, they show their prowess. Because you are talking much, it appears that you are assured of your death in this battle." (Lord Krishna, Krishna, The Supreme Personality of Godhead, Vol 1, Ch 49)

As the Supreme Lord is the greatest at everything, He in particular has no need to assert His dominance. He is already the owner of this and every land created, so what need is there to remind people? If, on the other hand, the dependents by constitutional position realize where they fit in and what line of work will give them the most lasting happiness, then only will they derive true pleasure. And from that happiness, the served entity, the one person constitutionally fit to accept an endless amount of affection from an unlimited number of people, feels pleasure as well.

Though Rama owns everything, He allows His children to borrow sections of His property for their own use. The sanctioned freedom is so great that the conditioned souls can even mistakenly believe that the property belongs to them, though they never did anything to create it. Though it's expected that maybe God would be forgotten at the time of birth, at the very least the parents should get the credit for the hard work required to create the circumstances that exist when we emerge from the womb. Therefore the pitrs, or forefathers, are immediately owed a debt upon birth. With a proper understanding, the living entity can hopefully realize that all property belongs to God. Using our possessions for the Lord's pleasure makes the temporary ownership fruitful.

Rama is also the strongest. With His impersonal energy He holds afloat the numerous planets. The sun is His creation, and it gives off so much heat and light that people are affected from thousands of miles away. Should the sun not be visible on a particular day, life on that specific section of the earth is drastically affected. Yet Rama never boasts about His strength, though He is stronger than anyone else. After much effort in the gym and a difficult to follow eating regimen, a human being may be able to lift a car or do something else physically extraordinary, yet Rama as a young child in the form of Krishna can lift up a hill without a problem. He can hold it up for seven consecutive days without breaking a sweat, though He ordinarily chooses to mask His strength to allow the offering of innocent affection from others.

Rama is the most famous. During His time on earth He was known throughout the world. His activities were so splendid that Maharishi Valmiki wrote about them before they took place. The sages of the time lived in the forests and thus they were not privy to the day-to-day news of the famous people around the world. There were no nightly celebrity shows or paparazzi to take pictures, yet everyone still knew about Rama and His wife Sita Devi. How their marriage was arranged became so famous that exalted personalities delighted in hearing the story again and again. Anasuya, the wife of Atri Rishi, asked to hear about the accounts directly from Sita, though the sage's wife already knew what had happened.

"I have heard, O Sita, that your hand in marriage was won by the renowned Raghava on the occasion of the self-choice ceremony [svayamvara]. O Maithili, I wish to hear that story in detail. Therefore please narrate to me the entire sequence of events as you experienced them." (Anasuya speaking to Sita Devi, Valmiki Ramayana, Ayodhya Kand, 118.24-25)

Though Rama is the most knowledgeable, He still bows down and pays obeisance to the respected elders. Rama kindly offered service to Vishvamitra Muni in the forest, though He had no need to take any instruction from anyone. As Krishna, the Supreme Lord accepted the loving affection from the parents Nanda Maharaja and mother Yashoda. A parent best offers their service when they think the child is dependent. As God is the embodiment of independence, who is there who can properly attend to His needs? Yet Krishna played the role of a dependent child to enhance the loving exchanges with His most cherished devotees.

On the battlefield of Kurukshetra, Krishna sung the famous Bhagavad-gita only after Arjuna, the hesitant warrior, asked the Lord to settle his doubts. One could say that Krishna sat on that information for too long, but then again one has to be eager to listen to the highest truths of life in order to understand them. Krishna is the most knowledgeable, but He will not waste His time distributing knowledge to those who have no desire to act upon it. Arjuna was the perfect candidate, so the Lord kindly dispelled his doubts.

Rama is also the most renounced. During His time on earth, He gave up the throne of Ayodhya without any reservation. The order came from His father, but Rama was the rightful heir. The Lord's younger brother Lakshmana even suggested taking over the throne by force, but Rama has no need for a high position. In the garb of an ascetic, roaming the forests Rama retained His resplendence. His two favorite companions, Sita and Lakshmana, were also extremely beautiful. That is the test to see if one is truly divine. Rama shines in all His glory wherever He is. He possesses renunciation to the fullest degree, so when stripped down from a higher post, the Lord is still Bhagavan, or the possessor of all opulences.

Rama's beauty is His feature which He arguably downplays the most. The fruitive worker, mystic, and mental speculator are all searching for Rama, as they are attracted by His beauty. Yet the Lord doesn't let this position affect His behavior. He is comfortable with who He is, so He doesn't need to flaunt any of His gifts. With this humility, His beauty increases all the more, embarrassing those other objects in life that are considered naturally beautiful.

In the above referenced verse from the Janaki Mangala, Goswami Tulsidas is again making a comparison to the Sharad Purnima, or the full moon of the autumn season. This moon is especially auspicious, as it shines bright in the night sky. It is the emblem of natural beauty, but Rama's facial features and entire body seated in a throne in King Janaka's kingdom were so beautiful that they embarrassed that full moon of the autumn.

Rama was seated in a guest's throne, as Vishvamitra had brought the brothers to Janaka's kingdom to observe a ceremony. Janaka's daughter Sita was to be given away in marriage to the first person who could lift Lord Shiva's extremely heavy bow. Again, Rama is the strongest person, but out of humility, staying in line with His character, He did not volunteer to step up. He had no desire to embarrass the other kings who were confident in their ability to lift the bow and win Sita as a wife.

As reserved as Rama was, seated alongside His brother Lakshmana His distinguishable features could not be fully masked. The onlookers started to notice His beauty and how it defeated the pride of millions of cupids. The god of desire, Kamadeva, is the Vedic equivalent of cupid. The arrows he shoots instill desire for sense gratification in the struck targets. Rama is more powerful than cupid, and His beauty defeats anyone else's.

Rama's strength would soon defeat the pride of the invited princes, who had previously tried but failed to lift Shiva's bow. In a swift motion, Rama would lift, string and then break Mahadeva's bow, showing the world that only He was fit to marry Janaka's daughter. That sort of humbling was good for everyone involved, as the more one learns about the Supreme Lord and their own position respective to

Him, the better chance they will have to take up devotional service, the soul's constitutional engagement.

VERSE 53

उर बिसाल बृष कंध सुभग भुज अतिबल।
पीत बसन उपबीत कंठ मुकुता फल।।53।।

ura bisāla bṛṣa kandha subhaga bhuja atibala |
pīta basana upabīta kaṇṭha mukutā phala ||53||

"…A broad chest, shoulders like a bull, mighty arms, wearing yellow clothes, a sacred thread, and a pearl necklace…" (53)

Essay - Painting the Picture

Goswami Tulsidas previously mentioned just how enamored everyone in the assembly was over the two youths brought in by the exalted Vishvamitra Muni. They couldn't believe what they were seeing, and Janaka himself started to doubt whether his decision was correct. Was there really a need for a contest anymore? Previously the king believed that his daughter was so beautiful and virtuous that no man existed in the world who was deserving of her companionship for life. Though it was standard for a daughter to take on the role of a supporting wife in marriage, in this situation the pressure was put on the male to give protection.

A beautiful woman will garner much attention from males, as the urge for sex is especially strong in men. A human being has potency, and within the male it manifests through sex life, the ability to create another living being. To this end, the natural relationship with the opposite sex is sought out. Biologically, the woman tends to have different priorities and can have interactions with a man and not be tempted towards conjugal relations. If you put a beautiful woman into a room with many men, even if the men are in committed relationships, they will give the beautiful woman much attention. There is typically a purpose as well: to increase the closeness of the ensuing relationship. In the reverse situation, the man can turn into a friend or confidante of the group of women. Plus, being naturally stronger, the male has a better ability to fend off the advances than a woman does.

Janaka knew that his daughter's beauty was extraordinary. She was an ideal daughter for the king, who was known throughout the world for his piety. He held a strong affection for her, but this did not preclude him from following protocol. When Sita reached an appropriate age, the king knew he had to arrange for her marriage, to find someone to protect her for the rest of her life. Janaka decided that a proper match couldn't be made in the traditional way, so he decided to instead hold a contest.

For a pious king, your word is everything. Janaka made a vow to give Sita away to whoever could lift an extremely heavy bow originally coming from Lord Shiva, the god of the mode of ignorance. Every behavior we see can fall into one of three modes: goodness, passion, or ignorance. In the short description goodness leads to higher knowledge, passion to a neutral state, and ignorance to degradation. As the aim of the evolutionary process of reincarnation is to move upwards, towards a perfect consciousness, people who fall into the different modes are given religious rituals and regulations, which have an accompanying worshipable deity. The mode of ignorance lacks high knowledge of the self and also a temporary reward of fruitive activity that has some benefits. Ignorance doesn't lead to anything tangible, so one shouldn't desire to stay in that mode for too long.

"There are eleven Rudras, of whom Shankara, Lord Shiva, is predominant. He is the incarnation of the Supreme Lord in charge of the modes of ignorance in the universe." (Shrila Prabhupada, Bhagavad-gita, 10.23 Purport)

Lord Shiva, as a divine and worshipable personality, is not in the mode of ignorance, but he is assigned the status of worshipable figure for those in this mode. He grants benedictions to those who worship him properly, though he has no interest in such gifts. He lives like a recluse, with the holy name on his tongue serving as his wealth. He constantly recites the name of Rama to feel pleasure, and when he's not chanting, he's describing the glories of the Lord to his wife Parvati, the mother of the universe.

Lord Shiva also takes pleasure in glorifying God's many incarnations and expansions, like Lord Vishnu and Lord Krishna. In the Padma Purana, Mahadeva glorifies the twelfth chapter of the Bhagavad-gita in a discussion with Parvati. The Bhagavad-gita is a famous work describing a conversation between Lord Krishna and his friend Arjuna that took place on a battlefield some five thousand years ago. The work was subsequently divided into chapters based on the subject matter, and the twelfth chapter is considered the best one by Mahadeva, as it expounds on devotional service, which is a discipline above the three modes of nature.

As Lord Shiva's intent is to stay in pure goodness and constantly connect with the Supreme Personality of Godhead, things directly relating to him are auspicious. His bow thus represented him in Janaka's kingdom, and it served as a nice way to determine the suitable husband for Sita, the king's daughter. But then Vishvamitra Muni came to town unexpectedly, with two handsome youths as his escorts. Word spread throughout the world about the bow-lifting contest, but Vishvamitra lived in the forest, and he didn't have any sons that were candidates.

Rama and Lakshmana were sons of King Dasharatha of Ayodhya, and they were both unmarried. At the time they were in the forest with Vishvamitra defending against attacks from night-rangers. The brothers appeared in Janaka's kingdom seemingly by chance, though the arrangement was made by higher authorities. Rama was the same worshipable figure of Mahadeva, and the same Krishna who would later deliver the Bhagavad-gita to Arjuna. Lakshmana was Rama's younger brother to the eyes of the world, but in spirit he was the Lord's number one protector and friend.

Because of their divine qualities, Rama and Lakshmana garnered much attention when they entered, though they weren't explicitly looking for it. They did not arrive like the other guests, who brought their royal clans with them. Think of an official state dinner hosted by the President of the United States. Now imagine that the dinner is in honor of every world leader. This sort of gives an idea of what was occurring in Janaka's kingdom on this day.

Now, here came two boys who were not opulently dressed, as they were living in the forest. Yet they were so naturally beautiful that people couldn't believe what they were seeing. Being God Himself, Rama especially garnered attention, though Lakshmana was practically a mirror image of Him, with the slight difference being that Rama was dark in complexion while Lakshmana was fair.

When Janaka saw the two boys, he thought that perhaps the impersonal Brahman he had previously worshiped had taken the form of two youths. He then heard about the boys' ancestry and how they had protected the sage against the enemies of the demigods. In this way Rama, who was elder and thus eligible for participating in the contest, was the perfect match for Sita. He belonged to as famous a dynasty as you could get, the Ikshvakus, and He had such tremendous strength at a young age that He fought off the vilest creatures in the world.

Ah, but there was one slight problem. The king swore to give Sita away to whoever could lift Mahadeva's bow. He couldn't now go back on his word. Janaka held it together and decided to show the trio around the grounds, giving them thrones to sit on to watch the festivities. The above referenced verse describes how Rama looked while seated on that throne, when everyone else was looking at Him.

Previously we were told of the reaction others had, and in this verse we get an idea of what caused that reaction. Rama had a broad chest, shoulders like a bull, and mighty arms. These three features indicate strength, which is required in a fighter. Violence and force are only harmful when used improperly. When in line with religious principles, they help to protect the innocent, thereby creating peace when it is otherwise threatened. Rama was of the royal order, which held many responsibilities, with fighting enemies included among them.

Rama wore yellow clothes, as is standard for Lord Vishnu. The Vedas describe the Supreme Absolute Truth as having no form and a form. The formless aspect is a sort of energy that pervades space. Every living being has a spark of the spiritual force within them, though we can't see it. The results validate the fact that there is something amazing within each of us. As that force pervades all of space, it can be thought of to be a singular collection. The individual spirit is Brahman, and the Supreme Spirit is Parabrahman, though we can't necessarily see either one.

The formed aspect is the original, and something can only be without form if something with form exists. That spiritual form is inconceivable in its brilliance, especially to eyes that can be tricked into mistaking a rope for a snake. The spiritual forms of the Supreme Lord are many, with Lord Vishnu being one of them. Sometimes Rama is considered an incarnation of Vishnu, while other times He is described as the original Lord. In the Narasimha Purana, the half-man/half-lion incarnation of Vishnu is described to be the original personality, but there is no contradiction. Vishnu, Krishna, Rama, Narasimha and the other avataras are equally the original Lord, whose personal expansions are non-different from Him. In all of these forms, the Supreme Lord wears yellow garments.

"Lord Narasimhadeva is here, and He is also there on the opposite side. Wherever I go, there I see Lord Narasimhadeva. He is outside and within my heart. Therefore I take shelter of Lord Narasimhadeva, the original Supreme Personality of Godhead." (Narasimha Purana)

Rama wore a sacred thread across His body. The brahmanas, the priestly class, are known as dvija, or twice-born. The first birth is from the parents and the second takes place during initiation with a spiritual master. Initiation marks the beginning of accepting the sublime instruction of Vedic teachings, and for the brahmanas the instruction applies to the mode of goodness, which leads to the highest knowledge. Formerly, the kshatriyas and vaishyas would also receive sacred threads, and they took instruction from brahmanas as well. Since their occupational duties involved fighting and trade, the instruction they received was slightly different. Nevertheless, the sacred thread marked the sign of a second birth for the eldest son of King Dasharatha, thus showing that He was cultured and not living like an animal. The ability to practice religious principles is what separates the human beings from the less intelligent animals.

Rounding out the sweet vision were the pearls worn around Rama's neck. That mental picture is nicely painted by the poet in this verse, and regularly keeping that vision in the mind can only do good things for one's mood. The people in Ayodhya couldn't keep their eyes off of Rama, and they would receive the fruit of their existence when He would lift Lord Shiva's bow and wed Sita.

VERSE 54

कटि निषंग कर कमलन्हि धरें धनु-सायक।
सकल अंग मन मोहन जोहन लायक॥५४॥

kaṭi niṣaṅga kara kamalanhi dhareṁ dhanu-sāyaka |
sakala aṅga mana mohana johana lāyaka ||54||

"With a quiver around the waist, and the lotus hands holding a bow and arrow, all the parts of their bodies enchant the mind which has a look at them." (54)

Essay - Take a Look

Take a look at the beloved sons of King Dasharatha. You won't see anyone like them in the world again, and you certainly haven't gazed upon such beautiful youths before. Today is the day to look upon the contestants of a grand competition. You scrutinize their features, seeing if they measure up to the divine qualities of the princess whose hand will be given away as the prize to the winner. You take into account the family heritage, the dedication to chivalry, and the overall demeanor of each candidate. These two youths don't appear to be here for the contest, and yet their bodily features all enchant the mind. The objects they carry with them also have divine qualities, only increasing the overall beauty.

The two youths have quivers tied around their waists. The quivers indicate that they hold arrows to be used to defend the innocent. These are young boys, yet they are the protectors of an elder muni who calls the forest his home. The muni is the teacher, the preceptor, but the students are the defenders. The paradox is furthered by the fact that these defenders are so beautiful in appearance. They wear sacred threads around their necks and have hands that are lotus-like.

The lotus flower is the symbol of purity and grace; you wouldn't necessarily equate it with fighting. In the time period in question, fighting took place with bow and arrow, with the objective being the death of the enemy. Dying while in combat was considered noble, as you sacrificed your life for a higher cause. The sacrifice was for the interest of the party you represented. If you are willing to give up your life to defend the innocent, why shouldn't you be rewarded with residence in heaven afterwards?

"O Partha, happy are the kshatriyas to whom such fighting opportunities come unsought, opening for them the doors of the heavenly planets." (Lord Krishna, Bhagavad-gita, 2.32)

The warriors qualified by internal qualities welcome the chance to show their skills. They are not afraid of meeting death at the hands of the enemy. In fact, for them running away from a fight is considered much worse. Infamy in that regard is the equivalent of death, while dying honorably in battle is the height of sacrifice, a high achievement, an indication of a life dedicated to someone else. Real love must involve sacrifice, and these two boys were willing to sacrifice everything for the protection of their spiritual master.

The bow and arrow set carried in the lotus-like hands enhanced the beauty. Princes carry weapons all the time, but the beautiful features of these boys enchanted the mind, and the weapons inherited the properties belonging to the owners. Thus the residents of this town could not take their eyes off of the two sons of King Dasharatha, who were seated on thrones as guests of the host, King Janaka.

Anyone who would see the two youths in this setting would feel the same way. The elder was dark-skinned and the younger lighter. The elder was Lord Rama, the jewel of the Raghu dynasty, and the younger Lakshmana, His dedicated brother. The muni Vishvamitra specifically asked for Rama's protection in the forest, and his insistence proved to be necessary when Rama later killed the wicked female night-ranger Tataka. Lakshmana always follows Rama. You get one, you automatically get the other. The muni derived tremendous pleasure from having their association, and he did not consider their youth and inexperience to be negative assets.

On the contrary, their external beauty matched their internal purity, their dedication to protecting the innocent. In fact, it was their father who had reservations about them going to the forest to fight off the world's wickedest creatures. Rama and Lakshmana unhesitatingly left home to tend to the muni. They guarded the sage's sacrifices, which ensured that auspiciousness would abound both locally and in the neighboring communities.

The night-rangers, on the other hand, were committed to thwarting those religious practices. Rama and Lakshmana were like guards of a church, where the attackers weren't arriving to pick apart sections of scripture or argue with the person giving the sermon. They weren't so wise in these areas. They instead wanted to kill the priests and then eat their flesh. Thus Vishvamitra required an expert bow warrior who was not afraid to fight off evil forces.

If anything, Rama and Lakshmana were worried about pleasing the sage properly. This concern would cause them to give greater attention to their work, which in the process pleased Vishvamitra very much. After proving their worth in the forest and removing the fears of the many hermits assembled there, Rama and

Lakshmana were led by Vishvamitra to Janakpur, where the goddess of fortune's hand in marriage was to be given away.

King Janaka instantly held affection for Rama and Lakshmana. Rama was especially intriguing because He was eligible for the contest. The younger, unmarried Lakshmana would not show up his brother by trying to lift the bow. If Rama won, Lakshmana would automatically become part of the family, so all interests were served in that regard.

The mind is enchanted by the appearance of the two brothers sitting innocently with their weapons. The mind likes to be enchanted because normally it is filled with so many worries. "Did I pass the test I took yesterday? Will my favorite team win the big game? Did I get that job that I interviewed for yesterday? Why has no one called me? I can't stand the anticipation."

The personal forms of the divine help one break free of these worries. Instead of hankering after things you want or lamenting over those things you failed to achieve, let your mind bask in the beauty of Rama and Lakshmana. Let your mind be enchanted by their beautiful bodily features and their weapons which are extensions of their mercy. Rama's strength would delight the onlookers when it would be used to lift Lord Shiva's bow, signaling the end of the contest. The winner was the delight of King Dasharatha and Queen Kausalya. Lakshmana and Vishvamitra were thrilled but not surprised, and the enchanted minds in Janakpur gazing upon the two boys felt relief and elation at the same time.

It should be remembered that at this gathering were the most famous princes from around the world. Janaka's daughter Sita was the most beautiful woman in the world, and her virtue rounded out her divine features. She was Janaka's daughter after all, so there could not exist a hint of sin in her. The fact that she was available for marriage presented such a tremendous opportunity for other royal families. If the wife is chaste, of good character, and from a family of good values, her presence within a new family is a godsend.

The large assembly of kings dressed in royal garb made Rama and Lakshmana's beauty stand out even more. The boys were escorting a hermit in Vishvamitra, so they didn't have a royal entourage with them, though one could be found back home in Ayodhya. Their presence was not announced with pomp, and yet everyone noticed them anyway. There was something special about Rama and His younger brother, and it could be noticed immediately.

Rama's features were so enchanting that many people, including Janaka himself, worried that Rama might not be able to lift the bow. The concern was over the potential of a missed opportunity. If the contest would prevent Rama from marrying

Sita, the contest must be bogus. And the person who came up with the contest and vowed to uphold its rules should also be cursed for making such a horrible decision.

All of this added to the anticipation, making the end result one to never be forgotten. As Rama lifted Mahadeva's bow, He broke it in half, creating a sound that travelled throughout the three worlds. That fissure also cracked the tension and fear over the wrong outcome occurring. The enchanting elder brother of Lakshmana, who was worthy of marrying Sita, fulfilled destiny, to the delight of the devoted onlookers.

VERSE 55

राम-लखन-छबि देखि मगन भए पुरजन।
उर आनंद जल लोचन प्रेम पुलक तन॥55॥

rāma-lakhana-chabi dekhi magana bha'e purajana |
ura ānanda jala locana prema pulaka tana ||55||

"Looking at Rama and Lakshmana's beauty, the people of the city became so happy. From love their hearts are filled with bliss, their eyes with tears, and their bodies with excitement." (55)

Essay - Filled With Love

The vision of the transcendental body of the Supreme Personality of Godhead has an enchanting effect on others. The same potency exists in the Lord's immediate expansion, His number one servant. This notable pair was seated on thrones in the kingdom of Janakpur at an assembly many thousands of years ago. Some were far away and others closer, but because of their internal clarity of vision, the observers showed symptoms that can only come from seeing God and recognizing His transcendental features.

Is it possible to see the original creator and have an improper reaction? Think of it another way. Is it possible to look at something and not recognize it for what it is? This already takes place with theatre and drama. If you turn on the television and flip to a channel that is showing a movie, depending on the position in the story, from watching the present scene you may or may not know what is going on. If it is at the end and you haven't seen the movie before, there may be no reaction at all. But consider this: if you watch the movie from the beginning, that identical scene, viewed with the exact same set of eyes, can bring tears to your eyes. Or it can make you extremely happy and thrilled throughout the body.

If you're looking at a painting and not wearing your glasses, you may not appreciate all the intricacies of the piece. If you're driving and your vision is obstructed by the setting sun or the headlights of oncoming traffic, you may not notice the street signs that you need for guidance. Your eyes in these instances are the same, but there are distractions that lead to a different effect when viewing.

The people in Janakpur were not meditational yogis, experts on theology, or first-class teachers. The majority of them were simple townspeople, who lived their lives according to the standard set by their leader, King Janaka. Whatever a great man does, others will follow. This fact is confirmed in the Bhagavad-gita, the guidebook of guidebooks. King Janaka followed righteousness so closely that he even held a ceremony to give away the daughter he didn't want to part with. Her qualities were so extraordinary that there wasn't a prince in the world worthy of her hand in marriage. At least this is how Janaka felt.

To see if he could find a worthy match, Janaka decided to hold a contest, where the first person to lift Lord Shiva's bow would win his daughter's hand in marriage. Janaka would find the ideal match, but ironically enough it wouldn't come from the invited guests. Instead, the prince was a sort of standby passenger, admitted entry at the last second because of the people He knew. Vishvamitra Muni, as a recognized spiritual leader, led two sons of King Dasharatha to Janaka's kingdom after they had successfully defended the sages residing in the forests from the attacks of wicked night-rangers.

Janaka, as he was known to do, welcomed brahmanas to his kingdom. Vishvamitra was treated like an honored guest, and so were his escorts, Rama and Lakshmana. But these were no ordinary boys. They had just defeated the staunch enemies of the demigods. Their ability to protect was so great that Vishvamitra used them for protection. If Rama and Lakshmana could protect the priestly class from wicked creatures who could change shapes at will and use illusion to kill their enemies, then surely the boys could protect a king's daughter.

The family ancestry of the boys was perfect, and so were their bodily features. Given thrones to sit on, Rama and Lakshmana glowed in the assembly. The townspeople could not take their eyes off of them. In the above referenced verse from the Janaki Mangala, the people of the town became happy at seeing the beauty of the two boys. Depending on the object viewed, sometimes beauty can lead to unhappiness. If it belongs to a member of the opposite sex who is already committed to a spouse, that beauty only causes pain, for you know that you can't go beyond external viewing.

Rama and Lakshmana's appearance brought happiness because that is the natural effect that God and His personal expansions have on kind-hearted people. The deity and the picture representations of the Supreme Lord are beautiful and awe-inspiring for a reason. Their transcendental features are not ordinary. Show a young child a picture of Lord Rama and they will instinctively know that the image depicts something divine. They know that it is different from an ordinary picture.

Rama and Lakshmana's divinity is revealed in the sacred Ramayana and many other Vedic texts. Their status is also confirmed in the reactions aroused in onlookers. The onlookers felt bliss in their hearts. Ananda, or bliss, is the reason for living. It is the only thing that gives life meaning. Without bliss in the heart, what is the point to working so hard day after day for so many years of your adult life? What is the point to getting out of bed in the morning if you can't find bliss?

And know for certain that the bliss the heart desires exists. It is not a myth. It was taken from the vision of Rama and Lakshmana, and the people kept it with them. They received the fruit of their existence just through sight, without any other method of implementation. Life's meaning is revealed to those who apply the right attitude towards the Supreme Lord and His servants.

The eyes of the onlookers filled with tears. This can only happen when viewing something extraordinary. The tears were a result of amazement as well. "How could two people be so beautiful? And they are so kind too. They protect the brahmanas, the people who practice religious principles and kindly disseminate Vedic wisdom to others." The entire Ramayana poem of Valmiki brings such tears to the eyes simply through sound vibration. The qualities of Rama and Lakshmana are so extraordinary that the enemies of the saintly class try to discount them as made up or part of mythology because they can't wrap their minds around them.

The bodies of the onlookers also filled with excitement, an emotion which goes hand-in-hand with anticipation. They saw the two beautiful boys and they immediately hoped that something good would come of it. Rama was the elder brother, so only He was eligible to marry Sita. They saw the beautiful vision and immediately became greedy. They wanted those youths to never leave their sight. They wanted Rama to win the contest and marry Sita.

These reactions were due to the love the people of the town felt. Nothing more than a glance at the two boys caused that love. The divine features elicit these reactions in sinless people, those who are not distracted by desires for personal gain. The aim of religious life is thus revealed in this verse. Follow the principles of bhakti-yoga, avoiding the most mentally distracting behaviors of meat eating, gambling, intoxication and illicit sex. And always chant the holy names, "Hare Krishna Hare Krishna, Krishna Krishna, Hare Hare, Hare Rama Hare Rama, Rama Rama, Hare Hare". Soon thereafter, the same body that was previously distressed and fatigued from the daily grind will be filled with excitement over the prospect of seeing the Supreme Lord and serving Him without motivation and without interruption. That excitement was warranted on that day in Janakpur, when Rama would eventually step up and lift Mahadeva's bow, fulfilling the destiny everyone was waiting for.

Essay - Gauging the Reaction

To know that a particular method is having a tangible effect, one must see a difference, either in their personal emotions or in their physical wellbeing. The barometer is based on the specific benefit desired, but irrespective of the specific circumstance the result must manifest for the original system to be considered effective. This principle applies to devotional activities as well, as through the vision of the Supreme Divine Being one should fill up with certain emotions, which are by constitution pleasurable.

Think of the natural reactions that occur in the course of everyday dealings. Say perhaps a new child is born in the family. You've never met this person before, as they have only been alive for a few days. Just from a single glance you swell with loving sentiments. Why didn't you feel this way before? What could one person have inside of them to elicit this type of emotional response from others?

The Vedas, the ancient scriptures of India, reveal that the essence of identity is filled with a blissful potency. The spirit soul is full of knowledge and bliss and is eternal in its existence. The bliss already exists within everyone, but depending on the circumstance it can get suppressed. Love is meant to be offered to others, and in the form of a small child the living entity can best extract that loving sentiment from others.

The claim that the newborn carries the most potent form for extracting love is validated by the noticeable reaction of parents and other elder family members. Without the noticeable reaction, the claim wouldn't be valid. Just as when you eat a meal, you know that there was a tangible result when you feel full afterwards, when following the highest path of religiosity the benefit doesn't have to come in the afterlife. By seeing the real thing, even by hearing it, the individual swells with love, which in turn fills the various body parts with pleasure and excitement.

A long time ago, innocent townspeople got a look at the Supreme Lord and His younger brother seated in thrones in an assembly to determine a marriage arrangement. According to the Vedas, the brothers in question were divine incarnations of the Supreme Personality of Godhead. Again, any claim can be made by any person. I could say that I am God and you could say that you are God. No one is authorized to make such claims, and thus either person can be refuted rather quickly.

The Vedic texts, which purportedly descend from the Supreme Lord Himself, can be greeted with similar skepticism, but through the reactions that result from following the recommendations, we can see whether or not the works are genuine. If they are for real, the statements about the Supreme Personality and the need for connecting with Him in a mood of love are also valid.

In the assembly in King Janaka's court, the two princes of the Raghu dynasty were first spectators. The contest was to determine who would marry Janaka's daughter Sita. Rama was the elder brother and Lakshmana His devoted follower. The two brothers were inseparable, so when Vishvamitra Muni asked to have Rama's protection in the forest, Lakshmana had to come along as well. No harm there, as Lakshmana is equal to his brother in strength, beauty and overall opulence. The difference between the two is subtle, as Rama is dark-skinned and Lakshmana fair.

The people in Tirahuta looking at the brothers couldn't believe what they were seeing. "Who are these two youths? Where did they come from? The elder Rama is so beautiful that we can't take our eyes off of Him. The fair, younger brother is just as beautiful. We have received the fruit of our existence by being blessed with this splendid vision today." Just from that vision the people wanted Rama to win the contest. He was the elder brother, and since He was not yet married He was eligible to try for Sita's hand.

There was only one rule to the contest: lift Lord Shiva's bow. Whichever prince could do this first would win. Seems easy enough, but none of the many princes could even move the bow, let alone lift it. You would think this would ease some of the tension in the onlookers, but it actually made them more nervous. Obviously the bow had an enormous weight. What if Rama couldn't lift it? Janaka made the vow, so he could not go back on his word now. This meant that if Rama failed, He would be eliminated as a candidate.

The above referenced verse from the Janaki Mangala tells us that Rama is God and that Lakshmana is practically equal to Him. Upon first sight at this stranger and His brother, the townspeople became so happy. It was the beauty that caused this reaction. The Supreme Lord is the most beautiful. In His original form He is described as all-attractive; hence He is addressed as Krishna. That all-attractive form gives transcendental pleasure to others; therefore He is also known as Rama. The original personality has many expansions, and Lakshmana is one of them. The living entities are also expansions, but they are separated, sort of like tiny samples of the original.

This means that there is an inherent link between God and us. If we see Him, we should have the same reaction that the townspeople had. Their minds were distracted by the event taking place, but that did not stop them from appreciating the beauty of Dasharatha's beloved sons. The brothers weren't specifically invited to the contest because they were away from home when the news went out, escorting Vishvamitra in the forest, where he and other sages were being attacked by night-rangers.

The level of selflessness of Rama and Lakshmana was unprecedented. They were young children at the time, so if anything the elders should have been protecting them. They left home not to play or have fun, but to offer protection against the world's most powerful fighters. They didn't complain, and they didn't itch to return home. Rama had Lakshmana with Him, so how could He be unhappy? Wouldn't you be pleased to have your number one caretaker by your side, especially if they are an expert warrior capable of defeating any enemy?

These qualities made Rama and Lakshmana all the more endearing. If Rama could protect the exalted sage Vishvamitra, He most certainly could protect the goddess of fortune, the beloved daughter of Janaka who had delicate features. She had soft skin, beautiful limbs, and an internal character that was spotless. Sita was the perfect match for Rama, and that the two would be in close proximity at the svayamvara was no coincidence.

When there is love for a newborn upon first sight, that love leads to other reactions and behaviors. When seeing Rama and Lakshmana and feeling happiness over their beauty, love overcame the townspeople as well. From that love their hearts filled with bliss. To feel bliss is the reason for our existence. The long hours you put in at the office and the time you spend taking care of responsibilities are meant for experiencing the highest pleasure, even if you're not consciously aware of the fact. The living being has a vital force capable of action for a reason. The vitality of the living being is best used for connecting with God, as that activity is the most efficient in terms of realizing the purpose to life.

Not surprisingly, the love in the townspeople caused their eyes to fill with tears. Crying can be cathartic depending on the cause. Tears filling the eyes represents a release of the barriers erected by the living entity who is afraid of getting hurt. From the transcendental love felt from seeing Rama and Lakshmana, the onlookers felt free to cry, to appreciate the vision in front of them.

In addition, their bodies filled with excitement. Seeing God is not the end of activity; it is the beginning of the real life intended for the spirit soul. The endless engagement of devotional service begins with excitement, the anticipation of knowing that bliss will continue to arrive as long as the destined husband for Sita Devi is remembered.

From the reaction of the onlookers in Tirahuta know that Rama is God. Extract the same love from within by regularly chanting, "Hare Krishna Hare Krishna,

Krishna Krishna, Hare Hare, Hare Rama Hare Rama, Rama Rama, Hare Hare", and following the devotional activities of hearing, remembering, and associating with devotees. That love will then fill your heart with bliss, cause tears to flood your eyes, and make you so excited that you'll wake up every day anxiously awaiting the next time you get to see in your mind the beautiful Rama seated in Janaka's kingdom alongside His devoted brother.

VERSE 56

नारि परस्पर कहहिं देखि दोउ भाइन्ह।
लहेउ जनम फल आजु जनमि जग आइन्ह।।56।।

nāri paraspara kahahiṁ dekhi do'u bhā'inha |
lahe'u janama phala āju janami jaga ā'inha ||56||

"The ladies say to each other, 'Look at those two brothers. They brought with them the fruit of our existence today, the reason for our coming to this earth.'" (56)

Essay - The Purpose to Our Existence

The women look upon the two brothers seated on beautiful thrones in the assembly. Rama and Lakshmana are special guests of King Janaka, the host of this ceremony. The sage Vishvamitra brought the brothers, two sons of King Dasharatha, to Janakpur to witness the ceremony, and Janaka, seeing an exalted brahmana accompanied by two beautiful youths, gave them a warm reception. The attention was supposed to be on the contest relating to a bow, but the onlookers, which included the women who were talking amongst themselves, couldn't take their eyes off of the enemies of the enemies of the demigods.

Why the attention on Rama and Lakshmana? What was so special about them? Why not focus on the contest? Ah, but the contest was very important; it was the context for the talking within the crowd. Janaka's beloved daughter Sita was to be given away in marriage on this day. But since she came from the earth and thus didn't have biological parents, the foster-father Janaka needed another way to find a suitable match for a husband. He decided to hold a bow-lifting contest, where the first person to raise Lord Shiva's bow in the air would win his daughter as a wife.

The contest seemed pretty fair. This bow was rather heavy, proof of which was seen in the many princes who arrived in Janakpur who couldn't even move the bow. They stepped up to the plate, ready to show their strength to the massive gathering, only to be humbled in the end. They would bow down to the bow, bested by its immense weight. After a while it seemed like no one would win Sita as a wife. If that were the case Janaka would be off the hook, as he hadn't purposefully tried to keep his daughter unmarried.

With such an amazing contest going on, it would take something extraordinary for the attention to be diverted elsewhere. But with the Supreme Personality of Godhead, regardless of the external circumstances He can enchant anyone. In the Vedas the embodiment of lust is known as Kamadeva, who is the equivalent of a cupid. Kamadeva is very beautiful and he can enchant others with his beauty. Yet the Supreme Lord's beauty is so great that He is known as the enchanter of cupid, or Madana-Mohana.

Sita Devi, the goddess of fortune, the eternal consort of the Supreme Lord in any of His personal forms, is so beautiful that she enchants Bhagavan Himself. Bhagavan is another name for God and it references the full possession of the attributes of beauty, wealth, strength, fame, renunciation and wisdom found within the original Divine Being. In this famous ceremony you had both Madana-Mohana and Madana-Mohana-Mohini.

Ah, but there was another player there as well. Rama is the same Lord Vishnu, the opulently adorned, four-armed form of Bhagavan, and Lakshmana is Vishnu's protector and dedicated servant. Lakshmana is identical in qualities to Rama, except his complexion is fair while Rama's is dark. Think of twin versions of the Supreme Lord in front of you in forms that are innocent, beautiful, and powerful at the same time. This sort of explains the image of Rama and Lakshmana in Janaka's court.

They were known to be powerful because they were escorting Vishvamitra through the forests. Though they were quite young, the boys assumed the occupational duty of warriors, protecting the innocent from attack. In the adult human society, no one is more innocent than the brahmana, or priest. They don't participate in the feverish competition of fruitive activity; they don't try to best anyone in terms of opulence. They are strictly focused on religious activities, helping others, regardless of their specific position, aiming to attain the ultimate goal of life, that of becoming God conscious by the time of death. The brahmanas require extra protection because their presence adds the most value to society.

Okay, so Vishvamitra was an important character, but why didn't he get King Dasharatha's direct protection or the entourage that was the royal army in Ayodhya?

If you held an exalted position that enabled you to get whatever you wanted and you had the chance to have the Supreme Lord personally protect you, wouldn't you take it? It wasn't as if Vishvamitra was taking Rama away from home forever. He just needed some protection against the Rakshasas, who were headed at the time by a fiendish character named Maricha.

"Please allow Rama to protect me during those times when I am observing religious functions and trying to keep my concentration. O chief of mankind, a terrible fear has befallen me on account of this Rakshasa Maricha." (Vishvamitra speaking to Maharaja Dasharatha, Valmiki Ramayana, Aranya Kand, 38.4)

Dasharatha didn't want to part with Rama, but the pious kings never turn down the requests of the brahmanas. Lakshmana came along because he never leaves Rama alone. The two brothers together would fight off powerful Rakshasas and externally earn the favor and trust of both Vishvamitra and the entire brahmana community living in the forests.

In the scene referenced above, the brothers are in the middle of the assembly on the day of the svayamvara, and the people can't keep their eyes off of them. This verse from the Janaki Mangala shows that the women in the town weren't idly gossiping about trivial matters. They were delighted by what they were seeing, and at the same time they knew that the boys weren't ordinary.

When looking at something beautiful, to say that you have received the fruit of your existence, the reason for your coming to the earth, is likely the highest compliment you can pay to the object in question. Implied in the statement is that all the previous days of your life have basically not amounted to much. You didn't realize this until today, when you saw the object in question that is so beautiful.

Two beautiful youths created this impression in the observant women, whose opinion was spot on. The women hadn't studied Vedanta extensively, and neither had they performed rigorous austerities in the forest. They were household women after all, so they weren't expected to be great scholars. But since they harbored spontaneous loving affection for the Supreme Lord and His direct expansion, they received the most wonderful benediction. They fulfilled life's purpose through a simple glance.

We are here on this earth to experience the same pleasure, to see the same youths kindly looking over the festivities. Their innocence made them even more endearing. Rama and Lakshmana were in simple clothes and they hadn't arrived on the scene with the royal pomp of the other guests. Surely they were accustomed to that lifestyle back home, but on this occasion their aura was subdued. Yet the divine qualities can never remain hidden to those who know how to recognize them.

How does one recognize divine qualities? The entire scope of religious activity is aimed at bringing about this recognition. Every authorized rule and guiding behavior that seems foolish or unnecessarily annoying is aimed at purifying consciousness, to help move the pure spirit soul towards a state of mind where they can see the two sons of Dasharatha seated together. More importantly, one should bask in that vision after reaching it, as everything one could ever need is found in those two princes. They protect, they defend, they give pleasure with their playful sport, and they rescue the fallen souls from the cycle of birth and death.

With laundry, the clothes remain in the dryer, spinning around, until they are completely dried out. In a similar manner, the spirit soul spins around the cycle of birth and death until it no longer desires a material body. The up or down vote is taken at the time of death by polling the mood of the consciousness. To make sure that the proper vote is cast, follow bhakti-yoga, whose principal activity is the chanting of the holy names, "Hare Krishna Hare Krishna, Krishna Krishna, Hare Hare, Hare Rama Hare Rama, Rama Rama, Hare Hare". Simultaneously, avoid the dangerous pitfalls concentrated in the activities of meat eating, gambling, intoxication and illicit sex.

The women in Janakpur talking amongst themselves were correct. There was no argument that the fruit of their existence was met on this blessed day. At the same time, the tasting of that fruit only marked the beginning of many more wonderful things to come. The elder brother would win the contest and join the family by marrying Sita. Though He would take Lakshmana and Sita back to Ayodhya with Him, the residents would never forget that scene. Whether in happiness, danger, or distress, they would remember that scene and relive the same pleasure.

CHAND 7

जग जनमि लोयन लाहु पाए सकल सिवहि मनावहीं।
बरु मिलौ सीतहि साँवरो हम हरषि मंगल गावहीं।।
एक कहहिं कुँवरु किसोर कुलिस कठोर सिव धनु है महा।
किमि लेहिं बाल मराल मंदर नृपहि अस काहूँ न कहा।।7।।

jaga janami loyana lāhu pā'e sakala sivahi manāvahīṁ |
baru milau sītahi sāṁvaro hama haraṣi maṅgala gāvahīṁ ||
eka kahahiṁ kuṁvaru kisora kulisa kaṭhora siva dhanu hai mahā |
kimi lehiṁ bāla marāla mandara nṛpahi asa kāhuṁ na kahā ||7||

"Everyone is getting the fruit of their eyes for having taken birth. They all pray to Lord Shiva, 'May that beautiful, dark youth marry Sita so that I can happily sing about the auspiciousness.'" (Chand 7.1)

"One person is saying: 'This person is an unmarried youth, while Lord Shiva's great bow is heavy and hard. How can a childlike swan carry a mountain? Why hasn't anyone told the king about this?'" (Chand 7.2)

Essay - Grant Our Wish

The women can't believe what they are seeing. "Where has such a beautiful youth come from? He looks so innocent. He is completely different from the other princes gathered here today. He possesses features in paradoxical combinations. He is kind and sweet, and yet it appears that He can rid the entire world of the demon race. He is in such a youthful figure, but His long arms show signs of immense strength. He is dark in complexion, but this has done nothing to take away from His beauty. He is seated on a throne as a welcomed guest, but He is unmarried, so He is most certainly eligible to marry Sita, which is the reason we are all gathered here today. He has a younger brother who looks like an identical twin except for the skin color. Therefore there is something unique about this boy. He must win this contest and wed our beloved Janaki."

The women received the fruit of their eyes; a benefit that results from taking birth. The bodily features exist for a reason and they develop after one exits the womb. It is difficult to keep track of this fact, that we have a higher purpose to fulfill, because life in a material existence involves constant fear. "Am I going to do well in school? Will I pass the test? Will I get a good job when I get older? What about my position relative to others? They look like they are so happy making the amount of money they do. I'm equally as smart, if not smarter, so why shouldn't I make as much money? But then what about my other priorities? How can I balance the need to provide for my family with actually spending time with them?"

As every living being who takes birth is headed for the same destination, that of eventual death, all that happens in between must have a tangible purpose, something which provides a lasting effect. As a mental exercise, think of yourself on your deathbed, knowing that you don't have much longer to live. What would you want to think about? No more concerns over work, money, school, or the pressing needs of the day. Instead, this is a time for retrospection, to look back on what you did, to see if you maximized the time you spent on this earth.

For the people in Janakpur on this famous day, they realized immediately why they had been given eyes and why those eyes were a blessing from the time of birth. The pleasure from seeing Rama and Lakshmana was so strong that these revelations naturally awoke. The delight to the eyes was heavenly and humbling at the same time. The women wanted to see the two youths every day for the rest of their lives, and just as the people in Ayodhya had previously prayed for the boys' welfare, the women here wanted the elder to emerge victorious in the contest.

The youths left home at the request of Vishvamitra Muni, who was being harassed in the forests by ghoulish creatures who changed shapes at will. Sort of like terrorists who don civilian clothes to lure in innocent people for attack, these night-rangers had no scruples. They would target the innocent, renounced sages of the forest, kill them, and then eat their flesh. King Dasharatha was a world famous fighter at the time, so he was ready to help Vishvamitra when asked.

Ah, but the sage wanted Dasharatha's eldest son Rama. No need for the entire army, just the jewel of the Raghu dynasty would suffice. If you get Rama, you get Lakshmana too. There is no way to avoid it. Lakshmana will not leave the side of his brother unless absolutely ordered to do so, and even then he will put up a fight. Not that he interacts with Rama in a spirit of friendship or that they spend hours on end talking with each other. Just Rama's company alone makes Lakshmana happy, as it does for the entire creation.

Rama is the Supreme Lord, the Absolute Truth in a personal form. The original feature of God is always personal, in spite of what may be taught by less intelligent spiritualists. That same original personal form kindly expands into the Supersoul to accompany every living entity in their travels through a material existence. The recognition of the Supersoul and the effort taken to connect with Him bring transcendental pleasure. Sometimes that same Supersoul appears in a personal form to give the eyes an idea of what God looks like and what results from that recognition.

The love offered to Rama and Lakshmana was innocent and heartfelt; the sentiments were genuine and not rooted in an awe-inspired viewpoint. As the brothers left for the forest, the people of the town of Ayodhya prayed for their welfare, that not a single hair from their heads would fall while bathing. They also prayed that they would return successful, as that would enhance the fame of the family.

After defeating many Rakshasas in the forest at the direction of Vishvamitra, the boys made it to Janakpur, where a contest was taking place. Vishvamitra brought them there, and King Janaka, the host of the ceremony, gave the trio a warm welcome and provided thrones for them to sit on and watch. The attention was on the extremely heavy bow belonging to Lord Shiva. It had to be lifted by someone if Sita were to be married. First come, first serve. Sudden death, if you will. The first person to lift the bow would win the contest and Sita's hand in marriage.

Lord Shiva is a primary divine figure of the Vedic tradition, and he takes on several different roles. For his own identification, he is a Vaishnava first, a devotee of the personal aspect of the Supreme Lord. Then there is his assigned role as the demigod in charge of the mode of ignorance, granting benedictions to those who don't know any other religion except asking for boons to carry out their wicked plots. He is also the worshipable figure for others looking for benedictions. Unmarried women worship him to get a good husband.

The women at the ceremony were so kind that they prayed to Lord Shiva to give Sita Devi, Janaka's daughter, a good husband. They wanted Rama to marry Sita for their own satisfaction as well. They prayed to be able to happily sing of the auspiciousness should the blessed event take place. The prayer to Lord Shiva was also significant because it was his bow that was to serve as the determining factor. These types of deals with divine figures are always nice to see, because they attempt to put the order suppliers in a sort of checkmate situation. "If you let Rama marry Sita, we will happily sing of the auspicious occasion. That is certainly a good thing, as who wants to live in misery? Everyone here will be happy as well." By phrasing the request in this way, the pressure was put on Lord Shiva to come through. If he didn't, it would almost be his fault for the situation turning from auspicious to inauspicious.

What would the result be? Upon seeing Rama the fruit of their eyes was tasted just slightly, and that pleasure would increase exponentially when the sweetheart son of mother Kausalya would try His hand at the contest. Lakshmana was the younger brother, so he was not eligible for the contest in Rama's presence. The youth with a dark complexion arose from His throne and easily lifted Mahadeva's bow, subsequently announcing to the world His victory by breaking the bow while stringing it. The women got what they wanted, as did Lord Shiva. The wish granted, that joyous occasion has been happily sung about ever since.

Essay - Alert the Authorities

"It's David versus Goliath. This bow is as hard as steel and so heavy that the most powerful princes in the world can't even move it. They have come from far and wide to participate in the contest, but the bow is besting them, like a formidable foe whose strength is too great to overcome. Now this beautiful prince, who is of a tender age and unmarried, is expected to try His hand at lifting the bow? He will get embarrassed. Can a young swan move a mountain? That is pretty much what the king expects this youth to do. Why hasn't anyone notified the king? He should not allow this to happen."

Some of the onlookers at the contest were so much in love with the jewel of the Raghu dynasty that they worried over His embarrassment and also His suffering. We would never expect a child to lift up an automobile. Forget the fact that they won't be able to move the car, the primary concern is over their safety. Why should they risk getting hurt doing something that is impossible? The Supreme Personality of Godhead gives off the innocence of a young helpless child, yet even within that form He can do wonders. The entire universe can be seen within His mouth, so why should He have difficulty lifting up a bow?

Though He was a youth during the time of this incident, before this event, when He was even younger, Lord Rama, King Dasharatha's eldest son, played happily in the royal courtyard in Ayodhya. Just as in Janaka's kingdom, the onlookers in Ayodhya were amazed at the sight of Rama. So beautiful, delicate, handsome and charming was He that none could believe that a human being could assume such a form. The devoted bird Kakabhushundi once came close to the young Rama. After being chased he was eventually swallowed by the boy. Rama did this both for His own fun and the bird's.

What the bird saw within Rama's mouth was astounding: the entire cosmos, the universal form - at least a version of it. The eyes can't properly fathom the length and breadth of the entire creation. Picture looking at the world's largest number and trying to decipher its value. With commas placed in the right positions the number would still be impossible to understand. As another exercise, try looking at a container of straws and then guessing how many are in there. Look at a box of jellybeans and try to come up with an accurate count. You could put forth a guess, but your eyes have really no way of ascertaining the count of unique items.

If that limitation exists with something in our immediate vicinity, imagine then how paltry our understanding of the universe is. The universe is far more complex than we think. A few automobiles driven in a particular area may have an impact on the surrounding environment, but climate as a whole operates on a much larger scale. More formidable than the earth is the galaxy, and larger than a galaxy is the universe. That entire creation is but one representation of the Supreme Lord, who appeared in Ayodhya as the young prince named Rama.

Many thousands of years later, the same Rama would return to earth in His manifestation of Shyamasundara, the beautiful Lord Krishna, the son of Yashoda and Nanda Maharaja. Similar loving feelings were directed at God this time around, and again the youthful appearance did not prevent the Supreme Lord from performing miraculous feats. There were the attacks by the Putana witch, the demon using the whirlwind, and the asura who took the form of a bull. These were but a few of the wicked characters who tried to kill Krishna while He was still a young child, but even in that form the Lord was able to defend Himself.

In Janakpur on this famous day, the people watching over the festivities worried that the young Rama, accompanied by His younger brother Lakshmana, would fail in the contest and maybe get hurt in the process. The delicate features of the youthful delight of mother Kausalya masked the known fact that the exalted sage Vishvamitra had previously insisted on Rama to be his protector. The sage was very powerful from his austerity. He knew very well of Rama's abilities, and he also knew that there were others around to protect him. King Dasharatha insisted on bringing his entire royal army into the forest to protect the munis, but Vishvamitra said that he only needed Rama. Lakshmana came along as well, for if you get Rama you get Lakshmana always. The two are like twins, with Lakshmana fair in skin color and Rama dark.

Some residents of Janakpur were so afraid of Rama failing to lift the bow that they wondered why no one had alerted King Janaka to the potential trouble. The contest was to determine the husband for his beautiful daughter, Sita Devi. A king is a protector first and foremost. If he were true to his role, Janaka would protect Rama from the heavy bow, which would overcome His strength. At least this was the feeling of the kind-hearted devotees observing the scene.

They hadn't been acknowledged devotees for long. Upon first sight of Rama and Lakshmana entering the kingdom with Vishvamitra the viewers could tell there was something special about them. These youths were so beautiful in appearance that they couldn't be of this earth. Rama was the perfect match for Sita, and for this match to materialize He had to win the contest. But if He lost, if Lord Shiva's bow bested Him, He would automatically become ineligible to wed the goddess of fortune.

The youthful form with its delicate features made the ensuing act of the Supreme Personality of Godhead all the more pleasurable to the eyes. Rama would calmly step into the arena and easily lift the bow. In the process of stringing the bow, He would break it. Has anyone heard of a swan breaking a mountain? With the Supreme Lord, these seemingly impossible feats are child's play. He can break things with His youthful figure, and He can smile gently while fighting with the enemy.

Rama's most remarkable strength is found within His name. Just by chanting the holy names, "Hare Krishna Hare Krishna, Krishna Krishna, Hare Hare, Hare Rama Hare Rama, Rama Rama, Hare Hare", the sweetheart who won Janaki's hand in marriage arrives on the scene to give pleasure. Those names form the subject matter of the couplets and verses which describe the original event. Hearing those verses paints the picture of the original scene within the mind, giving the eyes a feast of deserved delights.

How does Rama do it? How does His name carry His personal presence? Hearing is believing in the Vedic tradition. The ancient scriptures of India pass on sublime wisdom to be used in achieving the highest end. Through sound connect with the Supreme Personality of Godhead. Though to us the sound of the Absolute Truth is absent form, since it addresses a personality with divine features it can carry out the same miraculous feats that the original person can. Rama is always destined to be with Sita, despite what the external circumstances may portend. In the same way, no matter our plight or personal condition, the holy name can rescue us from the ocean of material suffering.

VERSE 57

भे निरास सब भूप बिलोकत रामहि।
पन परिहरि सिय देब जनक बरु स्यामहि॥57॥

bhe nirāsa saba bhūpa bilokata rāmahi |
pana parihari siya deba janaka baru syāmahi ||57||

"Looking at Rama all the princes became disappointed. 'Abandoning his vow, Janaka will give Sita to the dark-complexioned youth for marriage." (57)

Essay - Broken Promise

There was no way Janaka was going to break his vow. If he had been inclined to go that route, he wouldn't have arranged for the marriage ceremony in the first place. It was his commitment to dharma that brought all the princes from around the world to his kingdom for that special day, the event of events. Whoever could lift Lord Shiva's bow would win Sita's hand in marriage. This was the promise made by the king, and because of his truthfulness and the divine qualities of his daughter, the assembled princes from around the world were eager to participate in the contest and hopeful of emerging victorious.

Ah, but there was a newly introduced wildcard. This handsome youth with a dark-blue complexion arrived on the scene with His equally as beautiful younger brother and the venerable rishi Vishvamitra. You couldn't have created a better contrast if you painted the picture yourself. On the one side you had a line of arriving guests that looked like a conveyor belt. The princes didn't come alone. They had their royal entourages with them, which included priests and paraphernalia required for travel.

"Gather all essentials and pack them in securely so that we'll have whatever we need for the journey and the hopeful extended stay in Janaka's kingdom." The princes leaving home were on their way to a tournament-style venue. If you're a sports competitor participating in a tournament, the goal is to make it to the final rounds. This means that the longer you stay at the tournament site as a participant, the more successful you are.

There were no extended rounds at this contest. It was one and done. You had one shot at victory, and if you didn't win, you'd have to sit down and watch others make the same attempt. If you should happen to emerge victorious, you would get to marry the goddess of fortune in a grand ceremony. The wedding would likely take several days and you'd get to return home with the beloved princess and her maidservants. In this way there was a lot riding on the outcome of the event. The participants hoped to have an extended party, and the people back home wished for a triumphant and jubilant return.

Lord Rama, on the other hand, arrived at the event without much fanfare. He hadn't gone there to specifically participate in the contest. He and His younger brother Lakshmana had other pressing matters which warranted attention. The lives of the innocent sages residing in the forests were at stake, as they were troubled by the attacks of the fiendish night-rangers, who changed their shapes at will and paid no regard to innocent life. A priest is not bothering anyone if he lives by himself away from society. What need then did Maricha and his band of Rakshasas have to harass saintly ascetics?

Never mind their motives, for one can spend their entire life studying the behavior of miscreants and not get anywhere. The more important issue was to provide protection. For this King Dasharatha's eldest son was called to the scene. Though He was a youth with delicate features, there was not a single hole in His defensive capabilities. With His bow and arrow He could defeat an unlimited number of attackers. Add to the mix Lakshmana, who is equally as capable in fighting, and you get an impenetrable wall of protection.

After defending the sages in the forest, the unselfish brothers made it to Janakpur at the direction of Vishvamitra, who was welcomed kindly by King Janaka. The trio were given thrones to sit on to watch the festivities. Though they didn't arrive in large caravans, the two brothers drew attention from the onlookers. Rama was especially noteworthy because He was the elder brother, which meant that He was eligible to participate in the contest. Lakshmana was younger and since Rama wasn't yet married it would have been a sin for him to marry.

King Janaka initially didn't want to marry off his daughter. He found her through divine intervention, in a field of all places. She was a baby at the time, and since he was childless she was a true blessing in his life. He loved her so much that he didn't want to give her away to just any man when the time was right. But he knew that if he kept his daughter unmarried, he would invite ridicule from relatives and the citizens of the state.

As a suitable compromise, Janaka decided on the bow-lifting contest. He vowed to give Sita away to whoever could first lift the extremely heavy bow belonging to Lord Shiva. This vow combined with Janaka's respected standing in the world brought the many princes to his city. Though they were very powerful, they could not lift the bow. One by one they approached the sacrificial arena, made their attempt, and then paid respect to the bow as they left.

Now seeing Rama sitting there in all His beauty, the princes started to wonder if Janaka would break his vow. "We can't compete with this dark-complexioned youth of divine features. He is so enchanting that He defeats the pride of millions of cupids. Why is Janaka even going to waste time with the contest? This youth is obviously the perfect match for Sita, so we don't stand a chance."

Though they were rooted in defeatism, these kind sentiments served to praise Rama even more. It is one thing for devoted souls to offer praise, but these were competitors, people trying to win the contest before Rama could. The Supreme Lord's competitors can't help but acknowledge and praise His qualities. Previously, when the wicked night-ranger Maricha had attacked Vishvamitra, Shri Rama, without blinking an eye, without breaking a sweat, calmly strung His bow and shot an arrow that struck Maricha so hard that it flung him over eight hundred miles away. Maricha never forgot that incident, and he knew that he only remained alive because of Rama's mercy.

Now the contestants were watching Rama and they felt defeated already. The beauty of the Supreme Lord was so magnificent that they irrationally thought that Janaka would break his vow. Indeed, many of the town's women had hoped that Janaka would break his promise, for what if Rama couldn't lift the bow? In that case the king's vow would serve to prevent the match made in heaven. That wouldn't be good.

But things were arranged in this way for a reason. The fear of the competing princes should have been rooted in Rama's strength, which was seemingly overshadowed by His delightful, youthful appearance. Contradictory attributes exist in the Supreme Lord, and this fact is very hard to understand for the mind conditioned by the bounds of dry logic. Rama is both formless and with form. His formless feature lacks His personal presence, whereas His spiritual form brings sweetness in association. The sweetness of that form was so strong that Rama defeated the pride of the princes participating in the contest.

Rama's spiritual features can carry out any function. His delicate hands can lift a bow as heavy as iron. His sweet smile can instill both delight and fear. But best of all, the sound of His holy name can deliver the fallen souls drowning in an ocean of material suffering, where there is constant competition and uncertainty over the future. The holy names of, "Hare Krishna Hare Krishna, Krishna Krishna, Hare Hare, Hare Rama Hare Rama, Rama Rama, Hare Hare", bring the delight of the Raghu dynasty to the mind's vision. There was no reason to fear Janaka breaking his promise, for Sita and Rama were destined to be with one another. Shri Rama would win the contest, playing within the rules, and thus prove to the world that He is worthy of the affection of the goddess of fortune.

VERSE 58

कहहिं एक भलि बात ब्याहु भल होइहि।
बर दुलहिनि लगि जनक अपनपन खोइहि।।58।।

kahahiṁ eka bhali bāta byāhu bhala ho'ihi |
bara dulahini lagi janaka apanapana kho'ihi ||58||

"One person says: 'It will be good if Janaka breaks his oath to allow Sita and Rama to get married.'" (58)

Essay - Pardon

It's not good to break your promise, for otherwise people will not trust you. The next time you make a vow, no one will take you seriously. If you're in a position of authority and people don't assign any value to your word, how can you effectively wield that authority? If a police officer is laughed at for his inability to apprehend suspects, will the innocent people feel safe? What then will be the difference between a police officer and an ordinary citizen? The ordinary citizen would be in a better position because they at least don't pretend to be capable of defending the innocent. Yet sometimes it is considered good to break a vow, especially if the desired end is beneficial. This was the sentiment of a group of observers at a famous wedding ceremony a long time ago.

If I vow to only eat certain foods in order to lose weight, breaking that vow will not be good. The vow was taken with a specific purpose in mind, that of losing weight. If there is no will power, no ability to control oneself through a difficult time, how can the proper end be reached? Ah, but herein lies the key point. That proper end is what determines whether or not a particular action should be taken. If breaking my vow will help me to lose weight, then perhaps it isn't so bad.

As another way to think of the same principle, imagine driving along the street and then encountering a red light. The red light says that you must stop. In this particular instance, however, stopping is not an option due to the traffic situation that is ahead of you. If you go through the light, you are not only risking a collision with oncoming cars, but you are also breaking the law. But in some cases, it is better to go through the red light in order to avoid a dangerous situation. The stipulation to stop at the red light exists for the same purpose that is furthered by the special circumstance.

For a king a long time ago, a vow was taken in order to find the perfect match for his daughter. The king wanted a strong and courageous prince to take care of his daughter, who had delicate features and a level of virtue never before seen to the world at the time. Neither has that level of virtue been seen in a woman since. It can only exist in the eternal consort of the Supreme Personality of Godhead. Not surprisingly, the actions of Janaka were the will of Providence meant to join the devoted pair, Sita and Rama, together for the eyes to delight in.

Janaka made a vow relating to an extremely heavy bow he possessed that originally belonged to Lord Shiva. "Lift the bow and I will give away my cherished daughter Sita to you in marriage." This was a pretty safe vow, for if no one could lift the bow, Janaka would be let off from blame. It wouldn't be his fault that no one in the world was worthy of his daughter's hand in marriage. If someone could lift the bow, then obviously that person was exceptionally strong and would therefore provide good protection to the beloved Sita.

Shri Ramachandra's appearance in Tirahuta threw a wrench into the equation. Neither Janaka nor anyone else in the close inner circle knew that someone like Rama existed. They also didn't think that someone like Rama would be unmarried and eligible for accepting a new wife. Had they known these things prior there would have been no reason to proclaim the vow. If you're a manager of a business team and you know someone who is perfect to fill an open position, what need is there to put out an ad for the job? Why go through a detailed hiring process, where you interview candidate after candidate, if you already know of someone who is perfect for the job and eligible to be hired?

Lord Rama was so beautiful that people seeing Him for the first time couldn't believe it. His younger brother Lakshmana was equally as beautiful, and they both arrived in the city with Vishvamitra Muni. If as a man you tell a woman that you devote time to reading to the blind, feeding the poor, taking care of abandoned puppies, or some other good work, you are sure to get a positive response. It is thought that the typical adult-aged male enjoys drinking, partying, chasing after women, sports, video games and a host of other activities relating to personal sense gratification.

In ancient times, the kings enjoyed themselves quite well, as to the victor went the spoils. Yet this youth with a bluish complexion appeared on the scene without fanfare, and He wasn't roaming the forests out of His desire for fun or the need to practice His marksmanship with the bow and arrow. No, He was there to protect Vishvamitra, an innocent priest-like person, from the wicked attacks of terrorist-like night-rangers.

Add to the fact that Rama and Lakshmana were descendants in the famous Ikshvaku family and you get an idea of why there were new grumblings questioning the king's decision. The elder Rama was perfect for Sita. There was no flaw in Him. Looking at Him was enough to tell that He was someone special, but His character and dedication to fighting against the most powerful enemies sealed the deal.

In the above referenced verse from the Janaki Mangala, we get a sample of the statements of the people watching the contest. One group decided that it would be okay if the king broke his vow. No harm would be done, for the decision would allow Rama and Sita to be married, which is what everyone wanted anyway. Actually, the oath was taken for the purpose of finding for Sita a good husband, especially one who was fit to protect. Vishvamitra's faith in Rama was the only testimonial needed to vouch for the delight of the Raghu dynasty's ability to defend the innocent.

In the end, Janaka didn't break his vow. He wouldn't need to, as Rama would lift and break Shiva's bow. The people got what they wanted, a marriage which didn't relate to them personally. Just the sight of the perfect match joining in holy matrimony was enough to please the devoted souls watching the proceedings. That same vision can be created within the mind by regularly chanting the holy names, "Hare Krishna Hare Krishna, Krishna Krishna, Hare Hare, Hare Rama Hare Rama, Rama Rama, Hare Hare." A vow to chant these names every day with full faith, attention and reliance brings the cherished benefit of the divine consciousness.

VERSE 59

सुचि सुजान नृप कहहिं हमहि अस सूझई।
तेज प्रताप रूप जहँ तहँ बल बूझई।।59।।

suci sujāna nṛpa kahahiṁ hamahi asa sūjha'ī |
teja pratāpa rūpa jahaṁ tahaṁ bala būjha'ī ||59||

"The pure and gentlemanly kings are saying, 'For me, I understand that wherever there is splendor, fame and beauty, the strength will be there as well.'"
(59)

Essay - Where There is Smoke

The champions of the ancient art of bhakti-yoga say that through a single sound vibration one can get in touch with the Divine. More than just an abstract concept of a heavenly figure who has the power to give or take away rewards, this entity is a personality, where the names used to address Him call Him to the scene. And this personality possesses transcendental features which are purna, or complete, in their goodness. He is not lacking anything, a fact validated by the ability of His name to bring His aura.

The famous phrase, "where there is smoke, there is fire", says that if there are the trace attributes of a specific thing, it is likely that the specific thing is present as well. The smoke is the aftereffect of the burning fire. If you see smoke, then it must have an initial cause. That cause will be the burning of something, and in order to burn you must have fire. Therefore, simply from the result of visible smoke you can deduce that there is a fire somewhere nearby.

In a similar manner, by seeing the results of chanting the holy names, especially the names sequenced in the maha-mantra, "Hare Krishna Hare Krishna, Krishna Krishna, Hare Hare, Hare Rama Hare Rama, Rama Rama, Hare Hare", you can assume the presence of the divine personality. By chanting in the proper mood, with firm faith, attention and dedication, so many beneficial attributes are acquired. We'll start with the foremost among them, which is the continued loving dedication that lacks both motivation and interruption. This looks like a paradoxical combination, as how can you have dedication without some sort of motivation? What will get you over the hump, pull you across the finish line, if a motivating force is lacking?

Interruption is equally as important, for the unending commitment alone depresses enthusiasm in an endeavor. If I assign a task to someone, they might ask me how long it should take. If I respond with, "Oh, it'll go on forever. You'll never finish that job," will the worker want to accept the job? Who would want to take on a task that never finishes? Yet this is precisely what reveals the glory of bhakti-yoga, showing how it can break all combinations previously thought to be paradoxical.

The symptom of the pure devotee is the relentless attention to chanting and overall worship. They chant the holy names in a regimented fashion, preferably saying the specific mantra relating to God at least sixteen rounds a day on a set of japa beads. But there is also spontaneous devotion, where signs of transcendental love manifest at the mere mention of the beloved's name. The holy name brings to mind the transcendental features of the person being addressed. His sweet form, His cherished pastimes, and His vital instructions are all contained within His name.

As an added bonus that is almost considered negligible, the devotee also avoids sinful behaviors like meat eating, gambling, intoxication and illicit sex. One may argue that it is nearly impossible to avoid these staples of modern material life, but the benefit of avoiding them can't be discounted. A person who can avoid sinful life is always in a superior position, for they steer clear of the deepest pitfalls that prevent happiness.

So we have no sinful life coupled with a dedication to chanting, dancing, hearing, remembering, and worshiping in devotion. This combination cannot be found through any other endeavor. Mental speculation, fruitive activity, and mystic yoga cannot give the same benefit to the participants, as there is always a point of maturation. In fruitive activity, the reward doesn't provide lasting happiness, so pretty soon you're left searching for another endeavor. In mental speculation, the endpoint is void, where activity ceases. This goes against the natural inclination of spirit, for the soul is a vibrant force with a desire for activity. Mysticism provides a perfection of some sort, an ability that can be used but which doesn't necessarily bring the yogi to a better end.

As where there is smoke there is fire, where there are the amazing benefits of bhakti through the innocent chanting, there must be a higher power responsible for the outcome. Just chanting any word or series of words will not do the trick. The power in the holy name is its equivalence to the supreme person it addresses. In this sense the results reveal and validate the superior standing of the Supreme Lord, whose features are so nicely described in the Vedas.

That same Supreme Personality appeared on this earth many thousands of years ago to enact wonderful pastimes. One famous incident occurred in the kingdom of Tirahuta, which was ruled over by Maharaja Janaka. The king had an unmarried daughter who would be given away to whichever prince could lift the extremely heavy bow belonging to Lord Shiva. God in His avatara of Lord Rama appeared on the scene with His younger brother Lakshmana and the sage Vishvamitra. They supposedly were there just to watch, but as Vishvamitra, a brahmana, was well-respected, so too were his two disciples.

Rama and Lakshmana were of a young age, but they stood out. Their beauty was amazing. The attention focused more on Rama because He was the elder brother, so He was eligible for participating in the contest. In the above referenced verse from the Janaki Mangala, we get an idea of what some of the attendees were thinking when they saw Rama. In this particular statement, we see how someone can notice God's complete feature-set simply by noticing other divine features.

In the Vedas the Supreme Lord is addressed as Bhagavan, which is a word that indicates that He possesses all opulences to the fullest degree and at the same time. From the visual, the other princes in Tirahuta could tell that Rama was the most beautiful. They also saw that he had splendor, or tejas. Fame belonged to Rama as well because of the family He belonged to and His having protected Vishvamitra from powerful attacking Rakshasas in the forest.

The princes making these remarks are described as pure and virtuous. This means that their assessments were not clouded by jealousy, rivalry, or the desire for personal gain. Bias is only natural when we are competing with our fellow man for opulence, but in this case the pious princes were not partial in their assessments. They accurately noted that since Rama had the three aforementioned features, He would likely have strength as well. They were correct, as Rama would indeed lift the bow and win Sita's hand in marriage.

That same strength, beauty, fame and splendor are packed into the holy name cherished by the kind-hearted souls like Goswami Tulsidas, Shri Hanuman, and Rama's wife Sita Devi. They know that where there is supreme auspiciousness due to chanting, the presence of the Supreme Personality must be there as well. Knowing this, the wise and virtuous souls, irrespective of their occupational duty or societal standing, make the chanting of the holy name their primary occupation in life.

VERSE 60

चितइ न सकहु राम तन गाल बजावहु।
बिधि बस बलउ लजान सुमति न लजावहु।।60।।

cita'i na sakahu rāma tana gāla bajāvahu |
bidhi basa bala'u lajāna sumati na lajāvahu ||60||

"You can't even look at Rama's body. Your cheeks are just making sounds. You were already embarrassed by the strength from the creator. Now be wise and don't further embarrass yourself." (60)

Essay - The Empty Can Rattles The Most

Aside from the issue of politeness, it is not considered wise to brag, to be overly vocal about your abilities, because it really serves no purpose. If you can back up what you're saying, if your boasting legitimately speaks to your strengths, you should prove yourself in the subsequent exercise. What good does your boasting do? If I am a carpenter capable of cutting wood to match the specifications of the job in question, whether or not I talk a lot beforehand makes no difference in the final outcome. It is said in many places in the Vedic literatures that a true hero doesn't speak much; he lets his work do the talking.

"My dear King Jarasandha, those who are heroes do not talk much. Rather, they show their prowess. Because you are talking much, it appears that you are assured of your death in this battle." (Lord Krishna, Krishna, The Supreme Personality of Godhead, Vol 1, Ch 49)

There is also the issue of failure, which is more often the cause for the bragging. The person fond of boasting speaks so much because they are unsure of their ability. In talking, they hope to put down the opposition, to instill some fear in them. If the person were actually confident of their abilities, they would have no need to talk much. Therefore in either circumstance, avoiding bragging is a good idea. For many kings assembled in Janakpur a long time ago, the recommendation to remain free from bragging was made because of the imminent defeat to arrive from the strong hand of the Supreme Personality of Godhead, who was on the scene as the innocent, yet beautiful youth of the Raghu dynasty, the eldest son of Maharaja Dasharatha. Known by the name of Rama, the delight of mother Kausalya was seated in the assembly alongside His younger brother Lakshmana and the exalted sage Vishvamitra.

There was talk amongst the assembled princes because no one could keep their eyes off of Rama and Lakshmana. The brothers were just that beautiful. They had such delicate features that people couldn't imagine how they were sons of a powerful and capable fighter like Dasharatha. In those times the people most capable of defending the innocent took charge of the government. This fact reveals the primary aim of government. There will always be aggressors in society, regardless of the time period. The strong shouldn't be able to dominate the weak just because of their superiority in strength. A person has a right to the property that they lawfully acquire, and the innocent should not be harassed without cause. Therefore the government's primary duty is to provide protection against the aggressors, not to be the aggressors themselves.

Though Rama and Lakshmana were still too young to take an active role in the administration, they nevertheless proved their ability to defend the innocent. They were with Vishvamitra because of the attacks he and the other sages in the forest of Dandaka constantly faced from the evil night-rangers, who were known as the Rakshasa species based on their hideous features. The night-rangers would change their shapes at will and attack during the dark hours when it was difficult to see. They had only one thing in mind: eliminate the influence of the pious. The end justified the means, so they didn't care what codes of conduct they violated along the way.

Rama, for His part, was always attentive to pious principles. He and Lakshmana went to the forest because Vishvamitra asked them to. They got the permission of their parents first, and they never hesitated in performing their duty. Sometimes the attention to piety gives rise to doubt. How do we know what the right decision is in a particular area? For Rama, the first dilemma came from the attacking night-ranger named Tataka. She was a female, and kshatriya warriors never battled against females. Vishvamitra repeatedly instructed Rama to not pay attention to the gender, as Tataka had no concern for fighting fairly. Despite this fact, it wasn't until Vishvamitra urged Rama strongly that the Lord did away with the fiendish creature.

Now He and His brother were in Janakpur with Vishvamitra, quickly made welcomed guests by the host of the occasion, King Janaka. This ceremony was to be more peaceful; no conflict was foreseen. Kings from around the world were invited to come to try to lift Lord Shiva's bow. First come, first serve. Whoever could lift the bow first would win. Ah, but this was not an easy contest. The many kings who stepped up to the sacrificial arena already had to walk back to their seats with their heads hanging down. The bow bested them. This meant that the creator, Lord Brahma, had not given them bodies suitable for lifting this heavy bow.

In the above referenced verse from the Janaki Mangala, we see some advice given to the haughty kings. They are told to basically keep their mouths shut in relation to Rama. They are not qualified to even look at the handsome youth, as His beauty defeats the pride of millions of cupids. The expression relating to moving one's cheeks references bragging. This is the equivalent of saying that someone is "blowing smoke", "flapping their gums", or "running their mouth." The kings bragging about their own prowess was a wasted effort. Their cheeks were moving, but nothing worthwhile was coming out of their mouths.

The kings were already embarrassed by the bow, so talking further of their own prowess only embarrassed them more. When humbled in such a way, it is best to remain silent and not further degrade oneself. In this case the advice was also valid because Rama would step into the arena and lift the bow without a problem. He was destined to marry Janaka's daughter Sita, for she is the goddess of fortune. The pair can never be apart, even when it appears to the eyes that they are not together. Sita can never marry anyone else.

The humbling of the kings was beneficial for them, as it is symbolic of what is needed for every spirit soul who lands in the material world. The root cause for the growth of the tree of material existence is the flawed notion that the individual can imitate God and perhaps surpass Him in ability. Only through illusion can one think that they are so great that they brag about their abilities. Even if one is at the top of their field, at some point in their life they required diapers and the help of adults. Skill is given by the creator through the body type awarded at the time of birth, but the exercise of that ability is not perfect. As we cannot see in the dark, we are limited in our sight. We cannot see through walls either, so in this way the material nature has dominance over our abilities.

To be humbled directly by the Supreme Lord is a tremendous boon, because it is better to appreciate His abilities instead of someone else's or our own. If we remember Rama lifting and breaking the immensely heavy bow originally belonging to Lord Shiva, we will remember that He is the person most worthy of honor. He is the richest, wisest, most beautiful, most renounced, and most famous.

In the kingdom of Janakpur that famous day, He showed that He is also the strongest.

The person possessing these features simultaneously becomes worthy of the name Bhagavan. His strength is not displayed only in contests. The strongest person can also provide the best protection, something needed by every person who is constantly tossed by the raging waters of the ocean of material existence. Rama's strength is available to the surrendered souls when they regularly chant His names, "Hare Krishna Hare Krishna, Krishna Krishna, Hare Hare, Hare Rama Hare Rama, Rama Rama, Hare Hare". Shri Rama, Raghuvira, is the hero of the Raghu dynasty, and though He is quiet, He is the strongest person. He defends the innocent who try to connect with Him, and through His institution of bhakti-yoga, which is non-different from Him, His protection is available to all.

VERSE 61

अवसि राम के उठत सरासन टूटिहि।
गवनहिं रामसमाज नाक अस फूटिहि॥61॥

avasi rāma ke uṭhata sarāsana ṭūṭihi |
gavanahiṁ rāmasamāja nāka asa phūṭihi ||61||

"It's assured that when Rama gets up, He will break the bow. Embarrassed by that, all the assembled kings will leave here with their noses broken." (61)

Essay - Egg On Their Faces

"Egg on your face; tail between your legs, sheepish feeling", these are some of the expressions used to describe embarrassment. The specific terms are referenced in the hopes of more accurately quantifying the emotion. If we just say that we're embarrassed, the statement doesn't say much. We could feel shame over having forgotten an appointment or having used the wrong translated word in a foreign country. These are simple mistakes that you shouldn't really feel bad about. The aforementioned expressions are used when the pride of the individual has been humbled, when they thought they were better than they were. A Hindi equivalent of the same emotion is invoked in the above referenced verse from the Janaki Mangala, and it was an appropriate way to describe how the assembled kings would feel.

You get egg on your face when you're sure about something happening and then it doesn't pan out. Say, for instance, that you predicted a specific outcome to an upcoming election. Beyond just speculating on how the votes would align, you went on television on a daily basis and argued against the competing viewpoints, calling them silly. You pointed to your own polling research and knowledge of election trends to emphatically support your contention.

On election day, however, the votes go just the opposite way. If you had just made a guess as to how the election would pan out, you might not feel so embarrassed now. People make incorrect predictions all the time. If this weren't the case, the bookmakers in Las Vegas would have been out of money a long time ago. Indeed, the point spreads for professional sporting events are determined by finding a number where the person taking the bets will have an equal distribution of people wagering. The aim is to have just as many people betting on one outcome as there are on the other side. This way, the house will not run out of money if a specific outcome occurs.

The person who invested so much in the wrong outcome to the election feels like they have egg on their face, that they have a food substance smearing their otherwise beautiful countenance. A noted political strategist actually went on a nationally syndicated Sunday morning talk show several years back and broke a raw egg on his face after he was incorrect about a particular outcome. His wife, who happened to be a guest on the show with him, couldn't believe what he was doing, but the act was done to make a point, to show that he knew he had made a gross miscalculation of the sentiment of the voting public.

In Tirahuta many thousands of years ago, there was a huge throng of warriors full of pride. They couldn't be blamed, for if you are in charge of a government and not confident of your ability to protect the innocent, how will you do your job well? If you have confidence in the task ahead of you, it will be a lot easier to work. If you're constantly doubting yourself, at the first sign of trouble your resolve will crack.

The kings were assembled on this day to try to lift an extremely heavy bow which originally belonged to Lord Shiva, the deity in charge of the mode of ignorance. The ghosts, goblins and those into black magic have a deity they can worship. The Vedic tradition provides every type of person with a system of religion, a way to curb harmful behavior in the hopes of purifying consciousness. Restraint is a negation on an active tendency, but it has the underlying purpose of shaping behavior for the better. As eating animal flesh that is the result of unnecessary violence is a tendency that should be curbed, for those who are addicted to such behavior there are worshipable deities to whom they can offer obeisances. Through this method, a gradual purification can occur.

Lord Shiva is devoted to the Supreme Personality of Godhead, but he still takes care of other functions. He is the worshipable figure of the human beings mired in the mode of ignorance, which is noted by any activity bereft of both knowledge and passion. The mode of ignorance brings you down to the hellish planets and to the lower species, both of which are destinations the sober and rationally thinking adult would want to avoid. Since only someone who doesn't know any better would purposefully take steps that lead towards the wrong direction, the behavior in that category is described by terms such as ignorance and darkness.

On this occasion, Mahadeva's bow was to play a pivotal role in an event of pure goodness. The Supreme Lord had descended to earth to enact wonderful pastimes, one of which was about to take place. King Janaka had gathered famous princes from around the world together to take part in this contest. It wasn't known who, if anyone, was going to lift the bow. The princes understandably felt good about their chances, for they had proven their strength by administering their own governments.

There was one slight problem, though. A handsome young prince and His younger brother arrived on the scene with a renounced brahmana. The brahmana had a beard and had not come to participate in the contest. He was accompanied by the two brothers, who had protected him from attacking night-rangers in the forest. Those ghoulish creatures were steeped in the mode of ignorance, so they thought they could continue attacking the innocent sages and get away with it. Shri Rama and Lakshmana, the brothers in question, showed them the error of their ways.

Following the sage Vishvamitra, the brothers made it to Tirahuta, where they were received very well by King Janaka. He seated them in nice thrones, which gave everyone a chance to see them. You couldn't glance at Rama and Lakshmana and miss their transcendental features. They both sparkled, and the attention shifted especially towards Rama because He was older. He would be the one to try to lift the bow. The prize was the hand in marriage of the king's daughter. Neither one of the brothers was married yet, so it would have to be Rama to go first.

In the above referenced verse from the Janaki Mangala, we see some advice given to the assembled kings. It is said that Rama is sure to break the bow when He gets up from the throne. It should be noted that the contest did not stipulate that one break the bow after lifting it. Up until this time, so many princes had approached the sacrificial arena, tried to lift the bow, and then sat back down after having failed. There was no guarantee that anyone was going to lift it.

In this instance Rama's strength is deduced from His other transcendental features. As when there is smoke there is fire, when there is beauty, fame and a pious nature, there is likely strength as well. Rama appeared to have delicate features, but it was known that He and His younger brother had just defeated so many of the fiercest creatures on earth. Though they were youthful in appearance they didn't lack anything in skill. Therefore it was assumed that they would have immense strength as well.

It is surmised here that when Rama will break the bow, the kings will have their noses broken. This references the pride of the kings, as through the symbolically broken nose they will have to go home in shame. For a fighter beaming with hubris, to be bested by a youth is shameful. This was a contest after all, and for a youth who was travelling through the forest to lift and break the bow would be quite amazing.

If Rama is the Supreme Lord, why would He symbolically break other people's noses? Actually, to be humbled by Rama is a tremendous blessing. The phrase, "If you can't beat em, join em", has some relevance here. God can never be beaten. You can try to ignore His existence and chart out your own territory through applying techniques you had to acquire through your many days in the present life, but nothing is stable. The more powerful forces of nature will check you in the end, despite your best attempts.

The Supreme Lord is more powerful than that nature, so He can never be defeated. For this reason one of His many names in the Vedas is Ajita, which means one who is unconquerable. Rama would not fail on this occasion, as He would fulfill the destiny He previously created. He would lift Lord Shiva's bow and win the contest, marrying Sita Devi. That divine couple is the savior of the surrendered souls, who in humility bask in their brilliance and celebrate their triumphs.

VERSE 62

कस न पिअहु भरि लोचन रूप सुधा रसु।
करहु कृतारथ जन्म होहु कत नर पसु।।62।।

kasa na pi'ahu bhari locana rūpa sudhā rasu |
karahu kṛtāratha janma hohu kata nara pasu ||62||

"Why don't your eyes drink fully that pure, nectarean form? Get the most out of your human birth; why live like an animal?" (62)

Essay - The Human Birth

The human birth is the most auspicious because of the potential it carries for the purification of consciousness. There is no difference between souls. An animal's soul and a human's soul are the same, but differences arise in the type of body accepted. Indeed, even within the human form there are varieties to consider with respect to the output of energy. The body of a child is not nearly as capable as the body of an adult, yet we don't consider the two body types to have different souls. For the human birth there is only one way to reach a successful end, to make the experience fruitful. The greatest welfare workers are those who know this hidden gem of knowledge and then kindly pass it on to as many people as possible.

That task isn't always easy. One of the subtle elements of material nature is ego, which in its tainted form deludes the otherwise intelligent living being into thinking that they know everything. The property of "all-knowing" can only exist in someone who is all-pervading. Think of it in terms of a computer server. Only if you have a machine capable of holding every observation ever made by every person to have ever existed can you have a chance at perfect knowledge. The database doesn't guarantee you the perfection in thought, however, for you still have to know how to look up information and properly make use of it. You need the ability to recognize patterns in experiences and then know how to implement the resulting mental conclusions to alter behavior for the better.

The human being cannot be all-knowing because he cannot remember what happened a day or two ago. A few hours ago is also a little fuzzy with respect to exact timings. How then can the human being think that they are supremely wise or not in need of instruction from others? The answer is that the ahankara, or false ego, takes over and uses pride as a way to block off the good counsel others offer.

The kind-hearted saints distribute the proper information regardless of the reception. Does it really matter what someone else thinks? If we know that we are correct, isn't it our duty to instruct others on the proper way to act? Why should we pay so much concern to how others treat us, for unkindness and intolerance should have no bearing on our decision to speak the truth?

In the above referenced verse from the Janaki Mangala we have an instance of where good instruction is offered with emphasis at a time when the only all-knowing being was within eyesight. The Supreme Personality of Godhead in the avatara of Lord Rama was on the precipice of a remarkable feat. The most famous and capable kings from around the world had gathered in Janakpur to take part in a contest that would determine the husband of Janaki, the daughter of King Janaka.

She was found as a child while in the ground that the king had planned on ploughing. Because of the strange circumstances of her birth, the girl was named Sita and raised by the king as his daughter. When the time came for her marriage, Janaka decided to hold a contest, where whoever could lift an enormously heavy bow originally coming from Lord Shiva would be declared the winner.

The princes called to Janakpur were eager to show their prowess and prove their worthiness to have such a beautiful and chaste woman for a wife. Yet they were humbled by the bow, unable to even move it. Then Rama, Lakshmana and Vishvamitra arrived on the scene. Rama and Lakshmana were brothers belonging to the Ikshvaku line led at the time by King Dasharatha of Ayodhya. Vishvamitra was a venerable rishi residing in the forests at the time. The two beautiful brothers were with him to protect him from the attacks of ogres.

Shri Rama's form is described above as nectarean. If we should come upon nectar, something with a heavenly taste, it would make sense to taste it. The reference to the eyes points to the fact that the nectar from Rama in this instance came from His beautiful form. The eyes would do the drinking by looking upon Rama, getting their fill of the pure nectar. Shuddha refers to the Supreme Lord, who is above the modes of material nature. Everything about His personal self is pure, including His transcendental body.

It is also advised that one should drink this visual nectar as a means of getting the most out of the human birth. To understand and love God represents the purpose to an existence, and since the human being can take the steps to rationally understand this need, they have the most auspicious birth. The spirit soul in the human form has spent many lifetimes in previous wombs and lived the life of the animals, birds and beasts. Those lives revolve around eating, sleeping, mating and defending.

"The foolish cannot understand how a living entity can quit his body, nor can they understand what sort of body he enjoys under the spell of the modes of nature. But one whose eyes are trained in knowledge can see all this." (Lord Krishna, Bhagavad-gita, 15.10)

The human being follows the behavior of the animals when there is no attention given to worshiping God. Instead of drinking nectar with the eyes, the mouth tastes the poison that brings intoxication. The flesh of the innocent animals killed to satisfy the taste buds only further binds one to the cycle of birth and death. The itches for sense gratification are regularly scratched through illicit sex and gambling, rounding out the life of sinful behavior.

The sin is designated as such because of the effect the behavior has on consciousness. As Rama is shudda, or pure, interaction with Him is by definition sinless. Through service to Him the human being can avoid wasting the precious human birth on activities already patronized during the many previous lives.

It should be noted here that the recommendation for worshiping God relates to tasting nectar, not just to refraining from bad behavior. The call for worshiping God is not strictly tied to sitting quietly and forcing restraint on oneself. To truly transcend the animal instincts, the beautiful mental picture of Shri Rama innocently awaiting His turn in the contest comes to the rescue. Though He has the most to be proud of, Rama does not falsely inflate His ego. He is the most capable, so He doesn't need the fanfare that the other kings require prior to their attempt. He and Lakshmana are in youthful figures who have just arrived from the forest, an austere setting. The wilderness is no place for a prince, something the infamous King Pratapabhanu once found out. He accidentally ventured out into the forest one time and had the misfortune of meeting one of his old rivals, who had since taken the false guise of an ascetic. The rival then tricked the king into insulting brahmanas, which in turn caused Pratapabhanu to be cursed to take birth as a ghoulish creature named Ravana in the next life. Dasharatha's eldest son Rama would defeat that same Ravana later on.

The animal drinks up maya, or material nature, not knowing any better. The birth from the womb of the mother for the human being is like an animal birth, but with the entry into spiritual life under the guidance of the spiritual master, the second and more important birth takes place. That existence ideally culminates with the sweet vision of the Supreme Lord, a mental picture which can be created and maintained through the regular chanting of the holy names, "Hare Krishna Hare Krishna, Krishna Krishna, Hare Hare, Hare Rama Hare Rama, Rama Rama, Hare Hare".

Essay - Stop to Smell the Roses

Your life is filled with pressure. The workplace environment is especially tough, for the boss constantly asks you for things. He's not really sure what he wants every time, so when you do present the final work, he immediately makes corrections, points of fact that would have helped you more at the beginning. If you were given the proper instructions from the start, you could have done the job right the first time. Oh, and don't think that your life at home is any picnic. One of the cars won't start, or maybe someone else in the family has been in a minor car accident that requires attention. You haven't cleaned your room in a long time and bills that need to be paid are mounting up. The front button just fell off from your favorite pair of pants, so you have to get that fixed. So many issues keep coming up that you don't have any chance to breathe. But there are roses out there, pleasant things in life that can go unnoticed. A long time back, in a very tense situation the recommendation was made for the worried participants to break away from their concern to instead delight in the sweet vision of the jewel of the Raghu dynasty.

As the main character from the famous Ferris Buehler's Day Off movie noted, life moves pretty fast; if you don't take the time to stop and look around once in a while, you might miss it. In the same vein, if you don't stop to smell the roses, you won't get any delight from having them. It is easy to forget the finer things in life because of the constant worry over the future. Yet the human being has the ability to use discrimination in both thought and action. Therefore, from only a cursory review of past activities, it is seen that the little worries aren't really necessary in the end. So you have a big deadline approaching at work? In the past you had deadlines and you either met them or didn't. In the end, did it matter that much? Was the constant worrying a major factor in the outcome?

Let's say that the worrying enabled you to complete the task successfully. In that sense the attention helped you to reach the desired end. But what did that end get you? On a more abstract level, what does victory in a competition bring? Are you the superior person of this world? Are you the best at everything? Even if you do excel in a particular field, where does it lead? The loser also eats, sleeps, mates and defends, so in that sense no one is really superior to anyone else. The animal lives the life dedicated to sense gratification without all the worry. They are more efficient machines in the game of sense gratification.

The animals also compete from time to time, with the victory often coming at the cost of the opponent's life. Is this a behavior the rational thinking human being should aim to imitate? What good comes from the victory in competition, especially if there is ample food to eat in either case? The concerns over temporary achievements take primary focus in the less developed consciousness. The auspiciousness of the human birth comes from the ability to direct the essence of existence towards the root of existence. The Supreme Lord, the person most of the world refers to as God, is already superior, so why not bask in His glory instead of trying to mask it?

This was the precise issue raised many thousands of years ago. Kings from around the world had assembled in Janakpur to take part in a unique contest. A bow lay in the middle of a sacrificial arena, and it was to determine the husband for the daughter of King Janaka, who was the host of the ceremony. You may be tempted to think that the order of the participants would influence the outcome. For instance, in many of the reality television series that have contests, in each round it is usually a disadvantage to go first. The other contestants can see how the game is played by watching the first people to go, thereby gathering intelligence on what to do and what not to do. By the time the last team goes, there is familiarity with the game, which boosts performance.

With the contest in Janaka's kingdom, the ordering really didn't matter. This bow was so heavy that none of the kings could even move it. Oh sure they tried to, but one by one they were humbled by this divine weapon that initially belonged to Lord Shiva. Shri Rama, though not formally a participant in the contest, caught the eyes of the assembled people. He and His younger brother Lakshmana were there as guests of Janaka, as they had entered the city following the exalted Vishvamitra Muni.

In his Janaki Mangala, Goswami Tulsidas mentions some of the idle chatter that was going around while Rama and Lakshmana were seated on thrones watching the contest. Some of the people couldn't believe how beautiful the two sons of King Dasharatha were. Others worried that Janaka had made a grave error in taking the oath to give Sita away to whoever would lift the bow. What if Rama failed? He then would automatically be disqualified from marrying Sita.

They wanted Rama to win because His features were stunningly beautiful, as was His character. His beauty would defeat the pride of millions of cupids, and His kindness was seen in His unflinching protection He and Lakshmana offered to Vishvamitra and the other sages who resided in the forest. The eyes of the onlookers became truly valuable upon seeing Rama. Previously, the eyes were used to look upon so many other things, but now they were really paying off. "It is worth it to have a vision in order to see the beautiful Rama and Lakshmana," is what some onlookers thought.

Then there was the perspective of the competitors, the princes who had travelled from far and wide to attend the contest. Some of them noted that where there is beauty, fame and good family lineage, there is strength as well. This meant that it was inevitable that Rama would lift the bow. Since Rama was the elder brother, Lakshmana would not participate in the contest. None of Rama's other features had any flaws in them, so naturally His strength would be flawless as well.

The above referenced verse advises the competitors to give up their jealousy. Instead of fighting with God or worrying about losing the contest, let the eyes drink up fully the pure nectar that is Rama's beautiful form. To relish such a vision is the true purpose of the human birth; otherwise one remains just like an animal. The comparison applies to all aspects of life, not just competition to earn the hand of a beautiful princess. The life of sense gratification is dull and full of misery. The ills of society are all rooted in forgetfulness of God, so the only solution is to turn the eyes towards the Supreme Personality of Godhead and look upon Him with love.

How do we do that when we don't believe in God? What if we're not sure of which religion to follow? Isn't Shri Rama a personality of the Hindu faith? Actually, we can use the attributes described above as a litmus test. Obviously, if your mind is racing from the fever of material competition, you will have a difficult time appreciating God's features, as was the case with some of the competitors at the contest. Yet, at the same time, enough interaction with pure goodness, exposure to transcendental beauty and sweetness, will bring about a lasting change. The results will be so beneficial that the doubts over the divine nature of the personality in question will vanish as well.

The starting and ending points are the same: the chanting of the holy names, "Hare Krishna Hare Krishna, Krishna Krishna, Hare Hare, Hare Rama Hare Rama,

Rama Rama, Hare Hare". Association with others who can never get enough of the sweet vision of Shri Rama or one of His other Vishnu forms, including the original personality of Lord Krishna Himself, is a tremendous boon, as such devotees make recommendations similar to the one noted above. Some of the onlookers on the scene in Janakpur were so devoted to Rama that they started to chide the king for his oath. Through their sentiments alone they showed others how to live and how to fulfill the primary mission in life.

Essay - Don't Miss Your Chance

The thrill of the moment makes us forget the fact that the predicament we are so worried over will likely arise once again in the future. The nervousness over the imminent aftermath is due solely to the fear over what will happen should the result not be in our favor. Because of this short-sightedness so much attention is repeatedly given to tasks that amount to nothing in the long run, while those things which are really important, which are right in front of us, are tossed aside as being insignificant. A long time back the stakes seemed a little higher, as the outcome would determine if a beautiful princess would be brought into the family, but again there was something more important worth noticing. That beautiful gem was so rare that it wasn't guaranteed to come around again; so the observer was well-advised to really take note.

Think of the nervousness over taking an exam. Perhaps you have prepared well to take a road test to get your driver's license in a particular state. You put in the time behind the wheel, got used to the turns and how to handle the brakes, and even mastered the art of parallel parking. Now comes the time for the test. You're very nervous because you know that one slip up and you'll fail. In this particular state, you don't get to take the test every day, which means that failure to pass on this day means that you won't get another chance for a few months.

Ah, but this is actually a benefit, a fact to take comfort in. You will get another chance! Though it may take a while, though it may be after several months, eventually you'll again have the opportunity to try for the driver's license. Nevertheless, because you're not sure how you'll handle failure, you get nervous both before and during the exam. You're so worried about passing because you know that a license will open up a whole new world for you. You can drive to wherever you want without asking others for a ride. You can rent a car if you should have to travel somewhere, and you can maybe even purchase your own car and feel independent in that way.

In the game of life, these sorts of obstacles appear all the time. To be swayed by them is not very wise, for the rise of happiness and distress operates on a pattern similar to the onset of the winter and summer seasons. This notable truth is presented by Lord Krishna in the Bhagavad-gita as a way to get His cousin, Arjuna, who was hesitating to fight prior to a great battle, to understand how to remain steady in both happiness and distress.

"O son of Kunti, the nonpermanent appearance of happiness and distress, and their disappearance in due course, are like the appearance and disappearance of winter and summer seasons. They arise from sense perception, O scion of Bharata, and one must learn to tolerate them without being disturbed." (Lord Krishna, Bhagavad-gita, 2.14)

It is strange if you think about it. If the sun is not out on a particular day, you may feel sad, but you know that the clouds will part eventually. The sun was just out the day before, so why shouldn't it return? Moreover, once it does come back, there may come a time when you want it to be blocked again, for it can give off scorching hot rays that cause discomfort. The reaction to the seasons is similar. If it's really cold in the winter you long for the comforting heat of the summer, but in the summer the heat may get to you as well.

The person of steady mind is not distracted by these temporary ups and downs. Life is full of opportunities for sense gratification, so a loss on a particular day isn't so important. The same goes for victory, for we know that winning a championship in a particular sport doesn't insulate one from heartache and pain caused by failure in subsequent years. There is one aspect of life, however, that doesn't always come around, and when it does you should make the most of the rare occurrence.

"In order to deliver the pious and to annihilate the miscreants, as well as to reestablish the principles of religion, I advent Myself millennium after millennium." (Lord Krishna, Bg. 4.8)

The Supreme Personality of Godhead pervades the entire space in His unmanifested, impersonal form. This means that wherever we are we can get a glimpse of God through His external energy, as within that external force is an internal energy that has a higher potency. The living beings are considered part of the marginal potency because they are by constitution the same as the internal energy but they can be deluded by the external energy. Sort of like choosing sides in a game, the individual spirit souls can pick which energy they want for association.

On rare occasions, due to outside circumstances and also His own personal desire, the Supreme Lord descends to earth in a personal form, one that has features visually identifiable to even those who are otherwise enamored by the material nature. As Lord Rama, God took on the guise of a handsome, valiant and chivalrous warrior prince. He and His younger brother Lakshmana once made it to the town of Tirahuta, where a grand ceremony was taking place to determine the marriage for the daughter of King Janaka, Sita Devi.

Rama is known as Bhagavan because He is the most fortunate, and so anyone who has the opportunity to see His personal form is also very fortunate. At the gathering in Tirahuta, so many people from around the world got to see Rama, but there was a pretense. Famous families were in Janaka's city to take part in a contest, to see who could first lift Lord Shiva's amazingly heavy bow. Rama and Lakshmana actually arrived there as an afterthought, following the lead of the venerable Vishvamitra Muni.

King Janaka welcomed all of his guests very well, and his behavior was no different towards Vishvamitra and these two handsome youths, who were protecting the sages in the forests from the attacks of night-rangers. Janaka gave the trio thrones to sit on to watch the ceremony, which allowed the spectators to gaze upon the beautiful two sons of King Dasharatha of Ayodhya.

The observers noticed something special in both Rama and Lakshmana, and since Rama was older, they hoped that He would win the contest. He was eligible to marry Sita, but the rules stipulated that the groom must lift the bow. All sorts of emotions arose in the spectators, with some worrying whether Rama would win and others cursing the king for having taken such a vow. If that vow prevented Sita from marrying Rama, what good was it?

There were also the other princes on the scene, competitors to one another and to Rama, though the Lord was not worried in the least. He wasn't even there to compete; He just followed whatever the spiritual master Vishvamitra said. Some competitors realized that since there was beauty, fame and splendor in Rama, there was surely strength as well. This was a wise assessment that would later prove to be accurate as well.

In the above referenced verse from the Janaki Mangala of Goswami Tulsidas, the rival kings are advised to give up the competitive attitude of the animal species and instead drink up the beautiful nectar that was Rama's form sitting so innocently for everyone to see. Animals compete with each other for food, sometimes fighting to the death. But the human being has a higher intelligence, and he can gather food without having to limit resources for anyone else. Moreover, victory and defeat arrive on their own, like the coming and going of the seasons. Why put so much emphasis on something that will occur again in the future? Why not take the opportunity to bask in the rare vision of the Supreme Lord standing before you?

The ability to have this vision and take advantage of it give the human being a leg up on the other species. Just as the opportunity to take pleasure in Rama's personal presence shouldn't be missed, so the wonderful chance to regularly recite His names, "Hare Krishna Hare Krishna, Krishna Krishna, Hare Hare, Hare Rama Hare Rama, Rama Rama, Hare Hare", should not go to waste. Every person has a chance to recite this sacred formula, if not congregationally then at least to themselves. There is no cost in this most potent method of the discipline of bhakti-yoga, or devotional service, and the benefits are long lasting. Through the holy names, the same nectarean vision of Shri Rama on the precipice of marrying Sita can arrive in the mind to give supreme comfort and pleasure.

VERSE 63

दुहु दिसि राजकुमार बिराजत मुनिबर।
नील पीत पाथोज बीच जनु दिनकर।।63।।

duhu disi rājakumāra birājata munibara |
nīla pīta pāthoja bīca janu dinakara ||63||

"The princes are on the two sides of the muni, like blue and yellow lotuses with the sun in between." (63)

Essay - Daymaker

This is another reference to the sun made by Goswami Tulsidas to describe the son of Gadhi, Vishvamitra Muni. The spiritual master is the sun to brighten up the unfortunately dark consciousness of the conditioned living being. The source of the sun's effulgence is unknown to the spiritually disinclined, but the brightness of the spiritual master shines from his belief in the Supreme Personality. More than just a faith directed towards a figure of a particular spiritual tradition, in full intelligence the guru serves the Supreme Being regularly, with every thought, word and deed. Because of this his life is a symbol of sacrifice.

In this particular instance, the two young disciples accompanying the sage were already all-knowing. They had no need to accept a spiritual master, and so they voluntarily assumed the role of disciples. They were quite young, so youthful that their guardians worried about their welfare in the forest, even while under the care of the expert teacher Vishvamitra. The boys were capable bow warriors, specifically requested to quell the threat of violence that had plagued the peaceful saints residing in the forest.

What was that threat exactly? On the one side you have peaceful saints and on the opposite end are the miscreants who are more than just averse to spiritual traditions and the principles followed in them. One person may be unaware of something foreign to them, but they won't have the hubris to proclaim that they know what is going on. The miscreants, who are committed to their way of life, will go one step further and denounce the pious, proclaiming that they are a threat to society. Since they don't follow an authorized system of maintenance themselves, these fools make up dharmas on a whim, and because of this they are capable of anything.

The miscreant class was concentrated on the island of Lanka during this particular time period. They had decided that it was pious behavior to attack the sages residing in the forest. Mind you, these ascetics had no possessions, just the bark for their clothes and the thatched huts for their residence. They had no money and they weren't trying to get any. They wanted to live in peace, to stay detached from material affairs.

The night-rangers from Lanka decided to attack the saints in the dead of night, when it was hardest to be detected. They would also change their shapes at will, thereby first appearing innocent to a person who would otherwise suspect foul play. In the vulnerable state the sages were being attacked, killed, and then eaten by these vile creatures.

Vishvamitra went to Ayodhya to get the help of one particular fighter. King Dasharatha was the ruler of the town and thereby the leader of the army. The king received Vishvamitra well and promised to offer his personal protection, which would be accompanied by his massive army. But the son of Gadhi wanted only Dasharatha's eldest son Rama, who was not yet twelve years of age. On to the forest went the jewel of the Raghu dynasty, taking His younger brother Lakshmana with Him.

"Travelling along the way with the rishi they are looking so beautiful. That beautiful image lives within Tulasi's heart. When the trio was going, it looked like the sun travelling north, taking with it the spring season." (Janaki Mangala, Chand 4.2)

In his Janaki Mangala Tulsidas compared the scene of the trio departing Ayodhya to the sun travelling in the north, taking the two months of the spring season with it. The sun was referred to as dina-natha, or the lord of the day. That Rama and Lakshmana would be compared to spring is not surprising, as they would bring renewed life to an area that had suffered a winter-like period due to the attacks of night-rangers headed by Maricha.

Rama and Lakshmana would do their part, and then later at the direction of Vishvamitra they would make it to Janakpur, where a svayamvara was being held for the king's daughter, Sita Devi. King Janaka received the trio hospitably and gave them thrones to sit on. It was while they were seated that they looked like the sun rising with a blue lotus on one side and a yellow lotus on the other.

The sage and the boys weren't purposefully placed in thrones for everyone to see, but their beauty was such that no one could fail to notice them. The residents were so enchanted by Rama and Lakshmana that they knew that the reason for their existence had been met that day. They worried over the outcome of the event, wanting Rama, the elder brother, to win the contest, which required lifting an enormously heavy bow. The winner would gain Sita's hand in marriage and thus enter the family. Through their beautiful appearance, the two sons of Dasharatha had already entered the people's hearts.

Aside from being the symbol of purity and beauty, the lotus flower is notable for its behavior with respect to the sun. As soon as the sun rises in the sky, the lotus flower sprouts open and shows off its beauty. When the sun sets later on, the same lotus closes back up, as if to shun the association of anything besides its precious sun. The comparison is appropriate for this situation because Rama and Lakshmana were so dedicated to Vishvamitra. One would never think that the boys were in the superior position, though they were the Supreme Lord and His number one servant respectively.

Rama was dark in complexion, so He was like the blue lotus. Lakshmana was golden colored, so He was like the yellow lotus. In this situation Vishvamitra was the maker of the day, the sun, because he brought the vision of the two flowers to the assembly. The boys acted at the direction of the sage, just as the lotus flowers are dependent on the sun for their movements.

Through His actions the Supreme Lord pays the highest honor to the spiritual master, who is His representative on earth. That maker of the day would ask Rama to participate in the contest, to curb the pride of the many princes who had gathered there on that day. The blue lotus would easily lift the bow and win Sita's hand in marriage, automatically bringing huge smiles to the faces of the devoted onlookers, who were like lotuses to the sun of the sun-dynasty, Shri Rama.

VERSE 64

काकपच्छ रिषि परसत पानि सरोजनि।
लाल कमल जनु लालत बाल मनोजनि।।64।।

kākapaccha riṣi parasata pāni sarojani |
lāla kamala janu lālata bāla manojani ||64||

"Vishvamitra has his lotus-like hands affectionately over their hair, like red lotus flowers on baby cupid." (64)

Essay - Attention to Duty

To properly paint a picture with words, reference points are often used. They prove to be helpful, especially if the terms invoked are known to most people. In the Vedic tradition, the best picture of the Supreme Lord in all His beauty is painted through the many verses of poetry, both in the Sanskrit language and its derivatives. For issues of beauty, Kamadeva, the god of love, is often referenced, as his beauty is well-known. He is the equivalent of the commonly known cupid, so to help him instill lusty desires in others, he has lotus flowers around him. The arrows he shoots from his bow also have flowers on them, as the beautiful fragrance and sight of these natural wonders help to create an amorous mood. A long time ago, the transcendental affection shown by a spiritual master towards his child disciples could be better explained through a comparison to a young Kamadeva.

The scene in question was a grand sacrifice in the kingdom of Janakpur. A religious sacrifice is for the benefit of the Supreme Lord or one of His deputies. With a sacrifice you dedicate some time to an issue not relating to your personal interest. Even if you want to acquire something for your own comfort or you are establishing a rite of passage, the attention to religious life is there all the same, at least in the case of the pious. For instance, in the Vedic tradition the birth of a new child is celebrated with a sacrifice, for the desire of the parents is to bring auspiciousness to the occasion, to ensure that the child no longer has to suffer through birth and death.

Notice that the plea for auspiciousness does not have to relate to only personal wellbeing. The ability to have all of your amenities provided for in life does not represent the summit of existence. Rather, the advanced species that is the human being has a higher purpose to fulfill. They are the elder brother of the animal community, so they are to set a good example of tolerance, kindness, and dedication to piety. That piousness leads to a benefit for all, not just the person adherent to it. The benefit of following your occupational duty may not be readily known to someone who is sensually driven, but if we see some examples of different roles properly fulfilled, we can figure out the reason for the dedication and also the purpose behind the pleas for auspiciousness made by others.

A long time back, two sons of a famous king were on their way out into the wilderness for an indefinite period of time. They were quite young, and though they were young enough to still require adult supervision, their purpose in the forest was to defend against the attacks of the wickedest creatures on earth. The son of Gadhi, Vishvamitra Muni, had come to Ayodhya to request the protection of Shri Ramachandra, the delight of the Raghu dynasty and eldest son of King Dasharatha. After the king reluctantly agreed to allow Rama to leave, Lakshmana, the Lord's younger brother, also accompanied the group.

"They pray to God to grant them blessings: 'May You garner fame and return victorious. May You not lose a single hair while bathing.'" (Janaki Mangala, 29)

As they were leaving, the residents prayed for Rama and Lakshmana's welfare. They did not want a single hair from their heads to fall while bathing, but they also wanted them to return successful in their duties. Children are the essence of innocence, and on this occasion, they left home because of the request of a respected sage. The citizens would have been excused for only thinking of the boys' welfare, but they knew that to fulfill the higher purpose is more important.

The dedication to chivalry would create a peaceful condition in the forests for others who were carrying out their occupational duties. The brahmanas live by religious principles, and from their ability to worship God they can grant so many benedictions to the rest of society. If that dedication to piety is jeopardized by ill-motivated thieves and rogues, then the entire fabric of society crumbles.

Rama and Lakshmana successfully carried out their duties and then made it to Janakpur, where another highly pious person was carrying out his obligations. King Janaka was the host of a grand sacrifice to determine the husband for his beautiful daughter Sita. Marriage is also a religious tradition, meant to create a stable bond that can benefit both parties in terms of advancement in consciousness. The husband supported by a chaste wife can carry out his occupational duties as delineated by the Vedas and explained by the priestly class. The wife, at the same time, gets the protection she needs from her right-minded husband.

Oh, but if only finding the right boy for your daughter were easy. Janaka knew that his precious Sita deserved only the most righteous prince. Rama fit the position perfectly, as He had already protected Vishvamitra and the other munis in the forest from the worst attackers, so protecting Sita should not have been a problem for Him. Oh, and there was His beauty as well. Both Rama and Lakshmana seemed like creatures that didn't belong on earth. It seemed like the creator took all of the beauty from his palette and placed it in their forms and then used whatever little beauty he had left over for the rest of the population.

The sacrifice in Janaka's kingdom involved a contest with a bow, which originally belonged to Lord Shiva. Whoever could lift the bow first would win the contest. Many princes had already tried, but they couldn't even move it. As if on a conveyor belt, they each walked up to the bow, tried to lift it, and then offered respect to it after having failed.

Now these two handsome youths were on the scene with the sage Vishvamitra. Everyone was looking at them, for their beauty was indescribable. The affectionate sage at one point caressed their heads with his lotus-like hands. Goswami Tulsidas compares this to red lotus flowers touching baby Kamadeva, or cupid. Kamadeva is beautiful to start, but in a childlike form he is more endearing. The child is innocent, and when decorated with nice flowers the innocence is enhanced even further.

All of the related parties who followed their occupational duties would be rewarded through Rama. The pious king of Ayodhya allowed Rama and Lakshmana to leave at the insistence of the sage. Vishvamitra gave powerful mantras to the two boys after they defeated the wicked Tataka demon. And now King Janaka was going to be rewarded for holding a contest to determine the husband for his daughter.

Shri Rama, in a young form that surpassed the beauty of millions of cupids, lifted the bow easily and won Sita's hand in marriage. The goddess of fortune herself then further decorated the beautiful youth with a bluish complexion by placing the flower garland of victory around His neck. And for all of time she stays by His side as His beautiful and devoted wife. The perfect devotee Lakshmana also remains with Rama, and their number one servant, Shri Hanuman, completes the picture. That beautiful group remains with the devotees who always think of them.

CHAND 8

मनसिज मनोहर मधुर मूरति कस न सादर जोवहु।
बिनु काज राज समाज महँ तजि लाज आपु बिगोवहु।।
सिष देइ भूपति साधु भूप अनूप छबि देखन लगे।
रघुबंस कैरव चंद चितइ चकोर जिमि लोचन लगे।।8।।

manasija manohara madhura mūrati kasa na sādara jovahū |
binu kāja rāja samāja mahaṁ taji lāja āpu bigovahū ||
siṣa de'i bhūpati sādhu bhūpa anūpa chabi dekhana lage |
raghubansa kairava canda cita'i cakora jimi locana lage ||8||

"' Those sweet forms melt your heart and steal your mind, so why don't you respect it? Without accomplishing your work you come to this royal assembly, and renouncing shame you seek to ruin yourself.'" (Chand 8.1)
"Having given that advice, the saintly kings started to look at that unique picture of the moon of the lily-like Raghu dynasty, making their eyes like a Chakora bird looking at the moon." (Chand 8.2)

Essay - Have You No Shame

The picture is so sweet. Two young boys taken care of by a much older muni, all while watching a ceremony to be remembered for thousands of years into the future. The observers at the time didn't know it, but history was about to be made. The precious daughter of King Janaka was to be given away to the strongest prince in the assembly, for immense strength was required to lift up the heavy bow belonging to Lord Shiva. King Janaka had stipulated the rules of the contest, vowing to bequeath his daughter to whoever could lift this bow first. The youthful delights seated on opposite ends of the sun-like Vishvamitra were ready to join this family shortly, with the elder Rama eligible to participate in and win the contest.

This presented an issue for the other contestants. Rama and Lakshmana were no doubt beautiful. In fact, you couldn't find a flaw in them. This was the assessment made from the initial glance. We can't really tell much about a person's character by looks alone, but we can get an idea of whether or not they are favored by the creator. Nothing happens on its own. Every reaction is the result of a past action. The pistons in the car start firing at the turn of the key by the operator of the vehicle. That engine cannot roar unless there is gasoline in the tank, which requires human effort for transport.

The womb gives shelter to the embryo which eventually matures to the point that it exits into the world. That embryo could not exist without the combined action of the mother and father. Therefore nothing happens on its own, including the workings of nature. There is intelligence behind results, though we may not always see or know who that intelligent force is. The animals also don't act randomly, as they scour the land for food based on personal desire. They may look like they are running around for no reason, but they have a purpose to their actions. Though their intelligence isn't nearly as sharp as the sober human being's, there is nevertheless a specific impetus for action.

On this particular day, by noticing the beauty of the two boys escorting Vishvamitra one could tell that the creator was favorable to them. If we have natural beauty, good parentage, and strong intelligence, it is to be understood that these are the rewards of good deeds from a previous life. The spirit soul exists within all species and continues its existence after the present body is discarded. It also had a form in a different individual in a past life. The cycle continues on for as long as the desire to remain separated from the good graces of the spiritual land remains.

"Those who worship the demigods will take birth among the demigods; those who worship ghosts and spirits will take birth among such beings; those who worship ancestors go to the ancestors; and those who worship Me will live with Me." (Lord Krishna, Bhagavad-gita, 9.25)

The same point is subtly addressed in the above referenced verse from the Janaki Mangala. Even with the rival kings Rama and Lakshmana's beauty was noticed and appreciated. Rama is God, so wherever He goes He carries a glaring effulgence, a transcendental beauty that no one has ever seen before. Just the interaction, the personal presence, however, is not enough to effect change in others. It is what one does with that association that matters.

Think of being stranded in a desert without any water. It's so hot that you can't move anymore. You think that you won't survive long enough to make it to an area where there is water. Now, let's suppose that you come upon an oasis, a large supply of fresh, drinking water. The potential for the benefit exists with the water, but unless you actually drink it, you won't be in a better situation. It's sort of like looking for your car keys when you are holding them in your hand the entire time.

The admonition in the verse quoted above relates to making the best use of the divine vision standing in front of the kings. It's understandable that the rivals would be proud of their entourage, good work, and kingdom. Indeed, the more opulent your kingdom is, the better it is believed to be. King Janaka was wealthy as well, though he was known more for his perfection in mysticism, his equal disposition. He had not a hint of sin in him, and his daughter followed in his footsteps. That is why there was so much attention paid to her svayamvara, or self-choice ceremony.

The pride that comes with working hard and securing valuable possessions should not prevent one from appreciating God, who is the source of everything. He is the original proprietor, so what we call our "possessions" are actually on loan from Him, meant to be used to help move our consciousness in the right direction. There is no easier way to purify consciousness than to direct it at the Supreme Lord standing in front of you. As if to make the emancipation of the soul easier, the exact form of Godhead on display for the people in Janakpur was one that best elicited spontaneous loving affection.

The child is the essence of innocence, and though Rama wasn't a baby, He wasn't a fully grown adult at the time either. He and Lakshmana had delicate features, yet they were still strong enough to be sought out for protection by Vishvamitra, who lived in the forest at the time. The hearts were already melting in the rival kings, and the minds were stolen by the enchanting vision, so what need was there to disrespect Rama and Lakshmana?

Respect for the Supreme Lord is the precursor to spontaneous loving affection that never dies. Renouncing shame, the kings that didn't respect Rama would have to honor His strength when He would later lift up the enormously heavy bow without a problem. That same bow that previously could not be moved by the proud kings was lifted, strung and broken in a blink of an eye by the jewel of the Raghu dynasty. The onlookers that respected the beautiful form, the murti of the Supreme

Lord, got to bask in the sweetness of the vision and celebrate the marriage of the divine couple, Sita and Rama.

That same beauty can exist within the mind of the sincere worshiper. The respect for it can be shown by regularly chanting the holy names, "Hare Krishna Hare Krishna, Krishna Krishna, Hare Hare, Hare Rama Hare Rama, Rama Rama, Hare Hare". All the possessions and relationships we have will disappear at the time of death, so rather than squander the wonderful opportunity we have to stop rebirth, why not follow the divine path and show respect for the beloved protectors of the saints? Rama and Lakshmana look beautiful with Vishvamitra, and that vision can melt the hardest of hearts and slowly bring about a sober understanding of the temporary nature of this world and reveal who the original owner of all objects is.

Essay - Good Embarrassment

Embarrassment is obviously something we look to avoid, as who wants to feel small in front of others? Our false ego inflates our pride even if we have no reason to feel proud. The pauper has just as much pride in what they do as the wealthy celebrity, so whichever path supports that pride is the one generally taken. Therefore, when it is rhetorically asked, "Have you no shame?", the implication is that shame exists for a reason, and when you abandon it, you are doing so for a reason that is not justifiable, or at least not understandable. A similar kind of question was put forth many thousands of years ago in relation to a famous royal assembly.

The kings were gathered to participate in a contest. They wanted to be the first one to lift up an extremely heavy bow. The bow was not to be used as a weapon, as it could hardly be moved. Getting it to the middle of the sacrificial arena must have been difficult enough, so trying to string it and shoot arrows off of it were not in the cards. Instead, any prince just had to lift it up. The bow was magical in a sense, as it originally came from Lord Shiva, the deity of the Vedic tradition who is charged with various tasks. He came from the forehead of Lord Brahma, the creator, but he is actually not an ordinary living entity. Lord Shiva is very easily pleased, as he would rather spend his time in meditation than on paying attention to requests for benedictions. A simple leaf offered to his deity form can make a person very wealthy quickly.

But Lord Shiva has a higher wealth, which he attains through his meditation. The object of his affection always stays with him, at least in consciousness. When objects relating to Lord Shiva are placed anywhere, there is still some relation to Mahadeva's worshipable figure. Therefore it shouldn't be surprising that this bow in Janaka's kingdom would act as a sort of magnet to bring the delight of Raghu's clan. The bow had a destiny, to be lifted by Lord Rama, the Supreme Personality of Godhead in His avatara as a warrior prince.

The kings assembled in Janakpur obviously didn't know this, but they did get to see Rama in a youthful form, looking charming as ever. Though this wasn't an official state visit, Rama was there nonetheless, escorting the exalted sage Vishvamitra. The muni was a forest-dweller in a sense, for he lived in the wilderness as a way to practice his penance and austerity. So many powers come through regulation, through controlling the senses and focusing the mind. The consciousness that sees clearly sees only God, and that divine vision provides the spiritual food necessary to remain alive. In a place where delights entice the senses at every moment, that vision can get blurry very quickly, so renunciation is a good way to go for a spiritualist looking to advance in consciousness.

Vishvamitra's reward for his penance was the personal protection of Shri Rama, who was accompanied by His younger brother Lakshmana. Lakshmana was like a twin to Rama, except He had a fair complexion, while Rama was dark. The muni took his twin protectors with him to Janakpur, where the group received a warm welcome from the host of the ceremony, King Janaka. The boys and their preceptor were given royal thrones to sit on to watch the ceremony, and it was during this time that others started to notice them.

The kings looked to size up their competition, to see what they were up against. The different sentiments of the kings are reviewed in the Janaki Mangala, a poem authored by Goswami Tulsidas that glorifies the event . In the above referenced verse, we get one style of sentiment, wherein kings who have not changed their hearts after looking at the beautiful boys are being admonished.

The vision was so sweet that it stole the mind and melted the heart. This reaction was instant, and it can only take place when one sees God. But seeing Him is not enough. From that beautiful vision should come a change in consciousness, and thus a different way of thinking. The kings who did appreciate the vision of Rama and Lakshmana admonished the kings who didn't. In their estimation, the people who weren't instantly devoted to those beautiful forms were wasting their time. They had come to Janakpur for no reason, as they would never win the contest. In addition, they were abandoning shame by not having respect for God, and they were ruining themselves in the process.

Seems like a rather harsh assessment for a single moment's transgression, no? Actually, our existence is meant for tasting the sweet fruit of the Supreme Lord's association. If after seeing Rama, who would surely win the contest, the other kings still thought they were better, why were they living? They wouldn't win because, as other kings noted, where there is fame, good family heritage, and beauty, strength will surely exist as well. So many princes had already tried to lift the bow, but none of them could even move it. If you know you're going to lose, and you see that the person who will defeat you is so enchanting and wears a sweet and innocent smile, why wouldn't you surrender and give up your competitive attitude?

In this situation, shame would have been a good thing. The embarrassment over the transgression of not appreciating Rama would lead to devotion to God. That is always a good thing, for if we can be defeated in our attempts to surpass the Supreme Lord's strength, we will gain a better understanding of our actual position. As knowing is half the battle, if we know where we really stand, we will be better informed when making future decisions. These kings were renouncing their shame and continuing with their obstinance, which in turn would ruin them.

The sweet association of Shri Rama is available in so many different ways, but the stipulation is that one must desire to appreciate it. I can show someone the most beautiful painting in the world, but if their vision is clouded by hatred, jealousy, intoxication, or some other strong negative influence, they will never appreciate what is in front of them. Despite the most ardent persuasion, they will not budge from their position of defiance.

Sadly, everything will be ruined if this willful defiance continues with respect to devotional service, which is man's real occupational duty. The objects of the senses are only temporarily manifest, and in the next life the cycle repeats itself. On the other hand, the Supreme Lord and His beauty and splendor never dissipate. Truth of this fact is seen in the Janaki Mangala itself, which continues to celebrate that wonderful day in King Janaka's court, where Shri Rama lifted up Shiva's bow and won the hand of the king's daughter, Sita Devi. That mind-stealing vision of Rama and Lakshmana manifests before the eyes of the devoted soul who listens to the pastimes of the Supreme Lord with a guileless heart, showing respect for the sages who follow in the mood of devotion shown by Vishvamitra Muni.

Essay - When The Night Has Fallen

The kairava flower is the white lotus, which is unique because it opens up at the sight of the moon. The lotus flower commonly invoked by poets of the bhakti school symbolizes spontaneous and dependent devotion to the Supreme Lord. During the day the sunshine causes the lotus flower to open up, and then at night, when the sun falls, the lotus closes up, as if to say it only lives for its beautiful sun, the giver of life.

In the dark night, it is the moon to provide the soothing rays of hope. The kairava, the white lotus, opens up at the sight of the bright moon, showing that nothing else in the night can give it happiness. In the dark night the Chakora bird also fixes its gaze upon the moon, not looking at anything else. In this way there is strict dependency and also loyalty. If we tell someone else that we can't live without them, to back up our statement, we will not look anywhere else for happiness. The exclusive devotion shows the object of affection that the attention they get is special, and at the same time that style of worship gives the worshiper pleasure, for they know that they are honoring the relationship they hold so dear.

A long time ago, a gathering of saintly kings made their eyes like the Chakora bird, except the moon they were looking at was a person. Since He was the moon of His dynasty, He was known as Ramachandra. Since He was the Supreme Personality of Godhead manifesting Himself in a seemingly human form, His activities were celebrated during His time. He continues to be remembered and honored to this day through the devotees who sing of His glories and chant His holy names, "Hare Krishna Hare Krishna, Krishna Krishna, Hare Hare, Hare Rama Hare Rama, Rama Rama, Hare Hare".

The Raghu dynasty itself was like the kairava flower, or water-lily, spreading its beauty throughout the world. In the above referenced verse, Goswami Tulsidas compares Rama to the moon of that lily-like dynasty because the glory, fame, strength, prestige, and protection of that dynasty opened up and spread with the appearance of Shri Rama, who was the moon of that dynasty, which happened to originate with the sun.

The kings looking at the beautiful son of King Dasharatha were gathered in Janakpur to take part in a contest. King Janaka was hosting the event and he promised to give away his beautiful daughter Sita to whoever could lift a very heavy bow. Some of the assembled kings viewed Rama as part of the competition, but then others developed a spontaneous attraction to Him, harboring love for both He and His younger brother Lakshmana, who were both there accompanied by the sage Vishvamitra.

Rama and Lakshmana must have presented a unique picture at which to look for the natural competitive attitude to subside in the kings. The royal dynasties from around the world were there for one reason: to win the contest. Think of competing in a sporting event that you've prepared for quite a while beforehand. You're ready to compete, you've trained hard, and you know that victory will prove that you are very capable in your particular sport.

The need to show off his strength is more important in a king. The winner of this contest would show that he was uniquely strong and that with that strength he could protect the new wife, who had delicate features and feminine beauty that was unmatched. For that competitive attitude focused on victory to vanish at the mere sight of something, that object had to have unique features.

The brothers had this effect on people, with Rama garnering more attention because He was to participate in the contest. Some of the kings advised other kings to give up their opposition and surrender to the beautiful image. They were admonished for abandoning their shame and not worshiping Rama, who was God standing right before them.

The saintly kings not only abandoned their competitive attitude, they kept looking at Rama with devotion. Their eyes were like the Chakora bird, which has no other source of sustenance than the moon. That dedication would not harm them in the end, though Rama would raise the bow and win Sita's hand. His accomplishment was more pleasurable to the saintly kings than winning for themselves. The unique picture of the Supreme Lord reuniting with His pleasure potency expansion is for the pleasure of the eyes, whose lens is cleared by devotion.

In the degraded state, the eyes can't see the influence of the Divine. Though not a single blade of grass can move without Rama's influence, the stubborn mind thinks that the individual is responsible for all the results seen in life. Because of this defective mindset, there can only be misery, as man cannot control every outcome. Try as hard as you can, but you can never get a complete handle on things. The kings assembled in Janakpur are an example to prove this fact. They thought they were strong enough to lift the bow, but none of them could even move it. Then along came this youth with His even more youthful younger brother. The brothers were not supposed to participate, as they only arrived there following the sage's lead.

The kings kept their eyes fixed on the brothers, considering the external surroundings to be like darkness. Can you stare at something that you can't see? In the dark night there are many other objects around, but they cannot be seen because of the absence of light. The Chakora bird points its eyes only towards the soothing light of the moon, ignoring the objects in the darkness. Even those things which are illuminated by the moon are considered unimportant by the devoted Chakora.

The eyes of the saintly kings were like a magnet naturally attracted to the beautiful form of Lord Rama, who was seated next to Lakshmana and Vishvamitra. The area of interest was packed with so many people, so it wasn't as if the kings were seated in a serene setting where concentration is easier to establish. But the vision of Shri Rama has that effect, creating a connection in consciousness with those who are pure of heart.

Where there is fame, beauty, and splendor, there is likely strength as well. Shri Rama is the greatest coordinator, and He planned this event to curb the false pride of the rival kings and delight the hearts and minds of the sincere souls gathered there that day. He continues to shine His bright rays to the population of this and many other planets through His holy names, the saints which chant them, and the pastimes recorded in Vedic literature.

VERSE 65

पुर नर नारि निहारहिं रघुकुल दीपहि।
दोषु नेहबस देहिं बिदेह महीपहि।।65।।

pura nara nāri nihārahiṁ raghukula dīpahi |
doṣu nehabasa dehiṁ bideha mahīpahi ||65||

"The men and women of the city are staring at the lamp of Raghu's family with love, while they give a bad look to the king of Videha." (65)

Essay - Shooting Daggers

On one side there is love, and on the other strong disappointment. One vision gives so much joy and happiness that the person opposing that pleasant vision is instantly blamed for his mistake. Of course there was no mistake, but due to strong affection the people of the town began to worry over what might happen. What if their newfound visitor, who became the joy of their life, emerged a failure due to the king's stubbornness? In that case the fault would lie with the king and not anyone else. Seeing this handsome youth, the king should have immediately taken back his word, and no one would have minded.

The word in this case was the vow to give away his daughter to whoever could lift an extremely heavy bow. King Janaka was the host of the ceremony in the kingdom of Videha, and aside from being known for his mastery over the senses, the famous ruler was known to never tell a lie. He lived by his word, so when it was declared that his beautiful daughter Sita would wed whoever would first lift a bow belonging to Lord Shiva, it was understood that the contest was legitimate. A simple measure of strength was all it would take; nothing else.

All seemed well and good until Shri Rama arrived on the scene. He is described through so many terms because He is the Supreme Personality of Godhead. Can one name suffice for the person who has limitless transcendental features? How can we only pick one way to describe Him, for through experiences our mind's preoccupation changes all the time? One second we are worried about finishing an assignment for school and the next we're concerned over the future of our financial situation.

The changes occur rapidly, and depending on how those changes manifest, we can take the same periods of time to be either long or short. For instance, four years spent in college seem a lot longer than four years spent at the same job as an adult. Expanding to an even larger scale, twelve years of schooling prior to college seem much longer than twelve years of working. The difference, of course, is in perspective, as the maturation process brings a more marked change in the individual when they are younger.

If you work at the same company or the same occupation for a long time, there aren't many external changes that allow you to gauge progress, or even notice it. In school there is always the beginning of the subsequent year, where you take new classes and interact with new people. That might not be the case with your occupation in adult life; thus making time go by a lot faster.

So depending on where you are in life, you may have particular things that interest you, items and issues that you take to be of paramount importance. As God is the supreme everything, He can be worshiped at any point in one's life. To the residents of the town hosting this ceremony, the focus was particularly on strength and qualities conducive to being a good ruler. Sita would be given away to a prince after all, and his duty would be to protect Janaka's precious gem.

Sita was just as qualified in truthfulness, austerity, cleanliness and mercy as her father. She is never bereft of these qualities because she is eternally the goddess of fortune, the consort of the Supreme Lord. She gives Him more pleasure than anyone else can, and as a byproduct of her position, she has all glorious attributes. Janaka was the right match to have as a father for Sita, who was found one day in the ground while Janaka was preparing for a sacrifice.

She was thus technically his adopted daughter, but that did not get in the way of his fatherly duties. If anything, the manner in which he found Sita made Janaka even more affectionate. It is one thing to love your biological offspring, for it is nature's way to have a bond with people who are connected to you in blood. But the adopted son or daughter didn't automatically belong to your family, so when you show them the same affection, the love is actually stronger.

Janaka didn't want to give Sita away, but the age was right for her marriage, and if he kept her unmarried he'd invite scorn to his family. The princes arriving in Janakpur were fully capable, but none of them could even move the bow. Then came Shri Rama, who in the above referenced verse is described as the light of the Raghu family. This is a significant statement because Raghu's family was already splendorous, as the dynasty originated from the sun-god, Vivasvan. His son was Manu, and his son was Ikshvaku, who in turn set the standard for good government.

Rama was considered the light of the Raghu family because He made it even more famous. His brightness spread through His transcendental features, which were all splendorous. When the sun shines bright in the sky, it's influence is impossible to miss. Even if you're not in direct contact with the sunlight, you know that the sun has an effect based on the heat that results.

In a similar manner, Rama's splendor was shown off immediately upon His arrival in Janaka's city. The residents with pure eyes could not get enough of the Supreme Lord, who was accompanied by His younger brother Lakshmana. The two were escorting Vishvamitra Muni, who outwardly acted as their preceptor. Their youth made the brothers more charming to look at, and since Rama was the elder of the two, He was eligible to take part in the contest and marry Sita.

In the course of day-to-day affairs, if someone really angers us, if they behave badly or insult us in some way, our dislike of them makes us automatically treat others better. This is just part of human nature, as the disliked's association creates a noticeable contrast with the people who don't behave poorly towards us. It's like tasting something really bitter one second and then something sweet the next. The sweetness of the second item is a constant, but since the bitter taste was just there, it feels like the sweetness is stronger while tasting.

For the residents in Janakpur, the situation was sort of reversed. The sweetness of Rama's vision was so nice that when looking at Janaka next they immediately felt dismay. They were angry that he had created a situation where this delightful youth could possibly lose the contest. Or worse yet, what if Rama got hurt trying to lift the heavy bow? His bodily features were so delicate that no one wanted any harm to come to them.

"They pray to God to grant them blessings: 'May You garner fame and return victorious. May You not lose a single hair while bathing.'" (Janaki Mangala, 29)

The residents of Ayodhya had a similar affection for Rama, whom they knew since His initial appearance on earth. When the delight of mother Kausalya left Ayodhya with Lakshmana and Vishvamitra, the people of the town gathered by the road and prayed for their welfare. They prayed to God to protect the two boys and allow them to return successful. They did not want a single strand of hair to fall off them while bathing.

The brothers left with Vishvamitra for the forest to protect the sages against the attacks of the night-rangers, who used illusion as their strongest weapon. They would change shapes at will and sometimes become unseen, making it easier to pounce on the sacrifices of the sages, who were looking for a quiet setting that was more conducive to spiritual advancement.

Rama would prove His ability by defeating the female demon Tataka. Though she tried her tricks of illusion, becoming invisible and then visible, just by using sound Rama was able to locate her and shoot her with His arrows. Though He was reluctant to fight with a female, at the insistence of Vishvamitra He ended her life and thus gave the sages the protection they desired.

In Janakpur, lifting the bow of Lord Shiva would be no problem for Rama, but the residents didn't know this. His beauty mesmerized them, and so they didn't want Him to leave their sight. "Let Him win the contest so that He can enter our extended family. This will make us happy."

Any strong leader will regularly take criticism, for that is part of life at the top. Sharp criticism from dependents is part of the league in which the leaders play, and it's an indication of the authority they wield. If these leaders weren't important, there would be no need for anyone to complain.

Janaka absorbed these daggers shot by the eyes of the residents who loved Rama so much upon first glance. He decided to continue on with the contest, though he was kicking himself a little too. Shri Rama, the savior of the fallen souls, who remains by the side of the devotees who cherish His association, would not disappoint. He would win the contest, marry Sita, and live happily in the hearts of the residents who looked upon Him with love. The same king who was previously cursed suddenly became the most celebrated person for having been the instrument to bring the light of Raghu's family together with Sita.

VERSE 66

एक कहहिं भल भूप देहु जनि दूषन।
नृप न सोह बिनु बचन नाक बिनु भूषन।।66।।

eka kahahiṁ bhala bhūpa dehu jani dūṣana |
nṛpa na soha binu bacana nāka binu bhūṣana ||66||

"One group is saying: 'The king is good and shouldn't be spoken of poorly. Just as a nose does not look good without a ring, so the king does not look good when his word has no meaning.'" (66)

Essay - Complementary Objects

The clothes go with the person wearing them. For a king the clothes correspond with his leadership, with the way that he administers the kingdom. The clothes are an ornament to complete the picture. Just like their integral paraphernalia, the word of the king is what establishes his high standing. Breaking that word is never good, and therefore the king shouldn't be overly criticized when he holds firm to his vow.

Many thousands of years ago King Janaka held firm to a particular vow, and this resulted in so many different opinions. The controversy first arose with the arrival of an enchanting figure, who was accompanied by His younger brother and His preceptor. The disciple in this case is actually the spiritual master of the three worlds, the original truth. He is the source of the ultimate system of knowledge known as Vedanta, which has truths not found in any other discipline.

The supremacy of Vedanta is rooted in its founder, who didn't concoct any information. He didn't have to learn anything, so whatever He first spoke was automatically flawless. Those who accepted Vedanta from Him or through someone in that chain of disciplic succession thus accepted conclusions to be utilized for finding the summit of happiness. In this sense Vedanta is all-encompassing; it covers every aspect of life. Whether one is large or small, young or old, or male or female is of no concern, because each individual is represented by their spirit soul, their basis for identity.

"I am seated in everyone's heart, and from Me come remembrance, knowledge and forgetfulness. By all the Vedas am I to be known; indeed I am the compiler of Vedanta, and I am the knower of the Vedas." (Lord Krishna, Bhagavad-gita, 15.15)

This kind youth accepted a spiritual master as a formality, to show others that high knowledge comes not from mental speculation but from intentional and humble submission before a bona fide teacher. This kind attention to the saintly class was one reason He was dear to the inhabitants of the city He entered.

There were also many more features to increase the transcendental delight of the onlookers. The youth was escorting the venerable Vishvamitra Muni because the sage required protection from nishacharas, or night-rangers. If you fight in the night it's difficult for your opponent to see you. Also, the nighttime is generally reserved for sinful activity and those who live by it. Thus the peaceful sages had the odds stacked against them in the forest that was suddenly infiltrated by these ghoulish creatures of the night.

Though of a young age, Shri Rama, the jewel of the Raghu dynasty, could still defeat these demons. Vishvamitra knew this, so that is why he went to Ayodhya to specifically request the king to part with Rama's company for a short while. The younger brother Lakshmana accompanied Rama, making for a sweet picture when the trio entered Janakpur, where a grand contest was taking place.

The contest was the source of the controversy amongst some in the assembly. The contest related to who would marry the daughter of King Janaka, the host of the ceremony. The first person to lift a massively heavy bow would be crowned the victor and be garlanded by Sita Devi, the precious daughter of the king. Therefore so many royal families traveled to Janakpur to try to win the contest and enhance the fame of their dynasty.

Yet when people saw Rama, His ability to defend, and His kind attention to the guru, they were taken with Him immediately. Add to the fact that Rama's beauty was out of this world and you can understand why so many started to worry over the outcome of the contest. "What if Rama doesn't win? What if King Janaka's vow results in Rama becoming ineligible to marry Sita?" Some in the crowd started giving Janaka a negative look, in a sense shooting daggers at him with their eyes.

In the above referenced verse from the Janaki Mangala, some are stepping up to say that Janaka doesn't deserve blame. He should not be spoken about negatively because he was virtuous. Prior to this event he was famous around the world for having a renounced attitude, carrying out his obligations without attachment. If it weren't for his fame and high standing, the many people who were there that day would never have bothered to show up. One person's arrival shouldn't change Janaka's standing. Whoever did or didn't come to the ceremony shouldn't figure in the character of the king.

It is said that a king without his word is like a nose without a ring. The ring in the nose gives special beauty to that part of the face, acting as an integral ornament, especially for women. If the king went back on his promise, it would be like losing part of his clothes, like being embarrassed in front of everyone. It is important for the leader to avoid embarrassment because he must be respected by the subjects. If an authority figure is not respected, they lose their authority and subsequently their ability to administer justice.

If Janaka suspended the rules and gave Sita away to Rama, his word would have been broken. It was his dedication to piety that caused him to hold the contest in the first place. That contest brought Rama, the Supreme Lord, to his kingdom, so in this sense his vow is what led to the potential for the transcendental bliss of having God's association. Therefore upholding his word and staying true to the rules of the contest was the right way to go.

Shri Rama would validate that decision by lifting the enormously heavy bow and winning Sita's hand. The symbolic ring of truth got to stay in the nose of the king, whose stature was enhanced by welcoming Shri Rama to his family. The devoted souls bask in the Supreme Lord's association, and so for them Shri Rama upholds their vows while carrying out His own desires in the process.

VERSE 67

हमरें जान जनेस बहुत भल कीन्हेउ।
पन मिस लोचन लाहु सबन्हि कहँ दीन्हेउ॥67॥

hamareṁ jāna janesa bahuta bhala kīnhe'u |
pana misa locana lāhu sabanhi kahaṁ dīnhe'u ||67||

"'I know that the king, the lord of the people, has done a very good thing, for his vow has brought the pleasing vision, the fruit of the eyes, to everyone here.'"
(67)

Essay - A Good Deed

Something previously thought to be unwise turns out to be a blessing when there is a benefit received. "If such and such had never happened, then I never would have met such and such person." Fill in the blanks with many such occurrences and outcomes to create variations of the same sentiment, but the general idea is pretty easy to understand. What you thought was harmful to you ended up to be in your favor, so the initial act itself was not bad. When that final outcome is the best one possible, then all past mistakes and experiences that were thought to be unpleasant turn out to be great blessings.

The ultimate benefit is to receive the fruit of your existence. A fruit is the result of work, the manifestation of the reward intended for a specific task. For instance, a plant is considered pious if it bears fruits. Strange to think, but in the Vedic tradition the trees that don't produce any fruits are considered sinful. This is because they serve no higher purpose. Perhaps they provide shade and oxygen to the world, but in general these trees don't make good use of their existence.

An existence is marked by the presence of spirit, which is a vibrant force that cannot be killed. You can't remove spirit, take away its existence, make it wet, cut it up, or change any of its properties. However, the spirit soul can travel into different forms, which in turn can limit the exercise of ability. This is only true of individual fragments of spirit, not of the original storehouse.

How can there be a difference between the two? If I have a clay pot and suddenly it breaks into thousands of pieces, is not the pot's existence removed? Don't I need to merge all the pieces together to get the whole again? Such laws exist in the material world, as the drop of ocean water is a sample of the entire ocean. At the same time, you take enough drops away and you no longer have an ocean.

With the storehouse of spiritual energy, every expansion does nothing to diminish its original size. In fact, that size is infinite, so there is no way to measure its aura. Since the fragments come from it, they are part of its definition, but they are still separate. Hence the true relationship between the individual fragments and the whole is described as achintya-bhedabheda-tattva, or the truth that there is a simultaneous oneness and difference between the spirit souls and the origin of spirit, a oneness that is inconceivable to the mind.

The fragments inherit the properties of the original, but to a smaller degree. There is also the defect in that the natural properties of blissfulness, eternity and full knowledge can be masked by the form accepted, sort of like how a shade can dampen the light emitted by a burning bulb. Nevertheless, the properties of the spiritual spark indicate a penchant towards activity, with an ultimate desire for happiness. To receive the fruit of one's existence is to taste transcendental sweetness through abilities given by nature.

Just as the tree that produces fruits shows that its ability to exist can create something that is enjoyable, the human being who is given eyes with which to see can produce transcendental sweetness internally by looking upon something out of this world. This is what occurred in a kingdom a long time ago, and some of the residents were keen to pick up on what was going on. There were differing opinions on the situation because of the nature of the day. A king's daughter was to be given away in marriage, but there was one particular person attending the event that everyone was focused on. They wanted Him to marry the precious daughter Sita, but due to the king's vow the desired result wasn't guaranteed.

The contest ultimately rested on the word of the king. Janaka said he would give Sita away to whoever could lift an amazingly heavy bow, one that took hundreds of men just to carry into the sacrificial arena. The problem was that King Dasharatha's son Rama entered the assembly accompanied by His younger brother Lakshmana and spiritual guide Vishvamitra. The brothers were identical in appearance except for bodily complexion. Rama was dark, while Lakshmana was fair, but both were extraordinarily beautiful. In youthful forms, they captured the attention of the pure-hearted citizens who had gathered to witness history.

As is understandable in a large gathering, there were murmurs in the crowd. Some people started to curse the king for having made the contest. What if Rama couldn't lift the bow? Then it would be Janaka's fault for preventing the marriage everyone wanted to see. If Janaka hadn't remained so truthful to his promise all his life, the contest could be called off and Rama could marry Sita. Even Janaka wanted this, showing how beautiful Rama was. The young prince of Ayodhya had every good quality imaginable, including chivalry and the ability to protect the saintly class from the vilest creatures of the world.

In the above referenced verse from the Janaki Mangala, we get a different opinion from some of the people in the crowd. This group says that King Janaka has done a very wonderful thing, for his contest created the condition that brought Rama and Lakshmana there. In reality, the boys were just following the direction of the forest-dwelling spiritual master, Vishvamitra, but if there wasn't something major going down, the sage would not have brought the boys to Janakpur that day.

The sight of the two brothers was so pleasing that it was like receiving the fruit of the eyes, tasting transcendental nectar in the form of a wonderful vision. Whoever was responsible for creating the situation deserved credit, whether they did it intentionally or not. Since it was Janaka's vow that allowed so many people to be gathered in one place and receive the fruit of their existence, the king could be thought of as a saintly character who spread the message of divine love inadvertently. There are many ways to find that transcendental connection, with one of the easiest being sight. Since there were so many people there, the reason for living got to show off His transcendental features to many people at one time.

In the same vein, if we should taste the fruit of our existence one day, we should know that whatever conditions that led to that auspicious end turned out to be beneficial. This means that the many days spent in misery and turmoil can be turned into a positive if they bring us to the lotus feet of a devotee of the same Shri Rama, who is the Supreme Lord in His manifestation as a warrior prince. We also know from the Vedas that the spirit soul travels through many bodies in what is known as reincarnation. This process continues for as long as the fruit of existence isn't tasted, so by having the divine connection we can also make the many previous births worth it. Going forward, in whatever womb we accept, in whatever land we call home, the divine connection remains.

The fortunate residents of Janakpur and the gathered attendees got to keep the divine vision of Rama in their minds by staring at Him. The happiness would increase further when Rama would lift and break the bow in question and win Sita's hand in marriage. To relive that wonderful experience in the mind, the wise souls regularly chant the names of Sita's husband found in the sacred maha-mantra, "Hare Krishna Hare Krishna, Krishna Krishna, Hare Hare, Hare Rama Hare Rama, Rama Rama, Hare Hare". The tongue, the eyes and the ears are all put to good use with this chanting, and the mind stays positively situated by tasting the fruit of existence in the form of God's vision.

VERSE 68

अस सुकृती नरनाहु जो मन अभिलाषिहि।
सो पुरइहिं जगदीस परज पन राखिहि।।68।।

asa sukṛtī naranāhu jo mana abhilāṣihi |
so pura'ihiṁ jagadīsa paraja pana rākhihi ||68||

"'Just as good deeds give people whatever their mind desires, so God will deliver to the people through the king's protecting his vow.'" (68)

Essay - Sukriti

The joke is sometimes made that no good deed goes unpunished, which can mean that once you do something nice for someone, you will likely be punished in the future by them approaching you to do something for them again. Either that or the good deed will go unappreciated, with the recipient complaining about what you did for them. If you had never stepped forward to offer your service out of kindness, you wouldn't have had to deal with the future inconvenience. Real sukriti, however, does not go to waste. Good deeds bring meritorious credits that lead to one's benefit. It's difficult to remember this truth while you're carrying out your good deed, but that is why it's helpful to have others around to remind you.

When would you need to remember this? When your commitment to righteous behavior is threatened through some unforeseen circumstance, the tendency is to bail, to take shelter of your immediate emotions. For example, think of fasting on a particular day to gain some benefit. Fasting is part of religious traditions around the world, and in the Vedas there are many fasting regulations recommended. If you control your urges to eat on a specific auspicious occasion, your mind will be better geared towards focusing on the Supreme Lord. That remembrance is the real boon of the human form of life, as with conscious thought developed to the max you can choose where to focus your efforts. If they are shifted towards a transcendental realm governed by an all-powerful figure of unmatched benevolence, then you're obviously making good use of your discrimination.

If the fast calls for total abstention from food, it is natural to get the urge to eat during the day. "What is it going to hurt me if I have one tiny thing to eat? Is God going to all of a sudden hate me? Will He punish me because I broke the rules of the fast out of intense hunger? I did make a vow this morning not to eat anything, but all this food around me is just too tempting to pass up." To injure oneself to the point that you can't function is never the intended aim of a fast, but at the same time, the original vow helps to bring one the auspicious merits they're looking for. As best you can, if you can carry through on your vow, especially in the spiritual context, you will achieve a good result.

King Janaka always stayed true to his vow. Not only in relation to fasting, but in all aspects of occupational duty, or dharma. He was a king, but this didn't mean that he was free of duties in righteousness. If anything, his enhanced stature made him a larger target. More people would scrutinize his behavior, so this meant that if he slipped from the pious path, his subjects would take that as license to break the rules in their own lives. The thief feels validated when they see higher authorities engage in theft. "If they are allowed to get away with stealing, why shouldn't I? I'm not doing anything they aren't doing."

On the flip side, when the king follows his vow to uphold righteousness through his own conduct, so many benefits accumulate, which then trickle down to the rest of society. Think of it in terms of the policeman or firefighter. These public officials have vowed to protect the innocent and put out blazing fires. In times of emergency, if they do their job, the citizens are satisfied. If they fail to uphold their vow, then everyone gets hurt. This is the general rule with dharma. You follow it and you're benefitted. If not, you're harmed.

The gray areas are what make this dedication difficult. What if you're in a situation that seems like it's okay to break the rules just one time? This is what the pious Janaka faced one time. Indeed, many of his citizens were urging him to break his vow previously announced to the world. The king had a beautiful daughter who had recently reached an age appropriate for marriage. She was of such splendid character that Janaka couldn't decide on a proper husband for her. After consulting with his royal priests, he decided to hold a contest.

Janaka vowed to give Sita away to whichever prince would be the first to lift an extremely heavy bow belonging to Lord Shiva. The king was famous throughout the world for his control over the senses and his dedication to piety, so everyone took his vow seriously. They packed up provisions, assembled the royal family members, and headed straight for Janaka's city. They knew that the king wasn't lying, so if a prince in their family could lift the bow, the beautiful Sita Devi would enter their family.

A chaste wife coming from a noble family is considered a great blessing. Through her own dedication to piety, the new wife ensures that the family life is supported and that the husband is happy in his daily affairs. The pious wife can even keep the husband on the straightened path, should he feel the desire to stray. Though the husband may feel like he's getting nagged, the closeness in the relationship allows the wife to correct errant behavior that would otherwise go uncommented on. This puts her in a unique and powerful position.

As an example, it is considered rude to chew food with one's mouth wide open. The sound that results is very annoying to others, and the behavior mimics that of animals like dogs, who are not civilized enough to know how to eat properly. A good wife who loves her husband will immediately correct this behavior, reminding him that eating in such a way is not good. The ability to chew is not hindered when the mouth is closed, so the annoying sounds from eating and sipping with the mouth open are not necessary.

Janaka made the vow, but things got really interesting when a beautiful youth with a bluish complexion entered the city. He wasn't there for the contest. Vishvamitra Muni was using this young boy and His younger brother Lakshmana as protection in the forest against vile rangers of the night who had been harassing the innocent sages for too long. Though the kind youths were only following their spiritual master, they looked prime to participate in the contest. Neither of them were married, and since Rama was the elder, He could try to lift the bow to win Sita's hand. Before any of these thoughts could enter the minds of the observers, the wonderful beauty of both Rama and Lakshmana was noticed. It was mesmerizing, and many of the people realized that they were tasting the fruit of their existence. At that very moment they were finally understanding why God gave them eyes.

With the intense attachment that formed instantly and spontaneously, many people started to worry about the contest. The elder brother Rama was so beautiful and youthful, so how could He lift the bow? Sure, He had just killed attacking Rakshasas in the forest, but His immediate vision was sort of a paradox. Everyone wanted to protect Rama when seeing Him, instead of the other way around. Lakshmana was identical in appearance except for complexion. So such a beautiful sight lay before the eyes of the pure-hearted residents protected by King Janaka, and now they wanted to make sure to never lose that vision again. Their joy could only be enhanced if Rama were to win the contest and marry Sita.

Ah, but that was the issue. The king made a vow. If not for his promise, all these people wouldn't have arrived in Janakpur. If not for the king's dedication to piety, Vishvamitra wouldn't have considered it necessary to visit him, taking Rama and Lakshmana with him. So many opinions thus circled, with some cursing the king for his vow and others standing up for him, saying that his vow is what brought Rama and Lakshmana to Janakpur.

In the above referenced verse from the Janaki Mangala we get another viewpoint that is sympathetic to Janaka. It says that pious deeds, sukriti, bring whatever the mind desires, so in the same way God Himself will ensure that happiness will abound by Janaka protecting his vow. The vow was a kind of pious deed anyway, and all deeds rooted in legitimate piety are initially instituted by the Supreme Lord. Therefore He is the distributor of good fortune to those who follow sukriti.

This viewpoint was indeed correct, for more than one reason. Shri Rama is the very same Supreme Lord, so He would personally protect King Janaka's vow. There was no need for concern, for even in a youthful figure Bhagavan exhibits immense strength. The youthful son of King Dasharatha would lift the extremely heavy bow without a problem, winning Sita's hand in marriage. The people would get what they wanted, and it was originally arranged by Janaka's vow. He stayed true to it in the presence of the Supreme Lord, and everyone was duly rewarded for it.

VERSE 69

प्रथम सुनत जो राउ राम गुन-रूपहि।
बोलि ब्याहि सिय देत दोष नहिं भूपहि।।69।।

prathama sunata jo rā'u rāma guna-rūpahi |
boli byāhi siya deta doṣa nahiṁ bhūpahi ||69||

"' If the king had first heard of Rama's wonderful qualities and beauty, he would have called for Sita to marry Him, and nobody would have faulted him for it.'" (69)

Essay - King's Oath

King Janaka was in the public eye. As the leader of a historic country, everyone watched his every move. This is the burden that accompanies leadership. If you're the leader, everything that you do is scrutinized, and since you have authority, people will complain about you a lot. It's only natural, for if something goes wrong you will get the blame. If things go well, then that is the norm, or at least the expected condition. Thus there is not as much attention given to the leader in good times, but when there is trouble, when there is doubt as to the proper course of action, all eyes turn to the leader to see if they can redress the situation. A long time ago the king was faced with a very difficult decision, a predicament that seemed to be of his own making.

Was there a foreign attack? Were the citizens suddenly without work? Was there a drought? These issues certainly are important, but for the group of spectators gathered at arguably the most famous event in history, the problem related to the future fortunes of the king's daughter. Known as Sita, she was the cherished possession of King Janaka. He and his wife Sunayana were childless for a long time until one day when Janaka found a baby girl in the ground while ploughing a field.

The field was to serve as grounds for a sacrifice, which is intended to please the higher authorities. The highest authority is the Supreme Lord, who is known as the lord of all creatures. At the beginning of the creation, He advised man to perform sacrifices so that they would find all good things in life. It is easy to get distracted by temporary pursuits. You let go of an object from your hand and it falls to the ground. You pluck a flower from a plant and now you have control of it. You take a banana from a tree and enjoy the resulting taste. In this way you start to think that you are the ultimate controller of your own fortunes, that you and you alone steer the ship.

"In the beginning of creation, the Lord of all creatures sent forth generations of men and demigods, along with sacrifices for Vishnu, and blessed them by saying, 'Be thou happy by this yajna [sacrifice] because its performance will bestow upon you all desirable things.'" (Lord Krishna, Bhagavad-gita, 3.10)

Of course lost in these sequences of action and reaction is the fact that these objects had to come from somewhere. Indeed, the body that we call home had to develop in someone else's womb. That initial placement and then subsequent development occurred without our sanction. We had no say in where we took birth or even in how we'd be protected in the early years. These and many other facts that prove how little control we have are recognized through discipline in spiritual practice.

Yajna, or sacrifice, is one of the central components of the eternal occupation known as sanatana-dharma because it takes care of many issues simultaneously. You perform a ritual to bring auspiciousness from higher beings. This automatically takes time away from sensual pursuits that further the erroneous thinking that you are the sole cause of your fortunes and the only person worthy of enjoying the most. The sacrifice also allows you to hear the holy names of the higher beings, including the chief, who is called Narayana among many other names. He is also known as Prajapati, or the lord of all created living beings.

Janaka found auspiciousness before the sacrifice ever took place. That young baby girl in the ground was so precious that the king, who was known throughout the world for his dispassion, immediately had parental affection for her as he held her in his arms. The higher authorities, awaiting the sacrifice from Janaka, arrived on the scene to confirm that the discovered baby was indeed his daughter. She was Janaka's in all righteousness, or dharma, which was something the king lived by.

"Since he was childless, and due to affection for me, he placed me on his lap and said, 'This is my child.' Thus he developed feelings of love and affection for me." (Sita Devi speaking to Anasuya, Valmiki Ramayana, Ayodhya Kand, 118.30)

Janaka named the girl Sita because she came from the ground, and with his wife he raised her to be just as pious as he was. She was not formally educated in the Vedas, but she knew all about dharma. Thus Sita was ready to be given away in marriage when the time was right. But Janaka couldn't find a suitable match. The unique circumstances of Sita's appearance in Janaka's family precluded the king from giving her away to just anyone. She truly was a fortune wrapped up in a bundle of joy, so only someone deserving of that fortune should be graced with her company.

Janaka made a fateful decision, one that would lead to a story that pure hearted souls never tire of retelling. They already know how the story begins and ends, and yet they won't miss an opportunity to hear about it again. If no one is around to act as an audience, the mind of the saint will go through the sequence of events again just to derive so much pleasure. And isn't that what life is about, being happy? Know that from the divine sports documented in the Vedas, the consciousness can reach a blissful condition under any circumstance.

The decision was made that Sita would wed whoever could lift an extremely heavy bow belonging to Lord Shiva. Just to bring that bow to the middle of the arena in Janakpur required hundreds of men. Therefore only a person sent from above, who was chosen by the higher authorities, would be able to lift it.

Hearing of the king's oath, princes from around the world came to Janaka's capital city. They were from different kinds of families, but they all seemed up to the challenge. They would be bitterly disappointed, as one by one they approached the bow only to be humbled by it. They couldn't even move it.

A trio arriving from the forest really caused a stir. They did not come with the usual fanfare of a royal assembly. In fact, they weren't specifically there to take part in the contest. The group was led by Vishvamitra Muni, an ascetic who called the forest his home. With him were two youths, sons of King Dasharatha. They were beautiful in every way, and despite having delicate features, they were known to be wonderful protectors. Vishvamitra had chosen them to act as escorts in the forest, to give protection against the attacks of the evil night-rangers who feasted on human flesh.

Rama was the elder brother and Lakshmana the younger. Both were unmarried, so it was protocol that Rama would have to get married first. Hence He was eligible to participate in the contest. The residents began to gripe to themselves when they saw Rama. He was so beautiful that they instantly knew that their eyes were tasting the fruit of their existence. With such a wonderful jewel in front of them, focus turned towards protection. How were they going to secure the vision in front of them? How were they going to make sure that Rama never left their sights?

They all wanted Him to marry Sita, but that little thing known as the king's oath was in the way. With such a strong affection for Rama, some of the residents took to giving the king dirty looks. The contest's rules now jeopardized the marriage everyone wanted to see. Why had the king done that? And why now was he sticking to his promise? Why not just call the contest off and give Sita to Rama?

In the above referenced verse from the Janaki Mangala we get a different viewpoint from within the crowd. Some of the people were understanding enough to know that the king hadn't really done anything wrong. If he had seen Rama prior to the contest, if he had noticed the Lord's wonderful divine qualities, he surely would have given Sita away to Him. And if Janaka had done that, no one would have faulted him at all. In fact, they would have praised him for making such a wise decision.

But you can't turn back the clock. The contest was already set, and since the king lived by dharma, he wasn't going to go back on his word. Not to fear, though, as his dedication to dharma is what initially brought the wonderful fortune of Sita Devi into his life, so now that same deference would bring her husband for life, Shri Rama, into the family. Sita is the goddess of fortune, and Rama is the person she serves without fail, the Supreme Lord. Thus the king's contest served as a way to glorify the lord of creatures, who would step up and effortlessly lift the extremely heavy bow. Sita would place the garland of victory on Rama, and the previously worried spectators would taste even more transcendental bliss.

VERSE 70

अब करि पइज पंच महँ जो पन त्यागै।
बिधि गति जानि न जाइ अजसु जग जागै।।70।।

aba kari pa'ija pañca maham̐ jo pana tyāgai |
bidhi gati jāni na jā'i ajasu jaga jāgai ||70||

"' If he now abandons his oath, after having announced it to the people, his infamy would spread throughout the world. No one knows the ways of the creator.'" (70)

Essay - Strange Are His Ways

The ways of the creator are a mystery. One baby is born completely healthy while another has defects. One child grows up to be just fine, escaping the dangers created by the threefold miseries of life, while another is constantly in trouble from disease, natural disasters, and the influence of other living entities. One king a long time ago had a particularly interesting life, especially in relation to his daughter. Coming to him under odd circumstances, the issue of her marriage would be equally as interesting. The anticipation reached a crescendo at the final moments, as it appeared that the king had made a mistake.

The daughter came to the king from the ground. We might tell our children that babies come from the mailman or the supermarket, but this is done to avoid the topic of the birds and the bees, sex life. King Janaka's daughter was indeed found in the ground. She was still alive, amazingly enough. The king was in the process of cultivating the field for a religious sacrifice. Obviously an odd place to find a human being, the king couldn't believe what he was seeing. He held her in his arms after wiping the dust from her face, and he immediately felt parental affection for her.

The next important moment in their lives was her marriage. She reached an appropriate age, and so the king had to decide who would protect her for the rest of her life. She was something special. He named her Sita because she came from the ground, and now it was time to part ways. In the Vedic tradition, the wife is considered to be part of the husband's family. She essentially renounces her ties to her original family, as her occupational duty is to serve her husband. The good king and his wife taught these principles to Sita during childhood, so she was more than ready to accept her responsibility.

But the king felt like a rich man about to become poor. He decided that no ordinary prince was worthy of his exceptional daughter. Therefore he took a vow in front of everyone that the lifter of Lord Shiva's bow would win Sita's hand. News spread around the world and royal caravans arrived in King Janaka's city for the contest. They did so on a matter of trust. The king took an oath, so there was no way he was going to break it. We board the airplane slated for an intended destination because we trust the airline. We believe that they will take us to the place they say they will. If we don't trust them, why board the airplane?

In a similar manner, these royal families believed Janaka. He had a proven track record on the issue of virtue. Thus they knew all they had to do was lift this enormously heavy bow. Seemed simple enough, no? The residents of the town gathered and watched as one prince after another attempted to lift the bow and then failed. No big deal, as everything was going according to plan. But as we remember, the ways of the creator, who is responsible for the bodies we assume and the circumstances we end up in, are impossible to predict.

Suddenly, two handsome youths appeared on the scene. Their entourage consisted of a sage who called the forest his home. The boys were princes, so they were eligible for the contest, but they had arrived there at the sage's direction. King Janaka was known to be hospitable to brahmanas, so he immediately welcomed the trio. Upon seeing the two brothers, Janaka's mind was taken. He became lost in an ocean of transcendental bliss.

This was due to the fact that the brothers, Rama and Lakshmana, were God and His number one servant respectively. Janaka's daughter Sita was the goddess of fortune, so unbeknownst to him, Janaka was involved in coordinating the reunion between God and His wife in the real-life play known as the Ramayana. Janaka's reaction is natural for a pure-hearted person who sees God. Indeed, he also had the proper reaction when he found Sita as a baby.

There were a few problems, however. Janaka did not know the divine natures of the people involved; nor was he confident that Rama could lift the bow. This meant that the vow, which was responsible for this entire assembly, could turn out to harm him. This boy Rama, the elder of the two and thus the one eligible for the contest, was perfect for Sita. If Janaka had known of Him beforehand, he never would have drawn up the contest. He would have given Sita over to Him immediately.

The people of the town talked amongst themselves as this was going on, and Goswami Tulsidas kindly eavesdrops to let us know what they were saying. One group was cursing the king for his vow, while another was empathetic to his plight. In the above referenced verse, we see that someone is saying that the king would awaken infamy for himself throughout the world if he should go back on his word. Moreover, the king had no idea that Rama, the perfect match, would arrive. The ways of the creator are impossible to predict, so we can't just change our mind later on to suit our whims.

Time and circumstance play an important role in Vedic rituals. The king's vow was also very important; it was in line with dharma, or virtue. To go off of sense impulses, without any consideration for the impact changes have on others, is not a very wise course. In this instance, Rama Himself coordinated the events, which meant that the last-minute dilemma served to enhance the fame of the event. If Janaka had just given Sita over to Rama, the marriage ceremony may not be as well remembered today. It was better for Rama, in a youthful and beautiful form, to lift an amazingly heavy bow without a problem, showing the world that He was the only match for the beautiful Sita Devi, the daughter of that virtuous king who held true to his vow and thus satisfied all the parties involved.

VERSE 71

अजहुँ अवसि रघुनंदन चाप चढ़ाउब।
ब्याह उछाह सुमंगल त्रिभुवन गाउब॥71॥

ajahuṁ avasi raghunandana cāpa caṛhā'uba |
byāha uchāha sumaṅgala tribhuvana gā'uba ||71||

"' Today Rama will definitely lift the bow, and the three worlds will sing of the supreme auspiciousness of the marriage with excitement.'" (71)

Essay - I Will Write You a Song

If you really want to honor somebody, how would you do it? Would you praise them in front of others? This is the method employed by winners at awards ceremonies. They feel humbled by the honor of receiving the award, and so to show their gratitude they offer up praise to those people they feel are deserving of it. The champion athlete thanks the members of the team, which include the trainer, the coach, the spouse, and the parents. The actor will praise the cast and crew of the production and the winning politician the members of their campaign staff. Such honor lasts for but only a moment, so one way to continue the praise going forward is to use song.

It should make sense if you think about it. As Shakespeare says, brevity is the soul of wit, so the less words you can use to convey a point, the better the presentation will be. The message will also resonate better; it will be easier to recall to the mind. Say, for instance, we want to praise the brightness of the sky. We can either write a four-page dissertation on the inner-workings of the elements in the sky or we can write a short two-line poem describing the same. The dissertation provides a lot more information; it is obviously more detailed. But the defect is that it will only be read once or twice. The poem, on the other hand, can be committed to memory. This means that you could hear the same poem day after day and derive pleasure from it. The person offering the praise feels pleasure, and to hear something of value praised by others is also pleasurable.

An even better method is to turn the poem into a song. A melody is much easier to remember than specific lyrics. So many songs we have memorized, but we likely don't know all the specific words. The melody is easier to recall, and thus the song is pleasing when we sing it from within. If the content is improved, that same tendency can be used to remember the glories of something that is noteworthy. No one is more noteworthy than the Supreme Lord, and so the exalted saints, those on the highest platform of transcendental knowledge, prefer the route of composing songs.

"While churning the butter, mother Yashoda was singing about the childhood activities of Krishna. It was formerly a custom that if one wanted to remember something constantly, he would transform it into poetry or have this done by a professional poet. It appears that mother Yashoda did not want to forget Krishna's activities at any time." (Shrila Prabhupada, Shrimad Bhagavatam, 10.9.1-2 Purport)

As an example, mother Yashoda a long time back would compose songs while she was working during the day. She was not a Vedic scholar or a poet by trade. She was a simple-hearted mother living in the farm community of Vrindavana. Her son happened to be the delight of the town and also the origin of the creation. As His enchanting form was all-attractive, He was known as Krishna. This is another name for God. There is no difference between any of the popular faiths with respect to the Supreme Deity. God is always the same; it's just that sometimes His features aren't described fully.

Krishna is considered the best name for God, because what can be better than supreme attractiveness? In Vrindavana this beauty shone through in the features of His tiny body and also in His activities. To better be able to remember those pastimes, Yashoda composed songs while churning butter in the daytime. The song is the highest honor to pay to someone, because it is a way to both give praise and ensure that the outputted item remains relevant into the future. Others can hear those songs, commit them to memory, and then sing them.

Many year's prior to Krishna's advent, the same Supreme Lord walked this earth in His incarnation as a warrior prince named Rama. There were many notable events in Rama's life, with one of them being His marriage to the goddess of fortune, Sita Devi. Sita was Janaka's daughter and her marriage ceremony was not ordinary in the least. She was an extraordinary princess, so the pious king decided to hold a contest to find a suitable husband for her. The rules of the contest were simple: lift an extremely heavy bow belonging to Lord Shiva. The first person to lift it wins.

There was some nervous conversation in the crowd on the day of the contest, however. One prince in particular caught everyone's attention, and His features were so wonderful that people started to wonder whether the contest was a good idea. "This youth named Rama is the perfect match for Sita. He is beautiful, charming, kind, and a protector against the worst kinds of enemies. He is accompanied by His equally beautiful younger brother Lakshmana and the sage Vishvamitra. If Rama can protect the sages in the forest from the attacking night-rangers, then surely He will be able to protect Janaka's precious daughter for the rest of her life."

But what if Rama couldn't lift the bow? Some in the crowd wanted Janaka to renounce his vow, while others knew that this wasn't a good option. The king was famous throughout the world for his dedication to the truth. The only reason so many princes arrived for the contest was their faith in Janaka's word, that he would indeed give Sita away to whoever could lift the bow. If he suddenly called off the contest and gave Sita to Rama, it would raise suspicions.

In the above referenced verse from the Janaki Mangala, one group in the crowd states that Rama will definitely raise the bow. With that amazing feat, the three worlds will sing of His glories with excitement. The three worlds are the heavenly planets, the earth, and the hellish planets. These areas are part of the material creation, meaning they go through the cycle of creation, maintenance, and annihilation. For fame to spread worldwide is certainly noteworthy, but as Rama is

God and capable of out of this world feats, news of His lifting of the bow would reach the heavenly and hellish realms as well.

This prediction would turn out to be true, as Rama's glories are still sung to this day. The Janaki Mangala itself is a songbook authored by Goswami Tulsidas for the purpose of glorifying the occasion of Sita and Rama's marriage. The central component of that marriage was the contest, which required the lifting of the bow by Rama. Thus the Supreme Lord offered help in the glorification process, as He knows that the soul's dharma, or essential characteristic, is service to the Divine. In the conditioned state, the Divine aspect is absent, and there is just service. Since no target is as perfect as God, the service jumps from one area to another, in lifetime after lifetime, until finally there is service to God in what is known as bhakti-yoga.

Singing of Rama's glories in pure love is bhakti-yoga; it never fails to bring pleasure to the singer. As the world today is full of diverse languages and cultures, a single mantra has been recommended for song. It can be spoken repeatedly on a set of japa beads or it can be sung out loud with others, in a call-and-response fashion. Whatever method preferred, the maha-mantra, "Hare Krishna Hare Krishna, Krishna Krishna, Hare Hare, Hare Rama Hare Rama, Rama Rama, Hare Hare", brings the soul the pleasure it craves.

VERSE 72

लागि झरोखन्ह झाँकहिं भूपति भामिनि।
कहत बचन रद लसहिं दमक जनु दामिनि॥72॥

lāgi jharokhanha jhāṁkahiṁ bhūpati bhāmini |
kahata bacana rada lasahiṁ damaka janu dāmini ||72||

"From their window perch, the wives of the royal court are peeking out. While talking, their shiny teeth look like lightning." (72)

Essay - Shining Like Lightning

In this scene the handsome youth of a dark complexion has captured the attention of the many people gathered in King Janaka's court. The boy, who is the eldest son of King Dasharatha and the elder brother of the fair-skinned Lakshmana, hasn't specifically done anything noteworthy yet. He is not even here for the contest; He was accompanying the exalted sage Vishvamitra in the forest. Yet His subdued nature combined with His amazing beauty has given birth to many a conversation within the audience, which includes the wives of the royal court. They can't help but peek out to see what is going on.

The topic of their conversation is King Janaka's daughter's marriage. This is a svayamvara, or self-choice ceremony. The wife gets to marry a prince from amongst a group. The marriage arrangement was not settled beforehand; so there was a choice to be made. During these times, princesses sometimes would get to pick the husband just based on looks. This is what occurred once with a svayamvara arranged by Shri Hari, God Himself.

Narada Muni, who can be likened to a mendicant space traveller, was once swelling with pride over having conquered lust. To defeat kama, or material desire, is very difficult, but it is possible with focus in bhakti-yoga, or devotional service. Narada is so accomplished in the yoga of divine love that he is an authority on its practice; he teaches others how to follow the same line of work. He carries around his vina and always sings the glories of Narayana, which is another name for God.

On this occasion, Narada's pride was a little much, so to bring him down a peg, Shri Hari used His energy to create a majestic city that was hosting a self-choice ceremony. The bride to be was so beautiful that she caught Narada's attention. He immediately forgot his previous triumph over kama and decided that he must have her. Despite the temporary fall from grace, Narada was always faithful to his occupational duty, devotional service. Though he knew he shouldn't desire the hand of this beautiful woman, he prayed to Hari for favor. He asked that the woman pick him from among the princes assembled. Hari, in a clever play on words, agreed to Narada's request, saying that He would do what was best for the sage.

What was best for Narada was to lose the contest, so when the princess saw him, she saw that his face was like a monkey. Immediately she turned away and chose another prince, who was Hari Himself. Narada later found out about the deception and became very angry. Only many years later would he find out the reason for Hari's intervention and how it was all done for his own benefit.

In Sita's svayamvara, the winner would be determined through a test of strength. King Janaka vowed that Sita would wed whoever could first lift Lord Shiva's bow. This was no ordinary bow; it took many men just to move it to the sacrificial arena. Sort of like pregame talk before the Super Bowl, the people gathered to watch the contest started to size up the many participants. They were interested to see who could lift the bow and who Sita would spend the rest of her life with. She was Janaka's pride and joy, his most valued possession. He didn't want to give her away, as he felt like a rich man about to lose his fortune. Nevertheless, his attention to dharma guided him in the proper direction.

The royal wives were watching from above, perched on the balconies with the windows open. They were especially taken by Rama, as they could tell He was something special. Depending on the mental disposition of a woman, she will find particular qualities attractive in a man. As these were pious women devoted to their husbands, they took chivalry, bravery and overall goodness to be very attractive. In Rama they found these qualities to exist at the highest level, so they couldn't stop talking about Him.

From that talk their mouths were open, and their shiny teeth aligned together to look like streaks of lightning from afar. The lightning is notable because its brightness contrasts with the darkness of the storm cloud. In the same way, this kind of lightning stood out, meaning that people could tell from afar that the women were talking. Based solely on His external features they wanted Rama to win the contest. Rama is God Himself, an incarnation of the Divine as pointed out by the Vedas, the ancient scriptures of India.

The attention on Rama also gave birth to some apprehension. What if Rama couldn't win? What if He couldn't lift the bow? He had proven His fighting ability previously in the forest, defending Vishvamitra from the attacks of the night-rangers, vile creatures who could change their shapes at will to fatally wound the most innocent members of society, the priests. But fighting was one thing; this contest relied completely on the strength of the arms. How was this beautiful youth going to lift the bow and win Sita's hand?

The teeth of the women that shone like lightning would remain visible to all when Rama would lift the bow and wed Sita. These gabbing women would have plenty to talk about for the rest of their lives. And so would all the people present on that day, as saints never tire of hearing of the Supreme Lord's triumphs, especially when they occur in unlikely situations. Goswami Tulsidas immortalized that chatter in his famous poems, and so we are fortunate to be able to go back in time whenever we want, to a moment when the eyes of the world were focused on God in a shining moment of glory.

CHAND 9

जनु दमक दामिनि रूप रति मद निदरि सुंदरि सोहहीं।
मुनि ढिग देखाए सखिन्ह कुँवर बिलोकि छबि मन मोहहीं।।
सिय मातु हरषी निरखि सुषमा अति अलौकिक रामकी।
हिय कहति कहँ धनु कुँअर कहँ बिपरीत गति बिधि बाम की।।9।।

janu damaka dāmini rūpa rati mada nidari sundari sohahiṁ |
muni ḍhiga dekhā'e sakhinha kuṁvara biloki chabi mana mohahiṁ ||
siya mātu haraṣī nirakhi suṣamā ati alaukika rāmakī |
hiya kahati kahaṁ dhanu kuṁara kahaṁ biparīta gati bidhi bāma kī ||9||

"Their faces shining like lightning are so beautiful that they defeat the pride of Rati. The queen and her friends are looking at the two princes with the muni, a picture that enchants the mind." (Chand 9.1)

"Staring at Rama's divine beauty made Sita's mother so happy in the heart. She says, 'This bow is heavy and this youth is tender, so the Creator desires the wrong outcome.'" (Chand 9.2)

Essay - Friends of the Queen

There are distinct ways to pass time depending on situation. Say, for instance, you are in a doctor's office waiting for an appointment. Waiting is invariably the case, as the doctor is almost always full with patients, accepting more people than they can handle. Thus the waiting room becomes your resting area for a certain period of time. While there you might watch what is on the television, read the magazines that are on the table, or talk to other people waiting for the doctor. Yet these activities aren't the primary focus, and once the situation is changed, you probably don't miss your previous experience. In a ceremony to determine a marriage a long time ago, there was much to look at to pass the time, but one vision was so wonderful that it would stay with the attendees for the rest of their lives.

We can think of it another way. Say that you work in an office with people who like to go out to eat lunch. You work hard during the morning, so you look forward to getting out and just relaxing in the afternoon. The problem, of course, is in choosing where to eat. Some people have dietary restrictions, while others refuse to go to certain restaurants based on their opinion of them. Perhaps you then settle on a compromise area, a place everyone can agree on. No one would consider this their favorite place, and they likely wouldn't eat there if the circumstances were different, but for the time being it will do.

The visit to the restaurant is a kind of interest, and these sorts of compromise interests exist in so many different situations. In Janakpur a long time ago it may have appeared that the interested women of the royal court were just passing the time staring at two handsome youths who were escorts to a respected muni, but it was more than that. The event was to determine the husband of the king's daughter. The king was named Janaka and his daughter Sita. Royal families from around the world arrived due to the unique way in which the marriage would be determined. The typical method of using horoscopes of the prospective bride and groom was not used. The family ancestries were not compared, and neither were the qualities of the princes taken into account. Rather, the eligibility for marriage relied solely on one thing: the ability to lift an extremely heavy bow.

Thus it was quite natural for the people watching the contest to size up the participants. "Oh, look at this person. They appear very strong. Oh, look at that person. They don't appear as strong, but see how beautiful they are. Oh, that person belongs to a wonderful family, so they would be an ideal match for Sita." Much fanfare surrounded the event, as so many royal entourages arrived in King Janaka's capital city. Yet it was the group that lacked any fanfare in arrival that garnered the most attention.

And from where were they coming? Did they bring a caravan? Was this like an official state visit? On the contrary, this group was led by a muni who called the forest his home. The peaceful setting of the wilderness is conducive to spiritual life, especially activity in the mode of goodness. The three modes of nature govern all material activity. In simple terms we can think of goodness as that which leads to true knowledge, passion to a neutral state, and ignorance to a degradation of the consciousness. As no one intentionally prefers to become less intelligent, the mode of goodness is always the preferred route. Ignorance and passion get in the way of cognizance of this fact, and so to be able to practice methods belonging to the mode of goodness is considered a boon.

"The mode of goodness conditions one to happiness, passion conditions him to the fruits of action, and ignorance to madness." (Lord Krishna, Bhagavad-gita, 14.9)

The muni in question, Vishvamitra, had a problem with man-eaters mired in the mode of ignorance who were disrupting his religious observances. The same went for the other munis who called the forest their home. Vishvamitra asked to have two sons of King Dasharatha as his bodyguards. They were quite young at the time, so they could be considered his disciples as well. To please the spiritual master is the quickest way to make progress in developing consciousness, and these boys never failed to follow Vishvamitra's requests. They actually didn't need to progress in anything since the elder was the Supreme Lord Himself and the younger the servitor God, the origin of all spiritual masters.

Rama and Lakshmana by name, the brothers came to Janakpur by following Vishvamitra. This was after they successfully removed the fears of the munis in the forest. They had to defeat and kill the man-eaters, and this was a noteworthy task. Rama and Lakshmana were up to it because they were expert bow warriors. When they arrived in Janakpur, people couldn't take their eyes off of them. The vision was a paradox. You had the innocence of youth, with delicate and beautiful features all across the body. And these boys were also fighters; so how were they able to protect the sages? And they had not a hint of pride or sin in them. They were protectors of dharma, or religiosity, so they never did anything that went against the standard moral codes.

In the above referenced verse from the Janaki Mangala, it is said that the females of the royal court were so beautiful that their faces shone like lightning. In the Vedic tradition, Madana, or Cupid, is said to be very beautiful. He can arouse amorous feelings in others through the arrows that he shoots, and the spring season is his most potent weapon to aid him in this task. Madana's wife is known as Rati, and she is also amazingly beautiful. Yet here it is said that the women of the royal court could defeat the pride of Rati with their beauty. Their shining faces added a nice touch to the scene.

They, along with Sita's mother and her attendants [sakhis], intently stared at the two princes from Ayodhya, who were with Vishvamitra. It is said that what they were looking at enchanted the mind. This vision wasn't merely a way to pass the time, to fill the void until the contest actually took place. Rather, in this oddest of settings, the people of Janakpur tasted the fruit of their existence. To see God and hold affection for Him is a wonderful boon, fulfilling life's ultimate aim. The human being can use discrimination, so when they see something that is divine, they can alter their behavior going forward to keep that vision in front of them. The necessary tool in this endeavor is the mind, which can conjure up any image, from any time period, at any time.

That we can go back to that famous day and bring to mind Rama and Lakshmana proves this fact. The saints write devotional literature to help facilitate this. The incident of Sita's wedding became famous throughout the world, and accounts of it are found in the ancient Sanskrit poem called the Ramayana. Tulsidas wrote the Janaki Mangala anyway as an exercise in remembrance of God. He painted a wonderful scene that could be used to both pass the time and derive pleasure at any moment. The Supreme Lord's beauty has a lasting influence, and to remember Him is the most worthwhile activity.

Essay - The Wrong Outcome

Though in this scene the laments of a woman give the impression that she is more simple-minded than most, her expressions of unhappiness actually reveal her high level of intelligence. Only a fool would think that the innumerable outcomes that occur every second are due solely to the individual's will. We may make the choice to act in a certain way, but the outcome is never guaranteed. There are other forces of nature, autonomous beings at that, and also the laws within the nature that one must abide by. Gravity is a simple force that is taken for granted, but the living being must operate according to its direction. Gravity is but one small example to prove the fact that there is a Creator who is responsible for outcomes. Sita's mother was well aware of this, and since the situation looked dire, she was not happy with the outcome the Creator had given.

"In the beginning of creation, the Lord of all creatures sent forth generations of men and demigods, along with sacrifices for Vishnu, and blessed them by saying, 'Be thou happy by this yajna [sacrifice] because its performance will bestow upon you all desirable things.'" (Lord Krishna, Bhagavad-gita, 3.10)

In the Bhagavad-gita, Lord Krishna says that at the beginning of time, the Lord of creatures set in place the system of sacrifice. Along with the items to be sacrificed were the honored personalities, the entities to enjoy the offerings. If God created the system, why would He appoint others to act as the enjoyers? Why not just have a single destination for all offerings? Why not create a single pathway for sacrifice?

The intent is to gradually build a high level of intelligence. In the immediate vicinity we see outcomes that seem to be affected by actions at the local level. For instance, I decide that I will lift my hand, and voila, my hand moves up. I decide to get up, and the next moment I arise. There is an illusion to this stream of cause-and-effect, as what is not seen is the initial cause. I am in my body right now, but my form was not always this large. At one point in time I was inside of my mother's womb, which meant that I required a smaller body in order to fit into that tiny space. Prior to that I was in another body, at a time and a place that remain a mystery.

To help us break away from the illusion, to understand that there are higher forces responsible for the results to action, the system of sacrifice was put into place. Sacrifice already exists in society to some degree or another. The electricity in the house doesn't appear by magic. One must pay tribute to the electric company in order to receive electricity. The same goes for the cable and internet services. In the community at large, there are the taxes paid to the government. The system of sacrifice instituted by Lord Krishna is the way to pay honor to the highest governing authority.

The government exists to carry out specific functions. They are not to enjoy the tax revenue for themselves. The money is supposed to be used for roads, bridges, schools, and most importantly, defense. In a similar manner, the demigods who accept the sacrificial offerings made by the living entities on earth are in charge of various departments. The topmost demigod is Lord Brahma, who is referred to as the Creator in the Vedas. He is the creator in that he is charged with populating the earth. He is not the original Personality of Godhead, nor is he immortal in his present form, but nevertheless all creatures on earth can trace their ancestry back to him.

As a painter has their palette of colors, so Lord Brahma has the three modes of material nature to use in creating. Depending on the species that is desired, more or less of certain ingredients are used. The animals are mostly in the mode of ignorance, while the human beings are mostly in the mode of passion. The governing officials, the demigods, are mostly in the mode of goodness. Thus the wise souls, who understand that God exists and that He delegates responsibilities to authority figures, know that every creature and every outcome is ultimately due to the will of the Creator.

In the circumstance in question, the wife of King Janaka was awaiting the outcome to a bow-lifting contest. The bow was very heavy. It took hundreds of men just to move it into the assembly. The winner would have to lift the bow. The first one to do this would win the prize of Sita's hand in marriage. Sita was Janaka's beloved daughter, and her qualities are so splendid that there are prayers offered to her in the same way that they are offered to God.

In the Vedic tradition, there are thousands of names assigned to God by the devotees. The devotees do this as a way to remember and honor Him. To remember God is the best activity, and so to create more avenues for remembrance, the pious souls give so many names to the Supreme Lord. Each name references an attribute or a specific activity performed by God. The attributes relate to features that we already know of, such as beauty, wealth, strength, fame, wisdom and renunciation. As attributes can be used in limitless ways, there are limitless names for God.

Sita is considered on an equal level with God because she is His eternal consort. She loves Him purely, without any personal motive. God is the energetic, and Sita is the energy. Krishna is God, and He has many expansions and incarnations, and in the same way, there are different forms of Sita, such as Goddess Lakshmi and Shrimati Radharani. There are limitless attributes in Sita that are referenced by the devotees when they offer prayers to her.

In this particular situation, Sita was on earth enacting pastimes to coincide with her husband Rama's. Rama was to be the future husband, as no one had lifted the bow yet. Janaka's wife saw the presently unmarried Rama in the assembly in Janakpur. He was a beautiful youth at the time, so the queen started to worry over the outcome. We don't expect young children to lift heavy objects. If anything, we worry over their safety when they are in front of something heavy. And now here was Rama ready to try to lift the bow that no prince had even moved an inch. How was He not going to get hurt?

The queen lamented the hand of fate, how the Creator had left them and desired an outcome opposite to what should have been. She was correct in remembering the Creator and how he is responsible for outcomes, but what she didn't realize was that Rama was the Supreme Lord, the destined husband for her daughter Sita. He and His younger brother Lakshmana had already defeated the most powerful ogres in the world when the innocent sages in the forest were attacked. The same Rama was ready to lift Shiva's bow to the amazement of the onlookers. The simple-minded queen would be wonderfully elated at the outcome she never thought was possible.

VERSE 73

कहि प्रिय बचन सखिन्ह सन रानि बिसूरति।
कहाँ कठिन सिव धनुष कहाँ मृदु मूरति।।73।।

kahi priya bacana sakhinha sana rāni bisūrati |
kahāṁ kaṭhina siva dhanuṣa kahāṁ mṛdu mūrati ||73||

"The queen lovingly said to her friends in amazement, 'How heavy is Shiva's bow and how soft and gentle is the form of this prince.'" (73)

Essay - Two Worlds Colliding

A youth is not expected to be strong. When the child first emerges from the womb, they are so helpless that you have to hold their head up and watch over them at all times to make sure they don't find danger. They can't feed themselves and neither can they move to any place on their own. The mother who nurtured the child while in the womb thus has an automatic tie of affection. No matter how mature the child later becomes, she always remembers the helpless infant that required constant supervision.

How was a young prince who had just arrived in the assembly going to lift a bow of a massive weight? The queen was amazed beyond belief at the dichotomy. Her daughter Sita was to wed the first prince to lift the bow, which belonged to Lord Shiva, a famous deity of the Vedic tradition. He is the god of the mode of ignorance, which means that the ghosts, goblins, and evil-doers worship him for benefits. Every person is provided religion by God; no one is shut out. Depending on their level of intelligence, they may not be open to the idea of worship in the mode of goodness, wherein one follows duty for the sake of virtue, not expecting a personal result for their dedication.

"Of sacrifices, that sacrifice performed according to duty and to scriptural rules, and with no expectation of reward, is of the nature of goodness." (Lord Krishna, Bhagavad-gita, 17.11)

The three modes of material nature are goodness, passion and ignorance. The bodies assumed by the living entities are composed of these modes, as are their activities. Worship is a kind of activity, as is charity, sacrifice, penance, etc. All acts that fall under the umbrella of religion fall into these three modes. In ignorance one pays no attention to proper time and circumstance. They desire their cherished boon right away, and for this they can approach Lord Shiva, who is known as Ashutosha because he is easily pleased.

Lord Shiva spends his time worshiping God. He doesn't like to have his meditation broken, so he quickly whisks away his worshipers, giving them whatever they want. The hope is that the worshiper will eventually be purified through their association with Shiva, who lives in complete renunciation, not requiring any of the opulence that he gives to others. His item of focus is the lotus feet of the Supreme Lord.

Those feet once roamed the earth. They belonged to the prince of the Raghu dynasty, Lord Rama. Sita's mother saw Rama enter her kingdom alongside His younger brother Lakshmana and the sage Vishvamitra. The occasion was the svayamvara contest, and so all the princes were assessed by the spectators.

In the above referenced verse from the Janaki Mangala, Sita's mother is remarking to her friends the difference between the youth, Rama, and the bow, which belonged to Shiva. She is speaking to her friends with affection and amazement. There is an automatic affection for Rama, as this is the effect the Supreme Lord has on the eyes that are not tainted by material attachment. The queen was qualified to receive that spontaneous emotion based on her affection for her daughter. Sita is God's eternal consort, His wife for all intents and purposes. To love her in devotion is to love God, and so it was not surprising that the queen was enamored by Rama.

That affection then led to worry, as the bow was very heavy. The child is not expected to move large appliances within the house, nor can they drive the much larger automobile. How was the youth Rama supposed to lift a bow that required hundreds of men just to bring in to the assembly? Rama is described as soft and gentle, while the bow is hard as steel and very heavy.

There was no need to worry, though, as the same youth had just protected Vishvamitra. Rama and Lakshmana defeated the enemies of the saints living in the forest, and so they were well-equipped for fighting, though still very young. This bow was destined to be lifted by Rama, and in this case the paradoxical vision made the outcome that much more delightful.

One of the Supreme Lord's names is Ajita, which means unconquerable. He is undefeated in the true sense of the word. Sometimes when He plays as a young child, He allows His friends to win, but this doesn't equate to defeat, as a loss is only meaningful when there is something on the line, when there is the desire for victory in competition. The desire in this case related to the queen, her attendants, Sita, Lakshmana, Vishvamitra, Janaka, and countless other pious souls anxiously awaiting the conclusion to the contest. Rama comes through in the clutch, delivering to His devotees their cherished desires, which always relate to His happiness.

VERSE 74

जौं बिधि लोचन अतिथि करत नहिं रामहि।
तौ कोउ नृपहि न देत दोषु परिनामहि।।74।।

jaum bidhi locana atithi karata nahim rāmahi |
tau ko'u nṛpahi na deta doṣu parināmahi ||74||

"' If the Creator had not given our eyes the gift of the guest Rama, then no one would have blamed the king for the result.'" (74)

Essay - Blaming the Creator

It's natural to lament when you're caught in an unfavorable situation. You didn't ask for this difficult circumstance; it just happened. If you are wise and understand that the Creator is ultimately responsible for distributing the outcomes to action, you can rightfully blame him for the circumstance, though in reality every individual has free will in their decisions. We can blame the law of gravity for the pain we feel from falling to the ground, but it is our choice to take steps, and with each step there is the potential for a misstep, which then causes a fall. The fall referenced here relates to the missed opportunity of finding the perfect match for your daughter, who is deserving of the most chivalrous prince in the world.

In the Treta Yuga, the second time period of creation, King Janaka was famous throughout the world. Just as the day is divided into different portions, such as morning, afternoon and evening, the duration of the creation gets split up into yugas, which not only indicate the amount of time elapsed since the initial birth of the universe but also point to the qualitative makeup of society specific to each time period. The Treta Yuga is like the afternoon; it is just after the initial moments of the creation. The people are still very pure; dharma, or virtue, stands on three of its initial four legs.

King Janaka was exemplary in his practice of dharma. A beautiful daughter belonged to the ideal king, and he did not want to let go of her. But protocol called for a marriage when she reached the suitable age. With the advice of his counselors, Janaka decided on a bow-lifting contest. The first prince to lift this heavy bow originally belonging to Lord Shiva would be garlanded the victor by Sita, Janaka's daughter. The oath was made in front of others, which meant that everyone would know if King Janaka went against his word later on. For a king in those times nothing was worse than being untrustworthy. If you couldn't stay true to your word, how could you expect anyone else to be truthful? And without truth what kind of a society will you have?

Janaka's dedication to virtue made his wife very nervous towards the end of the contest. A handsome youth who was perfect in every way for Sita had arrived at the assembly. The queen would have handed Sita over to Him immediately were it not for the oath taken by her husband. The main problem was that this prince was so youthful in appearance. He had delicate features, and beautiful and soft skin. He was accompanied by His younger brother Lakshmana and the sage Vishvamitra.

In the above referenced verse from the Janaki Mangala, Janaka's wife is lamenting over the situation and blaming the Creator for it. If Rama had never come to the scene, there wouldn't have been an issue. Either someone would have lifted the bow or no one would have, in which case there would have been no blame. "I tried my best", Janaka could say. "There is obviously no prince on earth worthy of Sita's hand." The exact sequence of events pertaining to this famous incident vary depending on the creation. In the original Ramayana of Valmiki it is described that Rama finally steps up to lift the bow after Janaka describes the bow's history. In the Ramacharitamanasa, which incorporates versions told in other Vedic texts like the Puranas, after seeing many princes fail Janaka proclaims that there is no suitable match for Sita, at which point Lakshmana angrily intervenes to proclaim that his elder brother can most certainly lift the bow.

The queen thought that since Rama was now here, people would blame Janaka for the oath if the outcome wasn't ideal. The lament is similar to meeting a person of the opposite sex, developing a strong affection for them, and not being able to marry them. If they had never come into your life, you wouldn't have felt the pain of rejection, the sting over the loss of a cherished object. But for some reason the Creator destined for you to meet that person, form an attachment to them, and then be forever separated from them.

Everything does happen for a reason, and on this occasion Rama's delicate features painted a nice contrast to the extremely heavy bow that was central to the contest. In certain situations it looks like the preferred outcome is just impossible. Perhaps the two parties in a romantic affair are too incompatible to make things last. In amorous relations, one party may be attracted to the other, but the other side may not feel the same way. If you want to hire a top notch employee, they might not be willing to come to your firm. You may want to eat at a certain restaurant on a specific night, but the establishment might not be open.

Here it looked like things weren't going to work out. Rama was too youthful in appearance. He didn't look as strong as the other princes, all of whom couldn't even move the bow. Ah, but with God the impossible is not only possible, but it can be made to look easy. With a single exhalation the Supreme Lord as Vishnu creates this and many other universes, and so even within the youthful figure of the prince of the Raghu dynasty He can easily lift a bow that takes hundreds of ordinary men to move. On that day He would live up to His stature as the rescuer of the surrendered souls. With nowhere else to turn, the queen and her friends left the outcome up to the higher authorities. No one is a higher authority than Rama, so He would swiftly deliver the desired outcome.

VERSE 75

अब असमंजस भयउ न कछु कहि आवै।
रानिहि जानि ससोच सखी समझावै।।७५।।

aba asamañjasa bhaya'u na kachu kahi āvai |
rānihi jāni sasoca sakhī samajhāvai ||75||

"Now in confusion, no words are coming to the queen. Seeing her worried and in thought, her friends are trying to make her understand." (75)

Essay - What Are Friends For

You're too invested in the outcome to think straight. Desire strengthens to the point that the mind no longer can think clearly. The telltale sign that you have temporarily lost your "marbles" is the crippling fear over a potential outcome. This is an unwise course because there were many outcomes in the past that you fretted over, and either way you came out okay. Whether you got what you wanted or didn't, you still managed to survive. The tiny, pressing issue of the time didn't mean the end of the world to you, though at the time you thought otherwise. In these instances, your friends are a good support system. They are more distanced from the situation, so they can lend a helping hand.

In the biggest picture, the best friend is the spiritual master, someone we may not have even met yet. The genuine spiritual master, or guru, lives devotional service, or bhakti-yoga. This service is a full-time engagement relying on the always available instrument known as the mind. In the morning while trying to get up out of bed, the mind engages in serving by thinking of God. During the morning hours, the tongue is used to chant the holy names, "Hare Krishna Hare Krishna, Krishna Krishna, Hare Hare, Hare Rama Hare Rama, Rama Rama, Hare Hare", and offer prayers to the deity in the home or temple. The ears are simultaneously utilized to hear the sounds of the holy name produced by the tongue. The eyes gaze upon the deity and the legs travel to places where the holy names are either heard or distributed.

"Although the Lord was present in Vaikuntha, He was present also in the heart of the brahmana when he was meditating on the worshiping process. Thus, we can understand that things offered by the devotees even in meditation are accepted by the Lord, and they help one achieve the desired result." (The Nectar of Devotion, Ch. 10)

The Nectar of DevotionIf the guru should find a situation that is not ideal for the outward display of devotion, within the mind they still chant the holy names, think of God, or plan some type of future service. In The Nectar of Devotion, which is a summary study of Shrila Rupa Gosvami's Bhakti-rasamrita-sindhu, it is said that once a brahmana simply desired to offer service to God by taking sacred waters and other paraphernalia for worship, and in that mental state the offering was as good as made. The sincerity of purpose is what counts most in the highest discipline of divine love, so just by planning out some type of service to God, the act is as good as done.

With respect to friendship, the guru is the well-wisher of everyone. Having studied the Bhagavad-gita and Shrimad Bhagavatam, two of the most important texts of the Vedic tradition, he can relate to pretty much any situation. Even if he hasn't been married, he can understand what it's like to have affection for someone else. The issues of dealing with someone else's desires, getting along with another person on a day-to-day basis, and figuring out where to steer the relationship are not foreign to the guru, who through his service to God acquires the requisite knowledge pertinent to practically any situation.

In Mithila a long time ago, the friends of the queen weren't necessarily spiritual masters, but since they had the same guiding sentiment, love for God, they could provide good counsel when needed. At one time the queen was swooning over the fear of losing the ideal match for her daughter Sita. The good mother wanted to give away her eldest daughter to an eligible suitor, who would be ideal in the categories of ancestry, appearance, strength and behavior.

The queen's husband knew the task wasn't easy, so he settled upon a contest. Whoever could lift an enormously heavy bow would win Sita's hand in marriage. So many princes arrived, but none of them could so much as move the bow. Now here was this youth that was captivating everyone, including Sita's mother. Named

Rama, He was the eldest son of King Dasharatha. Rama's trusted younger brother Lakshmana was with Him, as was the venerable Vishvamitra Muni. Sita's mother worried that Rama might not be able to win the contest because of His delicate features. He was so beautiful in every way, looking like the perfect youth to wed the young and beautiful Sita.

In the above referenced verse from the Janaki Mangala, the queen's friends are trying to make her understand that everything is going to be alright. For the mother it was difficult to think clearly when so much was at stake, but the wise sakhis knew that this youth had just come from the forest where He and His younger brother fought off the vilest creatures in the world. This wasn't a training exercise in military combat either; the stakes were real. The peaceful sages living in the forests had been harassed for too long by these night-rangers, who were enemies of religion. Vishvamitra knew of Rama's fighting prowess, and that's why he specifically asked for Him from King Dasharatha.

In the minds of the sakhis, if Rama, this youth who was so beautiful that He gave everyone the fruit of their eyes upon sight, was trusted by the sage for protection, He could surely lift Shiva's bow. The queen thus had very good friends, who knew just what to say to her at the right time. Also, like the queen they were obviously devotees of God, as they had an appreciation for Rama and Lakshmana. Amazingly, their understanding of Rama's features came from only seeing and hearing about them for a brief period of time. Know that the best friend in this world is the person who has the same love for the Supreme Lord and who kindly speaks of His glories to us. They provide the most valuable information, allowing us to think clearly in situations where we otherwise can't.

VERSE 76

देबि सोच परिहरिय हरष हियँ आनिय।
चाप चढ़ाउब राम बचन फुर मानिय।।76।।

debi soca parihariya haraṣa hiyaṁ āniya |
cāpa caṛhā'uba rāma bacana phura māniya ||76||

"' O Devi, leave aside your doubts and bring happiness to your heart. Have faith in these words: Rama will string the bow.'" (76)

Essay - Believe What I Say

The foundation of the Ramayana is the idea of investing full faith and confidence in the ability of God to deliver the proper outcome. This faith requires the release of worries, the removal of doubts, believing that the higher authority will make everything right. At the same time, this isn't a sanction for abandoning activity, as sitting like a stone will not accomplish much. Prescribed duties are set into place for the benefit of the worker, with the manager ultimately responsible for delivering the proper outcome. In this particular time of worry for the queen of Mithila, her attendants tried to assure her of the proper outcome, telling her to have faith in their counsel, which said that Rama would indeed string Lord Shiva's bow.

"But ignorant and faithless persons who doubt the revealed scriptures do not attain God consciousness. For the doubting soul there is happiness neither in this world nor in the next." (Lord Krishna, Bhagavad-gita, 4.40)

It's difficult to have full faith in God because the natural inclination is to think of ourselves as the doers. "I decide to get up in the morning, and bam, the next second I am out of bed. I made that happen. I had the seed of desire in the mind, and then my body parts made that desire a reality through work. If I want to graduate from school, I do the necessary work, which includes studying and completing assignments, to pass my classes. In adulthood, I have so much control over my actions that others are willing to pay me for my abilities. This then means that I get responsibilities placed upon me. I can't just pray to God to get this work done. I have to take action myself, so why shouldn't I assume that other outcomes are dependent on personal work as well?"

"The bewildered spirit soul, under the influence of the three modes of material nature, thinks himself to be the doer of activities, which are in actuality carried out by nature." (Lord Krishna, Bg. 3.27)

Of course lost in this narrow outlook is the higher scheme, which is influenced by so many aspects of life that are completely out of our control. With the example of working for a company, I may be capable of getting the job done, but this doesn't mean that I am guaranteed to get to work on time. My car could stall during the trip to the office. I could get into a car accident that is not my fault. There could be traffic on the road or a weather event could get in my way. Do I have any control over these factors? To say that I can control the traffic is ridiculous. The same holds true with the weather. Yet all of these factors have to be aligned just right on the days when I get a successful outcome to my work. This means that I am not the supreme controller. I have control over how my body works, and even that to a small degree, but nothing else.

Religious life begins with the acceptance of a higher authority. To know more about that authority is what drives the subsequent work. To be inquisitive is the human nature, and when that curiosity leads to the realm of spirituality, the benefits can be long lasting. In the Vedic tradition, the human birth marks the need for inquiry into the Absolute Truth. And the first fact to realize is that we are not our body. We are Brahman, or pure spirit, and the resultant actions that take place with the body are due to the laws of nature and also the Supreme Spirit, who is both all-pervading and localized within each individual.

A higher realization is to know Bhagavan, who is the entity that best equates to the term "God". He creates the giant system of cause and effect which is so amazing that it bewilders us into thinking that we have complete control over outcomes. As He is in charge, He can make any outcome possible. Sometimes He doesn't give us what we want, for He knows what is best for us. He only personally intervenes for His devotees, as the non-devoted ignore His presence. In this sense, they too are given what they want, namely continued forgetfulness of God.

"God has given independence to everyone; therefore, if a person desires to have material enjoyment and wants very sincerely to have such facilities from the material demigods, the Supreme Lord, as Supersoul in everyone's heart, understands and gives facilities to such persons. As the supreme father of all living entities, He does not interfere with their independence, but gives all facilities so that they can fulfill their material desires." (Shrila Prabhupada, Bg. 7.21 Purport)

The Ramayana is an ancient Sanskrit poem that is a gift from above, as through its accounts of historical incidents it provides us a practical application of the proper mood of surrender and when it is required. The poem begins with the dilemma of King Dasharatha, who is a pious ruler of the town of Ayodhya. He is missing one very important thing: a son. He approaches his counselors, religious guides who understand Brahman, to see how to solve the problem. In response, God Himself descends to earth in a human form to give Dasharatha a son. The original Supreme Lord also expands into three other forms to give Dasharatha three additional sons.

Later on, the sage Vishvamitra requires help in practicing his austerities in the forest. A band of evil-night rangers was attacking the sages who sought refuge in the pristine forest. Rather than cast spells in return, they simply surrendered to God, who is known as brahmanya-devaya, or the worshipable deity of the priestly class. Rama and His younger brother Lakshmana make the forest safe again, successfully terminating the reign of terror of the wicked night-rangers.

In the above referenced verse from the Janaki Mangala, which is a Hindi poem that describes a portion of the same events found in the Ramayana, we are given another instance of God's rescuing hand. King Janaka of Mithila wants to find the perfect husband for his precious daughter Sita. He decides to hold a bow-lifting contest, and everything seems to be going okay until Dasharatha's eldest son enters the arena accompanied by Lakshmana and Vishvamitra.

Rama was not an unruly guest. On the contrary, He was quite well-behaved. The problem was that His beauty was captivating. It had the effect of creating a transcendental attachment in the pure-hearted onlookers. Sita's mother was one of these spectators, and her love for Rama was so great that she could think of nothing else besides His potential for marrying Sita. She wanted Him to win the contest very badly, but oh yes, that issue of the contest got in the way. What if Rama couldn't lift the bow? He was too beautiful to be strong enough to lift something that required hundreds of men just to move.

We see that the queen's friends decided to step in and reassure her. They proclaimed that Rama would indeed raise and string the bow. He had a divine presence. God's potencies can never be fully masked, no matter what personal form He takes. He is enchanting whether in the body of a youth or an adult. On this occasion, the queen's sakhis were essentially telling her to trust in God, as Rama was God Himself. No other recourse was available, as Janaka could not cancel the competition after the rules had been announced. With nowhere else to turn, they relied on the strong hand of Rama, which has rescued the devotees from fear since time immemorial.

VERSE 77

तीनि काल को ग्यान कौसिकहि करतल।
सो कि स्वयंबर आनिहिं बालक बिनु बल॥77॥

tīni kāla ko gyāna kausikahi karatala |
so ki svayambara ānihiṁ bālaka binu bala ||77||

"' Knowledge of the three periods of time (past, present, future) Vishvamitra holds in his hand, so why would he bring to this svayamvara boys devoid of strength?'" (77)

Essay - Knowledge of Past, Present and Future

There is a section in the Shrimad Bhagavatam where Narada Muni approaches his father Lord Brahma to hear about the cause of all causes. Brahma is considered the creator, the grandsire, the original living being. Every creature can trace their ancestry to him, and since he is responsible for the population of creatures, he knows about the present. Since he is the oldest person in the world, he also knows about the entire past, as Brahma's original act of creating took place in what is the past for everyone else. He also knows about the future because it is due to his influence that future generations of creatures manifest. That same knowledge of the three time periods is found to some degree in the brahmana, who is the servant following in the line of devotional service established by Brahma.

"My dear father, all this is known to you scientifically because whatever was created in the past, whatever will be created in the future, or whatever is being created at present, as well as everything within the universe, is within your grip, just like a walnut." (Narada speaking to Lord Brahma, Shrimad Bhagavatam, 2.5.3)

Past, present and future are the three time periods, and they are different for each person. My past is different from your past, and my future will be different from your future as well. Narada Muni, who is himself very wise, once approached Brahma to know the cause of all causes. Only Brahma could really know this since he was around at a time when no one else was. Brahma wasn't the original cause, as he took birth from the stem of the lotus flower that grew out of the navel of Lord Vishnu. And Vishnu is a personal expansion of the Supreme Lord Krishna, who is thus known as the cause of all causes.

Brahma is provided knowledge of the Absolute through the medium of the heart. He then follows devotional service while simultaneously carrying out his duties as the creator. The first human beings are of the brahmana order, so they only know devotion to God. As such, they know of past, present and future through Brahma's influence. Narada is also a brahmana, and from approaching Brahma, who initially approached Vishnu, his knowledge is perfect. Vishvamitra is a brahmana in this line, and through austerity, penance, and acceptance of authorized information passed down through disciplic succession, he knows past, present and future.

In the above referenced verse from the Janaki Mangala, it is interesting to note that women of the court in Janakpur were well aware of Vishvamitra's knowledge. These sakhis, or friends to the queen, stepped in to reassure the worried queen about the outcome of a contest. This wasn't a friendly competition or a game to watch to pass the time. The winner of the contest would get to marry the queen's daughter Sita. She is the goddess of fortune, so whoever is blessed with her association is considered very fortunate. King Janaka and his wife got to raise her as their daughter, but when she reached an appropriate age, she had to be married off, lest she remain unprotected later on in life. The fortune of Sita's association was to be granted to a capable prince. To ensure that the prince was capable of adequately protecting her, Janaka set up a contest, where the task was to lift an extremely heavy bow initially coming from Lord Shiva.

Princes from around the world came to Janaka's capital city for the contest, and Vishvamitra arrived too, bringing two princes from Ayodhya with him. These youths captured the attention of everyone, both friend and foe alike. There were more friends than foes, as the innocent spectators of the town immediately took a liking to the two boys, who were named Rama and Lakshmana. The rival princes were on the opposite end, fearing over the potential outcome. Yet even those who were in favor of Rama and Lakshmana had cause for concern.

Rama was the elder brother, so Lakshmana would not participate in the contest. Sita's mother noticed Rama's delicate features and His exquisite beauty. She determined immediately that He was a perfect match for Sita; never mind the contest. The king had made a vow, however, so he could not now go back on his word. For Sita to marry this boy, the boy would have to lift up the bow, which previously required hundreds of men just to move. The queen began to worry, thinking that the desired outcome would not occur.

In stepped the sakhis to reassure her. They made a very good point by reminding her that Vishvamitra has knowledge of the three time periods in the palm of his hand. Narada Muni made a similar comparison when offering a prayer to Brahma. He said that Lord Brahma holds the information of past, present and future like a walnut within his grip. The walnut is rather small, so when it is inside the closed hand, it cannot move anywhere. Similarly, Vishvamitra knew of the past through study, was aware of the present through knowledge of his surroundings, and knew of the future based on proper assessment. Therefore he wouldn't bring Rama and Lakshmana to this svayamvara, or self-choice ceremony, if they were not strong.

Vishvamitra previously had proved his knowledge of the future when he went to Ayodhya to specifically ask for Rama's protection. Rama was quite young, and the father, King Dasharatha, did not want to let Him go off to the forest without protection. And yet Vishvamitra wanted this youth to protect him from the attacks of the wickedest creatures in the world. Lakshmana came along too, and the brothers showed that even with their beauty in youth, they could still defeat anyone in battle.

And now in Janakpur, Rama was slated to lift Shiva's bow and marry Sita. The sakhis relied on Vishvamitra's knowledge to allay the fears of the queen, and in a similar manner we can rely on the advice of the sages to know that bhakti-yoga, or devotional service, is the only way to win God's favor. Through chanting the holy names, "Hare Krishna Hare Krishna, Krishna Krishna, Hare Hare, Hare Rama Hare Rama, Rama Rama, Hare Hare", and hearing of Rama's triumph in the assembly in Janakpur, know that victory will ultimately arrive for you too in the form of ascension to the spiritual kingdom.

VERSE 78

मुनि महिमा सुनि रानिहि धीरजु आयउ।

JANAKI MANGALA

तब सुबाहु सूदन जसु सखिन्ह सुनायउ ||78||

muni mahimā suni rānihi dhīraju āya'u |
taba subāhu sūdana jasu sakhinha sunāya'u ||78||

"Hearing of the muni's greatness, patience came to the queen. Then her friends told her of Rama's feat of slaying Subahu." (78)

Essay - Slaying Subahu

Okay, so you've been working on something for a while now. This something can be anything, but for this example, we can pretend that it is some type of structure. It is complex in nature, so you had to be really careful while you were building it. The pieces had to be inserted in just the right sequence and spacing in order for the structure to remain sturdy and safe. There is one final piece, one last obstacle towards completion. Just as you are about to lay the last "brick" so to speak, an enemy comes to the scene and ruins everything. They knock down your building and take great delight in it, laughing in your face. They could have attacked at the beginning, but it is more demoralizing to the victim to wait until the very end. Something similar was a regular occurrence in the quiet forests of Dandaka many thousands of years ago, that is until the eldest son of King Dasharatha came to the scene.

The sage Vishvamitra knew of Rama's divine nature. That is why he specifically asked for Him from the King of Ayodhya. Maharaja Dasharatha was reluctant to part with Rama, who was his most cherished son. But the pious kings of those times never refused the requests of the priestly class, and so Rama, though young at the time, went off to the forest with Vishvamitra. Rama's younger brother Lakshmana came along as well, and in this way the sage had two great protectors with him.

It didn't seem that way to outside observers. It looked like the elder sage was walking around with young students who were full of exuberance. It is said in the Janaki Mangala that Rama would chase after deer in fun and pluck flowers to make garlands. His excitement would temper when He would remember the presence of the sage, who was to be treated like a father.

Though they were young, the brothers would nevertheless be called upon to provide protection that was not available anywhere else in the world. The first test was the female Rakshasa named Tataka. She had been harassing the sages in the forests for a long time, but since she was a woman Rama was reluctant to take up arms against her. He finally gave up His reluctance at the insistence of Vishvamitra. In tandem with Lakshmana, Rama killed the female demon in a fair fight. As a reward the brothers received powerful weapons as boons. These weapons were special arrows that had potent effects when used properly.

Killing Tataka earned Rama more than enough fame, but His stature would increase after the next episode. In Vedic culture, there are so many styles of religion and sacrifice, all depending on what your aim is. The ultimate aim is to have love and devotion to God, but as this is a difficult platform to reach, one requiring millions of births just to become aware of, there are other processes recommended for gradual advancement. The yajna, or sacrifice, is a central practice that helps one purify their consciousness. The sages during this ancient time would regularly perform these sacrifices in the quiet wilderness.

The issue was that the yajnas required a certain amount of time for maturation, sort of like planting a tree and waiting for the fruit to grow. Just because you plant a seed doesn't mean that the desired outcome will manifest immediately. You have to see the entire process through in order to taste the fruit. In a similar manner, in a formal Vedic ritual you have to recite the mantras properly and wait for the proper amount of time in order to get the desired benefit.

On one occasion Vishvamitra initiated himself for a sacrifice. He required concentration for six days and nights; no disturbances. Rama and Lakshmana were there to ensure that there were no interruptions. Sure enough, everything went smoothly until almost the very end, when two wicked creatures were ready to mount an attack from the sky. Vishvamitra could not break away from the sacrifice; otherwise the entire effort would have been for naught.

"Then I, resembling a cloud and having molten-golden earrings, made my way into Vishvamitra's ashrama, for I was very proud of my strength due to the boon given to me by Lord Brahma. As soon as I entered, Rama quickly noticed me and raised His weapon. Though He saw me, Rama strung His bow without any fear." (Maricha speaking to Ravana, Valmiki Ramayana, Aranya Kand, 38.16-17)

Without blinking an eye, Rama strung His bow and fired a powerful weapon at the demon Maricha. The force of the blow sent the night-ranger flying one hundred yojanas away into an ocean. Rama next took up another weapon and shot it at Subahu, Maricha's partner in crime. Subahu wasn't as fortunate, as this weapon killed him. Rama then killed the rest of the night-rangers that were part of the pack, allowing Vishvamitra to successfully complete his sacrifice. The sage was very pleased with Rama, telling the Lord that He had upheld the faith of Dasharatha and himself, both of whom believed in Rama's fighting ability.

This incident was related to the mother of Sita Devi during a time of grave doubt. Later on Vishvamitra would lead Rama and Lakshmana to the kingdom of Janakpur, where a contest was being held to determine Sita's husband. Whoever would lift the enormously heavy bow in the assembly of gathered princes would immediately be proclaimed the victor and win the hand of the beautiful princess, the daughter of King Janaka.

So many princes came and tried, but none of them could even move the bow. Then Sita's mother saw Rama and she immediately thought that He should marry her daughter. She worried over the outcome of the contest, however, as Rama appeared to be very youthful, possessing delicate features. How was He going to lift such a heavy bow? "He might even get hurt while trying," is what the mother thought.

The sakhis, the friends of the queen, reminded her of Vishvamitra's knowledge of past, present and future, and also of Rama's glory of slaying Subahu. The contest of the bow was also a kind of sacrifice, and Rama's presence was required for its successful completion. He would once again uphold the honor of the sage Vishvamitra by lifting the bow, thereby ensuring that Janaka's effort in preparing the sacrifice did not go to waste. The successful outcome arrived again, due to the grace of Shri Rama, the Supreme Personality of Godhead.

Essay - Protector of Sacrifice

A justifiable fear for a person starting out in devotional service, or bhakti-yoga, is that through surrendering, or sharanagati, other aspects of life will go unattended. To worship without attachment for material gain is the highest form of sacrifice, and to sacrifice something means to give it up, all for a purpose. Therefore if one is to give up something, are they not going to lose it? What if they don't want to lose it? More importantly, what if the sacrifice isn't successful? What if it gets destroyed at the last moment, leaving the worshiper with nothing? The incident of the slaying of the demon Subahu shows how the Supreme Lord is not only the enjoyer of sacrifice, but also its protector.

"All living bodies subsist on food grains, which are produced from rain. Rains are produced by performance of yajna [sacrifice], and yajna is born of prescribed duties." (Lord Krishna, Bhagavad-gita, 3.14) Bhagavad-gita As It Is

In the Bhagavad-gita it is said that at the beginning of creation, the Lord of all creatures instituted the process of sacrifice and said to man to be happy through its implementation. "All good things will come to you if you sacrifice," which implies that the opposite behavior leads to all bad things. This should make sense. If you are completely selfish all the time, after a while people aren't going to be so nice to you. You have to compromise a little in order to get along with others.

In the higher scheme, the elements we receive for our personal use were not created by us, so to completely ignore the power of the higher authorities is not very wise. We use the sun's light and heat, but to say that we created them is silly. It is even sillier to say that a few chemicals just collided to make the sun, for if that were the case then why not repeat the same process today? Just create a tiny sun, one that stays in your closet. It doesn't have to heat that large of an area, just the few feet inside of your room. Ah, but this is impossible to create, as every source of light and heat that we generate requires some sort of energy. That source will never burn in perpetuity without requiring some outside help. Yet the sun has been autonomous since the beginning of time and it will continue to burn well into the foreseeable future.

Sacrifice helps to curb the ego, which falsely tells us that we are everything and that everything is in our control. The exact implementation of sacrifice varies based on time and circumstance. In some traditions, the sacrifice is to give up eating meat for a certain period of time. In others it is to stay awake for a certain number of hours on a specific day. In the Treta Yuga, the sacrifices of the sages required completion in order to deliver the desired benefit. These sages took refuge in the forest because there were less distractions there. No one to bother them, and so hopefully nothing to interrupt their concentration once they initiated themselves for the yajna.

But there was a problem during a particular period of time. Night-rangers, creatures who could also change their shapes at will, would pounce on these sacrifices just as they were about to finish. This meant that all the effort went to waste. Who would do such a thing on purpose? What harm were the sages causing? Ah, but to one who thinks that there is no God, that man is meant to enjoy fully on this earth without consequence, the resources are finite. Therefore it's every person for himself, sort of like in The Hunger Games book but to the largest scale. These sages were pious and renounced, and therefore they didn't possess much. Through their sacrifices, however, the celestials, the demigods in charge of distributing life's essentials, were fed. The demigods were the enemies of the night-rangers, so the best way for the enemies to attack would be to go after the source, i.e. disrupt the sacrifices.

Vishvamitra was a different kind of sage. He would perform these sacrifices in the forest, but his primary aim was devotion to God. Thus it was not surprising that the Supreme Lord would arrive on the scene to personally protect his yajnas. In His incarnation as Lord Ramachandra, God once protected Vishvamitra's yajna as two notorious night-rangers prepared to attack at the last minute. Maricha and Subahu and their associates appeared just when the sacrifice was about to finish. They started raining down blood on the scene. Rama, though a youth at the time, prepared His bow and arrow for combat. His younger brother Lakshmana was with Him, and as if to predict what He was going to do, Rama explained His tactics to Lakshmana prior to enacting them.

Maricha was struck with an arrow from Rama that thrust him hundreds of miles away into the ocean. Subahu was then slain by Rama's arrows, as were the other night-rangers who attacked. In this way Vishvamitra's confidence in Rama was affirmed, as it was his idea to go to Ayodhya and ask the king for Rama's protection. This incident also proved that the devotees need not worry over losing out on other things when there is full dedication to sacrifice. If there is a desire for a personal reward, the yajna may not always complete successfully. This is the way of karma, as so many past results go into influencing future outcomes. The desire for personal enjoyment makes the sacrifice impure to a degree as well, and with impurity there is the chance of failure.

In pure bhakti, the only desire is to be able to continue to serve God. That service can take place in practically any situation, and the Supreme Lord makes sure that the tools and conditions necessary for that worship are provided to the devotee. In this present age of Kali, which is marked by quarrel and hypocrisy, the prescribed sacrifice is the sankirtana-yajna, or the chanting of the holy names. Anyone can chant, "Hare Krishna Hare Krishna, Krishna Krishna, Hare Hare, Hare Rama Hare Rama, Rama Rama, Hare Hare\", as a sacrifice to God and be assured of all good things. Shri Rama is always standing by with His bow upraised to protect the devotee from foreign attack.

VERSE 79

सुनि जिय भयउ भरोस रानि हिय हरषइ।
बहुरि निरखि रघुबरहि प्रेम मन करषइ।।79।।

suni jiya bhaya'u bharosa rāni hiya haraṣa'I |
bahuri nirakhi raghubarahi prema mana karaṣa'I ||79||

"Hearing those words with faith, the queen became happy in the heart. Staring at Rama's face so much, her mind is drawn to Him in affection." (79)

Essay - Prema Magnetic

Prema, or pure love, for the Supreme Lord is not like any type of love we have encountered. And neither is it something we will ever feel for another human being, as the relationships in the material world are contingent upon some level of reciprocation. We are friends with someone based on what they can give to us. If they cease to provide companionship or a helping hand, we will stop being friends with them. This only makes sense, for who would want to be around an acrimonious individual? The characteristic of "friendly" should mean something. With the Supreme Lord, however, the feeling of prema is not based on any reciprocation, because in fact He has been the individual's friend since time immemorial.

How can He be our friend if we have only come to know of Him recently?

Even if you knew about God since you were very little, that still is not a long time in the grand scheme. In the situation from the above referenced verse from the Janaki Mangala, the queen of Janakpur has only known the Supreme Lord's incarnation of Shri Ramachandra for a few brief moments. In that time she developed the same attraction to Him that exists within all of us.

But where was Rama before this?

In the Ramayana and other Vedic scriptures it is described that Rama holds a bow in His hands and wears a quiver tied around His waist. This is His garb while roaming the forests to protect the innocent sages. He is most famous as a warrior, the prince of the Raghu dynasty, so this vision of Rama is the one preferred by the devotees. But in other parts of Vedic literature, the same Supreme Lord is described as the four-armed Vishnu, the two-armed Krishna, or the half-man/half-lion Narasimhadeva. In other religious traditions He is not given a form or it is speculated that He is an old man who is vindictive.

To make light of the seemingly disparate pieces of information one should be familiar with their own identity. Actually, learning about the Supreme Lord's transcendental features enables one to know their own identity as well, but in the chance that the descriptions found in the Vedas are too much to take or are dismissed due to sectarian considerations, we can still learn about the difference between spirit and matter to increase our knowledge. This difference is at the core of spirituality. The spirit soul is not the body. Every individual life force is spirit at the core; the material covering is like a temporary set of clothes that gets put on and then taken off later.

The basic truth of the existence of the soul debunks any theories relating to a big bang of chemicals creating the universe. No matter what research is made or to whatever degree of certainty scientists may claim to have proven the "big bang", there is nothing they can do to reproduce their purported explosion. Where do we see an explosion create things? It always destroys. The terrorist bomber can't plead innocent and say that chemicals randomly collided to create the destruction of the blast attributed to them. No one will buy this excuse. If chemicals did collide to create the universe, from where did the chemicals come? No answer to this is forthcoming, as saying, "They were just there," is equivalent to saying that there is a God. If chemicals can create all of life, why can't human beings create something as simple as the sun? Not a giant solar body like the one we rely upon so much; just anything minute in scope that has an endless capacity to give heat and light without requiring an external source of energy will suffice.

The truth of the soul's existence makes a lot more sense, and the soul's properties are further discussed in the Bhagavad-gita. From that text we learn that each individual has two souls within them. One is the individual soul, or jivatma, and the other is the Supreme Soul, or Paramatma, who is God. The Supreme Soul is all-pervading, whereas the individual soul is localized. This means that God is always with us. He has always been with us in the past and will continue to be with us going forward. He is always our well-wishing friend, but through forgetfulness we search out other deities, descending to the point that we'll give deity status to chemicals that we've never seen.

Awareness of the Supreme Soul can come about through different paths, most of which are rather difficult to follow. The easiest path to follow, but also the most difficult to accept, is bhakti-yoga, or divine love. The bhakti process is accelerated when there is the direct audience of the Supreme Soul in a manifested form, as was the case with the queen of Janakpur. She saw Shri Rama, an incarnation of Bhagavan, who is the person most of the world refers to as God. Bhagavan is the origin of the Supersoul, and He is the same person that resides simultaneously within all of us.

The queen on this occasion was set to marry off her daughter Sita. There was a contest to determine her daughter's future husband. The queen's husband, King Janaka, drew up the contest. Now the queen saw Lord Rama and wanted Him to win. She was worried that He wouldn't be able to lift Lord Shiva's bow due to His youthfulness, but her friends assured her that Rama could do amazing things. Moreover, the sage Vishvamitra had full faith in Rama's ability; otherwise he wouldn't have brought the Lord to the contest.

The queen took faith in those words and she became happy in the heart as a result. She then stared at Rama, drawn to Him like a magnet due to affection she felt in the mind. When the outside distractions are removed, one is free to worship God without impediment. And that worship is tied to prema, or pure love. There is no question of reciprocation or a sought out state of maturity. There is just uninterrupted affection offered through the mind, which is an indication of consciousness. To purify our consciousness in this way is the aim of the human form of life, and Sita's mother reached that pinnacle of existence that famous day when she saw Shri Rama, who was on the precipice of lifting Shiva's bow.

VERSE 80

नृप रानी पुर लोग राम तन चितवहिं।
मंजु मनोरथ कलस भरहिं अरु रितवहिं।।80।।

nṛpa rānī pura loga rāma tana citavahiṁ |
mañju manoratha kalasa bharahiṁ aru ritavahiṁ ||80||

"The king, queen and people of the city are staring at Rama's beautiful body, with their hopes like a pitcher constantly filled and emptied." (80)

Essay - Filling and Spilling

To stare at a picture with rapt attention is not to stop your thoughts altogether. Rather, the thoughts flood into the mind anew, like rushing waves to constantly replenish that which has just departed. The more beautiful the picture, the more thoughts will come to the mind. There is the amazement, the awe in seeing something out of this world. Then there are the questions relating to the origin, such as wherefrom the image came. Then there is the fear, that at one time such an image might cease to please the eyes or that it will vanish from the scene. In a famous incident in the city of Janakpur a long time ago, such thoughts rushed to the minds of the people looking upon a handsome youth. Since He was the Supreme Lord Himself, the constant toggling between fear and safety did not hurt them.

What do we mean by this? To have a material existence means to lament and hanker. One day I want this, and the next day I'm lamenting that I don't have something else. I win today and lose tomorrow. This all stems from taking birth and then dying later on. That is the definition of material, after all, to have an existence tied to matter, which is mutable, transient, and ultimately not the source of identity.

"One who is thus transcendentally situated at once realizes the Supreme Brahman. He never laments nor desires to have anything; he is equally disposed to every living entity. In that state he attains pure devotional service unto Me." (Lord Krishna, Bhagavad-gita, 18.54)

In the Bhagavad-gita it is said that the Brahman realized soul does not hanker or lament. To realize Brahman means to know the spiritual nature, to understand that the individual is a spirit soul, part and parcel of God. If I know that I am not my shirt, why will I worry so much over what happens to it? If I tear my favorite shirt, I can just get a new one. Moreover, I usually don't wear the same shirt every day, so perhaps the loss of a single shirt will only affect me for one day out of each week. Nevertheless, I can easily get another one. Along similar lines, the decay and ultimate loss of the body is not that important, as a new one will be provided. We already know that this is true in our present dealings based on the shedding of skin. We are constantly losing skin cells, though we can't see it. If we get a cut on the skin, eventually the wound will heal. Thus there must be constant regeneration of the cells.

At the time of death, the entire skin covering is left behind, and a new one is accepted somewhere else. Although we can't see this it doesn't mean that it doesn't happen. We couldn't see the spirit soul injected into the womb, but we know it happened based on the end result. In the same way, we can understand reincarnation, believing more in its validity through accepting the authorized instruction of Lord Krishna and those who follow devotion to Him. Krishna is a personality, but it is also a word which describes God, the same divine figure worshiped in all faiths.

In the brahma-bhuta state, hankering and lamenting cease from the point of view of its effect on the state of mind. Think of it like getting pricked by a pin but not having it take you off your game. You might hear the annoying car alarm outside, but if you stay concentrated on what you're doing, it's as if the alarm isn't even blaring. Through realization of Brahman, you can stay immune to the swinging pendulum of hankering and lamenting. From there you can take up devotional service to God, which is the soul's constitutional engagement.

But these facts seem to contradict what occurred in Janakpur a long time ago. Rama is the same Krishna, a personal incarnation of the Supreme Lord who descended to earth to delight His devotees. On one occasion, He appeared in the capital city of the kingdom of Videha to take part in a contest to determine the marriage for Sita Devi, the king's daughter. Whoever could first lift Lord Shiva's heavy bow would win the contest. The people of the town were taken by Rama when they first saw Him. He was in a youthful figure, so His features were delicate and beautiful. This flooded the mind with thoughts of amazement, keeping the eyes attracted to the enchanting vision.

That meditation eventually led to fear. "What if Rama doesn't win the contest? How is He going to lift this bow? He is like a delicate swan and this bow like a mountain. They don't mix well together. If He doesn't win, then He won't marry Sita, and we will all be devastated." When these thoughts would arrive, they would vanish soon after, replaced by loving attraction to Rama. "This boy is not of this world. He must have been sent by the creator himself for our benefit. If He is here, then He must also win the contest. There is no doubt."

Then thoughts would later return to fear. This constant swinging between hope and despair is likened to a pitcher that is constantly filled and then emptied. This captive audience consisted of devotees, which meant that they were already Brahman realized.

If so, why were they lamenting? Also, why were they hankering for Rama to win? Isn't marriage a temporary thing, an aspect of the material existence?

Actually, offering rapt attention to God is the pinnacle achievement in a human birth. The sentiments of the people were pure, as the mood was one of support. The people wanted Rama to win because they loved Him. Fear also brings a kind of thrill, as we know patrons flock to the amusement parks with rollercoasters for this very reason. Horror movies are also popular because of the thrills they provide. With the thrills created by Rama, the outcome is always beneficial, as the attachment to Him only increases. On this occasion, hankering and lamenting were on the spiritual platform, ensuring that the mind's racing would not bring negative consequences. In fact, the event was so wonderful to behold that it is still talked about to this day. The devotees sing of that glorious occasion, and through their retelling the sincere listeners get a glimpse of the thrill of anticipation felt by the fortunate witnesses that day.

CHAND 10

रितवहिं भरहिं धनु निरखि छिनु-छिनु निरखि रामहि सोचहीं।
नर नारि हरष बिषाद बस हिय सकल सिवहिं सकोचहीं।।
तब जनक आयसु पाइ कुलगुर जानकिहि लै आयऊ।
सिय रूप रासि निहारि लोचन लाहु लोगन्हि पायऊ।।10।।

ritavahiṁ bharahiṁ dhanu nirakhi chinu-chinu nirakhi rāmahi socahīṁ |
nara nāri haraṣa biṣāda basa hiya sakala sivahiṁ sakocahīṁ ||
taba janaka āyasu pā'i kulagura jānakihi lai āya'ū |
siya rūpa rāsi nihāri locana lāhu loganhi pāya'ū ||10||

"Emptying and filling the pitcher, looking again and again at the bow and Rama they are thinking. The men and women are both happy and sad, and so with all their hearts they are praying to Lord Shiva." (Chand 10.1)
"Then Janaka came and asked the family guru to bring Sita. As she is a storehouse of beauty, the people received the fruit of their eyes." (Chand 10.2)

Essay - Shiva's Bow

"This is Lord Shiva's bow after all. He originally gave it to the family ruling over Janakpur, and it has since made its way down the succession of kings, now in King Janaka's possession. Such a pious ruler is worthy of such a wonderful bow belonging to a divine figure of a sterling character. Lord Shiva can make anything happen, as it is said that at the end of the creation he will ignite the fire to destroy everything. In Vedic literature references are often made to this fire of devastation as a way to describe a fiery onslaught of gigantic proportion. Now it is Shiva's bow to determine the husband for Janaka's beautiful daughter Sita. He must save us today, for our worry is too much.

"Why are we worrying, you ask? This beautiful youth from Ayodhya has captured our hearts. This contest is a test of strength, so naturally many princes from around the world have arrived. They brought their friends, family and priests with them. They wanted their close ones to be with them should they win the contest and marry Sita. Who could blame them for their presumptiveness? A king these days is determined by their strength in fighting more so than their ancestral link. If the king can't protect his citizens from foreign attack, he isn't much of a ruler. If he can't weed out the evil elements of society and bring them to justice, he isn't much of a protector.

"These are the best kings in the world, and they surely think that they can lift the bow. But thus far not one of them has been able to move the bow an inch. This must be Shiva's doing, as no one but he can understand the reason for its immense weight. It is like a giant mountain made of iron, and this youth from Ayodhya is like a delicate swan. He is so beautiful, and His innocence is further enhanced by the bow and arrow set that He dutifully carries. His equally as beautiful younger brother Lakshmana is with Him, and so we are hoping that both brothers will soon be united with Janaka's family.

"Normally, we wouldn't think there was any hope. We've never heard of a swan lifting a mountain. On the contrary, the swan would be greatly overpowered by the mountain, so much so that it wouldn't survive the clash. Thus even by Rama attempting to lift this bow there is the chance of harm. Yet there is one thing that gives us hope. Rama and His brother are accompanied by Vishvamitra Muni. This venerable rishi, the son of Gadhi, is their spiritual master at this time, and though he has taught them much, he has also relied upon them for protection.

"We have heard that Rama, with the help of Lakshmana, killed the wicked demon Subahu. He has also protected the sacrifice of the sage from the fiend Maricha, who as a Rakshasa is known for his affinity for disrupting sacrifices. Rama also killed the female Rakshasa Tataka who had been harassing the sages in the forest. This means that He possesses strength as well. This contest is also a kind of sacrifice, as it is to determine the religiously wedded husband for Janaki, our beloved princess. Rama must also protect this sacrifice and thereby ensure that Janaki receives the proper husband.

"As Rama is so beautiful, we can't help but stare at Him. One second we are confident that He will win, but then the next we look at the bow and fall back into despair. Our hopes fill into a kalasha, which then empties as soon as we look at the bow. We didn't have this worry before Rama arrived. We were actually eager to watch the contest, to see who could win. But now we have a vested interest. Rama must win. It cannot be any other way. But what if He loses? Then the perfect match will be foiled. Some will say that it is Janaka's fault for making the contest, while others will blame the creator for having made such a pitiable situation.

"At this time what else can we do but pray to Lord Shiva. He is a devotee of Shri Hari, the Supreme Personality of Godhead. This means that whatever Shiva asks for he will get. Others are known to worship Shiva as well, and since he is easily pleased he is known as Ashutosha. We're not asking for material opulence. We don't want to rule the world through some power to be used for evil. We don't ask for a long life or the elimination of distress. We simply pray for the bow to be made as light as a feather when Rama tries to lift it. He is the proper husband for Sita, and without Shiva's help we don't think the match can materialize.

"If Mahadeva grants us this wish, we will sing of the glorious occasion in all felicity. We think that the occasion will be so famous that sages, housewives and kings alike will fondly remember it going forward. Fruitive workers, mental speculators, yogis and devotees will all look back to this day and immediately get a smile on their face. As the bow will be a key instrument in the making of the marriage of Sita and Rama, Lord Shiva will be honored as well. Therefore it is in his interest to help us on this day, one we hope to never forget."

Essay - A Storehouse of Beauty

Shri Ramachandra's wife is the most beautiful. As they say, "Beauty is in the eye of the beholder", the eyes that gaze upon her lovely form make an instant decision. The beauty is so striking that the observer realizes that they have just then received the fruit of their eyes. Previously, the eyes were used to look at this thing and that, but nothing was so beautiful that it gave meaning to having eyes, making one thankful for them. This beauty in Sita is used to please her beloved, who is the Supreme Lord. Thus she is the best devotee, practicing devotion in the proper way.

Is there a wrong way to practice devotion?

Sure there is, though in those cases the word "devotion" may not be entirely appropriate. Let's say that I am devoted to my diet, which came to me from a fitness guru. I liked what they said initially, so I decided to listen to them. Whatever the diet, they all work. The health benefits may not be equal, but in any case one who follows a diet, wherein they limit their intake of food, will see the desired benefit of a shedding of weight, provided they are faithful.

This faithfulness is a kind of devotion, but what is the intention? What if the diet didn't work? Would I still follow it? Would I still give attention to the fitness guru who came up with it? Obviously my attention would go elsewhere, to someone with a valid message. Thus the original devotion wasn't really devotion; it was more of a bargain, an agreement. "I'll scratch your back and you'll scratch mine." There is nothing inherently evil with this arrangement, as the fitness guru has the same purpose. "You give me money and attention and I'll give you something in return."

Real devotion, which is known by terms such as bhakti and prema in Sanskrit, is not dependent on the object of attention's reciprocation. Then the obvious question is, "Why be devoted? If the corresponding party is not obliged to offer you anything in return, why waste your time?" These are indeed relevant issues, and they are kindly resolved by the qualities found in the corresponding object. Since only one person is capable of reciprocating properly through their qualities, of giving a benefit regardless of what the servicing party is expecting, bhakti can only be offered to them.

Not surprisingly, that person is God. Devotion to Him is never a waste. If we take the same diet example, if we should choose to only eat prasadam, or food first offered to God, as our diet, we may not lose weight. We may not get the specific health benefits that we want, but nevertheless there is still a benefit to us. How is this? The fruit of an existence is devotion to God. No matter what route is taken to reach that fruit, the taste at the end is so sweet that the past miseries are forgotten.

"The many past births you spoiled can be rectified right now, today, if you start chanting Shri Rama's holy name and renounce bad association, says Tulsi." (Dohavali, 22)

In his Dohavali, Goswami Tulsidas notes that the mistakes of so many past lives can be rectified immediately through devotion to Rama, or God. The fact that we took birth from a womb indicates past mistakes. The original sin for every person is the desire to challenge God, to compete with Him for supremacy and enjoyment. We may not remember having made this choice, but through our present efforts the original sin is validated. The competitive race in karma, or fruitive activity, indicates a desire to reach a state of full material satisfaction, where it is believed that enjoyment will be available without a problem. But in fact just the opposite happens. With no worries over money, there is nothing to do. With no job, left to sit around at home all day, there is a deep void to fill. One needs some way to find enjoyment, though previously they worked so hard to secure it.

In bhakti, the desire is to please God rather than compete with Him. This puts a stop to the cycle of birth and death, and it means that the past mistakes get erased. If I eventually reach the treasure, I may not dwell so much on the many hours of searching from the past. In the same manner, whether it takes me one or many lifetimes, indulgence in all the different yogas or excessive drinking and material sense gratification, if I reach devotional service and practice it in earnest, I will taste the sweet fruit of my existence.

In Janakpur a long time ago, the people assembled on a particular day got the fruit of their eyes a few times. First, they saw Rama and Lakshmana, two sons of King Dasharatha. Rama is the Supreme Lord in a personal form and Lakshmana is His younger brother, almost God Himself. The boys were in Janakpur following their guru Vishvamitra. The occasion was a svayamvara, a self-choice ceremony to determine the husband for the daughter of King Janaka.

In the above referenced verse from the Janaki Mangala, Janaka is asking his guru to call Sita, the princess whose hand will be given away. She would choose her husband based on a contest. Whoever would lift Lord Shiva's heavy bow first would win. When Sita arrived in the assembly, the princes got to see who they would be marrying. This added to the suspense, as the people of the town wanted Rama to win. The assembled kings this time got the fruit of their eyes when they saw Sita. They may not have felt the same way when they saw Rama, as He was their competitor. Many kings surely did notice the divine presence in Him, but the envious rivals only thought about how their chances had diminished. Some of them worried that Janaka would hand Sita over to Rama without even bothering with the contest.

Sita's beauty is used for Rama's pleasure, and so she is the best devotee. We too have various gifts given to us by God, talents and abilities that can be used for His pleasure. In that devotion there is no need to expect reciprocation, as just being able to practice bhakti is reward enough. Fortunate we are to have ears to hear about that wonderful incident in Janaka's kingdom, which saw the union in matrimony of Sita and Rama. More fortunate it is to have the works of Goswami Tulsidas to recreate that scene over and over again.

VERSE 81

मंगल भूषन बसन मंजु तन सोहहिं।
देखि मूढ़ महिपाल मोह बस मोहहिं।।८१।।

maṅgala bhūṣana basana mañju tana sohahiṁ |
dekhi mūṛha mahipāla moha basa mohahiṁ ||81||

"With auspicious jewelry and beautiful clothes on the body she is looking beautiful. Looking at her, the foolish kings are illusioned by the illusion." (81)

Essay - A Foolish Viewpoint

To believe that the nature around you exists solely for your personal enjoyment is the root cause of the initial descent and subsequent stay in the material world. The elements of nature, including those possessed by the temporary body, give off an illusion. For instance, we look in the mirror and think that the vision identifies us, but in reality the vision is constantly changing. We don't notice the change until a longer period of time has elapsed, but the shifts are subtly going on regardless. The embodiment of that illusion in its most mature state is described to us in the verse quoted above, which references a famous incident.

"It should be understood that all species of life, O son of Kunti, are made possible by birth in this material nature, and that I am the seed-giving father." (Lord Krishna, Bhagavad-gita, 14.4)

The material elements come from somewhere. In the Bhagavad-gita, it is explained that the Supreme Absolute Truth, the original personality, impregnated the material energy to populate the creation with creatures. The same distinction is visible at the local level within each individual. For instance, in my body there is an owner and a field. The local field is the body and the external field the material elements. The soul, myself, is the owner. It was the injection of the soul that led to the development of the body, not the other way around. There is no possible way to gather a collection of material elements, mix them together, and then get them to grow without outside intervention. The initial seed of existence must be present, and that seed is the purusha, or spirit. The matter that develops because of the presence of the purusha is known as prakriti.

In the larger view, the injector of the spiritual force is the father and the nature it enters the mother. But even before that there is a larger abstraction. There is the original Lord Himself and His accompanying energy. The energy belongs to Him; it is meant for His enjoyment. The energy has some independence, however, so there is a choice in behavior. The purified form of that energy is known as the hladini-shakti, or pleasure potency. Every living entity is part of God's energy, but not all choose to please God. The wayward spirit souls, who want to enjoy other aspects of the energy for themselves, are granted residence in a temporary land governed by illusion.

The illusion was on full display in Janaka's kingdom many thousands of years ago. The Supreme Lord had descended to earth as the warrior prince Rama, and His pleasure potency as Sita Devi, the daughter of King Janaka. At the svayamvara in Janaka's kingdom, many princes had assembled, wanting to marry the king's precious daughter. It was a contest; whoever could lift the bow first would win.

Towards the latter stages, when the contest was about to be decided, Janaka called to have Sita enter the assembly. She was wearing auspicious ornaments and a beautiful dress on her body. The pious people received the fruit of their eyes when they saw her. This is because they saw her properly, as someone meant to serve and please Shri Rama, the youthful son of King Dasharatha who was an attendee and a potential participant in the contest.

The foolish kings, however, were struck by illusion. They are described here by Goswami Tulsidas as mudhas, or fools. They saw Sita as a vehicle for enjoyment, someone they would get to keep. This illusion is the same as looking at the material energy as being solely for one's enjoyment. The eyes are given to us for a reason. In the verse previous to this one in the Janaki Mangala, it is said that the kings received the fruit of their eyes when they saw Sita; meaning that their eyes were used properly. These were obviously the saintly kings. The collection of material elements that formed their eyes was provided to them for the purpose of viewing God and His closest associates in the proper mood.

When the eyes are used for other purposes, such as for personal enjoyment alone, the fruit of the eyes is not tasted. Only in illusion would we take something for what it is not, and hence the material nature is often referred to as maya. But maya is God's maidservant, so the illusion exists intentionally. On this occasion, the foolish kings gave a wonderful example of how not to view God and His eternal consort. Sita was always meant for Rama, and the pious people in Janakpur hoped for their reunion.

That would eventually take place through Rama's lifting of the bow, but later on another foolish king would succumb to illusion. He would try to take Sita for himself, though he was already married to so many beautiful queens. It is said in the Kurma Purana that the version of Sita taken by the evil king Ravana was an illusory version. The effect was similar for the assembled princes in Janakpur, who didn't really see Sita as she is. The real Sita is always with Rama, and she can never be touched by the miscreants.

To receive the fruit of the eyes, and all the body parts for that matter, engage in devotional service, which begins and ends with reliance on the holy names, such as those found in the maha-mantra, "Hare Krishna Hare Krishna, Krishna Krishna, Hare Hare, Hare Rama Hare Rama, Rama Rama, Hare Hare". For the foolish kings their hopes created through illusion would break simultaneously with the bow of Shiva in Rama's hands, marking the triumph of God and His devotees.

VERSE 82

रूप रासि जेहि ओर सुभायँ निहारइ।
नील कमल सर श्रेनि मयन जनु डारइ॥82॥

rūpa rāsi jehi ora subhāyaṁ nihāra'i |
nīla kamala sara śreni mayana janu ḍāra'i ||82||

"Wherever Sita's beautiful form goes, others follow with their eyes, like blue-lotus arrows flying from Kamadeva's bow." (82)

Essay - Following Sita

One of the many names for God provided in the Vedas is Madana-mohana. This has special significance beyond the basic translation. Madana is the god of love, or the equivalent of a cupid. Mohana is an enchanter, so as Madana-mohana God is the enchanter of cupid. The common understanding of this name is that the Supreme Lord enchants cupid, who can enchant others. If one person is so beautiful that they can cast a spell on others, whoever can cast a spell on them is obviously more beautiful. But another name for Madana is Kamadeva, and kama can translate to lust. An enchanter is one who can defeat someone, so the Supreme Lord is thus also a conqueror of lust.

Why is this important to know? Lust is not a good thing. Even in the basic understanding, to lust after something shows a weakness of mind. If, for instance, I am lusting after a slice of pizza, the behavior is not justified. Pizza is just food after all. Sure it tastes great. The combination of cheese, sauce and dough is unique and flavorful. The one slice isn't enough either, as a few slices really hit the spot. Some like their pizza well done, while others prefer the softer crust, wherein the ingredients are not too hot. In either case, the pizza tastes great to the person lusting after it.

But why should I lust after pizza? I need food for survival and no other reason. I could get the same nutrients, in likely a healthier combination, from other dishes. Moreover, the satisfaction from eating the pizza, from giving in to the lusty demands, is short-lived. Pretty soon thereafter I will crave pizza again, and if I can satisfy my itches so easily this way, I will start eating pizza on a regular basis, which was not my original intention.

Lust after food is one thing, but in its more dangerous form lust targets illicit sexual connections. To achieve this connection requires more effort, and the consequences are more harmful as a result. You could end up with an eighteen year responsibility in the form of an unwanted child. You could end up with a relationship with a person of the opposite sex whom you don't like. You could end up doing something gravely sinful like killing an innocent child within the womb. You could be depleted of money while supporting your habit, and you could start running from partner to partner to satisfy your lust that never seems to go away. Indeed, studies in America have shown that one of the easiest ways to prevent poverty is to graduate from high school and wait until you are married to have children. These are both difficult to do when you are ruled over by lust.

As the enchanter of cupid, God is above the influence of kama, or lust. He also defeats the lust in others, whether they prefer it or not. This is the result of connection with Him, proving that yoga, or the link to the supreme consciousness, is never harmful. It is worthwhile in every case, as even with an improper attitude in the neophyte stage the divine influence itself will purify you of things that are bad for you. Case in point the lusty kings in Janakpur many thousands of years ago. They were not interested in yoga, but due to the divine vision consisting of both the Supreme Lord and His eternal consort, their lust led them towards purity.

The scene was a contest. Princes and rulers from around the world gathered in Janakpur to try to lift an extremely heavy bow originally belonging to Lord Shiva. The winner of the contest would win the hand of Sita Devi, the daughter of King Janaka, who was the host of this contest. Madana-mohana was there in His incarnation of Lord Rama, the prince of the Raghu dynasty. He appeared so beautiful that others could tell that He could defeat the pride of millions of cupids. The pious wanted Him to lift the bow and win the contest, while the impious were jealous of His beauty and the attention others gave to Him.

Then came Sita. Janaka called for her, and she walked through the assembly. The lusty kings kept staring at her. Wherever she went, their eyes followed. Goswami Tulsidas likens the situation to Kamadeva constantly shooting his blue-lotus arrows. Their lust was targeted at her, and yet they had to keep shooting because Sita was not affected by their attraction. She is eternally Rama's. She is the pleasure potency of the Supreme Lord, and so she can never be with any other man. She is never swayed by lust, and she is so beautiful that she enchants even Madana-mohana.

The lust of the kings would lead to purification because their eyes would next focus on the lifting and breaking of the bow by Rama. Because of their lust for the most beautiful woman in the world, they were led to the vision of one of the most famous incidents in history. Though their intentions were not pure to start, they received a wonderful benediction, one rarely achieved. Their arrows of lust had no effect on Sita and Rama, and in this way know that through the divine consciousness, through focusing on the Supreme Lord, all negative attributes we possess will lose their strength, sort of like a serpent losing its fangs.

The senses remain, but in real yoga they are used for continuous glorification of the wonderful couple, Sita and Rama. If in enmity the rival kings in Janakpur got the benediction of seeing Sita and Rama wed, imagine what reward awaits the yogi in devotion, who harbors love and affection for the Supreme Lord instead of envy. Through chanting the holy names, "Hare Krishna Hare Krishna, Krishna Krishna,

Hare Hare, Hare Rama Hare Rama, Rama Rama, Hare Hare", practice the yoga of devotion and defeat the dreaded enemy known as lust.

VERSE 83

छिनु सीतहि छिनु रामहि पुरजन देखहिं।
रूप सील बय बंस बिसेष बिसेषहिं।।83।।

chinu sītahi chinu rāmahi purajana dekhahiṁ |
rūpa sīla baya bansa biseṣa biseṣahiṁ ||83||

"Sometimes the people are looking at Sita and sometimes at Rama. Having beauty and respected ancestries, the people are praising the unique combination."
(83)

Essay - A Unique Combination

The tendency to get excited over the prospect of two perfect people meeting together in holy matrimony, to enjoy each other's company for life, is quite natural. It was even exhibited many thousands of years ago in the kingdom of Janakpur. The people were excited on an occasion where a match was to be determined for the daughter of the king. She could marry anyone, provided they could lift the extremely heavy bow belonging to Lord Shiva. One youth in particular looked like a perfect match, and so when He was visible at the same time as the princess in question, the eyes kept moving back and forth, like watching a rally in a tennis match.

When you watch tennis on television, the principal camera is situated behind one of the baselines. This provides for an optimal viewing angle, as you get a view similar to one of the players. They see north and south primarily, and they move left and right when they have to, but the opponent is still in front of them. By keeping the main camera behind the baseline, the camera doesn't have to move much, which means that the sightline for the spectators is easier to maintain.

When attending a live match, however, sometimes the seats are situated on the sides. In fact, due to the nature of the setup of the arenas, the majority of the seats are on the sides. The seats behind the baseline are more expensive precisely because they provide a more comfortable viewpoint. When you're seated on the sides, during the points you will have to move your head back and forth, left and right, in order to see the ball. As a spectator, you're not consciously aware of what you're doing, but to someone else it looks a little strange to keep moving the head back and forth, over and over again, for a few hours in fact. It is the attention which drives the movement. Without an interest in the point, there would be no reason to keep moving the head.

In a similar manner, in Janakpur a long time ago it was the attention garnered by two beautiful personalities that caused a momentary pendulum effect, wherein the heads toggled between looking at Lord Rama and looking at Sita Devi. The people sized up each of their qualities, and everything appeared to be a perfect match. To think of it in modern terms, it's like comparing two celebrities who have just started dating. The gossip columnists and the readers of the celebrity-focused magazines get excited when two beautiful people start a romantic relationship. "What will their children look like? How long will they stay together? Can they make it last?"

In Janakpur, the attention was similar, and the anticipation was heightened by the fact that Sita's husband was to be determined in this assembly. So many kings were there, so it was only natural for the spectators to choose favorites. Rama was the overwhelming consensus choice, as His beauty, ancestry and behavior were ideal. His beauty was unmatched. Though He was a fighter, a protector of the brahmana Vishvamitra in fact, His features were still delicate. His beauty defeated the pride of millions of cupids, and His shyama complexion was intoxicating to the eyes.

His ancestry was spotless as well. He was a descendant of the famous King Ikshvaku. Men in this line were known for their fighting ability, their deference to dharma, and their courageousness. These factors were well-suited for marriage, as a woman takes protection from her husband. Interestingly enough, Sita's features were comparable to Rama's. Her beauty was impeccable, and her family line went through King Janaka, who was famous throughout the world for his piety. She was also very polite just like Rama. Rama and His younger brother Lakshmana were there as escorts to Vishvamitra, who as a renounced ascetic required aide in protecting his religious sacrifices from the attacks of miscreant night-rangers in the forest. The two brothers left their home and nobly protected the sage.

Sita was deferent to brahmanas as well. Through such piety one acquires tremendous spiritual merits. This also meant that she was ready to be the ideal wife, to serve her husband without hesitation. A pious husband who can protect and a wife who is faithful create a potent combination that brings one closer to meeting the ultimate aim in life, becoming God conscious. The husband is pious and the wife supports him, which means that both share in the fruit of an existence, devotion to God.

Of course in this instance there was no need to meet life's aim for the participants, as Sita and Rama are the object of religious practice. Rama is the definition to the abstract conception of God. He is an incarnation of the original

Lord, a worshipable figure capable of granting His association to anyone simply through His name. Sita is Rama's energy, His eternal consort. Therefore just by saying their names, one is in their company. The fortunate attendees of the svayamvara in Janaka's court got to focus their eyes on those two beautiful forms, basking in the sweetness of the vision. We can create that same unique combination within our minds by always chanting the holy names, "Hare Krishna Hare Krishna, Krishna Krishna, Hare Hare, Hare Rama Hare Rama, Rama Rama, Hare Hare".

VERSE 84

राम दीख जब सीय सीय रघुनायक।
दोउ तन तकि तकि मयन सुधारत सायक।।८४।।

rāma dīkha jaba sīya sīya raghunāyaka |
do'u tana taki taki mayana sudhārata sāyaka ||84||

"When Rama looks at Sita, Sita sees Rama. Looking at both of them, Kamadeva sharpens his arrows." (84)

Essay - Eyes For Each Other

There was no need for Cupid to sharpen his arrows and release them on two parties who were simultaneously interested in each other. As if it were serendipity, Rama looked at Sita and Sita looked at Rama. Neither party had met before, and they weren't officially betrothed. Rama was there as a guest, and He was soon to participate in the contest, the winner of which would get Sita's hand in marriage. Yet seeing one another before Rama's try at lifting the bow created the seed of desire within each, as they wanted to be with each other. Rama was no ordinary competitor, and Sita was no ordinary prize.

Rama is God. He is the Supreme Personality of Godhead in His avatara as a warrior prince. Any person can claim to be God, and we can also tag any notable historical personality as an incarnation of God. Authenticity is required, though, and it is determined by the revealed scriptures and those who follow them. No people are more respected throughout history than the famous acharyas and saints like Narada Muni, Vyasadeva, Lord Chaitanya, Ramanujacharya, Shankaracharya, Shrila Rupa Gosvami, His Divine Grace A.C. Bhaktivedanta Swami Prabhupada, and Goswami Tulsidas. All of these personalities accept Rama as God, though they might not worship Him specifically. Some choose to worship God as Krishna or Vishnu, but both of them are the same Rama.

These personalities follow the authority of the Vedas, the oldest scriptures in existence. The Vedas discuss Rama's divine nature at length and also reveal that Sita is the goddess of fortune, who is the energy of God. The energy and the energetic are always linked, a singular entity in a sense. For this reason God in the Vedic tradition is always worshiped alongside His energy. There is Lakshmi and Vishnu, Radha and Krishna, and Sita and Rama.

If God is always with His energy, why were Sita and Rama involved in a marriage yet to be determined? The events that take place on this planet are sort of like a real-life play directed by the Supreme Lord, who kindly casts Himself in the leading role. Sita and Rama marry in the most amazing event, one talked about for thousands of years into the future. It becomes famous even during their time, where word is spread through stories from village to village rather than through newspapers or radio or television broadcast. The word travels all around, keeping others excited in anticipation each time they get to hear about the event.

In the verse quoted above from the Janaki Mangala of Goswami Tulsidas, the reference is made to Kamadeva, the god of love, to show that Sita and Rama had eyes for each other. Rama only wanted Sita as a wife, and Sita only wanted Rama as a husband. Sita's marriage was to be determined by a pious king, her father King Janaka. He decided that a contest was the way to go, as the show of strength required in lifting Lord Shiva's amazingly heavy bow would be an indication from above that a perfect match was found.

A match is important for the father because the daughter must be protected in marriage. A weak husband would not do justice to Sita, especially considering that she was the most beautiful woman in the world. Other princes would try to take her for themselves, and so the husband had to be able to fend off such villains. Indeed, Sita would be taken from Rama's side later on through a backhanded plot executed by the purported most powerful man in the world, Ravana. Yet his powers were overestimated, and simultaneously he underestimated Rama's. The Lord would defeat him and get back His dear wife.

At the occasion of the svayamvara, there was anticipation, as no one knew who was going to win the contest. Upon seeing Rama, who was a handsome youth who entered the city accompanying Vishvamitra Muni, the residents who loved Sita wanted Rama to win. The eldest son of King Dasharatha of Ayodhya was there with His younger brother Lakshmana also. Lakshmana could have participated in the contest, but as Rama was the eldest, he would not violate etiquette. In addition, he would never want to defeat Rama in a contest even if he were asked to.

Kamadeva operates on the mortals, instilling lusty desires in them by shooting his arrows. As God, Rama is obviously not susceptible to the influence of mundane lust, but the symbolic reference to Kamadeva is used to show that there was mutual attraction between Sita and Rama. Kamadeva gets ready to shoot his arrows when he sees there is a potential relationship between two parties. The arrows in this instance would have had to have been fired at both Sita and Rama, as it couldn't be determined who was more desirous of the match.

As Hari, God is one who can take away. He excels at taking away the fears of His devotees, and on this occasion He would not fail to live up to His name. Shri Hari would win the contest by easily lifting up the bow, making the desired union a reality. A feast for the eyes followed, and the match made in heaven would etch its mark in history. The divine couple is still celebrated and worshiped to this day, with Lakshmana and Hanuman, Rama's dearest servant, included in the picture. Just as Sita and Rama are meant for each other, all living entities are meant for worshiping the Supreme Lord. Through hearing about Sita and Rama's marriage, we take one step closer to reawakening our dormant love for God.

VERSE 85

प्रेम प्रमोद परस्पर प्रगटत गोपहिं।
जनु हिरदय गुन ग्राम थूनि थिर रोपहिं।।85।।

prema pramoda paraspara pragaṭata gopahiṁ |
janu hiradaya guna grāma thūni thira ropahiṁ ||85||

"You can see the love they have for each other, which they try to keep secret. Knowingly they erect a collection of stable pillars made of goodness within their hearts." (85)

Essay - City of Love

In an area that is more or less undeveloped, when you see a series of pillars placed in the ground, indicating that construction is going on, you know that some type of building is going up. The pillar goes with the foundation, and in order for it to serve its purpose it must be stable and remain in good standing [no pun intended] for quite some time. The pillars are not something to be knocked down right away. Ideally, they should last a very long time, providing stability to the building's occupants. Such stable pillars were erected within the hearts of two lovely souls ready to embark on a lifetime's journey together. The construction was seen not through yellow tape or hard hats, but through the looks they gave each other.

The pillars were made of goodness, or guna, which can also mean virtue. The more goodness you have inside of you the better. You hear the expression, "that person is just a good soul," which means that "good" has a higher presence within their body than "bad." It is very easy for the bad side to dominate. You just have to look at someone else to give rise to bad feelings. "Oh look at them. They think they are so great. They're really not. My stuff is better. Plus, even if they have more stuff, they are just wasting their money. I'm more intelligent with my expenditures. I don't need all that stuff to be happy. I'm not so materialistic."

It's harder to see the good in everything around us, especially in other people. It is for this reason that the highest transcendentalist in the Vedic tradition is known as a paramahamsa. The most elevated religionist if you will, the person who practices spirituality as it is meant to be practiced, does not suddenly find more and more people to tag as sinners. They do not find more and more people to criticize and make feel bad. Rather, the perfect transcendentalist is compared to a supreme swan. The swan is unique in its ability to separate milk from a mixture of milk and water. Basically, it grabs the essential item, the nectar if you will, out of something that isn't pure.

"If we give a swan milk mixed with water, the swan will take the milk and leave aside the water. Similarly, this material world is made of two natures - the inferior nature and the superior nature. The superior nature means spiritual life, and the inferior nature is material life. Thus a person who gives up the material part of this world and takes only the spiritual part is called paramahamsa." (Shrila Prabhupada, Teachings of Queen Kunti, Ch 3)

The supreme swan of a transcendentalist sees the good in everything. They know that God's energy is everywhere, and that not even a blade of grass can move without His sanction. They are not Pollyannaish or unreasonably happy. They know that karma works on everything, and so there isn't a pressing need to look at everything negatively. After all, every individual is a spirit soul, part and parcel of God. Eventually they will make their way towards enlightenment, even if it takes them many lifetimes. To preach to others, to give them instruction on how to remove all bad from within and acquire all goodness, the paramahamsa temporarily steps down from their lofty position to make distinctions, but all the while they maintain their pure goodness on the inside.

One way to foster that goodness on the inside, to erect pillars of good qualities within the heart, so much so that it looks like you have a neighborhood full of sturdy buildings made of goodness, is to hear about God and His pastimes. One of His most famous pastimes is His lifting of the illustrious bow belonging to Lord Shiva. This occurred in the kingdom of Janakpur, where a contest was taking place. At the time the Supreme Lord was there in His incarnation of Shri Ramachandra, the eldest son of King Dasharatha. Lord Rama is God based on His qualities, which are described in the Vedic texts. He is not a pseudo-incarnation created on a whim after the fact. His appearance and activities were described before they took place by Maharishi Valmiki, a self-realized soul, a paramahamsa in his own right.

The purpose of the contest was to find a husband for King Janaka's daughter Sita. The problem was that none of the kings could even move the bow. Rama was there as a guest with His younger brother Lakshmana and the sage Vishvamitra. Though a guest, He was eligible to participate in the contest, and when Sita and Rama saw each other, sparks started to fly internally. Just from looking at one another, pure love began to grow. They tried to keep this a secret, however, but others could tell what was going on. There was no hiding it, though neither party made any outward gesture.

The love was growing within their hearts. Goswami Tulsidas compares it to erecting a network of pillars made of virtue or goodness. This love was there to stay; it wasn't going anywhere. The only people leaving dejected on this day were the rival princes who had come to try to win Sita. Rama would lift the bow with ease and complete the construction of the buildings of goodness through wedding Sita in a grand ceremony.

How can hearing about this incident fill our hearts with goodness? Envy, especially of God, is the root cause of our residence in the material world. The envy we feel towards others indicates a lack of spiritual awareness. Think about it for a second. If someone else has more money than you, why should you feel threatened? They still have to eat. They still feel the sting of defeat. They still hanker for things. They also have to die. If you can eat just fine, why does it matter if someone else is better off financially? Since you know how difficult life in the material world is, shouldn't you be happy that someone else might be able to find some relief from the daily pressures?

Only through knowing the self, which is completely spiritual, can you get rid of envy, lust, greed, anger and all other negative emotions. To know God is to know the self, for He is the Supreme Soul, or the Superself. He is the origin of both matter and spirit, and so if you learn about Him as best you can, you will know yourself too. And when you know yourself, you will know others, and pretty soon you will see that we are all in the same boat, trying to find our way to eternal happiness.

Simply from hearing the Janaki Mangala, we can know God so well. He is very strong, pious, and kind. He also loves Sita, His eternal pleasure potency, very much. She loves Him without deviation, and He loves her back. Know that He always loves us too, and His mercy is already available to us in so many ways. Through regularly chanting the holy names, "Hare Krishna Hare Krishna, Krishna Krishna, Hare Hare, Hare Rama Hare Rama, Rama Rama, Hare Hare," we can start to take advantage of that mercy.

VERSE 86

राम सीय बय समौ सुभाय सुहावन।
नृप जोबन छबि पुरइ चहत जनु आवन।।86।।

rāma sīya baya samau subhāya suhāvana |
nṛpa jobana chabi pura'i cahata janu āvana ||86||

"Sita and Rama both are looking so beautiful that the atmosphere is very nice, like a youthful king bringing to the people a vision that they want." (86)

Essay - Giving Them What They Want

This was a contest with spectators after all. Spectators are pleased with a spectacle, especially if it gives pleasure to their eyes. If the spectacle relates to an image that remains within the mind, giving the individual a source of pleasure going forward, then it is all the better. Such an image was created when Rama and Sita were looked at simultaneously. The pairing was perfect, and so the scene looked as if a youthful king had brought to the town a perfect image that everyone wanted.

What image did the people want? How can we tell that? Don't desires change all the time? One second I want pizza and the next I want ice cream. One day I love playing baseball and the next I never want to play it again. This is the nature of a material existence; to hanker and lament. The mind hankers after something, and if it doesn't get it lamentation follows. Even if you do get what you want, your hankerings will not stop. And since not all hankerings can be met, lamentation will surely follow.

The unmarried man in his youth wants to get married. "Why can't I get a wife? I just want someone to love. I will be so faithful to her. I will treat her so well. Because of my love for her people will say that I am the best husband. Others are married, and they don't know how lucky they are. I might just have to go it alone my whole life. I will never meet the right person."

The seasoned veteran of marriage will have a different take. "When will I have my freedom? Every day she nags me about this and that. Wherever I go, there she is. Anytime I want to go anywhere, I have to check with her first. I can't even sit and watch television in peace. This is my home too, you know. I should be able to feel comfortable here. These single guys have no idea how good they have it. I would kill to have that freedom again."

"One who is thus transcendentally situated at once realizes the Supreme Brahman. He never laments nor desires to have anything; he is equally disposed to every living entity. In that state he attains pure devotional service unto Me." (Lord Krishna, Bhagavad-gita, 18.54)

Hankering and lamenting continue until one is Brahman realized. Brahman is the all-pervading spiritual energy, the impersonal force that ties us all together. We are all part of Brahman, which is truth. This is difficult to perceive because of the variation in outward appearance. We make classifications based on this variation, and with each differentiation we get further away from the realization of Brahman.

One way to become Brahman realized is to abandon attachment to the sense objects. Basically, deprive yourself of whatever you tell yourself you want. Limit your eating, sleeping, mating and defending. Study the Vedas, which describe the differences between matter and spirit in great detail. Stay focused on the Absolute Truth through your work, and one day you'll become detached.

An easier way, which actually leads to a better end, is to have devotion to God directly. He is the source of Brahman, so if you connect with Him, you'll not only see the oneness shared between all the species, you'll also feel a higher pleasure. This was the case in Janakpur many thousands of years ago. The people of the town weren't acknowledged Vedantists. They weren't considered Brahman realized. On the contrary, on the surface it seemed like they were way too invested in the outcome of a single event, the marriage of the king's daughter Sita.

They wanted Sita to marry a handsome and chivalrous prince. She deserved such a husband, as she was beautiful in every way and dedicated to the rules of propriety. Her marriage event was a contest, wherein princes from around the world would try to lift an enormously heavy bow belonging to Lord Shiva. The first one to lift it would win and thus get to marry Sita.

When the people saw Shri Rama, a handsome youth accompanied by His younger brother Lakshmana and the sage Vishvamitra, they wanted Him to win. They also saw the way Rama and Sita looked at each other, and this created a wonderful atmosphere. It was the perfect setting; everything was auspicious. It looked like a young king had arranged for the picture, creating a town that was perfect.

This was not ordinary hankering within the people. A Brahman realized soul can take the next step to devotion to God, as is pointed out by Shri Krishna in the Bhagavad-gita [18.54]. Krishna is God, the Supreme Personality of Godhead in fact. Rama is the same Krishna but in a different visible manifestation. The manifestations are described in the Vedic texts; they are not concocted on a whim.

People didn't just see someone special and then proclaim them to be God. In fact, the people in Janakpur did not know Rama's divinity. This ignorance helped their devotion, keeping it more genuine.

It should also be known that someone who reaches the platform of bhakti, or pure love for God, has already done the legwork in the past at some point. They satisfied the obligations pertaining to mundane piety, and they understood the Brahman energy as a result, even if they may not remember doing so. Therefore the hankerings of the people with respect to Sita and Rama getting married were not ordinary. They were spiritual emotions tied to a result that would never be forgotten.

That beautiful picture is still remembered to this day, showing that nothing about the event was material. Matter is dull, lifeless, and ever changing. Spirit is eternal, immutable, and imperishable. The spiritual event of Sita and Rama's meeting is celebrated by the wonderful saints like Goswami Tulsidas, who in their storytelling carefully lead the listener to the wonderful conclusion, the blessed marriage itself.

RAMA WITH THE BOW

VERSE 87

सो छबि जाइ न बरनि देखि मनु मानै।
सुधा पान करि मूक कि स्वाद बखानै॥87॥

so chabi jā'i na barani dekhi manu mānai |
sudhā pāna kari mūka ki svāda bakhānai ||87||

"That beautiful picture cannot be explained; it can only be felt. With nectar, a dumb person can only drink it, not explain its taste." (87)

Essay - Dumbfounded

Herein we get a metaphor for how devotional service, bhakti-yoga, operates. In trying to describe the beauty, wonder, glory, fame, opulence, and power of the Supreme Lord and His energy, everyone is dumb. Being dumb is bad if there is someone else who is wiser than you, but if everyone is dumb in comparison to the highest being, then it's not so bad. More importantly, those same glorious attributes can be experienced. Just because we can't explain them doesn't mean that we can't use them for deriving pleasure.

Can a dumb person explain how nectar tastes? More importantly, would they even care about explaining it? The explanation is helpful in trying to give others an accurate assessment of the drinking experience, but the drink itself is meant to be experienced by the sense of taste. Being dumb in this context means not having the ability to communicate effectively with respect to an experience. Think of a child who tells you that what they're eating is "yummy." They don't say that the salt mixes well with the sugar or that the perfect combination of spices adds an exotic flavor to the dish. They just eat and don't worry too much about poetic ability.

The same tact is taken by the wise saints who follow bhakti-yoga as their occupational duty in life. The biggest questions in life are indeed impossible to answer. For starters, we can't think beyond the bounds of time and space. Try to go back to the beginning of time. Now realize that there was a time before that, and a time before that. Keep going back and you'll never reach an end, because time's span is infinite. The same applies to space. Travel as far out as you can go, but where do you reach an end? Is there a barrier somewhere? Ah, but the barrier must have something on the other side, otherwise it wouldn't be a barrier. Therefore space continues beyond the limits of vision.

If we can't fully understand time and space, how can we explain them? How can we explain the Supreme Absolute Truth, that force which is beyond duality? No birth, death, old age or disease. No loss, no gain. No sadness, and no happiness. Just a fixture; a rock that is immune to the deficiencies that plague us. How are we to explain such a force? Is it a person or just an energy?

The Vedas say that the human birth is auspicious because it brings the potential for understanding these things, to some degree. This is key. We can only understand a little bit about that which is beyond our control. We can never have full knowledge. This should make sense because a force with full knowledge would never need to acquire it. If, at any point, I need to be taught something, it means that I am not perfect. If I am imperfect at any point in time, it means that I am not all-perfect.

Better it is to experience the Absolute Truth than to try to understand it esoterically. The highest experience is that which brings a transcendental taste, which means that there is enjoyment from connecting. In the above referenced verse from the Janaki Mangala, Goswami Tulsidas gives us an idea of what that taste is like and how it is impossible to explain.

But isn't this verse an explanation? By describing an event from a long time ago, the poet uses words to convey a thought. Therefore he is explaining something, not just experiencing it.

Through instruction, one can lead others towards a taste. For instance, I may not be able to tell you how this nectar I'm holding tastes, but I can advise you to give it a try and see for yourself. The Vaishnava saints, the devotees of the personal aspect of the Absolute Truth, guide us towards this taste test. If we repeatedly indulge in that taste under ideal conditions, we'll never want to give it up. And since it is the highest taste, it brings the highest pleasure.

In this instance, the taste is the vision of the Supreme Lord and His eternal consort. God is a singular entity, and so is His direct energy expansion which gives Him pleasure. Depending on the time and circumstance, they both appear on earth in different manifestations. In the Treta Yuga, God was the warrior prince Rama and His energy the princess of Videha, Sita. One time they were set to be married in King Janaka's assembly where many princes from around the world had gathered.

The divine natures of the personalities in question were unknown to the people observing. They just drank up the visual nectar instead. They speculated about Rama and His qualities and how Sita was the perfect match for Him. They could tell that Sita and Rama had eyes for each other, and paired together the entire scene became auspicious.

The poet stops at this point, however. He can't really explain anything more about the beauty. One has to just experience it. But how do we do that if we're not there? This event took place thousands of years ago, so why explain it to us and then tell us that it can't be fully explained? One of the many glorious features of the Supreme Lord is that His name carries His presence. He has many names assigned to Him based on His qualities. Rama is one such name, and Sita is a name for His energy. Hare also addresses the same Sita, and Krishna describes the same Rama in His original form of a beautiful youth with a blackish complexion, holding a flute in His hands. Thus by chanting, "Hare Krishna Hare Krishna, Krishna Krishna, Hare Hare, Hare Rama Hare Rama, Rama Rama, Hare Hare," one can taste the nectar of the beauty for themselves.

One of the definitions of kirtana is "to describe." By trying to describe the glories of God, one engages in kirtana, and through this method there is a taste as well. Though he couldn't fully describe the beauty of the scene in question, just by trying Tulsidas tasted the nectar. He was by no means dumb; the works he authored showed his mastery over Sanskrit and various dialects of Hindi. Nevertheless, the humble souls always consider themselves dumb in relation to the Supreme Lord, and so in full humility they follow bhakti-yoga. They know that to taste transcendence is better than to try to understand it solely within the mind. Because of their attitude, the Supreme Lord guarantees that they never run out of the nectar they desire.

VERSE 88

तब बिदेह पन बंदिन्ह प्रगट सुनायउ।
उठे भूप आमरषि सगुन नहिं पायउ॥88॥

taba bideha pana bandinha pragaṭa sunāya'u |
uṭhe bhūpa āmaraṣi saguna nahiṁ pāya'u ||88||

"Then Janaka's vow was announced to the people. The kings arose excited, but none could get the desired result of lifting the bow." (88)

Essay - Not Meant to Be

At the end of each week in the National Football League season, there is extensive analysis of all the games that just completed. This is one of the contributing factors to the profitability of the league. Since most of the games are played on a single day, and each team plays only one game per week, there is ample buildup for each upcoming game. The rest of the time is spent in contemplation of the previous week's games, increasing the anticipation over what lies ahead. An inevitable part of the review process is looking at the missed opportunities. What could have been done differently to receive a better outcome? From an incident a long time ago, we get another reminder of a harsh reality of life. If your desired outcome is not in the cards, if it is not meant to happen, nothing can be done to reverse the fortune. By the same token, that which is meant to occur by the divine will can never be prevented.

For the sports fan, a well-known indication of the ability of a single event to shape destiny is the last minute field-goal kick. In American football a field-goal is worth three points, and since the games are played under the direction of a sixty-minute game clock, you can ostensibly kick a field-goal as the last play of the game. If the addition of the three points puts your team in the lead, the kick essentially wins the game for you. On the flip side, if you're trailing and your team misses the last second kick, you lose the game.

In the postgame review, you can tell yourself, "Oh, if only we would have made that kick. It was so easy too. Our kicker never misses from such short distances. Man, if the kick was good we would have won, and with that win our record would be better." That win can shape the fortunes of the team going forward, and so you can analyze the kick forever and ever. Other plays from the game can be similarly analyzed. Perhaps something went your way at a pivotal moment. Perhaps the other team made a costly error at an inopportune time.

These close encounters show that preparation and ability are not the sole determining factors in victory. A victory is nothing more than a desired result, a successful end to the output of energy. There are all kinds of victories; they are not limited to sports. The same principle applies to those outcomes, wherein personal effort alone is not a guarantee for success. I can try as hard as I want in a particular endeavor, doing everything right, and still not get the desired outcome. On the flip side, sometimes I can do everything wrong and still end up on top.

Many thousands of years ago, famous royal dynasties from around the world assembled in a city known as Janakpur. They knew why they were there; they wanted to win the hand in marriage of the king's eldest daughter. News had gone out that the king was to hold a bow-lifting contest. The most powerful princes in the world were gathered there that day, but there was a brief distraction when Shri Rama from the kingdom of Ayodhya arrived. He wasn't there specifically for the contest, but His arrival was nonetheless noteworthy. His beautiful features indicated a divine presence, one so strong that people forgot about the contest for a moment. When they returned to normal consciousness, they still couldn't forget Rama. They tied the contest to Him, wanting Him to win it.

But a contest is a contest. After the visual attention paid to Rama, who was there with His younger brother Lakshmana and the sage Vishvamitra, King Janaka, the host of the ceremony, had the rules of the contest announced. It was an oath. The king vowed to give Sita, his daughter, to whoever would first lift the bow. Janaka was known around the world for his virtue, and Sita followed in his line. Therefore she was considered a great prize, a tremendous fortune to whoever would welcome her to their family.

The princes assembled there that day arose with excitement upon hearing the king's vow. It was "go time." This was akin to the gun in a race going off. No more sitting around and waiting. Here was their chance to prove to thousands of people that they were the strongest person in the world. The bow in the middle of the sacrificial arena was not ordinary. It originally belonged to Lord Shiva, a heavenly figure in charge of the mode of ignorance. The three modes of material nature are described in detail in the famous Vedic scripture, the Bhagavad-gita, which is also known as the Gitopanishad. In summary, living entities can adopt bodies belonging to the modes of goodness, passion, or ignorance. Sometimes the modes are mixed together in varying proportions, and so you have the many different species. People in each mode have a corresponding deity, and Lord Shiva is the worshipable figure of those in the lowest mode, wherein real knowledge is completely lacking.

But Shiva's actual position is devotee of the Supreme Lord, who is the worshipable figure of those in the modes of goodness and pure goodness. Therefore this bow couldn't be lifted by just anyone. It was, in a sense, Lord Shiva's representative at the contest. He could make the bow extremely heavy or light at a moment's notice. Though the princes assembled there wanted very badly to win, they couldn't even move the bow. All that anticipation, all that excitement on the way to Janakpur, was for naught, as they walked away defeated.

Rama was meant to lift the bow. He is the Supreme Lord, the worshipable deity for Lord Shiva. Sita is Rama's wife for life, the eternal consort of God. She is His energy, and He is the energetic. The two together make for a wonderful sight, and their reunion on earth took place at that contest in Janaka's kingdom. Victory was not meant to be for the rival princes, and it was guaranteed for Shri Rama. That same lifter of Shiva's bow guarantees to protect His devotees who always chant His names, "Hare Krishna Hare Krishna, Krishna Krishna, Hare Hare, Hare Rama Hare Rama, Rama Rama, Hare Hare."

CHAND 11

नहि सगुन पायउ रहे मिसु करि एक धनु देखन गए।
टकटोरि कपि ज्यौं नारियरु, सिरु नाइ सब बैठत भए।।
एक करहिं दाप, न चाप सज्जन बचन जिमि टारें टरै।
नृप नहुष ज्यौं सब कें बिलोकत बुद्धि बल बरबस हरै।।11।।

nahi saguna pāya'u rahe misu kari eka dhanu dekhana ga'e |
ṭakaṭori kapi jyauṁ nāriyaru, siru nā'i saba baiṭhata bha'e ||
eka karahiṁ dāpa, na cāpa sajjana bacana jimi ṭāreṁ ṭarai |
nṛpa nahuṣa jyoṁ saba keṁ bilokata bud'dhi bala barabasa harai ||11||

"Unable to get the desired result, some made an excuse and stayed where they were, while others went to see the bow. Like a monkey examining a coconut, they each sat back down with their heads hanging down." (Chand 11.1)
"Some were excited, but the bow was immovable, like the word of a saint. Looking at the bow, their strength and intelligence were forcefully stolen, like with King Nahusha." (Chand 11.2)

Essay - Fear of Failure

This bow was so intimidating that some were afraid to even try to lift it. The bow was the reason they were there in the first place. The princes came to try to win the hand of the most beautiful princess in the world. And to do that required lifting a bow in front of so many other people. But some were intimidated by the bow to the point that they wouldn't try to lift it. Their behavior set the table nicely for the ultimate triumph of the Supreme Personality of Godhead.

The famous fable relating to the fox and the grapes gave rise to the popular expression, "sour grapes." The fox tries to reach for grapes that are up high on a vine. After a failed attempt, the fox changes his tune, saying that the grapes are probably sour anyway. The fox doesn't know that for sure, but in order to massage its ego, to feel better about the failure, it dismisses the grapes as being poor in taste and thereby not worth attaining.

Some of the princes assembled in Janakpur took a similar attitude, except they didn't necessarily speak ill of the item in question. This bow originally belonged to Lord Shiva, a famous figure of the Vedic tradition. If the name Shiva is unknown to you, at least know that during this time period everyone knew who Shiva was. He was highly respected, even by those who didn't worship him specifically. This bow originally came from him, and since it was the centerpiece of the event in Janakpur, people knew that it wasn't ordinary.

King Janaka didn't call people to his kingdom to lift a grain of rice. Why would people even come for that? If they did, then they'd fight with each other to be the first in line. The lifting of the rice would be a given, as even an infant can pick up something as light as rice. This bow was not ordinary, and people knew that it wouldn't be easy to lift. Many princes came to Janaka's city because the winner would be a true gem, a tower of strength to be known throughout the world.

Some were too afraid to try to lift the bow, though, knowing its strength and wanting to avoid public shame. If you fail on the grand stage, it is sometimes worse than not trying at all. If in sports you consistently lose in the final round of a big tournament, it's worse than actually losing in the first round. No one remembers who played in the earlier rounds, but the finals are viewed by a larger audience. A perennial failure in the important moments then gets labeled a choker, which is worse than being known as incapable.

"People will always speak of your infamy, and for one who has been honored, dishonor is worse than death." (Lord Krishna, Bhagavad-gita, 2.34)

In the Bhagavad-gita, Lord Krishna tells Arjuna that for a celebrated warrior, dishonor is worse than death. This is because they were previously honored. They were known for some reason or another. Through dishonor, they tarnish their reputation. The eager journalists pay close attention to scandal for this very reason. If they can take down a celebrated figure through reporting their flaws, their story will be very popular. The dishonor will draw much attention because it is focused on someone who was previously honored. Dishonor to someone who was never honored isn't as important.

From the above referenced verse from the Janaki Mangala, we see that some of the princes made an excuse and stayed where they were. Think of it like the football player refusing to go into the game by faking an injury. "Oh my knee hurts. I don't think I can play, coach." Others got up and examined the bow, but they sat back down with their heads hanging low. Their behavior is compared to monkeys looking at coconuts. The inside of the coconut is what matters. It takes some effort to open the coconut too; it's not an easy business, even for human beings. Unless you make the effort, however, you will never taste the fruit that is inside, namely the water and the coconut meat.

Comparing these princes to monkeys is humorous and also harsh in a sense, but it is done to paint the right picture. This event is talked about to this day because Shri Rama would eventually lift the bow. He is the Supreme Personality of Godhead in an apparently human form. He performs superhuman acts witnessed by the parrot-like saints, who then document what they see and repeat the information to others, passing on the descriptions of the pastimes to future generations.

Whether they tried or not, these princes did not have the ability to lift the bow. The bow was like a coconut that no monkey could crack. It was destined to be lifted by Rama, who is Sita's husband for life. Janaka's daughter, the beloved Sita Devi, was fit for the most powerful prince in the world, and since no one is more powerful than God, only He is worthy of Sita.

Essay - Immovable

Goswami Tulsidas here makes a few references to Vedic history to describe what happened to the rival princes as they tried to lift the famous bow of Lord Shiva. The setting was a kingdom hosting an event with thousands in attendance. The main attraction, the final act on the bill if you will, was the lifting of the bow. Whoever could do it first would win. The fight would be declared over as soon as that bow went in a prince's hand and was raised to the sky. As destiny's will is impossible to subvert, on this day only one person was set to win, someone who has never lost anything in His life.

Do we know of anyone who has never lost? Famous political figures may have won the big election when they were on the ballot, but they definitely lost something prior to that. No one goes completely undefeated. Death is the greatest champion in this regard, as it defeats every single person, regardless of the effort they make to send it back from where it came.

To say that God is undefeated seems a bit obvious. "Oh sure, go the God route. You can just say that about anything. 'I will never win this. Only God could do this. It is hopeless for me. No one but God could succeed in these trying circumstances.'" The Vedas give more than just an abstract or utopian idea of God.

There are concrete details provided which are easy to remember, provided that one wants to remember them.

And why wouldn't we want to remember someone who is undefeated? To aid in the remembrance we get God's name of Achyuta. Just saying the name "Achyuta" over and over again brings God to the mind, allowing us to remember that He is undefeated. If that remembrance isn't giving enough pleasure, go back to an incident that proved that He is the strongest person in the world. For such an incident to take place, the undefeated figure known as God must have a form that is visible to the eyes.

There are debates among transcendentalists as to whether God is with form or without, whether He is a personality or just an energy. On a higher level, the arguments are a waste of time because we only think in terms of form and formlessness because of our limited abilities. On a cloudy day we say that the sun is not out, but the sun hasn't gone anywhere. We say that a person is gone after they die, but their soul still exists. They are still alive, though we can't see them.

To make an entity distinct, we refer to them as a person. A person possesses features but a person is also flawed. Therefore we think God can't be a person because that would mean He's flawed. He must also be without form because we can't see Him. Both of these are indeed not the case; His personality and form are different than how we know personalities and forms. He is the Supreme Person, and His attributes are divine. He can lift an extremely heavy bow while in the visible manifestation of a young prince.

Before that victory took place, other princes tried their hand. King Janaka hosted this contest to find a groom for the bride, his daughter Sita Devi. What better way to find a good protector than to hold a contest relating to strength? But this bow was originally Shiva's, and Sita is eternally Rama's. Rama is the Supreme Lord in His incarnation as a warrior prince. Rama appears before the eyes, but He is not an ordinary person. He possesses the attributes of beauty, wealth, strength, fame, wisdom and renunciation to the fullest degree and at the same time.

Shiva is a great devotee of Rama, and Sita, as Rama's wife for life, can only be with Rama and no one else. Janaka is also a famous devotee today, so we see that based on the players alone, the result of the contest was set. Of course no one knew this outwardly, as this is the fun the Supreme Lord likes to have. If all knew what was going to happen, why show up? And if everyone knew beforehand, why would we want to hear details of the event today? Why celebrate Achyuta's marvelous feat of lifting the bow if everyone there already understood what was going to happen?

In the above referenced verse from the Janaki Mangala, Goswami Tulsidas continues his description of the kings who tried to win the contest. Prior to this, some just stared at the bow and walked away, making an excuse. They were like monkeys looking at a coconut, not trying to open it because they were too afraid of the shame of losing. The kings mentioned above were so excited that they actually tried to lift the bow. But it is said that the bow was immovable, like the word of a saint.

A saint in the Vedic tradition is known as a brahmana, which can be likened to a priest. A brahmana lives by austerity and penance, and through their good deeds they acquire tremendous spiritual merits. As a result, when they say something, it must come to be. For instance, if they curse someone, the results of the curse must manifest. If they are supplicated after the fact, they can proclaim something else which will also come to be, but they will never take back their word of the original curse. This is a power granted to brahmanas by the Supreme Lord, who holds His devotees in very high esteem.

It is also said that by looking at the bow, the strength and intelligence of the kings were forcefully stolen, like with what happened to King Nahusha. Nahusha was a famous king during ancient times, and through his pious deeds he ascended to the heavenly realm. The three worlds are the earth, the heavenly planets, and the hellish planets. As they are all part of the material world, residence is not permanent for the wandering soul. You go to heaven if you are good in this life, but you don't stay there forever. Similarly, being condemned to hell doesn't mean that you are stuck there without any hope.

King Nahusha was in heaven, but while there he had lusty desires towards the wife of King Indra. Indra is the king of heaven and he cursed Nahusha to fall from heaven and be born as a snake for his impious thoughts. Material life is thus very tenuous; there is no certainty for anyone. These kings were previously considered to be very powerful and intelligent, but since this bow was destined to be lifted by Rama, they seemingly lost all their strength just by looking at it.

Fortunately, there is one discipline that is above the material nature, that brings permanent results in a permanent realm. Devotional service, also known as bhakti-yoga, is the soul's eternal occupation, and one of its primary methods of implementation is hearing. Just hearing about Rama's eventual victory in the contest, and how all the other kings were bested by the bow He was to lift, brings the consciousness closer to the transcendental realm. While the curse of a saint cannot be reversed and accumulated merits can vanish with a single transgression, know that through loving God spiritual strength increases in a manner that is irreversible. The undefeated Shri Rama makes sure of it.

VERSE 89

देखि सपुर परिवार जनक हिय हारेउ।
नृप समाज जनु तुहिन बनज बन मारेउ॥89॥

dekhi sapura parivāra janaka hiya hāre'u |
nṛpa samāja janu tuhina banaja bana māre'u ||89||

"With the people of the town and their families, Janaka was disappointed in the heart at seeing this. It was like a forest of the best lotuses being killed by a frost."
(89)

Essay - Like the Coldest Winter Chill

The farmer's worst nightmare is the frost. If you have a garden in the backyard, you probably don't rely on its output for sustenance. It's nice to see tomatoes and squash growing, but you still get the majority of your food from the supermarket. The farmers are the ones who supply these markets, and so their harvest is a lot larger. When the frost comes and wreaks its havoc, the toll it takes on the farmer can be devastating. This is what it looked like to King Janaka a long time ago when he saw the best princes in the world defeated by an amazingly heavy bow.

The chill was the bow. It was as hard as adamant; it could not be moved. It would just take one prince lifting it to end the contest. They would be declared the winner immediately. No more worry over what to do. No more sadness over seeing defeat. Even if it's your worst enemy, seeing them fail miserably in front of the world evokes some feelings of pity. Imagine then a host of proud kings bested by a bow while others watched. Janaka felt sad in the heart seeing this.

The princes were the lotuses. They were the best flowers to grow in the forest that was Janakpur. The host Janaka wanted the best princes to come to his city to try their hand at the contest. The winner would get to marry Janaka's daughter Sita. She was worth the effort. A good wife from a good family is a great fortune for the husband and his family. Through her support the man is energized, and then he is better equipped to carry out his obligations.

The frost of the bow was too formidable a force for these kings, so it looked like Sita would have to stay unmarried. But one person could handle the frost without a problem. He was a special flower in the forest, and for Him whether there was weight or not in the bow was of no concern. He is self-illuminating, so if you compare Him to a lotus, He acts as if the sun is always shining bright in the sky.

"That abode of Mine is not illumined by the sun or moon, nor by electricity. One who reaches it never returns to this material world." (Lord Krishna, Bhagavad-gita, 15.6)

In the Bhagavad-gita, the same lotus in His original form of Krishna says that in His realm there is no need for electricity. We know that the source of light within this planetary sphere is the sun. The further you get away from the sun in outer space, the darker it becomes. When the earth rotates temporarily out of the vision of the sun, there is darkness for the inhabitants. So the sun is the source of illumination, but in the spiritual world there is no need of a sun. The proprietor Himself, the king of the spiritual world, is so effulgent that there is no need for external light. Therefore one who reaches that realm never has to live in darkness.

That proprietor was there in Janakpur that day, ready to take a shot at lifting the bow. His splendor was evident in His facial and bodily features, and that splendor spread to His limbs as well. There was immense strength in Him, and so lifting the bow would not be a problem. Shri Rama, the eldest son of King Dasharatha, at the request of the sage Vishvamitra, stepped up and raised the bow without issue.

Why allow the frost to set in? Why didn't Rama lift the bow immediately? The sun's brightness is appreciated more after the dark night. The spring is welcomed after a harsh winter. On this occasion, the cold winter of defeat affected both the participants and the host. The lotus-like princes tried their best to lift the bow, but the chill was too much to bear. Janaka's hopes were sinking slowly with each successive defeated prince, and so it looked like all hope was lost.

And then came God to save the day. Rama is the Supreme Lord, the same person other faiths worship. In Rama the features are more clearly drawn out. He is Bhagavan, which means one who possesses beauty, wealth, strength, fame, wisdom and renunciation to the fullest degree and at the same time. The defeated princes were embarrassed by the bow, but in seeing Rama victorious, it was known that the proper result occurred. The miscreant princes who were still upset at their failure at least had their false pride checked.

Because of the preceding frost, the sun of the solar dynasty shone so bright that He is still remembered to this day. Word spread quickly of Rama's victory. The female sage Anasuya even once asked to hear about the event from Sita herself. The saints always delight in hearing about Rama, and since they are like lotuses as well, they look to Him as their sun. In the harsh winter of Kali Yuga, the sunshine is available through the chanting of the holy names, "Hare Krishna Hare Krishna, Krishna Krishna, Hare Hare, Hare Rama Hare Rama, Rama Rama, Hare Hare."

VERSE 90

कौसिक जनकहि कहेउ देहु अनुसासन।
देखि भानु कुल भानु इसानु सरासन।।90।।

kausika janakahi kahe'u dehu anusāsana |
dekhi bhānu kula bhānu isānu sarāsana ||90||

"Vishvamitra then instructed Janaka, telling him to allow the sun of the sun family to look at Lord Shiva's bow." (90)

Essay - The Sun of the Sun Family

There are many ways to describe the Supreme Personality of Godhead, and from each way a new path for glorification is found. It's like having a magic wand that can be waived to create endless discussions that warm the heart and inform the mind. In this particular instance, Goswami Tulsidas nicely set the table by first mentioning that the failure of many princes in a contest was like watching a forest full of the best lotus flowers killed by a chilling frost. And after the onset of that winter chill, the sun of the sun family was to have His chance, to show that someone could indeed lift this amazingly heavy bow.

Shri Ramachandra is a historical personality and also an incarnation of God. We are informed of this by the Vedas. His name says that He is the moon that gives full transcendental pleasure. His appearance took place in a dynasty that originated with the sun-god, Vivasvan. When hearing such facts, the tendency is to think that in a primitive era man didn't know much about things out of their grasp, so they just personified such things as the sun, the moon, and the rain. This seems plausible enough, but we also know that despite the wealth of material science and research over millions of years there is still no explanation given for the sun's origin. If there was a big bang of chemicals to create life, why can't we repeat the same explosion? Are chemicals more intelligent than us? How can chemicals randomly create an object that burns brightly without cessation, while we can't even keep a light bulb burning for as long as we want?

The ancient scriptures of India assign personalities to the sun and the moon not out of sheer conjecture, but as an accurate way to describe how all material bodies operate. There are three modes of material nature: goodness, passion and ignorance. Think of goodness as knowledge, passion as a neutral state, and ignorance as just that, stupidity, lack of knowledge. The elements belonging to these modes can then be combined into so many different proportions, resulting in 8,400,000 species. The sun is a divine figure, so it is mostly in the mode of goodness. It is a giver of life, and so it is to be honored.

The sun's body is composed mostly of the element of fire, whereas in some creatures fire is almost absent. The sun's family lineage is described in books like the Bhagavad-gita and Shrimad Bhagavatam. The sun's son was Manu, and his son was Ikshvaku, who took charge of government. These were not sense-gratifiers; they operated off of religious principles, or dharma. The princes who took birth in this line upheld the standard of government set by Ikshvaku. Yet Rama is described as the sun of this line because He was the brightest figure. He made it even more famous than it already was.

In the above referenced verse from the Janaki Mangala, Vishvamitra Muni is not exaggerating when He refers to Rama as the sun of the sun race. Prior to this, Rama was used as protection in the forest against wicked ogres who were attacking the sages. Think of retreating to the wilderness to find peace and quiet. You want to get away from the hustle and bustle of civilized life and just take it easy for a while. These sages took this attitude to the extreme and decided to make the forest their home. They just wanted to worship God, and the Vedas gave them plenty of rituals and regulations to follow. There would be fewer distractions in the forest, or so they thought.

Rakshasas, creatures who were mostly in the mode of ignorance, purposefully attacked these sages because of their respect for religious principles. If I live in ignorance I can't really successfully debate someone who lives in knowledge. My arguments will always fail, for deep down I know that I am engaged in the wrong activities. The only way I can emerge victorious is if I destroy my opponent. This is a principal tool of the politician who doesn't stand for anything in his campaign. Rather than tell people the truth, that he wants to stay in power so that he can distribute taxpayer dollars to his specific interest groups of choice, he will try to slander the opposition, using every fallacy of argument there is in order to sway voters.

These Rakshasas couldn't argue, so they just attacked. Therefore the sages required protection and so Vishvamitra went to Ayodhya to get the help of Rama and His younger brother Lakshmana. Though they were very young at the time, they still defeated the Rakshasas. The forest was previously chilled by these vile creatures, but the sun of the solar dynasty was there to bring the lotus-like sages back to life.

On this occasion in Janakpur, Rama would not revive the princes who had failed to lift the bow. They were trying to win the hand of Sita Devi in marriage. She was King Janaka's beloved daughter. Rama's transcendental warmth would revive the hopes of the people of the town, who wanted Him to win. They saw His beauty and were enamored by it. They had never seen anyone like Rama before. This is what happens when you see God, and in order to see Him right you must be pure at heart. Only then will your eyes notice the Divine when it is standing in front of you.

As a pious king himself, Janaka respected the priestly class, and so Vishvamitra was not out of place in instructing Janaka. It was at the sage's direction that the brothers went to Janakpur, for they were otherwise content staying in the forest and protecting him. Vishvamitra was doing the work of the demigods, the celestials who wanted Rama to rid the world of the head of the Rakshasas, Ravana. Through lifting the bow of Lord Shiva, the wheels were set in motion for the demon's demise.

VERSE 91

मुनिबर तुम्हरें बचन मेरु महि डोलहिं।
तदपि उचित आचरत पाँच भल बोलहिं॥91॥

munibara tumhareṁ bacana meru mahi ḍolahiṁ |
tadapi ucita ācarata pāṁca bhala bolahiṁ ||91||

"' O best of munis, your words can shake the mountains and the earth, but this situation requires the right behavior that will be for the good of the people.'" (91)

Essay - Questioning the Muni

In traditional Vedic culture, the order of the parents is never to be defied. If they tell you to do something, you do it. They are the first authority figures, after all. If it weren't for them, we wouldn't be where we are today. Even if one or both of our parents weren't around during our upbringing, someone was, and they are thus automatically afforded respect. The same respect should be offered to the guru, or spiritual guide. Yet on some occasions we think we know better and thus doubt their words. All works out in the end only if we eventually follow through on their advice, despite our misgivings.

A famous example that illustrates this fact is the first meeting between His Divine Grace A. C. Bhaktivedanta Swami Prabhupada and Shrila Bhaktisiddhanta Sarasvati. The guru is the representative of God. Since he is godly and treated on the same level as God, he is known as gurudeva. He is not God, but he is offered treatment as if he were. There is a reason for this. The respected guru unlocks the door to the spiritual kingdom, a place free of birth, old age, disease and death. The only requirement for winning the guru's favor is humility. If you are humble and sincere in wanting to learn from them, they will open up to you. And if they are part of an authorized chain of teachers originating from the Supreme Lord, the information they offer will help you reach the ultimate destination.

The acharyas are the notable gurus who lead by example. Both Shrila Prabhupada and Bhaktisiddhanta Sarasvati are known as acharyas today, and so they are not ordinary people. They are specifically empowered by the Supreme Lord to descend to earth to rescue scores of fallen souls. Nevertheless, they go through typical life cycles, where it appears that in their youth they are ignorant, to distribute their mercy more freely to others.

In his youth Shrila Prabhupada was not yet a recognized acharya, and his fateful meeting with his future spiritual master took place when he was in his early twenties. In this first meeting, Bhaktisiddhanta Sarasvati asked the young Prabhupada to preach about the glories of bhakti-yoga, devotional service to God, to the English speaking world. Bhaktisiddhanta Sarasvati was a recognized guru, and so his words carried tremendous weight. Basic etiquette called for following his advice. Yet the young Prabhupada was a little challenging during that first meeting, saying that the issue of India's independence needed to be solved first. Despite his stubbornness, that initial meeting eventually led to Prabhupada taking up the cause seriously. He protested a little at first, but later on the original advice was taken so seriously that today the name of Krishna is known throughout the world.

A long time before that, during an ancient time period, a notable spiritual master named Vishvamitra gave a suggestion to a king who was hosting a contest. The contest was related to a bow. Whoever could lift it first would win the hand of the king's daughter, Sita, in marriage. The contest saw royal families from around the world arrive in Janakpur. They wanted to win Sita and bring her into their family.

The problem, of course, was that the bow was impossible to lift. None of the powerful princes could even move it. The king, Janaka, became sad over this. To him, it looked like a forest of lotus flowers had been destroyed by a frost. Vishvamitra, who was there with two youths, Rama and Lakshmana, asked the king to give permission for the elder Rama to try to lift the bow. Vishvamitra wasn't Janaka's guru, but he was respected enough as a brahmana, or one in the priestly order. Rama and Lakshmana listened to his words. Those brothers had just protected Vishvamitra and other brahmanas from attacking night-rangers in the forest. If Vishvamitra had such wonderful and obedient disciples, princes from the Raghu dynasty, serving him, he must have been someone special.

Despite Vishvamitra's position, Janaka was a little hesitant to agree to his request. In the above referenced verse from the Janaki Mangala, we see that Janaka acknowledges the power of Vishvamitra's words. He says that those words can shake mountains and the earth. Brahmanas during those times could curse someone just by declaring it out loud. They could have fought back against the Rakshasas attacking them in the forest by casting spells, but that would have decreased their accrued spiritual merits. That is why Vishvamitra approached the king of Ayodhya to allow Rama to come to the forest. Rama and Lakshmana were of the royal order, so they were warriors by occupation.

"By the powers gained through our performance of religious austerities, we are certainly capable of killing these Rakshasa demons. But at the same time we don't want to waste our ascetic merits, which took such a long time to achieve, on these demons. Oh Raghava [Rama], these demons are always putting obstacles in the way, making it impossible for us to concentrate on our performance of austerity and penance. Therefore, even though we are being eaten away by the Rakshasas, we do not curse them." (Sages speaking to Lord Rama, Valmiki Ramayana, Aranya Kand, 10.13-14)

While acknowledging the power of Vishvamitra's words, Janaka also says that the words should speak of the proper behavior for the situation at hand. That behavior should be for the benefit of all the people. Essentially, Janaka thought that Vishvamitra's advice was improper. "How was the youthful Rama going to lift an extremely heavy bow that none of the other competitors could even move? How was Rama's failure going to please the people, who all wanted Him to win?"

This hesitancy was understandable on Janaka's part, but eventually Vishvamitra would win out. Those words would be followed, and they would benefit everyone, as Rama is the best well-wishing friend of every living entity. As the Vedas proclaim, He is the Supreme Lord in His personal incarnation as a warrior prince. He is the worshipable deity of the brahmanas, brahmanya-devaya, so they know what He is capable of. Vishvamitra gave the right advice to Janaka, and the doubtful yet respectful king eventually followed through, and the world was better off for it.

VERSE 92

बानु बानु जिमि गयउ गवहिं दसकंधरु।
को अवनी तल इन सम बीर धुरंधरु॥92॥

bānu bānu jimi gaya'u gavahiṁ dasakandharu |
ko avanī tala ina sama bīra dhurandharu ||92||

"' Like an arrow Banasura and Ravana came to the bow and then went. Who on this earth is as heroic as them?'" (92)

Essay - Requiring God's Sanction

It's easy to believe something if we've seen it happen before. Also, if what is to be seen is a derivative of other things in nature that we have witnessed, then we can also believe it. Doubt settles in when we can't conceive of something, when something is purported to happen that is beyond our range of perception. Yet just because we are limited in this way doesn't mean that the thing in question is impossible. This truth especially holds true with the Supreme Personality of Godhead, whose every personal feature is inconceivable. During a famous incident witnessed by King Janaka, the Lord showed that His strength is beyond understanding.

Perhaps you've seen the strong man competitions that air late at night on the cable television sports networks. These aren't your typical games. Rather than compete in a sport with a ball and a time clock, these competitors participate in strange events that uniquely challenge their strength. In one event they may have to lift a very large sack and carry it across a field. In another event they may have to pull an automobile using only their arms. In another event they may have to pick up a large weight and hold it above their head for a certain number of seconds.

If we didn't see these competitors successfully complete these challenges, we maybe wouldn't believe that it was possible. What's more, once we do see their abilities, we use them as a benchmark. If the strongest man in these competitions can pull a large truck for one hundred yards, to say that a single man could pull a truck one thousand yards would seem ridiculous. "No way any human being could do that. The world's strongest man can only pull the car for one hundred yards, and such a person is a freak of nature. A thousand yards increases the difficulty by a factor of ten, so there's no way such a thing is possible."

A long time ago, the strongest man competition related to a bow. During this time, the Treta Yuga, military combat took place using primarily bows and arrows. If the fighters were removed from their chariot, they would fight with clubs and daggers, and in the absence of any physical weapons they would fight by hand. As fighting with bows and arrows was commonplace, it wasn't all that difficult to lift up a bow and draw its string back with an arrow.

Ah, but this bow in King Janaka's court was not ordinary. It took hundreds of men just to move into the arena. It originally belonged to Lord Shiva, a principal deity of the Vedic tradition. He is known as the destroyer. With a discharge of a large fiery weapon he destroys the entire creation when the time calls for it. That weapon is akin to the sun becoming ten times hotter. It is no wonder then that his weapon effects the destruction of the creation.

Though Lord Shiva is the destroyer and also a worshipable deity for those in the material mode of ignorance, as a person he is fully devoted to the Supreme Lord, Vishnu. Vishnu is also Krishna, the Supreme Personality of Godhead. Vishnu is also Rama, an incarnation of the Supreme Lord who roamed the earth during the Treta Yuga. Shiva's bow was destined to be lifted by Lord Rama. The winner would get the hand of Janaka's daughter Sita in marriage.

In the above referenced verse from the Janaki Mangala, King Janaka expresses his doubt over Rama's ability to lift the bow. Vishvamitra Muni led the two brothers, Rama and Lakshmana, bow warriors themselves, to the contest area. After many princes had tried and failed to lift the bow, Vishvamitra asked that Rama be allowed to give it a try.

To Janaka, the ceiling of strength was seen in two powerful fighters of the time: Banasura and Ravana. Interestingly enough, both were devotees of Lord Shiva. Banasura had a thousand arms and Ravana ten heads. They were extremely powerful due to benedictions offered by Shiva. Mahadeva is only interested in devotion to Vishnu, so he quickly gives his devotees whatever they want. This way they will leave him alone. Material benedictions are limited anyway; they are not absolute in their ability to deliver desired outcomes.

Janaka saw that Banasura and Ravana came towards the bow, tried to lift it, and then went away in a flash. Their arrival and subsequent defeat was as swift as the flight of an arrow. To Janaka, there was no one on earth as heroic as those two. Ravana was feared throughout the world, and Banasura had Lord Shiva's favor. Many years later, Banasura would fight directly with the same Rama during His time on earth as Krishna. In that fight, which is described in the Shrimad Bhagavatam, Lord Shiva would help Banasura, but to no avail. Krishna would counteract both of them, and in the end it was Shiva's kind plea towards Krishna that saved Banasura's life. Krishna spared the demon by deciding only to reduce his number of arms from one thousand to four.

"My dear Lord Shiva, I accept your statements, and I also accept your desire for Banasura. I know that this Banasura is the son of Bali Maharaja, and as such I cannot kill him, for that is My promise. I gave a benediction to King Prahlada that the demons who would appear in his family would never be killed by Me. Therefore, without killing this Banasura, I have simply cut off his arms to deprive him of his false prestige." (Lord Krishna, Krishna, the Supreme Personality of Godhead, Vol 2, Ch 8)

That incident gave further evidence that nothing can happen without the Supreme Lord's sanction. Even if we see tremendous ability, we should know that it is only a partial indication of the supreme strength that exists in full in God. Material affairs are of no concern to Him, as dualities pervade a life devoid of devotion to God. If there is duality, there is no universally beneficial condition. What we think to be opulence today can turn out to be a curse tomorrow, and vice versa.

On that famed day in Janakpur, Vishvamitra was right in his insistence, and Janaka and the rest of the world would see that for God lifting an extremely heavy bow is a piece of cake. He can lift thousands of bows if He needs to. Since this contest dealt with reuniting with the goddess of fortune, Sita Devi, Rama kindly showed off His supreme strength.

As the sanction of the Supreme Lord is required to receive any benediction, the wise choice would be to follow activities that spark His interest. In devotional service, bhakti-yoga, the Supreme Lord takes a direct interest, and because of this He can make something as simple as the chanting of the holy names, "Hare Krishna Hare Krishna, Krishna Krishna, Hare Hare, Hare Rama Hare Rama, Rama Rama, Hare Hare," deliver even the poorest and weakest person in the world. If there is sincerity and full reliance on the Supreme Lord, His strong helping hand will be too much for the material energy to overcome.

VERSE 93

पारबती मन सरिस अचल धनु चालक।
हहिं पुरारि तेउ एक नारि ब्रत पालक।।93।।

pārabatī mana sarisa acala dhanu cālaka |
hahiṁ purāri te'u eka nāri brata pālaka ||93||

"' This bow is as fixed as Parvati's mind. This bow is from Lord Shiva, who observes the vow to accept only one wife.'" (93)

Essay - Shiva and Parvati

The celebration of the lifting of the heavy bow in King Janaka's assembly travels to all spheres, touching especially those who are intimately related to the Supreme Personality of Godhead. In the Vedic tradition, there are many gods, but not all of them are equal. There is only one Supreme Lord, and by worshiping Him, all other gods are automatically worshiped. If they should still feel slighted, the protection granted by the original Godhead to the worshiper is perfect; a fact proved during the famous incident of the first Govardhana Puja. The most elevated of the godlike figures are so exalted that the Supreme Lord requests their direct participation in His pastimes. No one is more dear to God than Shiva and Parvati, and so it was not surprising that their names came up quite often in Janakpur during a famous event a long time ago.

With so many gods, how do we know which one is the original? Also, some take the original to be one person, while others take Him to be someone else? How do we reconcile the differences?

The Vedic literature mentions different paths to attaining enlightenment, and with each path there are also different worshipable figures. In order to tell which worshipable figure is supreme, we have to compare the destinations of the paths.

But don't all paths lead to the same place?

Ideally, they should, but immediately they may not. The person graduating from first grade in elementary school is headed for second grade in the immediate term, while they are looking to eventually reach graduation. The person who has already reached graduation has no need for the second grade and its requisite assignments.

Depending on which mode of material nature you are in, you will follow a certain path towards transcendental enlightenment. The ultimate end goal is pure love for God. This is the only real definition of love, and it is known by terms such as prema, bhakti, and bhava in Sanskrit. What we consider love is more like kama, or material lust. Even when we offer love to parents, siblings, or children, the affection, or sneha, is a derivative of the original prema that we possess.

And prema can only exist for one person: God. God consciousness is the original consciousness. Every other kind of consciousness is a reflection or masking of the original consciousness. The question then remains: who is God? Is He a formless energy known as Brahman? Is He the Supersoul resting within the heart? Is He an angry man who looks to punish the sinners? Is He old?

Only the Vedas provide the most complete information about God. It is impossible to fully enumerate the qualities of the Supreme Lord. This is actually a good thing, as it allows prema to be directed through channels of endless glorification. If the qualities could be fully enumerated, then one person could expound on them and shut everyone else out of the fun. When we see award shows or ceremonies honoring a specific personality, there are multiple people who offer their insight. One person doesn't suffice for praise, as people have different viewpoints and different stories to share. In the same way, each individual can offer praise to God. If everyone in the world did this without end for the entire duration of their stay on earth, there would still be plenty left to glorify.

In the simplest definition, God is Bhagavan, or the Supreme Personality of Godhead. The word Bhagavan means one who possesses the opulences of beauty, wealth, strength, fame, wisdom and renunciation to the fullest degree and at the same time. He is the only person who possesses this feature, and so He is the only Bhagavan. Sometimes respectable personalities who are intimately related to Bhagavan in a mood of divine love are also addressed as Bhagavan, but again this is only because of their relation to the original Bhagavan. The word Bhagavan also means the most fortunate, and so that good fortune spreads to the devotees as well.

Lord Shiva is one person who is sometimes addressed as Bhagavan. This is because he is fully devoted to the original Bhagavan. In the Shrimad Bhagavatam and Bhagavad-gita, two famous Vedic texts which present wisdom so profound that every other philosophy existing past, present and future is explained, it is said that God's original form is Lord Krishna, who is also known as Shyamasundara, the youth with a blackish complexion and a stunningly beautiful face. A direct expansion of Krishna is Lord Vishnu, who takes charge of creating this and many other universes. Then there are further expansions of Vishnu, to the point that the material world is managed by Lord Brahma, Lord Shiva, and another Lord Vishnu.

All the Vishnu expansions are equivalent to one another; they are like identical candles lit from the original candle that is Krishna. Lord Brahma and Lord Shiva agree with this conclusion, so much so that they are original teachers of the philosophy known as Vaishnavism, or devotion to Vishnu. Along with the Vishnu expansions there are the avataras who descend to earth. Lord Rama, the eldest son of King Dasharatha, is one of the more famous incarnations, and He is the preferred form of Vishnu for Lord Shiva.

Lord Brahma and Lord Shiva are considered demigods, or elevated living entities who work at the direction of the Supreme Lord. There are other demigods as well, and each of them provides specific material benedictions to their worshipers. Just because they fulfill this role doesn't mean that they are completely immersed in material life themselves.

Worship of Lord Shiva and his wife Parvati is prominent in the Vedic tradition. The story of their marriage is described in many Vedic texts. Parvati is the daughter of the mountain king Himavata. Her name means daughter of the mountain. In her youth Narada Muni, a celebrated spiritual master and devotee of Vishnu, told her father that her destiny was to marry Lord Shiva. In order to effect this, Parvati went into the forest and did tapasya, or austerity, for a very long time. Her resolve was tested many times, including by her parents, who did not want her to marry Shiva. One time Shiva sent his attendants to entice her in the forest. They offered her Lord Vishnu as a husband, but Parvati's resolve was so strong that she stood by the words of Narada. Not that there was anything wrong with marrying Vishnu, but she was intent on following what her spiritual master had told her.

In the same way Lord Shiva is dedicated to Parvati. In her previous birth she was also Shiva's wife. Known as Sati, she died after her husband was insulted one time. Shiva only accepts one wife, and combined the two manage the material creation. Parvati is also known as Durga, which as a word means "difficult to overcome." Her material creation is like a fort with giant walls that are seemingly impossible to scale. Her devotees worship her so that the material creation will not be so painful to them. Durga carries a trident in her hand, which symbolizes the threefold miseries of life: those caused by the body and mind, those caused by the demigods, i.e. nature, and those caused by other living entities.

In King Janaka's assembly a long time ago, there was a contest to see who would marry the king's daughter Sita. So many princes from around the world came and tried, but none of them could even move the bow. The bow originally belonged to Lord Shiva, so it was special. Vishvamitra Muni, a noted brahmana of the time, asked the king if Lord Rama, who was there with His younger brother Lakshmana, could try His hand at lifting the bow.

In the above referenced verse from the Janaki Mangala, Janaka is responding to Vishvamitra with skepticism. He compares the bow's firmness to Parvati's resolve, and says that the bow is originally from Lord Shiva, who observes the vow to accept only one wife. Janaka is such a pious individual that when he wants to describe something that is immovable he references Shiva and Parvati. Today Janaka is known as one of the authorities on devotional service, which is the discipline that reawakens prema, or pure love for God. Lord Shiva is also an authority on devotional service. We see that Janaka had so much respect for Shiva and Parvati, which means that any genuine Vaishnava will also have respect for the couple who is so dear to Sita and Rama.

Janaka was indeed correct in describing the bow in this way, but what wasn't immediately known to everyone was that Rama is the very worshipable Lord of Shiva. And Parvati is devoted to Shiva, which means that she is part of a chain that worships Shri Rama. This bow was Shiva's representative at the ceremony, and since Shiva and Parvati are one, Parvati was there as well. Rama was destined to lift that illustrious bow and win Sita's hand in marriage. That amazing feat paid honor to Shiva and Parvati as well, showing that through worship of God all other respectable personalities are worshiped simultaneously.

VERSE 94

सो धनु कहिय बिलोकन भूप किसोरहिं।
भेद कि सिरिस सुमन कन कुलिस कठोरहिं।।94।।

so dhanu kahiya bilokana bhūpa kisorahiṁ |
bheda ki sirisa sumana kana kulisa kaṭhorahiṁ ||94||

"' You're asking for the young prince to look at the bow, but can a piece of a shirisha flower pierce through hard steel?'" (94)

Essay - As Delicate As Shirisha

Let's say that you're out at a restaurant. The food dish you order requires a knife and fork to eat. You could also use your hands and take advantage of your teeth, but then that would make a mess. You'd rather use utensils to make the eating experience more pleasant. But there is a problem at this restaurant. They only have plastic utensils. You're forced to use a plastic knife and a plastic fork to eat. This causes a problem because the plastic utensils aren't strong enough to cut through the food you've ordered. Every time you go to make a cut, the knife gets duller and duller. Also, just by placing the fork into the food, the fork starts to melt. It cannot handle the temperature of the food, so you're left with a deformed fork.

You'd rather have the steel utensils, which are strong enough to cut through the food. The firmer utensils are meant to cut through the less firm food. Now try to imagine it the other way around. What if you needed to cut through steel? You'd need something harder, no? Or perhaps you'd need an instrument that can reach a level of heat intense enough to break through the steel. A long time ago, a bow was compared to steel, and during a particular contest that bow need only be lifted. No one had to cut through anything. The king hosting the contest saw one prince in particular and was astonished that He would try to lift the bow. The king compared the prince to a piece of a soft flower, which has no chance of cutting through steel.

The shirisha flower is very soft. It is often invoked in Vedic literature to describe the softness of the skin of the Supreme Personality of Godhead. Though there are many gods in the Vedic tradition, there is still only one Supreme Lord. He is known by such names as Hari, Vishnu, Krishna and Rama, and there are endless ways to describe His transcendental features. His skin is of a bluish hue, and His smile is intoxicating. Everything about Him is attractive, and so Krishna becomes the best name to use in addressing Him.

Rama is also a great name, as it refers to the full pleasure that the Supreme Lord holds. Rama also describes His incarnation as a warrior prince who once roamed this earth many thousands of years ago. Lord Rama, the eldest son of King Dasharatha, also has extremely soft skin. He is very beautiful and not everyone knows that He is God. They don't need to anyway, as having affection for Him is enough to attain the goal of life.

And wouldn't you rather receive attention based on your qualities than your stature? You could say that your qualities make your stature, but it is better if someone appreciates your qualities first. The stature can bring respect even if you don't possess all of the qualities, but through your qualities someone can respect you for who you really are, even if they never know of your stature. With Shri Rama, His stature is set in the Vedic texts, which describe His endless glories.

And the qualities described are evident to the people who connect with Rama in a mood of love. Sometimes those qualities appear to contradict one another, as they did in the kingdom of Janakpur a long time ago. King Janaka was hosting a contest to determine the future husband for his daughter Sita. The king decided to make the contest one based on strength; this way the winner would be best equipped to protect Sita for the rest of her life.

Many princes came to the contest, but they all failed to even move the bow, let alone lift it. Then the respected Vishvamitra Muni asked Janaka if Rama could try lifting the bow. Rama was not there specifically to participate in the contest. In youthful forms, Rama and His younger brother Lakshmana were defending Vishvamitra and other sages from the attacks of vile creatures in the forest. The brothers came upon the contest through following Vishvamitra.

From the above referenced verse from the Janaki Mangala, which is a poem by Goswami Tulsidas that describes this sacred event, we see that Janaka obviously has appreciation for Rama. He compares the Lord to the shirisha flower, which is a very high compliment. To say that someone has skin as soft as a flower is to say something nice. Soft skin is a more attractive quality than hard skin.

Janaka then compares the bow to something very hard, like steel. As mentioned before, the harder object can easily cut through the softer object; hence the common use of silver utensils when eating. How then is the softer object going to do anything against the harder object? Janaka didn't think it possible for a youth like Rama to lift the bow, and he was especially worried about embarrassing Him. Many other princes had tried but Janaka didn't give them any warning. On this rare occasion, Janaka actually expressed doubts to a venerable brahmana, a member of the priestly class. Typically, the kings in those times listened to whatever advice the priests gave. Janaka's hesitancy only further confirms his love for Rama, who is God.

And that love never goes in vain. Janaka's affection for Rama shown through his doubt would be rewarded with Rama's victory in the contest. Today Janaka is one of the twelve highest authorities on devotional service, which is the best occupation for man. Loving God is the soul's constitutional occupation, and so it can be taken up at any time and at any place. The easiest method is the chanting of the holy names. Just as the soft-skinned Rama easily lifted the steel-like bow, know that the holy names, "Hare Krishna Hare Krishna, Krishna Krishna, Hare Hare, Hare Rama Hare Rama, Rama Rama, Hare Hare," can melt the hardest of hearts, making a lover of God out of anyone.

VERSE 95

रोम रोम छबि निंदति सोभ मनोजनि।
देखिय मूरति मलिन करिय मुनि सो जनि।।९५।।

roma roma chabi nindati sobha manojani |
dekhiya mūrati malina kariya muni so jani ||95||

"'Every part of that vision puts to shame the beauty of Kamadeva. O muni, please don't do anything that will sully that form.'" (95)

Essay - Protecting the Vision

The beautiful trophy should go on the mantel in the home. This way it will be on display for others to see. That setting is appropriate given the importance of the trophy; it is befitting its value. If you put the same trophy somewhere else, it won't be appreciated as much. You wouldn't want to place it next to the garbage can in the kitchen. You wouldn't want to place it on the floor. The object wouldn't lose anything in value, but appreciation of it would diminish. To the person who appreciates it, that loss in appreciation will not be good. The same sentiment exists with devotees of the Supreme Personality of Godhead, and so they do whatever they can to protect their beloved.

Why would you need to protect God? If He is God, He must be supreme. If He is supreme, He must not require any person's protection.

To understand the behavior of the devotees, we can again think of the trophy. That statue indicates a personal accomplishment, and so respect of the trophy is a kind of respect of the accomplishment. The Supreme Lord, who has an image that can rest internally within the heart and externally in front of the eyes of the devotee, is the embodiment of all good qualities. In fact, all qualities emanate from Him, and the good qualities are those which more closely represent Him.

"I am the strength of the strong, devoid of passion and desire. I am sex life which is not contrary to religious principles, O Lord of the Bharatas [Arjuna]." (Lord Krishna, Bhagavad-gita, 7.11)

In the Bhagavad-gita, Lord Krishna explains that He is the strength of the strong, the ability in man, the penance of the ascetic, and a host of other things. The references show that God is the life of everything. Strength is what makes the strong, and ability is what distinguishes the man from the animal. In the same way, the Supreme Lord is the life of an existence. That we have a consciousness shows that there is a God. In the purified consciousness, when all dirty things are removed, the life of the individual is understood to be driven directly by God, and He is appreciated as such.

If you disrespect God, you are essentially disrespecting yourself. Not that you are God, but He is the source of your identity. Your real identity is Brahman, which is pure spirit. Brahman emanates from God, who is known as Parabrahman. There is a relationship between the two that goes beyond which came first. Parabrahman is superior and Brahman is inferior. There is a relationship of oneness only when the inferior voluntarily acts to serve the superior. The superior party in this case elevates the inferior due to the love they show.

Because of the respect held for the Lord by the devotees, sometimes it is not easy to reveal divine love outwardly. Think about it for a second. As soon as you tell someone that you like something, they have an advantage over you. Let's say that you like a particular song by a particular band. If someone else finds out about it, they can criticize that song and the band who plays it. Anytime something happens to that band, they can bring it up to you. "Oh, did you see what your favorite band did? I can't believe they did that. Why would you like them? Did you hear how bad their last album was? They've lost it. They're just sellouts now."

This criticism will bother you since you like that band so much. If you had never said anything, the criticism from others wouldn't be so forthcoming. After all, they would have no idea that you're interested in that particular band. The same vulnerability exists with any preference declared openly, including politics and movies.

For the bhaktas, or devotees, the preference is at the highest level. Loving God is the most important commodity any person can possess. Driven by envy, someone else could criticize God in front of you and thus make you angry. Therefore devotees very carefully worship the Supreme Lord in the proper setting. This is with respect to external worship, as no one sees your internal worship. External worship takes place typically in a temple, where a deity representation of the Supreme Lord is honored with offerings of beautiful flowers and sumptuous food preparations. The place is kept clean, and the deities aren't visible all the time. Only during the proper times will others get a chance to see and worship the deity, automatically making the deity, the Supreme Lord, the chief resident of the establishment.

Sometimes the same Supreme Lord descends to earth and gives a more animate deity to worship. There is actually no difference between the Supreme Lord and His incarnations. The bodies of the incarnations, deities, and original Lord Himself are all spiritual. If they weren't, they would never be worshiped. Moreover, there wouldn't be any benefits derived from worshiping them. You can try to worship an ordinary tree as God, but it won't get you anywhere because the worship of the tree is not authorized. And neither is the tree ever declared to be equivalent to the Supreme Lord.

A long time ago King Janaka saw God in His incarnation of Lord Rama. Janaka immediately held affection for Rama, who came to his kingdom while He was still a youth. In worship in bhakti-yoga, there are offenses to be avoided. The offenses are listed out for the devotee's protection. There is no way to offend God, as He is self-satisfied. The devotees can be offended, though, especially when the deity is not properly respected. Janaka, as an ideal devotee, was worried on this occasion that Rama would be disrespected if He were asked to participate in the contest.

The contest was to see who could lift an extremely heavy bow belonging to Lord Shiva. The winner would get to marry the king's daughter Sita. Vishvamitra Muni, the spiritual master of both Rama and His younger brother Lakshmana, asked Janaka if Rama could have a try at the bow. Other princes had tried, but none of them could even move the bow. In the above referenced verse from the Janaki Mangala, we see Janaka comparing Rama's vision to Kamadeva, who is the equivalent of a cupid. It is said that every part of Rama's vision puts to shame the beauty of cupid. Janaka doesn't want to do anything that will sully that image. A defeated Rama would certainly tarnish the image, and so Janaka wanted to spare his eyes of that vision.

It was very nice for Janaka to think this way, as he was only trying to make sure that God wasn't disrespected. There was no reason to fear, however, as Rama would lift the bow without a problem. That feat created a new image to worship, one of a victorious Supreme Lord reuniting with His eternal consort, Sita Devi. The devotees continue to honor the Supreme Lord in the same way as Janaka did by carefully keeping discussions of Him limited to assemblies of open-minded, non-envious spiritualists, those who are sincerely interested in serving the source of Brahman. And since the devotees are harder to find in the present age of Kali, to spread the divine influence the same devotees now risk being offended by others by remaining humbler than the grass and more tolerant than the tree in their congregational chanting of the holy names, "Hare Krishna Hare Krishna, Krishna Krishna, Hare Hare, Hare Rama Hare Rama, Rama Rama, Hare Hare."

VERSE 96

मुनि हँसि कहेउ जनक यह मूरति सोहइ।
सुमिरत सकृत मोह मल सकल बिछोहइ।।96।।

muni haṁsi kahe'u janaka yaha mūrati soha'i |
sumirata sakṛta moha mala sakala bichoha'i ||96||

"Laughing, the muni said, 'O Janaka, this form is so beautiful that by remembering it one gets so many good merits that all bad elements caused by illusion get removed.'" (96)

Essay - Removing Illusion

Knowledge is power. A knowledgeable person immediately is able to fight off illusion in the form of ignorance. If you're lacking the requisite knowledge, it will be more difficult to tell that you're being fooled. An outsider can inform you that you are wrong in your assessment, that you're not looking at things clearly, but it is better if you actually know what is going on yourself. Rather than close your eyes to the deception, if you can shine a bright light to see through the thick illusion, you will be better situated. A similar point was made by the venerable Vishvamitra Muni a long time ago.

The illusion in question related to a king's worries over the outcome to a contest. It was his contest, so it would make sense that he would have concern over the result. A bow lay in the middle of an arena. Anyone who could lift it up with their arms would be the winner of the contest. Frantic jostling over who would get first in line wasn't necessary. It wasn't like fighting over some money that fell on the ground. This bow originally belonged to Lord Shiva, and it took hundreds of men just to move into the sacrificial arena. Therefore only one prince, if that, in the entire world could lift it. Each person would get their chance, but their chances of success were low.

Janaka fell prey to illusion when he suddenly had a favorite. The winner of the contest would marry Janaka's daughter Sita, so the king wasn't too concerned with the exact nature of the victor. As long as someone would win that would be good enough for Janaka. But when he saw this handsome youth arrive accompanied by His younger brother and spiritual guide, the king suddenly had a vested interest. He wanted this youth, named Rama, to win the contest and marry his daughter. After the many other princes at the assembly failed to even move the bow, the spiritual guide asked Janaka if Rama could take a shot at it.

Janaka replied with doubt. It's not that the sage Vishvamitra was wrong to make the request. Janaka certainly would allow Rama to try to lift the bow, but he was worried about the outcome. He didn't want Rama to lose and then get embarrassed. How was such a beautiful youth going to move something as hard as steel?

In the above referenced verse from the Janaki Mangala, we see Vishvamitra's reply. The sage playfully chuckles at Janaka's words and then offers some sound advice. Rama's vision is so beautiful that one need only think of it in order to have the bad elements caused by illusion disappear. The illusion in this case caused Janaka to hesitate in allowing Rama to try to lift the bow. Vishvamitra could have told Janaka that he was wrong and that one shouldn't be deceived by an external vision, but when you're so invested in an outcome it's hard to overcome opposing elements that feed your fear.

Vishvamitra offered the easier approach: remember Rama. "Just look at Him," the sage said. By doing that, the worry would disappear. Rama is God, the Supreme Personality of Godhead actually, as mentioned in the Vedas, the ancient scriptures of India. The point to take away here is rather obvious: think of God to overcome illusion. You just have to remember Him when you're feeling doubtful, and that remembrance essentially acts like a torchlight of knowledge. It helps you see in the dark.

"He [King Muchukunda] could see also that the dense darkness within the mountain cave had already been dissipated due to the Lord's presence; therefore He could not be other than the Supreme Personality of Godhead. He knew very well that wherever the Lord is personally present by His transcendental name, quality, form, etc., there cannot be any darkness of ignorance. He is like a lamp placed in the darkness; He immediately illuminates a dark place." (Krishna, The Supreme Personality of Godhead, Vol 1, Ch 50)

Rama is also Krishna, which is the original form of the Supreme Lord. Krishna's name means all-attractive, and that attraction inherently speaks of a form. That form itself is self-illuminating, a fact shown one time in an encounter with King Muchukunda. The king had been sleeping in a cave for a long time, but when Krishna entered suddenly there was a glowing light. The king could see Krishna without a problem, and so the self-effulgent Krishna acted to dissipate the illusion caused by darkness.

Rama is considered a personal expansion of Krishna, and so His transcendental body is also all-attractive. Looking at it alone can remove doubts, and the more qualified you are to look at that wonderful vision, the more benefits you will receive. Sukriti, or meritorious credits, can come through good work, that which is in line with virtue. In assessing merits, one would have to rank those which bring a greater reward to be superior. There is no better reward than thinking of God, as the soul's business is to be a lover of God. Therefore the sukriti that comes from remembering Rama is automatically the best. And the best merits always overcome demerits, which in the case of Janaka related to his fear that Rama would lose the contest. While Rama's vision originally caused the worry in Janaka, the same vision, repeatedly glanced at, would dissipate the bad elements. This was the point stressed by Vishvamitra.

In the material world we are daily a victim to the influence of the illusion known as maya. Know that remembrance of God is the easiest and most effective way to dissipate the illusion. Being able to see clearly, the devotee gets an unobstructed view of the most wonderful vision. Janaka and the rest of the pious souls assembled there that famous day would get to see the heartwarming image of a victorious Rama reuniting with His eternal consort Sita. Illusion cannot survive in that scene, and so anyone who makes it the home for their eyes will not be troubled by the dark elements of this world.

CHAND 12

सब मल बिछोहनि जानि मूरति जनक कौतुक देखहू।
धनु सिंधु नृप बल जल बढ़यो रघुबरहि कुंभज लेखहू।।
सुनि सकुचि सोचहिं जनक गुर पद बंदि रघुनंदन चले।
नहिं हरष हृदय बिषाद कछु भए सगुन सुभ मंगल भले।।12।।

saba mala bichohani jāni mūrati janaka kautuka dekhahū |
dhanu sindhu nṛpa bala jala baḍhayo raghubarahi kumbhaja lekhahū ||
suni sakuci socahiṁ janaka gura pada bandi raghunandana cale |
nahiṁ haraṣa hṛdaya biṣāda kachu bha'e saguna subha maṅgala bhale ||12||

"' O Janaka, just see His beautiful form, and know that it magically takes away all bad elements. This bow is like an ocean of energy belonging to the kings, and Rama is like Agastya who will drink it up.'" (Chand 12.1)

"Hearing this, Janaka became confused and started to think. Rama offered prayers to the guru's feet and then went, with neither happiness nor sadness in His heart. The good omens portended auspicious things to come." (Chand 12.2)

Essay - Kryptonite

As no one except God is all-powerful, each one of us has a weakness. That weakness takes full effect at the time of death, when there is nothing we can do to prevent the soul from exiting the body. There are smaller weaknesses too, as during times of strength we can be brought down to a subordinate position through the influence of only one or two elements. For the demon class in ancient times, a great source of weakness was the presence of a particular sage. Several times he brought them down from their position of power, and because of this the sage is often referenced when discussing the defeat of a formidable foe.

For the comic book hero Superman, the chief weakness is an element called kryptonite. It comes from a fictional planet called Krypton. Superman can fly through the air, hold large buildings in his hand, and see through walls. He is very powerful, but when in the presence of kryptonite, he immediately starts to weaken. His enemies exploit this weakness when they find out about it. Though Superman is fictional, his popularity has made the term "kryptonite" a synonym for that which weakens someone. It is also used to point to a singular weakness, one thing which weakens someone the most.

Kryptonite for the demon class is always the same: devotees of God. The most powerful devotee is the brahmana merged in an ocean of transcendental bliss through following bhakti-yoga, or devotional service. The brahmana is like a priest, and so commensurate with their position is a life of austerity and penance. Just as you can improve your performance in sports by controlling your food intake and following exercise, in spiritual life you can make tremendous advancement by limiting sense interaction and controlling the mind.

Agastya Rishi is one of the famous brahmanas of the Vedic tradition. His powers from austerity are so great that he can defeat others who are apparently more powerful. It's sort of like the David versus Goliath, where David is victorious because of using strengths not related to brute physical force. Agastya uses his mind, which is connected to God in a mood of love, to defeat enemies.

There are many stories pertaining to Agastya that are documented in the Vedas. One of them relates to the thwarting of a pair of demons who used to trick brahmanas. The demons were brothers, and their little game involved entering into food. One brother would enter food using mystical power, and when a sage would eat the food the other brother would call out to the brother who was now in the stomach of the sage. The sage would thus die from the demon piercing out of his stomach.

"The sage Agastya is of such a purified nature that in his hermitage a liar cannot live, nor a deceitful person, nor a wicked person, nor one that is committed to sinful activity." (Lord Rama speaking to Lakshmana, Valmiki Ramayana, Aranya Kand, 11.90)

The brothers tried this one time with Agastya Rishi, but the sage simply laughed at them when the moment of truth arrived. Agastya was not so weak spiritually. The brother in his stomach died immediately, and when the other brother went to attack Agastya, the sage burned him to death with a simple glance. Lord Rama, a famous prince of the Raghu dynasty, loved this story so much that He once related it to His younger brother Lakshmana while they were travelling through the forests.

In the above referenced verse from the Janaki Mangala, a poem that describes the marriage of the same Rama to the daughter of King Janaka, Vishvamitra Muni points to another famous incident relating to Agastya. One time the demon class took refuge in an ocean, insulating them from the attack of the pious demigods. Agastya then drank up the entire ocean, which left the demons vulnerable and eventually led to their demise.

In this instance, Rama is like Agastya and the bow, which represents the collective energy of the assembled kings, the ocean. King Janaka hosted a contest to determine the husband for his daughter Sita. Whoever could first lift an enormously heavy bow belonging to Lord Shiva would win. Janaka was worried when he saw Rama because the Lord had very delicate features. In a youthful form, Rama didn't look like He could lift a bow that no king up to this time had been able to even move.

Vishvamitra reassured Janaka, who wanted Rama to win the contest, by pointing to the famous incident with Agastya. Agastya was obviously much smaller in stature than a giant ocean. Yet he was spiritually powerful, which was more important. Similarly, if the bow represented the combined material strength of the competitors at the assembly, Rama represented the spiritually powerful Agastya. Rama is actually the source of all strength; as He is God. In the Bhagavad-gita, the same Rama in His original form of Krishna, confirms that He is the ability in man.

"O son of Kunti [Arjuna], I am the taste of water, the light of the sun and the moon, the syllable om in the Vedic mantras; I am the sound in ether and ability in man." (Lord Krishna, Bhagavad-gita, 7.8)

The reference to Agastya is also appropriate because Agastya is a great devotee of Rama. Agastya is part of a disciplic succession that passes on the story of Rama's life and pastimes. Tulsidas, the author of the Janaki Mangala, is a link in that chain, and so he also has immense respect for Agastya. Vishvamitra's analogy would prove correct, as Rama would lift the bow without a problem. The ocean of the energy of the kings was formidable, but its kryptonite was the Supreme Lord, whose presence is carried on today through the devotees who always chant His names, "Hare Krishna Hare Krishna, Krishna Krishna, Hare Hare, Hare Rama Hare Rama, Rama Rama, Hare Hare."

Essay - The Guru's Feet

Feet tread upon the ground. They therefore come in contact with all kinds of dirty elements. The ground is also hard; it contains rocks and other substances that can damage the soles of the feet. Therefore one often wears shoes or other kinds of protection to save the feet from damage. From this when we hear of worshiping someone's feet, paying honor to them by touching them before important moments, the practice seems a little strange. Though it may seem odd, the practice is most beneficial when the honored feet belong to an authority figure. This fact was validated by none other than the Supreme Personality of Godhead Himself one time.

Feet have a tendency to smell, especially if they are trapped inside of shoes for a long period of time. In houses of worship, footwear is often kept in an isolated area, away from the people gathered to worship. If the area housing the footwear is too close to the people, the foul smell of feet will permeate the air. This smell then taints the mood of worshipers, who try to keep a pure mind fixed in devotional thoughts.

Yet in Vedic culture the feet are an object of worship for those deemed inferior. For instance, when greeting parents and elder relatives, the younger parties touch the feet of the elders. The same goes for when departing. This practice has been going on since time immemorial, as it is enjoined in the shastras that the original objects of worship for the newborn child are the parents, followed by the spiritual master later on in life.

There is a benefit to the practice of honoring the gurus, or authority figures, in this way. Touching the feet is a show of humility. Humility when in the company of one who holds important information only makes them more affectionate towards you. If I worship my parents, they will be pleased. If they are pleased, they will protect me. They will be more enthusiastic to protect me as well. If I honor the spiritual master by touching their feet, they will share some of their wisdom with me. That wisdom is the source of their spiritual strength, and so by showing humility, their strength is shared with me. In any endeavor requiring force, it is better to have multiple sources of energy. Two heads are better than one, as the saying goes.

A long time ago, the exhibition of strength related to the lifting of an extremely heavy bow. The guru in this case knew that only one person in a gathered assembly could lift the bow. There were many prospective candidates, and they were all contestants vying for the hand of the daughter of King Janaka. The king had vowed to give away his daughter Sita to whoever would first lift the bow.

The guru Vishvamitra recommended Rama to Janaka. Other princes there had tried and failed in lifting the bow. Some were too afraid to even try. Janaka was very respectful to his own gurus. As a king, he relied on the advice and consent of the priestly class when making important decisions. It was not like him to question the advice of a wise sage. Yet this time Janaka was hesitant to accept Vishvamitra's counsel. Janaka was worried that Rama would lose like the other princes. Rama was delicate like a flower and the bow hard like steel. How was a flower petal going to pierce through steel?

Vishvamitra told Janaka not to worry and in the above referenced verse from the Janaki Mangala we see what happened after the advice was given. Shri Rama, being neither excited nor dejected, touched the guru's feet and then went towards the bow. Rama is God. God is a singular entity, the same person worshiped by all the various traditions that have been in existence since as far back as history documents. Rama is the personal form of God; the detail behind the abstract conception. His features are specific to the time and circumstance of the Treta Yuga in which the demon class headed by a Rakshasa named Ravana was prominent. Rama is an incarnation of the Supreme Lord Vishnu, who is an expansion of the original personality, Shri Krishna.

Rama was going to lift the bow without a problem based solely on His identity. God never loses if He wants to win; hence one of His names is Ajita. Yet Rama still touched the guru's feet prior to approaching the bow, as if to say that Vishvamitra was giving Him the necessary strength. This was a very nice thing that Rama did, and it illustrates to one and all the respect the bona fide spiritual master deserves. The guru's words were used to alleviate the worries in Janaka, and his feet were symbolically used to lift the bow and bring to Janaka the desired outcome of Rama marrying Sita.

For the spirit souls wandering through the cycle of birth and death that seemingly has no termination, the guru's feet bring the strength and wisdom necessary to achieve the supreme abode in the afterlife. The wisest guru teaches bhakti-yoga, or devotional service, which is the eternal occupational duty of the soul. By respecting the guru, we gain strength in the chanting of the holy names, "Hare Krishna Hare Krishna, Krishna Krishna, Hare Hare, Hare Rama Hare Rama, Rama Rama, Hare Hare," and we please God in the process. The guru gets their strength from their devotion to God and the disciple from devotion to the guru. The servant thus achieves everything desired based on their respect for the proper authority figures.

VERSE 97

बरिसन लगे सुमन सुर दुंदुभि बाजहिं।
मुदित जनक, पुर परिजन नृपगन लाजहिं।।97।।

barisana lage sumana sura dundubhi bājahiṁ |
mudita janaka, pura parijana nṛpagana lājahiṁ ||97||

"Then it started raining flowers from the demigods and drums played. Janaka, along with the city's people and families, became happy, while the rival kings were embarrassed." (97)

Essay - Happy For Others

It is a saintly quality to be happy for someone else when good fortune finds their way. You are a better person if you are happy when your friend wins the lottery as opposed to being jealous of them. Envy is nevertheless a quality all of us possess to some degree. The killer of envy, which is rooted in false pride, is the Supreme Lord. The mechanism for that destruction is His various triumphs, which the pious souls can then rejoice in. The lowest among mankind, however, will never find happiness even with God, whose existence they will continue to deny.

"Wouldn't it be so much better if God just showed up in front of us? Just remove the doubt already. Why does He make things so difficult? If He showed up right now, everyone could see Him and know that He is real. He would show to everyone that He is not a myth like Santa Claus or the Tooth Fairy. Then everyone could happily worship Him and believe in His words found in sacred texts like the Bhagavad-gita."

This lament is understandable, but it is incorrect in a few assumptions. For starters, implied is that God is not available to us right now. That is like saying that the sun doesn't exist when we don't see it. If we are in a dark room during the nighttime, there are no traces of the sun anywhere, or at least that is the accepted conclusion. If I were to then say that the sun doesn't exist, would that be very wise?

Secondly, the assumption is that just by seeing God in a visible and identifiable form everyone would believe in Him. This is certainly not the case, as the field of law shows that any truth will be challenged if someone sees fit. A good lawyer is one who has no principles; they don't have any system of authority. They change their accepted authority source based on their needs. For instance, if past case law supports their client's arguments, the lawyer will cite those cases as evidence for their claim. If they run into trouble, they will use other authorities to help them. When there is no other recourse, they will attack the character of the other side. They will look for any chink in the armor to exploit. This also explains why government becomes so chaotic when run by lawyers. By occupation they are not supposed to follow an absolute authority, so when they take over government they use their expertise in cheating the law to grant favors to various special interest groups.

The above referenced verse from the Janaki Mangala shows that the miscreants, the lowest among mankind, who have lost all intelligence, will not recognize God's presence even when seeing Him directly. Here Shri Rama, the Supreme Lord in His incarnation as a warrior prince, is approaching a bow central to a contest in a kingdom ruled over by a pious king. Many princes were assembled there who had tried to lift the bow. The bow was so heavy that some of the princes just walked up to it and then went back without trying. They didn't want to risk an embarrassing defeat in front of everyone.

Here there is embarrassment nonetheless. When Rama steps up to the bow, flowers rain down from the sky. Drums also beat to mark the occasion. This means that the residents of the heavenly planets have an interest in the game. They obviously want Rama to win. They didn't do the same for the other princes. This is embarrassing to the rival princes because Rama received honor that they didn't.

At the same time, Goswami Tulsidas tells us that King Janaka and the residents of the town were happy to see this. They were pure souls; people who had already performed rigorous austerities in past lives. In the present life they lived under the protection of the pious King Janaka. He was known throughout the world for his honor and dedication to the Vedas, the original scriptural tradition of the world. Though he received a daughter in a non-traditional way, he still followed protocol and looked for a suitable husband for her when she reached the appropriate age.

Janaka's innocent respect for the rule of Vedic law brought the many princes from around the world. He created a contest, and so everyone wanted to win it. The prize was the hand in marriage of Janaka's daughter Sita. Rama also came, following Vishvamitra Muni from the forest. The people of the town were interested in the contest, which required one to lift the extremely heavy bow of Lord Shiva. Since they were pious souls, they recognized Rama to be someone extraordinary. Therefore they immediately decided that He should win, that He should marry Sita.

They saw God, and though they didn't necessarily spot His identity right away, they didn't have to. They had a spontaneous love for Him, which was shown in many ways. They wanted Him to win, they were attracted to His transcendental beauty, and they were thrilled when flowers rained down from the sky prior to His attempt at lifting the bow.

And their love continued when Rama lifted the bow and married Sita. They never forgot Him even after He returned to His home of Ayodhya with His new wife. They worshiped Rama both when He was in their presence and when He wasn't. Such worship is only possible with God, who is Absolute. Remembering His physical presence is as good as seeing it in person. Also, saying His name is as good as seeing Him. Therefore the wise souls who follow the example of the thrilled residents of Janakpur always chant the holy names, "Hare Krishna Hare Krishna, Krishna Krishna, Hare Hare, Hare Rama Hare Rama, Rama Rama, Hare Hare." The miscreants will never believe in God despite all the evidence available to them. After many lifetimes of suffering, if they are fortunate enough to receive the blessings of a devotee, only then will their eyes open up, allowing them to join the party.

VERSE 98

महि महिधरनि लखन कह बलहि बढ़ावनु।
राम चहत सिव चापहि चपरि चढ़ावनु॥98॥

mahi mahidharani lakhana kaha balahi baṛhāvanu |
rāma cahata siva cāpahi capari caṛhāvanu ||98||

"Lakshmana tells the earth and Ananta Shesha Naga, 'Increase your strength. Shri Rama wants to lift Lord Shiva's bow and string it.'" (98)

Essay - Hold On To The Roof

Do we control the revolution of the earth? Do we control how the planets are held up in orbit? Do we control the seasons and when the sun rises and sets? These seem like silly questions, but actually the atheistic science culture is not too far off from affirming all of these preposterous suggestions. If the public can be made to believe that they can change the climate of the earth with their behavior, then surely it will be believed that something can be done to control the other aspects of nature, like the planets. From this verse from the Janaki Mangala we get the Vedic point of view, which also represents the truth in the matter.

If we can't hold something with our own arms for an indefinite period of time, how can we say that any person can control the planets? We take the law of gravity for granted, but someone had to make it. The mathematics involved in the rate of descent of an object indicates that there is intelligence to gravity. If there weren't such laws, then the gravitational force would be a random operation. We know that it is not, and we also know that the revolution of the earth is not random either.

The question them remains: how do we find out who holds up the planets? To respond with "God" seems like a cop out, the easy way out of a tough situation. "The term 'God' is so vague anyway, so you can invoke it to get your way out of any mystery." Ah, but the fact that there is a mystery tells us that there is a need to further delve into the concept of God. Just as we are curious about gravity, the climate, and outer space, we should be curious about the origin of the creation itself. We know that the origin is not chemicals, for if it were then we could use the same chemicals to create a large land mass and have it float in space without any external support. If chemicals were the original cause, we could then at least create a miniature version of the sun. But we are not even close to doing such things.

The need for curiosity with respect to the Absolute Truth is addressed in the Vedic aphorism, athato brahma jijnasa. This translates to, "Now is the time for inquiring about Brahman." The "now" refers to the time of birth for the human being, and Brahman refers to the Absolute Truth, that which is above the dualities of temporary conditions. That which is not affected by like and aversion, heat and cold, light and darkness, and happiness and sadness is Absolute. In the same collection of aphorisms we find janmadya asya yatah, which means "the Absolute Truth is the source of everything." From it have come the material nature and its population of creatures.

Our minds are incapable of thinking beyond the infinite time and space. We can't think of the real beginning of time, because there is always something before a beginning. Similarly, there is always something after an end. That is the meaning to sanatana, i.e. that which has no beginning and no end. There is also no end to space. You can keep travelling and maybe hit a wall, but there is still something beyond that wall.

If we can't think beyond infinity, how can we properly conceive of something that is absolute? This leads to the speculation that the Absolute Truth must be impersonal. It must be devoid of qualities, because a quality is a limiting feature. To say that I am tall is to say that I am not short. To say that I have blue eyes is to say that I don't have brown eyes. If the Absolute Truth is tagged with any attributes, it automatically removes its absolute nature. At least this is the conclusion of the mind that has given up hope for supremacy through material acquisition. It is said that the last snare of maya is the desire to merge into the Absolute Truth, to be one with the spiritual energy that is Brahman, declaring oneself to be God.

In the Vedas the recommended way to learn of the Absolute Truth is to hear about Him. And yes, He is a male in that He is the supreme enjoyer. The Sanskrit word "purusha" refers to person or spirit. It also refers to that which is predominating, like a male. Prakriti is matter, the covering of the person; it is dominated. Within each individual the purusha is the spirit and the outer covering is the prakriti. In the larger scheme, however, the living entities are prakriti, or that which is enjoyed by the supreme purusha, or God.

In hearing about the Absolute Truth from authorized sources, we also learn of His activities, which inherently require features. These features are not limiting;

they are beyond our conception of features. They can still be identified and enumerated to some degree, though. The above referenced incident is one such example of where features can be observed and lessons can be taken away on other aspects of the material nature from that observation.

In the scene in question, Shri Rama is about to lift an extremely heavy bow originally belonging to Lord Shiva. This bow lay in the middle of an arena that is central to a contest hosted by King Janaka of Mithila. The prize of the contest is the hand in marriage of the king's daughter Sita, who is the most beautiful woman in the world. From the Ramayana, a famous Vedic text, and other scriptural works we learn that Shri Rama is an incarnation of the Supreme Lord, the universal God who is known to some degree in all spiritual traditions.

Here Rama's younger brother Lakshmana is advising the earth and the holder of all planets to brace for the impact of Rama's feat. He says that Rama would like to lift and string the bow. Since Rama is God, whatever He wants to do is always accomplished. Therefore Lakshmana knows that the bow will be lifted and that Rama will break it while trying to string it. The resulting sound will be tremendous; it will travel throughout the universe.

By giving this command, Lakshmana informs us that the planets are held by a specific personality. His name is Ananta Shesha Naga. Naga refers to a serpent, shesha to ends or remainders, and ananta to unlimited. Taken together, this divine creature is a serpent with unlimited hoods. On these hoods the many planets of the universes rest. Interestingly enough, Lakshmana is considered an incarnation of that serpent, also known as Anantadeva. He is essentially commanding himself here. Ananta Shesha Naga is also the number one servant of the Supreme Lord in His form of Narayana, who is the source of all men. The unlimited hoods also serve the purpose of glorifying God endlessly.

The earth and other planets are living entities with intelligence. All of this borders on mythology, but if we follow Vedic teachings with a little sincerity in the beginning, the mythical aspect quickly gets removed. Just because we can't see or talk to something doesn't mean that it doesn't exist. Anantadeva is also the original spiritual master, who is the representative of God. This means that his words are the highest authority, which in this case was proven by Lakshmana's prescience. He knew what was going to happen, and so he gave the proper notifications as preparation.

In the current time period, Lakshmana's representatives know that without God consciousness society will be lost in an ocean of despair and chaos, where not even material opulence will do anything tangible for them. Therefore such kind-hearted souls, who follow devotion to the same Rama, ask everyone to make devotional service their priority. And this service is open to every person through a simple sound vibration, "Hare Krishna Hare Krishna, Krishna Krishna, Hare Hare, Hare Rama Hare Rama, Rama Rama, Hare Hare."

VERSE 99

गए सुभायँ राम जब चाप समीपहि।
सोच सहित परिवार बिदेह महीपहि।।99।।

ga'e subhāyaṁ rāma jaba cāpa samīpahi |
soca sahita parivāra bideha mahīpahi ||99||

"When Rama went walking towards the bow, worry came over King Janaka and family." (99)

Essay - The Minutes Seem Like Hours

"I know that I shouldn't worry so much about what will happen, but I am helpless in this situation. I really want this house. My wife and I were just kicked out of our other apartment. Not a forced eviction for any wrongdoing, it's just that the people who own it need the extra space for their family. They've given us a few months to find a new place, and I'd really like to buy a house this time. I don't want to throw money away on rent anymore.

"This one house looks perfect. It is ideal for our future plans. It fits with the number of children we'd like to have. I can also do some of the renovations myself, creating rooms suited for entertainment and comfort. I can also fix things so that if there is a power outage, we will have a backup generator in place that relies on gas. This way we won't miss a beat. Also, it will be nice knowing that I won't get suddenly removed from my home because of someone else's desires.

"This is all well and good, except there is competition for this new house. The people selling it really like us, but there is another bid. We're able to match the bid, and the seller has preferred us, but still this doesn't mean that the house is ours. As we are financing the purchase, the bank needs to give its approval. In order for that to happen, they must inspect the house. If something is not right, they will withdraw the money, which will immediately give the seller a reason to choose one of the competing bids.

"Common sense tells me that we have a pretty good chance of getting the house. More than likely, we will get it, but there is still the chance of failure. For the time being, I can't seem to think of anything else. All of my future plans rest on this single outcome, and until that outcome is settled, my mind will not be at ease. One way or the other, I'd like to have the issue resolved. I can't imagine living like this for much longer."

For a famous king a long time ago, the minutes seemed like hours because of the high stakes resting on an outcome. It wasn't a house that he was purchasing. He wasn't waiting to hear on a job he applied for. He wasn't anticipating an acceptance letter from the college of his choosing. There was nothing really related to his personal comfort. In fact, the worry was entirely over someone else's future. She would not live with him afterwards, so in essence the king's worry was rooted in love. To want more for someone else than you want for yourself is the accepted definition of love, and in this case the desire related to a suitable husband for the king's daughter.

The moment of tension wasn't necessarily expected. King Janaka knew that his daughter might get married, for it was his idea to hold a contest to determine her husband. There was still the chance that she wouldn't get married also. The contest required the lifting of an enormously heavy bow originally belonging to Lord Shiva. Janaka invited all the royal families from around the world to this sacred place. Because of Janaka's character and the beauty of his daughter, the princes were eager to try to win the contest.

Many of them tried, but they all failed to even move the bow. Janaka and family did not have so much riding on the outcome then. They watched, but they weren't overly worried. But now the situation was different. The worry was so intense that it sprung up from the competitor's moving towards the bow alone. An outcome was soon to arrive. If this moment were likened to a college course, it would be like hearing of the final grade, seeing whether you passed or failed. Shri Rama would either lift the bow or not. The people watching would know soon enough, but worry overcame them anyway.

And why were they suddenly worried? Of all the suitors, they thought Rama was the best. Sometimes this isn't the best way to describe a preference. If we're shown samples of carpet to go on the floor in our living room, we might not like any of them. Out of what we're shown, we'll pick the one that we hate the least. That is the point to the samples after all. If we knew the exact color and style we wanted from the outset, we would just order it.

In this instance, Rama was not merely the preferred prince out of the lot. As soon as the people saw Him, they wanted Him to win the contest. In fact, some in the crowd whispered that Janaka should call off the contest and hand over the beloved daughter Sita to Rama right away. "Why take any chances? He drew up this contest to find the worthy husband for her. No one is worthier than Rama. We can tell this by looking at Him. He is obviously some kind of divine figure. We also know that

His character is unmatched. As a humble youth, He has protected the religious observances of the sages living in the forest. He and His younger brother risk their lives to protect the innocent. In this way no one in society can match them in stature."

Janaka too wanted Rama to win when he saw Him. Now that the moment was approaching, the anticipation was too great. The future fate of Sita Devi was on the line. Since the people loved her, if she received bad fortune they would take it worse than her. And by the same token, if something good happened to her, they would be even more elated than she would be.

As Shri Rama is the Supreme Lord, an incarnation of the original Personality of Godhead, He never fails to deliver what His devotees want. And true to form, those spectators who agonized through the suspense felt so much elation that they never forgot about that moment for the rest of their lives. The saints who heard about it immortalized it in poem and song. Goswami Tulsidas relays the event to us in his Janaki Mangala poem, which was composed thousands of years after the fact. In this way if we shift our worries over to God, concerning ourselves with His stature, fame, honor and reputation, then the agony over uncertainty ends up benefitting us immensely.

VERSE 100

कहि न सकति कछु सकुचति सिय हियँ सोचइ।
गौरि गनेस गिरीसहि सुमिरि सकोचइ॥१००॥

kahi na sakati kachu sakucati siya hiyaṁ soca'i |
gauri ganesa girīsahi sumiri sakoca'i ||100||

"Unable to say anything, with a worried heart Sita laments. Remembering Shiva, Parvati and Ganesha, she prays." (100)

Essay - Worship in Tradition

Vaishnavas are often asked: "Why don't you worship Shiva and Parvati? Why don't you worship Ganesha? Why do you just focus on Krishna, Vishnu, or Rama?" The short answer is that the spiritual teachers in the present age of Kali have streamlined their teachings to suit the hustle and bustle of the modern society, where one is considered fortunate just to have a firm faith in God that goes beyond looking at the Supreme Lord as an order supplier. And of course there is also the truth that with worship of the personal aspect of the Supreme Lord, all other kinds of worship are automatically satisfied. Indeed, all other worship is meant to eventually bring one to the platform of pure love for God.

"Men of small intelligence worship the demigods, and their fruits are limited and temporary. Those who worship the demigods go to the planets of the demigods, but My devotees ultimately reach My supreme planet." (Lord Krishna, Bhagavad-gita, 7.23)

In the Bhagavad-gita, Lord Krishna says that those with little intelligence worship the demigods. There are many gods in the Vedic tradition, but there is still only one singular leader, an original personality. He is the same person addressed in other spiritual traditions, except the details of His names, forms, and pastimes may not be disclosed fully. It is said that Krishna, the Supreme Personality of Godhead, can award liberation, material opulence, and mystic perfections very easily, but love for Him will not be granted so freely. This makes the gift of love for God that much more special, and it requires that the individual be worthy of receiving it.

The requirement for qualification explains the many rules, regulations and rituals of religious life. In the Vedic tradition there are so many rituals that span from the time of birth all the way until the last rite at death. Consciousness is constant; it is an integral aspect of the individual, who is represented by the spirit soul. This soul is what animates us. In fact, it animates all life. Thus there is a soul in an animal as well, and also a plant. There are not different kinds of individual souls; just different kinds of bodies. There is a Supreme Soul, however, who is an expansion of the original Lord. This soul is all-pervading; it exists within everyone and has a consciousness that is singular.

Part of the Vedic rituals involves worship of divine figures known as devas, or demigods. But it seems that we've reached a contradictory point here. Part of the culture, which is millions of years old, is demigod worship, but in the sacred work that best describes the purpose of the Vedas, it is said that only the less intelligent worship the demigods. Why even have demigod worship then? Why allow the less intelligent to fall into a pattern of behavior that is not the highest worship?

Actually, the question answers itself. The less intelligent by definition will not be wise enough to follow the highest path that is pure devotion to God. But just because someone is less intelligent doesn't mean that they can't gather knowledge. One doesn't have to stay unintelligent forever. After all, we are all born ignorant. We have a consciousness that carried over from the previous life, but in the present life we still require education to reawaken our dormant consciousness. If no one teaches us, we'll stay as ignorant as the animals.

Demigod worship helps to awaken the spiritual consciousness. The less intelligent are allured by aims of temporary significance. For instance, if I'm concerned with getting married, it means that I give a lot of attention to having a life companion of the opposite sex. Yet even if I do get what I want, it doesn't mean that life's problems will be solved. You can be separated from your spouse and family at any moment. There are no guarantees. More importantly, the love everyone has inside of them is meant to be offered to God. Any other kind of love is a watered-down version of the pure form, which is known as prema.

Worship of Ganesha, Shiva, Parvati, and others who are not the Supreme Lord Vishnu, who is the same Krishna, is part of a culture in families who have had the tradition for too many past generations to even count. If I am born in the United States, I know that my ancestors have lived here for at most a few hundred years. Before that, maybe they lived in Europe, and before that no one knows. Yet if I am born in India, it is highly likely that my ancestors have been in the same area for several thousands of years. The culture stays with the family for that long as well, and so it is not surprising that the demigods continue to be worshiped by those born into the Vedic tradition.

The Vaishnava spiritual masters, however, don't recommend demigod worship and neither do they teach it to their students. Assuming the identity of a Vaishnava is the fruit of all past religious observances, from present and past lives. In other words, the Vaishnava is the most intelligent, so they don't require allegiance to traditions reserved for the less intelligent. And because they are so wise, they don't attempt to recreate the same level of tradition in their disciples. Instead, the sole focus is on worship of Vishnu, which means that the descendants in the chain of spiritual instruction won't even know how to properly worship the demigods.

In the above referenced verse from the Janaki Mangala, Sita Devi, who is Lakshmi, Vishnu's wife for eternity, is praying to Shiva, Ganesha and Parvati. Lord Shiva is the greatest Vaishnava. Though he plays the role of a demigod to those who are desirous of material rewards, he himself is only interested in worshiping the Supreme Lord. Parvati is his chaste and beautiful wife, and Ganesha is one of their sons. One could spend an entire lifetime describing the glories of that family, but just from this one incident with Sita we get an idea of how worthy of honor they are.

Sita here is playing the role of the daughter of King Janaka. Janaka has drawn up a contest to see who will marry his precious daughter. The first person to lift an extremely heavy bow, which not coincidentally belonged to Lord Shiva, will get to marry Sita. Shri Rama is the favorite of everyone in the family. He hails from Ayodhya, and He happens to be an incarnation of Vishnu. Thus Vishnu and Lakshmi were about to meet in the marriage of Rama and Sita.

It is said here that Sita is so worried that she is unable to say anything. She is worried in the heart, and in that helpless state she remembers Shiva, Parvati and

Ganesha. This remembrance is significant because of the powers they have. Shiva and Parvati are especially worshiped by those desirous of a good spouse, and Ganesha is known as the remover of obstacles. In this instance the weight of the bow was the obstacle, and Sita wanted that removed so that Rama would be able to win the contest. She had previously prayed to Parvati to get Rama as a husband, and Shiva was a de facto officiator of this contest through the presence of his bow.

Sita gives us an example of how to avoid the pitfalls of demigod worship while satisfying family tradition at the same time, if the situation calls for it. This event took place during the Treta Yuga, which is the second time period of creation. People were very pure during the second age, so the Vedic culture was vibrant. Through family tradition, people knew how to worship Shiva, Parvati and Ganesha. In this instance Sita prayed so that Vishnu, or God, would be successful. Thus she did not desire a temporary material reward. And what an honor it was to be worshiped by Sita. Of all the people who have walked this earth, none has a better character than her. And that wonderful person thought of Shiva, Parvati and Ganesha when she ran into trouble.

Today the Vaishnava can respond to the question of demigod worship by simply saying, "I'm sorry, but I don't know how to properly worship people such as Shiva, Parvati and Ganesha. My spiritual master never taught that to me, so all I can do is offer them my respect. Since Vishnu is loved by Shiva, I know that he will be pleased by my worship of Him through the chanting of the holy names, 'Hare Krishna Hare Krishna, Krishna Krishna, Hare Hare, Hare Rama Hare Rama, Rama Rama, Hare Hare'". And if we ever run into difficulty in our devotional service, we can always remember Shiva, Parvati and Ganesha as well, informally asking for their favor in pleasing the Supreme Lord.

VERSE 101

होत बिरह सर मगन देखि रघुनाथहि।
फरकि बाम भुज नयन देत जनु हाथहि।।101।।

hota biraha sara magana dekhi raghunāthahi |
pharaki bāma bhuja nayana deta janu hāthahi ||101||

"Afraid of a bad outcome, she was drowning in a pain of hopelessness while looking at Rama. Then she felt twitching in the eyes and left side, which acted like a rescuing hand." (101)

Essay - A Rescuing Hand

"God, I've been so faithful to You for so long. If You really cared about me, You would give me some kind of indication. I'm so worried about the outcome to this particular event that I can't even think straight. I need something to reassure me that everything will be alright. Yes, I realize that in the past I worried over such things and that later on they amounted to nothing, but for some reason I can't think beyond the present. I need some kind of sign from You that everything will be alright."

This sort of request is understandable, especially if we have been faithful to the "man upstairs" for a long time. Not that we offered Him our attention with a specific benefit in mind, but there is the implied understanding that if you do things the right way you won't fall into the depths of despair. In the Vedas such depression is considered a product of the mode of ignorance, which is the lowest of the three modes of nature.

"O son of Bharata, the mode of ignorance causes the delusion of all living entities. The result of this mode is madness, indolence and sleep, which bind the conditioned soul." (Lord Krishna, Bhagavad-gita, 14.8)

Depression is often tied to laziness or long periods of inactivity, both of which are also in the mode of ignorance. While the three modes of nature are discussed at length in Vedic texts like the Bhagavad-gita, we can understand them very quickly using the context of doing things the right way versus the wrong way. The right way is the mode of goodness, the wrong way is the mode of ignorance. Somewhere in between, with a little right and a little wrong, is the mode of passion. When we see murders, rapes, robberies and the like reported on television, those can be likened to the mode of ignorance. This is the stuff we would consider stupid. When we see worship of a higher power, kindness to strangers, charity to those who are in need, humility, and study of the meaning of life the behaviors fall into the mode of goodness. The mode of passion is anything in between, like say for instance starting a business, playing a sport, or chasing after members of the opposite sex.

It is important to rise to the mode of goodness because goodness equates to knowledge. And isn't it always better to be in knowledge than in ignorance? If I know how to drive a car, isn't that better than not knowing? Perhaps there is the detriment due to the increased attention that arises from other potential passengers looking for a ride, but this in itself doesn't make the knowledge of operating a motor vehicle harmful. The parent is superior to the child because they know what it is like to be a child and what it is like to be a parent. The teacher in the classroom is in a similar position, and therefore they are superior.

To reach the mode of goodness and stay there is not easy. Charity, sacrifice and knowledge can all fall into the three different modes. Just because I'm charitable doesn't mean that I'm charitable in the right way. I could give guns away to criminals, condoms to promiscuous children, and cash to drunkards to buy alcohol. None of these charitable donations are good in the long run. To follow sacrifice, charity, and knowledge gathering in the mode of goodness requires attention and guidance from an authority figure. For this reason the brahmanas are considered the brains of society. A brahmana by quality is someone who lives in the mode of goodness and who can therefore guide all other members of society.

In the scene from the verse quoted above, you have a woman who lived in the mode of goodness her whole life. She never did anything the wrong way. By the book she followed the code of conduct assigned to her, and her father was the same way. But now she was in a desperate situation, feeling as if she were sinking in an ocean of despair. On this particular day her husband was to be determined. From the many princes that came to her father's kingdom, one would be chosen as her future partner for life.

If such a thing were to happen today, a woman would understandably be upset prior to the ceremony even taking place. If you grow up with the hope of finding true love in an amorous relationship that is voluntarily entered into, the arranged marriage seems like a punishment. In Sita's case, the culture was such that she knew her husband would be chosen for her. She was fine with that aspect of it, but now that she was in the assembly, she was able to have a look at some of the candidates.

One in particular caught her eye. It is the general belief that in a society where men and women freely intermingle, the women who are more lusty prefer male companions who are expert at seducing women. In essence, they want someone who knows what they are doing in the romance department. On the flip side, the chaste women prefer someone who is more honorable in character, someone who will protect them for a long time. No one is more chaste than Sita, who is an incarnation of the goddess of fortune, the eternal consort of the Supreme Lord. Therefore she is only attracted to pure goodness, which exists in the highest degree in Shri Rama.

He was there as a participant in the contest to determine Sita's husband. King Janaka made the vow that whoever would first lift Lord Shiva's bow would win Sita's hand. This meant that even though Sita now had eyes for Rama, it wasn't guaranteed that He would marry her. He had to lift the bow, a bow which none of the other princes could even move thus far. The situation on appearance looks like ordinary lust, but in fact Sita wanted Rama as a husband. Based on her culture, she wanted to serve Him for the rest of her life. Since Rama is the same Supreme Lord that every tradition worships to some extent, her desire was above even the mode of goodness. She wanted to serve Rama not just for virtue's sake. She would serve Him no matter what the codes of conduct called for.

When she saw the bow, she knew that it would be difficult to lift. Therefore she started to worry very much. Fearing that Rama wouldn't win the contest, she fell into an ocean of despair. At this moment of trouble, however, a sign from above came to her in the form of involuntary movement in her eyes and left side [the word "bama" here can refer to arm or hand]. You can call this superstition if you like, but in the Vedic tradition there are specifics given as to which signs are ominous and which are auspicious. This twitching was auspicious and it gave her hope; it acted like a hand to rescue her from the pool of despair she was drowning in.

For those who are constantly tossed around by the forces of the dark age of Kali, by regularly hearing the holy names, "Hare Krishna Hare Krishna, Krishna Krishna, Hare Hare, Hare Rama Hare Rama, Rama Rama, Hare Hare," fortunate circumstances can be created rather than hoped for. This is a subtle rescuing hand that was passed on by Lord Chaitanya and His followers, and it is so wonderful because it can be created at any time, whenever one is in despair. The names reference the same Sita and Rama, the energy of God and the energetic, and so the good omens are sure to arrive.

VERSE 102

धीरज धरति सगुन बल रहति सो नाहिन।
बरु किसोर धनु घोर दइउ नहिं दाहिन।।102।।

dhīraja dharati saguna bala rahati so nāhina |
baru kisora dhanu ghora da'i'u nahiṁ dāhina ||102||

"On the strength of the good omens she has patience, but then she worries that the outcome won't happen. 'The groom is but a teenager and the bow is ghastly in weight, so the giver is not on the right side.'" (102)

Essay - Ghastly in Weight

We see that someone is strong. They can lift heavy objects very easily. They can hold these objects in their arms for an extended period of time. Jobs requiring intense manual labor are no problem for them. They don't get frustrated by the patience required and they don't get intimidated by the size of the project. We keep that person in mind as our reference point for strength. All other measurements for strength in a person are made against them. But when we see something as large as a tree or a building, we know that our strong person is no match for it. For such reasons it is difficult to conceive of a God, a supreme controller. We've never seen anyone strong enough to hold up a tree, so how can anyone even create something as large as a planet? Therefore God must be a myth, right?

Well, we know that the planets are suspended in the air. There is no visible fulcrum underneath. There is no rope holding the earth up. There is no visible person on whose shoulders the earth sits. As nothing stays in the air on its own, some force must exist to accomplish the task. Whether that force directly belongs to a person's body or is an external manifestation of their energy is not really important. I can drive the car myself or I can hire someone else to drive it. Either way, someone is taking the steps necessary to get the car moving.

As another example, let's take a computer program that does calculations. I can do complex calculations myself using pen and paper. This proves that I have the mental ability to do the calculations. A written program, which relies on a programming language, an operating system, and user input, can do the same calculations. By writing this program, I am not directly doing anything within my mind when a person needs to figure out the square root of sixty-four, but my energies are acting nonetheless. The energies in this case come from me, so they are an extension of my mental strength.

In the same way, the power of the sun, the suspension of the planets, the force of the wind, the chill in the air, and the heat in fire are all extensions of the Supreme Lord. He is the source of everything; therefore He is automatically the strongest. He holds up the planets. This is what is revealed in the Vedas, the ancient scriptures of India. The Vedas say that a separate personality named Ananta Shesha Naga holds up the planets on his many hoods. This person, who is also known as Anantadeva, is a direct expansion of the original Personality of Godhead. He is almost like God, but not completely the same. Nevertheless, since He acts at God's direction, He is non-different from Him in one sense. By his holding up the planets, it is as if God were holding them up.

Whether one knows that Anantadeva holds up the planets or not is not important as long as the acknowledgement of the higher authority is there. If you think the planets just hold themselves up, then you are not properly educated. Moreover, your logic doesn't make sense. Nothing else holds itself up. The earth is not only suspended in space, but it revolves and rotates at set intervals as well. The person who discovered these patterns is certainly wise, but is not the person who created them wiser? We know that life comes from life. Everything we see around us is created by some intelligent person, so the same should apply to all aspects of the material creation.

Despite the scriptural and logical basis for these truths, we are still hesitant to believe in God. We see things that are ghoram, or ghastly, and think that no force is capable of overcoming it. In the above referenced verse from the Janaki Mangala, we see a worrying princess who thinks that God, addressed here as "the giver," has turned against her because of a ghastly obstacle placed in front of a teenage prince. Her attitude shows that she wasn't foolish, for she attributed the situation to God's displeasure. He must not have favored her since the odds were so against this beautiful prince lifting up a heavy bow and winning her hand in marriage.

The worrying princess is Sita Devi, who is an incarnation of God's eternal consort. Therefore she is also His energy, technically known as the hladini-shakti, or pleasure potency. She knows that God is all-powerful and all-wealthy. In this situation, the energy known as yogamaya is acting over her to enhance the pleasure she will feel from the prince's triumph. The prince is Lord Rama, who is an incarnation of the Supreme Personality of Godhead. He is automatically the strongest person, so lifting up this bow shouldn't be a problem for Him.

We see that Sita at one moment draws patience from auspicious omens and the good qualities found in Rama, who is extraordinarily beautiful and chivalrous in every way, and the next she sees the bow and starts to worry. She describes the bow as ghoram, or ghastly, and Rama as a tender youth. Though she is acting under the influence of yogamaya, the behavior is instructive to those who are fooled by the influence of mahamaya, or the material energy. The material energy causes us to falsely identify with our body and forget the influence of God. We see something amazing in stature and think that no human being can overcome it.

This bow was so heavy that none of the other princes at the contest could even move it. Therefore it was natural to think that the bow was something like a large tree, an object impossible for a human being to move. Yet Sita's sentiment also shows that she understands that God exists. She knows that if no one can lift the bow, it is due to God's influence and not merely a lack of strength. The Lord is the strongest, and so He can move anything, including a planet. On this occasion, He would prove that fact by lifting a bow of a ghastly weight, winning Sita's hand in marriage in the process.

If Rama can lift Shiva's bow for Sita, He can move heaven and earth for anyone, provided that they desire His association. Sita only wanted to serve Rama; she didn't want Him as a husband just to derive personal pleasure. In the same way, if we desire God's association with an intent to serve Him eternally, He will remove all the obstacles in our path, no matter how ghastly they are in strength. That desire is best made known through the chanting of the holy names, "Hare Krishna Hare Krishna, Krishna Krishna, Hare Hare, Hare Rama Hare Rama, Rama Rama, Hare Hare."

VERSE 103

अंतरजामी राम मरम सब जानेउ।
धनु चढ़ाइ कोतुकहिं कान लगि तानेउ।।१०३।।

antarajāmī rāma marama saba jāne'u |
dhanu caṛhā'i kotukahiṁ kāna lagi tāne'u ||103||

"As antaryami, Shri Rama knows everyone's maladies. Raising the bow, in curiosity He is drawing the string to His ear." (103)

Essay - Rama Navami

Sugriva put all his faith in this one person and got everything he could want in return. Vibhishana trusted the same person and was also duly rewarded. Shabari, the boatman named Kevata, the residents of Ayodhya, King Janaka and so many others also invested full faith in the same man and were not disappointed. One time Janaka's daughter was frantic in fear over the uncertainty of her future, over how she might miss the chance to spend the rest of her life with someone very special. Not surprisingly, faith was extended in the same person, who can hear and answer innumerable simultaneous prayers. He responded to her faith by effortlessly lifting up an object of a massive weight. On the day of Rama Navami, we celebrate His name, fame and glories.

It's nice to have faith in someone else to do something extraordinary. It's like knowing that the job will get done despite all the formidable obstacles present. If you can't solve a math problem, you can at least say: "I may not be able to do it, but my friend can. He's so smart. He's smarter than all of you people. Watch when he sees this equation. He will put everything together in mere moments, making fools of us all." We have the same mentality with pretty much any issue of ability, such as with alluring members of the opposite sex, making sales, cooking, and fixing cars.

The Supreme Lord is the greatest at everything, so He can make any difficult task look ridiculously easy. And the exhibition of this ability is especially pleasing to those who have faith in Him. We all invest faith, regardless of whether we are religious or not. Thus religion's uniqueness cannot come from the issue of faith. Indeed, to think of religion only in terms of faith is a fallacy, the viewpoint of those whose knowledge has not yet been fully revealed by the Truth. We put faith in politicians, who are known to lie and disappoint us. We put faith in sports teams, who are guaranteed to lose many times over. We put faith in our friends and family, but they, like us, are destined to die.

Faith in the higher power may be invested with a similar attitude, but the difference is that the higher power never fails to deliver. In the material land there is competition over worship. The statists want the citizens to worship them instead of God:

"Put your faith in us. Why worship an imaginary figure? Tell you what, let's take these two plants. Give one of them to us and the other leave to God. See what happens in a few weeks. Our plant will come out just fine and the one left to God will wither and die. This proves that there is no God. Either that or He doesn't answer all of your prayers. We'll listen to you, while He, if He exists at all, won't."

If faith in Him is dependent on His ability to deliver on orders, like an online retail outlet, then the faith will not last very long. Since not all orders are fulfilled, one thinks that the faith is meaningless. But in actuality sometimes not getting what we want is better for us. In fact, this is the case many times. The faith in ordinary living entities, including the godless regimes, is different because the object worshiped is not capable of doing everything. They cannot even hear all of the faith extended to them, so how could they possibly respond to everything?

When the faith is extended in earnest, where there is no desire for personal gain, only for the ability to serve Him more, the Supreme Lord reciprocates in the best possible way. One time there was a contest in the kingdom of Janakpur. It related to strength. A bow of a massive weight lay in the middle of an arena. It's formidability was evident just upon sight, and its legendary stature increased as each prince approached it and failed to even move it. It soon became the greatest obstacle to the hopes of a beautiful princess.

Sita Devi, the daughter of King Janaka, saw Shri Rama at the assembly and wanted Him as a husband. This was an ancient time, the Treta Yuga, which is the second of the four time periods of creation. A wife in such a time was a faithful servant. Sita was especially pious since she was the daughter of Janaka, who was the host of the ceremony. So in hoping to have Rama as a husband, she desperately desired the opportunity to serve Him without motivation and without interruption. Indeed, through her actions after marriage she would prove to be the most chaste wife, an example of fidelity for all relationships based on trust.

Rama is God. He is the Supreme Lord in His manifestation as a warrior prince. The Supreme Lord is all-pervading. Some part of Him is always visible. If you can't see His personal form, you can at least see His influence. One who cannot perceive the influence thinks that He doesn't exist. In such cases, especially when there is a decline of religious practice and a sharp increase in irreligion, the Lord manifests in a personal form. Even then there is doubt over His existence, but those who have a pure heart can see Him and take further pleasure in attachment to Him. Rama is one such personal manifestation of Godhead. His body is spiritual. He doesn't take birth, though He emerges from the womb of Queen Kausalya, one of the beloved queens of King Dasharatha of Ayodhya.

Whoever would first lift the bow would win Sita's hand in marriage. Sita hoped that Rama would win, but she wasn't sure of the outcome. Think of the pleasure you feel when the person you put faith in comes in to save the day. Now just imagine how much greater that pleasure is when you are not as sure of the same person getting the job done. This is sort of how the devotees feel when the Supreme Lord swoops in to save the day. On this occasion, the bow was the great obstacle, but as Goswami Tulsidas describes in his Janaki Mangala, Rama took the bow in His hands and lifted it up as if it were child's play.

The toys for a child are not complex. They are not that heavy, either. This way the child can curiously look at the toy and do with it as they please. This bow was treated in the same way by Rama. "Hmm, what's this? This bow looks interesting. Let me pick it up to get a further look. Hmm, there's a string on here. I wonder what happens if I draw this string back to my ear." And just as the child may take their curiosity too far from time to time, Shri Rama drew the string back so far that the bow snapped in half. That object which was too heavy for even the mightiest of princes to move was easily broken by the beautiful and youthful Shri Rama.

Rama's army building a bridge with rocksRama had many similar pastimes. During a later time, after Sita would be kidnapped by the Rakshasa fiend named Ravana, it looked like Rama would have difficulty crossing over an ocean with His army. Yet through His same curiosity, triggered by the same faith extended in Him by the eager monkey-army from Kishkindha, rocks were able to float. Instead of sinking, they stayed on the surface of the water, allowing for a bridge to be made. Rama also once playfully defeated 14,000 of the greatest fighters in the world. They came to attack Him, His younger brother Lakshmana and Sita while they were in the forest. Again, all faith was put in Rama, and He responded by singlehandedly defeating the fiends sent from Lanka.

Sugriva was troubled by his brother Vali, who had driven him out of his kingdom. Vibhishana was also driven out of his kingdom by his brother. Bharata, one of Rama's younger brothers, had the guilt of knowing that his mother had caused Rama to leave the kingdom for fourteen years, when the kingdom rightfully belonged to Rama. In all such cases, the faith extended in Rama was rewarded with the removal of the obstacles. At other times, Rama descends in different forms, but He still shows the same ability to make child's play of a difficult situation. As Shri Krishna, He turned a massive hill into a pastime umbrella. As Lord Varaha, He lifted the earth planet with ease and saved it from a deluge. He invests similar potency in His devotees. Shri Hanuman, Rama's greatest servant, once lifted a mountain when he was in panic over saving Lakshmana.

Hanuman lifting a mountainSimilarly, devotees of today are invested with the ability to deliver Rama's presence through the simple sound vibration of: "Hare

Krishna Hare Krishna, Krishna Krishna, Hare Hare, Hare Rama Hare Rama, Rama Rama, Hare Hare." Faith in these words always delivers the best result, as Shri Rama personally arrives to show His strength. On Rama Navami, we remember that king of kings who once curiously lifted the famous bow of Shiva to make the beautiful Janaki His wife.

Essay - What's Bugging You

"In the Vedas it is said that the Supreme Lord is antaryami. This means that He is the all-pervading witness. At any time, at any place, whatever I am doing He can see me. He knows if I've been naughty or nice for not only the present year, but my whole life. The same holds true for every other person, existing past, present and future. As He is the greatest witness, He knows exactly what is bugging me. Therefore shouldn't He come to fix the situation? Why does anyone succumb to the effects of disease if the antaryami Supreme Lord knows their condition? How could He let them suffer like that?"

Indeed, such concerns are understandable once one learns that God resides within them as the Supersoul. The individual soul is what identifies us, but that soul is only locally residing. My soul is in my body but not in yours. My soul does not change, while my body constantly does. At the time of death, a new body is given to me to replace the one I just left behind.

"As a person puts on new garments, giving up old ones, similarly, the soul accepts new material bodies, giving up the old and useless ones." (Lord Krishna, Bhagavad-gita, 2.22)

Though my soul travels to different bodies, it is still only locally conscious. I do not know what you're thinking. I may witness your activities right now while you are in front of me, but I have no idea what you did before this. I can only find out through hearing, and in that I have to trust that what I hear is true. God, on the other hand, is everywhere. The Supersoul is our link to Him that is within close proximity, should we choose to take advantage of the situation.

This last point is what answers the question of why God doesn't stamp out bad conditions altogether. He certainly does know all of our maladies. If you think about it, He must be all-pervading. If He cannot witness every activity, it means that He has a defect. If He is deficient in any possible way, if He is not supreme in every single category, He is not God. Since He is the Supreme Lord, He knows all and has seen all.

If we don't want to connect with Him, He is not obliged to get rid of our ailments. To help us understand how and why, let's say that I have a small child. They don't know very much since they have only been on earth for a short while.

Though the soul is eternal, full of knowledge and full of bliss, in the conditioned state, where the soul accepts a temporary body, knowledge is covered and requires action in educational disciplines to become uncovered.

The young child's inherent knowledge is covered up and doesn't start to reveal until they mature. This means that I have to guide my young child in all of their activities. Let's say that they want to place their tiny hand into a blazing fire. I tell them not to. I know what the result will be. Their hand will get burned, and that is not good. When they are in my presence, I give a stern warning: "Don't place your hand in the fire! Get away from there! I don't want to see you anywhere near that fire." If they disobey me, I get in the way and use force to prevent them from getting injured.

Though the child is a dependent, they are raised to eventually become independent. At some point in time they will have to make their own decisions. This is true even while they are in the childhood years. Despite the best protection, I cannot control my child's every move. They will make many decisions on their own. If during a moment of alone time they decide to place their hand in the fire, an action which is prohibited, they will get hurt. Is it my fault then that they got the pain? Am I responsible for the burn on their hand?

Perhaps you can blame me as the parent when the child is young, but if they make the same mistake in adult life, it is solely the child's responsibility. I know what their potential action is and I also know the result of that action. And I did whatever I could to prevent the injury as well, but it came nevertheless because of the independence afforded the child. That same independence is granted to all of us to some degree.

If we do things the wrong way, and thereby neglect our inherent occupational duty of devotional service, or bhakti-yoga, then we'll surely fall into unpleasant situations. If I am offered soup to eat and someone gives me only a fork to use, obviously I will have a difficult time eating the soup. I need a spoon for the soup, not a fork. The fork is intended for something else. In a similar manner, the material nature can be used for endless activities, but as a spirit soul I am constitutionally fit to serve the Supreme Lord. This service doesn't have to be based on blind faith towards a particular personality. In fact, it is said in the Bhagavad-gita that the person who approaches the Supreme Lord with some knowledge of the Absolute is actually the most dear to Him.

"Of these [four kinds of people who approach to render devotional service], the wise one who is in full knowledge in union with Me through pure devotional service is the best. For I am very dear to him, and he is dear to Me." (Lord Krishna, Bhagavad-gita, 7.17)

There are various spiritual traditions and different grades of practice, but if the purpose is the same, that of loving God, then the recommended actions are valid. When operating under any other kind of consciousness, I will be misusing the material energy around me and the Supersoul's influence will be ignored. As such, I will be responsible for the misfortune that befalls me.

In the above referenced verse from the Janaki Mangala, Goswami Tulsidas reminds us that God is antaryami. He is the all-pervading witness. In this instance, God is seen as Lord Rama, the eldest son of King Dasharatha who roamed this land many thousands of years ago during the Treta Yuga. God is one, but He has many incarnations and expansions. There are too many to count, but the most prominent ones are enumerated in the Vedas.

Rama knows everyone's maladies, including Sita's. Here Sita is worried over the outcome to a contest that will determine her future husband. She wants Rama to win. She has eyes for Him and He for her. But rules are rules. King Janaka, Sita's father, vowed to give Sita away to whichever prince could first lift the bow. This meant that Rama had to lift this amazingly heavy bow originally belonging to Lord Shiva. Sita was worried because Rama was a youthful prince and the bow was ghastly in weight. The odds were very much in favor of the bow.

Knowing her worries, Rama lifted the bow with ease, like a curious child playing with a new toy. And then He drew the bowstring to His ear. That was it. He did it. He removed Sita's worry, which was the ailment causing her the most pain. Her worry was entirely related to serving Rama, who is God. She was afraid that she wouldn't get to serve Him as His wife. Rama made sure that she had nothing to worry about. And in a similar manner, if we are eager to serve God and wish to derive all the endless benefits that come with that service, Shri Rama will remove all obstacles in our way.

VERSE 104

प्रेम परखि रघुबीर सरासन भंजेउ।
जनु मृगराज किसोर महाराज भंजेउ॥104॥

prema parakhi raghubīra sarāsana bhañje'u |
janu mṛgarāja kisora mahārāja bhañje'u ||104||

"Examining her love, Rama broke the bow, like a young lion routing a great elephant." (104)

Essay - The Lion's Den

"Though this youth is very innocent in appearance, don't underestimate Him. He has already proven His fighting ability in the forest against the wickedest creatures. Maricha was very proud of the boon he received from Lord Brahma. Therefore when he attacked the sacrifice of Vishvamitra at the last moment, he thought that the destruction was a done deal. Unfortunately for him, he forgot about Rama. Though a young boy at the time, Rama, without hesitation, strung His bow and drove away Maricha. The demon's friends weren't so lucky. They did not leave the area alive. Now the same Shri Rama is here in Janakpur to lift the enormously heavy bow of Lord Shiva. Though He is still a youth with delicate features, He can roar like a lion when necessary."

In the above referenced verse from the Janaki Mangala, Goswami Tulsidas invokes a reference that is commonly used in Vedic literature to describe the Supreme Lord's activities. These acts described are heroic, and so the comparison to the lion is fitting. Mentioning the defeat of an elephant is also appropriate, as since the elephant is much larger than the lion, it is believed that it should have no problem in a conflict. Yet the lion can scare with just its roar, and thus it is the king of the jungle. Similarly, the Supreme Lord is the king of all kings, so no one can defeat Him. Moreover, He roars like the lion to protect His devotees like Sita, who love Him unconditionally.

God is compared to a lion several times in the Shrimad Bhagavatam, considered the crown jewel of the Vedas, which are the ancient scriptures of India. God is a person, but a supreme one. As a person, He has features. The abilities tied to these features are inestimable, so to give us a slight idea of what that means, God descends to the earthly plane every now and then to enact pastimes.

"Lord Hari then climbed onto the elephant with the ease of a mighty lion, pulled out a tusk, and with it killed the beast and his keepers." (Shrimad Bhagavatam, 10.43.14)

One of His many names given in the Vedas is Hari. This word has several meanings. It can mean one who takes away. Hari is the remover of the fears in His devotees. Hari can also mean a monkey or a lion. When Shri Krishna, the original form of the Personality of Godhead, battled an enemy elephant named Kuvalayapida, He was addressed as Lord Hari in the verses in the Bhagavatam. This use was intentional, as Krishna attacked the elephant like a powerful lion.

"Hiranyakashipu murmured to himself, 'Lord Vishnu, who possesses great mystic power, has made this plan to kill me, but what is the use of such an attempt? Who can fight with me?' Thinking like this and taking up his club, Hiranyakashipu attacked the Lord like an elephant." (Shrimad Bhagavatam, 7.8.23)

One of Krishna's most famous descents to earth was as His avatara named Narasimha, which means half-man/half-lion. Narasimhadeva is also known as Lord Narahari, which means the same thing. In this descent, God stayed on earth for a very short period of time, there only to rid the world of an evil king named Hiranyakashipu. This king was harassing his five-year old son named Prahlada. God's unique form kept the boons previously granted to Hiranyakashipu safe, while at the same time allowing for the demon to be killed. During the short battle that took place after Narahari arrived, it is described in the Bhagavatam that Hiranyakashipu attacked like an elephant. This means that he was eventually defeated by the lion, which is what happens often in the jungle with conflicts between elephants and lions.

"I am faithfully engaged in the service of Rama, who is a lion among men [nrisimham], has a broad chest and powerful arms, who treads the earth like a lion and who is like a lion in prowess." (Sita Devi speaking to Ravana, Valmiki Ramayana, Aranya Kand, 47.35)

The Ramayana is another Vedic work, and it describes the life and pastimes of Lord Rama, one of Krishna's most famous avataras. In that work, Rama is compared to a lion by His wife Sita. She makes this comparison when speaking to the evil King Ravana after he kidnapped her. Ravana thought that he was very powerful, but Sita wanted him to know that her husband was a lion among men. This meant that Rama wasn't afraid of anyone or anything, and that He had the might necessary to fight anyone.

With these references and more found in many places in the Vedic literature, it is not surprising that Goswami Tulsidas would make the same comparison to a lion in the above quoted verse from the Janaki Mangala. Here the same Shri Rama is in Janakpur ready to win Sita's hand in marriage. This took place before Sita and Rama were officially wed. Though Rama was only a youth at the time, He still acted like a lion. The strength and courage of a lion were necessary to win the contest.

The bow of Lord Shiva lay in the middle of the sacrificial arena. Many princes from around the world came to try their hand at lifting the bow, but none of them could even move it. The first person to lift the bow would marry Sita, the eldest daughter of King Janaka, who was the host of the ceremony and the person who came up with the idea of a contest.

As Rama is the Supreme Lord, He has many names. In this verse He is addressed as Raghubira, which in Sanskrit would be spelled as Raghuvira, which means the hero of the Raghu dynasty. Rama was a king's son, and not just of any ordinary king. King Dasharatha of Ayodhya was a famous ruler appearing in the ancestry of King Raghu, who himself was part of the ancestral line dating back to King

Ikshvaku, one of the first kings on earth. Rama was the hero of this dynasty because He was the best fighter. He was the most capable of protecting the citizens, and so He was naturally the greatest hero. He was also the jewel of that line.

Tulsidas purposefully uses the name Raghubira here because Rama's act of lifting and breaking Shiva's bow was heroic. Rama didn't do it just to show His strength. Rama is God, so He is above the need for cheap adoration. He broke the bow to ease Sita's fears. She was watching the contest and was very anxious. Though she only saw Rama for a few brief moments, she wanted Him to win. Her desire was so strong that she could think of nothing else. Rama knew her worries, and so by breaking the bow, He shattered her fears, which is what any good hero would do.

The bow was like a great elephant and Rama like a young lion. The contest looked like a mismatch, but with God anything is possible. Know that this present age of Kali brings cause for much fear, but if there is reliance on the same Raghubira, who can be called out through the holy names in the maha-mantra, "Hare Krishna Hare Krishna, Krishna Krishna, Hare Hare, Hare Rama Hare Rama, Rama Rama, Hare Hare," then the immediate vicinity turns into Shri Hari's den, with all unwanted elements shattered in the same manner as the wonderful bow in Janaka's kingdom.

CHAND 13

गंजेउ सो गर्जेउ घोर धुनि सुनि भूपि भूधर लरखरे।
रघुबीर जस मुकता बिपुल सब भुवन पटु पेटक भरे।।
हित मुदित अनहित रुदित मुख छबि कहत कबि धनु जाग की।
जनु भोर चक्क चकोर कैरव सघन कमल तड़ाग की।।13।।

gañje'u so garje'u ghora dhuni suni bhūpi bhūdhara larakhare |
raghubīra jasa mukatā bipula saba bhuvana paṭu peṭaka bhare ||
hita mudita anahita rudita mukha chabi kahata kabi dhanu jāga kī |
janu bhora cakka cakora kairava saghana kamala taṛāga kī ||13||

"When the bow broke, the sound that was heard was such a ghastly roar that the earth and mountains shook. The pearl of Rama's fame spread through all the worlds, like a box being filled with treasures." (Chand 13.1)

"The well-wishers were happy and the enemies had crying faces. The poets describe the scene of the raising of the bow as being like a pond in the morning

filled with so many chakava and chakora birds and kairava and kamala flowers."
(Chand 13.2)

Essay - So Much Space

In the modern age, where amenities are available at the click of a mouse, it is not uncommon for households to be filled with items that are unnecessary. The excess items are collectively referred to as junk, and some people have so much of it that film crews come to document their lives. "Why would anyone keep so much stuff?" is the question that piques the curiosity of the viewers. Though hoarding is generally considered a bad thing, space still exists for a reason. It is meant to be filled with something, and when the right something is found, it is anything but junk.

Let's say that I'm moving into a new place, perhaps a house. When I visit the house for the first time, it is empty. This means that there are endless possibilities with respect to interior decorating. If I am married, I will have to discuss with my spouse on how we will decorate. I will want my stuff, and they will want theirs. Hopefully there is room for compromise. Sometimes what the man wants is not what the woman wants, and vice versa. The husband may be excited to have a painting of dogs playing poker, while the wife thinks that the painting is ridiculous and should never be seen by anyone who enters the home.

At its essence, the space in the house is for living. Living at the basic level involves eating, sleeping, mating and defending. These four behaviors guide the primary actions of animals each day. The human being is animal-like, so they follow the same behaviors, though they require a more refined version of the lifestyle. To facilitate this, the ideal home is laid out to have a room for sleeping, a room for lounging, a room for eating, and rooms for external cleansing. There are also locks on the doors to take care of defense.

All of this still doesn't require that much space. So what do you really need in the home? Well, perhaps you can mimic what is required outside of home. At the office you need a desk and a computer. Maybe you can put that in the home too. At the nightclub there are places to sit so that you can relax and do nothing, like watch television. Maybe you can have an area for that in the home as well. You can also play games outside, so perhaps there can be a game room too.

The wise person will realize that every inch of space in the home should be filled with things that are valuable. This doesn't have to equate to high monetary value. The children, the spouse, and the guests are what make the home. None of them are purchased in a store. They are valued because of the association; they make the journey through life more enjoyable.

That which holds us together is even more important, and not surprisingly its association is the most enjoyable. In the Bhagavad-gita, Lord Krishna says that all the truths of the Vedas are like many pearls. They rest on the thread that is Krishna. This analogy is nice because it is easy to understand. You can have many individual pearls, but if you don't have a string to place them on, they aren't that useful. Who wants to walk around holding a bunch of loose pearls? The pearls are valuable and beautiful, but they take on their true significance when placed on a thread.

"O conquerer of wealth [Arjuna], there is no Truth superior to Me. Everything rests upon Me, as pearls are strung on a thread." (Lord Krishna, Bhagavad-gita, 7.7)

In the same way, all the objects of this world aren't so valuable when disassociated from their origin. Everything, both matter and spirit, is rooted in the Supreme Lord. Thus in one sense there is no way for anything to be separated from Him. This understanding of oneness is known as advaita, or non-dualism. Everything is God. It must be this way, otherwise God is not God. If He is not everything, then He is deficient, which automatically invalidates His supreme position.

At the same time, the objects that emanate from Him have an independent existence to some degree. Hence there is also non-dualism, or dvaita. The combination of the two properties gives us the highest truth known as achintya-bhedabheda-tattva, which was taught by Shri Chaitanya Mahaprabhu through the congregational chanting of the holy names: "Hare Krishna Hare Krishna, Krishna Krishna, Hare Hare, Hare Rama Hare Rama, Rama Rama, Hare Hare."

There is simultaneous oneness and difference between God and what He creates. The energetic is the source and the energy is that which the energetic generates. The relationship is inconceivable; it cannot be grasped through mental effort alone. Fortunately, we don't really have to understand the relationship empirically. Just acting off of it is enough to reach the highest position. One acts off of the relationship by using whatever they have for the Lord's pleasure. In bhakti-yoga, one fills whatever space they have around them with things and people that glorify God. To glorify the Supreme Lord is the most pleasurable activity, but unless one knows God they cannot glorify Him properly.

The verse referenced above from the Janaki Mangala tells us a little more about God. In this way Goswami Tulsidas, the author of the wonderful poem, gives every person an invaluable gift. From this verse we learn that God as Lord Rama broke a bow belonging to Lord Shiva to win a contest in the kingdom of Janakpur many thousands of years ago. The sound of the bow breaking was ghastly; it created such a thunderous roar that the earth and mountains were shaking as a result.

More powerful than that sound was the fame that spread as a result. Rama's fame, which is compared to a pearl, filled the three worlds. There are the heavenly planets, the earthly planet, and the hellish planets. These three worlds, with their fourteen planets in total, comprise the material creation, which is perishable. God is imperishable. His fame inherits the same property, so His fame is not bound by any material designation; a fact confirmed by this verse.

The spreading of Rama's fame was like a container being filled with treasures. The treasures in this instance were the pearls of Rama's fame. If we have a trunk full of junk, it is a great burden to us. We have to haul it with us if we want to move, and it takes up much space in the home. If we want to make room for something more important, we have to lift the heavy trunk and put it somewhere else.

If we have something valuable in the trunk, however, we are so happy to have the trunk. It becomes our prized possession. If the trunk is filled with pearls, we won't look at it as a burden so much. Rama's fame is like a pearl because it can be remembered and appreciated at any time, by any person, from any background. A person born in a poor family is just as fortunate as the rich person if they both have this pearl. Material designations are of no concern. God is for everyone, and so His fame is meant to spread through all the worlds, to all the creatures, whether living in heaven or hell.

Whether we have a lot of space to work with or just a little, we can fill it with the Lord's glories, which are too many to count. It is said that of the millions of verses in Vedic literature that glorify Rama, Lord Shiva takes only the two syllables that comprise Rama's name as his most valuable possession. He produces this name constantly to remember God's glories, thereby filling the space around him with auspiciousness. Through using the holy names handed down by the Vaishnavas we can find good things as well. The name of Rama reminds us of the time He lifted Shiva's bow to win the hand of the beautiful Janaki, Sita Devi, the daughter of King Janaka.

Essay - A Spirited Debate

You're at the local bar, watching the big game with a bunch of friends. There are strangers there as well. The game is the biggest of the year; all eyes are on it. Each person watching has their own interest. There are the fans of the respective teams. There are the gamblers who have money riding on the outcome. There are also those who know one or several of the participants in some way. Some have a positive viewpoint in this regard, while others have a negative one. When the event is over, when the outcome is known, there will surely be some discussion. And the opinions are sure to vary. Some will be happy, while others will not. A long time ago, with the cracking of a bow that was heard around the world, the same variety in opinion was seen. The wise poet compared it to what is seen in a pond in the morning.

Goswami Tulsidas is the poet here, and he refers to a poet describing the event. Tulsidas is famous in India, where he is hailed as a saint by many and appreciated by countless others for his poetic ability. He himself was only interested in devotional service, the highest occupation for man. Worship of God is not monolithic, and it is not exclusive to any one region. There are many worshipers of the Supreme Lord in His personal incarnation of Shri Rama, but not all of them follow the same path. Some choose to meditate quietly on Rama's form. Others like to remember His pastimes, while others enjoy describing His glories to others.

Tulsidas was so immersed in thoughts of Rama that he enjoyed writing wonderful devotional poetry about Him. As Rama's many names were required in this endeavor, the poet was automatically a dependent on the sound vibration representation of the Supreme Lord. As these poems described Rama's pastimes, Tulsidas also regularly remembered Rama's activities. As the poet injected his own opinions, which are merely new expressions on the same truths that exist eternally, he also participated in glorifying Rama.

From this verse from the poet's Janaki Mangala, we get a mental picture of what the scene was like when Rama lifted and broke Lord Shiva's bow. Why would Rama do such a thing? Actually, everyone assembled in Janakpur that day was waiting for someone to lift Shiva's bow. That darn thing was so heavy that no one could even move it. All any of the princes had to do was lift it and string it to win the contest.

The prize warranted the massive attendance. So many princes from around the world arrived so that they could have their chance to win the hand of Sita Devi, the beautiful daughter of King Janaka. The anticipation reached a crescendo when Rama, the eldest son of King Dasharatha, took His turn. Of all the princes there, Rama seemed the least likely to win. He was so beautiful, and young too. He was a teenager, while the bow was like a mountain. Granted, so many of the spectators, including Sita and Janaka, wanted Rama to win, but there was the quiet fear that it just wasn't going to happen.

With God, one should always expect the unexpected. When the unexpected does arrive, however, the emotions are always stronger. Since we know that Rama is God based on the statements of the Vedas and their authority figures, the tendency is to think first of the positive reactions to Rama's feat. He lifted the bow without a problem and broke it while trying to string it. This was the same bow that no one else could move. Obviously Sita was happy, as were the other well-wishers. The king, the queen and their attendants were thrilled. The people of Janakpur were happy as well. But there were enemies watching too. They weren't pleased. They had crying faces.

We get this mental picture from the first line of the above referenced verse. To give us more clarity, poets often invoke analogies. Here Tulsidas says that a poet would liken the scene to a pond in the morning. This particular pond would be filled with chakka and chakora birds and kairava and kamala flowers. These birds and flowers are referenced quite often in Vedic literature, especially with respect to the Supreme Lord and His pastimes. The saints who composed these works also often lived in the forests, so they would witness so much in nature and tie what they saw to God. This is how one truly becomes one with the nature around them. Everything is God, but at the same time everything is separate from the Lord. The simultaneous oneness and difference is best understood when everything around us is used in glorifying God, an act which is part of serving Him, which is the soul's constitutional engagement.

"Because the blue lotus flower blossoms with the rising of the sun, the sun is the friend of the blue lotus. The chakravaka birds also appear when the sun rises, and therefore the chakravakas and blue lotuses meet." (Shrila Prabhupada, Chaitanya Charitamrita, Antya 18.98 Purport)

The birds and flowers mentioned are opposite in behavior. The chakkas, which are often referred to as chakravakas, are like geese. These birds particularly prefer the morning time, when the sun rises. This is the time period used in the analogy. The chakoras, on the other hand, prefer the moon. Shri Rama appeared in the solar dynasty, and in this instance the breaking of the bow was like the sun rising for Janaka and family. It was also the beginning of the marriage of Sita and Rama. Therefore the well-wishers are like the chakkas, while the enemies are like the chakoras, who were upset that the sun rose.

The kairava is a water-lily that opens up at the sight of the moon. The kamala is the lotus flower, and it behaves in the opposite way. The kamala opens up at the sight of the sun, so the well-wishers were also like the kamala flower. The enemies here are like the kairava; both their pride and their hopes closed up once Rama broke the bow. He was like the dreadful sun to them.

The kairava and chakora are often used in glorifying Shri Rama as well, but here the references were befitting the occasion. Whereas in the outcome to material events all the opinions are more or less equal to one another, here the side of the well-wishers was better situated. They had the right reaction, one that has since been passed on to generations of saintly people who never tire of hearing of God's triumphs.

VERSE 105

नभ पुर मंगल गान निसान गहागहे।
देखि मनोरथ सुरतरु ललित लहालहे।।१०५।।

nabha pura maṅgala gāna nisāna gahāgahe |
dekhi manoratha surataru lalita lahālahe ||105||

"Auspicious singing, drums and sounds filled the air and the city. It looked like a desire tree blooming with whatever the mind desired." (105)

Essay - Green Tree

The Vedas describe something known as a desire tree. In Sanskrit the word is either kalpataru or surataru. The latter mentions the suras, or demigods. They are residents of the heavenly planets. When the term "heaven" is invoked it must relate to something. In this case the heavenly aspect relates to increased material sense gratification. One way this is facilitated is through the desire tree, which immediately grants whatever the mind wants. Goswami Tulsidas chose to invoke this tree when describing the felicity that followed the lifting of the bow by Lord Rama.

It's the winter. It's cold outside. It takes you ten minutes to warm up your car. If you don't have a remote starter, you have to run out into the cold, start the car, turn on the heat, and then run back into your house. Then you can get ready, eat something, and enter your car when it is warmed up. The car will be easier to drive, and there also won't be the discomfort of the cold conditions.

Depending on where you live, in the winter months it could be so cold outside that the high temperature doesn't even reach the freezing point. This is a little disturbing if you think about it. If you were to stay outside for an extended period of time, you would freeze to death. At least in the summer months if you stayed outside you would only be slightly discomforted. You could still survive. In the winter it is so cold that life cannot sustain itself without some means of heat generated by other forms of life.

As life outside cannot survive in the winter, the leaves fall off the trees. This is depressing because the tree is meant to have leaves. A plant's ideal destiny is to produce fruits. In the Vedas, the fruit-bearing trees are considered pious, and the ones without fruits are tagged as sinful. The fruit-bearing tree helps others to survive by providing food. The trees that only have leaves don't really do anything for others besides providing oxygen and perhaps shade. Granted, these are necessary to sustain life, but if the tree could give fruits someone could rely on it for their livelihood.

When the tree is blooming, it looks better. Think of it like having a home that is nicely decorated. The interior and exterior arrangements make everything look better. In Janakpur a long time ago, it looked like a desire tree was in full bloom. A desire tree gives whatever the mind wants. If you want to eat something, you go up to the tree and ask for some food. They say that money doesn't grow on trees, but if you go up to a desire tree, money will fall in bundles should you ask for it.

Now imagine that you had a city full of citizens kindly approaching a large desire tree. They simultaneously ask for their specific desire. The tree then responds by blooming all the things asked for. In this verse from the Janaki Mangala, Tulsidas says that beautiful singing and drums filled the air of the city. This was in response to the culmination of the contest of the bow. King Janaka vowed to give away his daughter Sita to whoever would first lift the bow of Lord Shiva. The prince of Ayodhya, the eldest son of King Dasharatha, Shri Rama, finally accomplished the feat, and everyone was so happy that joy filled the air.

The symbolic desire tree in this instance was not material. It was a tree that granted all the spiritual desires of the citizens. A spiritual desire is one that does not have any karma tied to it. If I ask for a tablet computer and I get it, the device then drives my actions. Since the device is related to matter, my subsequent actions are tied to matter as well, which means that I will have to accept a material body again in the next life. Lord Krishna, the same Shri Rama but in His original form, confirms this fact in the Bhagavad-gita, where He states that whatever state of being one remembers at the time of death, that state they attain in the next life.

"Whatever state of being one remembers when he quits his body, that state he will attain without fail." (Lord Krishna, Bhagavad-gita, 8.6)

Celebrating Sita and Rama's marriageTo accept a material body in the next life is considered inauspicious because we are all spiritual at the core. Why not accept a spiritual body in the next life? The spiritual body is actually our original body; it is tied to our original consciousness. That consciousness is God consciousness, where we only think of the Supreme Lord and His interests.

In Janakpur the celebrating citizens were thinking only of Rama's welfare, and also Sita's. They wanted the divine couple to reunite, to stay together for all of time. They also wanted to celebrate Rama's victory. Their desires were fulfilled by the only person who can fulfill all desires. By lifting and breaking that bow, Shri Rama, the Supreme Lord, fulfilled so many desires simultaneously. As that desire tree was in full bloom, the scene was beautiful.

VERSE 106

तब उपरोहित कहेउ सखीं सब गावन।
चलीं लेवाइ जानकिहि भा मन भावन॥106॥

taba uparohita kahe'u sakhīṁ saba gāvana |
calīṁ levā'i jānakihi bhā mana bhāvana ||106||

"Then the priest asked all the sakhis to sing wedding songs. They then went to bring to Janaki whatever her mind desired." (106)

Essay - The Perfect Day

If you could plan out your perfect day, what would it look like? Where would you go? What would you do? Who would be there with you? For many young women, this dream relates to their marriage. That will be the perfect day, when everything goes right. For one famous young lady in particular, her wedding was like a fairy tale, only everything about it was real. News of the reality spread throughout the world at the time. The same news was then immortalized in India's ancient texts, allowing for us to relive that most auspicious day.

What would be the perfect wedding? For the woman, obviously a suitable husband would be the first priority. How can you have an ideal wedding if you're marrying someone you don't like? This begs the question as to what makes the perfect husband. The word itself implies protection. In the Vedas, the term for husband is pati, which can also mean controller. Not to be confused with a domineering figure who forces other people to submit to his demands for sense gratification, the controller in this sense is one who runs the show with respect to a married life guided by religiosity.

What is the difference between marriage in religiosity and marriage in irreligiosity?

Without religiosity, one is guided by their senses. The sense impulses have dominance in the lower species, but in the human being those impulses can be ignored. For instance, we decide when and how much to eat. We could immediately shift to a diet of rice, vegetables, and fruits if we wanted to. We could eat meat, drink wine, and consume endless candy bars if we wanted to also. Each choice has consequences, and using the receptacle of information that is the mind, combined with the wonderful gift of an advanced intelligence, the human being can make wiser choices that will benefit them in the future.

A marriage based in sense gratification isn't really a marriage at all; it is more a formalized bond based on animal instincts. The animal is cold in its dealings with sense objects. Think of the two dogs that have sexual relations and then move on. There is no duty or honor; there is no conscience persuading one party to take care of the other for life. A marriage in sense gratification is similar to this, as it can break at any time should either party no longer feel sense stimulation. In the Vedas, the householder who lives without religiosity is known as a grihamedhi.

A grihasthi is the householder who lives with religiosity. All rules and regulations of religious life, which in its bona fide form is based on the laws of the spiritual science, are meant to culminate in God consciousness. To think of God is to have a taste of the original consciousness. To constantly think of God is to reach the aim of life, which automatically brings an end to the cycle of birth and death. As the sense demands are the strongest hindrance towards God consciousness, various systems of maintenance are suggested to help one gradually work their way towards the stage of bhava, or full ecstasy resulting from connection with the Divine.

Grihastha is an ashrama; it is a spiritual institution. The male in this system is the protector; he dominates in the sense that he will protect his wife from outside attack and also maintain the household so that the spiritual activities can be carried out without a problem. The woman looking to enter this religious institution would thus prefer the best protector. Someone who was religiously inclined would be the most helpful to fitting into the scenario of the dream wedding.

For your special day, you would also want your friends and family around. Life is no fun if you don't have anyone with whom to share your experiences. Sometimes it is actually more enjoyable to relive an event after the fact, telling your friends about what happened. If you go on vacation, it is better to visit so many places just so that you have something to talk about with your friends later on. "I went here and I went there. I ate at this place and relaxed over there."

For the daughter of King Janaka, the wedding was perfect. Everyone she loved was there. All her closest friends, along with her family priest, mother and father, celebrated the occasion. Sometimes the wedding situation is not ideal for everyone. For instance, perhaps the father of the bride doesn't like the groom. Perhaps the mother of the groom has objections to the marriage. In the end, they may give their blessings begrudgingly so that the wedding can go forward without a hitch.

In Janaki's situation, everyone was ecstatic. One couldn't tell who was happier. Was the bride more thrilled or the parents? Were the friends happier or the protected citizens, or praja? In this verse from the Janaki Mangala, Goswami Tulsidas provides further details about Janaki's special day. The name Janaki means the daughter of Janaka. She is more commonly known as Sita, the wife of Rama.

Here Rama has just fulfilled the qualification for marrying Sita, and so the wedding is all set to take place. King Janaka's family priest, Shatananda, told the sakhis, the friends of the princess, to sing felicitous wedding songs. They then went to get Sita, fulfilling all her desires.

Sita's marriage was perfect because all the conditions were met. Her husband is the best husband. He is the protector of the whole world. He is the Supreme Personality of Godhead in His spiritual form of a warrior prince. If you surrender to Rama, you will never be devoid of protection. Even if you somehow think He is absent from your life, you can simply chant His name and be reminded of Him. And more comforting than thinking of Rama is thinking of Sita, who is devoted to Him in thought, word and deed. She united with that beautiful son of King Dasharatha on the occasion of her perfect marriage, an event still talked about to this day.

VERSE 107

कर कमलनि जयमाल जानकी सोहइ।
बरनि सकै छबि अतुलित अस कबि कोहइ।।१०७।।

kara kamalani jayamāla jānakī soha'i |
barani sakai chabi atulita asa kabi koha'i ||107||

"Taking the victory garland in her lotus hands, Janaki is looking so beautiful. What poet is there who can describe such a grand picture?" (107)

Essay - Awarding the Victor

Here Sita Devi is ready to place the victory garland on her soon-to-be husband, Lord Rama. While the victory has brought joy to the entire town, to each person there is a unique happiness. It would be natural to assume that the triumphant party would be joyful, as would be His friends and well-wishers, but in this instance the happiness of the person giving the symbol of victory is specifically addressed. She was radiant with beauty from her happiness, and the picture was too wonderful for any poet to describe.

One way to understand what Sita was feeling is to repeat the same event in the present. "How can we do this? How can we go back to that famous moment in time when Lord Rama, the Supreme Personality of Godhead, broke the amazingly heavy bow of Lord Shiva? How can we recreate the suspense? The victory was more remarkable because it was surprising. It was astonishing because of the many previous princes who had failed to lift the bow. To recreate the scene would be like skipping to the end of a movie without having experienced the entire buildup, no?"

The fact that we know of this incident today shows that we can recreate the event to some degree. The poets glorified the event in song and thereby immortalized it in the process. From this one verse alone, Goswami Tulsidas has allowed us to travel back in time using the mind. We can try to picture the beauty of Sita's lotus-like hands as she held the garland of victory. We can imagine the joy she felt and the anticipation in her heart as she awaited placing that garland on the deserving victor.

She wanted Rama to win as soon as she saw Him. She knew that none of the other princes gathered there that day were right for her. Not that she wouldn't serve her husband regardless. Her father, King Janaka, taught her the principles of religion since her childhood. She was ready to accept a husband and dutifully serve him so that both of them could advance spiritually. She didn't need this advancement since she is eternally the consort of the Supreme Lord, but in this time period she set the proper example for all the people of the earth.

King Janaka drew up the contest to determine Sita's husband. Just as the princes assembled in Janakpur were eager to have Sita as a wife, Sita was invested in the outcome going her way. She wanted Rama as a husband, and so when she held the victory garland in her beautiful hands, she was one step closer to making her dream a reality. When someone finally achieves what they truly desired, especially when it looked like there wouldn't be success, the happiness is unmatched. The joy is so powerful that it cannot be contained. Therefore the poet here says that the picture of Sita holding the victory garland cannot be described accurately by anyone, no matter their superior eloquence.

One way to partially recreate the same scene is through worshiping the deity. Sita and Rama have been worshiped ever since their time on earth many thousands of years ago. They are known as incarnations of Lakshmi and Narayana. Lakshmi is the goddess of fortune and Narayana the source of all men. Narayana is also known as Vishnu and as Krishna. A Vaishnava is one who worships Vishnu or one of His non-different forms, as this kind of worship is directed to a personal God. The Personality of Godhead has transcendental features that the devotees, His fragmental expansions, can contemplate upon, worship, describe, and be fully immersed in.

The abhisheka is a central component of deity worship in the Vaishnava tradition. It is a bathing ceremony. The deity is not dirty; it is transcendental due to the authorized way in which it is constructed and then worshiped. The bathing ceremony is for the worshiper's benefit. It allows the souls that are servants by nature to serve. It's like a general being given a mission or a hockey player being allowed to play a game. There are temporary designations we accept throughout the journey of life based on our material capabilities, but every soul's original designation is servant of God. Any chance we are given to act on that designation should be capitalized upon. And someone who allows for that opportunity to materialize is to be known as a true saint.

The Vaishnavas are saints in this regard, as they pass on the tradition of deity worship. The tradition originates with the Supreme Lord, who is thus known as the most merciful. When performing the bathing ceremony, one takes the designated liquid and pours it from a conch shell over the head of the deity. When one is doing this they can immediately go back in time to when Sita held the garland of victory for Rama. They can pretend that they are declaring both Sita and Rama to be victorious, to be the most beautiful couple that is so kind to allow the fallen souls to worship them in such an intimate way. And that worship is key to the personal relationship, something no person can take away from us. Someone may teach us how to worship and how to understand God, but in the end the formation of the relationship is up to us. To make God our own is to realize the true boon of the human existence.

Rather than imagine what God looks like and what He does, we can rely on the words of the saints like Tulsidas, who from a single verse in his works gives us the chance to spend the entire day thinking about God. That beautiful garland lay in Sita's hands, awaiting its destiny of hanging from the neck of the beautiful Shri Rama. God is glorious, something which His triumph in Janakpur reminds us of.

VERSE 108

सीय सनेह सकुच बस पिय तन हेरइ।
सुरतरु रुख सुरबेलि पवन जनु फेरइ।।108।।

sīya saneha sakuca basa piya tana hera'i |
surataru rukha surabeli pavana janu phera'i ||108||

"With loving hesitation, Sita steals glances at the body of her beloved, like the vines around a desire tree going through its leaves by the blowing of the wind."
(108)

Essay - A Helpful Nudge

Sita's love for Rama is real. It is not something that will go away or change. The blowing of the wind causes objects to shift. One second they may be connected with one object and the next they are disconnected. One second the wind knocks off the hanging piece of siding from the house, clanging against the side and annoying the residents in the process. Another second the same wind blows the piece of siding away from the house, removing the noise. In our dealings in the material world, our constant toggling between like and dislike manifests in all areas, and this shift can be compared to the blowing of the wind or the swinging of a pendulum. In real love, however, the connection is there to stay, like vines of a creeper wrapping around a tree and not pulling back.

Love, as we define it, is flickering, and this shouldn't be difficult to understand. Just think of any couple you know who is married. Perhaps in the beginning of their relationship they are madly in love, always craving each other's association. After many years together that excitement fades, for they see each other every day. They see each other all the time, and they have no other option. They are essentially stuck with each other for a long time. If they have children, they have other responsibilities to deflect from their original flame of affection. If they both work for a living, they have even less time for interaction. Thus their life goes from excitement to dull routine.

The routine then represents a sort of disconnected state. If you're not at least thinking of each other all the time, then the physical separation due to the time spent at work only makes you further apart emotionally. Then, as soon as there is any disagreement, it becomes easier to separate permanently. Think about it. If you hardly see the person that you live with, how difficult would it be to live without them permanently?

This fact also explains how quarrels with family members who live elsewhere are so commonplace. If I see my family members once a year on Thanksgiving, what is the harm to me if I don't see them one particular Thanksgiving? If I barely have enough time for my spouse and children, how will I have time to spend with my friends and family who live nearby? If I get into any kind of argument with them, it is very easy to vow to never speak to them again and then keep that vow.

The Vedas explain why material love is tenuous. The foremost exponent of Vedic philosophy in the modern age is His Divine Grace A. C. Bhaktivedanta Swami Prabhupada, who teaches from the authorized line of disciplic succession that originates from Krishna, the Supreme Personality of Godhead. In this line of instruction not only is material love talked about, but so is spiritual love. The Bhakti-rasamrita-sindhu of Shrila Rupa Gosvami deals extensively with loving God, which is the soul's natural disposition.

From the bona fide teachings of acharyas in this line, we learn that what we know to be love is actually kama, which can be translated to "material desire" or "lust." Material desires change all the time, so what we know to be love isn't permanent. We love someone today, but tomorrow we could love someone else. We love our nephew today because they are so young, but when they get older the love might not be as strong since they are an adult, and thus deemed less innocent.

Real love is prema, and it can only be directed at God. You cannot have prema for anyone else. Seems like an unfair declaration, but in the Vedas there is no concern for how the truth will make others feel. Political correctness is simply a way to stifle speech because of how others are made to feel. Still, the truth is the truth. If our cat is dead, we shouldn't tell someone else that it is alive to spare their feelings. The death is a reality. Similarly, the fact that prema can only be directed at God is a reality, and the sooner one accepts this fact the sooner they will reach the ultimate aim in life.

We can try to offer prema to others, but something will get in our way eventually. If we keep our affection for someone else throughout life, which is indeed very rare, eventually their association will be lost. This is the influence of time, which is known as kala in Sanskrit. Kala appropriately also translates to death, which is the most obvious indication of the influence of time. Attempted prema can also be checked by others through their treatment. The lack of reciprocation is the easiest way to turn love to hate. Our own affection can go elsewhere based on the actions of others. Also, we are limited in this exercise of prema. If I am separated from my loved one and I think of them, they have no way of being affected by my thoughts. In this case the physical distance influences how my prema is offered.

Real prema cannot be checked because it is directed at someone who is omnipresent. Thinking of Him is as good as being with Him. The verse quoted here from the Janaki Mangala reminds us of this fact. Sita Devi is about to place the garland of victory around her future husband, Lord Rama. Rama lifted and broke the bow of Lord Shiva at the contest in King Janaka's kingdom. The first person to do this would win, and the prize was the hand in marriage of Sita, Janaka's daughter. Sita was thrilled that Rama won; she saw Him and knew that He was the right husband for her.

Her love was so strong, but since the marriage hadn't been officially performed yet, she couldn't do anything but stare at Rama. And yet that was good enough to be considered love, as her behavior is likened to a creeper wrapping around the leaves of a desire tree due to the influence of the wind. The creeper in this sense is too shy to go to the desire tree. Sita loves Rama, but protocol dictates that she not approach Him yet. She was a pious daughter of a pious king; so she would not violate the standard etiquette by showing too much affection in front of others.

Rama is not an ordinary tree; He is likened to a desire tree, which is found in the heavenly realm. From a desire tree you can get whatever you want. It is the only tree in existence that will grow money if asked. To be wrapped around a desire tree is to be in the presence of something that will always give whatever you want. Sita only wanted to be with Rama and serve Him. Her love for Him was without motivation and without interruption. Not even her shyness could prevent her from going to Rama. Her glances were like the wind pushing her towards Rama to steal a moment of affection.

We are all meant to love God. We may realize Him through different features, but the attraction is there all the time. When influenced by ignorance, we love His material energy, which is separate from Him. This kind of love is known as kama, and it results in repetition in the cycle of birth and death. When we love His impersonal feature, we merge into the Brahman effulgence, and thereby lose our identity. The loss of identity means the loss of the ability to love; hence residence in the Brahman effulgence is not permanent.

When we love God's personal form we actually offer prema. This is what the soul really wants, but due to the influence of the material nature, which changes our real ego into a false one, we offer our affection to so many other people and things. From Sita's example we should know that if we offer our love to God He will never reject it. He will allow us to wrap our vines around Him without any problem, no matter how far away from Him we may be. And the devotees of the Lord are so kind that they carry the winds of devotion to help the process along, giving us the necessary nudge when we are hesitant. They bring the information of Sita and Rama's marriage and they also always chant their names, as found in mantras like "Hare Krishna Hare Krishna, Krishna Krishna, Hare Hare, Hare Rama Hare Rama, Rama Rama, Hare Hare."

VERSE 109

लसत ललित कर कमल माल पहिरावत।
काम फंद जनु चंदहि बनज फँसावत।।१०९।।

lasata lalita kara kamala māla pahirāvata |
kāma phanda janu candahi banaja phaṁsāvata ||109||

"With her beautiful, lotus-like hands she is putting on the garland, like
Kamadeva placing the moon in a noose of lotuses." (109)

Essay - Garland of Love

"What is the purpose to that chain around your neck? Is it an ornament? Does it symbolize something? Why do you wear it? Who gave it to you? If someone offered it to you, why did you accept it? It looks very nice, and you seem to be happy wearing it, so obviously it must mean something to you."

In the Vedic tradition, it is customary to offer exalted guests a garland of flowers. Especially if the guest is a holy man who has come to speak on the glories of the Supreme Lord, the offering of the garland is almost compulsory. But what is the actual purpose? Why a garland of flowers and not something else? Why does the invited guest accept the offering? In this verse from the Janaki Mangala we see the purpose to not only the offering of the garland, but also the offering of any item in the proper mood. The garland in this case is compared to a noose, which means that the gifted party is bound in some way.

We don't usually think of binding the Supreme Lord. He is supreme for a reason; He cannot be bound. We, on the other hand, are bound to the cycle of birth and death based on our karma. We do some work today, and we may not realize it, but that work has consequences both in the short term and the distant future. I enroll in a four-year college today, and while presently my work may involve completing assignments for the specific courses I'm taking, in the future this work will help me to perform my job functions. Thus there is both a short and long term effect.

"The living entity in the material world carries his different conceptions of life from one body to another as the air carries aromas." (Lord Krishna, Bhagavad-gita, 15.8)

Our work influences our state of being when we quit our body. That state of being then determines where we will end up next. This fact is given to us by Lord Krishna in the Bhagavad-gita. The gross elements of earth, water, air, fire and ether make up our visible body, and the subtle elements of mind, intelligence and ego make up the portion that we can't perceive. These subtle elements come with us to the next life, like the air carrying aromas.

As work influences consciousness, it would make sense to fix our work right now so that we could have the best consciousness at the time of death. This is easier said than done, however. In the same Bhagavad-gita, Arjuna, the recipient of Krishna's instructions, compares subduing the mind to trying to control the wind. The mind is driven by the senses, which are like wild horses running in every which direction. The senses are influenced by the material energy, and so in this sense we are bound to the cycle of birth and death because of the material energy.

Krishna, or God, is the origin of matter and spirit. He has a transcendental body, so His features are not binding like ours are. He can even appear within the material energy and remain above its effects. Therefore when we say that we can bind God, it doesn't seem to make sense. If the material energy, which controls us when we are conditioned, doesn't control Him, how can we ever possibly do anything like bind Him?

In this verse from the Janaki Mangala the answer is given. Goswami Tulsidas compares the placing of the victory garland on Lord Rama to Kamadeva binding the moon with a noose of lotuses. A noose connotes a negative to the target. Who wants to be bound by a noose anyway? Here the noose is made of lotus flowers, so the experience isn't bad. The lotus is not only externally beautiful, but it smells very nice as well. The moon is very beautiful, so it is an apt comparison for Rama.

Kamadeva is the god of love, and in this instance Sita is the one acting as the romantically interested party. This is still only a comparison made by a devoted poet. There is no way to accurately describe Sita's love for Rama, so the comparison to the god of love helps us to understand her emotion a little. Since Sita here loves Rama, who is God, instead of kama, or material love, she feels prema, or divine love. While the conditioned souls are bound by kama, the Supreme Lord is bound by the prema of His devotees.

This should make sense if we think about it. Our children are in the inferior position. They have to listen to what we say. They are smaller in stature as well; a disposition that is very convenient for us. Imagine if our children were stronger than us. In the critical years where they need instruction, we wouldn't be able to provide it. Due only to their yet to be developed bodies and minds can we compel them to hear some words of wisdom, whether they like it or not.

The children don't always get pushed around, however. Sometimes we do things that they want. How is this possible if they are in the weaker position? The answer is love. From our love for them, we agree to their demands from time to time. Our love can be so strong in many cases that we allow them to do things that they shouldn't. This is typically the case when the parents are looking to find friendship with their young children.

In the case of the Supreme Lord, any offering made with love and devotion is accepted by Him. In Sita's case, the victory garland bound Him both in terms of social protocol and divine love. The garland was the symbolic trophy of the contest. Rama, who is the same Krishna but in a slightly different visible form, was in Janakpur while a contest to determine Sita's husband was taking place. Her father, King Janaka, decided on the rules of the contest: whoever would first lift Lord Shiva's heavy bow would win the hand of his daughter in marriage.

Rama did what no other king came close to doing: He lifted the bow and broke it while stringing it. This meant that Sita was now His wife. He was bound to her for life. The garland she placed on Him was an offering of love because she wanted Him to win and no one else. Rama was forced to accept that noose made of lotus flowers. Rama is the source of all light. In His transcendental abode there is no need for a sun or electricity.

"That abode of Mine is not illumined by the sun or moon, nor by electricity. One who reaches it never returns to this material world." (Lord Krishna, Bg. 15.6)

Since He is the source of all light, His brilliance does not diminish when wrapped in a garland of lotus flowers. The moon's brightness may be shielded by the clouds, but not Rama when in the presence of His devotees. The same type of garland is offered to the spiritual master and to respected Vaishnavas, devotees of the same Rama and Krishna. If made with love, the offering is accepted by the Vaishnava, who then agrees to talk about the Supreme Lord. They accept the offering and pass it up the chain of spiritual teachers, eventually reaching Shri Krishna.

VERSE 110

राम सीय छबि निरुपम निरुपम सो दिनु।
सुख समाज लखि रानिन्ह आनँद छिनु-छिनु।।110।।

rāma sīya chabi nirupama nirupama so dinu |
sukha samāja lakhi rāninha ānamda chinu-chinu ||110||

"Both the picture of Sita and Rama and the day were incomparable. In happiness, the society and the queen look at them and receive bliss moment after moment." (110)

Essay - Nirupama

"How can you describe God accurately? If He is everything, the complete whole, then aren't the words you use to describe Him part of Him? If even your words, which come out of your mouth moment after moment, are part of His definition, how can you ever completely describe Him? Every time you open your mouth to glorify Him you are further expanding the definition. By doing this you're also saying that the previous descriptions were not sufficient. If God is so impossible to explain, why even try? Why frustrate yourself?"

We use comparisons to try to accurately describe things. For instance, if we go to a new pizza restaurant and try out the pizza, we will explain its taste by comparing it to the pizza from other restaurants. "Oh, this is even better than that other place. Previously, that was my favorite, but not anymore." We can take the same approach when saying how bad something is. "This is worse than even that other place, and you know how much I didn't like that place. So just imagine how horrible this place is."

It is natural, then, to attempt to describe the Supreme Lord, the source of all things, by using comparisons. For the comparisons to be meaningful, they should reference objects which are known to the audience. I can explain how I make my decisions throughout the day by invoking references to computer programming and database querying, but if people aren't familiar with these disciplines, my comparisons won't mean much. The Supreme Lord is thus typically explained in terms of objects of which people know.

The radiance from His complexion is compared to the bright moon. His fragrance is compared to the beautiful lotus flower, as is the softness of His skin. His beauty is compared to Cupid, who is the god of love. His strength is compared to the lion and the elephant. His fighting prowess is compared to the leader of the heavenly realm, Lord Indra. The breadth of His fame is described in terms of known space, namely the three worlds. His longevity is compared to the time span of the living entity, which remains manifest between the times of birth and death. Though He is compared to so many things, He is actually incomparable, or nirupama. The same holds true for the image created when He unites with His eternal consort.

If He is incomparable, why do the scriptures give us comparisons? The reason is the constitutional position of the living entity. Whether we like it or not, we are inherently linked to God. And there is nothing we can do to permanently get rid of the link. We can try to forget it, and this is to our detriment. The forgetfulness causes us to fall into the material ocean, which is miserable due to the fact that everything exists temporarily. Whatever you have today will eventually be gone. Though you search for temporary fixes, trying to forget about imminent death, know that the end will approach all the same.

Death is the end of the current life, but the cycle repeats in the next life. In this way the forgetful soul continues to spin through acceptance and rejection, enjoying temporarily only to suffer separation in the end. The link, however, is available at any time. In order to get it back all it takes is a desire to reactivate it. It's like that book that you bought months ago that's remained on your bookshelf, gathering dust from remaining untouched. You mean to get around to reading it, but you've constantly put it off. Just because you put it off doesn't mean that the book ceases to exist. At any time you can open it up and get the experience you originally desired.

In the same way, the connection to God can be rekindled at any moment. The scriptures, such as the Vedas, make the process easier by explaining the glories of

God in terms that we can understand. Even if you have no interest in philosophy and get bored hearing about the difference between matter and spirit, you can get the same idea of God by listening to stories about Him. These stories describe factual occurrences, such as the time when the Supreme Lord incarnated on earth and lifted the extremely heavy bow of Lord Shiva to win the contest in King Janaka's court.

This is the event of focus for the Janaki Mangala poem by Goswami Tulsidas. Though not part of the original Vedas or their direct supplements known as the Puranas, the work is Vedic literature nonetheless, as it describes the glories of God as they are explained originally in the famous Vedic texts. The language may be a little different and the storytelling more streamlined, but since the focus is on the Supreme Lord and His activities, the work serves the same purpose as the original scriptures.

If you know nothing about God at all, from the verse referenced above you can at least know that He once lifted a bow to win a contest. The prize was the hand in marriage of Sita Devi, the daughter of King Janaka. God was in His incarnation of Lord Rama, and in that form He looked so beautiful. When He received the garland of victory from Sita's lotus-like hands, the picture was so beautiful that you couldn't compare it to anything else. The fact that the image was incomparable proves that it could only be about God, who is everything.

It is valid to say that the image was incomparable. It is said that the day was also incomparable. Nothing can compare to the marriage of Sita and Rama, which had all the drama of a Hollywood movie and the heroism of a competition of strength. Though the Supreme Lord is unlimited and can thus accept an unlimited number of devotees, as Rama He takes only one wife. They only get married one time in each creation, and on only one day. Thus to say that the day was incomparable is accurate.

Though words can't accurately describe the image or the day, Tulsidas does not throw his hands up and give up. The nature of a true saint is to try to bring that which is most valuable to as many people as possible. Never mind that the image was incomparable, the poet still gives us ways to understand what the image looked like. He says that the queen and her family were in total happiness and that they received ananda, or bliss, moment after moment by looking at Sita and Rama. In this way we know that the image was cherished by the eyes; it was so beautiful that no one wanted to look at anything else. The satisfaction came from the image itself; because the object of focus was splendid enough, there was no diversion of attention.

From their behavior know that immersion into the glories of the Supreme Lord, which are fortunately endless, automatically brings the focus necessary to stay away from the unwanted elements in life. "Don't do this and stay away from that." This we already hear from so many people, but what should we do all the time? What should we use our vitality for? Here the answer is given: look at God and His devotee. If you can't see them directly, hear about what they did and what they looked like on an incomparable day. This version of thought is known as vishno-smaranam, or remembering God, and just like its target it cannot be compared to anything else.

VERSE 111

प्रभुहि माल पहिराइ जनकिहि लै चलीं।
सखीं मनहुँ बिधु उदय मुदित कैरव कलीं।।१११।।

prabhuhi māla pahirā'i janakihi lai calīṁ |
sakhīṁ manahuṁ bidhu udaya mudita kairava kalīṁ ||111||

"Sita put the garland on Rama and then her friends took her away, like the kairava flower happily blooming from the bud at the sight of the moon." (111)

Essay - Spontaneous Devotion

"Who am I devoted to, you ask? You want to know who I offer my worship to? For me there is only Shri Rama, the eldest son of King Dasharatha. Automatically accompanying Him are Sita, Lakshmana and Hanuman. I only begrudgingly say that I am devoted to them because to call myself a devotee is to imply that somehow there is a choice in the matter. It implies that I have chosen them out of a host of worshipable objects. The fact is that they are mine, and I am theirs. There is no separating us. No matter what happens I will always be with Shri Rama and His family in mind. I derive happiness only from their company. Any other activity is tasteless to me, though I sometimes try to pretend that it is not. This is just to get by in society, for I don't want to draw attention to my relationship with Rama, whom I know to be God but never consciously think of in that way."

The difficulties in describing something constitutional are many. That which is constitutional exists perpetually. It is not created nor is it destroyed. Yet in our journey through life everything is temporary, so even when we engage in something that is actually constitutional, we feel the need to explain it in terms of a choice. The wise poets know how to accurately describe the constitutional by pointing to objects which are interdependent. The motions are true by definition; they cannot be changed.

"O Rama, You should know that just as fish cannot survive when taken out of water, neither Sita nor I can live without You for even a moment." (Lakshmana speaking to Lord Rama, Valmiki Ramayana, Ayodhya Kand, 53.31)

One of the most common expressions used to explain constitutionality is: "like a fish out of water." Interestingly enough, in an ancient Vedic text we find that this is used by Shri Lakshmana to explain devotional service. No one is keeping score, but Lakshmana's use has the chance of being the first time the phrase was ever uttered. He said it to his elder brother, Lord Rama, as a way to explain how neither he nor Sita, Rama's wife, could live without Him.

The poets have since used similar comparisons, but the fish taken out of water is still one of the more preferable ones. The fish cannot survive out of water. In this sense its love for the water is indescribable; it is part of the fish's being. The fish cannot be without the water, so it cannot live without its love. The water, the loveable object, defines the fish's existence.

The comparison is important to study because it helps explain the living entity's relationship to God. One may wonder how we could be compared to fish out of water when we are alive right now and not necessarily God conscious. Even if we are a sterling example of devotional service to the Almighty today, there was a factual point in history where we weren't. When we emerged from the womb, we didn't even know how to walk or talk, so how did we know anything about God? We know that we didn't consciously know about God back then and yet we remained alive. How, then, can the fish out of water comparison apply to any human being?

The comparison applies to the devotee, who is a living entity in the bhava stage. Bhava is devotional ecstasy and it is the constitutional state. We are eternally servants of the Supreme Lord. This is our original position as well, a fact kindly told to us by Shri Krishna Chaitanya Mahaprabhu, a preacher incarnation of the Supreme Lord who revived the bhakti-yoga tradition in the modern age. In the conditioned state, our bhava is covered up, like the sun shining bright but no one able to see it because of the thick cloud cover in the sky.

In the conditioned state we think in terms of "I" and "Mine." "I am an American; I am an Indian; I am black; I am white." "This is my house; this is my son; this is my God; this is my religion." Because we descend into temporary possessiveness and flawed conceptions of our personality, we understand religion only in terms of explicit devotional practices. When we see others in the bhava state, we tend to think that they are purposefully practicing devotion, when in fact they are constitutionally tied to the Supreme Lord in a bond of love. Nothing can be done to change their situation.

In the above referenced verse from the Janaki Mangala, Goswami Tulsidas makes yet another comparison with the kairava flower to explain spontaneous devotion. Here the kairava flowers are blooming from buds at the sight of the moon. The flowers are Janaki, the daughter of King Janaka, and her sakhis, or friends. Janaki is Sita, the eternal consort of Lord Rama, the Supreme Personality of Godhead in His incarnation as a warrior prince. It shouldn't surprise anyone that the moon referenced here is Rama, one of whose many names is Ramachandra.

The kairava is the water-lily. It is white and has a unique behavior. While the common lotus flower opens up at the sight of the sun, the kairava opens up at the sight of the moon. Like the fish attached to its water, the opened kairava is attached to its moon. There is nothing that can be done to change this relationship. The kairava doesn't open up to make the moon happy. It doesn't open up on purpose to make a show of devotion to the moon. Rather, the relationship is automatic; it is part of the flower's constitution. Nothing can be done to change this, and to outside observers the spontaneous devotion is a thing of beauty.

In a similar manner, the sakhis and their chief friend, Sita, are forever devoted to Rama. They sprout up in happiness from seeing Him. In this instance, Sita has placed the garland of victory around Rama's neck. The garland is made of flowers and it is the first reward given to the victor of the contest. Rama was the first person to lift Lord Shiva's bow in the assembly in King Janaka's court. His victory earned Him Sita's hand in marriage, a hand coveted by all the many princes assembled there that day.

Tulsidas here reminds us that Sita and her friends are spontaneously devoted to Rama. As flowers, they open up right away upon seeing Him. We living entities are actually the same way, though we don't realize it now due to so many births spent in the material existence. Yet just from hearing of Sita's devotion and the devotion of others associated with Rama, we can slowly work our way back to the bhava stage, where we love God so much that we don't even realize that we're serving Him. We always think of Him, and during times of inactivity we involuntarily recite His names, like those found in the maha-mantra, "Hare Krishna Hare Krishna, Krishna Krishna, Hare Hare, Hare Rama Hare Rama, Rama Rama, Hare Hare."

VERSE 112

बरषहिं बिबुध प्रसून हरषि कहि जय जए।
सुख सनेह भरे भुवन राम गुर पहँ गए।।112।।

baraṣahiṁ bibudha prasūna haraṣi kahi jaya ja'e |
sukha saneha bhare bhuvana rāma gura pahaṁ ga'e ||112||

"All kinds of flowers are raining down and in happiness everyone is saying, 'Jaya, jaya.' Love and happiness filled the world, and Rama went towards the guru." (112)

Essay - Testing the Material

"Dude, have you lost your mind? You're really celebrating that again? Haven't you had enough? I understand it was a big deal when it happened. We were all there. We celebrated with you. It was a remarkable achievement given what you had to go through. But that was then and this is now. Normal people don't remain stuck in the past. Most people forget about the occasion as early as a year later. If you keep celebrating it like this every day, people will think you are crazy."

What exactly is this person referring to? Actually, it could be anything of importance. A graduation, a promotion, an award, a trophy, a triumph in sports, or even getting a driver's license – these victories are celebrated on the day they take place, but soon afterwards they are forgotten. One can look back at those moments fondly, but to dwell on them every single day, expecting the same praise that others offered to you on the original day, is kind of silly. We mention this only because one person's triumphs can actually be remembered every day, with the celebration marked by the repeated voicing of "jaya, jaya." This uniqueness gives us another way to differentiate between the material and the spiritual.

For a spiritualist to discuss the material is quite normal. If you have no such interest for whatever reason then your knowledge hasn't reached its full potential. Put a book of logic in front of an animal and they won't know what to do with it. There is no possible way for them to understand. From what they inherited at the time of birth, the most they can do is eat, sleep, mate and defend. A human being, though, with the proper training can one day learn to open up that book and take away valuable lessons from it. That same book that looked like it was filled with gibberish soon speaks to the person on the inside, offering a way to hear what someone else previously said.

The most important books are those which discuss the difference between matter and spirit. Rare it is to hear such discussion, so one who is fortunate enough to get this information should take full advantage. The Vaishnava in the modern age feels that the information is so important that they try to distribute it to as many people as possible. The book of knowledge they rely on is the Bhagavad-gita, which chronicles an ancient conversation between a wise teacher and a sincere student. Right at the outset, the difference between matter and spirit is discussed.

"For the soul there is never birth nor death. Nor, having once been, does he ever cease to be. He is unborn, eternal, ever-existing, undying and primeval. He is not slain when the body is slain." (Lord Krishna, Bhagavad-gita, 2.20)

To illustrate the difference, the teacher makes mention of the most obvious indication of that difference. Death is what has bewildered man since time immemorial. On the particular day when the Bhagavad-gita was spoken, the same death perplexed a capable and knowledgeable warrior. The teacher, Shri Krishna, explained that the individual inside the body never dies. The soul is the identifying agent, and it is immutable, unchangeable, primeval, and not slain when the body is slain. That which appears to be destroyed is only the body, which consists of matter, or the material.

As the body is not spirit, it lacks the properties of spirit. The body changes all the time. It has a beginning and an end. Technically, it is eternal just like the soul, but that is because matter is rooted in spirit. For the purposes of our interactions, matter is temporary. One who knows the spiritual and the material can make the choice to associate with the spiritual. This choice is ultimately made through consciousness. The body is the vehicle to facilitate that association. From that decision, one also acts in such a way that their knowledge of the difference doesn't get lost.

The Bhagavad-gita is high philosophy that not everyone will want to hear. We can derive the same lessons, however, from studying the manner in which celebrations take place. By noting that the occasion of a graduation is only celebrated one time we can see that the occasion is material. Graduation is the completion of some kind. It is a moment in time where we have just finished our courses; therefore we celebrate. But my identity as a graduating student will soon change. Afterwards, I may become an office worker, a doctor, or a lawyer. Then I will have new things to celebrate.

I can look back to that moment of my graduation as often as I want to, but no one will want to celebrate it every single day with me. At the original celebration, perhaps many people came over to the house and my parents gave me an expensive gift. Yet they will not behave the same way ten years later. This proves that the event was related to matter, which is temporary. To think of it another way, try to keep in mind that today's celebration of something important will be forgotten very quickly. If you're attending a festival that you'll forget soon afterwards, how important can it really be?

The spiritual, being everlasting, can be celebrated millions of years into the future. The above referenced verse from the Janaki Mangala is one example of the fact. Here the same Shri Krishna, in His form as Lord Rama, has just been given the garland of victory by Sita Devi, His eternal consort. The Bhagavad-gita is important not just because of its lessons. It is spoken by the Supreme Lord, God for all of humanity. He may appear differently to different people, and He may not reveal Himself fully to those who are envious, but He nevertheless does exist and is a singular personality. Krishna and Rama are the same person, though they have slightly different appearances.

The verse above describes a celebration. Rama has just lifted an amazingly heavy bow to win a contest. None of the other princes gathered at the assembly could even move the bow. These were the most notable princes in the world. They all were in Janakpur to try to lift the bow. The prize was Sita's hand in marriage. She was the beloved daughter of the pious King Janaka. As Rama is God, it wasn't surprising that flowers rained down from the heavens after He won the contest. We see that the people repeatedly exclaimed, "Jaya, jaya," which means "all glories, all glories" or "victory to you."

Happiness and good feelings filled the entire world. After placing the victory garland on Rama, Sita went back to her place with her friends. Rama went back to the guru Vishvamitra, who was responsible for bringing Him to this contest. The "jaya, jaya," mentioned here is significant because it is the way God is still celebrated to this day. If you visit a temple dedicated to Krishna or one of His non-different expansions, there will surely be many times where "jaya, jaya" is repeated by the congregation. This is done to celebrate the Lord, His devotees, His activities, and His various holy places around the world.

The Bhagavad-gita was spoken some five thousand years ago and Rama's lifting of the bow took place many thousands of years before that, and yet we continue to celebrate both today. This means that the events couldn't be material. You could actually celebrate Sita and Rama's marriage day after day and not get sick of it. It is the constitutional position of the soul to be servant of God, and one way of serving is glorifying. This glorification provides so much pleasure that one wants to repeat it over and over again.

To be fixed in this glorification, to have dedication in devotion, one should be free of envy and know of the merits of the glorification. To hear is the best way to remove doubts and ignorance. Therefore the kind Vaishnavas have authored so much invaluable literature. They hope that everyone finds the ecstasy that is their birthright. That ecstasy comes when one is fully engaged in devotional service, where they repeatedly celebrate the spiritual.

CHAND 14

गए राम गुरु पहिं राउ रानी नारि-नर आनँद भरे।

जनु तृषित करि करिनी निकर सीतल सुधासागर परे।।
कौसिकहि पूजि प्रसंसि आयसु पाइ नृप सुख पायऊ।
लिखि लगन तिलक समाज सजि कुल गुरहि अवध पठायऊ।।14।।

ga'e rāma guru pahiṁ rā'u rānī nāri-nara ānaṁda bhare |
janu tṛṣita kari karinī nikara sītala sudhāsāgara pare ||
kausikahi pūji prasaṁsi āyasu pā'i nṛpa sukha pāya'ū |
likhi lagana tilaka samāja saji kula gurahi avadha paṭhāya'ū ||14||

"Rama went towards the guru, and the king, queen, men and women all filled with bliss, like thirsty male and female elephants entering a cool ocean of nectar." (Chand 14.1)

"Worshiping Vishvamitra, explaining things and getting his permission, the king became happy. Then the tilaka and wedding details were written on a decorated scroll and given to the family guru for being sent to Ayodhya." (Chand 14.2)

Essay - A Cool Ocean of Nectar

In the Vedas, there is often reference to purity. That which is pure is beyond contamination; it has no defect. Pure things are also the best; nothing is better. In a land governed by duality, everything is double-sided. Nothing is totally good or totally bad. What we generally consider good is that which brings us closer to the endpoint of complete purity, but this doesn't mean that the mechanism itself is free of flaws. For this reason, when making analogies to describe the behavior of those who get to personally witness God's glorious nature, the ever-attentive saints make sure to amplify the emotions by pointing to the best, the purest form of something.

In the above referenced verse from the Janaki Mangala, an analogy is made to elephants finding a cool ocean. Imagine male and female elephants living in a jungle. It is very warm. These are elephants, so they can't really think too far ahead into the future. They aren't expert at making plans. They can't tell themselves, "Okay, let me just tolerate the heat a little bit longer. This will be for my own good because then my senses will be trained to endure austere conditions. The stronger my senses are, the more capable I will be at handling adversity. As life is full of unexpected twists, sometimes bringing good fortune and other times taking away that to which we are attached, if I can survive through any condition I will be better off."

The animals are driven more by their impulses. This is why when we see someone eating uncontrollably, without giving concern to the future implications, we compare them to an animal. The same goes for uncontrolled sex life. The animals are less evolved in this way; it is their consciousness which is underdeveloped. They have no choice in the matter, as due to their body type inherited at the time of birth there is a ceiling to their intelligence. The human being's ceiling is much higher; in fact it goes to the highest level for living entities.

The elephants in the hot jungle could really go for a swim in a cold pond. Imagine, then, what they would feel if they found a large ocean full of cool, refreshing water. The satisfaction to the senses would be instant and great. The delight would be greater than that which is felt on an ordinary day when a cool pond is found. Think of it like sitting down for a sumptuous feast when you are really hungry. Think of it like getting a cold soft drink when you're really thirsty and suffering from the heat.

This comparison to the elephants is made by Goswami Tulsidas to describe what the men and women of the town of Janakpur felt when they saw Rama approaching His guru. The king and queen felt the same way. They were all happy to officially welcome Rama into their family, which was the result to His winning the contest of the bow. Rama lifted a bow that was so heavy that no other prince could even move it. His reward: the hand of Sita Devi in marriage. Sita was the king's daughter. She was so beautiful that any prince would do anything to have her. Yet the rules made by her father, King Janaka, stipulated that Sita would only marry whichever prince could lift the bow in the arena.

Seeing Rama, who is the Supreme Lord in an incarnation as a warrior prince, the people became filled with ananda, or bliss. The ananda was the pleasurable reward, and since the comparison was made to the thirsty elephants, it means that the people were highly desirous of that reward. They wanted very badly for Rama to win. They didn't want any other prince to succeed. They were so invested in the outcome that they feared what might happen should Rama be unable to lift the bow. As Bhagavan, Rama possesses the opulence of beauty to the fullest degree. At this time, He was a charming youth with delicate features. The people worried that His tenderness wasn't a good match for the hardness of the heavy bow.

Just as the thirsty elephants finally get water from a cool ocean, so the people of the town desirous of Rama's victory got an ocean of ananda in His vision. At the same time, Goswami Tulsidas makes sure to say that the ocean is made of nectar. Nectar is the best drink; it is akin to the purest beverage, as nothing is better than it. Rama is the best because He is God. The bliss the residents received was unlike any other. This wasn't the normal happiness that comes from relief. Rama's image gave them purity in bliss at the time, and the memory of His image would stay with them forever.

The material existence is likened to an ocean of suffering. Sometimes there is scorching heat and other times there is biting cold. Sometimes we are with friends and sometimes we are alone. The conditions always change, as that is the nature of the world. Despite our sufferings, we too can find an ocean of nectar to quench our thirst for ananda. That nectar comes in the form of the Supreme Lord's association, which is available through something as simple as a sound vibration: Hare Krishna Hare Krishna, Krishna Krishna, Hare Hare, Hare Rama Hare Rama, Rama Rama, Hare Hare.

This verse passed on by Tulsidas is a sound vibration as well, and just through hearing it one can experience some of the same sweet bliss that the men and women of the town of Janakpur felt. What's so wonderful about Rama's image is that it really is like an ocean. The material ocean is full of suffering, so its vast length poses a formidable obstacle for the bewildered soul. On the other hand, the ocean of nectar produced by Rama's association is full of bliss, so its unimaginable length is a welcome blessing that guarantees that there will be endless opportunities for happiness.

Essay - Finding What You Want

"This life has been unfulfilling. When I was younger I was told that I could be anything that I want to be. I could grow up to be a policeman, a firefighter, a baseball player, a stock broker - the sky was the limit. Though I didn't go for any lofty position, now in adulthood I have a steady job that provides a sufficient income. I can more or less eat whatever I want, whenever I want. When I'm not working I can do anything my heart desires.

"And yet I'm still not satisfied. I tried playing recreational sports for a while. I joined this league and that, for I thought that since I enjoy these sports with my friends, it would be even better to have a regular meeting of the sorts. The result was just the opposite. I hated having yet another engagement to pay attention to. Showing up on time for work is enough of a burden for me; I don't need any additional pressures relating to time.

"I've tried reading different books. I like philosophy and government. I love to read biographies, to see how other people weave their way through life. The philosophical works kind of bore me after a while and the biographies always make me sad at the end. I'm left thinking, 'Is that all there is to life? Even these very successful people didn't really seem to do much. At the end of life they were left with the question of what to do with their time.'

"I think there is something out there that I really want, but I can't seem to pinpoint it. I know that I haven't found it yet, because if I had I would never look back. I wouldn't doubt anymore. It's sort of like how they say you can tell you're in love when you don't have to question it. If I know that I have found what I'm looking for in life, I won't have to jump from one thing to another. I will only want that one thing and nothing else. It will bring me so much happiness."

The people in Janakpur a long time ago might not have gone through the same series of events in their quest for the one thing missing in their lives, but they found that invaluable treasure nonetheless. It was so wonderful to them that it was like they became filled with bliss upon receiving it. A famous Vaishnava poet compared the amount of bliss to an ocean, the gift itself to nectar, and the people to thirsty elephants.

"Seems like an odd comparison, no? When would thirsty elephants ever find an ocean of nectar? Nectar is a premium beverage, so by definition it isn't available in large quantities. To use modern terms, it would be like finding an outdoor pool filled with Cristal champagne. That is highly unlikely, as the beverage is too expensive for anyone to buy in that large a quantity for only filling a pool."

Interestingly, the comparison made by Goswami Tulsidas actually does not go far enough. Sudha, or nectar, is mentioned because it is what we would consider the best drink for quenching thirst. The more thirsty you are, the more you will appreciate a higher quality beverage. If you are already full from drinking, being presented with nectar might not do so much for you. If you are thirsty, you will appreciate the wonderful beverage all the more. Still, nectar is just a drink; it is not necessarily required for maintaining life. You could survive on just water.

Similarly, the ocean may be very large, but it is still finite in size. The comparison is used here only to help the listener understand to some degree what it is like to see the Supreme Lord wearing a garland of victory after you thought you wouldn't see Him in such a garb. In this scene He is also walking towards His guru, showing respect to someone else when He Himself is the most worthy of it.

God is impossible to fully understand, and so the parrot-like devotees love to discuss His glories endlessly. The impossible makes the endless glorification possible, a fact which adds on to God's glories, thus increasing the magnitude of the impossibility in fully understanding Him. In simpler terms, talking about God in a loving way is fun, and since God is endless, the fun never has to end.

In this instance, the male and female observers at the assembly in Janakpur were like thirsty elephants finding an ocean of nectar. Water would have sufficed, but Rama is the best of everything. He explains the same truth in the Bhagavad-gita in His original form of Krishna. There He says that He is the taste of water, the fragrance of the earth, the penances of the ascetic, and so many other things. He also says that among the warriors, He is Rama.

"Of purifiers I am the wind; of the wielders of weapons I am Rama; of fishes I am the shark, and of flowing rivers I am the Ganges." (Lord Krishna, Bhagavad-gita, 10.31)

The latter point has added significance to the discussion here. The king and queen in Janakpur, along with their protected citizens, were interested in finding the best prince for Sita, the king's daughter. As Krishna says in the Bhagavad-gita, He is Rama among those who use weapons, which means that if one wants to find the best protector in the world, they have to get Rama. King Janaka was very pious and devoted to spiritual life. For his efforts, he received the goddess of fortune as a daughter. Sita thus can only be with Rama. Externally she received the best prince in the world when Rama lifted the bow of Shiva in the assembly. Constitutionally it could not have been any other way. Sita has only one husband: Rama. And Rama has only one wife: Sita. As Krishna He can accept unlimited consorts, but as Rama He accepts only Sita.

The king, queen and residents were well-wishers to Sita. They took her happiness to be theirs as well. When they saw Rama win the contest, especially after so many other princes had failed to move the bow, they were elated. Due to the other failures, they thought that Rama might not win either. If He didn't win, He couldn't marry Sita, and thus their cherished desire would be left unfulfilled. This is the condition that created the thirst. They became elephants in the sense that they wanted very badly for Rama to win. Their emotions raged, similar to the way they do in an elephant in the hot jungle.

They found the ocean of nectar in the vision of Rama, who was garlanded by Sita herself. That nectar filled them up, but since it was an ocean, there was no way to run out of it. The cool beverage of the vision was soothing to the eyes, and it filled the people with bliss. That bliss is what we're all actually looking for, though it may take us many lifetimes to find it. There are different aspects to the Supreme Lord, who has unlimited names, forms and pastimes. The nectar doesn't come only through the vision of Rama wearing the garland, but it alone is sufficient to fulfill the purpose of life. Such visions and more are given to us through the words of the Vedic texts. And more potent than the actual descriptions is the name of God.

The best names to recite for this age are kindly given to us by Krishna Himself. The most munificent avatara, the golden complexioned Lord Chaitanya, freely distributed love for God, which automatically includes God's association through various visions from the past. Lord Chaitanya distributed this gift through the chanting of the holy names: Hare Krishna Hare Krishna, Krishna Krishna, Hare Hare, Hare Rama Hare Rama, Rama Rama, Hare Hare.

Essay - Contract Talks

In professional sports, when a player's contract is up, negotiations begin for a renewal. Since the player is a public figure and someone who knows the management and its affiliates very well, often times he won't negotiate the contract himself. Everything will go through the agent. The two parties have different interests. The owner's side wants to limit the value of the contract. They also want to avoid getting locked into an expensive long-term deal that could leave them stuck with a bad player. The player wants to make as much money as possible, for as long as possible.

Each party will have to talk down the other if they are to be successful. The player may say, "Well, look at what other players in the league make. They aren't as good as me, so why shouldn't I get paid more? Such and such is the price tag now for a player of my caliber." The owner's side will say things like, "This was your best year so far, but other years haven't been so good. We're ready to make a fair offer, but we don't think that you will be so great. Take this deal now and perhaps we can renegotiate in the future."

Rather than let tensions mount to the point that both sides dislike each other, the agent is inserted into the equation. Representing the player, he can say pretty much whatever he wants and not have it affect the relationship between the player and the team. The agent looks out for the player's interests. The player trusts the agent to get him the best deal.

A similar thing took place in Janakpur a long time ago, except all of the parties involved were pure. There was no haggling necessary, but since the parties were so pious, they went through the proper channels as a mere formality. This tells us that someone whose piety is rooted in real religious principles is automatically respectful. They don't have to separately endeavor for acquiring the trait of respectfulness.

The agreement in question did not relate to a contract to play anything. The agreement related to something as old as man himself: marriage. King Janaka vowed to give away his daughter Sita to the first prince who could lift an extremely heavy bow originally belonging to Lord Shiva. Many princes tried, but only the prince of Ayodhya, Lord Rama, managed to lift it. When the bow subsequently broke in Rama's hands, the sound of victory filled the air. Everyone on Janaka's side was thrilled, as were the residents of Janakpur. The rival princes were sad in defeat, but Rama's side was happy too.

While Janaka had his whole family around to celebrate the occasion, Rama's entourage consisted of only His younger brother Lakshmana and the famous sage Vishvamitra. The guru became the representative in this instance. In the Vedic tradition the guru is the representative of God; he speaks the Lord's message based on the authority of the disciplic succession he belongs to. The genuine disciplic succession originates in God, so the bona fide guru's message is always valid.

Here the guru also acted as Rama's representative, but in His direct presence. Rama is the Supreme Lord in the spiritual manifestation of a warrior prince. Rama and Lakshmana served Vishvamitra like respectful disciples just to show the proper code of conduct to the world, but Vishvamitra's role as representative couldn't be masked completely. After Rama lifted the bow, the marriage could have started immediately, but King Janaka followed protocol. It was Vishvamitra who brought Rama and Lakshmana to the contest. He was the elder as well, so Janaka wasn't going to follow through on something without his permission.

From the above referenced verse from the Janaki Mangala, we see that Vishvamitra gave his consent after being duly worshiped by the king. The sage then drew up the announcement of the wedding and gave it to Janaka's family priest, Shatananda. That announcement was then sent to Ayodhya. In the Valmiki Ramayana, which contains the original accounts of this most glorious wedding, Sita recounts how Rama first got His father's permission before proceeding with the marriage. Rama's representative in this instance was the catalyst for receiving that permission.

Rama participated in the contest after Vishvamitra got permission from King Janaka. Now Sita would marry Rama after Janaka got Vishvamitra's permission and Rama got Dasharatha's permission. Very respectful were all the characters associated with Rama. Later on, after several years of marriage, Rama would be exiled from His kingdom for fourteen years. Sita very badly wanted to come along and she was finally able to do so after taking permission from the superiors. Lakshmana accompanied Rama after getting his mother's permission.

"After obtaining the permission of the elders, I must go accompany You. If I am separated from You, O Rama, I will surely renounce my life." (Sita Devi speaking to Lord Rama, Valmiki Ramayana, Ayodhya Kand, 29.5)

So much respect was shown during this ancient time, but today the channels of communication aren't nearly as strong. Families can easily go many years without talking to one another. If something good happens to you, then it is easy to proceed without notifying others. Despite the degraded condition of the modern age, the respect shown to the spiritual master is still required. The compulsory nature of the approach towards a bona fide guru is mentioned quite often in Vedic literature because it especially prevents one from mentally speculating about God. Without approaching a guru, one is left to their own imagination to think of God and how to connect with Him.

The guru follows authority. Vishvamitra was worshiped by Janaka, but that alone didn't suffice for consent in the marriage. Even Vishvamitra, a brahmana, gets permission from others, so who are we to think that we can approach God without first learning about Him from someone who represents Him? And the kind representatives of the Lord, who are the real saints of the world, are more than happy to divulge information about Bhagavan, the Supreme Lord who is full of opulences. They make one stipulation, however. They ask that we be sincere in our inquisitiveness. If our desire is to deceive the world with a concocted form of religion, the guru's words will not be so forthcoming. We won't even be able to properly understand their message should it come to us in written form. The respect offered by the interested parties at Sita's svayamvara teaches so many lessons, including on how to make the most out of life.

Essay - A Little Discomfort

The easiest thing to do is give in to your emotions when they flare up. If you are angry, just let it all out. If you're upset with someone, let them have it with a verbal tirade. If you don't like someone else, don't offer them any respect. Don't even think for a moment that anyone else could be superior to you. As is often the case, the easier route isn't always the best one. Conforming to the proper code of conduct, even if it sometimes might bring a little discomfort, serves to better our condition. Such was the case with a famous king a long time ago.

"That country is looking so beautiful, and the Vedas have described its purity. Known in the three worlds, Tirahuta [Janakpur] is the tilaka of the earth." (Janaki Mangala, 4)

The king in question was named Janaka. He ruled over the territory known as Mithila. This area still exists. It is also known as Tirahuta, and as Goswami Tulsidas kindly informs us, it is the tilaka of the earth and known throughout the three worlds [heavenly, earthly and hellish realms]. The place was sacred before Janaka ruled over it, and based on what would happen there on one particular day its fame would increase even more.

"From Hrasvaroma came a son named Shiradhvaja [also called Janaka]. When Shiradhvaja was plowing a field, from the front of his plow [shira] appeared a daughter named Sitadevi, who later became the wife of Lord Ramachandra. Thus he was known as Shiradhvaja." (Shrimad Bhagavatam, 9.13.18)

Janaka was one king in a long line of kings known as Janaka. He was also known as Shiradhvaja. He was very famous during his time even before he received any children. Kings in those times were selected not simply off birthright. If I am a doctor by profession and so is my wife, if we have children then they will be predisposed to the physician's culture. They will grow up in a household of doctors, so they will be exposed to various aspects of medicine.

Birthright alone, however, won't anoint them with the title of Doctor. That they will have to earn in the same way that the parents did. They will have to go through years of schooling, pass the necessary board examinations, and complete training under the tutelage of other doctors. Only then will they be known as doctors.

In the same manner, kings during the Treta Yuga, the second time period of creation, ascended to the throne after they received the proper training. This implies that there were qualifications necessary. Some of those qualifications are provided to us in the Bhagavad-gita, which, among many other things, summarizes the ancient Vedic culture. The kings had to be noble, chivalrous, brave, and impartial. They were the administrators; the people in charge of administering justice. Justice is supposed to be blind; in its constitutional form it cannot play favorites. The same should hold true for the person administering it. If we walk into a courtroom and see the judge fraternizing with one of the attorneys, we have a feeling that the case will not be judged fairly. Sadly these unfair trials are quite commonplace, but in the ideal situation the people in charge of determining guilt and innocence shouldn't have any bias.

"Heroism, power, determination, resourcefulness, courage in battle, generosity, and leadership are the qualities of work for the kshatriyas." (Lord Krishna, Bhagavad-gita, 18.43)

Janaka met all the necessary qualifications for a leader. He had a few special distinctions as well. He was a rajarshi, which is a saintly king. He was well versed in the Vedas, the ancient scriptures of India. He was also expert at meditational yoga. He could withdraw the mind from the senses and thus remain unattached to what was going on around him. Despite his expertise in transcendentalism, he still did all the necessary work in his kingdom. He didn't use his status as a yogi as an excuse to shirk his responsibilities.

As a result of his behavior, Janaka was well-respected throughout the world. No one could really surpass him in character. When the time came to determine the husband for his beautiful daughter Sita, Janaka decided on a self-choice ceremony. This self-choice would be made for the bride through the vehicle of a contest. Whichever prince attending the ceremony could lift the extremely heavy bow of Lord Shiva would win Sita's hand in marriage.

Against all odds, after it looked like no one would win, Lord Rama, the eldest son of King Dasharatha of Ayodhya, lifted up the bow. This delighted Janaka and his wife. It also thrilled Sita and all the residents of the town. At this point, Janaka easily could have just handed Sita over to Rama and started the wedding ceremony.

He could have said, "To heck with all this protocol and tradition. Rama is my preferred choice anyway. He won the contest, and Sita obviously is fond of Him as well. What is there to stand in our way? I'm a very respected king. No one can say a bad word about me. Why should I have to listen to anyone else right now?"

From the above referenced verse from the Janaki Mangala, we see that Janaka did not think this way at all. Though for all intents and purposes the marriage was already determined, Janaka still worshiped the feet of the guru Vishvamitra, who had brought Rama and His younger brother Lakshmana to the ceremony. Janaka also got Vishvamitra's permission for the marriage. Though Janaka had all the power in the world, he did not abuse his position. With great power comes great responsibility. Part of that responsibility is setting a good example for others. If someone like Janaka makes the voluntary choice to pay homage to saintly people like Vishvamitra, who are we to not respect those who are worthy of it?

Even if our pride is swelling and the bad voice inside is telling us to toss aside the standard code of conduct, the slight discomfort of showing respect to the proper authorities will benefit us in the end. Janaka showed respect to Vishvamitra at the beginning of the ceremony. When the sage arrived, Janaka offered beautiful thrones to sit on. After the contest was over, Janaka again showed respect. As a result, an auspicious time for the wedding ceremony to take place was drawn up. The written announcement was then given to Shatananda to take to Ayodhya. Shatananda was Janaka's family guru, and so he would represent the king's family in the talks with Rama's family in Ayodhya.

Lord Rama is the Supreme Lord, and Vishvamitra was His representative in this situation. The same kinds of representatives exist in the world today. We can identify them by the signs of Rama they carry with them. Rama is also known as Vishnu and Krishna. These are the personal forms of the Supreme Lord. The representatives today sometimes wear an image of Rama's footprint on their forehead. They may also wear a necklace made of beads from the sacred Tulasi plant, which is very dear to Rama. Even if these signs are absent, there is still an easy way to spot them. They are always talking about Rama and chanting His holy names: Hare Krishna Hare Krishna, Krishna Krishna, Hare Hare, Hare Rama Hare Rama, Rama Rama, Hare Hare.

They ask only one thing from others: to chant the same names of their beloved. To chant the names just one time with full sincerity is the best way to offer respect to the Lord's representative. And the more respect we offer, especially in the form of a formal interaction between guru and disciple, the more benefits we receive. In Janaka's case he received Rama as a son-in-law. Later on Rama would leave the kingdom and take Sita with Him, but Janaka never forgot about either of them. His devotion to God makes him known today as one of the twelve mahajanas, or authorities on devotional service.

The chanting of the holy names, which may be a slight inconvenience in the beginning, brings us the same association. Chanting these names is also a way to respect the Vaishnava authorities. The chanting, which is part of the transcendental engagement known as bhakti-yoga, also gives respect to Janaka, who gave respect to Vishvamitra, who is Rama's representative. In this way know that a little respect offered in sincerity to one belonging to the chain of devotion that originates with God brings so much auspiciousness.

PREPARING FOR THE MARRIAGE

VERSE 113

गुनि गन बोलि कहेउ नृप माँडव छावन।
गावहिं गीत सुआसिनि बाज बधावन॥113॥

guni gana boli kahe'u nṛpa māṁḍava chāvana |
gāvahiṁ gīta su'āsini bāja badhāvana ||113||

"The king asked the qualified people to erect a mandapa. The married ladies sang songs and auspicious music played." (113)

Essay - A Dream Wedding

This verse from the Janaki Mangala serves the purpose of building anticipation for the blessed event. Thus far there was already much anticipation, fear, uncertainty, triumph, joy, victory, and relief. Nevertheless, with the Supreme Personality of Godhead's pastimes, the thrills are never-ending. Just because one part of a particular pastime completes doesn't mean that there is boredom to follow afterwards. Just as the bride-to-be in modern times gets excited over planning every detail of her upcoming wedding, so the residents of Janakpur got thrills at every moment in preparing for the marriage of Sita to Rama.

Ideally, you only get married once. The event should thus be as glamorous as possible; at least that is the hope. For the woman especially, the marriage day is the one thought about for many years. Pictures will be taken, so many friends and family will attend, and a new life will begin. Why not make it as special as possible? Why not go all out and find the best hall to host the reception?

In that hall you will want a certain theme. The plates and table settings must conform to the chosen theme. The flowers should be profuse and of the right kind.

The guests should be seated in such a way that they will get along with each other. The food should be so good that no one will leave the place hungry. There should also be enough options to satisfy all the different tastes. The music should be perfect too. Either get a DJ or a live band to come and play festive songs. The hall should be in a nice area. If it has an outdoor section in the back, that's even better. This way people can lounge outside during the appetizer portion of the evening. Let no one be bored at the wedding.

All of this shouldn't really matter, as all that is happening is the acceptance of marriage vows by two people. Yet the hosts go the extra mile to enhance the joy from the occasion. With a marriage ceremony you have an excuse to invite your friends over. If it were an ordinary day, they may not be so willing to travel to wherever you live. Also, it would be difficult to get all of your friends and family to come on the same day. If you have the occasion of the marriage, why not take full advantage of it? What is the harm in celebrating?

For King Janaka, the occasion had more meaning. He was to give away his precious daughter Sita. Her future didn't look so bright just a few moments before. Janaka knew that Sita was not ordinary. Her bodily features were auspicious, as was the way in which she came into his life. He found her one day while ploughing a field to perform a sacrifice. What an odd way to welcome in your first child. Janaka was thrilled nevertheless, and he named the newly found baby Sita because she came from the ground.

He couldn't arrange her marriage in the traditional way, through matching up the qualities of the prospective grooms. He decided instead to hold a contest of strength. Whoever could first lift an amazingly heavy bow would wed his beautiful daughter. Only one man did. Named Rama, He hailed from Ayodhya, where His father was the king. Rama was the preferred choice upon first sight, so everyone in Janaka's family was happy that He won.

Here Janaka orders that the mandapa be prepared. This is the architectural structure that hosts important ceremonies in the Vedic tradition. It looks very nice from the outside, and it acts as a sort of temple. Marriage is based in religion. If it weren't, it would have no purpose. The only reason the definition of marriage is up for debate today is because its use has been widely non-religious. No one has to teach a male and a female how to get together. The animals already mate without anyone instructing them. They have children and families without requiring marriage.

The marriage institution is passed down from God for the purpose of regulating behavior. Sex life is the greatest impediment towards understanding the living entity's true nature and his purpose for living. The more sex life goes uncontrolled, the more into ignorance one falls. You don't need to hear from the Vedas to understand this. Just see how quickly relationships in sense gratification dissolve. The difference between the relationship and the casual date is that sexual relations ideally occur more often in the relationship. And so even with regular sexual engagement available, there are disagreements, to the point that the two parties no longer can stand each other. If uncontrolled sex life were beneficial, then the opposite would hold true; the parties would become happier and happier as the marriage went on.

Of course it is possible to increase your happiness through marriage, but only when the aim is right. The marriage should help both parties advance in their spiritual awareness. At the same time, they get license to have children and become productive members of the community. Others are thus also benefited through their union. Sita would be Rama's queen, and since Rama would one day take the throne, through marriage He would get an heir to keep the family line going. In finding Sita a husband Janaka would satisfy his duty of protecting his daughter.

Thus so many things would be taken care of through the auspicious occasion of the marriage. The ceremony would take place in a beautifully erected mandapa, and in the background would be auspicious songs sung by married women. Everyone was excited, as they waited for Rama's family to arrive from Ayodhya. Janaka spared no expense for this occasion, making possible the dream wedding.

VERSE 114

सीय राम हित पूजहिं गौरि गनेसहि।
परिजन पुरजन सहित प्रमोद नरेसहि॥114॥

sīya rāma hita pūjahiṁ gauri ganesahi |
parijana purajana sahita pramoda naresahi ||114||

"They prayed to Ganesha and Parvati for Sita and Rama. The king, the relatives and the people of the town were all happy." (114)

Essay - Gauri Ganesha

If someone tells you that they are praying for you, you know that it is a really nice gesture. Especially if they are actually praying and not just saying so, it means that in their most vulnerable state, where they submit to the will of the divine creator, they ask Him to bestow His welfare upon you. They could ask for so many other things; be it money, fame, fortune, or good health. Within that time of prayer, they instead think of you, and so to hear such a thing is very flattering. The people of Janakpur a long time ago were so innocent that they actually prayed for the welfare of the Supreme Lord and His wife. The divine figures who were petitioned for help are themselves devotees, so surely the prayers would not go unanswered.

Have we ever heard of such a thing? It's like going to church and saying:

"Oh God, I love you so much. I think you're the best. You're the only one I'm devoted to. I prayed today for your fame and fortune to continue. I want you to be glorified all the time. I want that you should always remain with the people you love the most. I pray that whatever events you want to unfold go down without a hitch, to your liking. I know that these seem like silly requests, but they are what I want. I know that you give the devotees whatever they ask, that you will stop at nothing to please them. If you are really true to your nature, you will hear my prayers."

In Janakpur, the prayer was even better because the people didn't know the divine natures of Sita and Rama. There is only one God. No need to belabor the point, as the fact is obvious to any rational thinking human being who is not too puffed up with false pride. There is a singular controller, a guiding hand to the non-randomness we see in the nature around us. How to address such a person and how to know Him may be difficult to accept with confidence, but there is still the inherent understanding that there is a God. Even the staunchest atheist succumbs to the forces of nature at the time of death. In their case that very death represents their God. Thus everyone is a servant of a higher nature.

The Vedas say that there are many forms of the original Godhead. This is because so many activities take place through the desire for divine sport. And those activities are tied to specific features. In some forms the features aren't as clearly laid out. Some forms exhibit more of the features, while others exhibit less. Some forms are more attractive to some, while others attract a different kind of worshiper. The idea is that no one should be shut out from worshiping, irrespective of where they live, who their parents are, or what language they speak.

Sita and Rama are God's energy and the Supreme Lord respectively. This information is given in the Vedas. The bona fide spiritual traditions that emanate from the original person sometimes have different ultimate conclusions. Some take Sita and Rama to be the original, others take them to be incarnations of the original Lakshmi Devi and Lord Vishnu, while others take them to be incarnations of the original Shrimati Radharani and Shri Krishna. In whatever tradition you follow, Sita and Rama are still not ordinary. Their qualities alone make them worthy of worship.

The residents of Janakpur can attest to this. They knew nothing of Sita and Rama's true identities. They were won over simply by their qualities. And what were those qualities? Rama was kind, sweet, chivalrous, brave, respectful, handsome, beautiful, and a firm protector of propriety, or dharma. Sita was the most beautiful woman in the world, very shy in her behavior, and a copy of her father Janaka in adherence to dharma. Thus Sita and Rama were a perfect match. When the opportunity arose the people in Janakpur wanted the two to wed.

Lo and behold, Shri Rama was the only prince to lift the bow in the contest at Janaka's assembly, qualifying Him to marry Sita. In the above referenced verse from the Janaki Mangala we get further descriptions of what went on in the town in preparation for the marriage ceremony. It is said that the people prayed to Gauri and Ganesha. They did so for Sita and Rama, not for their own benefit. Gauri is another name for Mother Parvati, who is also known as Durga Devi. She is the wife of Lord Shiva and she takes charge of the material creation. The material nature is like a fort that is difficult to overcome; hence the name Durga. The threefold miseries of life are symbolically represented in the trident held by Durga Devi. Those who want to feel less of a sting from the effects of the mind and body, the natural forces under the control of the celestials, and the influence of other living entities pray for Durga Devi's kindness.

Ganesha is the respected son of Parvati and Shiva. He is pretty much the face of Hinduism, as he is known to so many. The reason his worship is so common is that he removes obstacles for his worshipers. And who wouldn't want obstacles removed? Ganesha is a dedicated son, as he considers his blessed parents to be his life and soul. He is so respected by God that he is granted the high honor of being the first personality worshiped in all Hindu ritualistic functions.

The tricky part of worshiping Gauri and Ganesha alone is that, by definition, they only grant material benedictions. The material relates to the temporary body within the current lifetime. The spiritual relates to the integral animating force within all living beings. The spiritual relates to the soul, which is eternal and thus of higher importance. It is better to seek out the welfare of the soul than the body.

Were the people in Janakpur ignorant of their true identity, then?

Actually, during this time the Vedic culture was still very strong, so everyone worshiped Shiva, Parvati, Ganesha and other divine figures as almost habit. The people were so pious that if anything good happened, they immediately attributed the success to the blessings of Shiva and his family. In this instance, they did not seek out personal rewards. They cannot be considered to be in the material consciousness, for they wanted the pleasure and safety of Sita and Rama.

Goswami Tulsidas, the author of the Janaki Mangala, is of like mind with the people of Janakpur. In his writings he often offers prayers to Ganesha as well, and he asks only to have the obstacles removed so that he can keep Sita and Rama in his heart. The people of Janakpur essentially asked the same thing, and in this style of worship there is no danger of material contamination. Shiva, Parvati and Ganesha act at the behest of Shri Rama, but they are devotees in their own right. They are more than happy to see the marriage of the divine couple, the glories of whom Shiva constantly describes to his chaste and beautiful wife.

VERSE 115

प्रथम हरदि बंदन करि मंगल गावहिं।
करि कुल रीति कलस थपि तेलु चढ़ावहिं।।११५।।

prathama haradi bandana kari maṅgala gāvahiṁ |
kari kula rīti kalasa thapi telu caṛhāvahiṁ ||115||

"First applying turmeric, they are singing of the auspiciousness. They are doing the family rituals, filling the kalasha and applying oil." (115)

Essay - Haldi Kalash

"In Hindu marriages the bride and groom get covered with dirt beforehand? They essentially put mud all over their bodies? What is the reason for this? How about all the pots that get laid out and the singing? Why such a big deal over a marriage? In a few years they're going to despise each other anyway. I can see why people prefer the city hall marriages. Less fuss; no making a big deal out of nothing."

Each tradition has their own rituals related to a wedding, and the Vedic tradition is no different in this regard. As it is the most ancient, it uses articles that are still commonly found today. There needn't be a costly ceremony if basic things like turmeric, oil and pitchers are around. Regardless of the tradition, the purpose of the pomp is the same: to make the occasion more festive. And in Janakpur a long time ago, they had a lot to feel festive about.

You could go with the simple marriage. The bride and the groom show up in front of a judge, get their marriage license, and then go their merry way. You save a lot of money this way too. Of course the parents likely aren't involved in such a ceremony. If they had any say, they would want some kind of celebration. After all, marriage is a lifelong journey, one not to be entered into lightly. Why not celebrate it? We have parades when our sports teams win championships. We have graduation ceremonies for people successfully completing school. We have a celebration when a new president enters the Oval Office. Is it too much to ask for a celebration for a wedding?

The wedding referenced above took place a long time ago. The arrangements were made by the King of Videha, Janaka. The two people getting married had no say in the arrangements. This event was for their parents, relatives and people of the town. Everyone in Janakpur knew Sita Devi, King Janaka's beautiful daughter. They were very happy that she was marrying Rama, the beloved prince of Ayodhya.

From the verse above we see that the ceremony started with the applying of haldi, or turmeric. Seems strange to put mud all over your body, but such a practice is meant to bring auspiciousness. We see that in the background was the sound of auspicious songs. We get these descriptions from the Janaki Mangala, a poem authored by the famous Vaishnava saint, Goswami Tulsidas. Mangala means auspiciousness, and in this case the auspiciousness relates to the marriage of Janaki, which is another name for Sita.

All the family rituals also took place, with kalashas filled and oil applied. Haldi and kalasha are staples of the wedding in the Vedic tradition. Thus nothing was held back. The people of the town got to join in on the festivities. In an ordinary wedding, if we don't know the participants very well, the most we can contribute is showing up to the actual ceremony. We sit through the religious part of the wedding and then enjoy the reception by eating and mingling with other attendees.

As this wedding related to God and His eternal consort, everyone got to participate. Never think that because you lack skill or notoriety that somehow you are then shut out from worshiping. There is no such thing as a big devotee or a small devotee in the eyes of the Supreme Lord. Sincerity is what matters most. In school, we can give identical sets of building blocks to students and then ask them to build something. The student who builds a castle will be praised more than the student who builds something much simpler, but in devotional service the distinctions are made based off the effort alone. As God says in the Bhagavad-gita, He is the ability in man.

"O son of Kunti [Arjuna], I am the taste of water, the light of the sun and the moon, the syllable om in the Vedic mantras; I am the sound in ether and ability in man." (Lord Krishna, Bhagavad-gita, 7.8)

As He is the ability, one person may be blessed with more skill than another. Yet it is how that skill is utilized that matters in the end. In Janakpur, some people helped with the actual arrangements, while others just stayed in the background and sang. Their singing was just as important as the other work going on. In the same way, know that today any person can celebrate Sita and Rama's marriage by remembering them and repeating their names over and over again. Rama is also known as Krishna in His original form. Sita is His energy, so she can be referred to as Hare. The maha-mantra thus addresses them both: Hare Krishna Hare Krishna, Krishna Krishna, Hare Hare, Hare Rama Hare Rama, Rama Rama, Hare Hare.

All the effort may seem a little over the top, but in worshiping God there is no wasted effort. Every time His name is recited, one becomes purer. Every time one travels back in time and gets excited over the prospect of the most virtuous man in the universe uniting with the most beautiful and chaste woman, the consciousness goes one step closer towards reaching its constitutional position of servant of God.

VERSE 116

गे मुनि अवध बिलोकि सुसरित नहायउ।
सतानंद सत कोटि नाम फल पायउ।।116।।

ge muni avadha biloki susarita nahāya'u |
satānanda sata koṭi nāma phala pāya'u ||116||

"After the muni reached Ayodhya, he took bath in the auspicious rivers. Shatananda achieved the fruit of reciting a billion holy names." (116)

Essay - One Billion Holy Names

If you want to become a better runner, you should run on a regular basis. No big surprise there. If you want to cook something very nicely, you'll need some practice. The first time you try it might get burned. Perhaps you'll cook it for too long, you won't mix it well enough, or you'll forget a key ingredient. The ovens can vary, so whatever recipe you took, it might not be suited towards your situation one hundred percent. Practice makes perfect, especially if the practice is ideal. Therefore it shouldn't surprise us that in order to increase our spiritual strength, practice of a particular method is recommended. That practice brings such a wonderful fruit as well. Whereas in ordinary strength training exercises, there is fatigue and vulnerability of burning out and having all the effort go to waste, such is not the case in the highest discipline of spirituality.

If my goal is to run a marathon and I currently don't run at all, perhaps I'll start off with running only one mile as my routine. The first day will be very difficult. I might be huffing and puffing my way through the exercise. The whole time I will be thinking of when it will be over. "I can't wait until I get home. I'm going to sink into the couch and do nothing. From this day forward runners have my utmost respect. I don't know how they can do this on a regular basis."

The next day I will be very sore throughout my lower body. I will likely have trouble walking down the stairs. Nevertheless, through enough practice, things will get better. Pretty soon I won't be so frantic while running. A single mile will seem as easy as taking a walk. My body won't get fatigued so quickly, either. I will thus become stronger in a particular field through practice. The same holds true in other areas as well.

When we shift the focus to spiritual life, the obvious question is what goal we should try to achieve. In running, the end is pretty simple: work up to the point that you have enough endurance to run long distances. In basic exercise the point is to get a lean and fit body. In cooking the goal is to be able to prepare sumptuous dishes without worrying so much about ruining them.

In spiritual life, to know the proper aim one must first know who they are. One route towards answering this question is to go through every single spiritual book ever authored and see what you can decipher. Another is to accept the basic truth of achintya-bhedabheda-tattva so kindly presented by Chaitanya Mahaprabhu. He is a famous saint from India during the medieval period. He is believed to be non-different from God Himself. This fact is corroborated in sacred texts like the Mahabharata and Shrimad Bhagavatam.

Even if you are skeptical of the claims of His divinity, that doesn't bar you from scientifically analyzing His philosophy. If you break down the words, you get a translation of "simultaneous oneness and difference, a relationship that is inconceivable to the mind." As it is achintya, or inconceivable, you don't need to wrack your brain trying to understand how it is true. It is better to just act off of the relationship, where the validation will come later on, as an eventual realization.

The oneness and difference is in comparing the individual's identity to the higher power's. The individual is spirit, or Brahman. The individual is not their temporary body. That means that while I'm in a human form right now, I won't be forever. Previous to this life I was in a completely different body. After this life, I will be in a different body again. Throughout the shifts, my identity doesn't change. The higher power is described as Parabrahman. Both His body and His spirit are changeless. He also expands to reside within every living being; thus He is all-pervading. He is simultaneously individual and collective.

From achintya-bhedabheda-tattva, we get the ideal relationship of servant to master. We are the servants and the higher power is the master. We can try to ignore this all we want, but it will only be to our detriment. Once we make the acknowledgement, however, our fortunes can turn around. The aim of the practice in the highest discipline of spirituality is thus twofold. First, one should truly accept the relationship of servant to master. After that, one should stay in that relationship, never breaking from it. This is for the benefit of the individual. All the rituals, regulations, funny dresses, odd-sounding chants, and places of pilgrimage are ultimately meant for bringing pleasure to the individual; there is no other purpose.

One of the best ways to serve the higher power is to constantly repeat His name. In an objective analysis, one would have to conclude that this is the superior method of all practices in spiritual life. That is because it can be practiced by any person, at any time and at any place. You are never precluded from chanting the holy names. Based on your country of origin, you may not be allowed in a specific temple. If you are not very intelligent, you won't be able to understand the high philosophy that helps one to empirically come close to the conclusion nicely presented by Chaitanya Mahaprabhu. If you live in an oppressive regime where the government tries to play the role of God by handing out gifts to citizens by first confiscating wealth from the producers, you will have a hard time practicing spiritual life.

In any of these situations you can still chant the holy names. Which names should we chant? There are billions of names, too many to count really. This should make sense, because if the higher power is really supreme, His features would have to be unlimited. If there is no limit to His glories, there would be no limit to the number of names used to describe Him. Lord Chaitanya says that the best names are Krishna and Rama and that the energy of God should be addressed at the same time. For this reason He recommends the maha-mantra, "Hare Krishna Hare Krishna, Krishna Krishna, Hare Hare, Hare Rama Hare Rama, Rama Rama, Hare Hare," as the best mantra to chant, the best way to realize the relationship to God and stay connected to Him in service.

In the Vedic tradition there are practices based on this chanting of the holy names. There are the thousand names of Lord Vishnu, which when chanted bring great auspiciousness. The result of saying any one of the names is an increase in spiritual strength, which is namely due to the potency of the name itself. The name is non-different from the person it addresses. This only works with God. Someone from thousands of miles away can call our name, but that doesn't mean that we'll rush to where they are. With God that is not the case. He immediately arrives when His name is chanted.

In the above referenced verse from the Janaki Mangala, the sage Shatananda has reached the city of Ayodhya, which at the time was the home of King Dasharatha. Dasharatha is the chosen father of Rama, who is an incarnation of God. Rama is one of the names in the maha-mantra, and it can refer to Rama, the son of Dasharatha, Rama, the elder brother of Shri Krishna, or just the Supreme Lord Himself, who is the source of all transcendental pleasure.

Shatananda went to Ayodhya to tell Dasharatha the news that his son Rama had won the bow contest in Janakpur and was thus slated to marry the daughter of King Janaka. We see that upon arrival the sage bathed in the holy rivers. In Ayodhya the holiest river is the Sarayu. By so doing, Shatananda received the fruit of chanting one billion holy names. One billion holy names obviously takes a while to recite, especially if one hears the names as they are recited. That chanting represents one billion steps taken towards the Supreme Lord; so the fruit is not chump change. The same was granted to Shatananda upon arriving in Ayodhya. This was due to the holiness of the city, which at the time was inhabited by pure devotees. All the residents there, including the king, lived the master-servant relationship with God. Though they may not have known that Rama was God, they nevertheless served Him. Even the father, though in an apparently superior position, was a great servant. To act as the Lord's father during His pastimes on earth is a wonderful service, performed in the mood known as vatsalya-rasa, or parental affection.

The same fruit that Shatananda, Janaka's family priest, received by arriving in Ayodhya and bathing in the rivers certainly comes to those who hear the accounts given by Goswami Tulsidas in his Janaki Mangala. The mood is especially what made the benediction come to the priest, as he was so happy travelling to Ayodhya to report on the festive occasion. Similarly, if one recites the holy names regularly with love and attention, they will get to be in the association of Rama's closest devotees. Indeed, hearing from Tulsidas is just as good as being with him, and his association is just as good as being in Ayodhya during that sacred time.

VERSE 117

नृप सुनि आगे आइ पूजि सनमानेउ।
दीन्हि लगन कहि कुसल राउ हरषानेउ।।117।।

nṛpa suni āge ā'i pūji sanamāne'u |
dīnhi lagana kahi kusala rā'u haraṣāne'u ||117||

"When the king heard, he came forward and worshiped his guest and welcomed him. Given the letter, the auspicious news was heard and the king became very happy." (117)

Essay - Good Tidings

Parents with children in the military have a unique struggle. As the material body is mortal, death can come at any moment. This is effected by natural forces, among which is disease. The terminal illness can be discovered at any moment, and an accident can end life in an instant. Old age takes longer to develop, so its impact isn't as sudden. As these are the harsh realities of life, if your son or daughter serves in the armed forces, at any time you can get sad news, information that will take your breath away. A king a long time ago faced a similar situation with his beloved eldest son. The news he received one time was so auspicious, however, that he couldn't help but feel elated.

The issue of sudden-death is also faced by the police officer's family. If your father is a cop, you know that he faces danger every day. When you come home from school, there is the chance that he might have been injured during the day. When he goes out at night for a late shift, there is the chance that he might not come back. Surely there is the possibility of the same occurring for any person, but the law enforcement official is in the thick of criminal activity, where guns and nefarious characters who wield them are present. Therefore the risk is increased.

The parents are typically more apprehensive because they are supposed to protect the children throughout their lives. When the child enters into military combat the risk of losing life is the greatest. And since the parents aren't on the field of battle with them, they can only hope to not hear bad news. Anytime someone from the military comes to them, anytime they get news of their deployed son or daughter, they have to hold their breath.

King Dasharatha's son Rama did not volunteer to go into combat, but He was groomed since childhood to defend the innocent. Dasharatha himself was an expert fighter. His name means one who can fight in ten directions with a single chariot. As he graced this earth many thousands of years ago in the Treta Yuga, military combat took place using bows, arrows and swords during his time. You got around on a chariot driven by horses.

A ratha is a chariot, and in military combat it represents a single foe. The more expert fighters could go against multiple rathas at a time. Think of it like the handicap match in professional wrestling, where you have one guy going against two or three other guys. Dasharatha was special because he could fight simultaneously in ten directions: north, south, east, west, the four corners, and up and down. He was also on the side of the good guys. He only fought against wicked characters dedicated to flaunting the code of morality passed down since time immemorial. Because of his good nature and fighting ability, Dasharatha was the ideal man for ruling over the sacred city of Ayodhya.

Though he had four sons, Dasharatha's favorite was Rama. Isn't it just like the hand of Providence to snatch away someone we're so attached to when we least expect it? The sage Vishvamitra one day came to Ayodhya and asked Dasharatha to have Rama accompany him in the forest. The vile night-rangers were harassing the most innocent in society. Fiends who masked their real appearance, cannibals with no scruples, were attacking the peaceful sages during their religious observances. Vishvamitra wanted the best protector, and so he asked for Rama.

The request was a little strange, as Rama was not yet a teenager. Dasharatha was ready to bring his whole army into the forest to give protection, but Vishvamitra insisted on Rama. As a pious soul, Dasharatha always deferred to the counsel of the priestly class. He reluctantly allowed Rama to go. Rama's younger brother Lakshmana went along too. Whenever you get Rama, you get Lakshmana also. Lakshmana is just as capable a fighter, and he never leaves Rama's side.

So we can imagine how Dasharatha must have felt afterwards. He not only lost the personal association of his favorite person in the world, but he had to live knowing that they were in constant danger. Rama and Lakshmana were going to fight these wicked creatures, and the only comforting thought was that Vishvamitra would guide them. All faith was invested in the sage, and without that faith Dasharatha would have nothing to give him comfort.

In the above referenced verse from the Janaki Mangala, Dasharatha is welcoming another priest into his home. This time Shatananda from Janakpur has arrived. He is the family priest of King Janaka. After being worshiped, he gives Dasharatha a scroll, which when read aloud brings the king so much joy. The scroll has news of Rama's upcoming marriage. No news of any harm to the king's eldest son. No news about Rama never returning. No news about any injury to Lakshmana. Rather, Rama has accomplished the amazing feat of lifting an extremely heavy bow in a contest in Janaka's kingdom. No other prince in the world was able to move the bow, and yet Rama lifted it with ease. He won the hand in marriage of the beautiful Sita Devi, Janaka's daughter. Thus Dasharatha was proud of his son and also excited to attend the wedding. He gladly gave his permission as well, which we know from Sita's recounting of her marriage story in the Ramayana.

"Thereupon, after inviting my father-in-law, the elderly King Dasharatha, to Mithila and receiving his approval, my father gave me away to Rama, the knower of the self." (Sita Devi speaking to Anasuya, Valmiki Ramayana, Ayodhya Kand, 118.52)

The pious leader of Ayodhya got news that day that sent the entire city into a joyful frenzy. Many years later, separation from the same Rama would cause him to leave his body. Death is inevitable, however, and one who thinks of Rama at that time has the most auspicious end to life. Rama is the Supreme Lord, non-different from the original. From Dasharatha's character, we see why God chose him as His father during one of His plays on earth.

VERSE 118

सुनि पुर भयउ अनंद बधाव बजावहिं।
सजहिं सुमंगल कलस बितान बनावहिं।।118।।

suni pura bhaya'u ananda badhāva bajāvahiṁ |
sajahiṁ sumaṅgala kalasa bitāna banāvahiṁ ||118||

"When the city heard, they became blissful and started singing congratulatory songs. They decorated auspicious kalashas and constructed pavilions." (118)

Essay - A Temple In Every Home

The purpose of bhakti-yoga, or devotional service, is to change consciousness. Without a notable shift in the way we think, practice of the yoga of divine love will not be any different from any other kind of practice. One person goes to the store, rents a movie, and then comes home and watches it. Another person attends a gathering where the holy names are sounded, discussions are conducted to delve into the meaning of such a practice and the names contained within the chanting, and sanctified food is eaten. If in both instances the consciousness does not change as a result, the practices are nearly identical. The verse quoted above from the Janaki Mangala gives us one way of telling whether or not consciousness has changed for the better.

If you spend time with miserable people on a regular basis, will you not eventually become miserable too? If they take alcohol and drugs all the time, will not you be swayed into their behavior a little bit? Perhaps if you are strong willed you will not imitate their actions, but your consciousness will still be focused on such a lifestyle. It would make sense then that if you wanted to become pure of mind, increasing your knowledge in the process, you would look to change the type of association.

The mind is the measuring stick to see whether the association is having an effect. The association doesn't necessarily have to involve physical presence. Television and radio are examples that show how this works. Just by hearing or watching something, our outlook on life can change. If we constantly hear and see these things, then they will be at the forefront of our thoughts. Our thoughts then drive our activities, which are the final indication of the shift in consciousness.

In bhakti-yoga, one should start thinking of the Divine. Why? Because from that thought process all other unwanted things go away. Anartha is the Sanskrit word for an unwanted element. At its root, it means the negation of artha, which means that which is profitable. Everyone desires profit. This doesn't have to be of the financial variety, wherein you start a business and make money selling a good or service. The worker is as much interested in profit as the owner of the establishment. The profit for the worker comes in the form of a salary. For the farmer it is the yield of the crops. For the loving mother it is the protection of her children. For the husband it is the blissful association of his wife. For the leader of the country it is the satisfaction and wellbeing of his citizens. Since everyone wants profit, everyone inherently tries to avoid anarthas, or things which are not profitable.

An anartha is like having a leak in the roof. If you erect a building to live in, it will have a roof on top. The roof protects you from the scorching rays of the sun in the summer and the chilling snow and rain in the winter. If the roof has a leak in it, its profitability diminishes. Imagine if you did all the hard work to install the roof yourself. The desired profit is a stable and secure home. If the roof is faulty, then your work was not profitable. It ended up being a waste of time.

Similarly, to live a life full of hatred, anger, despair, envy, chaos, tumult, and dread is not profitable for the living spirit, who is full of vitality. We have a life force for a reason, and it is not to eat, drink and be merry. The seemingly magnetic pull of intoxicants shows a desire to escape from the life solely devoted to sense gratification, which provides no lasting happiness whatsoever. Chemicals will not change the situation, though. Only a genuine shift in consciousness, towards an object who is completely pure, will eliminate anarthas and keep one steadily balanced in thought.

We can tell whether practicing bhakti-yoga, as it is passed on since time immemorial by the keepers of the faith who are not envious of the Supreme Lord and who consider Him to be the best well-wishing friend, is having an influence based on our outward behavior. To see how this works, we can look to the example of the residents of Ayodhya. A long time ago, they got the news that their beloved Rama had won a contest of strength in the kingdom of Janakpur. He was set to marry Janaka's daughter Sita.

Rama was the eldest son of King Dasharatha, and so He was to one day take over the throne. By getting married, He would have a beautiful wife to help Him in His religious observances. Ruling over a kingdom is considered a religious duty if one follows protocol. Even farming and doing menial labor are aligned with spiritual life if the consciousness is properly situated. Such was the case in Ayodhya, as the people started singing auspicious songs, filling up kalashas, and erecting pavilions upon hearing the good news.

From this verse from the Janaki Mangala, we can tell that everyone in Ayodhya tasted the fruit of bhakti-yoga practice. They essentially had a temple in every home. If you were a passing stranger, you could knock on any door and meet a person who was God conscious. As a result, any person would be kind, sweet, humble, generous, and extremely knowledgeable. They may not have known the theory of relativity, but they knew that Shri Rama was great and that His happiness equated to their happiness. That was more than enough knowledge for them. They knew that service to Him was the highest occupation for any spirit soul.

Rama is God, an incarnation of the original Personality of Godhead. He is the detail behind the abstract conception. He is ever youthful, extremely beautiful, and full of transcendental features. Thinking of Him is bhakti-yoga. To start thinking of Sita and Rama all the time is the best way to change consciousness. Keeping them in the mind is the effect from chanting the holy names, "Hare Krishna Hare Krishna, Krishna Krishna, Hare Hare, Hare Rama Hare Rama, Rama Rama, Hare Hare," and maintaining good association. It is the fruit of hearing from the Ramayana and other Vedic texts which describe their activities.

In Ayodhya, the people had the best association in Rama's company and the influence of His brothers and parents. Today, we can keep the same association by hearing about Rama's activities. Even hearing of this reaction in the people of Ayodhya is a way of keeping good association. And when that association leads us to start thinking of God all the time, worshiping Him in our home, thereby making it a kind of temple, then we'll taste the fruits of bhakti-yoga practice.

VERSE 119

राउ छाँड़ि सब काज साज सब साजहिं।
चलेउ बरात बनाइ पूजि गनराजहिं।।119।।

rā'u chāṁṛi saba kāja sāja saba sājahiṁ |
cale'u barāta banā'i pūji ganarājahiṁ ||119||

"King Dasharatha left aside all work and began making all the wedding preparations. Making the barata procession, he first worshiped Lord Ganesha."
(119)

Essay - The Best For Your Son

The father tries his best to ensure that his son avoids the same mistakes that he made. The father has more experience than the younger dependent, so he can pass on knowledge that the child can use to steer clear of discomfort, pain, heartache, sadness, and risky situations. This type of transfer of knowledge is known as the descending process, and it is superior to the ascending process, especially with respect to spiritual life.

Can a father pass on spiritual wisdom to his son? Does not the fact that he has a son indicate that he is not fully enlightened in the spiritual sense?

What we generally know as love is referred to as kama in Sanskrit. Kama is actually desire, or, in the perverted sense, lust. Kama is what keeps the population of the earth intact. Without a desire for relations with the opposite sex, life would not continue. Actually, only the visible manifestation of life would cease. The spirit soul is the operating force within each living being, and it does not ever die or take birth. What we refer to as birth and death are merely visible appearances and disappearances, sort of like the sun rising and setting each day. The time interval between those periods for the sun is very small in comparison to the typical lifespan of the individual human being, but the duration has no bearing on the existence. Whether the human being lives for one day or one hundred years, the comparison to the rising and setting of the sun is still appropriate.

"I am the strength of the strong, devoid of passion and desire. I am sex life which is not contrary to religious principles, O Lord of the Bharatas [Arjuna]." (Lord Krishna, Bhagavad-gita, 7.11)

In the Bhagavad-gita, Lord Krishna says that He is the sex life that is not devoid of religious principles. This means that sexual relations for the purpose of raising children who follow dharma, or religiosity, is itself religious. It cannot be classified as kama in the normal sense. Therefore we see that there is most certainly a way to keep the population of creatures visible on the earth while simultaneously staying free of the influence of lust.

A father can thus also be truly enlightened and still have children. Famous Vaishnava saints of recent times included householders, people who were married and had children. While maintaining a family, they still were able to author wonderful books on bhakti-yoga, which is the highest dharma, bhagavata-dharma. They were able to distribute information about bhakti-yoga both locally and to the larger communities around them. They were never accepted to be normal human beings; they were enlightened souls sent to this earth by God Himself to help the people.

Bhaktivinoda Thakura, a householder spiritual masterKing Dasharatha was also a householder saint, though he wasn't necessarily in the religious order. This means that one can be enlightened both as an ascetic and as a father living at home, and also as a priest and as a non-priest. Lord Krishna says in the Bhagavad-gita that the sublime wisdom He passed on to Arjuna was originally passed on in a chain of disciplic succession beginning with saintly kings. They followed the teachings of the Bhagavad-gita, which is considered the essence of Vedic wisdom, and then passed on that tradition to their descendants. Though they were in the royal order, the proper guidelines were put into place by the brahmanas, or priests, who advised them. Thus the kings listened to, understood, and protected Vedic wisdom.

"This supreme science was thus received through the chain of disciplic succession, and the saintly kings understood it in that way. But in course of time the succession was broken, and therefore the science as it is appears to be lost." (Lord Krishna, Bg. 4.2)

King Dasharatha was in the line of kings coming from Ikshvaku, who heard the Bhagavad-gita from his father Manu, who heard it from his father Vivasvan, who heard it from Krishna. Thus Dasharatha was no ordinary soul, and neither was he an ordinary father. He wanted the best for his eldest son Rama, who came to him in an unusual way. As a pious king, Dasharatha was not swayed by kama, so even if his sons did come to him through the conventional method, that wouldn't disqualify him from being considered enlightened. Rama and His three younger brothers appeared in Dasharatha's family as a result of a sacrifice. The three queens ate the remnants of a particular sacrifice, and from that food they got pregnant.

Rama is the same Krishna, but in an incarnation form. He is the Supreme Lord for all of mankind. He is not a sectarian figure reserved for the Hindus. Dasharatha, nevertheless, wasn't aware of Rama's real identity, which was fine because it allowed him to act with parental affection, which is a mood of devotional service. Dasharatha wanted the best for Rama, and so he always took good care of Him. In the above referenced verse from the Janaki Mangala, he is preparing for a wedding. He has heard the news that Rama will marry Sita, the daughter of King Janaka. Upon hearing that news, Dasharatha dropped everything and focused only on his beloved eldest son's upcoming marriage.

Here it is said that he set up the barata procession. This is the portion of the marriage ceremony where the groom's family travels together to the bride's home, which is where the wedding will take place. There is great pomp; sort of like a large procession with a marching band. The notable participants ride on elephants, and everyone is in a festive mood. Prior to arranging this, Dasharatha worshiped Lord Ganesha, who is a famous divine figure of the Vedic tradition. He removes obstacles from the path of his devotees. In this case Dasharatha prayed to have Rama's marriage go smoothly. The king just wanted the best for his son.

The Ramayana and other derivative works give many such examples of worship of divine figures for the benefit of the Supreme Lord. We tend to ask God for things for ourselves or for other people. "O Lord, please take care of my children. My friend is really sick, please see him through this. I'm in danger right now, please save me." This attitude is very nice, and certainly prayers to the original Personality of Godhead never fall on deaf ears. But as the material nature is temporary in its position, nothing will last forever. And neither is any condition universally auspicious. Therefore sometimes we don't get what we want after praying. Karma, or fruitive activity, has its own results to provide. Also, the temporary wellbeing of me or my family doesn't solve all the problems of life.

The ultimate aim is bhagavata-dharma, devotional service. When following that dharma, the mood is so pure that you actually pray for God's welfare. You approach powerful personalities and ask them to be favorable to the Supreme Lord. While this seems illogical, the sentiment is so much appreciated by the Supreme Lord that He never allows such a sincere soul to fall out of His favor. Dasharatha is always with Rama in mind, and this is due to Rama's grace, who is the king's favorite son.

VERSE 120

बाजहिं ढोल निसान सगुन सुभ पाइन्हि।
सिय नैहर जनकौर नगर नियराइन्हि।।१२०।।

bājahiṁ ḍhola nisāna saguna subha pā'inhi |
siya naihara janakaura nagara niyarā'inhi ||120||

"Playing the drums and sounding the auspiciousness and goodness of the occasion, they were getting close to Sita's native city of Janakpur." (120)

Essay - That Sound Around the Corner

When you're eagerly anticipating the arrival of someone else, you can't help but look out the window or wait by the phone. Any indication of their approach will make you even more excited than you already are. In Janakpur a long time ago, the indication of the arrival of anticipated guests was the beautiful sound of drums, which also sounded to mark the auspiciousness of the occasion. And auspicious it would be, as news of Sita and Rama's marriage would quickly spread throughout the world.

"I have heard, O Sita, that your hand in marriage was won by the renowned Raghava on the occasion of the self-choice ceremony [svayamvara]. O Maithili, I wish to hear that story in detail. Therefore please narrate to me the entire sequence of events as you experienced them." (Anasuya speaking to Sita Devi, Valmiki Ramayana, Ayodhya Kand, 118.24-25)

Anasuya, whose name means one who is not envious, many years later asked Sita, the bride, to describe the details of her marriage. Anasuya already knew these details, but since the event was so glorious, more auspicious than any other occasion, she wanted to hear the story again, this time from Sita, who was a key participant. Anasuya lived during a time where there was no radio or television. Newspapers did not exist, and there was no easy way to broadcast messages to a large population dispersed thousands of miles apart. She lived in a hermitage with her husband, Atri Rishi, and they one day had the good fortune of meeting Sita and Rama.

She knew of the story prior because news of God always manages to spread. That is because it is the most auspicious news, information that never becomes old or stale. Today's newspaper is discarded once tomorrow's is released. If the newspaper had valuable information, it wouldn't be tossed aside so quickly. Even the clothes we wear have a longer shelf-life. Yet the newspaper's temporary value is what makes it intriguing in the first place. Real news that will have a meaningful impact isn't so sought after. It is not until one has exhausted all of their material desires that they truly take an interest in that which goes beyond birth and death.

"Persons who have acted piously in previous lives and in this life, whose sinful actions are completely eradicated and who are freed from the duality of delusion, engage themselves in My service with determination." (Lord Krishna, Bhagavad-gita, 7.28)

Imagine then how qualified one must be to actually participate in the events that generate the headlines that remain relevant millions of years into the future. The people of Janakpur were all pious souls during this particular time period. They relished Sita's wedding. She was the daughter of the king, Janaka, and the king was loved and respected by all, as was Sita. She was marrying the right man; someone who had no blemishes. If there were any negative aspects to Rama's image, it was in the worry His seemingly contradictory features caused. How can a flower penetrate through steel? How can a youthful body with delicate features display immense strength? This caused worry in the citizens because they wanted Rama to win the contest that would determine Sita's husband. That worry quickly turned to felicity when Rama effortlessly lifted the bow. This was the mark of strength required to win the contest drawn up by Janaka.

In the above referenced verse from the Janaki Mangala, the bridegroom's party is approaching Janaka's city, where the wedding will be held. Rama's family was from Ayodhya, and when the people there heard what had happened, they were thrilled as well. King Dasharatha, Rama's father, stopped everything to give full attention to the wedding. The parties arrived in typical fashion, with elephants and loud drums letting everyone know of their arrival.

If you're stuck at home without any car to take to go to the place you need to go, you will anticipate the time that the car returns. Perhaps a family member has taken it without your permission. Perhaps they told you they would return at a certain point in time and they then were running late. Instead of just waiting patiently, you'll likely peep out the window, trying to edge your face against the glass so that you can see as far down the street as possible. This way you'll know right away when they are about to come home. Every car you see gives you hope, but not until it is the car you're looking for do you feel happy.

The people in Janakpur were just as anxious, except they were waiting for Shri Rama's family. In this way they had an eagerness to see God and share in His triumphs. Such desires never go unmet. Holding the same desires today will get you association with the same event. Physical separation is of no issue and neither is the long gap in time. Shri Rama, as the Supreme Lord, is timeless, and so are His events. His name, form, qualities and pastimes also extend to all of humanity, to every single person, irrespective of their religious tradition inherited at the time of birth. Men, women, children, priests, servants, and royalty alike heard the sound around the corner of Rama's family arriving, and with that sound their excitement grew even further.

Similar sounds are generated today by those who are devoted to the same Rama. He is also known as Krishna in His original form, and Sita is addressed as Hare, for she represents the Supreme Lord's energy. Devotees play mrdangas and kartalas, and chant the holy names, "Hare Krishna Hare Krishna, Krishna Krishna, Hare Hare, Hare Rama Hare Rama, Rama Rama, Hare Hare," to give everyone the good news that the Supreme Lord has arrived on the scene. Though He is all-pervading, we can't recognize His presence unless our consciousness is pure. Hearing of Him is the most effective way to clear consciousness of all dirty things. Hearing of Him is also a way to directly connect with Him. Thus one who hears these sounds, which are non-different from the Lord, knows that auspiciousness is right around the corner, like it was in Janakpur a long time ago.

CHAND 15

नियरानि नगर बरात हरषी लेन अगवानी गए।
देखत परस्पर मिलत मानत प्रेम परिपूरन भए॥
आनंदपुर कौतुक कोलाहल बनत सो बरनत कहाँ।
लै दियो तहँ जनवास सकल सुपास नित नूतन जहाँ॥15॥

niyarāni nagara barāta haraṣī lena agavānī ga'e |
dekhata paraspara milata mānata prema paripūrana bha'e ||

ānandapura kautuka kolāhala banata so baranata kahaṁ |
lai diyo tahaṁ janavāsa sakala supāsa nita nūtana jahaṁ ||15||

"As the barata procession approached the city, the people happily came to welcome them. Looking at each other and meeting, it was like love became complete." (Chand 15.1)

"The spectacle and the noise in that city of bliss were so great that it is difficult to explain. The barata party was taken to their living quarters, where they received everything you could want, new and arriving constantly." (Chand, 15.2)

Essay - The In-Laws

Few situations in life are more awkward than the initial meeting with the in-laws. They are your new family. Though you may know your future spouse, you likely don't know their family as well. No matter what you do, no matter how you act, they will always love your spouse more than they will love you. They are not guaranteed to like you, either, as they are naturally protective of their family member about to get married. In Janakpur a long time ago, strangely there were no awkward motions or inhibitions when the in-laws met each other prior to the wedding. This was due entirely to the nature of the participants.

In a traditional marriage, undoubtedly the bride-to-be has a tougher task ahead of her as it relates to the relationship with the in-laws. The groom may get a hard time from the bride's father, but her father isn't expected to live with them. The term "being given away" is not merely symbolic. The husband takes charge of protecting the woman once she gets married. She leaves the family of her father.

The wife, on the other hand, must coexist with her husband's family. Tensions can especially rise with the mother-in-law. For the mother, her whole life her job has been to care for her son. Now a new person is expected to take over that role. The bride wants to make sure she does a good job, but at the same time she doesn't want to diminish the importance of the mother-in-law. As a mother's love for her son is very strong, any apparent deficiency in the bride's duty to her husband becomes prone to correction. And in adulthood who likes to be corrected by anyone else, let alone your husband's mother?

Sita and Rama had the ideal marriage in so many ways. She was going to enter a family that had three mothers for the one groom. There was only one biological mother, but kings during those times often had more than one wife. This was not a problem since the wives were protected. They were happy living with the king, so who was to say that it wasn't pious? Indeed, to protect a woman in marriage is a highly chivalrous act on the part of a ruler.

The groom's party, for their part, didn't know the bride's side very well. They hadn't specifically arranged the marriage. To the eyes of the world, Sita and Rama were joined by chance. Sita was so beautiful and precious that her father decided that she couldn't be wed in the ordinary way. A contest of strength would determine her future husband. Rama, the eldest son of King Dasharatha of Ayodhya, happened to be at the contest. At the insistence of the sage Vishvamitra, He tried His hand at lifting the bow in the arena. And wouldn't you know it, He won.

In the above referenced verse from the Janaki Mangala, the barat procession that came from Ayodhya is approaching the city of Janakpur. The barat procession is the marching of the bridegroom's party towards the site of the wedding, which is typically the bride's home. Here we see that the bride's party welcomed them with great enthusiasm. It wasn't a formal gesture, either. The two parties were so genuinely happy to see each other that it was like love became complete.

Indeed, Rama is the Supreme Lord and Sita His eternal consort. They appear in the earthly realm every now and then to enact pastimes. I may not always live with my brothers, but wherever we are, we always stay brothers. In the same way, Sita and Rama may not always be together physically, but they are still eternally linked. When they meet, others feel so much happiness. They are overjoyed because they are devoted to the divine couple. They know how much Sita loves Rama and how much Rama loves Sita. They know how pious King Janaka is and how courageous King Dasharatha is.

Dasharatha's name means one who can fight ten chariots coming from the ten different directions [north, south, east, west, the four corners, up and down]. Dasharatha is a protector of dharma, or virtue. Similarly, Janaka is famous for being self-realized. He carries out his work, but he is not attached to the results. This is how we should act, because we don't have control over the outcomes to action. Two people may both be morally situated, but they will not always find equal circumstances. Two people may work hard at running their businesses, but both of them are not guaranteed to be successful. Better to carry out your prescribed duties with a cool head. No one was cooler than Janaka, and so it was fitting that his family would be joined with Dasharatha's.

The same joyful greeting is given by devotees who worship Sita and Rama in the temple. The same greeting is given daily by Shri Hanuman, who chants their names nonstop. The same joyful greeting is given by the devotees to other devotees, for they carry the message of Godhead with them. Goswami Tulsidas here beautifully depicts a wonderful scene, where love comes to life through the meeting of the energetic Supreme Lord and His energy.

Essay - First Class Accommodations

It is standard etiquette to treat your guests with the utmost hospitality. In Vedic culture, the hospitality is to be extended to even your worst enemy. You should think that your home is the home for the guests as well. This way you don't get puffed up with all the stuff that you have. You don't think that you are better than anyone else because your house may have more square feet than another's. In this instance, the hospitality related to a marriage, and the groom's party felt so welcome that it was like they were staying at a first class hotel.

"Is their house bigger than ours? What about their sound system? I bet we can crank ours up even louder. How many bedrooms do they have? Do they have central air conditioning? I still think our house is bigger. We did good in buying this place. I am very satisfied with all that we have."

This competitive attitude is beneficial if it leads to the offering of good hospitality. This hospitality is the primary purpose to the home. This is the injunction of the Vedas, the scriptural tradition that is the basis for the modern-day religion known as Hinduism. The Vedas present eternal truths, which are like scientific principles. They apply to all people and to all time periods. Human tendencies do not change with time. There may be a higher occurrence of sinful activity in a given age, but the tendencies with respect to likes and dislikes, attachments and aversions, do not vary. This is because the scientific makeup of the core feature in an animate creature is always the same. That core feature can never be cut up, made wet, created, destroyed, or altered in any way.

"The soul can never be cut into pieces by any weapon, nor can he be burned by fire, nor moistened by water, nor withered by the wind." (Lord Krishna, Bhagavad-gita, 2.23)

A key Vedic principle for the householder is the offering of hospitality. Householder life is unique from the other three spiritual institutions, or ashramas. A householder is allowed sex life, and they also have a significant possession called the home. Even with this possession there is the call to offer hospitality, to give in charity, and to generally serve others. This is not a once a year occurrence, like say volunteering at a soup kitchen on Thanksgiving. Think of how good the volunteers feel on such a day. Now imagine feeling that same goodness all the time. If you feel such a way for a long enough stretch, you eventually purify your existence.

If you have a large home, that means you have the opportunity to serve more guests. Whatever they want is what should be provided. Even if you don't like a particular food dish, if your guest does then it should be served. This only makes sense if you think about it. If you were a guest at someone else's home, would you want to be served things that you don't like? "Oh, but this is healthy for you. My husband and I are on a diet, so this is all that we are eating right now. Don't worry, it doesn't taste that bad." This wouldn't sit very well with us.

In the above referenced verse from the Janaki Mangala, a scene is described where a party arriving to a wedding is shown to their living quarters. This is sort of like a staging area, a place to stay before the actual wedding takes place. We see that the meeting of the two parties, the bride's and the groom's, was a wonderful spectacle with great noise and jubilation. The city became one of ananda, or bliss, and so the whole experience was difficult to describe.

"That country is looking so beautiful, and the Vedas have described its purity. Known in the three worlds, Tirahuta [Janakpur] is the tilaka of the earth." (Janaki Mangala, 4)

In the living quarters, the bridegroom's party received everything they could want. Every day they got new clothes and other such items. This wasn't required, but King Janaka, the host, did not want to hold back. He was the leader of a sacred land called Tirahuta, which is famous in the three worlds. Therefore he had a lot to offer, and he wasn't going to be miserly in the least. The wealth of the recipients wasn't taken into account, either. The arriving party was from Ayodhya, and it was the family of the king, Maharaja Dasharatha. Therefore they had immense wealth to offer themselves. Yet protocol dictated that Janaka provide everything to his guests.

The incident is noteworthy because it relates to the divine couple, Sita and Rama. Janaka is the chosen father of Sita and Dasharatha of Rama. Sita appeared from underneath the ground. Janaka found her while ploughing a field one day for a sacrifice. Rama appeared in the womb of Queen Kausalya after she ate the remnants of sacrifice. Thus in both cases the births were not in the conventional way. Sita and Rama appeared; they did not take birth. They can do that because they are God and His eternal consort.

God is one, though He can take many forms. In the Bhagavad-gita, He says He appears in every millennium to annihilate the miscreants and protect the pious. The pious filled the streets and the apartments in Janakpur when Dasharatha's family met Janaka's at the wedding of all weddings. That same hospitality can be offered by anyone today by making God the preferred guest in the home. Deity worship is a central practice of Vedic culture for this very reason. Rather than rely on a weekly trip to a house of worship, where you might only pray for material things, one can worship every single day by presenting the best offerings. You do this by having a statue or picture representation of God that you keep in a special place in the home. Through authorized methods of worship, such as the offering of flowers, the chanting of mantras, and the preparation of pure food, you show hospitality to the invited guest, the Supreme Lord.

Just like Dasharatha's family, Rama doesn't need such hospitality offered by us, but He accepts it anyway. Through such practice, we purify ourselves, becoming filled with goodness in the process. And purification of our existence is the real purpose to action. In the purest state, there are no miseries like birth, old age, disease and death. There is only constant celebration, like what was seen at Sita and Rama's wedding.

VERSE 121

गे जनवासहिं कौसिक राम लखन लिए।
हरषे निरखि बरात प्रेम प्रमुदित हिए॥121॥

ge janavāsahiṁ kausika rāma lakhana li'e |
haraṣe nirakhi barāta prema pramudita hi'e ||121||

"Then Vishvamitra went to the guest area, taking Rama and Lakshmana. The barata party became extremely joyful looking at them, with love filling their hearts." (121)

Essay - Meeting the Ultimate Objective

Harsha is a word used often in Vedic literature. The Janaki Mangala is rightly classified as Vedic literature because it describes the pastimes of the Supreme Personality of Godhead, especially focusing on His marriage to the daughter of King Janaka during an ancient time period. Harsha is the happiness specific to obtaining the ultimate objective. It is a joy like no other, and not surprisingly it is properly used here by Goswami Tulsidas to describe the happiness of the people from Ayodhya.

"Harsha is described in the Bhakti-rasamrita-sindhu. Harsha is experienced when one finally attains the desired goal of life and consequently becomes very glad. When harsha is present, the body shivers, and one's bodily hairs stand on end. There are perspiration, tears and an outburst of passion and madness." (Shrila Prabhupada, Chaitanya Charitamrita, Madhya 3.127 Purport)

The exact events of the Ramayana aren't always the same. The universe goes through cycles of creation and destruction. Just like you may go to the office for five days out of each week and not every day will feature the same events, the creation sees the appearance and disappearance of the Supreme Lord in various ages. Mostly the events are carried out in the same fashion, but sometimes there are slight differences. Sometimes more details are given in certain written versions as well. The accounts available to us today are not limited to the present age. We get descriptions from past and future ages as well. There are innumerable universes, and everywhere some pastime of Rama's is going on. Somewhere right now He is appearing on earth in His original form of Krishna. Somewhere right now He is lifting the mighty Govardhana Hill to save the residents of Vrindavana from the wrath of the king of heaven. And somewhere right now He is entering the guest tent set up by King Janaka for the marriage of his daughter.

With respect to the timeline of the current creation, the original telling of Rama's pastimes is found in the Ramayana, a Sanskrit poem authored by Maharishi Valmiki. In that work it is said that Rama didn't marry Sita, Janaka's daughter, right away because He didn't know the opinion of His father, King Dasharatha of Ayodhya. Rama won the bow contest, lifting the bow before any other prince could. Many of them tried, but they all failed. This was a big achievement, and Sita was certainly beautiful in all respects. And yet Rama still didn't make the decision for marriage on His own. He is God, so He doesn't need anyone's permission to do anything. But as Rama He especially pays attention to social etiquette, setting a good example for others to follow.

"Though being offered to Rama, I was not accepted by Him at the time, for He did not know the opinion of His father Dasharatha, the King of Ayodhya." (Sita Devi speaking to Anasuya, Valmiki Ramayana, Ayodhya Kand, 118.51)

In other areas of Vedic literature, more details of the event are given. It is described that Janaka's priest goes to Ayodhya to notify King Dasharatha of Rama's accomplishment. This is what is told here by Goswami Tulsidas. After Dasharatha gave his consent, the barat party, the group from the groom's side, arrived in Janakpur and were greeted with the utmost hospitality by the bride's side. They were shown to tents that were guest houses and then given every amenity imaginable.

And yet their harsha didn't come until they saw Rama and His younger brother Lakshmana with the guru Vishvamitra. They experienced the joy that comes with attaining the ultimate objective because for every person in this world the highest goal is to have love for God. And when you love someone, do you not long to see them? This longing was there in the barat party, and so they were overjoyed to get the vision of Rama again. He had left for the forest with Lakshmana to protect the forest-dwelling Vishvamitra from the attacks of vile creatures. The residents of Ayodhya understood that the mission was a success when they heard of Rama's victory in the assembly, and now they got to see Him again.

Rama looks more beautiful when He is with Lakshmana. This is because there has never been a better younger brother in the world. Lakshmana loves Rama so much that the Lord cannot do anything to control it. Rama cannot tell Lakshmana to stay home. This will not work. We initially view God with awe and reverence, and so in that mood of devotion we likely will do whatever He tells us. Lakshmana's love is pure, so he thinks he knows how to please Rama better than Rama does. The same attitude exists in Sita, who thus made a perfect match for Rama.

The vision was again more beautiful since it included the spiritual guide Vishvamitra. The two brothers faithfully followed him. He was the one who first led them to the assembly in Janaka's kingdom. Thus he played an important role in this great day becoming a reality. The people of Ayodhya were so happy that Rama was going to get the perfect queen. The couple would protect them in the future, and so the people were so happy for their good fortune.

From harsha comes love. You cannot be this happy if you don't love the party that causes your happiness. And upon attaining your objective, if you are directly connected with that person, their innocent vision will fill your heart with more love. The barat party travelled all the way to Janakpur, happily singing the entire time. Now they saw Rama and Lakshmana and their love for them increased all the more. Thus in devotional service the reservoir of emotion can never be filled. Its depths are fathomless, as are the glories of Sita and Rama.

VERSE 122

हृदयँ लाइ लिए गोद मोद अति भूपहि।
कहि न सकहिं सत सेष अनंद अनूपहि॥122॥

hṛdayaṁ lā'i li'e goda moda ati bhūpahi |
kahi na sakahiṁ sata seṣa ananda anūpahi ||122||

"Taking them in his lap, the king was very happy in the heart. His incomparable bliss cannot be explained even by Ananta Shesha Naga." (122)

Essay - Hundreds of Ways

The famous brothers Sanatana and Rupa Gosvami had a younger brother named Anupama. He was a devotee of God as Lord Ramachandra, therefore he felt that he couldn't properly worship Shri Krishna along with Radha, who were the worshipable figures of choice for his elder brothers and their spiritual master, Lord Chaitanya. He was still very blessed and considered Mahaprabhu to be none other than Krishna Himself, who is God. The Lord is ananta-rupam, or with unlimited forms. This doesn't mean that everything and everyone is God Himself, but there are still many non-different forms that are worshipable. In this instance the worship is directly engaged in by King Dasharatha, and the bliss he felt in that worship was incomparable.

Anupama means incomparable, so here it is applied to the brother Anupama's worshipable object of choice, Shri Rama. The scene in question is a marriage ceremony from an ancient time. Though this marriage took place many thousands of years ago, there was nothing lacking. Accustomed to our present surroundings, we think that we need electricity, large screens, limousines, speakers, and a grand banquet hall in order to have a fancy wedding, but actually through nature's arrangement all necessary opulence is supplied. What you really need to make a good wedding is love. And love in its purest form exists only with God. When it's His wedding, there is ample love to go around. In any time period, that wedding is enjoyed, even by those who only hear about it.

King Dasharatha was the father of the groom. His son Rama was going to marry Sita, King Janaka's daughter. The bridegroom's party arrived from Ayodhya and everyone in both families was thrilled beyond belief. In this scene Dasharatha is taking Rama and His younger brother Lakshmana on his lap to show them affection. He was a good father who was so happy to see his sons after a long time spent apart from them.

Family ancestry, physical proximity, and country of origin are of no concern in ordinary love. Love as we know it crosses all boundaries. Why, then, shouldn't it be the same with God? Why can't you love someone immediately upon seeing them, especially when they are full of all good qualities? Dasharatha was so happy when he saw the two brothers, and his heart became filled with bliss. That bliss could not be described even by Ananta Shesha Naga.

Think of the breaking news story. Perhaps a new spiritual leader has been announced. You tune to one television network to see what's going on. They have their reporters on the scene giving you the play by play. Then they have the analysts discussing what just happened. After that, they more or less speculate. The news filters out slowly, so to fill the time the on-air talent has to talk. If you don't have many facts to go off of, the only way to keep the conversation going is to speculate about this or that.

Now imagine if all the other television networks were covering the same story. You could flip from channel to channel and hear from their reporters. The media is typically centrally located. The newsmakers give their information in press releases and press conferences. This way there usually isn't just one media source that gets an exclusive. Each bureau hears the same things and then reports on it in different ways. After surfing a few channels, you notice that there isn't much new to report. Eventually, the coverage starts to get boring, and you are left to wait for the next big story.

With the Supreme Lord and His devotees, all things are so significant that a thousand networks wouldn't suffice for proper coverage. And this can be said of describing just the joyous emotions. This isn't necessarily to report on a specific action or event. Here Dasharatha hugged Rama and Lakshmana. How many ways are you going to describe that? Ah, but if you want to talk about Dasharatha's emotion, his unrivalled happiness, you couldn't properly explain that even if you had a thousand mouths all talking at once.

That is the opinion given here by Goswami Tulsidas. Ananta Shesha Naga, or Anantadeva, is a divine serpent who has a seemingly endless number of hoods. He constantly engages in glorifying God, and in that glorification he never reaches an end. He is also at this scene, having incarnated on earth as Lakshmana. Lakshmana is always with Rama, so he has the best information to use in glorification. Through his example he shows what the best implementation of bhakti-yoga, or devotional service, looks like. That occupation is the original one, which has a corresponding original consciousness. And in that consciousness there is no end to the glorification of God, which brings incomparable bliss.

Dasharatha felt so happy to be with the beautiful, chivalrous, courageous, strong, and pious two brothers from Ayodhya and to have them with him again. His happiness makes the devotees happy, since they know from his example that no other reward can compare to the association of the Supreme Personality of Godhead. And that reward brings the great gift of endless glorification, which ensures that there will never be a poverty of available activity for the devoted soul.

VERSE 123

रायँ कौसिकहि पूजि दान बिप्रन्ह दिए।
राम सुमंगल हेतु सकल मंगल किए।।123।।

rāyaṁ kausikahi pūji dāna bipranha di'e |
rāma sumaṅgala hetu sakala maṅgala ki'e ||123||

"King Dasharatha worshiped Vishvamitra and gave charity to the brahmanas. For the sake of Rama's great auspiciousness, he performed all the auspicious rites."
(123)

Essay - Bless You My Son

"O my child, you are so precious. You look so innocent today. How will you remain safe? You can barely keep together just laying down. Someone has to hold your head when they pick you up. They have to feed you when you get hungry and clean you when the time is right. Still, I have never been happier than today. I will love you with all my heart. You are my life now. I vow to protect you until my dying day. I will do whatever it takes to make your life successful."

There's no doubt that becoming a father changes a person. The miracle of birth brings newfound feelings of protection and caretaking. In the case of a famous king a long time ago, the fruit of his eyes was received with his new son. This son would one day take over the throne. It was the son who almost never arrived, as the king had been childless for so long. As soon as the child emerged from the womb of the eldest queen, the king vowed to protect Him for the rest of His life. And he most certainly did, though the child required not this protection. The king kept his son on his mind until his very dying day, bringing the most auspicious end to life.

"But I've heard from the Vedas that having attachments is bad. This information is found in the Bhagavad-gita, which is the scripture most often used for lecturing by swamis and panditas. You're not supposed to be attached. You're supposed to carry out your work as a matter of fact, out of obligation. Whatever the results may be, you should not mind them. This way your consciousness will be clear. If this king was so attached to his son, isn't that a bad thing?"

"Be steadfast in yoga, O Arjuna. Perform your duty and abandon all attachment to success or failure. Such evenness of mind is called yoga." (Lord Krishna, Bhagavad-gita, 2.48)

Attachment and aversion will always be there. Let's say that I read the verses from the Bhagavad-gita, a Vedic song originally put into written word some five thousand years ago but whose truths are eternally relevant, that describe the need to stay detached from outcomes and I take them to heart. "Okay, from now on I will not sweat the small stuff so much. From this Gita I understand that the body identifies neither me nor anyone else. The soul inside is our essence. Just as the central processing unit is what gives life to the computer, without the soul no being can be considered alive. I will not be so concerned with birth and death, because such things are only temporary, like the rising and setting of the sun. I will follow my work without attachment. I will stay level-headed. The speaker of the Gita, Shri Krishna, says that one who follows this path is very dear to Him. As He is the origin of matter and spirit, the Supreme Personality of Godhead, being dear to Him should be to my benefit."

"One who neither grasps pleasure or grief, who neither laments nor desires, and who renounces both auspicious and inauspicious things, is very dear to Me." (Lord Krishna, Bg. 12.17)

Ah, but even in this situation there is an attachment. Namely, it is to the principle of staying detached. Seems like circular logic, but it is nevertheless true. If I constantly tell myself to stay detached, and then I get upset when I become attached to something, that strict adherence to the principle is itself an attachment. So in this sense there is always some attachment and aversion. The principles put forth in the Bhagavad-gita apply specifically to karma, or work that has a material effect. Material means the body and not the soul. Thus to have attachment to work that benefits the soul does not violate the principles of the Gita.

"Okay, but this king was attached to his son. The son is just a bodily relation. The soul can appear in any family. There is nothing really special then about this relation or that. Why was the king taken in by maya, then, which is the illusory energy that covers the spiritual presence in the eyes of the conditioned souls?"

This king's son was the very same Krishna. That is why His appearance in the king's family was the happiest day in the life of the king. And that is why thinking of this son was the best ending to the king's life. The king was named Dasharatha and his eldest son Rama. Rama is a name for God and also a way to reference the personality who appeared as King Dasharatha's eldest son. Rama is a genuine incarnation of God, not one created on a whim. He was not assigned deity status after His time on earth. He was God before, during and after the events of the famous Ramayana.

In the above referenced verse from the Janaki Mangala, we get further details on the nature of Dasharatha and his affection for Rama. The scene here is Rama's marriage to the eldest daughter of King Janaka. Dasharatha pays obeisance to the spiritual guide Vishvamitra. The king was very powerful. His name means one who can fight ten chariots simultaneously. The chariots come from the ten different directions, and he can battle them all. Thus he was a superior fighter, and therefore perfectly eligible to rule over the wonderful kingdom in Ayodhya.

And yet Dasharatha still bowed down and worshiped someone who had nothing. Vishvamitra was not a fighter. He called the remote wilderness his home. Still, the sage's strength was so great because of his devotion to God. He was a brahmana, or priest, and so he could guide everyone in society. The king protected and the priest guided. Vishvamitra also had a major hand in making this marriage a reality. He had previously taken Rama and His younger brother Lakshmana with him to the forest. He wanted the boys to protect all the sages from the attacks of wicked night-rangers. The brothers were mere teenagers at the time, and yet Vishvamitra knew that no one could defeat them in battle. They made the sages proud as well as the father Dasharatha. It was no surprise that a king who could fight ten chariots would have sons who could fight ghoulish creatures who could change their shapes at will.

Dasharatha also gave in charity to the brahmanas who were there. Under ideal circumstances, the priests don't work for a living. They don't need much to survive, and whatever they need is provided by society. Giving charity to brahmanas by quality and occupation is the only legitimate form of charity. It yields the best results in the future. Dasharatha did all the auspicious rites, all for the sake of Rama's auspiciousness. He wanted everything to go right for his son. If he had to, the king would give up his own life for Rama's welfare.

That same dedication would be there in his son, who would renounce the throne and live in the wilderness for fourteen years just to save the honor of His father. Thus there was mutual adoration. The level of affection between father and son could not be measured. From this we understand that Rama was a fit son for Dasharatha and Dasharatha the most worthy father. Here he protected Rama by performing the auspicious rites.

Dasharatha was a famous king with access to great wealth to give in charity, but any person can perform similar rites to effect the same purpose. Rama is God, so He doesn't require protection, but if one tries to offer it anyway, who is He to reject it? In fact, such an offering will make Him so pleased that He will guarantee that person's protection in the future. He does this by staying within their mind, which is the best way to live. The most auspicious rite for the present age is the chanting of the holy names, "Hare Krishna Hare Krishna, Krishna Krishna, Hare Hare, Hare Rama Hare Rama, Rama Rama, Hare Hare," which brings supreme auspiciousness to both Rama and all those associated with Him.

VERSE 124

ब्याह बिभूषन भूषित भूषन भूषन।
बिस्व बिलोचन बनज बिकासक पूषन।।124।।

byāha bibhūṣana bhūṣita bhūṣana bhūṣana |
bisva bilocana banaja bikāsaka pūṣana ||124||

"He put the wedding ornaments on Rama, who is the ornament of ornaments. The lotus that was the eyes of the world bloomed at the sight of Him, who is the sun." (124)

Essay - The Ornament of Ornaments

"Everyone else in this room worships Him. They bow down as soon as the curtains open. They repeat these Sanskrit verses while their heads are on the ground, and they then rise and sing in ecstasy. They tell me that this chanting is the best way for self-realization in the modern age. They hail the glories of their spiritual master, speaking endlessly about the need to preach and how so many others need to be saved from the pitfalls of material life. Despite their sincerity, for some reason I just don't want to go along. I don't want to be like a sheep. I'm an individual, why should I follow everyone else?"

This attitude is only natural, as when we see so many others doing a particular thing, there is one of two reactions. One is to follow the pack. Join in with everyone else. In the path of least resistance, you're not making any waves; you're going with the flow. The other option is rebellion. Do something different just because. You're an individual, so you think for yourself. You don't have to follow what everyone else says. You make up your own mind. From the above referenced verse from the Janaki Mangala, we see that real devotion to God is constitutionally sound. It is part of us. Whether we are the only ones following that devotion or part of a group that includes the entire world, the reaction is still instinctual. The object of devotion is so important to us that what others do is of no concern.

How does the verse above convey this message? It is done through the analogy to the lotus flower. The lotus flower is the symbol of beauty. It comes from nature. The most brilliant artist in the world could not conjure it up on their own. Indeed, in painting beautiful pictures, one can include one or many such flowers to enhance the image; the lotus is that beautiful.

Though its beauty is naturally occurring, there are different looks to the flower. Just as we may not appear our best in the morning right after waking up, the lotus flower isn't as wonderful to look at when it is closed up. You don't need to pry the petals open, though. You don't need to chant a sacred formula to get it to open its eyes. This occurs naturally as soon as the sun comes out. Then the flower looks even more wonderful. It is like when we fully cleanse ourselves and then put on ornaments. This process is mechanical, while the transformation for the lotus flower is automatic. It is spontaneous and also without flaws. A machine may turn on properly for one hundred consecutive days and then suddenly fail, but the lotus flower will always sprout open when it sees the sun.

The flower doesn't look at other flowers to see if they are opening up too. Its relationship to the sun is not changed by the relationship other flowers have to the same sun. The love is pure. Without the sun, the flower will not open up. It will not reveal all its glory; it waits until the sun shines its light. If the entire garden is full of lotus flowers, each flower will still hold dear its relationship to the sun.

The same holds true for all of us in our constitutional relationship to the Supreme Lord. In the scene of the verse quoted above, Shri Ramachandra, God in His avatara as a beautiful warrior prince, is being seen after His father has placed wonderful wedding ornaments on Him. Lord Rama is about to get married to the princess of Videha, Sita Devi. King Dasharatha of Ayodhya has arrived to witness the marriage ceremony of his son. The good king is also a vital participant, making sure everything from the groom's side is done properly.

Shri Rama is described to be the ornament of ornaments. He is Himself an object of beautification. Put Him in your mind and your mind will always be pure. Put His presence in your food and you will never eat sin. Put the sound of His holy names on your tongue and what you say will always be pure as well. And that supremely pure object was being decorated by His loving father. Power, beauty and fame can quickly go to our head, causing us to be puffed up with pride. From the Supreme Lord's example, we see that loving service from others should be allowed in any situation. No one is too big to be loved by their parents.

The eyes of the world opened up at the sight of Rama. He is compared to the sun. His family ancestry also traced to the sun-god, Vivasvan. Here the eyes of the world are like a lotus flower. They didn't care what others were thinking. They didn't care if everyone else was taken by Rama as well. Each individual was supremely delighted to see Rama dressed up in such a way. They were so happy to see Him about to marry the daughter of the pious King Janaka.

VERSE 125

मध्य बरात बिराजत अति अनुकूलेउ।
मनहुँ काम आराम कलपतरु फूलेउ॥125॥

madhya barāta birājata ati anukūle'u |
manahuṁ kāma ārāma kalapataru phūle'u ||125||

"The barata procession in the middle of the road looked very appropriate, like Kamadeva taking rest underneath a desire tree in a garden." (125)

Essay - The Wedding Garden

Here Goswami Tulsidas continues his description of the festivities that took place just prior to the marriage ceremony of Sita and Rama. The bridegroom party had arrived in Janakpur, where the host King Janaka was set to give away his daughter to the eldest son of King Dasharatha of Ayodhya. The groom, Shri Rama, was appropriately adorned with beautiful ornaments by His father. The Lord looked like the bright sun that opened up the eyes of the lotus-like world. Here the same

Rama is once again compared to the god of love, Kamadeva, and His attendants to beautiful flowers within a garden.

Kamadeva is extremely beautiful, which is the reason for the reference. Similar references are used in ordinary talks. If we want to say that a woman is very beautiful, we'll compare her appearance to that of a famous actress. The same goes for a beautiful man. The celebrities are used as frames of reference, objects for comparison. Kamadeva is described in the Vedas to be very beautiful, capable of enticing other women to enjoy with him. He also instills amorous feelings in others through the arrows that he shoots from his bow.

Kamadeva lives in the heavenly realm, which is filled with trees. These trees are not ordinary, however. They are referred to as kalpatarus and suratarus, which mean desire trees. Like a wishing well or a magic lamp, you go up to one of these trees and ask for whatever you want materially. The reward is granted immediately, making the tree like a large umbrella to give shelter. Even the lower trees, which haven't grown to be very tall, are famous in the heavenly realm. This is because they are also desire trees, capable of granting whatever the wisher wants.

"By remembering Shri Rama's holy name, even those who are born into a low caste become worthy of fame, just as the wild trees that line the streets in the heavenly realm are famous throughout the three worlds." (Dohavali, 16)

The Barat procession featured Shri Rama in the center. In traditional Vedic marriages, the groom arrives riding on an elephant. There is a canopy above him, and in this scene the shade from the canopy is compared to the shade of a desire tree. The person resting underneath is compared to Kamadeva because of His beauty. The scene thus looked very appropriate, as Shri Rama is the most beautiful. This is one of the features of God.

God is also the most renounced, the most intelligent, the most wealthy, and the most famous. And on the occasion of Sita's svayamvara, He proved that He is also the strongest. He lifted a bow that no other prince in the world could lift. This earned Him Sita's hand in marriage, in accordance with the rules of the contest drawn up by King Janaka.

The people around the barata procession were looking very beautiful. This is the effect of devotional service enacted without motives. What did the people want for themselves? They had travelled far from Ayodhya just to see their beloved Rama get married. They wanted Him to be happy with Sita. They rejoiced as He approached the scene of the wedding. In their ecstasy, they looked like the flowers that surround the desire trees in the heavenly realm.

Rest is meant to be a state of comfort. You offer someone a nice seat or a bed so that they become more comfortable. In this sense Rama was very comfortable travelling to the marriage. His position made the revelers all the more joyous. Since He is the wealthiest, God does not require any gift from any person. He rests in the spiritual sky on the bed made by Ananta Shesha Naga, so He sleeps whenever He needs to. Nevertheless, He accepts the kind service offered to Him by the devotees. Their service makes Him very happy, and His pleasure is passed back to them.

To the people of Ayodhya, Rama especially deserved the best accommodations. He never played favorites in the kingdom. As the king's eldest son, any perk was available to Him. He could live in the largest palace, drink the finest wine, and enjoy with any woman. And yet since His very birth all He was interested in was the welfare of the citizens. The people He punished from time to time couldn't find fault with Him. They knew that Rama never violated dharma, or religiosity.

While still a teenager, He left home for the forest. This was at the request of the sage Vishvamitra. Rama took His younger brother Lakshmana with Him. The people of Ayodhya prayed that the brothers wouldn't get harmed while with the sage. They had good reason to worry. Vile creatures known as Rakshasas were attacking the sages in the middle of the night, killing them, and then eating their flesh. What would the people do if Rama and Lakshmana didn't return home?

The brothers provided ample protection for Vishvamitra, and their journey eventually led them to Sita's svayamvara. The blessed Rama made everyone so happy, including King Janaka. He deserved the best of everything. Here He travels to reunite with Sita Devi, His eternal consort. The couple is divine according to the Vedas. They are the Supreme Lord and His wife. Marriage is a spiritual institution meant for bringing the two parties closer to their original consciousness. Sita and Rama are the object of that consciousness, so their marriage is a little different. It represents the unbreakable link between the energetic and the energy. The energy like Sita never separates from Him, while the energy like us tends to alternate between devotional life and material life. Through remembering the love they have for each other, which was shown at the great ceremony that saw Rama arrive looking like the beautiful Kamadeva, the final decision in favor of devotional life can be made without reservation.

VERSE 126

पठई भेंट बिदेह बहुत बहु भाँतिन्ह।
देखत देव सिहहिं अनंद बरातिन्ह॥126॥

patha'ī bheṇṭa bideha bahuta bahu bhāṁtinha |
dekhata deva sihāhiṁ ananda barātinha ||126||

"Janaka sent so many gifts of all different kinds. Seeing this, the demigods became envious over the bliss of the baratis." (126)

Essay - Different Kinds of Envy

We know that envy is a negative emotion. We know this from the fact that it can cause us to do things that are unwise. We also know that envy is not grounded in logic. Just because someone else has something that we don't, it doesn't necessarily mean that we are worse off. Even if they are better off in that sense, there is no reason to feel displeasure. We would be happy if we were in the same situation, so why should we not take delight over someone else's good fortune? As the material world is full of dualities and is a reflection of the purified form of everything, envy also exists in spiritual matters. Its nature is different, however, which is seen in what it leads to.

Wasn't King Indra once envious over Shri Krishna? Didn't this lead to something bad? How is that spiritual then?

One time the celestial named Indra became jealous over worship offered to someone other than himself. The worship traditionally went to him, but one year it didn't. It was instead directed to a hill, with the residents not holding anything back. They cooked every delightful preparation, poured all their love into the festival, and then were supremely delighted in the outcome. Indra was so envious that he decided to retaliate. He tried to cause harm upon the citizens who ignored him.

This is the wrong way to react to envy. It shows the darker side to the emotion. In this instance, the envy was still spiritually related because it ultimately led to a glorious act by the Supreme Personality of Godhead, Shri Krishna. To defend the innocent people given unwarranted torture from Indra's wrath, Krishna lifted the worshiped Govardhana Hill and used it as an umbrella. This saved the sacred town of Vrindavana from the devastating flood. Thus Indra's wrath led to something wonderful. Govardhana Puja is now an annual occasion, and the hill itself is considered to be non-different from Krishna, who is God. He is the real thing, not just a sectarian figure who is exclusive to the Hindus. He is the detail behind the abstract concept of a Supreme Lord mentioned in every spiritual tradition.

On another occasion, there was again envy from the celestials, but it didn't lead to any harm. If anything, it made their longing to associate with the Supreme Being stronger. The envy is described in the verse from the Janaki Mangala quoted above. The same Shri Krishna was on earth as the jewel of the Raghu dynasty. Known as Rama, He was famous throughout the world for His family ancestry and His transcendental qualities. In this particular scene, He is about to get married to the beautiful daughter of King Janaka. Rama was famous for having lifted the bow in Janaka's assembly. Being the victor in that contest qualified Him to marry Sita, as stipulated by the rules set by Janaka.

Janaka welcomed the groom's party with the utmost hospitality. Goswami Tulsidas tells us that Janaka gave so many gifts to the baratis, the arriving party of the groom. Janaka didn't give an overabundance of just one kind of gift. Considering it in modern terms, he didn't hand out one million Rolex watches. Instead, he handed out thousands of jewels, necklaces, rings, and so many other items of opulence as gifts. The bliss of the baratis was so high that anyone viewing from afar would be jealous.

If I see my friend after a long time, and they have suddenly lost a lot of weight, looking real sharp, I will surely be a little envious. I have a choice in how to deal with this envy. I can intentionally offer them doughnuts and other decadent things to eat, hoping that they will get fat again, or I can take the impetus to improve my own health. The latter option is better because it brings a positive outcome to the envy.

In the same way, if we envy the closest associates of the Supreme Lord for the bliss they feel in His association, it can challenge us to purify ourselves to the point that we'll get the same association. This association is a reward guaranteed by Krishna Himself in the Bhagavad-gita, where He says that one who thinks of Him eventually will come to Him. He recommends that all of our actions be done as an offering to Him.

"O son of Kunti, all that you do, all that you eat, all that you offer and give away, as well as all austerities that you may perform, should be done as an offering unto Me." (Lord Krishna, Bhagavad-gita, 9.27)

The offerings have to be authorized. We cannot go up to animals, kill them and then present them to Krishna. This is a mentally concocted style of offering, and it is indicative of impure motives. If we're told to not do something, and we do it anyway, we can't think later on that we'll purify it by somehow connecting it to Krishna. The Lord doesn't accept offerings of meat. He does accept grains, fruits, flowers, and water.

The best offering is thought. How nice is it if someone tells us that they're thinking about us? Imagine then, the pleasure God feels when others always think about Him. An easy way to think of Him is to say His name. An easy way to say His name is to repeat mantras that contain those names, like the maha-mantra: Hare Krishna Hare Krishna, Krishna Krishna, Hare Hare, Hare Rama Hare Rama, Rama Rama, Hare Hare.

The demigods were envious of the bliss of the participants at Rama's marriage, but they still kept watching. They dropped flowers from the sky when the time was appropriate. Thus they had their own kind of service. They too had an enviable position, as they were able to watch the glorious wedding of Sita and Rama from above.

THE MARRIAGE

VERSE 127

बेद बिदित कुलरीति कीन्हि दुहुँ कुलगुर।
पठई बोलि बरात जनक प्रमुदित मन।।127।।

beda bidita kulariti kīnhi duhum̐ kulagura |
paṭha'ī boli barāta janaka pramudita mana ||127||

"Both family priests did the rituals according to the family traditions and the Vedas. Calling for the barata party, Janaka's heart is full of joy." (127)

Essay - Non-Sectarian

There is a God and He is for everyone. He is not the exclusive property of any sect. He does not only reside in one area of the world. He does not only hear prayers made in a specific language. His position is scientifically explained and at the same time His qualities are so great that they cannot be measured by any instrument. From the scientific aspect, we can understand that His properties involve laws, which apply to all situations. Just as the law of gravity does not take into account a person's income, race, ethnicity, or level of intelligence, so the Supreme Lord's presence is not dependent on any outside factor. At the same time, since our brains are limited, namely by the bounds of time and space, God is beyond our conception as well.

The family traditions help us to understand God to some degree. Complete understanding is impossible. Think about it for a second. If you had complete understanding, then you would know why you ended up being in a position to need complete understanding. After getting some knowledge, you could prevent yourself from needing complete understanding again. Ah, but there was a point where you needed complete understanding; therefore something must have happened previously. You'll never be able to find that out, so therefore complete understanding is unavailable to you.

Just a slight understanding of God is good enough to make a huge impact. Take two people. Both have no clue how an automobile works. They don't know what a carburetor is. They have no idea about how to change oil, check the fluid levels, or change a tire. They are clueless in car maintenance. One person knows how to drive the car while the other does not. Does this make a difference? Neither one has complete knowledge of the car, but one knows enough to be able to use the car. Therefore the more knowledgeable person is superior; they can get the best use out of the car.

In the same way, if we know a little about God, we can use that knowledge to better our lives. But that knowledge is difficult to come by. Starting from the time of birth, our perception leads us to think that there is no God. Our parents take care of us and then our teachers instruct us. In adulthood we act seemingly independently and see the results of that independent action. Therefore we think that we are the sole cause to the consequences. If we eat right, we'll change the way our body looks. If we read, we'll get smarter. If we relax a little, our stress levels will go down. Therefore everything is in our hands.

In actuality, in every result there is a higher authority who gives sanction. We need to eat, but where does the food come from? Does the government create it? Does the farmer generate it? Actually, without nature's arrangement, the farmer could not grow food. He needs nature to provide the earth, water and sunlight. And where do these things come from? It is easy to say God, but how do we know who He is? How will we even know to be conscious of the divine presence?

This is where family traditions come in. Purificatory rites start from the time of birth in all traditions. Whether the family knows the purpose to the rites isn't so important; as the attention creates a foundational culture. At least there is the consciousness of a higher power, the recognition that not everything is solely within one's control.

In the above referenced verse from the Janaki Mangala, we are reminded of the importance of family traditions. In this instance, there is no insistence that one family's tradition is superior to another's. Mind you, the families joining were both very pious and respected. They also belonged to the same Vedic culture, which is the original spiritual tradition of the world. The Vedas have no date of inception; they come from God, who spoke the truths at the beginning of known time. They existed prior to that as well; hence religion in the Vedic definition is known as sanatana-dharma, or the eternal occupation of man.

The daughter of King Janaka was marrying the eldest son of King Dasharatha. Janaka lived in Tirahuta and Dasharatha in Ayodhya. Each family had their specific ancestry and related traditions. They each also had their own priests. Here the priests are performing the rituals according to the Vedas and family tradition. Why not just rely on the Vedas? Well, it was the family tradition that led to the current situation. The attention to the tradition was a sign of respect. Neither party insisted that their family tradition was the only way.

Know that there are many paths to God, but the key in determining whether following a tradition is successful or not is to see if there is love for God. Without this love, the rituals are essentially a waste of time. The litmus test for love of God also gives a way to spot cheating religions and bogus religious acts. Blowing up innocent women and children in the name of God is not a religious act. It is pure ignorance. Such a tradition is not legitimate at all; it is a mental concoction.

The rituals performed by the two families here were not drawn up on a whim. They had been performed since time immemorial. When Janaka called in the barata party, he had so much joy in his heart. This meant that he had love for God, as Dasharatha's family had an incarnation of God as their jewel. Rama was marrying Sita, so the wedding here involved the union of the Supreme Lord with His eternal consort, His energy. Sita and Rama are always together, but sometimes they go through a marriage ceremony in the earthly realm to give pleasure to others.

The culmination of all religious traditions is bhakti-yoga. This is the original consciousness of the soul, to love God all the time. The traditions in Dasharatha's family allowed the Supreme Lord to appear there, and in Janaka's family the result was the appearance of the goddess of fortune. In this age of Kali, where so many traditions are vanishing or are completely lost, an easy tradition to create is the chanting of the holy names, "Hare Krishna Hare Krishna, Krishna Krishna, Hare Hare, Hare Rama Hare Rama, Rama Rama, Hare Hare." Chanting this mantra is so potent that one doesn't have to wait many generations to see the Supreme Lord in their family. The name itself is non-different from Him, making this chanting the best tradition to introduce and maintain.

VERSE 128

जाइ कहेउ पगु धारिअ मुनि अवधेसहि।
चले सुमिरि गुरु गौरि गिरीस गनेसहि॥128॥

jā'i kahe'u pagu dhāri'a muni avadhesahi |
cale sumiri guru gauri girīsa ganesahi ||128||

"The muni said, 'Go and bring the King of Ayodhya here.' The king then started, remembering the guru, Parvati, Shiva and Ganesha." (128)

Essay - Disciplic Succession

When we watch movies with our friends it's not uncommon to have a discussion afterwards. "You know, I noticed that the car was really important to that old man. I think it was symbolic of his attitude. The car was just like him. It was a classic. It was old, but still in great condition. Everything around it was changing, but the car was always the same. It was trusted. It was reliable. That was a pretty deep point the film tried to make." And then we can present countering viewpoints. Everything is up for interpretation. One person's view is just as valid as another's, as who is to say who is right? The tendency is to apply the same critical eye to the words of revealed scripture, but this is not a wise path. The Supreme Absolute Truth is neti neti, or "not this and not that." He is not of this world, and so an endless amount of words does not suffice in accurately describing Him. Yet at the same time, mental speculation can never get anyone close to knowing Him. Information of Him is passed on through authorized channels, including personalities who through their important role become worshipable figures.

What is the harm in mentally speculating with the words found in scriptures? What is wrong with offering a personal interpretation?

We can take the Vedas as an example. From the root meaning of the word, we see that the scriptures are not intended to be sectarian. Veda means knowledge. It does not mean knowledge for only the Hindus. It does not mean knowledge to apply only to an ancient time period. It does not mean knowledge that must be accepted out of fear. It is straight truth. Just like the law of gravity is scientifically understood, so too the knowledge of matter and spirit presented by the original system of knowledge, the Vedas, is meant to be accepted by the rationally thinking mind.

There is no ambiguity in the information transfer of the Vedas either. Today likely the most famous work of the Vedas is the Bhagavad-gita. It is widely known through its many translations that are available. The Bhagavad-gita is basically a conversation, one that took place on the battlefield of Kurukshetra between a hesitant warrior and his charioteer. The charioteer later revealed Himself to be God. He explained His position in terms understandable to the audience, which includes both Arjuna and future generations of mankind. He explained Himself to be the origin of the creation, the seed-giving father to the population, and the ultimate shelter for all forms of life. He even showed His universal form to dispel any doubts others would have.

"Furthermore, O Arjuna, I am the generating seed of all existences. There is no being - moving or unmoving - that can exist without Me." (Lord Krishna, Bhagavad-gita, 10.39)

Krishna showing the universal formSo, where is the room for interpretation? The charioteer is named Krishna, and He is described in so many other Vedic texts as well. The Bhagavad-gita was passed on through an oral tradition. Its inception and subsequent transfer are both described in the Gita itself by Shri Krishna. Nowhere does the Lord say that He suddenly had a revelation and that the knowledge appeared to Him. He doesn't say that He concocted the system on His own through trial and error. He does say, however, that saintly kings held on to the information and passed it on. Arjuna was to be a new link in the chain, someone who could be trusted with the information.

If I tell you something today and you remember it, you can repeat it verbatim to someone else in the future. To that person, the information is as good as coming from me. They may not have direct contact with me, but since the mechanism for transfer was not tampered with, they received the exact same message that I gave to you. In the same way, we can today hear from Krishna directly, though to us it seems like the message is coming indirectly. We simply have to approach someone in the chain of disciplic succession. They give us the only valid interpretation of Krishna's words. They may present it differently based on time and circumstance, but the basic message does not change. Today I may hear the Bhagavad-gita translated into the English language, and I know that originally it was spoken in Sanskrit, but if the person translating the words understood the truths properly, there is nothing lost in the transfer.

On the other hand, if I simply pick up a Bhagavad-gita, read the verses, and then apply my own interpretation, the meanings will be lost. There is no way for me to conceive on my own the concepts of birth after death, the changing bodies, and the modes of material nature. I could never realize on my own that the vital force within all life forms is the exact same in quality. I could never figure out that spirit never dies and that death as we know it is only the changing of bodies. My interpretation of the Gita would be like eavesdropping on someone else's conversation and taking everything out of context.

Disciplic succession brings the necessary context for understanding, and since the understanding is of the highest knowledge, those within the chain are worshipable. King Dasharatha of Ayodhya shows the importance of honoring those in the chain in the above referenced verse from the Janaki Mangala. Here he is being summoned to the wedding ceremony by King Janaka's priest, Shatananda. Janaka's daughter Sita was marrying Dasharatha's son Rama.

Dasharatha had just arrived and was staying at the guest quarters in Janaka's kingdom. Here he gets word that the time for marriage is approaching and that his presence is needed. Rather than haphazardly travel, Dasharatha first remembers his guru, Parvati Devi, Lord Shiva and then Ganesha. The guru is Vashishtha. He was the guru of the Raghu family, and so he was very important. He kept knowledge of the Vedas with him, and so his counsel was always appropriate.

Parvati, Shiva and Ganesha are important here specifically because of the nature of the participants of the wedding. Krishna is also Rama, the Supreme Lord in His incarnation as a warrior prince. Lord Shiva is the greatest Vaishnava, or devotee of the personal form of the Supreme Lord, which is the original. Shiva's preferred Vishnu form of worship is Rama. While there are many forms of Vishnu, we shouldn't mistakenly consider any divine form to be God. The Vishnu forms are spelled out in the Vedas.

Parvati is Shiva's wife. She is the controller of the material nature and also a devoted wife. She is the most chaste wife. Their son is Ganesha, and he serves his parents. Thus all three are linked to the Supreme Lord. Remembering them, combined with the guru, is always beneficial. Dasharatha prayed for their favor in the upcoming ceremony. He wanted his son and his future daughter-in-law to always be happy together. He specifically wanted that they adhere to dharma together. That is the point to marriage after all. If you degrade marriage to the point that it acts only as a sex contract, then surely others will want to have the chance to sign such a contract for themselves, even though they may not be of the proper gender combination.

Marriage is a religious institution, and religion is meant for advancing one towards pure God consciousness. Animals satisfy their desires for sex on a whim; they don't need marriage. Marriage exists to curb sexual desires, to sanction it in a way that promotes the continuity of the population, providing for good children at the same time. A good child is one who knows God. One who doesn't is animal-like, and so the business of the parents is to elevate their children from the animal consciousness.

Lord Shiva is one of the highest chains in the disciplic succession that knows God. He says that Rama is God, and so based on his position we can accept that as fact. Parvati Devi and Lord Ganesha also accept Sita and Rama, further buttressing the validity of the same truth. From Dasharatha's example, we see that there is no need to speculate on truths. Follow the real guru, who will inherently be linked to Sita and Rama.

In the modern age, there are four primary sampradayas, or disciplic successions, that teach the true message of the Bhagavad-gita. Consulting a teacher in this line brings us the right information, freeing our mind from the burden of having to reach the proper conclusion on its own. This is the heaviest burden, as without the grace of the guru there is no hope for transcendental perfection.

CHAND 16

चले सुमिरि गुर सुर सुमन बरषहिं परे बहुबिधि पावड़े।
सनमानि सब बिधि जनक दसरथ किये प्रेम कनावड़े।।
गुन सकल सम समधी परस्पर मिलन अति आनँद लहे।
जय धन्य जय जय धन्य धन्य बिलोकि सुर नर मुनि कहे।।16।।

cale sumiri gura sura sumana baraṣahiṁ pare bahubidhi pāvaṛe |
sanamāni saba bidhi janaka dasaratha kiye prema kanāvaṛe ||
guna sakala sama samadhī paraspara milana ati ānaṁda lahe |
jaya dhan'ya jaya jaya dhan'ya dhan'ya biloki sura nara muni kahe ||16||

"They remembered the guru as they went. The demigods rained down flowers and carpets were rolled out. Every kind of welcome was offered by Janaka to Dasharatha, as love overwhelmed his heart." (Chand 16.1)

"Full of all good qualities and equal in all respects in the relationship were the two fathers. When they met they felt tremendous happiness. Looking at them, the demigods, men and sages kept saying, 'All glories!' and 'Wonderful!'" (Chand 16.2)

Essay - Building a Lasting Relationship

It is the accepted custom to show hospitality to a guest. The guest is away from their home. That home may be many miles away or within just a short-distance, like next door, but still they are not in their comfortable environment. Therefore the host tries every which way possible to make the guest feel at home. It is just the polite thing to do. King Janaka a long time ago was indeed very polite, but based on the love he felt we know that his gestures were genuine; they went beyond mere protocol.

There were gestures made from above as well. First, the guest-party remembered the feet of their guru. Through his advice, the eldest prince Rama went to the forest with the venerable Vishvamitra Muni, a sage living in the forest at the time. The king, the father of Rama, did not want to let his son go. Rama was barely a teenager. Why should He go off and defend anyone at such a young age? Why should He be put into harm's way? It wasn't that Vishvamitra was asking that Rama be part of an army. He wasn't asking for Rama to be trained up and then learn by following others on the job. No, Vishvamitra wanted Rama to be the sole defender against the wickedest creatures in the world. More than just fighting a lion or tiger with your bare hands, Rama was expected to use His bow and arrow to ward off creatures who were expert in black magic. These fiends had no qualms about killing innocent sages either. They would eat human flesh regularly, so fighting dirty was not an issue for them. The young Rama was expected to fend off these fighters all by Himself. Why would the father Dasharatha sanction that?

Unable to give a blanket denial, the king was first speechless. Then he tried persuading Vishvamitra in another direction. Finally, the guru Vashishtha advised Dasharatha to not fight it any longer. Vishvamitra knew what he was doing; he wasn't making this request on a hunch. He knew that Rama would defend him. He also knew that Lakshmana, Rama's devoted younger brother, would come along as well. And so Dasharatha reluctantly gave in.

And now here he is walking towards the marriage ceremony for his son Rama. This was the first time seeing Rama since He left home. A lot had happened in the meantime. Rama and Lakshmana cleared the worries of the sages in the forest by slaying wicked characters like Subahu and Tataka. They earned the favor of Vishvamitra, and through following him they ended up in King Janaka's home. There Rama lifted the bow of Shiva and won the hand in marriage of Janaka's daughter Sita. It was for the marriage occasion that Dasharatha and family were called from Ayodhya.

Dasharatha went from intense worry to unbridled joy. In his happiness it was not surprising that he remembered the guru, along with Lord Shiva, Parvati Devi, and their son Lord Ganesha. The demigods, for their part, were so thrilled that they started dropping flowers from the sky as Dasharatha approached the marriage ceremony. He was the chosen father of the Supreme Lord Rama, who had descended to earth to enact wonderful pastimes. The demigods are all devotees; they worship God. They know that He exists and they work at His direction. They don't foolishly turn a blind eye towards the unexplainable phenomenon that is spirit. They don't think that the sun and the moon came into existence on their own. They inquire into why things in nature work, rather than try to exploit its presence.

Devotion incorporates more than just knowledge. A sign of devotion is thrill and delight at the chance for others to take part in devotional acts. Though they were envious of the bliss felt by Dasharatha and the other wedding participants, the demigods still dropped flowers as a sign of honor. King Janaka rolled out the red carpet for his guests. He was so happy to get Rama as a son-in-law. Who better to protect his precious Sita? Dasharatha was the father, so all the accolades owned by Rama increased the king's fame as well.

Welcoming his beloved guest, Janaka felt so much love in his heart. What a joy to get to see Dasharatha, a person who was famous for his defense of the demigods. His name was earned from his ability to fight chariots coming in the ten directions. He could fight them simultaneously. Though he was powerful, he too was very pious. Imagine having the best person in the world as your defender. Imagine that they are also unbeatable in battle. Wouldn't that make you feel good? Wouldn't you feel pleased to have the association of such a person?

Since Janaka felt love, the hospitality he offered was more than just a formality. It was a sincere offering directed to a wonderful family. And such an offering never goes in vain. We may try to make entreaties with our enemies just for the sake of getting along, but sometimes this approach doesn't work. They may not want a resolution. In the famous Bharata war, Shri Krishna, who is the same God but in His original form, tried to negotiate a peace settlement with the Kauravas, but they would have none of it. They were set on ruling and wouldn't budge unless they were physically forced to.

The result of making an offering to God is that love fills your heart. And wouldn't you rather live with love? Hate eventually destroys everything in its path, while love builds lasting relationships. The eternal relationship is the connection to the Supreme Lord, which is every person's birthright. Through devotional service, which includes kind offerings like the one made by Janaka, that relationship is reawakened. And through the love in the heart, the relationship only strengthens with the passage of time.

Essay - All Glories

If you visit a Vaishnava temple, you will often hear the exclamation, "Jaya." This means "all glories" or "victory" and it is usually preceded by a name or place. The person leading the offerings says it first, and then the members present follow along. Similar to the practice of singers on stage at rock concerts, this call and response type offering allows others to voice their love and appreciation for the objects in question. In the above referenced verse from the Janaki Mangala, the spectators and participants got to directly offer their joyous congratulations to the people involved. They didn't have to wait until afterwards, and since the people involved were so wonderful, the offerings kept coming, from all different directions.

"Amen, my good brother." This means "I agree. I wholeheartedly support what you are saying." "Jaya" goes a little beyond that, as it is both a sign of agreement and a way to offer praise. In the temple, the congregation members are obviously worshipers of a similar mind. They see the deity or picture representation of the Divine and then automatically feel appreciation. When it comes time to glorifying that Supreme Person, they are more than happy to follow along. They may also give support to the glories offered to the spiritual master, the holy places, and the people assembled there for the worship.

The ceremony referenced above didn't take place in a temple. It wasn't an explicit religious function either. And yet the entire culture at the time was rooted in spiritual life. If you advise that people keep religion and science separate, you will get many supporters. "Religion is faith, and so it has no place in science. We believe in God, but that should have nothing to do with how we use science." If you think of religion only in terms of faith, then surely this logic makes sense to you. But as more rational thought is applied, the advice loses its legs.

For starters, religion is intended to be about God. This shouldn't be a controversial point. If we're talking about God, then we're talking about the person who is the source of everything. The name you use for that source isn't so important here. The acknowledgment is there that life came from a higher form of life. The creation didn't just evolve from elements randomly colliding.

Now, if we're saying that God is the origin, why should He be shut out of any aspect of His creation? If He is really God, He must have a place in all aspects of life. Life is made by Him. Without His presence, there is no such thing as life. We are spirit too, and when we are somewhere, the neighboring collection of matter has life. When we are absent, the previously animate covering immediately turns inanimate. This transformation goes by the name of death, which is the exit of life from a specific area.

I may have faith in this person or that, but faith has nothing to do with the spiritual science. The sun has specific scientific properties. This is true of the overall nature too, which science seeks to understand. If you ignore the hand of the creator of the nature, then your study will always be deficient. Indeed, the desire to keep God out of your scientific discussion proves that you have no understanding of God. It is an obvious indication that you want to use science to manipulate matter for your own personal enjoyment, keeping God out of your life. If this weren't the case, you would have no problem including in the discussion the creator of the nature. And that creation must have a purpose as well, as the non-randomness to the properties of the creation shows an intelligence. If even unintelligent actions of ordinary people are done with a purpose, then surely the work of the most intelligent being would have a tangible purpose. And surely it wouldn't be to have His own influence later be ignored.

Though the people in Janakpur were celebrating a marriage, they did anything but keep God out of it. They knew that marriage wasn't merely a contract for sex life, a way to put into writing the amorous feelings shared by two people. If you think about it, what reason is there for God to include discussions on eating and sex life in any of His scriptures? Animals already follow these behaviors without a problem. They don't know anything about God, marriage, sacrifice, or charity. They go off their animal instincts. For God to include these things in written word means that there is a purpose to these activities in the human species that goes beyond furthering animal life.

Marriage is a sanction for sex life. It is a way to curb it. It is also a way to properly use it. The human being has potency, after all. The potencies are different for the male and the female. If the potency of the male is matched with the potency of the female in a marital relationship, the result is good progeny. Given the choice, isn't it better to have children who are wanted, loved and nurtured?

In the Vedas marriage is known as a spiritual institution, the grihastha ashrama. It is a way for both parties to continue in their spiritual advancement, which ideally started from the time of birth. Therefore marriage is a joyous occasion, where the well-wishers can rejoice in the beginning of a future journey for the bride and groom. The parents of both families also join in the celebration, and if they are an ideal match, the union means a wonderful way to extend the families.

Here the men, demigods and sages kept saying "Jaya" and "Dhanya" while observing the meeting of the two fathers at the marriage ceremony. King Dasharatha's son Rama was marrying King Janaka's daughter Sita. It is said by Goswami Tulsidas that both men were full of good qualities, or gunas. The relationship between them was equal; neither one was superior. And this is a difficult thing to say considering the gloriousness of both men. Who would think that you could find an equal to King Dasharatha, one of the leading fighters for the demigods? And who would think that you could find an equal to King Janaka, known throughout the three worlds for his dispassion and his dedication to dharma?

The people weren't in a temple specifically, but they offered their obeisances nonetheless. They repeatedly shouted "all glories" to express what they were feeling. Rama is the Supreme Lord, the very origin of the creation that scientists are so interested in. Sita is His eternal consort, His energy. When the two meet, the area turns into a temple-like ground, a place of pilgrimage. And the time surrounding that meeting becomes one to remember through the ages.

VERSE 129

तीनि लोक अवलोकहिं नहिं उपमा कोउ।
दसरथ जनक समाज जनक दसरथ दोउ।।129।।

tīni loka avalokahiṁ nahiṁ upamā ko'u |
dasaratha janaka samāja janaka dasaratha do'u ||129||

"In the three worlds, nothing could compare to the two. Dasharatha was equal to Janaka and Janaka equal to Dasharatha." (129)

GOSWAMI TULSIDAS

Essay - The Two Fathers

In order to have the perfect wedding, the parents must be there. You can't control events, for the world we live in is temporary. This means that the things you want the most may not be around when you need them. You may want your parents there on your special day, but if circumstances dictate otherwise, you are bereft of the cherished association. A famous marriage a long time ago was perfect in every way, as it was arranged by the master coordinator, the person who passively directs the movements of the material creation and passionately takes the helm for the affairs of His devotees.

There are two sets of parents in the ideal wedding; the bride's side and the groom's side. So many things can get in the way. Perhaps the bride's parents are not happy with the choice the bride has made. Perhaps the groom's parents think the son is making a terrible mistake. Then there are class distinctions to consider. What if the bride comes from a rich family and the groom from a poor one? If the bride is accustomed to a certain lifestyle going into marriage, how is she going to survive on the modest income of the groom?

There are social conventions in play as well. The classes generally stick together. If the classes are determined by income level, then it would make sense that those with a low income would spend more time around those with a low income. The same for those in a higher income group. Friends are made among equals, so it is difficult when there are differences in stature. If the statures of the two families going into a marriage are markedly different, how are the bride and groom supposed to form a friendship?

In Janakpur a long time ago, the match for a beautiful bride was left up to a contest. Forget trying to find the perfect husband through family tradition and horoscopes, which were the tried and tested methods during this particular time period. This bride had special circumstances surrounding her birth. Her father essentially adopted her. She didn't belong to anyone before. As a baby, she was found in the ground. The king was ploughing that earth with the intention of performing a religious sacrifice, a kind of worship. What he didn't know at the time was that he found the most special girl, the best object of worship for those who have real intelligence.

Holding affection for her immediately and then taking her into his family, with time the king knew that she was something special. Therefore he decided that her wedding wouldn't be arranged in the traditional way. Instead of worrying over finding the ideal match, he decided to hold a contest. Strength would be tested. In this way the victor would prove to be the most capable of protecting the precious daughter, who was named Sita because she was found in the ground.

Since the husband was to be determined from a contest, there was every possibility of a non-traditional match being found. Janaka was the king, and he was famous around the world for his character. He had the highest stature imaginable. A king is a ruler, and Janaka was no slouch in this area. He could protect his citizens very well. He also gave high deference to righteousness. He never committed a sin. He followed his occupational duties with detachment. He wasn't swayed one way or the other by personal desires or worries over missing out on fun. He knew what was right, and in that way he set the best example.

What if the winner of the contest came from a family that wasn't so high in stature? What if the father of the groom was evil and wicked-minded? It wouldn't be a good match for Sita. Janaka wasn't so worried on this front, as the contest was very difficult. The winner would be the first person to lift an extremely heavy bow. There was every chance that no one would be able to do it.

From the above referenced verse from the Janaki Mangala, we see that the match in family for Sita could not have been more perfect. Here the two fathers are meeting. Shri Rama from Ayodhya won the contest. His father was King Dasharatha, who was invited to Janakpur to attend the marriage ceremony. Goswami Tulsidas says that there is nothing in the three worlds that can compare to that image of the two fathers meeting.

Imagine if you found the perfect person. Alter the definition of perfect to suit the circumstance. In this instance, Janaka was the perfect king. He had no flaws in him, and his daughter was an extension of his greatness. Now imagine that you found an identical match and had him meet Janaka. It's like getting a pitcher in baseball to pitch two perfect games in a row. It's like having a bowler bowl two consecutive games of 300. Actually, this meeting was even more difficult to imagine, as both Dasharatha and Janaka were equal to one another. Dasharatha was pious like Janaka, and Janaka had wonderful children like Dasharatha. It was as if God had ordained that the two families should be joined.

Of course that is exactly what had happened. Rama is the Supreme Lord and Sita His wife. Rama is an incarnation of the original Personality of Godhead, who is all-attractive and thus known as Krishna. Krishna can accept an unlimited number of wives, while Rama accepts only Sita. As Sita and Rama thus have a unique relationship, the relationship between the two fathers is not surprisingly unique as well.

Essay - Five-Star General

"Whom should we select as our leader? I want a five-star general, someone who is a war hero. War isn't good, but if the other side is not willing to compromise, what choice is there? Should the innocent just roll over and give up? Should we allow others to come into our homes and seize our possessions? We may not be willing to fight, but our protectors most certainly should be.

"The general who has been recognized for his accomplishments proves that he is willing to sacrifice everything for others. The leader of the nation must show this dedication. If he isn't this dedicated, who will be? The military hero will also act as a great deterrent. Enemies will have to think twice before attacking. They'll know not to mess with us, because we have someone who is ready, willing and able to defend.

"I also want someone who is impartial to lead our country. It is very easy to be partial. I love my wife. I love my children. I love my friends. They are so good to me. They pick me up when I am down. They celebrate with me when I am happy. They are there for me when I need them. Why wouldn't I be partial to them?

"But actually, every person is the family member of someone else. Every person is also the friend to someone else. Therefore my partiality shouldn't take precedent over someone else's. I love my family and you love yours. Is my love more important than yours? It shouldn't be. This is especially true for the governing body, for their implementation of favoritism is much more harmful. They control the purse-strings. They say that the single largest collection of wealth in the world is found in the national treasury. This is the sum total of all taxes, fees and service charges. Therefore when the government plays favorites, it can use a lot of money and make a large impact.

"When the leader is impartial, we know that he is fair. Fairness is beneficial for everyone. Not that there will be an equality of outcomes. One person works hard and another does not. They shouldn't artificially be made to have the same salary, especially if the output to their work is different. The fairness should apply to the enforcement of the law. The leader shouldn't have anything invested in the outcome. Whether the pauper commits a crime or the wealthy businessman, the attention of the law should be the same. Otherwise the leader will set the wrong example."

The wishes mentioned above seem impossible to come true. Who is actually impartial and courageous at the same time? Who isn't swayed by the power of government? Who doesn't get caught up in taking care of their political friends and family? From the above referenced verse from the Janaki Mangala, we get an example of when such conditions were met. They existed in two kings, who happened to meet each other at a marriage ceremony. As they were both full of the best qualities necessary for leadership, the image was indeed unique. Nothing in the three worlds could compare to it.

The three worlds are the heavenly, earthly and hellish realms. Think of it like up, down and middle. We are in the middle right now. Sometimes we enjoy heavenly life and other times our journey is hellish. One minute we're enjoying pizza with our friends and family and the next we are staying late at the office to meet a deadline. One minute we are enjoying a peaceful walk in the woods and the next we are trying our best to get over a crippling disease.

The heavenly realm is where the enjoyments come nonstop, all the time. The hellish realm is where the miseries exist in full. Residence in any of the three realms is temporary. You can go here to there based on your work, or karma. The results of your work are temporary, so you can't remain in any of the worlds permanently.

Here the reference to the three worlds is made in the context of space. One world is large enough. When there is a top athlete or sports team, we refer to them as the best in the world. This is only with respect to organized competition; as we haven't really tested every single person or team to see if they indeed are not the best. With the meeting of King Janaka and King Dasharatha, you could actually search the three worlds and not find anything comparable.

Dasharatha was the father of Rama and Janaka the father of Sita. Dasharatha was famous as a ten-chariot fighter. Using only a single chariot, he could go against ten other chariots at the same time. He performed his tasks while fighting for the good guys, the demigods. He was thus the best protector anyone could ask for. He deserved to have Rama as a son, who was just like Him in fighting prowess. At the time of this meeting, Rama had already defeated several of the world's most powerful fiends.

Janaka was known for his dispassion. He didn't hold a grudge. He didn't play favorites. He had no interest in riches, fame, or personal enjoyment. He ruled because that was his duty passed on to him from birth. He was also trained in how to be a king; therefore he was qualified in every way. People knew that he was a standup guy. Therefore princes from around the world gathered in Janaka's city to stand up to the bow, which was central to a contest. The winner of the contest would get Sita's hand in marriage.

Since these two kings met to celebrate a marriage, we know that Rama won that contest. People were very happy to see Sita and Rama wed, as they were a perfect match for each other. The fathers were perfectly matched as well. Neither one was superior or inferior. In the same way, Sita and Rama are equal. One is male and the other female, but neither one is lacking anything. Rama is the Supreme Lord and Sita is His eternal consort. Worship of either one in the proper mood qualifies as bhakti-yoga. Since they are always together, they are generally worshiped together as well. They are both referenced in the famous maha-mantra: Hare Krishna Hare

Krishna, Krishna Krishna, Hare Hare, Hare Rama Hare Rama, Rama Rama, Hare Hare.

VERSE 130

सजहिं सुमंगल साज रहस रनिवासहि।
गान करहिं पिकबैनि सहित परिहासहि।।130।।

sajahiṁ sumaṅgala sāja rahasa ranivāsahi |
gāna karahiṁ pikabaini sahita parihāsahi ||130||

"In the queen's palace they are decorating for the auspicious occasion. With voices like cuckoos, they are singing and joking." (130)

Essay - Keeping with Tradition

In each culture there are specific traditions involved in a wedding. Not all wedding ceremonies are the same, and the different traditions date back to previous times. Vedic culture is no different in this regard, as the traditions go so far back that one can't even trace their origin. The setting of the above referenced verse from the Janaki Mangala is a kingdom from many thousands of years ago. The culture during that time was steeped in tradition, which the people followed with faith.

The people are preparing for a marriage. The participants had just been settled upon. The host of the ceremony, King Janaka, knew that his daughter would be the bride, provided that a groom was selected. If no groom fit the bill, then there would be no wedding. To find the perfect groom, Janaka set up a contest. Thus there was naturally some anticipation. There was excitement, as anything could happen.

The different sports bring their unique moments of tension. In basketball, there is the last second shot. Just one shot, one toss of a ball, can determine whether a team wins or loses. If the shot goes in, the player who shot the ball scores a victory for his team. If it misses, then his team loses. In American football there is the last second field-goal kick, and in baseball there is the bottom of the ninth inning.

In hockey there is the sudden-death overtime. When the score is tied at the end of regulation in a playoff game, the two teams skate an extra period. The period is twenty minutes, but the clock is irrelevant; it is more for bookkeeping. As soon as someone scores, the game is over. This means that if a player heads down the ice on a breakaway, all by himself, there is a chance that he can end the game right then. But if he doesn't score, the game could continue on for another hour. Nobody knows. For this reason, the overtime period is exciting. If the first overtime ends, then another one commences. This repeats until one of the teams finally scores.

In Janakpur the day started with the hope that Sita would get married. There was anticipation. Her husband would be determined by a contest. Whoever could first lift a heavy bow in front of others would win. As the day continued, it looked like Sita might not get married. None of the princes could even move the bow. How was anyone going to lift it?

Making matters worse, in entered a beautiful prince. He was so handsome, and His character matched His beauty. He was youthful as well. It was said that He was very capable in battle. The sage Vishvamitra relied on Him for protection. The younger brother Lakshmana too took shelter of the same prince. Thus this youth, who was named Rama, was perfect for Sita in every way. Now if only there wasn't that darn contest getting in the way.

Not to fear, as Rama ended up lifting the bow with ease. The Vedas reveal Him to be the Supreme Lord, the God for all of humanity. In the tradition we inherit at the time of birth, we may only know of God as a blank canvas, an all-powerful figure who can do pretty much anything. In the Vedas, some details to the abstract are provided. He is described to be all-powerful for sure. And if someone asks, "How powerful?" the response can be, "Powerful enough to lift the extremely heavy bow in Janaka's contest to win Sita's hand in marriage."

Rama's family arrived from Ayodhya and met Janaka's family. The princess, Sita, placed the victory garland around Rama and then returned to her palace. In the above referenced verse we get an idea of what was going on leading up to the eventual marriage ceremony. In the queen's palace, people were putting in place all the decorations. These decorations were auspicious, or sumangala, to match the occasion. The poem containing this reference is known as the Janaki Mangala, which translates to the "auspiciousness of Janaki," who is the daughter of Janaka. The "mangala" here specifically refers to her marriage, as it was an auspicious occasion due to the nature of the participants. It wasn't merely a codification of a relationship in sense gratification. It wasn't done at the desire of Sita or Rama. It wasn't done to show the world that they loved each other. It was an auspicious occasion because it marked their union on earth. Sita would serve Rama and Rama would protect Sita. The two would forever be happy in each other's company.

In preparation, the people in the queen's palace sang and joked, sounding like cuckoos. The cuckoo's call indicates that spring has come. In this instance, their cuckoo-like voices announced the presence of the spring of their lives. The cold winter represented by the uncertainty of the contest gave way to the spring of Rama's victory. In that joyous time, Sita would come to life, as she would join with her ideal match. The joking and singing was commonplace for a wedding of the Vedic tradition, showing that everything about the occasion was perfect.

The devotees of Sita and Rama are similar to the cuckoo, as they sing nice songs about them. These songs announce the presence of the divine couple as well. In that ancient time, the singing in the queen's palace signaled the beginning of Sita and Rama's wedded life on earth, and today the singing of the holy names, "Hare Krishna Hare Krishna, Krishna Krishna, Hare Hare, Hare Rama Hare Rama, Rama Rama, Hare Hare," signals the arrival of the Supreme Lord and His eternal consort into the lives of the devoted souls, who always look for ways to celebrate them.

VERSE 131

उमा रमादिक सुरतिय सुनि प्रमुदित भईं।
कपट नारि बर बेष बिरचि मंडप गईं॥131॥

umā ramādika suratiya suni pramudita bha'īṁ |
kapaṭa nāri bara beṣa biraci maṇḍapa ga'īṁ ||131||

"Hearing this, Parvati, Lakshmi and the wives of the demigods became very happy. After disguising themselves as ordinary women, they went to the mandapa."
(131)

Essay - Staying in the Background

"Hey, nice to see you. It's been so long. Where have you been? Have you been hiding? We've been here every week and we haven't seen you. We missed you. Tell us all about what you've been doing. Why haven't you been showing up? Is your job stressing you out? Is it something that we said? Did you get into an argument with someone over here? Whatever it is, we are so glad that you are back. Now hopefully we will see you all the time."

When a major event is going down, it's sometimes nice to just blend into the background. This way no one will bother you. You will get to enjoy the event, soaking in all the precious moments. Think of it like being a celebrity who attends a big game in sports. You want to watch the game. You don't necessarily want the attention. There is nothing you can do, however, as everyone will recognize you. In Janakpur a long time ago, celestials were anxious to attend a blessed event, to get up close to see and hear what was going on. Knowing that they would be recognized and thus garner attention, they decided to disguise themselves.

When the President of the United States goes anywhere, he needs the entire security detail to accompany him. If he's in New York City to give an address at the United Nations, so many streets are closed to accommodate his travel. If he is going to attend a sporting event, the security team needs to check out the area beforehand. He doesn't walk in like an ordinary person. Presidents in the past have sometimes avoided attending certain events precisely because they didn't want to take any attention away from the main participants. They didn't want to steal the glory for themselves.

If the event is of greater significance, like a marriage or a religious observance, you don't want to turn it into a social event. At least you don't want that to be the most important thing. You don't want to have to socialize while everything is going down. Maybe afterwards, in order to not appear rude, you will talk to various people. You will meet up with your friends. You will maybe make new friends while mingling. During the event, however, you're there to experience everything. That's the reason you attended.

"Lord Shiva is the husband of Durga, the controller of the material energy. Durga is personified material energy, and Lord Shiva, being her husband, is the controller of the material energy. He is also the incarnation of the mode of ignorance and one of the three deities representing the Supreme Lord. As His representative, Lord Shiva is identical with the Supreme Personality of Godhead." (Shrila Prabhupada, Shrimad Bhagavatam, 3.14.29 Purport)

For Parvati Devi and Lakshmi Devi, there was no way to attend a famous event without getting spotted. Both of them are worshiped figures of the Vedic tradition. Parvati is the beloved wife of Lord Shiva. Another one of her names is Durga, which means difficult to overcome. She manages the material creation, and her husband is charged with destroying it at the appropriate time. Through her various forms she is worshiped for so many different things, all of them relating to material life. She makes the difficult stay in the material land a little less painful, temporarily, for those who worship her. Thus if anyone sees her, they will immediately honor her and seek a benediction.

Lakshmi Devi is the goddess of fortune. The fortune belongs to her husband, Narayana, who is a non-different expansion of the Supreme Lord. Lakshmi manages that fortune for Him. She liberally distributes it to those who worship her. The fortune is to be used for pleasing Narayana. Any other use is a misuse. She would have the same problem as Parvati if she were to attend the famous event. People would ask her for fortune.

There are many demigods, who are godly personalities but not quite the Supreme Lord Himself. They have their wives, who are thus goddesses. Any of these goddesses appearing at this famous event would draw some type of attention. That is not what any of them wanted. They heard the singing of auspicious songs from above. That sound drew them towards the ceremony.

The auspiciousness related to Sita's marriage. For this reason, the work that describes these events is known as the Janaki Mangala, or the most auspicious occasion for the daughter of King Janaka. She was known as Sita, and is considered an incarnation of Lakshmi. From this verse Goswami Tulsidas tells us that Sita is more than Lakshmi, though she is non-different from her. Lakshmi herself is drawn to attend Sita's marriage. In the same way, although Narayana is the same Rama, still Narayana is interested to see Rama's marriage to Sita. In the spiritual world, such differences are not contradictory, while in the material sphere they are difficult to comprehend.

Lakshmi, Parvati and the wives of the demigods decided to go in disguise. They would look just like the other women in the mandapa, which was the structure under which the marriage was to take place. In addition to allowing them to enjoy the festivities without being bothered, this masking was also a kind act. The women that were already there weren't upstaged in beauty by Lakshmi and Parvati, who are beautiful beyond compare. If the two goddesses appeared as is, they would outshine all the other women. Thus we see how kind and respectful Lakshmi, Parvati and the wives of the demigods are.

They were drawn in by the singing of auspicious songs, and their interest was maintained by seeing Sita wed Rama. No one bothered them at the time, and afterwards they were able to go back to their posts as worshipable figures. They got to see the beautiful Sita, who was without flaw. They got to see the lovely Rama, who was perfect for Sita in every way. They got to see the pure-hearted residents of Janakpur rejoice in the day soon to be known as their favorite.

They stayed in the background so that nothing could break their focus. Their behavior reveals what is most important to them. They are of the godly nature, and they are powerful as well. They grant wonderful benedictions that the mind can't even fathom. And yet to them none of these benedictions are important. These personalities are not puffed up by having so many worshipers, either. They simply enjoy seeing and hearing about God and His eternal consort. From their attendance at the wedding they also showed great intelligence in figuring out how to allow that worship to continue. From their behavior we learn the true meaning of life: to be immersed in the devotional consciousness.

VERSE 132

मंगल आरति साज बरहि परिछन चलीं।

जनु बिगसीं रबि उदय कनक पंकज कलीं ॥१३२॥

maṅgala ārati sāja barahi parichana calīṁ |
janu bigasīṁ rabi udaya kanaka paṅkaja kalīṁ ||132||

"They then went to welcome the groom with an auspicious arati on a decorated plate. They were happy like the golden lotus blooming at sunrise." (132)

Essay - Mangala Arati

The arati is well known to followers of the Vedic tradition. It is an offering of light to a respectable personality. It is a central paraphernalia item in any ritual. The mangala-arati is most auspicious, as it occurs in the morning right before the sun rises. The sun is the maker of the day, and so without it we couldn't begin our work for the day. Work is necessary for finding all other kinds of auspiciousness, and so the sun should get some of the credit for whatever benefits come later. To honor the sun is a nice gesture, and so it is a central part of the tradition that worships a personal God. In the above referenced verse, the very same person is offered worshiped directly, under the pretense of a marriage ceremony. The symbolism inherent in the gesture did not get overlooked by the wise poet.

If there is a God, we should worship Him. Is it not true? Who would argue against such a point? God, in whatever way one would define Him, would have to be the ultimate order supplier. Since He gives everything, it would make sense to say "thanks" for that. If you're going to say "thanks" once in a while, why not every day? If you're going to do it every day, you're going to need different exercises to fill the various timeslots. Otherwise you'll go through the motions for five minutes and then go back to doing whatever you were doing. Then the worship becomes more conducive to forgetfulness.

The mangala-arati helps to start the day just right. Throughout the day we should worship God, but we have to work in order to maintain a living. We work to eat; there is really no other purpose. If we work to satisfy our senses, we will never be completely happy. This is because the senses are never truly satisfied. In fact, conditioning the senses to do with less is the better option. We condition the senses in order to lose weight. We do the same to keep the blood flowing strongly inside of the body. If we just went for straight satisfaction whenever there was an itch, we would not be happy at all.

If we have to work to eat, it means we shouldn't have to work very hard. This is easy in theory, but in modern times the implementation is much more difficult. We do have to work hard just to survive. Bills pile up, costs for goods and services rapidly rise, and one brief bout of hardship can leave someone financially ruined. Therefore work is so important; at least that is how it is seen.

If you're going to work hard to maintain a living, at least worship God in the morning. This is the start to your day. It sets the tone for how the rest will pan out. If you work first instead, then later on you might be too tired to worship. If you forget to worship, it'll be easier to continue in that forgetfulness going forward. Pretty soon you'll think that there is no God and that life is destined to be miserable.

The arati, which is the offering of fire usually emanating from lamps, is most auspicious in the morning; hence the name mangala-arati. The morning is the most auspicious time for all religious practices. Those practices shape your consciousness, which is the ultimate aim. In the Bhagavad-gita, Lord Krishna states that whatever state of being one remembers at the time of death, that state they will attain without fail.

"Whatever state of being one remembers when he quits his body, that state he will attain without fail." (Lord Krishna, Bhagavad-gita, 8.6)

In the above referenced verse from the Janaki Mangala, the term "mangala-arati" is used, but not in the context of the morning ritual. There are different aratis throughout the day, which are especially observed in Vedic temples. The temple is where the deity resides, and the deity is considered the visibly manifest incarnation of the Supreme Lord. The deity allows us to understand what God looks like in His various non-different forms. It discredits the weak attempts by the mental speculators to define God. It strengthens the conviction of the devotees, who know that God exists and that He is all-attractive.

Here the arati is offered directly to God in His incarnation as a warrior prince named Rama. With the personal form there are activities, which are known as lila in Sanskrit. Ordinary lila may or may not interest us. If it does hold our interest, it will only be for a brief while. God's lila is known as nitya, or eternal. It is enjoyable today, tomorrow, a week from today, a year from tomorrow, and a thousand years into the future. This arati was offered to Rama thousands of years ago, and it is still wonderful to hear about.

The arati was a lamp placed on a decorated plate. It was offered directly to Rama from the women on the bride's side. Rama was the groom in this instance, set to marry Sita Devi, the daughter of King Janaka. From this verse we also learn what happens when devotion is offered in the proper mood. Not surprisingly, it should make one happy. How happy? So happy that the reaction is spontaneous; not mechanical.

The spontaneous reaction is described through the comparison to the golden lotus. In the morning, this flower opens up. It does so at the sight of the sun. Thus the sun's rising is what makes the lotus happy; otherwise it remains closed up. In the same way, in worshiping God and making an auspicious offering of a lamp, the face should brighten.

The women here were golden-complexioned; hence the comparison to the golden lotus. Rama was a prince who appeared in the solar dynasty; hence the comparison to the sun. The lotus flower is also the perfect symbol of beauty. It is strictly God's creation. No mind could ever come up with something like it. No factory could produce it using a single seed. The flower can only be attributed to God. It is so pure that it spontaneously reacts to the vision of God's representative, the sun.

Here the origin of all light and heat was seen, and the lotus-like devotees naturally reacted in joy. In devotional service, which is the highest form of religion, the aim is to be happy. When the worship is proper, when both internal and external impurities are removed, the happiness comes automatically. Something as simple as an offering of a lamp can brighten one's day.

VERSE 133

नख सिख सुंदर राम रूप जब देखहिं।
सब इंद्रिन्ह महँ इंद्र बिलोचन लेखहिं।।133।।

nakha sikha sundara rāma rūpa jaba dekhahiṁ |
saba indrinha mahaṁ indra bilocana lekhahiṁ ||133||

"When seeing Rama, they notice His beauty from head to toe. As all parts of Rama's body are so wonderful, they thought of Indra and his many eyes." (133)

Essay - Not Enough Eyes

"If only I had eyes in the back of my head. Then I could see what is going on behind me. If I was a football player, I could see the defense coming up from behind me to make the tackle. I could then get away from them. If I played hockey, I wouldn't be duped into a big hit. I would be able to avoid the defense creeping up from behind me. In school, I would see others making funny faces at me. When pictures are taken, I could see if someone was mocking me behind my back. More eyes would thus help me."

In Janakpur a long time ago, a section of women wished for more eyes, but not necessarily to see things behind them. They already liked what was in front of them. It was so beautiful that two eyes were not enough to soak in the beauty. They thought of Lord Indra and his thousand eyes. Even that wouldn't be enough, but at least it would be better than two.

A similar lament is there with the bhakti poets. They wish they would have more ability in glorifying God. They wish they could spend the entire day glorifying the Supreme Lord with their gifted poetic ability. Despite their knack for putting phrases together in just the right way, they can only write so much in a given day. They still have to sleep. They still have to eat. They have to follow their sadhana, or regulative practice. If they don't chant the holy names a sufficient number of times, they feel that they won't be able to properly glorify God. No matter how much they want to, if the dedication to the holy names is absent, then the rest is merely academic.

Glorifying God is not an academic exercise; at least not to the devotees. It is the one thing that brings the highest pleasure. It causes everything else around them to increase in quality. Ordinarily, if we see a flower we may not notice it. We see flowers all the time, so what is the significance in seeing another one? However, if you've spent the whole morning glorifying God, when you see a flower later in the day, your mindset might be different:

"Look at how beautiful this flower is. Only God can create something like this. By His arrangement, something so perfect is born from a tiny seed. No factory could produce this. It takes so much intelligence and engineering in order to manufacture an automobile. Even then, the particular model isn't perfect. There is always something missing. There are also flaws that arise later on. Therefore the carmakers constantly look for ways to improve their product. Despite all their effort, the car is never perfect.

"But this flower most certainly is. It is created through nature's will. No computer designs the flower. In fact, the computer tries to copy the flower, using it as a reference. The artist tries to draw the flower to the best of their ability. The lover plucks a flower to give to their beloved. The host places flowers on tables so that guests will feel welcome. All of this is due to God's grace. His magnificent intelligence is beyond compare. I could meditate on this one flower for hours, because it reminds me of God."

The personal form of the Supreme Lord is the origin of all beautiful objects. As much as the flower is impossible to describe fully, the transcendental body of God is infinitely more beautiful. The poet therefore feels more incapable of properly describing it. The twenty-four hours in each day are not enough. A limitation is there also with the one hand used for writing or the two hands for typing. Four hands would be better. This way glorification could continue on two paths simultaneously. One set could glorify God's beautiful feet, while the other could focus on His face.

Here the female party in a wedding has direct access to the Supreme Lord in His incarnation as Shri Ramachandra. They notice that Rama's beauty is wonderful from head to toe. Looking at His feet is just as blissful as looking at His waist. All parts of the body are beautiful, and so they think of Indra, the king of heaven. Due to a curse, Indra was given a thousand eyes. This many eyes on a person makes them look odd, as if they have some disease. At the same time, this many eyes enhances the power of sight. "If only we had so many eyes. Then we could really enjoy this vision," is what the women thought.

Ananta Shesha Naga, the original spiritual master and protector of the Supreme Lord's interests, laments that even with his thousands of mouths he cannot properly glorify God. Since the beginning of time, he has been praising the divine features found only in the original person. Still, he has yet to reach an endpoint. As time and space are both infinite, so is the glorification of the Supreme Lord, who is worshiped today most prominently through the chanting of the holy names: Hare Krishna Hare Krishna, Krishna Krishna, Hare Hare, Hare Rama Hare Rama, Rama Rama, Hare Hare.

VERSE 134

परम प्रीति कुलरीति करहिं गज गामिनि।
नहिं अघाहिं अनुराग भाग भरि भामिनि।।१३४।।

parama prīti kularīti karahiṁ gaja gāmini |
nahiṁ aghāhiṁ anurāga bhāga bhari bhāmini ||134||

"With supreme love, they are doing the family rituals while walking like a great elephant. Not satisfied, the fortunate women continue to fill up with devotion." (134)

Essay - Never Satisfied

Lack of satisfaction with the consumption of something can lead to damaging effects. For instance, if in consuming adult beverages you are not satisfied, pretty soon you will be heavily intoxicated. That is never the real intent, as who wants to be so out of it that they don't remember what they did the next day? Who wants to be made dumb enough to get behind the wheel of a car and risk their own life as well as the lives of others? If you are not satisfied from eating, you will risk gaining weight. You might also jeopardize your health. In all areas, not being satisfied can get you in trouble. With devotion to the Supreme Being, however, the situation turns around. The negative turns into a positive.

Thankfully we have our body to stop us. Eventually the body malfunctions to the point that we can't drink anymore. Our stomach can only hold so much food, so eventually we have to stop eating. On the other hand, a subtle aspect belonging to that same body is what tempted us to overindulge in the first place. The mind previously processed various sense perceptions, and the intelligence, which should have known better, then sanctioned the indulgence in adult beverages. The mind previously gave us information to tell us that overeating wasn't good, and yet the intelligence gave the green light to overeat again.

So are we helpless? The mind and intelligence are part of the body as well. If they can't stop us from overindulging, what will?

Devotion is the only area where overindulgence due to lack of complete satisfaction is a good thing. Devotion is also guided by intelligence. To outside observers, the actions of the devoted soul may seem to be mere sentimentalism. "As passion steers you into an amorous relationship, so the devoted soul leaps into worshiping God with full vim and vigor. The passion will eventually fade, for that is the way of relationships."

Ah, but the inability to be fully satisfied just makes the passion continue elsewhere, showing that the passion is infinite in nature. Intelligence guides the devoted soul too, and in their case the intelligence is accurate. Therefore we know that the devoted souls are the most intelligent. Their past sense perceptions are duly recorded, and the intelligence knows how to properly process them.

If I eat something that is not tasty, the distaste will reach my intelligence. If the next time I reach to eat the same dish, my intelligence should stop me. If it doesn't, it means that the intelligence is defective. Think of it like a computer that doesn't work properly. The GPS device should give us the proper directions to lead us to our intended destination. If it gives us the wrong directions, it means that it isn't working properly.

We can get an idea of how devotion works from the verse referenced above. It comes to us courtesy of the Janaki Mangala, which is authored by Goswami Tulsidas, a famous saint from the medieval period in India. In this verse, women from the bride's side of a wedding are doing the family rituals. The wedding is all set. Sita will wed Rama. Sita is King Janaka's daughter. Rama is King Dasharatha's son.

From the Vedas we learn that Sita Devi is the goddess of fortune. The fortune belongs to her husband, who is the Supreme Lord. They are both personalities, and so they act. In simpler terms, they like to do stuff. The stuff they do is not ordinary, and so it is pleasurable to remember even thousands of years after the fact. Here Sita and Rama are getting married during their time on earth. Theirs is the best wedding to look back on. In weddings today, if there is a video taken it might be shown only when guests come over to the house. Even then the viewing experience is rather boring, as you most likely just sit there and watch people dance the whole time.

The wedding of Sita and Rama is so wonderful that you never get tired of hearing about it. This is especially true if your intelligence is clear. From the behavior of the participants themselves, we see that there is never full satisfaction. In performing the family rituals, the women were walking like great elephants. This indicates that the women were very beautiful in all respects, including in how they walked. We see that they were not satisfied in their actions. In our childhood, perhaps our parents compelled us to attend various religious functions. They seemed boring to us, so we couldn't wait until they were over. In this instance, as there was direct participation for the benefit of Sita and Rama, the women didn't want to stop worshiping. They enjoyed performing these rituals. They were very fortunate to be taking part in this, as their devotion continued to fill up.

There is no such thing as too much devotion. Maharishi Valmiki compares the ears of a devotee to a great ocean. This ocean is filled by rivers represented by stories of the Supreme Lord and His devotees. Though the rivers continually rush in, astonishingly the ocean never swells up; it is impossible to overfill. This analogy was made just with respect to hearing, but it applies to all aspects of devotion.

In this instance, the women were worshiping. In that worship they were not satisfied, giving a valuable lesson for all of humanity. Though today we may not be able to attend the marriage of Sita and Rama, we are not shut out from devotion to them. Though we may not be able to travel to a temple, we are still not prohibited from worshiping. Thanks to the kindness of the Vaishnava saints, we know that all potencies in worship are invested in the holy name itself. From chanting, "Hare Krishna Hare Krishna, Krishna Krishna, Hare Hare, Hare Rama Hare Rama, Rama Rama, Hare Hare," one can have their share of devotion. Since they will never be satisfied with that share, they will continue to chant, constantly filling their devotional reservoir.

VERSE 135

नेगचारु कहँ नागरि गहरु न लावहिं।

निरखि निरखि आनंदु सुलोचनि पावहिं ||१३५||

negacāru kahaṁ nāgari gaharu na lāvahiṁ |
nirakhi nirakhi ānandu sulocani pāvahiṁ ||135||

"When distributing gifts to the people of the town, they are not delaying. Looking again and again at His beautiful eyes, they receive bliss." (135)

Essay - Removing Miserliness

Like staying on a boat that has a leak, when living in Kali Yuga there seems to be a rapidly depleting supply of funds. There is always some bill that needs to be paid. As soon as money is earned, it vanishes. There is the bill for food, the bill for water, the bill for taxes, and so many others. Thus it is not surprising that miserliness would become almost a virtuous quality in such a time period. Know, however, that devotional service cures all ailments. When in the direct presence of the original person, who has beautiful eyes, instead of constantly worrying about the bank balance, fortune is liberally distributed to others.

Why is miserliness bad?

In the Shrimad Bhagavatam it is said that one who is miserly lives a hellish present life and is forced to suffer a hellish afterlife. The first part should make sense if we think about it. If my mind is consumed with thoughts on how to save money, get a deal, get something for free, cheat another person, etc., is that good? What does success in these endeavors really get me? If I am going to worry about something, that something should at least be worthwhile. If I get two doughnuts for the price of one, and in getting that I had to take so much effort, what is the use?

"Generally, the wealth of misers never allows them any happiness. In this life it causes their self-torment, and when they die it sends them to hell." (Lord Krishna, Shrimad Bhagavatam, 11.23.15)

The existence is accurately described as hellish because being consumed with worry is not the right way to live. We go on vacation precisely so that we'll have less worries. The good manager delegates responsibility so that he can stay more focused. If I am to focus on this thing or that all the time, when all those things relate to saving money, I am obviously missing out on life.

The afterlife will be more hellish because nothing in this world really belongs to us. I travel to some destination, find a spot that I like, and then mark the territory as mine. But I haven't really done anything. The spot was there before. It will be there long after I am gone. This isn't to say that the concept of property rights is invalid, but it should be inherently understood what it means to own property. Property is just a collection of matter - earth, water, fire, air and ether. We don't create these elements. When we lay claim to something, it should be known to be on lease from higher authorities. We have to eventually give it up.

One who doesn't understand this mistakenly acts like a miser, and thus they go against the standard code of conduct. Fortune is known as Lakshmi in Sanskrit, and it is named after the goddess of fortune. She has a unique character; she only serves God. She has no other interest. Her service is so pleasing that God keeps her with Him all the time. This is God in His personal form; His impersonal, unmanifest form pervades the entire universe.

"By Me, in My unmanifested form, this entire universe is pervaded. All beings are in Me, but I am not in them." (Lord Krishna, Bhagavad-gita, 9.4)

The personal forms all have the original goddess of fortune or one of her incarnations with them. One who takes fortune and doesn't use it for serving God, who is also known as Narayana, essentially steals Lakshmi. This theft is not good; it leads to bad things in the future. Whether we believe this or not, just see the same concept within our own sphere. If you take something that doesn't belong to you or if you use it the wrong way, will you not meet difficulty eventually? So the same applies to the broader category of property on loan from the Supreme Lord.

Charity is one way to remove miserliness. The different kinds of charity are laid out in the Bhagavad-gita, which is a flawless presentation of Vedic teachings, which are the oldest in existence. Oldest in this case does mean best, as the ancient works from India speak to the constitutional properties of the living entity. Societal conditions evolve and change with time, but core properties of individuals do not. Pizza is pizza, whether it is baked today or in one hundred years. Similarly, the living spirit is the same in qualities whether living today or one thousand years ago. Therefore teachings which address these properties never become outdated.

In the above referenced verse from the Janaki Mangala, we see an instance of where miserliness is tossed aside. Not that the people involved could ever be accused of being miserly, but here they nevertheless do not delay in distributing gifts. The occasion is a sacred wedding, the union of the daughter of King Janaka and the son of King Dasharatha. So many rites and rituals are associated with a traditional wedding, and in this case one aspect involved giving gifts to the people of the town. It is said that charity given to the proper recipient, at the proper time, and with no expectation of return is charity in the mode of goodness.

"That gift which is given out of duty, at the proper time and place, to a worthy person, and without expectation of return, is considered to be charity in the mode of goodness." (Lord Krishna, Bg. 17.20)

We can think of goodness as the right way to do something. Devotion is higher than goodness because it is more than just the right way; it is the best. The right way may land us in a better position materially, whereas the way of devotion sometimes appears to put us in a worse position. In charity in goodness, the understood benefit is that eventually the same money will come back to the donor multiplied by a large factor. In charity in devotion, there is no guarantee of the money ever coming back, but then it doesn't really matter. In devotion there is love for God, which is the most valuable gift to have.

This verse from the Janaki Mangala explains the same truth. After not delaying in distributing gifts, the people in Sita's wedding party received bliss over and over again by looking at the beautiful eyes of Shri Rama, the groom. Rama is Narayana and Sita is Lakshmi. Thus their wedding performed on this earth was a mere formality; the two are always together. In carrying out the wedding, the participants followed protocol. They gave charity when the time called for it. They were not miserly because they had both Sita and Rama there in front of them. Of what use is huge sums of wealth when you have the goddess of fortune in front of you? She is happiest when serving Rama. Would she not then be pleased with those who helped to make the union with Him a reality? If she is pleased, then there is no need to fear over destitution. She provides the devotee whatever they need to carry out their devotion. Here only the eyes were necessary, as the enchanting vision of Shri Rama was there for all to see.

VERSE 136

करि आरती निछावरि बरहि निहारहिं।
प्रेम मगन प्रमदागन तन न सँभारहिं।।136।।

kari āratī nichāvari barahi nihārahiṁ |
prema magana pramadāgana tana na saṁbhārahiṁ ||136||

"They are distributing gifts and doing arati while looking at the groom. They are so overwhelmed with love that they are not concerned about their bodies." (136)

Essay - Touching Up

"She's always late. Whenever we have to go somewhere, I am the one who is ready first. It's habit for me. I plan my day around the specific event of importance. If I have to be somewhere at 7:30 pm, I'll start preparing a few hours in advance. I'd much rather be early to something than late. I don't like the pressure of missing a deadline. To me it's not a game. I'm not trying to limit the amount of time spent waiting by being early. I am more than happy to be the first one there.

"My wife, on the other hand, takes her sweet old time. Not that she walks around here and there; she is preparing the whole time. She's trying on this dress and that. She's applying makeup and then taking it off, only to reapply it. She needs her shoes to match her dress. Her hair has to be a certain way. Everything has to be just right. She would rather be late and look perfect than on time and not so perfect. I can't stand it. One of these days I'm going to leave without her. That will teach her a lesson."

Indeed, a famous American television sitcom portrayed this exact scene in an episode. In the show, the father of the anxious husband had many years prior instituted a rule, wherein if the children weren't in the seats in the car at a certain time, the car would drive off without them. The husband decided to implement this rule one time, with the prior consent of the wife. Lo and behold, she wasn't in the car at the allotted time, and so the husband drove off to the event without her. Needless to say, the wife wasn't too pleased with him.

These are the stereotypes, that men don't pay as much attention to cosmetics and appearance as women do. This is nature's arrangement. Men and women are different in their behavior. They each have their tendencies and characteristics. Knowing that women generally pay more attention to their bodily appearance makes the above referenced verse from the Janaki Mangala especially significant. These were the most beautiful women in the world, and through offering devotion to a particular bridegroom, they completely cast aside attention to their bodily appearance.

The bridegroom in this case was the Supreme Lord, Shri Ramachandra. He appeared on earth because He desired to do so. There were also ancillary concerns relating to nefarious characters dispersed throughout the world. Typically these characters are dealt with through the Lord's impersonal forces. His most potent force that isn't directly under His supervision is time, which is also known as death. No matter how big a person may be, death will eventually knock them down. Thus Rama had no particular reason to knock down foes who were already slated for destruction by death.

He appeared more so to give pleasure to others. Those who would take pleasure in His vision had first priority at seeing Him. This only makes sense. Why waste your time with enemies? They will never turn your way, despite endless well-wishing and insightful words. Better to spend time with those who will appreciate you, for they are deserving of the rewards that accompany your association.

One of the benefits of associating with God is that you pay less attention to things that aren't so important. Maintenance of the body is necessary for keeping the internal vital air intact, but beyond that there is really no difference between a good appearance and a bad one. One person wears an expensive suit, while another wears rags, but the two people are identical in their constitution. The clothes are just part of the physical appearance. They don't change who the person is. The wise don't pay so much attention to appearance. From a simple life, where there is high thinking about the true meaning to an existence, the body looks fine enough.

This sounds well and good in theory, but it must be difficult to implement in practice. When there is such difficulty, it always helps to see the implementation in those we normally wouldn't associate with the practice. If the guy on television selling us a weight loss supplement is super thin and has been so their whole life, we may not be so tempted to buy their product. After all, the person is already in good shape. What need do they have for a weight loss supplement? If, however, we see that the same person was previously overweight, then we know that some difference was made. The overweight person is considered less likely to lose weight, so by seeing that they used a certain product, we can understand that maybe it might work.

In the scene of the above referenced verse from the Janaki Mangala, beautiful women are casting aside concern for their bodies. This is due to the love they feel while worshiping the Supreme Lord. They are offering Him an arati, or welcoming light, and showering Him with gifts. While doing this, they are filled with love. This means that they are not following these rituals as a mere formality. They are very happy to do them, as they get to worship someone who has everything. They get to make offerings to someone who is never in need of anything. Since He is following through on a marriage ceremony, with the intent of joining the daughter of King Janaka, He is compelled to sanction the offering of gifts. In other words, there is nothing He can do to stop the ladies from worshiping Him in such a way.

Through the love they feel for Rama, they immediately cast aside concern for their bodies. Whether their makeup was right, whether their dresses were properly in line, whether their hair was tightly knotted - these were not of concern since they got to love Rama. If an ascetic were to have the same emotion, then it wouldn't be so remarkable. After all, an ascetic has a simple garb. They likely don't have long hair to worry about. Their dress consists of a single cloth. They already give little attention to their body, so to say that worshiping Rama makes them feel less concern isn't that significant.

When you take women who are always attentive to physical appearance and illustrate the same principle of detachment in them, then you get a real idea of how powerful devotion to God is. Rama is God. He is the Supreme Lord with the features drawn out. He is not an old man who is vengeful towards those who defy

His will. Everyone who doesn't love Him in consciousness right now is going against His will. This would mean that God would be the angriest person in existence. In the Vedas, it is said that He is just the opposite. Since He has all transcendental pleasure, He is known as Rama. Since He is all-attractive, He is known as Krishna. On this particular occasion, He would marry Sita, the beloved princess of the town of Mithila. Through that bond Rama would also be known as Janakinatha and Sitapati.

CHAND 17

नहिं तन सम्हारहिं छबि निहारहिं निमिष रिपु जनु रनु जए।
चक्रवै लोचन राम रूप सुराज सुख भोगी भए।।
तब जनक सहित समाज राजहि उचित रुचिरासन दए।
कौसिक बसिष्ठहि पूजि पूजे राउ दै अंबर नए।।१७।।

nahiṁ tana samhārahiṁ chabi nihārahiṁ nimiṣa ripu janu ranu ja'e |
cakravai locana rāma rūpa surāja sukha bhogī bha'e ||
taba janaka sahita samāja rājahi ucita rucirāsana da'e |
kausika basiṣṭhahi pūji pūje rā'u dai ambara na'e ||17||

"Not caring for their bodies, in staring at the beautiful picture it is like the enemy of the blinking of the eye has run away. Their eyes were like the chakravaka bird in staring at Rama's beautiful form; they enjoyed the happiness that comes from having a good ruler." (Chand 17.1)

"Then Janaka offered the king and his entourage beautiful and appropriate seats. Worshiping Vishvamitra and Vashishtha, he offered the king new clothes." (Chand 17.2)

Essay - Conquering Limitations

"I have this important test tomorrow. I've been so busy with my other classes and also my regular responsibilities that I haven't had time to study. And then today I was occupied with so many other things throughout the day. I have no other option: I need to pull an all-nighter. It's going to be tough particularly because I will be so tired. I know I'm fighting a losing battle, but if I have enough coffee and if I find the right setting, I'll be able to stay up all night."

"My body says to stop, but my mind says to keep going. This isn't fair. Why do I get so tired all the time? Why does my body not allow me to have fun? It's not right. I need to work out some more. I need to keep going. My goal is to lose weight. If I just sleep because I'm so tired, that won't help me much. Afterwards, I get really hungry too. How am I supposed to stop eating when my body starts giving me pain in the stomach?"

Eating and sleeping are two aspects basic to an existence. They are present in both the animals and humans alike. Who can conquer over them? They are limitations imposed on the body. No matter the objective we may have, we eventually have to eat and sleep. The student cramming for the exam can try to delay that sleep through artificial means, but eventually their fatigue will catch up with them. The person trying to lose weight may successfully avoid food for a long time, but eventually they will have to eat. They will also be forced to take rest instead of exercise.

Along with the larger limitations like eating and sleeping, there are smaller ones as well. One of them is blinking. It is an involuntary movement of the eyelids. Though we can control blinking if we try, that control only lasts for a short while. This is because we don't have to think about blinking. It happens on its own. It's sort of like the breathing with the lungs or the beating of the heart. We don't have to tell ourselves to breathe. It just happens.

These things are good for us. If we don't blink for too long, the eyes can get dry. This is a common symptom for people who wear contact lenses. Unlike glasses, contacts rest directly on the eyeballs. Therefore when you blink, the reaction is different. It is much easier for the eye to get dry while wearing contact lenses. When the contacts are taken out, the eyes get a chance to catch up, but with prolonged use one can find a situation called "dry eye," which affects vision.

Nevertheless, even with contacts the blinking still occurs. As it is an involuntary movement, when we hear that someone has conquered over blinking through looking at something, we should know that the something is really special. This was the case a long time ago at a marriage ceremony. The people looking at the something were so mesmerized that they stopped blinking for a while. This helped them enjoy the moment; it allowed them to soak up the beauty.

Of course that beauty can only be found in the Supreme Personality of Godhead. He is not a mean person who tells people to do this and that. He is not vengeful against those who ignore Him. The pain from turning away from Him is automatic; sort of like when the hand is put into a fire. The hand is not meant to touch fire. This is just the way things are. If you put your hand in fire, the fire is not to blame and neither is God.

In the same way, when there is residence in a land that sees only death as the culmination to everything, God is not to blame. The residence is a choice, though the residents may not remember having made that choice. Memory alone doesn't determine fact. If I do something stupid and I don't remember being told not to do it, the stupid thing will still hurt me. Someone else may have told me not to do that a long time ago, and if I forgot their sound words of advice, it is my fault, not theirs.

Residence in the material land is caused by ignoring God. To love Him is the constitutional position of the spirit soul. To not love Him is to create a conditional existence. The condition is forgetfulness, and the result is residence in a land that is temporary, where no existence is permanent. If nothing is permanent, it means nothing can live forever. If nothing lives forever, it means everything dies. If everything dies, some will not be so happy from time to time; as they are guaranteed to lose whatever they have. Thus the ultimate result is only misery.

In God's company, there is no misery. Just the opposite occurs, in fact. The eyes are so happy in looking at God that they are able to conquer over blinking. The victors in this instance were women at a marriage ceremony. They were well-wishers to both bride and groom. The bride was Sita Devi, the daughter of King Janaka. The groom was Shri Ramachandra, the sun of the solar race, or the dynasty of kings that started with the sun-god. Shri Ramachandra is also the Supreme Lord in His incarnation as a warrior prince.

In this verse from the Janaki Mangala we are again told how the ladies in the marriage ceremony cast aside concern for their bodies. If we are out of a job or feeling down on our luck, we may not shower on a given day. For women to do this is more rare, as they generally pay more attention to physical appearance. Here the concern was given up due to intense transcendental pleasure. They were so happy to see Rama that they didn't worry about anything else.

In staring at the beautiful picture that was the handsome groom, the enemy known as blinking ran away. It was an enemy in this instance because it would periodically get in the way of the enjoyment of the ladies. It is also said that the eyes of the ladies behaved like chakravaka birds. These birds come to life in the morning, when the sun rises. The analogy is appropriate because Shri Rama is often compared to the sun. Additionally, His family ancestry is tied to the sun-god.

The women felt the enjoyment that comes from having a good ruler, or suraja. If you have a good ruler, you are protected. You know that things will be alright. Everyone is looking for such a ruler, but none can compare to God Himself. The citizens want protection; they want to feel safe. They want to know that economics will be accounted for, that they will have enough to eat and a place to live. They want to know that foreign enemies will be dealt with. If the ruler can take care of such things, the citizens will be happy.

Rama was indeed like the sun, as He dispelled the darkness of doubt that hovered above the marriage ceremony in Janakpur. As Sita's husband was to be determined by a contest of strength, there was no telling who would marry her, if anyone. Rama arrived with His younger brother Lakshmana and the sage Vishvamitra and won the contest, bringing His good protection to all the joyful party.

Essay - For the Sake of Others

One of the reasons you should follow etiquette when you are a public figure is that others will be harmed if you don't. It is natural to make fun of this person or that, to find fault with others, when you are having a casual conversation with friends. In journalist speak, these are known as "off the record" conversations. The content is not fit to print. You say things that you otherwise wouldn't, for people would be watching you and get the wrong idea. A public figure should know better; they should know not to mess up when the lights are on or when the cameras are rolling. In a famous marriage ceremony a long time ago, all the spotlight was on the host, King Janaka. The cameras represented by the eyes of the spectators were rolling and the journalists in the form of the poets had their tape recorders on. Since Janaka is of the purest character, he makes sure never to offend others.

What's the big deal about offending? Isn't that someone else's problem? If I say or do something, shouldn't the other person know that what I speak are just words? Why should I care so much about what they think?

A great man is a leader. This is true whether he knows it or not. If he does know it, he wants to set an ideal example because he knows others will want to follow him. In this sense offending others will cause them to not follow him. And this is more tragic when the offense is made unnecessarily. Think of it this way: If you really respect someone and value their association, you will want to hear what they have to say. If they should constantly criticize your parents and best friends, will that not offend you? If that offense continues for long enough, eventually there will be a breaking point. You will have to choose. Since your parents and friends don't offend you in this way, you will naturally side with them.

Both parties lose out when this choice is made. The respected person misses the opportunity to guide someone else along the proper course. The offended party loses the chance to gain valuable association. Indeed, critics of great leaders will look for any statement that might be deemed offensive to discredit their stature. If the critics can find anything that was said off-camera, during a casual conversation, or during a speech intended for a smaller audience, they will bring it to the limelight when the time is right. This way others will think: "Oh, I don't like that person. Did you hear what he said about such and such? He's no good."

"One who is thus transcendentally situated at once realizes the Supreme Brahman. He never laments nor desires to have anything; he is equally disposed to every living entity. In that state he attains pure devotional service unto Me." (Lord Krishna, Bhagavad-gita, 18.54)

The easiest way to avoid such offenses is to be of pure character. One who sees the spirit soul within every living being is equally disposed. He neither hankers nor laments. In that state he takes up devotional service, or bhakti-yoga, because that service is meant to please the origin of all spiritual beings. Such information is presented to us in the Bhagavad-gita, a famous Vedic text. That text provides the theoretical information, and the practical implementation is found in the example of King Janaka of Mithila.

Janaka was on this earth a long time ago. There were many kings named Janaka in his family ancestry, and so he was particularly known as Shiradhvaja, for he found his beautiful daughter Sita while ploughing a field. Though he was known as a Brahman-realized soul [someone who sees the spiritual equality of all living beings], he is today more famous for being the father of Sita. Sita is a special lady; she is the eternal consort of Lord Rama, who is a divine incarnation of the original Personality of Godhead.

In the above referenced verse from the Janaki Mangala, we get further accounts of Sita's wedding to Rama. It took place in Janaka's kingdom. Here we are in the middle of the actual marriage ceremony, and we see that all protocol is being followed. Janaka is the host, so he brings King Dasharatha and his entourage to the ceremony and offers them appropriate seats. Dasharatha is Rama's father. He had travelled from Ayodhya to attend the marriage ceremony of his beloved son Rama.

Janaka then worshiped Vishvamitra and Vashishtha, two great sages. Vashishtha was the family priest in Ayodhya. He was Dasharatha's counselor as well as Rama's. Rama's three younger brothers also took instruction from Vashishtha. Vishvamitra was Rama's teacher particularly in the advanced military arts. He gave special mantras to Rama and His younger brother Lakshmana and took protection from them in the forest. It was at Vishvamitra's direction that Rama ended up in Janaka's city, where a contest to determine Sita's husband was taking place. Janaka also offered brand new clothing to Dasharatha.

If Janaka had failed to do any of these things, he would have committed offenses. The many spectators would have noticed those offenses. So would have the devoted poets who were set to immortalize the events in sacred texts like the Ramayana. Tulsidas is one of those poets, and he can travel back in time with his mind to relive the event. He does so not to find fault. Even if he did, he would not find any. Knowing full well the character of Janaka, the poet takes great delight in relaying Janaka's behavior to all the world.

Such attention to etiquette was part of what made Janaka worthy of having Sita as his daughter. His devotion to God drove his actions, and so we see that one of the symptoms of devotion is careful attention towards avoiding offenses. If you love God's wife, you will love God as well. You will love God's father as well. Though the Lord has no father, in His descents to the material land He assigns various elevated living entities the roles of mother, father, friend, and so forth. More than anything, those associates with Rama are devotees, and so Janaka made sure never to offend them. He thus set the ideal example.

VERSE 137

देत अरघ रघुबीरहि मंडप लै चलीं।
करहिं सुमंगल गान उमगि आनँद अलीं।।137।।

deta aragha raghubīrahi maṇḍapa lai calīṁ |
karahiṁ sumaṅgala gāna umagi ānaṁda alīṁ ||137||

"Offering arghya water, taking Rama to the mandapa they went. There the sakhis sang auspicious songs with excitement and bliss." (137)

Essay - The Best Friend's Wedding

Sita's friends strongly approved of her marriage to Rama. They witnessed His accomplishment in the contest in King Janaka's assembly. They saw that He was the only person capable of lifting the mighty bow of Lord Shiva. They saw His amazing beauty, which was apparently a contradiction. How could such delicate features reside in a person with more strength than the fiercest bow-warriors in the world? How could such strength belong to someone with so much compassion that He would leave home at a young age to protect innocent forest-dwelling sages? The only way to answer these questions was to get to know Him better, a chance they received through their best friend's wedding.

If your best friend is marrying the wrong person, you may feel compelled to say something. "Hey man, this girl is not right for you. You are kind and sweet, while she is mean and manipulative. She will walk all over you. You don't really like her anyway. You're doing this for all the wrong reasons. You will come to regret this decision." Another friend might want to say, "He is totally the wrong guy. He is unfaithful and unclean. He will never appreciate you. You will be miserable having to wake up next to him day after day."

In such instances, though the temptation is strong to offer an objection, one likely won't be forthcoming. If in the ensuing session, the friend decides to go ahead with the marriage anyway, there will be resentment. After all, they will spend more time with the new spouse than with you. If they remain friends with you, it could hurt their marriage. If they choose in favor of the spouse and lose your friendship, they at least can survive on a daily basis. So rather than lose your friend, you remain silent, keeping your objections to yourself. At the wedding, because of your misgivings you won't be able to celebrate so much. You won't be into it emotionally.

In Sita's wedding, we see that the friends were so in favor of the chosen groom that they happily sang auspicious songs. They first worshiped the groom with arghya water, which is an essential aspect of deity worship. Offering such water is a great sign of respect, so much so that it is used when worshiping God in a temple on a daily basis. Even if one isn't at a formal temple, the same water can be offered in the home. The value of bhakti-yoga, or devotional service, is so high that no one is shut out from it. Regardless of what you may or may not know about the Vedas, the ancient scriptures of India, you can always offer something as simple as water to the Lord and have Him gladly accept it.

"If one offers Me with love and devotion a leaf, a flower, fruit, or water, I will accept it." (Lord Krishna, Bhagavad-gita, 9.26)

Here the person worshiped with water is actually God Himself, an incarnation of the Supreme Lord. Sita is His eternal consort. Thus Sita's friends are not ordinary souls, though they played well-wishers to a princess on earth. After offering water, they escorted Rama to the mandapa, the tent-like structure to house the various rituals of the wedding ceremony. The friends sang songs with full bliss, or ananda. This means that they were into the wedding. They sang happily because they were themselves happy. They knew that Sita was getting the best husband. Since they were real well-wishers, they were thrilled over her good fortune. They took her marriage to be like theirs, for that is how dear she was to them.

Your friends also give an indication of the kind of person you are. Rama and His family could thus tell that Sita was pretty special. Janaki, which means the daughter of King Janaka, had friends who were very respectful towards Rama. She had friends who were in favor of the wedding taking place. Since Rama is full of good qualities, this meant that Janaki's friends were very wise. Not clouded by the ignorance of the material world, which causes one to lament over another's gain and rejoice at their loss, they could see Rama properly. They could recognize His divine features. Though He did not speak much, they knew that He could protect their beloved Janaki. Though He was not brash, they knew that He would not be shy in defending her honor.

They also knew that by serving Him, Janaki would meet the best end in life. The partnership of their marriage would be beneficial to both. Rama would get a beautiful queen who would support Him in His exercise of religious duties. Years later He would practically say as much. In thanking Sita one time for her good counsel offered with affection, Rama made sure to describe her as a sadharma-charini, which means a chaste wife who helps the husband in his adherence to dharma, or religiosity.

"My dear beautiful wife, what you have said is befitting the occasion and also indicative of the greatness of your family heritage. You are dearer to Me than My life, for you are My companion in the performance of religious duties." (Lord Rama speaking to Sita Devi, Valmiki Ramayana, Aranya Kand, 10.21)

A marriage is meant to be in dharma and not kama. A marriage in kama is equivalent to a standard amorous relationship, which even the animals engage in. Dharma is unique to the human species, and its range of applicability is full. Dharma is the source of marriage, and not the other way around. Sita and Rama were always mindful of dharma, though as the goddess of fortune and God Himself they had no need to be. The sakhis were mindful of dharma as well, and they accepted the duty of welcoming Rama with great enthusiasm, making Janaki's wedding even more memorable.

VERSE 138

बर बिराज मंडप महँ बिस्व बिमोहइ।
ऋतु बसंत बन मध्य मदनु जनु सोहइ।।138।।

bara birāja maṇḍapa mahaṁ bisva bimoha'I |
ṛtu basanta bana madhya madanu janu soha'I ||138||

"Everyone is enchanted by the groom sitting inside the mandapa, looking so beautiful, like Kamadeva in the middle of the woods during the spring season."
(138)

Essay - Painting Assignment

Let's say you're taking a painting class in college. You have some artistic ability, and you want to see how far you can go. If you can refine your skills through the instruction of those who are already talented, you can get the most out of the wonderful gift that God gave you. Now let's say that one of your assignments is to draw a beautiful person sitting in the woods. These two points combine for the lone stipulation. The rest is up to your imagination.

The person can be anyone. The range of possibilities in this area is infinitely vast. The scene of the forest is a little more limited. You have only a few options. You can choose either day or night. You can choose a heavily wooded area or one that is close to outlets like ponds, rivers and pathways. The most important decision will likely relate to the season. The forest is filled with life. The trees, plants and flowers are living entities in bodies that are incapable of movement. These forms do take birth, remain for some time, and then eventually die. Thus they exhibit the same symptoms as other living beings.

Let's say that you decide to use a beautiful man for your person. He is fresh in his youth. He has features which are attractive to both male and female alike. Your painting will be viewed by all audiences, so you are not trying to slant the content towards a particular viewpoint. Now that you have the idea of the beautiful youth, where is he going to sit? What is the background going to look like?

The forest is most beautiful during the springtime. The other seasons present their own unique pictures, but the spring gives all signs of life. It is like the infancy of the human being. The young child is full of innocence and a zest for life. They are new to the world, and so there is so much potential for good things. Similarly, in the forest in the spring the flowers start to blossom, creating a wonderful aroma. The setting is so nice that the moving creatures start to happily frolic about. The peacocks, the deer, and the parrots enjoy the springtime the most.

If one were to look at a painting that had the beautiful youth set in the springtime of the most beautiful forest, all the eyes of the world surely would be enchanted. This is the analogy used by Goswami Tulsidas in the above referenced verse from the Janaki Mangala to describe how Shri Rama looked when He entered the mandapa at His marriage ceremony. He was a youth of the perfect age. He was set to get married, and His beautiful features were incomprehensible. The eyes of the admirers kept glued to Rama's form precisely to try to understand how one human being could be so beautiful.

The mandapa looked like the forest in the springtime. The family members and well-wishers from both sides accounted for the life of that forest. The sun is what causes the beautiful lotus flowers to open up, and in this case Shri Rama was the sun to the creatures of the forest that was the mandapa, which is a canopy-like structure under which the majority of the marriage rituals in the Vedic tradition take place.

Shri Rama is the Supreme Personality of Godhead in an incarnation form. He is the original brain behind the magnificent creation. The lotus flower, the peacock feather, the sweetness of the birds humming - all these come from God originally. He is the painter with the greatest artistic talent combined with an unmatched imagination. It was not surprising, then, that He created a wonderful scene with Himself situated in the center. Kamadeva is known to be the most beautiful living entity to one who understands the Vedic tradition. Kamadeva is the equivalent of Cupid, but he is still a living entity with a temporary body.

Rama is Bhagavan, which means He has all opulences all the time. His body never deteriorates. His beauty therefore is incomparable, or anupama. The reference to Kamadeva is made simply as a way to help us understand how beautiful Shri Rama is. That same beauty extends to His glories, His fame, and His holy names, which the devotees always chant: Hare Krishna Hare Krishna, Krishna Krishna, Hare Hare, Hare Rama Hare Rama, Rama Rama, Hare Hare.

VERSE 139

कुल बिबहार बेद बिधि चाहिय जहँ जस।
उपरोहित दोउ करहिं मुदित मन तहँ तस।।139।।

kula bibahāra beda bidhi cāhiya jaham̐ jasa |
uparohita do'u karahim̐ mudita mana taham̐ tasa ||139||

"All the rituals were done exactly in accordance with family tradition and the Vedas. Both priests here and there did everything with a happy mind." (139)

Essay - Beyond Reproach

Bhagavan is the Sanskrit term to describe the entity most of us refer to as God. It is a compound word that means one who possesses all fortunes. Someone is fortunate if they escape danger in the nick of time. One is fortunate if they get good things without having to strive for them. The more complete definition of "fortunate" spreads to the categories of beauty, wealth, strength, fame, wisdom and renunciation. One who possesses any of these opulences is considered fortunate. Indeed, if someone is wealthy alone and lacking all the other opulences, they get so much attention in society.

God has all of these opulences. He doesn't have some of them some of the time, either. He isn't beautiful one day and renounced the next. He isn't wise one time and then stupid another. He holds these opulences all the time. And by the way, He holds them to the fullest degree. The jocks in school may have gotten all the girls, but they likely weren't very smart. The nerds could do well in physics, but in beauty they weren't much of a match. The person who is renounced, living peacefully in a remote area, doesn't have much wealth. The wealthy man has a difficult time coping without someone to meet his every demand at every second. In this way we see that the opulences are often contradictory; possessing one means lacking another.

Not so with the Supreme Lord, who is thus known as Bhagavan. Since He holds all opulences simultaneously and to the fullest degree, He has no need to follow any protocol. I tell my kids to study in school so that they can get a good job when they grow up. I tell my employees to arrive to work on time every day so that the business runs smoothly. If they fail to do these things, there are negative consequences. When you are the most fortunate person, however, you can skip whatever function you want and not have it affect you.

In the case of Shri Rama, Bhagavan gives extra attention to protocol. This is Rama's special mercy. As an incarnation of Bhagavan described in the Vedas, the original books of knowledge of the world, Rama doesn't need to follow anyone or anything. If He fails to listen to someone, by definition He cannot be hurt. He still follows protocol better than anyone else, just to set a good example. That example spreads to all of His activities, including His marriage to the beautiful daughter of King Janaka.

In the above referenced verse from the Janaki Mangala, which is the wonderful poem of Goswami Tulsidas glorifying that sacred marriage, we see that all the rituals were done in accordance with the Vedas and family tradition. Deference to each can be logically understood. The family tradition is what brings us to the current position. Even if our family happens to be almost animal-like, there is still some tradition that is followed. Maybe everyone meets together on Thanksgiving. Maybe everyone exchanges gifts on Christmas. These may be small traditions, but they are important nonetheless, as they set a moral standard that serves to better the individuals growing up in the family.

The Vedas are the ultimate authority, so anytime you follow them it is to your benefit. The Vedas specifically address the needs of the soul. As every living being is a soul at the core, the Vedas benefit everyone. They are not just for the fruitive workers looking to make money. They are not just for the yogis looking to find mystic perfection. They are not just for the human beings, either. The humans are the only ones capable of adhering to Vedic principles, but in so doing the rest of society, including the protected lower species, are benefitted simultaneously.

One of the quickest ways to destroy a stable societal structure is to remove family traditions. The surefire way to destroy family traditions is to have a society filled with unwanted children. A famous warrior once worried over this possibility. His thoughts are recorded in the Bhagavad-gita, which is itself a Vedic text. With wanted children, which are produced through following the Vedas and family tradition, you help to ensure that the family structure remains solid in future generations.

"Due to the evil deeds of the destroyers of family tradition, all kinds of community projects and family welfare activities are devastated." (Arjuna, Bhagavad-gita, 1.42)

The institution of marriage is itself rooted in the Vedic tradition. Family tradition then adds little nuances here and there. In ancient times, each family had their own worshipable deity. These were authorized divine figures; they were not made up on a whim. In the marriage of Sita and Rama, the deities of both families were worshiped. Each tradition specific to each family was also followed. Such traditions are not completely necessary, but by showing respect, the individuals remain centered around godly life. They realize that marriage is meant to be in dharma, or religiosity, and not kama, or sense gratification. The animals live in kama and they don't have anything like a marriage.

The two family priests, Shatananda from Janaka's side and Vashishtha from Dasharatha's side, performed these rituals with happy minds. They went through all the different aspects, taking care of things here and there in the mandapa, the structure under which the ceremony took place. Since everything was done properly, the marriage ceremony of Sita and Rama was beyond reproach. No one could point out a flaw in what was done. Neither was there a flaw in either of the participants, who are perfect beings, ideal for being worshiped. Indeed, any couple who keeps the image of Sita and Rama with them throughout life will have the best marriage in dharma.

VERSE 140

बरहि पूजि नृप दीन्ह सुभग सिंहासन।
चलीं दुलहिनिहि ल्याइ पाइ अनुसासन।।140।।

barahi pūji nṛpa dīnha subhaga sinhāsana |
calīṁ dulahinihi lyā'i pā'i anusāsana ||140||

"The king worshiped the groom and offered an auspicious throne for sitting. They then gave the order to the sakhis to bring the bride." (140)

Essay - Worshiping the Groom

In modern times, where men and women freely intermingle and marriages are therefore often determined on mutual consent of the two parties, the groom-to-be naturally feels hesitant to approach the father of the bride. The father knows what young men have on their minds, and so they can predict how the prospective groom intends to enjoy with the daughter. Thus the boy naturally fears the contempt of the father, whose job it has been to protect his daughter throughout life. The groom-to-be treads lightly when in the company of the father of the girl, making sure that nothing is done to offend him.

Keeping this behavior in mind, it is strange to hear how in ancient times the groom would be worshiped by the father of the bride. This is exactly what is described in the above referenced verse from the Janaki Mangala. The father was King Janaka and the groom Lord Rama, the prince of Ayodhya. From the Vedas we learn that Rama is God, the Supreme Lord in an incarnation form. Therefore Janaka's worship of Him shouldn't be so strange. But actually such worship is customary in a Vedic marriage ceremony.

The daughter is given over to the groom. It is like a transfer of ownership, with the responsibility for providing protection shifted to the groom. It is a major gamble on the part of the father. Think of your most cherished possession. Think of that object or person that you treasure the most. Now imagine having to part with it. What will you do? Will you not be overprotective? Will you not go the extra mile to make sure that the new person assuming control is full of good attributes?

If you are virtuous, you follow the proper code of conduct without thinking about it; it is second nature to you. If you are lusty, then your mind goes the opposite way. Driven by your desires for eating, drinking, gambling, or sex life, you cast aside what you know to be right in order to get enjoyment in the short-term. Maybe if you want to harm yourself in this way it is fine, but I don't want my loved one getting in the middle of it. If you can't control your desires and thus can't take care of yourself, how are you going to take care of my cherished object?

On the other hand, if you are virtuous I can trust that you will know what to do. I can put my faith in you because you have proven in the past to be trustworthy. Such was the case with Rama. Previously He set the right example by following the orders of His teachers in Ayodhya, where King Dasharatha took great enjoyment from having Rama as a son. Since Dasharatha belonged to the Raghu dynasty of kings, one of Rama's names was Raghunandana, which means one who gives pleasure to the Raghu dynasty.

Rama retained His virtue when He was away from home as well. He protected the powerful sage Vishvamitra from attacking night-rangers. He never asked for anything in return. Sometimes we have to give remuneration to our kids for doing chores. They won't want to work otherwise. Rama never asked for anything and neither did His younger brother Lakshmana. They were completely virtuous; they followed the right path for the sake of doing things properly. They had trust in their gurus, which consisted of their elders and teachers.

Janaka's most cherished possession was his daughter Sita. She too was virtuous; a pure lotus flower in both vision and character, perfectly matched for Rama. Janaka didn't choose Rama as the groom, however. Rama won a contest of strength. It so happened that Providence brought Rama into the family, and Janaka was very happy about this. It was protocol to worship the groom because such a gesture would convey the importance of the daughter. Janaka worshiped Rama as a matter of etiquette and also as a way to please Him. If Rama is pleased then He will do anything for you.

Worshiping Rama's lotus feet just one time eliminates all past sinful reactions. From simply touching those feet the cursed wife of Gautama Rishi returned to his side. The boatman, Kevat, was afraid to touch those feet because of what had happened with Ahalya. He therefore washed those feet before allowing Rama onto his boat. Sita was also afraid to touch those feet for the same reason, for she would rather be by Rama's side than leave Him for the heavenly realm.

Janaka worshiped those feet and retained eternal devotion to them. As an added bonus, Rama always protected Sita. Even when she was in danger later on, Rama did not let her go. He put up a massive fight, one that the evil king of Lanka never expected. Rama rounded up uncivilized forest dwellers to help Him. He did not care who or what came with Him; He was going to do whatever it took to rescue Sita. From the time of Janaka's worship Rama vowed to protect Sita, and so that worship did not go in vain.

From this tradition of worshiping the groom by the father, we get another reminder of how in Vedic culture the emphasis is always on humility. When there is cause for celebration, charity is distributed. Rather than celebrate good news by buying something for yourself, make sure that others are benefitted first. When there is the occasion of the marriage, rather than instill fear in the groom, worship him so that your daughter will be protected for life. Better still it is to worship the Supreme Lord all the time. Through the occasion of the marriage of his daughter, Janaka got this opportunity, and he made the most of it.

VERSE 141

जुबति जुत्थ महँ सीय सुभाइ बिराजइ।
उपमा कहत लजाइ भारती भाजइ।।141।।

jubati jut'tha mahaṁ sīya subhā'i birāja'i |
upamā kahata lajā'i bhāratī bhāja'i ||141||

"Sitting amidst the group of young ladies, Sita looked so beautiful. In trying to compare that beauty, even Sarasvati Devi shyly runs away." (141)

Essay - Blessed in Speech

In the Vedic tradition, Sarasvati is known as the goddess of speech. One may be proud of their writing ability, but they should know that it doesn't come on its own. Without even mentioning divine figures, to be skilled in writing one obviously has to learn. They have to learn how to communicate in the language, first of all. They have to learn the alphabet and its proper use. They have to attempt to describe events and emotions first before perfecting the art.

When success does come, it only makes sense to appreciate those who helped you. When watching awards ceremonies honoring professional athletes, it's not uncommon to see parents and coaches thanked. The athlete is the one receiving the award, but they are not so foolish as to think that they suddenly developed great ability on their own. In cases where they can't think of who to properly thank, they pay homage to God, for they know that their ability is an opulence, a sign of good fortune.

In the verse quoted above from the Janaki Mangala, there is an irony of sorts. Goswami Tulsidas wrote the Janaki Mangala as a way to glorify God and one of His most famous pastimes. The title translates to the "auspiciousness of the daughter of King Janaka." That auspiciousness particularly related to the daughter's marriage. The groom in this case was God, the Supreme Lord in a famous incarnation. The incarnations are the same as the original; just the appearance and behavior may be more finely shaped. The incarnation doesn't mean that God is a human being, a fish, a boar, or a half-man/half-lion. The incarnation means that such forms can be transcendental when on the Personality of Godhead, for the material of the covering is actually non-different from the storehouse of spiritual qualities. Spiritual and material is only a dichotomy for anyone who is not God.

Anytime one is successful in glorifying God in written word, it should be understood that they have received the blessings of Sarasvati Devi. She is the wife of Lord Brahma, who is the first created living entity. We are all brothers and sisters because we can all trace our ancestry back to Brahma. Even if we've lost track of who our relatives were four and five generations ago, since Brahma created everyone, we at least know that we are related to him.

As Sarasvati Devi is related to Brahma, she accepts his interests as her own. Brahma is a devotee of God; he understands that God exists and that there is a purpose to body, mind and speech. Sarasvati Devi is specifically the goddess of speech and learning. Students growing up in India often pray to her for success. Since the material is ultimately not separated from the spiritual, even the material sound of speech is meant to be dovetailed with spiritual activity. The attempts of Goswami Tulsidas show this, as all his works are glorifications of God.

"[obeisance to]Guru, Ganesha, Shiva, Parvati, Brihaspati, Sarasvati, Shesha, Shukadeva, Vedas, and the sincere and intelligent saints." (Janaki Mangala, 1)

Sarasvati Devi obviously showered blessings upon him. In his other works, including the Janaki Mangala also, he specifically seeks her favor at the outset, as do many other famous Vaishnavas, or devotees of the personal God, in their works. Because she favored him, Tulsidas was able to write the Janaki Mangala, which included the verse above. In this verse it is said that Sarasvati herself cannot compare the beauty of Rama's wife sitting amidst a group of young girls to anyone else. Because of her inability, she flees in embarrassment or shyness. What this means is that Sarasvati herself enabled Tulsidas to write a verse that says Sarasvati, the goddess of speech, is incapable of describing Sita.

This is a very nice compliment paid to Sita, and it is not an insult to Sarasvati. Actually, it is not even a deficiency. If we are deficient a certain mineral in our body, eventually an unhealthy condition might arise. If I am deficient the funds necessary to purchase a house, I am somewhat hurt. A deficiency is typically taken as a negative; one wants something and they either don't have enough of it or are lacking it completely.

Sarasvati's inability to accurately compare Sita's beauty to anything else means that no glorification of Sita is ever complete. I could spend the entire day writing eloquent poetry in praise of Rama's beautiful wife. I could go on and on about her virtues. I could keep my mind immersed in her pastime of dutifully staying by her husband and following Him into the wilderness. I could speak for hours and hours about how she is well versed in the Vedas and knows right and wrong better than anyone else. I could write pages and pages about how happy she makes Rama with her devotion.

Even after doing that, I still wouldn't properly describe her. Sarasvati Devi, who is herself expert in all speech from all languages, is too shy to even try. Nevertheless, she and devoted saints like Tulsidas eventually cast aside that shyness for their own good. Their courage also benefits others, as hearing about God and His devotees is a blessing to the ears. Here Sita did stand out amidst the ladies, for it was her wedding after all. She is always with Rama, and on this day they joined in an official ceremony. That wonderful day could not be compared to any other, but thankfully Tulsidas, utilizing the blessings of Sarasvati Devi, took the time to try to describe it.

VERSE 142

दुलह दुलहिनिन्ह देखि नारि नर हरषहिं।
छिनु छिनु गान निसान सुमन सुर बरषहिं।।१४२।।

dulaha dulahininha dekhi nāri nara haraṣahiṁ |
chinu chinu gāna nisāna sumana sura baraṣahiṁ ||142||

"Looking at the bride and groom, the men and women were so happy. Again and again, songs and drums played and the demigods rained down flowers." (142)

Essay - Again and Again

Of course everyone was happy. Why wouldn't they be? Two people were about to embark on the journey of a lifetime. They had each other as support. This world can be a lonely place. Even if you are surrounded by other people, if in your mind you don't connect with anyone, you might as well be living in a secluded cave. The two people getting married weren't ordinary, and so the celebration for their nuptials wasn't ordinary, either. Though so many were looking on, each held a unique affection for the couple.

The affection is actually unique in all of us. The body we have right now does not represent our true form. It doesn't take a rocket scientist to figure this out. Take a picture of yourself right now, store it somewhere, and then look at it again in ten years. The same picture will seem very old. Right now it doesn't seem old at all. It is the present. It is what has just occurred. Through nothing else but the passage of time the same image will seem outdated in the future.

This means that this body is destined to be outdated. As it will expire at some point, it cannot represent our true identity. The difference between the two points in time of comparison for the picture is the change in bodies. The individual is still the same. It is the same "I" when looking at the picture. That "I" is thus constant. In the two images the "I" is surrounded by different collections of matter. You put on one shirt today and a different one tomorrow. The shirt doesn't define you. You define you.

That "you" has an eternal form, known as a svarupa in Sanskrit. In that svarupa there is a relationship to the original spirit, who is more commonly referred to as

God. As Lord Chaitanya Mahaprabhu, a famous saint from the medieval period in India, says, the svarupa of the living entity is servant of Krishna, or God. He doesn't say exactly what that form looks like. He doesn't say that the svarupa is identical in appearance for everyone. The mindset, or consciousness, is identical and it manifests in service.

Service can take place in different moods. You can serve someone as a friend. You can also serve someone as a lover. You can offer service by giving protection. You can serve someone just by appreciating them. The svarupa of the living entity can follow any one of these kinds of service. The mood is not forced upon everyone. Every individual has their original mood, and when in the presence of God they get to act on it.

In the scene referenced above, many men and women are happily looking at the bride and groom, Sita and Rama. Rama is God and Sita is His energy. God is masculine because the Vedas say so. The Vedas are the original scriptural tradition of the world. The claim of masculinity is supported through a scientific explanation. God is the original purusha, or enjoyer. Purusha dominates. The enjoyed is known as prakriti. The energy of God is meant to be enjoyed by Him, so naturally in its purest form it would be feminine.

We see males and females all around us, and so in various circles there are dominant living entities and those which are dominated. Ultimately everyone is dominated by the Supreme Enjoyer. This means that ultimately everyone is prakriti, which is meant to be enjoyed by God. He takes enjoyment through friendship, service in reverence, and parental affection as well. This means that the prakriti living entity doesn't necessarily have to assume a female body in the svarupa.

Here both men and women were in their forms fit for devotion. The men got to serve through appreciation. They watched as Sita and Rama joined in an official ceremony. Some took delight as parents and caretakers. Some took delight as friends. Some took delight as dependents. The same held true for the women there. There were friends of Sita who took care of her every need since childhood. Sita was the king's daughter, affectionately known as Janaki as well, for whom the poem by Goswami Tulsidas is named.

Some worshiped God by singing songs over and over again. Those who were more rhythmically inclined played drums. Not everyone has to sing in order to please God. If you play a basic percussion instrument to accompany singing of the glories of God, then you are equally as valuable in service. In sankirtana parties where the chanting of the holy names, "Hare Krishna Hare Krishna, Krishna Krishna, Hare Hare, Hare Rama Hare Rama, Rama Rama, Hare Hare," takes place, not everyone accepts the same role. Sometimes one person is playing the harmonium, while another is playing the karatalas, or hand cymbals. Sometimes the members switch roles to experience a different taste. In all respects they are engaged in serving God from the position of prakriti.

Even those who are extremely powerful in the material sense get to worship God through their post. The demigods are akin to saints of the Christian tradition. They can grant special favors when worshiped properly. They can give money, wealth, fame, beauty, learning, etc. Here they are serving in their desired capacity, that of showing reverence. They rained down flowers from the sky. It may seem like a trivial service, but imagine how great it would be if suddenly flowers fell from the sky as you were getting married. You would certainly appreciate the people responsible for it.

Sita and Rama were of a beauty without compare. Not even Sarasvati Devi, the goddess of speech, could accurately describe it. All the participants, whatever their level of ability and whatever their status in society, were included in the celebration. They got to appreciate the divine couple in their unique way, showing that love of God, bhakti-yoga, is the only religion for one and all.

VERSE 143

लै लै नाउँ सुआसिनि मंगल गावहिं।
कुँवर कुँवरि हित गनपति गौर पुजावहिं।।143।।

lai lai nā'um̐ su'āsini maṅgala gāvahim̐ |
kum̐vara kum̐vari hita ganapati gaura pujāvahim̐ ||143||

"Taking the names of each, the married women sang auspicious songs. They worshiped Gauri and Ganesha for the wellbeing of the prince and princess." (143)

Essay - Making the Ideal Song

You don't need much to practice bhakti-yoga. You don't need a yoga studio, an introductory membership that allows you to attend an unlimited number of classes in the first thirty days, a yoga mat, a bottle of water, an ability to endure one hundred degree heat for over an hour, or a lot of money. You don't need ability in exercise, dance, or advanced breath control. You don't even have to be that intelligent. All you need is consciousness, which is shown in the ability to think. A simple way of thinking is singing, which is something most people can do.

Bhakti-yoga translates to mean "the linking of the individual soul with the Supreme Soul in a mood of love and devotion." That is the actual meaning, not an interpretation. Yoga does not have to be about exercise or physical health. It does not have to be about wearing tight outfits and straining your body. That kind of yoga is more technically known as hatha-yoga or ashtanga-yoga. Since the term yoga is still there, there is the ultimate objective of linking with the Supreme Soul, the higher consciousness. That consciousness pervades the entire space; it is not limited to the local area. My consciousness only resides within me; no one else is privy to it. The same goes for your consciousness. The Supreme Consciousness is everywhere, and it belongs to a singular entity who is separate from both you and me.

Just as love for others is not restricted to a specific implementation, so the yoga of love and devotion does not have strict requirements. It is the attitude which matters most. And since it is the only yoga that has no pre-qualifications, it is the superior form of yoga. Since yoga is above any kind of material activity, bhakti-yoga is the supreme occupation. The same bhakti-yoga often goes by other names such as bhagavata-dharma and sanatana-dharma, both of which are sometimes mistakenly taken to mean religion. Indeed, these meanings serve as a way to find some equivalent to the modern term of religion, which is a kind of faith. Yoga is as much about faith as are gravity and the sunlight; namely there is only a marginal dependence on it. Yoga is a scientific discipline and so it applies to everyone.

You can practice bhakti-yoga through eating, sleeping, playing, exercising, reading and the like, but it is still the consciousness that requires altering. Therefore no one specific activity is a necessity; anything that changes consciousness to the point of creating the link to the Supreme Consciousness with love and devotion suffices for bhakti-yoga. From the above referenced verse from the Janaki Mangala we see how simple bhakti-yoga is to practice and how the attitude of the people practicing it is so heartwarming.

Here married women are singing auspicious songs at a wedding. They are already married, so they are singing of the auspiciousness of the couple that has just joined. The auspicious songs are created on the fly using the names of the bride and groom. This simple act constitutes bhakti-yoga, as the names of the individuals are Sita and Rama respectively. Sita is the name of the incarnation of the perfect energy of God and Rama is the name of the incarnation of God specific to the time in question.

We are also part of the energy of God, but we are not always perfect. Sometimes we choose in favor of personal conquests. We sometimes want to only think about where to eat, what to play, what to watch, and with whom to enjoy. In these pursuits, we forget God entirely. Therefore we are not always pleasing to Him. The perfect energy, however, is always engaged in bhakti-yoga. They are so immersed in love and devotion to God that they don't even know what the term bhakti-yoga means. They only have one way of living, and it is not a choice for them. If they didn't love God, they would cease to exist, like the fish out of water.

Singing a song is a nice way to pass the time and improve one's mood. So what exactly makes a good song? Is it the melody? Is it the words? Is it the arrangement, such as the shifting of time signatures to create a dynamic sequence? Is it the ability to change levels of energy so that the listener will want to go on the same emotional ride over and over again?

Actually, for the perfect song all you need is the names of God and His energy. Here the names are Sita and Rama, and the people who created the songs were more than happy to continue to sing them. The same names have been happily sung in songs ever since. Sita and Rama are so kind that they give us other names as well. The name Hare also describes Sita, and Krishna tells of Rama's original form as an all-attractive youth. So just by singing a mantra like, "Hare Krishna Hare Krishna, Krishna Krishna, Hare Hare, Hare Rama Hare Rama, Rama Rama, Hare Hare," you make the perfect song.

The names of Gauri and Ganesha are typically taken by those who are still desirous of enjoyment outside of God's association. Gauri and Ganesha are divine figures, but they fit the needs of those who want protection from the threefold miseries of life and the removal of obstacles. When in bhakti-yoga, the focus shifts towards God and His perfect energy. At the same time, the mood of the devotee is so nice that Gauri and Ganesha are not forgotten. Their abilities to grant rewards are shifted towards the divine couple. The married women here prayed for the wellbeing of Sita and Rama, and since Gauri and Ganesha give rewards to even the materialists, they were more than happy to answer the call of the devoted ladies who sang the perfect songs.

VERSE 144

अगिनि थापि मिथिलेस कुसोदक लीन्हेउ।
कन्या दान बिधान संकलप कीन्हेउ॥144॥

agini thāpi mithilesa kusodaka līnhe'u |
kan'yā dāna bidhāna saṅkalapa kīnhe'u ||144||

"Going in front of the fire, King Janaka took kusha grass and water. According to ritual, he made the oath and gave away his daughter." (144)

Essay - As Fire As My Witness

Everything at Sita's wedding was done according to tradition and the Vedas. Nothing was overlooked. By following tradition and the Vedas to the letter, you hopefully mitigate any potential problems that may arise later on. Think of it like tightening all the screws when constructing something within the home. Think of it like following a recipe when making a food dish. It's like dotting all your "i"s and crossing all your "t"s. Why leave any vulnerabilities, especially with something so important?

The burden here was on King Janaka. Though it was a marriage, it was Janaki's mangala, or her auspiciousness. Janaki is the daughter of King Janaka. This name especially speaks of how dear she is to King Janaka. And Janaka is dear to the people of Mithila, which means that Janaki is dear to them. Imagine having to part with someone whom you love so much. You have to give them away in a ceremony, one which has rules and regulations. If you really love that person, you will take great attention and care.

Here Janaka went before a fire and took kusha grass and water. All three items are common to a Vedic sacrifice. The fire is the witness to the ceremony. Personified, the fire is Agni Deva. In the name of his wife, Svaha, he accepts oblations poured into him. Those items are then passed on for enjoyment by the heavenly figures. The fire consumes whatever is placed into it; so you visibly see that whatever you are giving is being taken somewhere else.

In Vedic culture, taking an oath in front of fire is as good as signing a contract. Holding sacred kusha grass and water, which is purifying, Janaka here takes the oath to give away his daughter. She is leaving him to live with her new husband, Shri Rama. Rama will protect her now. Rama will make sure that she is safe. Rama will create conditions suitable for her happiness. Such things are easy for Rama to do since He excels in every single category we can think of. Sita's happiness was secure because every person is happiest when in God's company. Rama is the personal form of Godhead especially dear to those who value righteousness.

Rama upholds the vows of the pious. In an ancient time, a priest takes an oath to live an austere life in the wilderness so that they can better worship God. They survive on bare essentials like fruits, roots and bulbs. They wear torn rags for clothing and live in a thatched hut. Obviously there is no air conditioning. The scorching hot days of summer must be tolerated. The same goes for the pouring rain of the monsoon season. The chilling winter has to be endured by the ascetic who has taken a vow for a life of penance.

"I am the original fragrance of the earth, and I am the heat in fire. I am the life of all that lives, and I am the penances of all ascetics." (Lord Krishna, Bhagavad-gita, 7.9)

As God, Rama is the life of everything. Therefore He is the penance of the ascetic. Without some kind of austerity, the renunciate living in the forest is a pretender. Think of it like putting on the jersey of your favorite hockey player. It has their name and number on it. You can also put on the rest of the gear, like the shoulder pads, shorts and skates. But does this mean that you can skate on the ice in a real game for that team? Obviously not, for you don't have the skill to play at the level of the athlete whose jersey you wear. You could even try wearing a jersey with no name, but still you are not a real hockey player.

At the time of Sita's wedding, Rama had already shown how He protects vows. Vishvamitra Muni and other sages were living in the forest and being harassed by night rangers. These were wicked creatures who changed shapes to aid in their clandestine attacks against the innocent. Vishvamitra Muni was especially of strong vows, and now these night-rangers were hampering his ability to stay true to his nature. Rama was asked to come to the forest, and He did so along with Lakshmana. Though the boys were very young, they successfully defended against demons like Tataka and Subahu. Rama's protecting Vishvamitra was a precursor to Him being led to Janakpur, where the self-choice ceremony for Sita's marriage was taking place.

And now here was Rama ready to protect Janaka's vow. The father was charged with protecting his daughter, and so if he found her an unsuitable husband he would be partially liable for any misfortune that came her way. Rama made sure that would never happen. If anything, through having Rama as a husband, Sita's fame would only increase, thereby raising Janaka's stature as well.

In the future Rama would uphold the vow of truth of His father King Dasharatha of Ayodhya. Caught in a pickle, King Dasharatha either had to banish Rama to the forest for fourteen years or be validly labeled a liar by his youngest wife. Dasharatha didn't have the heart to give Rama the order; the words could not come out of his mouth. Since he had a son like Rama, they didn't have to. The protector of the vows of the devotees took it upon Himself to protect the good name of His father. He voluntarily left for the forest, despite the objections of His well-wishers. Sita, showing again how she was Janaka's daughter, insisted on following Rama. She would help Him uphold His vow to uphold Dasharatha's vow.

In giving Sita away Janaka did everything properly, but what actually held everything together was the nature of the husband. Since He was at the center of the rituals, there was success. Know also that in any activity you take up, if the Supreme Lord is the beneficiary, then everything will be considered done properly, even if there are a few innocent mistakes made along the way.

CHAND 18

संकल्पि सिय रामहि समरपी सील सुख सोभामई।
जिमि संकरहि गिरिराज गिरिजा हरिहि श्री सागर दई।।
सिंदूर बंदन होम लावा होन लागी भाँवरीं।
सिल पोहनी करि मोहनी मनहर्यो मूरति साँवरीं।।18।।

saṅkalpi siya rāmahi samarapī sīla sukha sobhāmaʼī |
jimi saṅkarahi girirāja girijā harihi śrī sāgara daʼī ||
sindūra bandana homa lāvā hona lāgī bhāṁvarīṁ |
sila pohanī kari mohanī manaharyo mūrati sāṁvarīṁ ||18||

"Taking the oath, Janaka gave away Sita to Rama in all politeness and happiness in a beautiful scene that was reminiscent of when the king of mountains gave away Parvati to Shiva and when the ocean gave away Lakshmi to Vishnu." (Chand 18.1)

"Applying the sindura, performing the homa, offering rice, circumambulating the fire, touching the stone - in doing all of this the enchanting murti of the dark-skinned groom stole the mind." (Chand 18.2)

Essay - Famous Marriages

The marriage of Sita and Rama is likely the most famous of them all, so what comparisons can be made to try to accurately describe it to someone else? Even the following description isn't sufficient: "Wow, this marriage was better than anything ever before seen. The uniqueness was in the beauty of the scene, especially at the culmination, when the bride was given away to the groom by the father. Everything in the scene was perfect. There were no reservations. Everyone was happy. The father took an oath in front of fire to give up protection of his daughter and hand that responsibility over to the new husband. He did everything properly, with attention to etiquette, and with a happy heart. That scene was so beautiful, but what can I say to describe it?"

Goswami Tulsidas understands this dilemma, and so he invokes other famous marriages. These marriages come close to the fame of the marriage of Sita and Rama, and they are also of the divine nature. These marriages were safe ground; using them as comparison points would not sully the image of the beautiful Janaki joining with the handsome Rama. In the process, the mind gets to remember those blessed events, which is always beneficial.

Tulsidas says that the beauty of the scene of Janaka giving away his daughter Sita to Rama was like when the mountain-king gave away his daughter to Shiva. This marriage is described in many places in the Vedas, including by Goswami Tulsidas. The Janaki Mangala is the song glorifying the marriage of Sita and Rama and the Parvati Mangala is the work of the same author glorifying the marriage of Parvati and Shiva. Also, in his most famous work, the Ramacharitamanasa, the same author very nicely summarizes the same wedding, glorifying Shiva, Parvati, Ganesha and Himavan in the process.

Himavan is the Himalayan mountain range. Though we think of mountains as inanimate objects, according to the Vedas they are powerful personalities. The famous Govardhana Hill is also a personality. The same goes for the Mainaka mountain, which was once petitioned by the ocean to provide respite to Shri Hanuman on his difficult journey to Lanka.

"O Sita, see the golden lord of mountains [Mainaka], which is golden-peaked and which rose up, piercing the ocean, to provide rest to Hanuman." (Lord Rama speaking to Sita Devi, Valmiki Ramayana, Yuddha Kand, 123.18)

That offering took place well after the marriage described here of Sita and Rama. Nevertheless, from the Ramayana we get evidence of how mountains are personalities too. Even if one is skeptical of the claim, they can at least acknowledge that the larger collections of matter don't suddenly appear on their own. The mountains give so much to humanity, so to show respect for them shouldn't be so odd. We give respect to famous sports trophies like the Stanley Cup, when we know that they are nothing but collections of different metals. It is what they represent that brings the attention, and so the mountain ranges like the Himalayas can be appreciated in the same light.

Himavan and his wife had a beautiful daughter who was named Parvati. This name means the daughter of the mountain, just as Janaki means the daughter of King Janaka. Another name for Parvati is Gauri, which references her beautiful fair complexion. She is also known as Durga, as through her union with Lord Shiva she manages the material creation, which is difficult to overcome. Goddess Durga acts as a fort who uses the threefold miseries of life to keep others from climbing over the walls. Those who propitiate her are able to tolerate these pains a little easier.

Parvati was actually Sati in her previous life. Sati was Lord Shiva's first wife. Since he would later marry Parvati, technically Shiva only has one wife, eka nari vrata. Sati burned herself in a fire after her husband was insulted. In the next life she would not accept any other husband but Shiva. Since Shiva also has the most chaste wife, Parvati performed tremendous austerities to earn his favor. In her youth the famous Narada Muni told her father that Parvati would be fit for marrying Shiva. Gauri took these words to heart, considering them as coming from her spiritual master, who is a representative of God. Shiva's attendants tested her commitment several times, once even offering Vishnu as a husband. Parvati kindly declined and held firm to her vow.

As a result, one day Himavan arranged for her marriage to Shiva. Since he was getting the most chaste wife, Shiva was very fortunate. Since the mountain-king's daughter was completely in favor of the marriage, the scene was beautiful. Though her lady friends and elders felt sorry for her that she had to marry someone who is so renounced, Parvati did not pay any attention. Lord Shiva's only desire in life is to meditate on the lotus feet of Vishnu, who is the personal form of the Lord dressed in full opulence and having four hands.

Vishnu's marriage is referenced here as well. Once the demigods and demons churned a large ocean of milk in order to get various items from it, including an elixir to grant immortality. One of the objects that emerged from that churning was Goddess Lakshmi. She appeared from the ocean, so she is considered the ocean's daughter. In actuality she eternally stays by the side of her husband Lord Vishnu, but in the material realm it was seen that she came from the ocean. The proud father, the ocean, then gave Lakshmi away to Vishnu in a very beautiful scene.

Only those two marriages could rival the beauty of Sita and Rama's. From the comparisons made by Tulsidas we see that nothing was missing in the union of the divine couple. Everything was extraordinary, including the final act of Sita leaving Janaka's custody and entering Rama's. Rama is the same Vishnu and Sita the same Lakshmi. They are God and the goddess of fortune respectively, and so naturally their marriage would be the most famous of them all.

Essay - Still I Stand

"These wedding ceremonies are interesting and all, but who actually follows the vows they make? They go through this giant production, following whatever the priest says, and then afterwards they get into so many fights. A squabble here and a squabble there - they are always fighting. In whatever tradition the wedding took place, the wife is generally asked to obey the husband. But come on? Are you kidding me? We all know that the wife runs the show. If she's not happy, he's not happy. He could be unhappy too, but that doesn't matter. So why the attention on all the rituals then? Why so much attention to detail? Wouldn't it be better to have a quick ceremony that changes the status of the people from single to married?"

Indeed, so many vows in life are broken, and the marriage vows are no different. To see an example of where they are upheld, however, look no further than the marriage of Sita and Rama. As this marriage is more about Sita than Rama, the poem to describe it written by Goswami Tulsidas is appropriately named the Janaki Mangala. In the verse above the author says that the ceremony took place exactly according to Vedic tradition, and in the process the dark-complexioned groom enchanted the mind.

As the husband to protect her, Rama applied sindura on Sita's head, where the hair parts. Sindura is a vermillion powder or paste and by applying it to the wife's head the husband promises to protect her. Both husband and wife sat through the fire sacrifice, the homa, in order to have the proper witness to their vows. All Vedic rites involve fire in some way, as the fire locks in whatever oaths are taken. Rice was offered at various times, and both husband and wife took the seven steps that are customary in a Vedic marriage ceremony. Sita also stepped on a stone to signify that her resolve in serving Rama would be as hard as stone. It would never break.

First there are the vows and then there are the actions that show whether or not the vows are followed. If the latter action supports the former, then both are forever linked. If I train very hard to run a marathon, the end result is not guaranteed. If I complete the marathon later on, then the training is tied to the accomplishment. It is part of the complete picture. If the marathon isn't completed, then the training is considered almost useless. It's an isolated event of little significance.

Sita and Rama showed how the marriage vows can be upheld. It's easy to have adherence when there are no difficulties. Husband and wife live peacefully together in a luxurious home with a steady income. As they always have money, they have no reason to fight. The wife is satisfied with the gifts the husband buys for her, and the husband is satisfied having his wife around. There are some children as well, so there is always something to do. Both husband and wife are not bored.

The example of Sita and Rama is not like this. They had everything thrown at them, every possible disturbance to provide an easy excuse to renounce their vows. As described in the verse above, when Rama married Sita people were enchanted by His vision. It stole the mind, meaning the people who were watching couldn't think of anything else. A murti is a statue that is worshipable when placed in a temple, and since Rama is an incarnation of the Supreme Personality of Godhead, His spiritual form manifest before the eyes is rightly described as a murti. Since it is all-beautiful, it steals the mind of the pure-hearted soul who gazes upon it.

Rama was a prince, the eldest son of the King of Ayodhya. Thus Sita, who came from royalty herself, married into royalty. Seems pretty easy to serve your husband when you're living the good life, no? It's not easy, however, when the same prince is banished to the forest for fourteen years, where He must live like a homeless man. It's not so easy when later on you're taken to an enemy land against your will and told that you'll never see your husband again. It's not so easy when this fiend who kidnapped you is trying to bribe you with material enjoyments and a high status within a very opulent kingdom. It's not easy when after reuniting with your husband later on, others think that you weren't true to your vow, when indeed you were.

Sita stayed true to Rama through it all. She did so not merely as a wife, but as a lover of God. She cannot live in any other consciousness; only God consciousness for her. Sita serves through the covenant of marriage. She vows to serve Rama in an official ceremony, but actually the ceremony is there just to show others how to take a vow that mimics Sita's eternal devotion. The stone is hard and seemingly unbreakable, but actually Sita's vow of service to Rama is harder than the stone. It is an object that is impossible to break. Not even Rama can stop her from serving Him. After being banished to the forest for fourteen years, He told her to stay home and be safe. She refused. In the end, there was nothing He could do to stop her from serving Him in the manner she preferred.

"I shall go with you today to the forest. There is no doubt about it. I cannot be prevented, O greatly fortunate one. I am ready to go." (Sita Devi speaking to Lord Rama, Valmiki Ramayana, Ayodhya Kand, 27.15)

In the marriage ceremony, she stood tall on the stone to show that she would be faithful to Rama, and after the many trials and tribulations she endured later on, she still stood tall. As such, she is the best wife, the most worshipable devotee, and the dearest to Rama.

Essay - Like Father Like Daughter

The Ramayana is filled with characters who are true to their word. Lest they be accused of miserliness or failing to repay good deeds done for them, so many figures make sure that their behavior is beyond reproach. They take the necessary steps to ensure that others, be they friend or foe, cannot find anything to criticize. The easiest way to dismantle your reputation is to be dishonest. If you fail to do what you say, especially if you give an oath, then why should you be trusted in other matters? Why would anyone believe what you say? King Janaka is one of the characters from the Ramayana with dedication to truthfulness, and in the scene referenced above his daughter lives up to his good name.

"Okay, I'm down for lunch tomorrow. I can't wait to go there. It's been a long time since all of us have been out together. This restaurant just opened too, filling the void that was created when our previous favorite restaurant closed down. I know that you don't have one of these where you live, so let's make the most out of your visit. Fortuitous it is that you stopped by here for work matters. Now we can all hang out like old times. It's going to be great."

…a little later on

"Sorry man, something came up. The wife wanted to go to the beach. Plus, I wasn't really hungry anyway. We ate so much last night. I couldn't stomach the food at that place. And yeah, I couldn't really read my phone when we were at the beach. That's why I didn't respond to your texts. When you called earlier I was still sleeping. Oh well."

In this situation, the person has broken a promise, though a subtle one. The intention was that the group of friends would go to eat at a restaurant on a specific day. The one friend decided not to go; he changed his plans at the last minute. He came up with excuses for sure, but then those excuses weren't put on the table at the beginning. He didn't say, "Maybe we'll go tomorrow. Let's see what happens." A de facto promise was made, and it was later broken. Hence the word of such a person loses its value a bit.

Now skipping a planned lunch isn't really going to cause the world to end. The word in this case was compromised, but since the person who made the promise didn't think it was so important, it's not the best way to judge their truthfulness. With King Janaka, one time his vow related to the most important person in his life, his precious daughter Sita. This vow was with respect to her marriage, meaning it was a word given about which person would assume the duty of protecting her for the rest of her life.

You can consider this to be the most important issue in Janaka's life, and despite so much worry, he remained true to his word. He vowed that whoever would first lift a heavy bow at a contest in his kingdom would marry Sita. The initial concern was that no one would lift the bow, and then there was worry that one prince in particular would fail. Janaka wanted this prince to win so badly that the thought of cancelling the contest crept into his mind. Since he gave his vow in front of so many, he wasn't now going to go back on his word.

As Janaka's eldest daughter, Sita followed the example of her father. Shri Rama of Ayodhya won the contest. It turned out that the prince that Janaka preferred did indeed get to marry Sita. In the Vedic marriage ceremony, the bride steps on a stone and makes a vow to always serve her husband. The stone is symbolic of the resolve required by the bride. So many obstacles will come along the way. Marriage is not easy in the least. You always have to worry about someone else. They may or may not be nice to you. They may or may not want what you want. Still, you have to make the relationship work, especially if your marriage is in dharma, or duty. The marriage lacking dharma is driven by kama, or sense desire. As even animals are driven by sense desire, without dharma there is no purpose to the marriage. The casual relationship suffices when the sole desire is sense gratification.

Janaka's vow was attacked from within by fear over the uncertain future. With Sita, never for a minute did she want to go back on her vow. Her issues came from outside attack; others who wanted to prevent her from serving her husband. The outside attack is considered an adhibhautika misery, while fear and nervousness is adhyatmika. Along with adhidaivika, these are the threefold miseries of life. They attack everyone, irrespective of their desires. Whether you are religious or not, these miseries will come after you.

The difference with the divine associates of the Supreme Lord is that these miseries don't have an effect; it's like being attacked by snakes who have no fangs. The fear from within could not break Janaka's vow, and the fiendish Ravana and his cohorts could not stop Sita from serving Rama. In the worst case, where there is no ability to exercise any kind of outward devotion, one can at least think of Rama, who is non-different from God. One can say the holy names, "Hare Krishna Hare Krishna, Krishna Krishna, Hare Hare, Hare Rama Hare Rama, Rama Rama, Hare Hare," as an offering, a way to serve.

The stone is the best representation to gain a slight understanding of Sita's resolve in serving Rama. We don't know anything that is completely unbreakable, so in this world there is nothing that accurately compares to Sita's resolve. She always loves Rama; no matter what. Her father is just as fixed in devotional service. He is a king, so his vows relate to ruling over a kingdom and managing a family. Sita is Rama's beloved eternal consort, so her vows relate to serving Him in that capacity. Each individual has their svarupa, or eternal form, which follows some type of service to God. In regaining that svarupa through practicing bhakti-yoga, the resolve in serving God becomes unbreakable.

Essay - The Uniqueness of Bhakti

If you've never heard of bhakti-yoga before, some of the practices, regulations and stated objectives may appear to be very similar to other religions. In this sense, it is easy to discount as mere sentiment, a kind of faith. And who are we to judge faiths? "One person likes the sports team from New York and another the team from Los Angeles. In the end it is just support without meaning, so there is no reason to compare the two. People who worship God want stuff. We can't really judge what one person wants since every person is in a different circumstance. Therefore all religions are more or less the same."

In the above referenced verse from the Janaki Mangala, in becoming aware of the context we see how bhakti-yoga separates itself from the pack. It stands tall above even other practices in the category commonly known as Hinduism. Those who practice bhakti-yoga never consider themselves to be followers of a Hindu religion, for religion suggests faith. "Hindu" says that I am part of a particular family lineage that does certain things with respect to faith. Bhakti-yoga is a compound term that is explainable in scientific terms. If I tell someone I am looking at the sun, appreciating its properties, there is nothing sectarian in my practice.

There is no "Hindu sun" or "Christian sun." The sun is the sun; it is there for everyone. Similarly, bhakti-yoga is a practice for all spirit souls. Since every living being is a spirit soul at the core, bhakti-yoga is the only practice that breaks through the barriers of separation created by age, gender, ethnicity, culture, prejudice, and fear of unknown traditions.

"As the embodied soul continually passes, in this body, from boyhood to youth to old age, the soul similarly passes into another body at death. The self-realized soul is not bewildered by such a change." (Lord Krishna, Bhagavad-gita, 2.13)

It is customary religious practice to ask God for stuff. "Give me this, give me that. I'm in trouble, so help me out. I have nowhere else to turn." In one Hollywood film of recent times, the main character is humorously assigned the post of God for a brief period. On his first morning as God, he hops on the computer to check his email and is greeted with a nice surprise. His inbox is flooded with requests. All these people are asking God for things. And the emails keep coming. Once he opens one email, another fifty arrive. Thus he gets overwhelmed.

As God is the all-powerful, He does not get overwhelmed in receiving the infinite number of requests coming from His children, but the scene in the movie gives us an idea of how God is generally viewed. Here Sita Devi takes a different approach. She steps on a stone and vows to always serve God. She will stay by His side no matter what. Whatever obstacles come her way, she will not be deterred. No material opulence will change her mind. This means that even if she had the ability to get whatever she asked, she still wouldn't constantly ask God for things.

Interestingly enough, she can indeed get whatever she asks for in the material sense. Bhakti-yoga comes from the Vedic tradition, which is the more accurate name for Hinduism. Hindu is a cultural term, while Vedic is a Sanskrit one. Vedic means coming from the Vedas, which mean knowledge. Following the Vedas means following a system of real knowledge. Knowledge is not sectarian. If I know that two plus two equals four, my understanding is not limited to my cultural surrounding.

In the Vedic tradition you worship people who are not God in order to get material rewards. These people are highly elevated personalities; they are divine in nature. They can give you rewards such as the ability to live thousands of years and beauty to make you attractive. And yet these rewards don't last forever, which shows that the people granting them cannot be God. One who practices bhakti-yoga automatically is entitled to the material opulence and abilities of these divine figures.

"All the demigods and their exalted qualities, such as religion, knowledge and renunciation, become manifest in the body of one who has developed unalloyed devotion for the Supreme Personality of Godhead, Vasudeva. On the other hand, a person devoid of devotional service and engaged in material activities has no good qualities. Even if he is adept at the practice of mystic yoga or the honest endeavor of maintaining his family and relatives, he must be driven by his own mental speculations and must engage in the service of the Lord's external energy. How can there be any good qualities in such a man?" (Shrimad Bhagavatam, 5.18.12)

Since Sita took a vow to be as strong as stone in her service to God, she was automatically entitled to different material rewards. A few times in her life it even looked like she asked for them. One time she prayed to the goddess who is a famous river to give protection to her husband. Another time she prayed to the presiding deities of the different directions to protect her husband along His journey. Another time she prayed to the god of fire to allow a fire on the tail of a monkey to feel as cool as ice. All of her requests were for someone else's welfare, and namely for someone who was either God Himself or acting directly in service to Him. These divine figures had to oblige; they could not deny her. If they did, they would be accused of getting in the way of her devotional service, which was her avowed occupation.

In bhakti-yoga you vow to make God happy. How does one please Him? Why does He need our service if He is so great? In works like the Bhagavad-gita, He tells us how to please Him. He says to always chant His names, like those found in the maha-mantra, "Hare Krishna Hare Krishna, Krishna Krishna, Hare Hare, Hare Rama Hare Rama, Rama Rama, Hare Hare." He tells us to worship Him at all times and to sacrifice all of our activities for His benefit.

"O son of Kunti, all that you do, all that you eat, all that you offer and give away, as well as all austerities that you may perform, should be done as an offering unto Me." (Lord Krishna, Bg. 9.27)

In asking God for so many things, it is easy to forget the role personal responsibility played in creating the present circumstances. If I made the choice to eat that extra slice of pizza and I later pray to God to relieve my indigestion, is that very wise? Among all the possible rewards the Supreme Lord could grant, I chose to have stomach pain removed; pain that I brought on myself. When in the consciousness of serving God, be there pain or pleasure, the resolve to continue to please is strong. If the same God can relieve indigestion, He can most certainly ensure that the service to Him continues. In fact, in Sita's case the resolve is so firm that God Himself, who acts as Sita's husband in His incarnation as Rama, cannot do anything to stop her. Only in bhakti-yoga does one become even greater than God.

VERSE 145

JANAKI MANGALA

एहि बिधि भयो बिबाह उछाह तिहूँ पुर।
देहिं असीम मुनीस सुमन बरषहिं सुर।।१४५।।

ehi bidhi bhayo bibāha uchāha tihūm̐ pura |
dehiṁ asīma munīsa sumana baraṣahiṁ sura ||145||

"As the marriage ceremony happened like this, the three worlds were in happiness. The munis gave their blessings and the demigods rained down flowers."
(145)

Essay - To Do Good For All

"Good luck." It is common to say this to someone else, as it is a kind gesture. When opponents are set to square off in a competition, they may say this to be polite. In fact, the good fortune is not really desired. If the opponent indeed gets fortune in their favor, it doesn't redound well for the other side. If one side gets a fortuitous bounce that is beneficial, it is not beneficial for the other side. With one person in particular good luck always benefits all. This applies to His wife as well, and so during a famous marriage the three worlds rejoiced, and those who could grant good fortune were more than happy to shower their blessings on the new husband and wife.

The celestials can grant boons. Think of it like asking Mother Nature to be kind. "Please pour down some rain for my farm. This land is my livelihood. I work so hard to make sure crops can grow. The final piece of the puzzle is the rain, which I know only you are responsible for. If you make it rain, I will be so pleased. I will honor you every day with my thoughts."

Saints can also grant boons. Think of it like getting the blessings of a priest or religious person. They have a preferred status since they dedicate their life to serving God. They are not interested in worldly pursuits. Sure, they could get a job in the marketplace if they wanted to. Then they could haggle over salary and benefits, looking to move up every few years so that their lot improves. Instead, they choose a life of service to God. This is a sacrifice, one for which so many others are benefitted. Getting the blessings of such saintly people is always good.

Then there is the issue of who is eligible for the blessings. If a sinful person wants boons from celestials, should they get them? If someone is intent on breaking into an innocent person's home and stealing their things, should the person in authority hand over the money necessary to carry out the crime? The criminal considers the money a great blessing, and the person beseeched is surely capable of providing it. In this case whatever auspiciousness is granted is limited; it is not absolute.

The saintly person can also give blessings to someone who doesn't deserve it. The recipient could then use those blessings as an excuse for sinful behavior. "Oh, such and such person died for my sins. Therefore I can do whatever I want. I can kill animals, lie, cheat, steal, and have sex with anyone, even outside the bounds of marriage. I am absolved since I have the blessings of this high personality."

Duality was absent in the case of the blessings showered upon Sita and Rama. The divine couple is benevolent to all. They are more than just saintly. They are also more than just powerful. As Sita is the goddess of fortune originally, she can donate any amount of wealth to any person. Rama is the Supreme Lord originally, so He is the owner of all matter. He can grant any material benediction to anyone very easily. Rama is beyond duality, so He knows that sometimes a material benediction can turn out to be a curse. Consider getting a drum set for Christmas as a kid. You think it's great since you can play drums all the time, but the noise will really bother your parents.

Sita and Rama are benevolent to all through their association. They are the best friends anyone could ask for. Do we not prefer to spend time with good people? Who wants to be around misers, cheats, frauds, liars and obnoxious blowhards? No one is kinder than Sita and Rama. Sita especially is of the highest character, and no sin exists in her. Rama is the same way, but since He takes on the role of a warrior sometimes it appears that He does things which are unkind. He prefers to fight from time to time against wicked characters, and so the wives of the slain foes then lament their loss. But even this is beneficial, as death at the hands of Rama is glorious. The wives share in the meritorious end of their husbands, and so Rama gives everyone a boon even through His ferocious form shown on the battlefield.

In the above referenced verse from the Janaki Mangala, Goswami Tulsidas describes the emotions of the world right after the rites had concluded at the marriage ceremony of Sita and Rama. He says that the three worlds were in happiness. The earth was certainly happy, as so many of its inhabitants had gathered in Janakpur to witness the beautiful ceremony. Residents of the heavenly realm were thrilled as well, as Rama was their life and soul. Sita was dear to Rama, so she was automatically dear to them too. Even the residents of the hellish realm were thrilled, as every person, no matter how far sunken they are in consciousness, retains a link to the Divine, for that is in their constitutional makeup.

The munis, or sages, gave their blessings very liberally. This wasn't required, but it kept in line with tradition. Sita and Rama usually grant benedictions, as they are in the superior position. But it is still very nice to be able to wish them well. This practice is unique to bhakti-yoga, showing another way in which it stands above all other kinds of yoga. In bhakti you pray for God to do well, for Him to have good luck. His luck is in the form of Sita's association. The couple is always together, but sometimes the devotees worry that they may have to be separated. The young child might pray for the parents' safety prior to falling asleep at night, though the parents are the ones who are charged with maintaining the children. The child's love explains the sentiment.

The love of the sages explains their liberal distribution of blessings upon Sita and Rama. The celestials once again rained down flowers, giving their approval to the proceedings. All were joyful on that day, which is one that can be celebrated infinitely into the future through the timeless works of saints like Goswami Tulsidas.

VERSE 146

मन भावत बिधि कीन्ह मुदित भामिनि भईं।
बर दुलहिनिहि लवाइ सखीं कोहबर गईं।।146।।

mana bhāvata bidhi kīnha mudita bhāmini bha'īṁ |
bara dulahinihi lavā'i sakhīṁ kohabara ga'īṁ ||146||

"With the rituals done just as the mind desired, the women became happy. Taking the bride and groom, the friends of the bride led them to the nuptial chamber." (146)

Essay - Worshiping God Together

"What is the purpose to a marriage? Is it to facilitate sense gratification? Instead of chasing after woman after woman, hoping that they like you enough to spend time with you, you get one woman for life. This way you won't have to go far to satisfy your urges for conjugal relations. You won't have to worry about dying alone. Is this all there is to a marriage? Why not just find a companion and forgo the formality?"

In the Vedas we get answers to these questions. These answers represent the truth as well, as marriage is indeed there to fulfill a higher purpose. The objective for every living entity is the same, but in the human form the opportunity for meeting it is the best. The animals don't have nearly the same potential, therefore things like austerity, penance, renunciation, knowledge, and rituals are absent in their lives. They are allowed to live like protected children, roaming here and there. Sin and piety do not apply to them. Righteousness is for the human species, and in the above referenced verse from the Janaki Mangala we get an instance of a very pious rite, one that is meant to help both parties involved.

The two parties are the groom and the bride. They start as a man and a woman. When they unite in holy matrimony, they become a singular entity, while maintaining their individual natures. Essentially the marriage allows two parties to help one another in advancing towards the ultimate objective of God consciousness. Not to be reached out of fear, this consciousness is what provides lasting and real happiness. The bliss that everyone is after only comes from intimate union with the Divine, a bond so strong that no one can accurately explain it in words.

To reach the point of creating that bond one has to eschew all other favoritism. Every exclusive affectionate relationship, every like and dislike, every attachment and detachment, must be cast aside. Otherwise the bond to the Divine will not be pure. Seems strange then that a relationship that is built on trust for another entity is meant to help one to advance towards God consciousness. If one is supposed to relinquish attachment to this person and that, how are they supposed to reach the vital objective when they accept a partner for life through marriage?

The living entity in the human body automatically has a tendency to form attachments to members of the opposite sex. Marriage, therefore, is a way to curb that tendency. It fixes the attachment on only one individual. In ancient times, some men did accept more than one wife, but again the attachment was limited.

Even in that fixed attachment, there is a singular objective. Like a wife who works to maintain the household and a husband who works to pay for the home's expenses, the marriage in dharma allots duties to each party. The objective is to maintain a devotional consciousness, one tied to the Supreme Lord. Thus there is work in both instances, but the marriage in dharma has a higher objective; therefore the work is more worthwhile.

Here Sita and Rama, the new bride and groom, are led to the nuptial chamber by Sita's assistants. Her friends were part of the royal court in Janakpur. Sita's father, King Janaka, was the leader of the country and the host of the marriage ceremony. Rama was the groom chosen through a contest, and here the rituals relating to their marriage have just completed.

Everything went according to the mind's desire. A marriage is a stressful occasion for those in charge of organizing it. The parties each have their specific desires. They want a certain place setting, menu, and banquet hall. They want different kinds of entertainment also. In Sita's wedding, everything that anyone could want was there. The most important element, happiness in celebration, was there at a level never before seen in the world. Sita is the goddess of fortune, who is the eternal consort of the Supreme Lord. Rama is that Supreme Lord in an incarnation specific to a time and circumstance many thousands of years ago.

Sita became a wife through the happily executed rituals, and the first destination for the new husband and wife was the bedroom. This was more than a place for sleeping or enjoying intimate relations. There they would worship the family deities, who had passed on the vital spiritual traditions that allowed everything in life to be ideal. The families were both happy through following dharma, or duty, and so the new members who would carry the torch forward would continue the tradition of worship.

Having someone by your side to support you is always better than going it alone. Perhaps one can get lazy if they don't have to do things on their own, but provided that one is enthusiastic to work having a partner is beneficial. Sita and Rama are equal in their respect for dharma. They are paragons of virtue, and so they set the ideal example for wife and husband. Shri Rama even remarks in the Ramayana how Sita is His partner in following religious principles. She is a sadharma-charini.

"My dear beautiful wife, what you have said is befitting the occasion and also indicative of the greatness of your family heritage. You are dearer to Me than My life, for you are My companion in the performance of religious duties." (Lord Rama speaking to Sita Devi, Valmiki Ramayana, Aranya Kand, 10.21)

As they are the objects of worship for the householder, Sita and Rama don't require advancement towards a final objective. Still, they set the proper example of how one can happily live in the company of a spouse. The Supreme Lord is all-attractive, and by extension the householders who work together to worship Him on a daily basis are as well.

VERSE 147

निरखि निछावर करहि बसन मनि छिनु छिनु।
जाइ न बरनि बिनोद मोदमय सो दिनु॥147॥

nirakhi nichāvara karahi basana mani chinu chinu |
jā'i na barani binoda modamaya so dinu ||147||

"Looking at the bride and groom, they again and again gave away clothes and jewels in charity. There is no way to explain the happy feelings and jovial nature of that day." (147)

GOSWAMI TULSIDAS

Essay - Not For Me

God is one. There is not a separate God assigned to each region or a separate worshipable figure specific to which book you follow. Some may think in this way, that "their" God is different from everyone else's, but in fact the same entity is described just in different terms. In the Vedas so many details are given about this singular divine entity. From these ancient works we learn that He is universal and that there are different ways to know Him. In the above referenced verse from the Janaki Mangala, we learn one way to recognize when His physically manifest form is within sight.

Imagine something good happening to you. Let's say you just got a new job. You are so excited. No more do you have to work for the tyrant you've called a boss for the last many years. No more will you have to deal with his lying straight to your face. He tells you one thing today and something totally opposite the next. He tells you that he and the company have no money to spend on salaries, and yet he just purchased a brand new car. He didn't need this one, either; it was just for fun.

At your new place of employment things will be different; at least you hope. To start this job you have to buy new clothes. You want to look good. To celebrate the switch, you want to take your friends and family out for a good time. From this example we see that when something good happens to you, you have to add possessions and expenses. Imagine that your good fortune is a wedding. Again, there is tremendous expense, with the added bonus of the worry over how to fill the brand new home. Even in modern times when the bride and groom often live together before marrying, there is never enough stuff; so the wedding provides a way to bring more things into one's life.

Here we see the celebratory behavior unique to viewing the Supreme Lord and His beautiful eternal consort. The women gazing upon the just married couple are continuously distributing gifts of dresses and jewels. This was part of a marriage ceremony, and there wasn't any running tally of the losses incurred. There also wasn't an expectation of return from the gift. Seeing God makes you act this way. No longer are material possessions important. Better it is to part with those items, donating them to the deserving people of society. Why not donate some nice clothes and jewelry to people who don't have much and who don't really require much to be happy?

The recipients here weren't expected to bring cash gifts to the wedding. They weren't expected to give anything back. This didn't matter to the women distributing the charity, for they were surrendered to Sita and Rama, who are the goddess of fortune and the Supreme Lord Himself. In Lakshmi, God has the most faithful and beautiful wife. As Narayana, the Supreme Lord is opulently adorned and worshiped in reverence. He is also known as the source of men. Thus Narayana is not a sectarian figure; He is not a God to be worshiped only by the Hindus.

The more one goes beyond the opulent aura of Narayana, the more the loving feelings within an individual can take over. As Sita and Rama, the same Lakshmi and Narayana appear in enchanting forms that evoke the natural penchant for service found within all of us. To serve them one need use only their mind. They don't require money. They don't require wealth. Objects can be used in service, for sure, as they are used here in distributing wealth. At the same time, the worshipers are not concerned over their personal fortunes. If you have the beautiful vision of Sita and Rama in front of you, you are naturally not attached to anything else.

The famous saints of the Vedic tradition provide further proof of this concept. None of them are known for their wealth, fame or number of possessions. In addition to their strong devotion, the example they set is of renunciation. The most knowledgeable of thinkers, who accepted supreme wisdom from their teachers and then further elucidated it in beautiful written word, lived on practically nothing. When their devotion was at its most mature stage in the eyes of others, the renunciation was quite pronounced. They didn't require much in chanting the holy names, "Hare Krishna Hare Krishna, Krishna Krishna, Hare Hare, Hare Rama Hare Rama, Rama Rama, Hare Hare." They didn't need so much money to maintain their writing and distribution of literature. Since they didn't require so much, they didn't have to work very hard to maintain a living. Absent the difficult labor that repeats day after day, their time was freed for worshiping God, which brings the most pleasure to any person.

Renunciation is superior to attachment to so many possessions. Thus from seeing Sita and Rama one reaches a better position automatically. This is one test for determining who is God and which activities are devotional. In a material existence, increased success brings increased burdens. In devotional life, the more one serves God, the more renounced they naturally become. They become extremely liberal in distributing gifts, including with the most wonderful gift of all: devotion.

VERSE 148

सिय भ्राताके समय भोम तहँ आयउ।
दुरीदुरा करि नेगु सुनात जनायउ।।148।।

siya bhrātāke samaya bhoma taham̐ āya'u |
durīdurā kari negu sunāta janāya'u ||148||

"At that time, Sita's brother came there from the earth. Performing the rituals and giving blessings, he made himself known." (148)

Essay - Son of the Earth

The wedding in Janakpur a long time ago was so important that the most powerful personalities in the world arrived there to witness it. One would think they had more pressing matters to attend to, but when it comes to witnessing beautiful moments shared between the Supreme Personality of Godhead and His eternal consort, everything else takes a backseat. Here we see that the personality who is the planet Mars arrived on the scene to offer his blessings.

Previously, the goddess of fortune and the personality in charge of guarding the material nature arrived there. The wives of other celestials came as well. They came disguised so as to not distract from the festivities. They were there to enjoy the scene, not to hog the glory. In the Vedas we learn that the higher forces of nature are controlled by intelligent beings. The most intelligent being is God, and everything surely does emanate from Him. This means that all that is bad and all that is good is originally sourced in God.

From hearing this one would be tempted to blame God for all the calamities of the world. After all, if He's going to get credit for everything good, as being the author of all that is blessed and sacred, why shouldn't He take the blame for the tragedies and painful situations people encounter on a daily basis? The root cause of this temporary creation gives the answer to this puzzling question. The Supreme Lord creates, but that doesn't mean He invests interest in the outcomes to the actions and results seen in that creation. He creates to satisfy the desires of the independent living beings who choose to not have His direct association.

His apathy in material interests is seen in how the creation is effected. Powerful personalities are put in charge of the various elements of nature. The sun is a person, though we find this hard to believe. The person is purusha, or spirit. Spirit is seen in the fish, the dog, the cat, and the human alike. Why can't it be in the sun as well? The body type is all that is different. Spirit is still there, so the combination of material elements surrounding that spirit just makes for a different kind of living being.

Good and bad are relative in the material sphere. We can use the sun again to test this theory. The sun diffuses heat and light. It does so perpetually. It does not require an external fuel source. It does not require maintenance. Now, depending on where you live, you either bask in the sunshine or fear its dreaded heat. In the summer months, you're not pleased with the sun, but in the winter you crave its warmth. The sun is identical in both situations. It does not choose to be favorable or unfavorable upon anyone.

From this example we see that what is good for one person may be bad for another. This concept extends all the way into the afterlife, where one person goes to a heavenly realm and another to a hellish one. Indeed, the present life is the afterlife to a previous term in a material body. And right now we see both heavenly and hellish situations, which means that we don't always get good and don't always get bad.

Real good is everlasting, extending beyond the foreseeable and unforeseeable futures. Real good belongs only to the Supreme Lord and by extension those who are tied to Him in service. The occasion of Sita's marriage is an example of all good. The personalities in charge of the material creation took great delight in the occasion. Though they are residents in a realm of duality, here they momentarily cast aside their duties to witness the beautiful spectacle.

Sita is God's wife in a unique spiritual form. For her earthly pastimes, she appears from the ground of the earth. She has a father in King Janaka, who finds her in the field one day, but she is an adopted child. Janaka has no sons at the time, so it seems as though Sita does not have any brothers. When it comes time for her wedding rites, the different aspects traditionally performed by the brother of the bride would seemingly not occur.

From this verse from the Janaki Mangala, Goswami Tulsidas says that Sita's brother did indeed appear at her wedding. He is known as Bhauma, or Mangala. He comes from the earth, and since Sita arose from the earth as well, Mangala is her brother. Everyone knew who he was when he started performing the rituals and bestowing blessings upon the newly married couple.

Mangala is the planet known in English as Mars. Like all other planets, Mars intrigues the mind. Its climate and appearance are studied by scientists in great detail. Of course even with so much invested in researching it, nothing of value is really known. One can see the color of the planet and perhaps analyze its atmospheric conditions, but what is gained from such information?

Here we get a better understanding of Mars. It is a personality who was originally nurtured by the earth. Bhauma took great pleasure in seeing Sita and Rama. Rama is the origin of everything in His form of Vishnu, who simply exhales to create innumerable universes that emanate from the pores on His body. Vishnu is opulently adorned and thus worshiped in reverence. The worship through offering service in a marriage is more intimate, and so fortunate personalities were able to serve in greater ecstasy through attending the marriage of Sita and Rama.

The ordinary living entities, who have a difficult time maintaining a job let alone even thinking of managing a planet, can stay very close to the same Sita and Rama by remembering their wedding, taking delight in the fact that so many well-wishers were on the scene, and always chanting their names, like those found in the mahamantra, "Hare Krishna Hare Krishna, Krishna Krishna, Hare Hare, Hare Rama Hare Rama, Rama Rama, Hare Hare."

VERSE 149

चतुर नारि बर कुँवरिहि रीति सिखावहिं।
देहिं गारि लहकौरि समौ सुख पावहिं॥149॥

catura nāri bara kumvarihi rīti sikhāvahiṁ |
dehiṁ gāri lahakauri samau sukha pāvahiṁ ||149||

"The clever ladies taught the bride and groom all the rituals. Giving curses to the other party in fun, feeding morsels of food to each one equally, they are very happy." (149)

Essay - Feeling Like Family

There are many benefits to having a sibling, and one of them is that you have someone with whom you can share your frustrations relating to your parents. If the mother or father consistently does something to irritate you, you can tell one of your friends for sure. But the discussion ends there. If your friend makes any derogatory remark whatsoever, even if it is a sentiment first urged on by you, you will get offended. "Who are you to speak about my parents that way? What gives you the right?" The sibling has the same set of parents, and so not only are you free to voice your complaints, but you can even make jokes about your parents without it hurting anyone. In the scene of the above referenced verse from the Janaki Mangala, all the parties involved indeed felt like family, though they had only been tied together for a short time.

If your grandfather has a peculiar habit that you find hilarious, you can discuss it with your brother or sister. If your mother has a tendency to fly off the handle, you can't bring it up with people outside of the family. They will get the wrong impression of your mother. They will think that she is tyrannical, whereas you only brought up the interesting behavior because it was a source of humor. In the material world there is duality in every sphere, which means a simple joke can cause both laughter and anger.

The person who is outside the circle of the joke will take offense. Especially if the person making it isn't a close friend or family member, what else are they supposed to think? If they don't have the full context of the conversation, they will get the wrong understanding. Indeed, taking humorous statements out of context is a principal tool of destruction used by political opponents. The "camera is always rolling," so to speak, with a person running for political office. If they should make a joke to their friends while they think the microphone is off, and then someone else picks up on that comment, it can be distributed widely to the public. Others who are not privy to the context will get the wrong impression.

To the person in the know, the jokes are very pleasing. Here the clever ladies at the marriage ceremony of Sita and Rama are giving verbal jabs to the opposing side. The bride's side is making fun of the groom's side and vice versa. At this marriage everything was done according to tradition. There was no expense spared, as the host was the wealthy and pious king of Mithila. The marriage took place according to dharma, or religiosity. There was no kama, or sense gratification, involved.

The parties felt comfortable making jokes at each other because they were all family now. If you can't make fun of your family members, who can you make fun of? If you're not going to enjoy with the people you trust the most, then you are devoid of any enjoyment. All had a good time since Sita was now married to Rama. Indeed, the joke-making made the event more joyous. Sort of like having a band at your wedding or a fully stocked buffet at your get-together, the jokes were very appropriate to the occasion.

The clever ladies also taught Sita and Rama the appropriate rituals, such as feeding a morsel of food to each other. The food consisted of yogurt and rice, and the exchange is customary in a wedding ceremony of the Vedic tradition. It is said that everyone was so happy as a result. Wouldn't you be thrilled as well? Where else do you hear about God being taught how to feed His wife? Where else do you learn about the beautiful eternal consort of the Supreme Lord being given instructions on how to offer food to her husband in love?

Indeed, such variety is present in the spiritual world, and that variety is replicated when the Divine and His associates appear on this earth in apparently human forms. With variety in form, the many children of God get the opportunity to engage in direct service. Here there was no fear on the part of the clever ladies. There was only boundless love. That love manifested in instruction and the offering of verbal jabs, thereby showing that the all-merciful Supreme Lord allows all to engage in devotional service in the mood of their choice.

Of course the prerequisite is the familial bond. We don't like it when our friends say anything bad about our family, even if their statements are accurate. The friends are not part of the family, so they don't get a free pass to lob abuses. The brother and sister are allowed to since there is a lasting bond with them. With God, there is the chance to enter the family since everyone is already in it. Through a lack of the proper consciousness only does one think that God doesn't exist or that man is evolved today through natural selection of the strongest species. That evolved man no longer has to worry about God, which is a foolish mindset.

With the proper consciousness, one is allowed to reenter the family and from there engage in these wonderful pastimes, the likes of which fill up the voluminous pages of Vedic literature. The ladies took delight in this ceremony and so do the pure-hearted souls who hear with rapt attention, paying homage to the author who took so much time and effort to describe these events that his mind was so immersed in.

VERSE 150

जुआ खेलावन कौतुक कीन्ह सयानिन्ह।
जीति हारि मिस देहिं गारि दुहु रानिन्ह।।150।।

ju'ā khelāvana kautuka kīnha sayāninha |
jīti hāri misa dehiṁ gāri duhu rāninha ||150||

"The wise ladies taught them how to play the wedding games. Winning and losing, they made accusations and gave a ribbing to both queens." (150)

Essay - Hear Our Jokes

When Sita loses, her mother gets made fun of. When Rama loses, His mother takes a ribbing. "Who taught you how to play? It's as if your family doesn't know anything. You lost this one time, and you will lose again going forward." Such jokes are allowed at the festive occasion of the wedding, and surprisingly here they are directed at the divine couple, Sita and Rama.

"O father, hear our prayer." This is a common refrain when making requests to the man upstairs. He is the Almighty. He can create universes without a problem. He can then destroy them without even thinking about it. Just to build a house we require so much effort. We have to plan. We have to gather the materials. We have to chart out the construction, keeping a close eye on the schedule. Without the schedule it is difficult to do things in a timely manner. We complain about having to wake up early for school or work, but if the pressure wasn't there we likely couldn't get our work done on time. Thus the schedule helps to keep us active.

The Supreme Lord doesn't require all of this. He doesn't need an alarm clock to wake up. In an apparently sleeping state, just by His breathing in and out, so many universes manifest and then disappear. Since He is so powerful, it would make sense to seek His blessings. If we are in trouble, we go to Him for help. If we really want a loved one to be safe and protected, and we know that we can't do so much on our own, we pray to the Lord to intervene.

The wedding is especially a time suitable for prayer. We see our loved ones entering a sacred covenant, a relationship to ideally last a lifetime. We pray to God that the newlyweds remain dedicated to each other, that they never forget their commitment to the relationship. We pray that God will protect them and allow them to enjoy family life.

Reverential worship of God is certainly superior to foolishly ignoring His existence, but the taste of interaction is sweeter when there is less fear. The leader of the nation certainly enjoys hearing praise from the citizens, but he takes greater pleasure in hearing the jokes from his friends and the loving complaints from his wife. Here the Supreme Lord is playing games with His eternal consort. In traditional Vedic weddings, the bride and groom don't know each other going in. As a way to break the ice, to spend time with each other without it being awkward, the newlyweds play games. The intelligent ladies in the wedding party teach them how to play.

The enjoyment is enhanced through commentary, from both those witnessing and those participating. In basketball, there is the common practice known as "trash-talking," where the opponents exchange verbal barbs in good fun. A player doesn't want to perform poorly in fear that the other side will lob jokes. This is meant to be in good fun, as ideally afterwards everyone shows respect for one another.

Here the ladies showing Sita and Rama how to play the games offer abuses at the two queens after the outcome of the game. If Sita wins a particular round of a game, they make fun of Rama's mother. If Rama wins, they make fun of Sita's mother. Who would ever think of making jokes at the Supreme Lord's family? Only those in the same family can do so. The enemies of God are not permitted, since they hold an inimical attitude. Those who only see God as an Almighty figure are also shut out from these delightful pastimes.

Only the devotees with pure motives can participate in such delightful joke-making. Such words enhance the pleasure of Sita and Rama, who like any other people enjoy the association of their friends and family. They are not conservative in this regard. They consider everyone eligible to be a friend, as they are intimately related to everyone. In each individual there reside two souls. One represents the person itself, and the other the Supreme Lord. This means that we all have God inside of us. We are not God Himself, but we are like Him and always tied to Him.

When we choose to ignore His presence, we miss out on His association. We think that He doesn't exist or that He is a person to be feared only. Why fear Him when He is always with us? Why think that we could be God when we can't even get what we want all the time? Better to be dedicated to Him in thought, word and deed. Better to be immersed in thoughts of Him. Better to please His dearmost associates, like Sita, Lakshmana, Hanuman, and the many who follow their example of devotion.

The women in the marriage ceremony associated with Sita and Rama in a wonderful way. The divine couple blessed them with further association, for this is the best reward that can be offered. Both men and women alike can receive these blessings. Shri Hanuman, a being with perfect intelligence and unmatched strength, gets the same blessings in the form of support for his devotion from Sita herself. He delights in the wonderful marriage ceremony by hearing the beautiful poetry of Goswami Tulsidas, a person whom he personally inspired.

VERSE 151

सीय मातु मन मुदित उतारति आरति।
को कहि सकइ आनंद मगन भइ भारति॥151॥

sīya mātu mana mudita utārati ārati |
ko kahi saka'i ānanda magana bha'i bhārati ||151||

"With a happy heart Sita's mother waved the arati lamp. Who can describe that pleasure, for even Sarasvati was overwhelmed by the moment?" (151)

Essay - Overwhelmed by the Moment

If there is an important event taking place, camera crews and reporters from various news organizations rush to the scene. Similar to how the emergency personnel must behave, these workers must not be affected by the event. They cannot be swayed one way or the other, for they are supposed to describe what is going on to others who are not there. In modern times there is the reporter on the scene who gives a live, eyewitness account. There are also those who will put their description to pad or computer screen.

Obviously the journalists are expected to be capable at their craft. They should have a way with words. They should know how to describe what's going on in a succinct manner, but not missing any of the vital details. They should answer the five questions of who, what, where, when, why and how. If they get too absorbed in the moment, then there is no one to properly describe what is going on. This is similar to what occurred in the scene referenced above, except the reporter on the scene is the most eloquent speaker in the world and the subject of the scene the most enchanting vision.

In the Vedas there is a goddess of speech and learning. You worship her in the hope that she can share some of her gifts with you. Though she distributes her rewards very liberally to anyone who pleases her properly, she still would like to see her gifts utilized in a certain manner. If you manufacture smartphones for a living, you are pleased when the purchasers use the phone to speak to their loved ones. You are pleased when they can send a text message very quickly or snap a picture of a crime scene to help catch a criminal. You are pleased if they can use the phone to be productive at work so that they can support their family.

You are not pleased, however, if the purchasers use your product to commit a crime. If they use the smartphone to organize a large scale drug run or the robbing of a bank, you will lament the tragedy and the small hand you played in it. Your product is still sold to anyone. You can try to have the purchaser sign a statement promising to use the device a certain way, but there is no means of enforcement. Thus you choose to conduct the transactions blindly. As long as there is payment made, the ownership transfers legally.

In the same way Goddess Sarasvati distributes the gift of learning and speech to anyone who pleases her. Still, there is an ideal use for her gifts. From this scene we see what catches her eye. Here she is absorbed in the moment of a bride's mother waving the arati lamp in front of her daughter. The arati lamp is a common component of worship in the Vedic tradition. It is a sign of welcome, a way to heartily greet someone. Here the mother prays that her daughter's marriage to her new husband will be auspicious.

The mother does this out of love only. She is not looking for wealth. She is not looking for fame. She likely may never see her daughter again, as the daughter now belongs to a new family. Thus the waving of the lamp is for the daughter's benefit. The mother has so much love that she wants God to always protect her beautiful daughter. That wouldn't be a problem, as the daughter's new husband was God Himself in His incarnation of Shri Rama.

It was the nature of the participants that caused Goddess Sarasvati to be absorbed in the moment. A person may manufacture and sell smartphones for a living, but at night they could take pleasure in something else. The business is their "day job," a way to carry out their obligations to their society and family. Just because they work in a certain way doesn't mean that they limit their enjoyment.

Sarasvati is a divine figure, so she possesses the quality of goodness to a very high degree. In ignorance one doesn't know what to do. They do such things as break useful objects out of anger and curse important people only to repent later. In passion one works very hard for a temporary result; thus reaching a neutral position. In goodness one sees things as they are, and so they are better situated for appreciating the glories of the Supreme Personality of Godhead.

Think of it like sitting in church and watching the proceedings. If you're intoxicated, you are more prone to being disrespectful of things that warrant the highest respect. If your mind is consumed with thoughts on how to make money and enjoy later on in the day, you will also not relish the nectar of topics of Godhead. If your mind is rightly situated, appreciating everything you have around you and knowing the common spiritual force that pervades everything, you will get more out of the experience.

The experience here is in bhakti, which is above even goodness. The poet says that the pleasure of Sita's mother cannot be described accurately, for even the goddess of learning herself was absorbed in the moment. If the person who has the most ability to describe something is fully absorbed in an event, who else can even come close to properly describing it?

In God's pastimes there are many such moments, but the saints immersed in bhakti still try their best to describe them. Sarasvati is more than happy to see her gifts utilized properly in this manner. The life-giving works of the saints of the bhakti tradition bring so much glory to the world that the benefits return back to Sarasvati as well, who delights so much in the marriage of Sita and Rama.

VERSE 152

जुबति जूथ रनिवास रहस बस एहि बिधि।
देखि देखि सिय राम सकल मंगल निधि।।152।।

jubati jūtha ranivāsa rahasa basa ehi bidhi |
dekhi dekhi siya rāma sakala maṅgala nidhi ||152||

"The group of young girls and queens stayed there in this way, receiving every auspicious treasure looking at Sita and looking at Rama." (152)

Essay - A Treasure Mine

The vision of the couple just married is a treasure. Therefore in a traditional wedding ceremony in modern times, there is the reception that follows the religious portion. The taking of wedding vows in front of a man of the clergy is enough to satisfy the requirement for marriage, but the well-wishers desire more time with the new couple. They wish to see them again and again in their wedded bliss. The same held true a long time ago in the marriage ceremony performed in the earthly realm for the Supreme Lord and His eternal consort.

To hold on to the memory of that special day, there are pictures and video taken. The day after, the attendees recount what happened the previous night. "Oh, did you see that person on the dance floor? Did you hear what that other person told me? What did you think of the food? Wasn't the church ceremony so nice? I couldn't believe all the nice things the bride had to say about the groom. She must really love him very much. The pair is a perfect match. They complement each other in qualities. One is bold and assertive and the other is calm and steady. I can't wait to see the wedding video to again experience the festive occasion. If only we could relive that night again and again."

Understanding the importance of the moment, the young ladies and queens at the marriage of Sita and Rama kept stealing glances at the divine couple. Normally, it is considered impolite to stare. "Would you like it if someone were looking at you all the time? After a while it would be a little creepy, wouldn't it? Therefore you shouldn't do that to someone else."

Sita and Rama didn't mind. They possess every virtue, every quality in goodness imaginable. If there is any object worth staring at, it is them right after they have officially been joined in the sacred city of Tirahuta. The women in the wedding party had a unique enjoyment due to their level of access. They got to lead Sita and Rama to the wedding chamber, where the couple got to know each other through playing traditional games. The women had the chance to make fun of the two mothers, ribbing them when their child lost a particular round.

Most importantly, the women were able to look at the bride and groom over and over again. Since Sita and Rama are divine, the goddess of fortune and the Supreme Lord respectively, others are not only allowed to stare at them, but encouraged to do so. Physical proximity is not a requirement for having the vision. Here the women got to stare at the couple sitting directly in front of them, but others have the same opportunity in visiting the temple.

Rather than speculate as to who the heavenly father is, and rather than remember only the sacrifice of life given by a son of God, in the temple one can see the transcendental features of God drawn out. There is no limit to these features, so the rendering is never completely accurate. Moreover, man is limited in the materials he can use to create the worshipable form. For instance, if God is everything, His height cannot be limited. And yet when making a statue of the original Lord or one of His many incarnations, the height must have a limit.

The form is still worshipable if it is created and installed in an authorized way. The deity is the mercy of God, giving the individual a chance to worship Him. That individual is not God; so it has limitations. He has a difficult time seeing the presence of the divine that is everywhere. Goswami Tulsidas, the author of the above referenced verse from the Janaki Mangala, in his Dohavali explains how the personal form of God is superior to the impersonal precisely because the personal form eliminates room for error. The comparison is made to the number, and how it looks different based on how it is presented. The numeral form looks different than the written out word. Both forms represent the same number, but the numeral can more easily be distorted. This is why both versions are presented on a check payment.

In the same way, the deity version of the incarnation removes the doubt in the mind of not knowing exactly who God is. The deity allows for the eyes to continuously stare, receiving every auspicious treasure in the process. The jewel of a reward in this life is devotion to God. Devotion is strengthened by attraction, and attraction automatically comes from opulence. The deity is worshiped in all opulence, attracting the mind with its features, activities and qualities.

"After having rested on the worshiped arm of the Lord of the world, how can I now take rest on the arm of any other?" (Sita Devi speaking to Ravana, Valmiki Ramayana, Sundara Kand, 21.16-17)

The deity of a just-wedded Sita and Rama attracts the mind to the sacred time in Tirahuta when Shri Rama, using His most powerful arm, which is the only worshipable arm for Sita, effortlessly lifted the heavy bow to win Janaka's contest. It attracts the mind towards Sita's undying devotion to Rama. It attracts the mind towards the kind attendants of Sita, who took so much pleasure in her auspicious day. Most importantly, it attracts the mind towards devotion itself, which is life's ultimate reward.

CHAND 19

मंगल निधान बिलोकि लोयन लाय लूटति नागरीं।
दइ जनक तिनिहुँ कुँवरि कुँवर बिबाह सुनि आनँद भरीं।।
कल्यान मो कल्यान पाइ बितान छबि मन मोहइ।
सुरधेनु ससि सुरमनि सहित मानहुँ कलप तरु सोहई।।19।।

maṅgala nidhāna biloki loyana lāya lūṭati nāgariṁ |
da'i janaka tinihuṁ kuṁvari kuṁvara bibāha suni ānaṁda bharīṁ ||

> kalyāna mo kalyāna pā'i bitāna chabi mana moha'i |
> suradhenu sasi suramani sahita mānahuṁ kalapa taru soha'ī ||19||

"Stealing the auspicious treasures by looking at the divine couple, the people of the city received the benefit of having eyes. When they heard that Janaka gave away brides for the other three princes, they became filled with bliss." (Chand 19.1)

"Auspiciousness on top of auspiciousness, when that happened [all four marriages] the picture enchanted the mind. The amazing beauty was like having a heavenly cow, the moon, a heavenly jewel, and a desire tree all together." (Chand 19.2)

Essay - Stealing Treasures

"How is no one else taking advantage of this? Though there is so much available in the material world to use for so-called enjoyment, nothing equals the reward of bhakti. To be able to glorify and worship the Supreme Personality of Godhead day after day is the real treasure of life. You don't need a secret map to find this gem. It is not hidden from people. In fact, from what I have learned, the treasure is as close by as the heart in the chest. It can be found through repeatedly creating a sound vibration with the tongue.

"By enjoying God's association on a daily basis, by basking in His transcendental qualities that bring me so much happiness, I feel as if I'm getting away with something. How are others not availing themselves of the same opportunity? I worry for them, as based on their personal testimony I can see what is missing in their lives. Though they are much more capable than me in all important areas, though they have so much in terms of potential for action, they are not meeting the true objective in life. They are not receiving the benefit to having an existence. I feel as if I am hoarding a treasure all to myself. Though I mostly fail even when trying my best to tell others where to find this treasure, I still won't give up enjoying it. If others want to snooze, they will undoubtedly lose out on the real enjoyment that life has to offer."

This is the general sentiment of the devotee who is immersed in bhakti-yoga, which is devotional service. The important things in life are abundantly available and inexpensive, relatively speaking. Milk and grains are easier to procure than wine and steak. At least this is how nature arranged it. When the opposite condition exists, it means that the actions of the people are guided by atheistic tendencies rather than the authorized words of scripture, which are available to one and all across different lands and in different languages.

Bhakti-yoga is the most readily available form of spiritual practice. It reaches more people than knowledge gathering, sitting in gymnastics postures, and working for a gain to be renounced later on. Indeed, its availability is greater than all other forms combined. Bhakti-yoga is like the sun of spiritual practice, dispersing its effulgence everywhere. The sun is but a tiny representation of God's potency. Since the sun goes everywhere, it is like God. In the same way, since bhakti-yoga awaits utilization by every single spirit soul, it is non-different from God. All other forms of spiritual practice come from God, but don't represent Him fully.

In a typical adventure film featuring a treasure hunt, the goal is to find the treasure chest and open it up. The seeker is rewarded with whatever is inside. The first person to find it owns it. "Finders keepers," as the saying goes. Pirates then try to steal the map or the treasure itself, understanding the value of the jewels and gold that are likely inside. The devotee who worships God in His personal form on a regular basis feels as if they have found the real treasure in life. Through some good fortune, which actually comes from God Himself and His representative, the means for finding the treasure are revealed.

"According to their karma, all living entities are wandering throughout the entire universe. Some of them are being elevated to the upper planetary systems, and some are going down into the lower planetary systems. Out of many millions of wandering living entities, one who is very fortunate gets an opportunity to associate with a bona fide spiritual master by the grace of Krishna. By the mercy of both Krishna and the spiritual master, such a person receives the seed of the creeper of devotional service." (Chaitanya Charitamrita, Madhya 19.151)

Then through even more good fortune, namely in the form of further association and dedicated practice in bhakti-yoga, the treasure arrives in the palm of the hand. They then own it. They make the best use of it, not wanting to give it up. Since it is from God, this treasure is available to every single other person as well. If I find a treasure chest in the desert, once I lay claim to it no one else can. When I take possession, others lose out. Not so with the treasure of devotional service. If I find it, others can as well. When others don't take to it, I will feel as if I am stealing, but that is actually a good sentiment, showing a level of appreciation necessary for truly loving God.

In the above referenced verse from the Janaki Mangala, the people of the town continue to enjoy the treasure of the vision of Sita and Rama. That image gives to them the fruit of their eyes. Eyes are used to see. To make the best use of the eyes, it would make sense to always look at the best thing. Nothing beats the vision of the personal form of God sitting next to His eternal consort. Sita and Rama fit that vision, though there are other non-different forms of Godhead and His energy as well.

The people appreciated what they had in front of them. Since only a select few were there, they felt as though they were stealing these treasures. Sita's father then announced that three more girls would be given away, to Rama's three younger brothers. This made the people even happier. In the Vedas it is said that Rama and His brothers are all expansions of Lord Vishnu, who is the Personality of Godhead in His manifestation of opulence. While Vishnu wears glittering gems and has a glaring effulgence that causes others to view Him with reverence, Rama and His brothers have human-like forms, which elicit stronger loving sentiments from the devotees.

The consorts of Rama and His brothers bring out even more loving feelings, as these beautiful women are dedicated to the brothers in thought, word and deed. The treasures from that day continue to be stolen by the sincere poets of the bhakti tradition, who give countless others the opportunity to time travel and enjoy that wonderful scene. That same opportunity is available to one and all today through the chanting of the holy names: Hare Krishna Hare Krishna, Krishna Krishna, Hare Hare, Hare Rama Hare Rama, Rama Rama, Hare Hare.

Essay - Take Your Pick

Those who are uncultured or not very mature in consciousness may chuckle at various statements made in scripture. While attending church if a priest reads a passage from the Bible, they may find the descriptions of different enjoyments and purposes to be ridiculous. The voluminous Vedic literature would serve as great fodder for such folks, but upon further study even that which seems out of the realm of possibility is actually assigned only secondary status in importance. The above referenced verse from the Janaki Mangala gives one instance.

If you're a good person you go to heaven. If you're a bad person you suffer in hell. This is the basic understanding of those who are not intimately familiar with the purpose to religion, and more importantly, the meaning of life. Indeed, even some who are supposedly very devout don't know much beyond this. In heaven you're supposed to enjoy. In hell you're supposed to suffer. The Vedas, the original scriptural tradition of the world, give more details into the exact nature of that enjoyment. Since they also deal with the essence of individuality, they put that enjoyment into the proper context.

"Those who study the Vedas and drink the soma juice, seeking the heavenly planets, worship Me indirectly. They take birth on the planet of Indra, where they enjoy godly delights." (Lord Krishna, Bhagavad-gita, 9.20)

In the Bhagavad-gita, which is the best summation to Vedic teachings, one learns that in the heavenly planets there is tremendous material enjoyment. There is a beverage called soma-rasa, and one is allowed to drink it at their leisure. All the beverages are higher in taste than what is found on this earth. One of the heavenly planets is the moon, which modern science believes to be uninhabited. In the Vedic definition, just because the living entities cannot be seen with the human eye doesn't mean that they are not there. The many planets are considered heavenly personalities, which means they govern using intelligence.

There are also heavenly cows and desire trees. Both fulfill the same purpose. The heavenly cow, known as the suradhenu or kamadhenu, provides whatever one asks for. The trees are all kalpatarus, which means they grant whatever material desire one has. If you go up to one of these trees and ask for gold, you will get it. If you want a drink of water, it will appear on the spot. All the trees are like this, including the small and strange looking ones. On our way to work in the morning, we may pass by hundreds of trees and not notice them. On the roads in heaven, however, even the tiniest trees are most significant and thus honorable.

"By remembering Shri Rama's holy name, even those who are born into a low caste become worthy of fame, just as the wild trees that line the streets in the heavenly realm are famous throughout the three worlds." (Dohavali, 16)

To round out the enjoyment there is the heavenly jewel, suramani, as well. Again, you can get whatever you want from this jewel. While all of this may seem like mythology or symbolism to the less intelligent, even if accepted as just a theoretical exercise one can take away valuable lessons. While there is so much material enjoyment in heaven, residence in that realm is not permanent. Reaching that land is never purported to be the ultimate objective in life. It is simply the reward to pious behavior. Piety is doing something the right way. If you play the game right, you might get a reward, like a trophy. Next year, the trophy is given to someone else if you don't win it again. Life in heaven is sort of like this. The duration of residence there is commensurate with the number of pious credits one accumulates. Once the time is up, the individual must fall back down to the earthly region, forced to work again for their so-called enjoyment.

Here Goswami Tulsidas puts the heavenly enjoyments into the proper context. He says they sort of resemble the image of the four couples newly married in Janaka's kingdom. He indeed compares a single image to having a wish-fulfilling cow, a desire tree, a magical jewel, and residence in the heavenly realm of the moon all at once! Strangely enough, this barely suffices as an accurate comparison. Rather than come close to the side of exaggeration, it leans more towards the side of underwhelming with respect to accurately describing the value of the image of the four couples.

This is because the couples are all God Himself and His immediate expansions. Rama is the leader; the eldest brother. He is the Supreme Lord Vishnu in an incarnation who appeared on this earth many thousands of years ago. Rama's three younger brothers are also expansions of Vishnu. Vishnu does not reside in the heavenly realm. His position is fixed, so He never has to leave His home. In His realm the enjoyment comes through association with Him and serving Him.

Material enjoyment has no place there since the residents have rightly cast it aside as being insignificant. In the highest realm Vishnu lives in His original form of Shri Krishna. There the residents roam a beautiful forest, where materially there is not very much, but everything is spiritual in nature. Therefore everyone is supremely blissful all the time.

A sampling of that bliss is available in the earthly region during the time of the divine descents. Rama and His brothers have the most beautiful wives, whom they accept at the occasion of Sita's svayamvara in Janakpur. That event puts the material rewards into the proper perspective, teaching one and all that no reward conjured up by the materially afflicted mind could ever compare with the association of the Supreme Personality of Godhead and those who love Him.

VERSE 153

जनक अनुज तनया दोउ परम मनोरम।
जेठि भरत कहँ ब्याहि रूप रति सय सम।।153।।

janaka anuja tanayā do'u parama manorama |
jeṭhi bharata kahaṁ byāhi rūpa rati saya sama ||153||

"The two daughters of Janaka's younger brother were supremely beautiful. The elder one, whose beauty equaled hundreds of Ratis, married Bharata." (153)

Essay - Manorama

There are different kinds of drunks. One is morose. They may be a happy person normally, but after a few adult beverages they tend to sit in the corner and sulk. Then there is the aggressive drunk. While they are mild and gentle during normal times, it's as if their beers are cans of spinach going into the mouth of Popeye. They think they can fight anyone in the bar, perform any strongman feat, and endure any pain just because they've had a few drinks.

Another kind is the happy drunk. Their love for the world comes out once they are intoxicated. They go up to everyone and hug them. They run through their contacts on their phone, calling each of them and telling them how they feel. From the king of education that is the science of self-realization we learn that deep down the soul wants to love. This is its feature of bliss, which is known as ananda in Sanskrit. Intoxication brings out the perverted form of the genuine sentiments belonging to the pure spirit soul. The soul is in its ideal state when loving God. That love manifests in service, and so when there is a chance to serve and the mood is pure, one is extremely happy. The purest form of the happy individual then gets shown to the world.

If you are genuinely happy and feeling so much love for someone else, you can't stop in your offering of service. With the householder this mentality manifests in the continuous offering of food. "What, that's all you're going to eat? You didn't like the food? No, you have to eat more. Here, take some more of this. You didn't have enough of that, either. Here, now your plate is full again."

With the member of a team, the love is shown in the offering of praise. If a player on a sports franchise is retiring after many solid years of service, it is not uncommon to hold a retirement ceremony for them. If the player is really special, he'll be shown honor by all the teams that he played against. Past players will come out to offer praise and gifts. The fans will give standing ovation after standing ovation. The honor paid will reach the point of excess, where the honored will have to ask others to stop, lest they further embarrass them.

In ancient times, one of the ways to pay honor to someone else was to give away your daughter to them. Known as the kanyadana, or the donation of a maiden, this was a very nice gift for the groom. These marriages were in dharma and not kama as they are today in most cases. Dharma is duty. In its original meaning it is an essential characteristic. It takes on the meaning of duty when the principles followed help to maintain that characteristic. Dharma is thus also known as religion and righteousness.

In a marriage in dharma, both parties follow duties that will help to make the relationship fruitful. The sought after reward is not a happy home, time enjoyed in each other's company, or even good progeny. Surely those things can be good, but the real objective is God consciousness. This is the real fruit of an existence, and it is also the most difficult to taste. There is the illusory energy known as maya that gets in the way. Maya tells us to chase after sense gratification instead. Earn so much money, find the spouse of your dreams, care for your young children and pets, find a hobby to lose yourself in - do anything except think of God.

One of the English translations for the Sanskrit word maya is "that which is not." Maya is specifically not Brahman, or the truth. Dharma is for finding the truth and going beyond it to Parabrahman, who is the entity most of the world scantily knows through the term "God." The path of dharma is not limited to renounced asceticism. It is not limited to study of esoteric truths found in a high philosophy. It is not limited to the difficulties of mystic yoga. Any aspect of life can be part of dharma, including marriage.

In the marriage in dharma, the chaste wife is a wonderful gift. She helps the husband stay on the righteous path. She supports him. He, in turn, protects her. The relationship is beautiful. As any relationship is difficult to maintain, if each party understands their role and the higher objective, the chances for maintaining that relationship and having it blossom increase.

In the above referenced verse from the Janaki Mangala, we have an example of a person in total bliss. He is in ananda because he is getting to serve God directly. Parabrahman has appeared on earth in His spiritual form as a beautiful prince from Ayodhya. King Janaka is the fortunate soul here given the chance to serve. His essential characteristic visible to the world is adherence to righteousness. This was tested when he decided upon a contest for the marriage of his beautiful daughter Sita. Janaka vowed to give Sita away to whichever prince would first lift the amazingly heavy bow of Shiva.

By divine arrangement, Rama attended the contest and lifted the bow. Thus Janaka was able to give away his most precious Sita to God. But that wasn't enough. His bliss was too high to be limited by a single offering. Rama had three younger brothers, all equal to Him in beauty, good character, and strength. They were chivalrous princes as well, and since the custom of the time was for the elder to marry prior to the youngers, these princes were without supporters.

Janaka took care of that by then giving away the daughters of his younger brother. The eldest daughter married Bharata. She was supremely beautiful, parama manorama. Manorama means "to please the mind," and the adjective parama indicates that she was the best at pleasing the mind of another. This came from her beauty alone, which rivaled that of hundreds of Ratis. Rati is the consort of Kamadeva, who is the equivalent of a cupid. Kamadeva is the god of desire, and he is very beautiful. His wife is naturally very beautiful as well.

Not meant to be an insult but a way to praise further, the beauty of Bharata's wife was like one hundred times that of Rati's. This was fitting for Rama's next younger brother. Bharata was of a dark complexion, just like Rama. Janaka had already given everything to Rama, so the brothers were next to be showered with gifts. They are also partial incarnations of the Supreme Lord, so in this act Janaka's devotional service continued. Whether one is a king or a pauper, whether they are wealthy or modest, if their desires in devotion are pure, know that the Supreme Lord will create endless opportunities for their service to continue and flourish.

VERSE 154

सिय लघु भगिनि लखन कहुँ रूप उजागरि।
लखन अनुज श्रुतकीरति सब गुन आगरि।।१५४।।

siya laghu bhaginī lakhana kahuṁ rūpa ujāgari |
lakhana anuja śrutakīrati saba guna āgari ||154||

"Sita's younger sister, who was also very beautiful, was given to Lakshmana. Shrutakirti, who had every virtue and good quality, was given to Lakshmana's younger brother." (154)

Essay - A Liberal Donor

Any parent with multiple children around the same age knows the issue with gift-giving. As soon as one child gets something, the other one wants it. Typically the younger voices their displeasure more than the older. As the younger ones get what they want more often, rather than explain the triviality of the issue, the parents get the same toy for the younger one. Then the older one naturally complains: "It's not fair. Why do you always give them what they want? This is my toy. I got it for my birthday. Why should they get the same thing? When I used to cry for things you would just tell me 'No.' Now they do the same thing and you give in."

Such are the ways of sibling rivalries, and not much can be done to stop the competition. The best bet for the parents is to always purchase the same toy in pairs. Another way is to designate a specific toy for the enjoyment of all, a sort of shared ownership. The parents behave this way because of the love they feel for the children. They don't want any particular child to feel slighted. Though the parents may be more lenient with one than another, it does not mean that they love any one of the children more than the others. It would be like someone asking you if you loved your father more than your mother, or vice versa. In a typical situation, you love both of them equally.

The parents don't choose which one of their children to love more, and so they try their best to not show favoritism. This attitude in its purest form was exhibited by a father with his new son-in-laws a long time ago. The sons belonged to the King of Ayodhya, Maharaja Dasharatha. They were four brothers who loved each other equally. What guided the three younger ones was their utmost respect, compassion, and concern for the eldest, Shri Rama. They were more than thrilled at His marriage ceremony, which was not arranged in the typical fashion.

In the time period in question, the Treta Yuga, kings would give away their daughters to other princes for marriage. This was how the marriages were arranged. There was no free intermingling between men and women. This was done to protect the women. Rather than leave them vulnerable to the perils of illicit sex, where one is more or less used for the bodily pleasure they can provide, the fathers would find a lifelong protector for their daughters when the age was right. This system also helped to keep the men focused, as they didn't have to worry about how their family lines would continue. They didn't have to worry about finding someone to support them in their religious efforts, which were taken to be the most important duties in life.

Rama would have been the ideal choice for any king looking to marry off his daughter. Rama was kind, sweet, gentle, strong, brave, courageous, and very respectful. These seemingly contradictory qualities appeared in Him in full. King Janaka, who had the most beautiful daughter named Sita, would have chosen Rama in a second, had he known that the eldest son of Dasharatha was roaming this earth.

Unaware of Rama's presence, Janaka held a contest instead. This way the chosen husband for Sita would be known to be the strongest person in the world. As his daughter was very attractive, winning this contest would at least give pause to other kings who might think of stealing her away. A beautiful woman is a magnet for men; this is just nature's way. If she likes, she can fend off suitors more easily by wearing a wedding ring. The presence of her husband will serve as the strongest deterrent for others looking to go beyond friendship with her. To win this contest required lifting an extremely heavy bow originally belonging to Lord Shiva. Thus the winner would have the most strength to use in defending Sita.

Rama won that contest. He got to marry Sita. For the ceremony, His family from Ayodhya came to Janakpur, the city ruled by King Janaka. The king was so happy to give Sita away to Rama that he felt the need to be more generous. Sita has every good quality. Think of every virtue you would want in a person. Now imagine that they exist at the highest levels and are always on display. Though this combination seems impossible, it is found in Sita, who was thus the perfect daughter for the righteous Janaka.

Janaka didn't want to part with his precious daughter, but he did so to follow protocol. Moreover, Shri Rama is the Supreme Personality of Godhead in His avatara as a warrior prince. A sincere offering to God never goes in vain. One is never a loser by sacrificing something for the pleasure of the Supreme Lord. Indeed, Sita is Rama's eternal consort, so it was due to the benevolence of the couple that Janaka got the chance to make the offering to Rama.

Janaka didn't want the three younger brothers to feel slighted. Janaka's younger brother had two beautiful unmarried daughters. They were then given away to Bharata and Shatrughna respectively. Bharata's wife is described as parama manorama, which means "supremely pleasing to the mind." Here Goswami Tulsidas says that Shatrughna's new wife, Shrutakirti, had every virtue and good quality. While all four brothers were sons of Dasharatha, Lakshmana and Shatrughna were the youngest two and they appeared from the womb of Queen Sumitra. Therefore here Shatrughna is referred to as Lakshmana's younger brother.

Lakshmana, who was with Rama during the contest of the bow, received Sita's younger sister Urmila as a wife. It is said here that she was also very beautiful. The brothers were already so happy for Rama to wed Sita. There was no sibling rivalry amongst them. If there was ever any competition, it was in how to please Rama. Janaka treated all four brothers like his sons, and so he made sure that none of them would feel slighted. All four brothers were matched with ideal wives. The generosity of Janaka knows no bounds, as he gave everything to Rama and His family. In the process, his devotion continued to flourish, which is the best possible reward to any activity.

VERSE 155

राम बिबाह समान बिबाह तीनिउ भए।
जीवन फल लोचन फल बिधि सब कहँ दए॥155॥

rāma bibāha samāna bibāha tīni'u bha'e |
jīvana phala locana phala bidhi saba kahaṁ da'e ||155||

"Just as Rama was married, so the three brothers became married in the same way. Through all the rituals they were given the fruit of their lives and the fruit of their eyes." (155)

Essay - The Fruit of an Existence

If you see a new child emerge from the womb, typically you hope for good things for it. Especially if the child is yours, you want it to experience all that life has to offer. You want it to reach the ultimate objective. But what if you don't know what that objective is? What if you have been searching for transcendence your whole life and have yet to find it? No need for panic, as the Vaishnava saints reveal to us the mature fruit to an existence. Within that existence are other gifts, such as eyes, ears, legs, a nose and a face. There are specific fruits tied to each of these things as well.

"Just try to learn the truth by approaching a spiritual master. Inquire from him submissively and render service unto him. The self-realized soul can impart knowledge unto you because he has seen the truth." (Lord Krishna, Bhagavad-gita, 4.34)

In the Bhagavad-gita, Lord Krishna says to approach a spiritual master. "By inquiring from him submissively and rendering service unto him, the self-realized soul will impart knowledge unto you." The specific qualification of the spiritual master mentioned here is that he has seen the truth, tattva darshinah. A byproduct of seeing the fruit is tasting it. I can see the pizza pie that's fresh out of the oven sitting on the kitchen table, but that isn't really experiencing it. I'll only know the wonderful taste once I decide to eat part or all of that pie.

The spiritual master has tasted the fruit an existence has to offer because they took to serving the Truth after seeing it. This truth is absolute. It is beyond duality. As such, it is not the truth only for the Hindus. It is not the truth only for the intelligent. It is also not the truth only for the human beings. It is the truth in all time periods and all situations.

The living entities face dual conditions and circumstances. One child is born into wealth, considered to have a silver spoon in their mouth. Another child is born into poverty, living in squalor. One person is given the chance for a good education, while another is forced into difficult labor at a young age. Regardless the circumstances, the Absolute Truth can always be seen.

The benefit of seeing Him is serving Him subsequently. Service takes place through one or all of nine different methods that belong to the discipline described as bhakti-yoga, or devotional service. Seeing the truth is one step, but serving Him is far superior. Following bhakti-yoga allows even the conditioned soul blinded by ignorance to one day see the truth. And hopefully from that vision their resolve in serving Him only becomes stronger. Shri Hanuman, likely the most famous of the deities of the Hindu tradition, saw God face to face. He saw the Absolute Truth in His incarnation as Shri Ramachandra. Hanuman then didn't end his life. He didn't consider his work to be done. In fact, he took even more initiative in serving the Supreme Lord, essentially pouncing on the opportunity.

That service is the true boon to an existence. In the above referenced verse from the Janaki Mangala, the people of the city of Janakpur all received the fruit that life has to offer. They accepted this wonderful gift through the performance of marriage rituals. Seems odd, for sure. After all, we've never been too keen on attending a marriage ceremony for someone we don't know very well. Even if we know one of the parties, the other may be a mystery to us.

Here the people felt supreme love because the women getting married were daughters to the king and his younger brother. These princesses were like the children of the community. They were cared for and loved by everyone under the protection of King Janaka. The fruit of their lives came from the fact that these princesses got to marry Shri Rama and His three younger brothers. The wives were ideal in every way. They had beautiful features and the perfect behavior suitable for marriage. The men were ideal as well, chivalrous princes who never shirked responsibilities. They never were afraid to fight to defend righteousness and righteous people.

The loving sentiments of the people were a kind of offering. Thus this qualified as devotional service, which is the fruit to an existence. They also received the fruit of their eyes by witnessing the marriage ceremony. Just as we may wish to be temporarily deaf on days when there is a loud car alarm outside or someone sitting next to us chewing their food with their mouth open, depending on what we see sometimes we may wish to not have eyes. Just because we can see doesn't mean that everything within our vision will be pleasant. Indeed, so many visions can be traumatic, things we wish to purge from our memory.

The fruit of having eyes is getting to see God. Seeing His marriage ceremony during His appearance on earth as an incarnation is the same as seeing Him. His absolute nature is passed on to those who serve Him as well. This explains why there is so much joy in meditating on pictures of Shri Hanuman, who is always involved in some kind of devotional service. Thanks to Goswami Tulsidas, here the mind can concentrate on the wonderful marriage ceremony for the four brothers and how everyone who witnessed it became supremely delighted.

VERSE 156

दाइज भयउ बिबिध बिधि जाइ न सो गनि।
दासी दास बाजि गज हेम बसन मनि।।156।।

dā'ija bhaya'u bibidha bidhi jā'i na so gani |
dāsī dāsa bāji gaja hema basana mani ||156||

"From the in-laws they received too many gifts to count. Included were male and female servants, horses, elephants, gold, clothing and jewels." (156)

Essay - A Generous Dowry

External features alone do not distinguish a material existence. One may be rich, poor, young, old, male, or female, but it is the consciousness which gives the real indication on the type of existence. In a material existence one is always fearful. Consider the animals. They are in a precarious condition since they don't have great intelligence to use in defending themselves. A dog cannot make a call to the local security company to install an alarm system to surround the perimeter of its home. The cat cannot pick up a rifle to defend itself from attack. The human beings have these advantages, but in the material existence they are also fearful. This fear permeates all aspects of life, including marriage.

In looking around, you think you have good reason to fear. Where are the jobs? Where is the security? Just one accident while walking outside could leave you stuck with a debt in medical bills impossible to pay off in a single lifetime. Financial hardship is a moment away, and when it comes how is one expected to cope? Even if you pay off the mortgage on your house, you still have to pay taxes annually. The larger your house and the more affluent the neighborhood, the larger the burden that must be paid each year. In effect, the beginning portion of the work year is spent in just paying the debt of taxes. Who says slavery is abolished, as one must work in order to be allowed to live in the area they do?

Therefore, not surprisingly, money is a major concern. "How will I save money? Let me clip these coupons. Let me shop where there are deals. Even if this deal is supposedly expired, let me haggle with the salesperson to see if they can cut me some slack. Let me threaten to cancel my phone service so that the company will lower my monthly bill. Let me purchase items from a big box retailer, use them for a while, and then return them to the store. The store has a very liberal return policy, so in this way I'm renting things for free instead of buying them outright."

As the fearful soul in a material existence is constantly concerned with money, they can't help themselves when it comes to marriage arrangements. Vedic marriages are notorious for the concept of a dowry, which today is taken to mean a payoff. "I'll only allow your daughter to marry my son if you pay me a certain amount. Make me an offer I can't refuse. Without a handsome dowry, this marriage isn't going to happen."

From the above referenced verse from the Janaki Mangala we get the real purpose to a dowry. It is nothing more than a gift. Indeed, even in weddings that are not arranged by the parents, there is still great concern for money. The hosts of the reception, typically the bride and groom, eagerly anticipate the gifts that are to come in, often openly stating their preference to receive cash instead of items.

The dowry in the original sense is a gift from the father of the bride to the newlyweds. A gift is better if it comes from the heart, if it's given out of love instead of obligation. Janaka had the most love in his heart for his beautiful daughter Sita. He was so pleased that she was marrying the eldest son of King Dasharatha, Shri Rama. The first hint of Janaka's enormous generosity came when he gave away three more beautiful princesses to Rama's brothers. Thus four marriages took place simultaneously. Rather than fret over what gift to give or how much he had to pay, Janaka then liberally donated so many things.

Here it is said that the gifts were too many to count. There were servants, both male and female. We can think of these people to be like butlers and maids, but more well-wishers than hired help. Instead of simply getting a paycheck for their work, they received a sustainable livelihood in a royal kingdom. They were very happy to serve the new couples. These servants were very close to the members of the kingdom. Sita had her own attendants as well, and they always looked after her.

There was gold, jewels, horses, elephants and clothing. Janaka gave the best gifts to the new couples. Since the men who were getting married were the Supreme Lord originally and three partial incarnations of Him, Janaka's offering was one in devotion. In pure devotion, bhakti-yoga, or Krishna-prema, there is no motivation and no interruption. Nothing can check someone who wants to serve God. The abundance of gifts wasn't required here, but Janaka had it to offer. He was not afraid of losing anything, for by serving God one gains the whole world.

Whether one has a lot or a little is of no concern to the Supreme Lord. It's the thought that counts, and here Janaka showed how pure his thoughts were. Even in the material existence, where circumstances give cause for constant fear, one can still make kind offerings simply through chanting the holy names, "Hare Krishna Hare Krishna, Krishna Krishna, Hare Hare, Hare Rama Hare Rama, Rama Rama, Hare Hare." A single instance of chanting the holy names purely, without motive, is more valuable than any material offering that could be made.

VERSE 157

दान मान परमान प्रेम पूरन किए।
समधी सहित बरात बिनय बस करि लिए॥157॥

dāna māna paramāna prema pūrana ki'e |
samadhī sahita barāta binaya basa kari li'e ||157||

"With love he offered charity, respect and supreme respect to completion. Dasharatha and the barata party accepted everything politely." (157)

Essay - Charity and Respect

So many interesting truths one learns from a single review of the Bhagavad-gita, the short ancient Sanskrit text nestled inside a massively comprehensive work known as the Mahabharata. The fundamental lesson, the most basic truth required for understanding the higher truths, comes from the opening remarks of the speaker, teacher, and always realized soul, Shri Krishna. He declares that all living entities are equal in their original constitution, for they are spirit souls.

"It is said that the soul is invisible, inconceivable, immutable, and unchangeable. Knowing this, you should not grieve for the body." (Lord Krishna, Bhagavad-gita, 2.25)

What does it mean to be spirit? For one thing, it means that the individual never dies. Just as the body changes from boyhood to youth to old age, the same soul similarly passes into another body at death. This individual is thus constant. This makes sense if we think about it. We don't consider ourselves to be different today than we were yesterday. Perhaps this morning there is a muscle spasm in my left leg that wasn't there the day before. Perhaps I don't have as much hair on my head as I did five years ago. Yet from these changes alone to think that I am a different person is silly. Just as I have not changed my identity from five seconds ago, I am the same person I was when I was the size of a tiny pea in my mother's womb.

All living entities are souls. We think others are different because of the outward covering. Sort of like a Halloween costume party, where everyone is dressed differently, from the perception granted to us by the eyes we make distinctions based on outward appearance. There is another similarity to all creatures as well. In addition to having the individual soul residing within, there is something known as the Supersoul. In Sanskrit the word for soul is atma. Atma can also mean body or mind, but it is generally used to reference the soul.

Though all souls are spiritual, there can be different types. The individual soul is known as jivatma. This other soul is paramatma. One is ordinary and the other supreme. An ordinary soul is obviously still amazing, for it retains its vibrancy throughout the changes in life, including the greatest change known as death. Paramatma is more amazing because its influence spreads to all creatures. Moreover, Paramatma, though residing within all the countless living entities, is still singular. Paramatma is one person. This means that I have something else in common with you. We both have Paramatma living inside of us.

"The Supreme Lord is situated in everyone's heart, O Arjuna, and is directing the wanderings of all living entities, who are seated as on a machine, made of the material energy." (Lord Krishna, Bg. 18.61)

From further study of the Bhagavad-gita, whose principles are not limited by faith and sectarian boundaries, we learn that the Supreme Lord is the very paramatma; it is one of His features. It is not His complete feature, though, for His actual transcendental attributes are not visibly manifest to the conditioned soul. From hearing I can get perfect knowledge. If someone tells me that putting my hand in fire will burn my hand, that is perfect knowledge. If I accept it, then I possess some knowledge that is free of flaw. In the same way, if I hear about the paramatma living inside of me and every other creature, I have perfect knowledge of it.

However, I still can't necessarily see what Paramatma looks like. To get a vision of the attributes of the Supreme Lord, I need Bhagavan. Bhagavan is the same as Paramatma; the distinction between more complete and less complete is with relation to our external vision. On a cloudy day we can't see the sun as clearly, but this has no bearing on the sun. The sun is always the sun, regardless of whether we can see it or not. So the same holds true with the Supreme Lord.

Since Paramatma is within everyone, we might make the mistake of treating everyone exactly the same. In mind I can understand that God is in the heart of the dog and in the heart of the priest, but to treat each the same way is silly. I wouldn't ask the dog about the key questions of life and death. I wouldn't go up to a priest and start rubbing its belly and asking it to go fetch a tennis ball.

In the above referenced verse from the Janaki Mangala, King Janaka exhibits behavior that follows realization of the divine vision. He is self-realized, so he both knows about Paramatma and can see it. Still, his behavior is tailored to the time, circumstance, and person. Here it is said that he offered charity, respect, and supreme respect to completion. This was right after his daughter married the eldest son of the king of Ayodhya. Janaka was the host of the ceremony, and from Ayodhya came a large contingent. They were so happy to see their beloved Rama wed the daughter of King Janaka, Sita.

Janaka too was so thrilled, and so he gave away beautiful brides to Rama's three younger brothers as well. After the ceremonies were complete, he gave charity to those who deserved it. Charity is to be given to those who are in an inferior position. This only make sense. One of the common complaints of citizens living in democracies is the practice of handing out government money to wealthy businesses and businessmen. Commonly known as corporate welfare, this practice is frowned upon and yet still employed to maneuver power in government.

To those in the superior position, one offers respect, or mana. Dana is for the inferior and mana for the superior. Janaka also offered paramana, or supreme respect. There was a diverse crowd at this wedding. Dasharatha was in an equal position with Janaka, but the king from Ayodhya also had his family priests and his royal attendants with him. Janaka did not offer each of them the same treatment. He knew they had God living inside of them, and so he respected them in the proper way. We respect our teachers by hearing from them and carrying out their requests. We respect our children by guiding them, by imposing limits and protecting them. There is respect in both instances, but the implementations are different.

Janaka's behavior was indicative of his high consciousness. To have God consciousness is to reach the pinnacle of a material existence. It is said that a life form is superior to matter, something which shows signs of life superior to that, something with consciousness superior to that, something with sense perception superior to that, and so on. When you reach an object that has God consciousness, true awareness of the Supersoul and its origin, then you have reached the height of the evolutionary chain. In that supreme state, one offers respect to God through so many ways, including with how they treat others. It is no wonder then that the supremely intelligent Janaka received Rama, Bhagavan in His avatara as a warrior prince, as his son-in-law.

VERSE 158

गे जनवासे राउ संगु सुत सुतबहु।
जनु पाए फल चारि सहित साधन चहु।।158।।

ge janavāse rā'u saṅgu suta sutabahu |
janu pā'e phala cāri sahita sādhana cahu ||158||

"The king returned to the guest house with his sons and their wives, like getting the four rewards in life along with the four sadhanas." (158)

Essay - He That Would Thrive

Having paternal affection for four sons who are expansions of the Supreme Lord Vishnu is a much higher reward than anything the material world can offer. Love gives meaning to life. It is the reason for living. Without love, there seems to be no reason to get up in the morning. The issue, of course, is where to repose that love. Where should one's undying affection turn? If the affection is undying, then it would make sense to find a corresponding object that never ceases to be. That object should remain in its attractive state for as long as the affection is offered. This qualification belongs only to the Supreme Personality of Godhead, and so Dasharatha's affection represented the greatest boon in life.

To reach the state of loving God is very difficult. It can take millions of lifetimes even. The allures of the material world are very strong. There is an illusion that strengthens the attraction to all things "not God." To help the individual in their struggle to find transcendental love, religious doctrine is passed on. Not everything is revealed in the opening pages. The spiritual master, who keeps the information safely with him, not selling it for money and cheapening its value, tests the disciple first to see if they are sincere. Even then, the information is shared slowly, with more value coming from the realization of knowledge after hearing the principles and truths.

To one who has not yet achieved the mature fruit an existence has to offer, four rewards in life are taken to be paramount. They are dharma, artha, kama and moksha, which translate to religiosity, economic development, sense gratification and ultimate liberation. To receive all of these rewards in one lifetime is very difficult. Sometimes one reward gets in the way of another. To be religious means to suppress your pursuit of money. To be wealthy means to want to enjoy a lot, which leaves less time for religion. And after spending a lifetime enjoying the rewards of hard work, how is one supposed to get liberation, which is the relinquishing of not only everything accepted during this lifetime but also the desire to ever go through the cycle of birth and death again?

So to achieve these rewards in one lifetime is very rare. To help the process along, there are the four sadhanas, or means to achieving the reward. The four means are being able to tell the difference between material and spiritual things, renouncing material things, developing six qualities conducive to godly life, and desiring liberation. These sadhanas help one to achieve the four rewards. So as rare as it is to obtain the four fruits of life, getting the four sadhanas to help you along at the same time is even more rare.

Goswami Tulsidas references these four fruits and their sadhanas in the above quoted verse from the Janaki Mangala to show how rare it was for someone to get such a gift as that which came to King Dasharatha. The king's eldest son Rama was married to the daughter of King Janaka. Sita and Rama married in a grand ceremony in Mithila, and here the festivities have just completed. Dasharatha was the guest party; he had travelled from Ayodhya. Janaka was the host. Dasharatha had three other sons as well, and Janaka was so liberally minded that he arranged for their marriages as well.

Rama is God; an incarnation of the Supreme Lord who holds a bow in His hands, wears an enchanting smile on His face, and is always ready to defend the innocent who are practicing their spiritual life. Loving Him is the highest fruit of an existence. Love for God is known as bhakti, and the exercise of that love is known as bhakti-yoga. Bhakti-yoga is above dharma, artha, kama, moksha, sadhanas, attachment, detachment, humility, kindness, strength, nonviolence, peacefulness, truthfulness, and other such virtues and objectives. One who practices bhakti may have one or many of these qualities or rewards, but it is their love for God which dominates.

Nevertheless, the comparison made by Tulsidas is very informative. The brothers are the four rewards and the wives are the sadhanas, which means that the wives help to bring and maintain the rewards. It is considered a great boon to have a faithful wife who is dedicated to helping her husband in his quest for spiritual enlightenment. Great statesmen like Benjamin Franklin quoted the proverb, "He that would thrive must first ask his wife," which has a similar meaning. As these were wives of the Supreme Lord Vishnu and His expansions, they weren't ordinary and thus not required to follow duty in the traditional way. Still, they set the proper example by supporting their husbands, who were tasked with upholding dharma, or righteousness, in society.

From this verse we also learn that love for God automatically incorporates every other reward.

So does this mean that if we love God, we automatically get a brand new flat screen television? If we chant the holy names, "Hare Krishna Hare Krishna, Krishna Krishna, Hare Hare, Hare Rama Hare Rama, Rama Rama, Hare Hare," will we get to eat pizza every day prepared by the world's most famous chef?

Though there may not be a specific material reward received, the enjoyment is superior. With whatever thing we desire, it is the enjoyment from obtaining it that really matters. The four fruits and the four sadhanas bring different kinds of enjoyment, and one who has bhakti automatically receives these enjoyments. In fact, their pleasure is far greater, to a degree immeasurable. Dasharatha had the four fruits and the four sadhanas and so much more, for his mind was always fixed on the lotus feet of Shri Rama.

VERSE 159

चहु प्रकार जेवनार भई बहु भाँतिन्ह।
भोजन करत अवधपति सहित बरातिन्ह।।159।।

cahu prakāra jevanāra bha'ī bahu bhāṁtinha |
bhojana karata avadhapati sahita barātinha ||159||

"With the four types of food, of so many different varieties, the King of Ayodhya and the barata party took their meal." (159)

Essay - Bhojana

There is no doubt that one of the top sensual enjoyments in life is eating. For those living in industrialized nations, where food is easy to find and so much of it is around, where and what to eat often make for the most pressing questions of the day. "Where will I get lunch today? I had pizza the last two days. I had Mexican food for dinner last night. I could pick up something quick, like a bagel, but then that is only one item. I've noticed that eating full meals is better. I especially like to pick at different things, alternating between the items. I am actually able to control my eating better this way. I don't have to eat as much when there is variety." For a host a long time ago, there was great satisfaction in feeding the guests. He gave them every kind of food dish imaginable, and in large quantities. Though the guests took part in the meal, the bhojana, and thus enjoyed themselves, the real pleasure was for the host.

If you are a host, you feel good when your guests eat to their satisfaction. You feel this way based simply on your own experiences. That one time you visited someone's home when you were hungry and they offered you a nice meal made you feel so good that you won't forget it. You weren't expecting it, and since the food was offered as part of the most genuine welcome, it made the eating process that much more special. When we were younger, perhaps many times we didn't think the occasion called for food. And yet that time when our mother showed up with a sandwich and a drink after we had just completed an important exam is something we'll never forget.

Indeed, one of the principal ways for an affectionate mother to offer her protection is to hassle the children about food. One of the most famous mothers in history, Yashoda, used to constantly worry about her son's nutrition. He was a precocious young child who loved to play in the field all day with His friends, who were of or around the same age. The boys had the basic task of tending to the young calves of the farm community. As is common with young children, something that an adult would take to be work is viewed as good fun. Since Yashoda's son was with them, everyone was happy. The mother was blissful as well, but in a different way. She always worried that Krishna had not eaten enough. Therefore she would feed Him very well when He would come home. She would offer Him the best food in the world, of many different varieties, and then take Him to a comfortable place to rest.

Here King Janaka has similar sentiments, including affection in a friendly way. He has just welcomed four new sons into his family, for they have married his daughters and those of his brother. Janaka hosted the ceremony initially only to get his daughter Sita married. So pleased was he in her choice of Shri Rama that he decided to get Rama's three younger brothers married as well.

A Vedic ceremony is not complete until there is the taking of prasadam. The Sanskrit word means "the Lord's mercy," and in this special occasion the food was offered directly to God. The mercy was in the chance to feed Him and take great pleasure. Rama is the Supreme Lord in His incarnation as a warrior prince. He is the same Krishna loved without motivation and without interruption by mother Yashoda. He is the same Vishnu who is always served by the goddess of fortune Lakshmi. He is the same impersonal Brahman which the spiritualists in the mode of goodness try to understand. He is the same Supersoul residing within the heart whom the meditational yogis wish to see.

Janaka's connection was superior since He got to see God and serve Him. There were four kinds of food offered, chatur-vidha. There was food that could be licked, food that could be sucked, food that could be chewed, and food that could be drunk. Goswami Tulsidas says that there were so many kinds in each category. The variety helps in both enjoyment and the ability to consume more. If you are at a restaurant and told to eat so many pancakes in one sitting, it will be quite difficult. You can put as much maple syrup and butter on it as you want, but you will still have a hard time. If you throw in some other items, however, like toast, potatoes, cereal, and the like, you will have an easier time consuming everything.

So the four kinds of food allowed Janaka to offer as much as he could to his beloved guests. Their bhojana was very enjoyable, and through their eating Janaka was spiritually satisfied. The Vaishnava is unique in their attitude to always seek God's pleasure first. Rather than ask for this thing or that - fame, money, wealth, women, wine - they want only that God be satisfied. If He is pleased, then they are pleased. Based on Janaka's supreme happiness, we can understand that his offerings were wholeheartedly accepted by Rama's father, the king of Ayodhya, and his party.

VERSE 160

देहि गारि बर नारि नाम लै दुहु दिसि।
जेंवत बढ़ािो अनंद सुहावनि सो निसि।।160।।

dehi gāri bara nāri nāma lai duhu disi |
jenvata baṛhaio ananda suhāvani so nisi ||160||

"From both directions, taking the names of the grooms and brides the ladies kept offering different jokes while they were eating, and this flooded that night with beauty and joy." (160)

Essay - Human Joke Machines

In the early history of American television, there was one actor in particular who was famously known for his skill at making jokes. Affectionately known as the "human joke machine," he could take any word, phrase or subject and immediately come up with a suitable joke. This talent was valuable in that time period, as many homes did not have television. Therefore get-togethers and dinner gatherings often featured live entertainment, where some of the guests would perform sketches, act out plays, and sing and dance. From this verse from the Janaki Mangala, we get an example of a similar practice, where the names of the brides and grooms in a marriage ceremony were taken and jokes made at their expense.

Who likes to be made fun of while having their meal? Just hearing someone else speak with food in their mouth is annoying enough, so to be constantly jabbed at by others while trying to enjoy food seems like harassment. The scene referenced above can be likened to a meal outside at a restaurant with friends and family today. To lighten the mood, surely some jokes will be made. Not everyone will be serious on a night out, where the goal is to have fun.

In this scene, the newlyweds and their wedding party are being fed by the host of the reception, King Janaka of Mithila. The custom in these kinds of weddings is to offer delectable food dishes of different varieties. The dishes were of the variety that could be sucked, licked, chewed, and drunk. The food kept coming too, so there really was bhojana, or enjoyment, from this eating.

During this time, the ladies assembled started taking the names of the brides and grooms. There were four of each. Originally, there was only one couple to be joined. Janaka held a contest of the bow in Mithila to find a suitable husband for his daughter Sita. So pleased was he by the victor in the contest, Janaka arranged to have Sita's husband's three younger brothers get married at the same time.

There were four couples to choose from, and the people taking the names then used those names to make songs. These songs were in jest; they made fun of the people named. This is an art that requires skill. A joke of the wrong tone can offend. And who can make an appropriate curse of someone else using only their name? Those assembled that day most certainly could and from the descriptions of Goswami Tulsidas we see that the curses only increased the bliss of the moment. Everyone was quite pleased, especially those who were the target of such jokes.

Taking the names and making curses out of them is appropriate in an intimate setting. But in places where the divine natures of the targets are not known, the practice is to take the names and make informative discourses out of them. These lectures praise the spiritual attributes of the people in question. Along with lectures and discussions, there are melodious songs of praise as well.

A famous spiritual master of recent times, who was known as the lion-guru for his fearlessness in spreading and defending the timeless principles of divine love, was known as a kind of human verse machine. On a whim, without reaching for any book, he could quote an appropriate verse from the Vedas that served to support his argument. His arguments were always in favor of devotional service, or bhakti-yoga, which means that he was always praising God in some way. Without any advance notice he could find a verse suitable to the discussion, a verse that would ultimately praise the Supreme Lord and His personal form.

From this verse from the Janaki Mangala we get another reminder of how powerful the name of God is. There can never be one name, as no one aspect known to our limited understanding could ever completely describe God. From famous texts like the Brahma-samhita and Shrimad Bhagavatam, we learn that Krishna is the most complete name for the Absolute, as it means all-attractive. Still, other names are used as well. Govinda, Gopala, Rama, Janaradana, Keshava, Achyuta, Damodara, and so many other names are also spoken by those who are favorable towards God. Though no name ever suffices to completely describe everything, one single authorized name uttered is enough to bring God's presence.

Accompanying the presence of God is His unlimited potency. Therefore from the name itself one can create a perfect discussion on some aspect of nature. From the name itself one can compose a beautiful song that reminds others of the divine sports of the Supreme Personality of Godhead, who always enjoys with those who love Him without conditions. And from the name itself one can even make verbal jabs that increase the joy the guests feel at a famous wedding, one where the host arranged everything just right.

CHAND 20

सो निसि सोहावनि मधुर गावति बाजने बाजहिं भले।
नृप कियो भोजन पान पाइ प्रमोद जनवासेहि चले।।
नट भाट मागध सूत जाचक जस प्रतापहि बरनहीं।
सानंद भूसुर बृंद मनि गज देत मन करषै नहीं।।20।।

so nisi sohāvani madhura gāvati bājane bājahiṁ bhale |
nṛpa kiyo bhojana pāna pā'i pramoda janavāsehi cale ||
naṭa bhāṭa māgadha sūta jācaka jasa pratāpahi baranahīṁ |
sānanda bhūsura bṛnda mani gaja deta mana karaṣai nahīṁ ||20||

"On that beautiful night, they played sweet songs with melodious music. The king took his meal, received betel nuts, and then happily returned to the guest house." (Chand 20.1)

"Actors, singers, soldiers, sons, and the people who were watching all praised the king and spoke of his deeds. The king, with joy and without hesitation, gave away jewels and elephants to the groups of brahmanas." (Chand 20.2)

Essay - A Satisfying Meal

What a day for King Dasharatha. He started by taking the long journey to Janakpur after learning that his eldest son Rama had won the contest of the bow. The king was previously worried when he gave permission to Rama to leave the kingdom for a journey into the woods with the venerable sage Vishvamitra. For young children to wander about in great fun is not out of the ordinary. It was Rama's task in particular that caused worry in the father. From the joyous satisfaction described above, we see that the end result turned out to be very favorable.

Not like letting your kids play baseball in the street until the sun goes down or even letting them venture into the woods for a camping trip, Dasharatha gave consent for Rama, who at the time barely had any signs of manhood on His face, to act as the guardian to an elder and wiser brahmana. A brahmana is a priest by trade, but their main qualification is the Brahman vision. We teach our young children not to discriminate. "Don't make judgments based on race. Just because she is a woman doesn't mean that she can't do everything just as well as a man can. Just because this person speaks a different language doesn't mean that they are less intelligent. Don't judge a book by its cover. Find out what's on the inside before you make judgments."

The brahmanas extend this vision out to the largest scope. They see the spiritual equality in ALL beings. They don't have affection for one kind of animal and then disdain for another. They don't sanction the unnecessary killing of one kind of animal and then the protection of another. They see the spirit, or Brahman, within all creatures, and so they are generally nonviolent. They know that not every being will have this same vision, so they don't always offer the same treatment. Nevertheless, they maintain that vision of Brahman. They can see past the cover and into the heart, where the soul resides.

Vishvamitra had issues with others attacking him. There were other brahmanas living in the forest who had the same problem. Night-rangers of the lowest consciousness would regularly attack them, kill them, and then eat their flesh. The lower consciousness means more discrimination. It means not seeing Brahman. It means judging everything simply based on appearance. It means being fooled by vision and ignoring words of wisdom that are best accepted through hearing.

Vishvamitra asked Dasharatha to have Rama protect him. Therefore the brahmana knew something about Rama. He wouldn't have made the request if he thought Rama would be in danger. But still, it was certainly an odd request to make. How was Rama going to take care of Himself, let alone defend against the worst creatures? These night-rangers already had no issue with killing innocent priests, so they certainly wouldn't have mercy for Rama, an adolescent.

Rama's younger brother Lakshmana came along. And so two of Dasharatha's four sons left home to head into danger. They were trained in the military arts, which meant that one day they would defend the kingdom. What better test could there be for them? The king made a huge sacrifice, and he put all faith in Vishvamitra to make sure the outcome was favorable.

The next thing he heard was that Rama was going to marry Janaka's daughter. Thus everything did turn out well for Dasharatha. He and his family were received wonderfully by the hospitable host, King Janaka. After leaving home, through a series of events Rama had made His way to Mithila, where a contest was being held. The winner of this contest would get to marry Sita, Janaka's daughter. She is also known by the affectionate name of Janaki. This name honors both Janaka and Sita. Janaka is famous for his dispassion; he never lets his emotions get the better of him. Emotions often override the intellect, and if you're in a position of power you don't want to allow this to happen. If your emotions win, so many others could lose. Even with his strong affection for his beloved daughter Sita, Janaka still followed his intellect in devising a plan to arrange for her marriage. Since his heart was properly situated, the Supreme Lord guided Him from within on the proper course.

"I am seated in everyone's heart, and from Me come remembrance, knowledge and forgetfulness. By all the Vedas am I to be known; indeed I am the compiler of Vedanta, and I am the knower of the Vedas." (Lord Krishna, Bhagavad-gita, 15.15)

Dasharatha's heart was in the right place when he allowed Rama and Lakshmana to accompany Vishvamitra. Janaka's heart was equally as situated in righteousness when he arranged for the contest of the bow. The Supreme Lord rewarded both their choices by bringing them together in a family. Janaki joined with Rama, who then earned a new name, Janakinatha, to accompany His many others.

After the festivities were over, Dasharatha and his party had a satisfying meal full of variety. Others made jokes while they were eating, and at the end they sung wonderful songs that were accompanied by melodious music. The king received betel nuts afterwards, as was custom to complete a meal. He then returned to the guest house, feeling so happy.

Dasharatha's example shows that in life the decisions aren't always easy. There are many forks in the road, and deciding which way to turn isn't so obvious. Janaka had similar issues, and since both kings were situated in righteousness, their decisions always favored them in the end. The root of their righteousness was their love for God. Dasharatha had love for Rama and Janaka for Sita, and since Sita and Rama are the energy and the energetic Supreme Lord respectively, the love the kings had was pure. The divine couple guided them along the proper path, as they guide any who are devoted to them in thought, word and deed.

Essay - Bhusura

The English term "demi-god" used by Thomas Jefferson in describing the group of men who assembled for the Constitutional Convention in 1787 gets a more complete definition in the ancient texts known as the Vedas. Demigod is the English term, while in Sanskrit the word is "deva," which just means "god" or "godly." The term "demigod" is a more accurate translation for "deva" because an ordinary god is always subordinate to the superior and singular Supreme Personality of Godhead. A godly entity is one who has more opulence and abilities than the majority of the rest of the living entity population in a particular region. The demigod possesses more of the qualities of the original God than do others.

When we hear that someone is godly, we immediately think of greatness. "Oh, they must live for a long time. They must have so much enjoyment where they reside. They must be able to grant wishes. If I'm in trouble, I should be able to pray to them for help. If I need guidance, a healing hand, or someone to rescue me from darkness, I should be able to go to them and find my way out through their intervention."

"Those who study the Vedas and drink the soma juice, seeking the heavenly planets, worship Me indirectly. They take birth on the planet of Indra, where they enjoy godly delights." (Lord Krishna, Bhagavad-gita, 9.20)

These are natural expectations of the demigods. In order to deliver on the requests of the not as godly living entities, the demigods should have extraordinary powers. Therefore the demigods have designated for them a separate residence, a heavenly realm. When we contemplate the idea of ascending to heaven after death, it would be to the region of the demigods. There one gets to enjoy more, in their preferred fashion.

In the verse quoted above from the Janaki Mangala, we see that there can be demigods on the earth as well. The term used here is "bhusura." This is a compound Sanskrit word composed of the words "bhu" and "sura". "Bhu" refers to the earthly realm, i.e. where we currently reside. "Sura" refers to demigod. A sura is distinct from an asura, or one who is not a demigod. The foundational characteristic of a sura is their belief in God. They have some idea of realized knowledge and some faith in the highest power to accompany it. Their devotion may not always be entirely pure, but whatever deviations they have are innocent enough. They are not envious of God, and nor do they think that He doesn't exist. The material nature is difficult to overcome, so even demigods have a difficult time remaining pure in their devotion. The asura is the opposite in qualities of a demigod; their foundational characteristic is their envy of God or their flat out denial of His existence.

"But ignorant and faithless persons who doubt the revealed scriptures do not attain God consciousness. For the doubting soul there is happiness neither in this world nor in the next." (Lord Krishna, Bg. 4.40)

The demigods of the earth are the brahmanas. Interestingly enough, they are typically not very powerful materially. They may not even live for very long. In some areas of the world, they live like homeless beggars. The famous Sanatana Gosvami of the Gaudiya-Vaishnava tradition would often survive on a little amount of flour which he would beg for every day. He would then take that trivial amount and mix in some water from a sacred river. Having something that resembled dough, he would then bake the compound in a makeshift oven. The resulting preparation would then be offered to God and eaten as prasadam, or the Lord's mercy. This was certainly less food than what is found in the modern day practice of "dumpster diving" of the homeless. Though the amount was little, it was more than enough for the very powerful saint, who worshiped the Supreme Lord in thought, word and deed, writing so much about the science of devotional service, or bhakti-yoga, in the process.

The work of such a brahmana is what makes them a bhusura, or a demigod of the earth. Though they may live completely renounced, not having a possession in the world, they can grant tremendous benedictions to others. One who approaches them humbly and inquires from them submissively can learn the truth. This is because the self-realized soul has seen the truth. They didn't demand to see it right away, either. They didn't insist that someone else show it to them. They instead followed the same process, accepting knowledge from a self-realized soul. By accepting that knowledge and carrying out the recommended practices, they were able to see the truth themselves. They acquired the eyes necessary to see the divine influence in everything.

To such demigods of the earth, King Janaka donated so many elephants and jewels. He did this after the wedding of his daughter was arranged and all were singing the glories of the occasion. In his royal kingdom, Janaka had supporters in singers, actors, poets, soldiers, sons, daughters, and everyone in the town practically. They were so happy that Janaka's beloved daughter Sita found the perfect match in a husband. Rama is the Supreme Lord, the truth that the self-realized souls have seen. Through Janaka's good character, Sita appeared in his family. Through his good works, Rama married into it. Thus the king's glories know no end.

By giving gifts to the brahmanas, Janaka pleased them. They in turn were able to better carry out their duties, which are the most important in a society. Though perhaps paltry in physical stature, the demigods of the earth can give the whole world to a disciple who is sincere. They can give the benediction of devotional service, which allows one to feel happiness that transcends the bounds of birth and death. There is no proper way to repay the brahmanas for this gift, but pious souls still give away whatever they can at the appropriate times. Any person, whether they are a king or not, can at least attempt to repay the debt owed to the bhusuras by chanting the holy names continuously: Hare Krishna Hare Krishna, Krishna Krishna, Hare Hare, Hare Rama Hare Rama, Rama Rama, Hare Hare.

DEPARTURE TO AYODHYA

VERSE 161

करि करि बिनय कछुक दिन राखि बरातिन्ह।
जनक कीन्ह पहुनाई अगनित भाँतिन्ह॥161॥

kari kari binaya kachuka dina rākhi barātinha |
janaka kīnha pahunā'ī aganita bhāṁtinha ||161||

"Again and again he requested the barata party to stay a few more days. Janaka continued to offer hospitality of so many kinds." (161)

Essay - A Welcome Never to Wear Out

"Oh, they're coming to stay with us for a week? That is going to be so great. I'm very excited right now. I'll help you prepare their room, dear. We can go to this place on the first day they are here. We can go to that place on the second day. We have to eat at this restaurant, as since they moved away they haven't been able to get their favorite dish. How great will it be to have them back in our home?"

…a week into their stay

"Man, they're still here? I feel very bad for saying this, but I can't wait until they leave. I haven't been able to do anything. It's like I'm trapped in my own home. I have to entertain constantly. I don't get any alone time. My routine is entirely thrown off. Their visit gives me pause to reflect on how my life is in general. I guess I don't really like idleness at all. I'm always doing something, and I prefer it that way. It's been great seeing these guests, but now I'm through with sitting around. I want to be doing things on my own terms again."

In the famous Poor Richard's Almanack, a publication which was released yearly for a while in colonial America in the 18th century, there is a particular saying from the author that has relevance to hosting and dealing with guests. It says that guests and fish both start to stink after three days. Fish is a kind of flesh, and so naturally it starts to rot if not eaten very quickly. There were no freezers during that time, so it wasn't like the food could be preserved for very long.

The guests don't literally stink; but their presence starts to become a nuisance after three days. This is not a knock on the guests or the host; it is just the general situation. If the guest stays longer, they are more permanent residents, which means that everyone else has to adjust to having new people living in the house. From this sagacious advice from Poor Richard, we see how to both plan trips to the homes of our friends and family and how to deal with hosting them ourselves.

If anyone could buck the trend, it would have to be the Supreme Lord. Indeed, in the above referenced verse from the Janaki Mangala, we see that when He visits some place, He never wears out His welcome. Indeed, what starts to happen is the host gets nervous at the Lord's impending departure. He begs and begs for the preferred guest to stay a few more days.

The beseeching host in this instance is King Janaka. The guest party consists of Shri Rama, His three younger brothers, His father, and the accompanying royal entourage that travelled to Janakpur. They were there to witness the marriage ceremony of Sita to Rama. Sita was Janaka's beloved daughter. So in this case Sita was now a guest as well; she was ready to depart back to Ayodhya where Rama lived.

In Vedic culture, it is the etiquette to always ask the guest to stay longer. "You can't leave right now. I will make some food to eat. Why do you have to leave tonight? Spend the night here and leave in the morning, when you won't be as tired." There is religious merit earned from being a good host. It is a shared value also, as the same practice is present in other cultures as well.

Here Janaka went beyond the etiquette of asking Rama to stay longer. He kept providing hospitality in different ways. The ways were uncountable, as Goswami Tulsidas notes. If I entice you to stay at my house for a day longer by promising to take you to a Broadway show, that might work for only a day. But what am I going to do after that? I will have to come up with another way to keep you interested in staying. In Janaka's case, there was full variety. He made the guests so happy that they didn't want to leave.

Alas, Rama and His family would eventually have to return. It is not possible for them to overstay their welcome, and so one never tires of hosting them. For this reason in the homes of the devoted souls are found deities of God and His family that are worshiped daily. This way the Supreme Lord becomes the permanent and most exalted guest in the home, someone who never has to leave. He is not expected to lift a finger either, just stay there in His sweetness, which is immeasurable. And just as there is spiritual merit from serving guests, by loving and honoring the permanent resident of the Supreme Lord and those closest to Him the worthy householder ascends to the supreme destination in the afterlife, all the while enjoying the company of the most beloved during their time on earth.

VERSE 162

प्रात बरात चलिहि सुनि भूपति भामिनि।
परि न बिरह बस नींद बीति गइ जामिनि॥162॥

prāta barāta calihi suni bhūpati bhāmini |
pari na biraha basa nīnda bīti ga'i jāmini ||162||

"When the king's wife heard that the barata party was leaving the next morning, being so sad that sleep couldn't come to her the night passed." (162)

Essay - Insomnia

Insomnia is the disorder where one cannot sleep. It is an identifiable disorder since usually the body goes to rest at night. After a hard day of work, study, play or a combination of all three, the human being needs to completely shut down, escaping from the gross body and taking shelter of the subtle body for upwards of eight hours. When this sleep doesn't come naturally, there is something wrong. In the case of a queen a long time ago, the insomnia was due to worry over parting with her beloved daughters and their new husbands.

An easy way to have trouble sleeping is to psyche yourself out.

"Wow, when I shut my eyes and then open them several hours will have passed. All I have to do is fall asleep and then tomorrow will come. This is going to be great. But wait, now I can't fall asleep. I keep thinking about tomorrow and that event that I am anticipating. If I don't sleep, however, I will be too tired to enjoy that event. This is not fair. I just want to relax. I don't need this pressure."

A queen a long time back was worried over losing her daughters. She heard that the party of the groom was set to embark for home the next morning. They had stayed as long as the king could keep them. He was a gracious host. He offered them all sorts of hospitality. It was a genuine sign of affection, too. He never wanted them to leave. Now news broke that they were preparing to finally go home, where the town of Ayodhya would welcome their four handsome princes and their beautiful new brides.

Two of those brides were daughters of the queen in Janakpur, and with the eldest particularly capturing the hearts of everyone there. In thinking about losing her daughters, the queen could not sleep. It just wouldn't come to her. And wouldn't you know it, soon enough it was morning.

While typically insomnia is very troubling, this sort of sleeplessness is actually blissful. We have to think about something. As Descartes said, "I think, therefore I am," if you're not thinking then you're not living. Even in the dreaming state the mind is fast at work. The process of falling asleep involves the mind working much faster, processing so many thoughts, jumping from one thing to another until there is no more control over the consciousness.

If you can spend your waking hours thinking of God, you are on the right path. Even if the thinking is in concern, it is to your benefit. It is difficult to explain precisely why this is the case. We know that water quenches our thirst on a hot day. We know that the space heater in the room makes us feel so good on a cold winter's day. We can't really explain why things are this way, but then again it doesn't really matter. The reaction is there, and we can perceive it. What more is there to know?

In the same way, constantly thinking of Sita with loving concern is blissful. We can try to explain the fact by pointing out how Sita is the goddess of fortune. She is the eternal consort of the Supreme Lord. God has a partner. He is not limited to one, but there is a single individual who excels in devotion and so is thereby eligible to always be by His side. God is also not limited to a single manifestation. He is an individual, like you and me, but He can appear at different times and different places with forms to match the occasion.

Sita is tied to Rama. Symbolically the bond is through marriage, which takes place in the kingdom of Janakpur. The affectionate mother, Queen Sunayana, prepared Sita for entering the bond of holy matrimony. At the first day that Janaka brought home the baby Sita from the field, she knew that eventually she would have to part with her beloved daughter. Then when Rama, the Supreme Lord walking the earth, lifted up the heavy bow to win the contest, she was again reminded how Sita would soon leave her.

Now the moment was fast approaching. Another mystery of devotional service is that thinking is as good as seeing. And seeing is as good as being by the side of. This means that in staying awake all night in worry over losing Sita, the queen never really lost her. Though the daughter was moving away to live with her new husband in Ayodhya, she remained in the mother's heart.

In a similar manner, the divine couple always stays in the heart of Shri Hanuman, who is the greatest servant of Rama. The couple stays in the hearts of all the devoted souls who adjust their days in such a way that they're always thinking of Sita and Rama. Thus whether sleeping or awake, Sita and Rama are always with them to stay.

VERSE 163

खरभर नगर नारि नर बिधिहि मनावहिं।
बार बार ससुरारि राम जेहि आवहिं।।163।।

kharabhara nagara nāri nara bidhihi manāvahiṁ |
bāra bāra sasurāri rāma jehi āvahiṁ ||163||

"Being restless, all of the men and women of the city prayed to the demigods. Again and again they asked when Rama would come again." (163)

Essay - Return Trip

The scene is quite common to film. A young child eagerly anticipates Christmas. On the eve, they leave cookies and milk for Santa Claus by the fireplace. They try to stay awake through the night, but they usually can't fight off sleep. Then suddenly they awake, as if by fate, and see Santa Claus in person: "Santa, it's really you. I knew you would come. You must be so busy. Thank you for visiting my home."

Then Santa replies with a few kind words of his own. After a brief conversation, it's time for St. Nicholas to leave, to the sadness of everyone. The young child then innocently asks, "When will you come back? When will I see you again?" The audience can feel the distress, and it is due to a fear of separation. The fear is stronger because the meeting is rare; it is not expected. A long time back residents in Janakpur, both male and female and young and old, met the origin of matter and spirit. After His brief stay in their town, they too wondered when He would return.

In His avatara of Rama, the Supreme Lord doesn't come bearing physical gifts. Children are enamored with toys, video games, puzzles and the like, but adults tend to value other things. Association is what they most cherish, and in that association they hope to engage all their senses to the full. Shri Rama gave this gift of association only briefly, and everyone was supremely thankful for it.

The lasting gift was His divine vision. It was accompanied by the equally as blissful vision of Rama's younger brother Lakshmana. The wise human seeks after this vision, even if they are unaware. As the Vedanta-sutra says, the human birth carries with it the call to know the Absolute Truth, athato brahma-jijnasa. The human birth is not the time for only accumulating a lot of wealth. It is not meant for enjoying the senses to the full, without limits and restrictions. It is not meant for sitting idly by as the years pass on.

These things can be done in other bodies. While wealth may be absent in the animal species, the fruit of wealth surely is present. If I have a large home filled with lavish furniture, to enjoy everything I must sit and do nothing. Taking rest, leisure time, is the enjoyment from having acquired so many things. As recently as two hundred years ago, the majority of today's leisure activities weren't even invented. There wasn't television. There were no sports. If people played games, it was likely chess. There was no arguing over the saga of a baseball player accused of cheating the system. There was no outrage over a pop singer's behavior at an awards show.

So the heralded progress of the human civilization has brought on much more time for idleness. Indeed, how to spend the idle time is of great concern today. But there is idle time in the animal species as well, as the bear hibernates for many months. Idleness thus does not require intelligence. The human being has an advanced intelligence, and it is earmarked for searching after the truth. That truth should be above national, racial, gender, and religious lines. It should be above blind faith and cheap sentiment. It should explain the meaning to everything and also enlighten the individual as to how to act going forward.

While it may not seem like it, in the scene referenced above the residents of a town have found the truth and are behaving accordingly. They have seen Rama and Lakshmana, who are not the exclusive property of any religion. Rama is Bhagavan and Lakshmana serves Him for all of eternity. Rama is beauty, wealth, strength, fame, wisdom and renunciation personified. Lakshmana is the service personified to such an owner of all opulences.

In seeing the truth before their very eyes, the residents hoped to see it more and more. They prayed to the gods they had previously satisfied for trivial matters such as good health, righteousness, economic development and dispassion. All traditions from all cultures and from all time periods have had such kinds of worship. Here the desire is finally purified, as it is for Rama's association alone.

Rama, Lakshmana and their two other brothers were set to leave that day from Janakpur. They had all been married through King Janaka's arrangement. Thus they would be returning home with beautiful new brides. The residents prayed to have Rama visit them again, to please their eyes with His enchanting vision. The magic of God is that His physical presence is not required for creating that vision. Just as a television image can show what is happening thousands of miles away, the holy name can create the association of the Absolute Truth very easily. The mood of the worshiper is what counts most, and in Janakpur the mood was as pure as it could be. So simply by saying the name "Rama" they would see Him again. We too can meet the objective of the human life by always saying Rama, as that wonderful name is included in the most sacred of formulas, the maha-mantra: Hare Krishna Hare Krishna, Krishna Krishna, Hare Hare, Hare Rama Hare Rama, Rama Rama, Hare Hare.

VERSE 164

सकल चलन के साज जनक साजत भए।
भाइन्ह सहित राम तब भूप-भवन गए।।164।।

sakala calana ke sāja janaka sājata bha'e |
bhā'inha sahita rāma taba bhūpa-bhavana ga'e ||164||

"Janaka did all the rituals and made all the preparations for the departure. Then Rama with His brothers went to the king's palace." (164)

Essay - A Long Running Tradition

This verse from the Janaki Mangala provides a hint into just how long a current tradition in Vedic culture has been in place. Though times change, the attitude of the saintly people of the world does not. Though carts pulled by horses are no longer the primary mode of transportation, the tradition referenced here still remains. Whether there is extra room or not, the departing guests should expect to bring back a lot of stuff with them.

This situation may sound familiar to some:

"Auntie, please. I don't need to take anything. Yes, the food was very good, but who will eat it at my home? Okay, fine. I will take it. What about the sweets, you ask? No, I've already eaten too much. Okay, well, since you just put it in my hands, I guess I will have to bring this home also. No, no, my sister doesn't need any more jewelry. That sari isn't necessary for my mother. You're giving me too much to take back; there won't be any room on the plane."

Another similar situation:

"Oh, you're going to visit such and such next weekend? Make sure to take this shirt and give it to their son. They will like it. I bought these bangles for your aunt. Give them to her. If you don't have room in your carry-on, take a bigger suitcase.

Give this shirt to your uncle. If it's the wrong size, then maybe his son can wear it. I've thrown a few shirts in there. See which ones they like; let them choose. Here are some sweets as well. Give this to them for eating as prasadam. They can offer it to the Lord first and then everyone can partake."

Prior to going on a trip, you can be so enthused about travelling lightly, about not carrying so many things through the airport. Even if you're just driving somewhere, it's a pain to pack the trunk up with so many things. But those insistent on keeping with tradition will not take "no" for an answer. They are more than happy to burden you with extra tasks for your visit. On the other side of things, the good host feels insulted if you leave their home empty-handed.

In a famed city a long time ago, a wonderful king prepared so many gifts to be taken home by his most beloved visitors. Whether they liked it or not, these gifts were leaving with them. The guests were not poor by any stretch. They hailed from the kingdom of Ayodhya, where everyone lived happily under the protection of Dasharatha. He was a leader famous for his ability to fight attacking enemies coming from ten different directions. When there is government tyranny we long for freedom through elections and the sort. But if a single person can rule justly, fairly and effectively, there is no need for voting. Everyone follows their duties without issue. Such was the case with the rule of King Dasharatha.

The guests who were leaving had just been married. There were four marriages arranged in that kingdom by its leader, Janaka. His eldest daughter Sita was the initial person getting married, but in his happiness Janaka arranged for her new husband's three younger brothers to get married as well. So four couples were heading back to Ayodhya, and Janaka made sure to pack their caravans with heaps of gifts. Janaka had plenty to give, and the departing guests had no way of refusing anything.

There is a saying in Hindi which means "The name of Rama is the truth." The name "Rama" addresses an individual who is beyond duality. He is beyond the temporary manifestations that bewilder us. We know that we are not our body, for our body continuously changes. We were once young and enthusiastic. Now we are older and more jaded. We have difficulty getting out of bed in the morning and a tough time breaking from the daily routine. We have been the same person throughout, however. It is only rather difficult to see.

As difficult as it is to see our true position as spirit, seeing the entity who is beyond all the duality of this world is much harder. Therefore the name comes into play. Rather than fret over personal and impersonal, matter and spirit, illusion and reality, simply say the name of Rama. That name gives understanding even to the less intelligent. It provides the vision of the Truth even to those who are blind. Even those who have no desire to see it are blessed with it just by saying the name constantly.

"[O mystic] First know yourself, then realize the Supreme Absolute Truth, and then see the material nature standing in between. O wretch, without seeing these how can you understand what the unmanifested [invisible] feature of the Absolute Truth [alakh] actually is? Chant Shri Rama's holy name instead, says Tulsi." (Dohavali, 19)

Rama, the eldest son of Dasharatha, never refuses a gift made in earnest, without motive for gain. Janaka was a king in a wealthy kingdom, so he had nothing to gain from giving gifts to the four new couples. He did so simply out of love. Rama couldn't refuse. He had to take everything back with Him. He also had to love Sita, who had the same amount of affection for Him. From this episode, we know that in the kingdom of God it is always the "era of good feelings." That kingdom exists in the spiritual sky, but it can also be replicated here at any time and place, as it was in Janaka's land a long time ago.

VERSE 165

सासु उतारि आरती करहिं निछावरि।
निरखि निरखि हियँ हरषहिं सूरति साँवरि।।165।।

sāsu utāri āratī karahiṁ nichāvari |
nirakhi nirakhi hiyaṁ haraṣahiṁ sūrati sāṁvari ||165||

"The mother-in-law did the arati and offered gifts, following tradition. Looking at His dark face again and again, she felt happiness in the heart and great attachment." (165)

Essay - When It's Polite To Stare

Sunayana's eldest daughter had a beautiful, golden-like face. She was extremely fair, and so her countenance is often compared to the moon. The moon is kind to all, offering its soothing rays in the dead of night. For one stuck in the forest, this light is the only hope; without it wading through the wilderness at a time that is otherwise considered dangerous becomes impossible. The thieves prefer darkness to perpetrate their crimes, and the pious prefer light to carry out their prescribed duties. Being like the moon, Sita was a friend to the pious.

Her new husband, however, had a dark face. It is of the shyama color. This Sanskrit word typically translates to "dark-blue," like the color of the raincloud about to pour down water. There is an atasi flower that also has the same color. In Vrindavana especially there are tamala trees, which has a color that so matches the face of Sita's husband that it is often mistaken for His body.

"The shyama color is not exactly blackish. Shrila Bhaktisiddhanta Sarasvati Thakura compares it to the color of the atasi flower. It is not that Lord Krishna Himself appears in a blackish color in all the Dvapara-yugas. In other Dvapara-yugas, previous to Lord Krishna's appearance, the Supreme Lord appeared in a greenish body by His own personal expansion. This is mentioned in the Vishnu Purana, Hari-vamsha and Mahabharata." (Shrila Prabhupada, Chaitanya Charitamrita, Madhya 20.337 Purport)

Shyama can also refer to green. There is no contradiction, as in some cycles of the creation Sita's husband appears on earth in a greenish color, and in others in a dark-blue. Regardless, His is not the same as Sita's wonderful complexion. And yet from this verse from the Janaki Mangala, we see that it was equally as pleasing to the mother, who felt so much happiness in the heart.

She looked at it again and again. It is impolite to stare. Our parents may have told us this when we were younger. We don't need someone to explain it to us to realize why it is so. Would we like it if someone stared at us? If we were eating out at a restaurant and suddenly noticed a piercing eye pointed our way from a table across the room, would we be pleased? Perhaps if the person was attractive we may not think it so bad, but after a while even that would get annoying.

Hey, can I help you with something? Why are you staring at me constantly?

Well, I think you're so beautiful that I can't help it.

Thank you. That's very flattering, but you need to quit it. Would you like it if I stared at you the whole time?

It was not impolite on the part of the mother in this instance since she had the excuse of offering an arati lamp. Rama was about to leave for home. He was going to take the mother's daughter with Him. Sita was His new wife. The mother-in-law did not give Rama a hard time. She did not lecture Him about how to take care of her daughter. She instead worshiped Him, wishing Him only the best. She made offerings of coins and other gifts, similar to how rice is thrown in modern day wedding ceremonies. More important to her was the happiness she felt in her heart. Looking at Rama's dark-blue face again and again filled her heart with happiness. She had tremendous attachment for Him.

Attachment to Rama is the only one worth having. In some traditions and time periods He is known as Shri Krishna, who also has the same complexion. Sometimes He is known as Vishnu, who appears more opulently dressed but again has the same beautiful bodily hue. In some circles He is known only vaguely, as the "man upstairs" who is in charge of everything. In some areas He is barely known at all, and so people debate whether or not He even exists.

We see that the attachment in Sita's mother came from looking at Rama again and again. This proves that the personal form is superior to the impersonal. It is practically impossible to be attached to something that we consider to be lacking distinguishable features. It's like being attached to air or ether. It's like being in love with the wind. These things don't happen; attachment is to the corporeal.

With Rama, the corporeal is the same as the spiritual; hence the happiness it creates in the person who stares at it. Rama is so kind that He arranged for situations that sanctioned the otherwise rude behavior of staring. With great difficulty one finally accepts the personal form of God, and the reward is equal to the effort. In this age, where believing that God can be blue is very difficult, the personal kindly manifests through the sound of His name. When this name is chanted with faith, attention and resolve, the same attachment is sure to take form.

The name "Rama" references the dark-blue youth at whom Sita's mother stared. The name "Krishna" addresses Rama's original form of Krishna, and "Hare" humbly calls out to the beautiful Sita, who is always with Rama. As Shrimati Radharani, she is always with Krishna, and as Lakshmi she is always with Vishnu. One who always chants, "Hare Krishna Hare Krishna, Krishna Krishna, Hare Hare, Hare Rama Hare Rama, Rama Rama, Hare Hare," sees Sita and Rama through the power of sound. With that enchanting vision, love fills the heart and the best attachment forms.

VERSE 166

मागेउ बिदा राम तब सुनि करुना भरीं।
परिहरि सकुच सप्रेम पुलकि पायन्ह परीं॥166॥

māge'u bidā rāma taba suni karunā bharīṁ |
parihari sakuca saprema pulaki pāyanha parīṁ ||166||

"Then when she heard Rama ask for permission to leave, she became filled with sadness. Without hesitation and with much love and ecstasy she touched His feet." (166)

Essay - Ecstasy in Loss

A material life can be likened to a swinging pendulum. You are never in a steady position. One minute you accept something and the next you reject it. In Sanskrit, the two corresponding terms are bhoga and tyaga. I enjoy the ice cream someone offers me so much that I don't stop them from serving me more and more. The next day I'm in such great physical discomfort that I swear off things like ice cream for a long time. "Never again," I tell myself, only to break my rule the next time the same enticing dish is placed in front of me.

The acceptance and rejection isn't exclusive to personal desire. It can relate to comings and goings as well. One minute we are sad and the next we are not. One second we accept something wonderful and soon after we have to part with it. We don't want the latter, as the former gave us so much happiness. But these are the ways of the world, so we have no choice. In the above referenced verse from the Janaki Mangala, it appears that there is the sadness of parting that immediately followed the ecstasy of a welcome. The difference, however, is that the interaction is spiritual, so even the moment of parting is a time of ecstasy.

Consider this situation: You are a new homeowner. You and your spouse decide that you want to have a dog in the house. The dog will provide someone besides each other to love unconditionally. You go out and pick the one that you both agree on. You are enamored by it, but at the same time you don't want to spoil it. You need to train the dog. Your day now revolves around the care of this beloved pet.

The initial days are filled with excitement, and though that tapers off, the affection remains strong for many years. Then one day your dog falls ill. You try your best to treat it, but the veterinarian gives you the dreaded prognosis: there is no hope. The dog will die. The previous excitement now doesn't come close to matching the intense sadness. You haven't felt this bad in a long time. You can't imagine going through this again.

From here it is quite easy to predict the next option: get a new dog. You repeat the whole cycle. You just replace the object of affection. You don't think to yourself that the initial affection was essentially forced on a random object and that since the object can be replaced maybe the affection isn't so real. You just push on. After a loss, you work again for another gain. Never mind that the gain will eventually vanish, leaving you sad once more.

In spiritual life, physical proximity isn't required for association. This means that once gained, the company of the Supreme Lord never leaves you. In fact, He is always with us; we just don't have the eyes to see Him yet. God is present in the rising of the sun, the falling of the leaves, the blowing of the wind, the onset of the winter and summer seasons, and the birth of a new child. He is the life of everything, so anywhere we look that gives signs of life automatically reveals the presence of the Almighty.

There are times when there is a physical manifestation that makes it easier to notice and develop an attachment to Him. Such was the case with the movements of Shri Rama, who appeared in Janakpur to win the contest of the bow and marry the daughter of King Janaka. In the scene referenced above, Rama is about to leave for home, taking His new wife Sita with Him. Sita's mother immediately becomes filled with sadness upon hearing Rama's request to return home.

Juxtaposing this verse with the preceding one in the Janaki Mangala, we see that one moment the mother was filled with happiness and the very next with sadness. An interesting thing happened with the sadness, though. She did not look to replace Rama. She did not bemoan fate and how it was now torturing her. Instead, she immediately reached for Rama's feet. She did this with love and ecstasy. So even in apparently losing the most precious gift of the association of the Supreme Lord, there are good feelings.

This is the meaning to Absolute. Happiness and sadness, acceptance and rejection, apply only to a material existence. In a spiritual existence, all is good. This doesn't mean that variety is absent. You get supposed birth and death, comings and goings, but they are not of the same nature. Indeed, in apparent separation from God the ecstasy is stronger than in association.

As the mother reached for Rama's feet when He was in front of her, she remained attached to them even after He left. Rama took her precious daughter with Him. The mother was now all alone; having sort of an empty nest. She and her husband would only have the memory of their beloved daughter, who came to them in the most unexpected way. But they would be comforted by knowing that she was with Rama, whom she would serve without motivation and without interruption. They would remain in ecstasy by keeping attachment to Rama's lotus feet, from which emanate the sacred river Ganga.

VERSE 167

सीय सहित सब सुता सौंपि कर जोरहिं।
बार बार रघुनाथहि निरखि निहोरहिं॥167॥

sīya sahita saba sutā saumpi kara jorahiṁ |
bāra bāra raghunāthahi nirakhi nihorahiṁ ||167||

"Entrusting Sita and all daughters to Him, again and again looking at Rama, with folded hands she requested:" (167)

Essay - From Taking To Giving

In the Bhagavad-gita, Lord Krishna says that four kinds of people approach Him when they are initially interested in devotional service, or bhakti-yoga. Some want money. Some are distressed and want to attain peace. Some are genuinely inquisitive, and some actually know things as they are and want to know more about God Himself. Regardless the initial reason for entering genuine spiritual life, once safely inside the constitutional engagement, the attitude changes from wanting to giving. Here we see the queen of a famous land entrusting her most precious daughters to the Supreme Lord, and she would not be the loser for it.

"O best among the Bharatas [Arjuna], four kinds of pious men render devotional service unto Me - the distressed, the desirer of wealth, the inquisitive, and he who is searching for knowledge of the Absolute." (Lord Krishna, Bhagavad-gita, 7.16)

It is quite natural to ask for things from God. "O Lord, please give me the strength to fight through this. O Lord, hear our prayer for the wellbeing of our friends and family. O Lord, this person is really struggling. Please shower your mercy upon them and lift them up from peril." A step above asking for things is giving thanks for what you already have. "O Lord, thank you for the wonderful feast that sits before us. Thank you for our kind family. Thank you for our health. We pray that we may never forget what You have done for us." Along these lines, there is the weekly visit to the house of prayer. Just following a basic practice like this makes one unique in society.

In bhakti-yoga, the attitude reaches the pinnacle of perfection. Never mind what we seek from the Lord for our personal benefit. Never mind giving thanks for what He has already provided us. In pure devotional service, the attitude is to offer everything that one has for the Lord's satisfaction. And whether He directly reciprocates or not, the offerings continue. In fact, there is nothing He can do to stop the outpouring of affection. There is no way for Him to repay the deeds of His devotees, who thus earn a very exalted status. They control God instead of the other way around.

In this scene from the Janaki Mangala, the queen Sunayana looks like she is about to ask God for something. So does that put her in the neophyte category? Does she want money? Does she want good health? Actually, here she is entrusting the care of her daughters to Shri Rama, the Supreme Lord in a personal form so kind that He walked this earth and allowed noted biographers like Maharishi Valmiki and Goswami Tulsidas to employ their mastery over poetry to preserve those sacred deeds for all future generations of man to reference.

Those daughters, headed by Sita, were the most important people in the world to the queen. Sita was the eldest and she was marrying Rama. As the new husband, Rama was to protect Sita for the rest of her life. No more could the mother give guidance on a daily basis. Sort of like seeing your kids off to their first year of college away from home, the queen would never have her daughters living in her home again. With love in her heart she offered everything to God, and she did not lose anything.

Here she is about to ask Him to remember her and all the people in Janakpur. If the devoted soul is willing to make such a kind offering, then how is it possible for the Lord to ever forget? Indeed, just a sacrifice of time is enough to catch His eye. The souls who have passed through the stages of asking for things from God and merely thanking Him employ their time in chanting the holy names: Hare Krishna Hare Krishna, Krishna Krishna, Hare Hare, Hare Rama Hare Rama, Rama Rama, Hare Hare. They act in such a way that Rama will never forget them. They entrust their thoughts, words and deeds to Him, and He not only takes care of them but grants them His association in the consciousness, an association to remain forever.

"If one offers Me with love and devotion a leaf, a flower, fruit, or water, I will accept it." (Lord Krishna, Bg. 9.26)

As recently as a few hundred years ago, land ownership was quite common, even encouraged. As the poorest person still had a small plot of land, they had the ability to make a genuine offering to the Supreme Lord. A flower, a leaf, some fruit, or even a little water offered in honesty and love is wholeheartedly accepted. In the so-called advanced times, where land ownership isn't as common, one can still go to the local supermarket and pick up a single piece of fruit for an offering. It is the sentiment which counts most, and in the mother of Sita the love for Rama was completely pure.

VERSE 168

तात तजिय जनि छोह मया राखबि मन।
अनुचर जानब राउ सहित पुर परिजन।।168।।

tāta tajiya jani choha mayā rākhabi mana |
anucara jānaba rā'u sahita pura parijana ||168||

"' O son, don't forget our love for You; keep us always in Your heart. Know that the king, his relatives, and this entire city are Your servants.'" (168)

Essay - Dependent On The Son

The new child is a bundle of joy. You can't get enough of it. How God could create so beautiful a creature, with its delightful features, limitless exuberance, and endearing gestures, is beyond you. You just want to stare at the new child all day, but then you also know that it cannot do anything on its own. It can't feed itself. It can't move to anywhere; not yet anyway. It can't communicate its emotions. Therefore you and the elders must provide complete care. The child is fully dependent on you.

The not-so-hidden secret, however, is that the elders are the servants. They are the ones who depend on the child. Though seemingly helpless, everyone is more than ready to offer it assistance. The person in adult life won't receive the same treatment. If others walk past it on the street, they won't even say "hello." Indeed, if we get stranded on the side of the road with a flat tire and someone comes up to us, we are likely suspicious. "Who are they? What do they want? They know I'm stranded, so that leaves me vulnerable. Hopefully they are being kind and want to help me, but I can't be sure."

Though the child is in the inferior position, it is the one being served. The parents, relatives and siblings are the servants, especially if they have love in their hearts. Through love in service, the child is able to reach maturity, hopefully acquiring values like honesty, cleanliness, compassion and austerity along the way. There is no ego in the servant-like adults. They are more than happy to cater to the child's every whim. This service is what makes them happiest.

Along similar lines, an entire community, including its king and queen, were servants to a newly welcomed son. He wasn't a baby, though He exhibited all the beautiful features of youth. He wasn't helpless, but He didn't talk very much. He spoke when necessary, and then only words that were appropriate.

The son already had a family. He came to the city accompanied by His younger brother, who was just like Him in features and demeanor, with the lone exception being that his skin color was golden while this new son's was dark. The son already had a loving father back home. That father had three wives, giving the son three loving mothers. They had so much affection for the son that it was difficult to tell which one was the biological mother.

The son also had an entire city that loved Him. When He and His younger brother left for a brief time to accompany a notable sage in the forest, the people of the town prayed that the boys wouldn't get hurt. They asked the higher powers to not let a single hair on their heads be harmed.

"They pray to God to grant them blessings: 'May You garner fame and return victorious. May You not lose a single hair while bathing.'" (Janaki Mangala, 29)

Despite everything the boy had going for Him already, the people of this sacred town of Janakpur eagerly served Him. He was welcomed into their lives through winning the contest of the bow. That made Him the favored son-in-law to King Janaka and his wife Sunayana. Here the queen makes a heartfelt plea to the new son-in-law, Shri Rama, just as He leaves for home. Rama was returning with His new wife Sita, the daughter of Janaka and Sunayana.

The mother asked Rama to never forget their love for Him. She did not give Him demands as to what He should do at home. She did not order Him to take care of her beloved Sita. Just the opposite in fact; she asked Rama to consider all the people in Janakpur to be His servants. Whatever He would want, they would do, without hesitation. Though He was younger than them, a newlywed in fact, they were ready to protect Him, take care of Him, and make life enjoyable for Him in every way.

The Janaki Mangala is the story of the marriage of Sita, who is also known as Janaki, to Rama, the beloved son of King Dasharatha of Ayodhya. It is of importance due to the nature of the main characters. Rama is the Supreme Lord in an avatara specific to the second time period of creation. Sita is His eternal consort; she is otherwise known as Lakshmi Devi and Shrimati Radharani. Sita is the goddess of fortune, always linked to the Supreme Lord, who is the husband of the goddess of fortune.

Now that we know the nature of Rama, we see that the people of Janakpur considered themselves to be servants of God. They asked nothing from Him; they only offered to give more and more. They asked only that He keep them in His heart. If Rama can create billions of universes simply by exhaling, how difficult is it for Him to remember His devotees? It is His most pleasurable duty to always protect the surrendered souls, remembering all they have done for Him. And so the queen's request was most certainly granted, and the same is available for all souls, regardless of age, income, ethnicity, race, or gender. While Rama was apparently their son, He was their beloved Lord and master, whom they would serve without motivation and without interruption.

CHAND 21

जन जानि करब सनेह बलि, कहि दीन बचन सुनावहीं।
अति प्रेम बारहिं बार रानी बालिकन्हि उर लावहीं।।
सिय चलत पुरजन नारि हय गय बिहँग मृग ब्याकुल भए।
सुनि बिनय सासु प्रबोधि तब रघुबंस मनि पितु पहिं गए।।21।।

jana jāni karaba saneha bali, kahi dīna bacana sunāvahīṁ |
ati prema bārahiṁ bāra rānī bālikanhi ura lāvahīṁ ||
siya calata purajana nāri haya gaya bihaṁga mṛga byākula bha'e |
suni binaya sāsu prabodhi taba raghubansa mani pitu pahiṁ ga'e ||21||

"'O You who know the people, please keep love for them who are offered to You', were the loving words sounded by the downtrodden mother. Again and again the queen brought the children to her heart and hugged them." (Chand 21.1)

"As Sita was leaving, the people of the town, the women, the horses, the cows, the birds and the deer became restless. Having heard the request of the mother-in-law, the jewel of the Raghu dynasty kindly solaced them and then went to where His father was." (Chand 21.2)

Essay - Judging Offerings

"I can't believe how dedicated that person is. You know that they've been a pujari at this temple for almost three decades. Every day, without fail, they've gotten up at the appointed time and tended to the wonderfully resplendent Lordships of the building. They bathe the deities, change their clothes, offer flowers and lamps, and make sure they look beautiful for the many visitors who walk through the gates every year. Can you imagine having that level of dedication? This person is so much better than me. All glories to them."

"I can't believe how much that mother cooks for her Lordships. She prepares a grand feast every week, and all by herself. So many guests come to her home throughout the week, and then on that one day reserved for the formal gathering, she cooks for hundreds of people. She first makes the offering to the Supreme Lord, who then happily accepts it. And why wouldn't He? He must love her so much. The mercy from the remnants of that offered food cannot be measured. I have trouble making a pot of herbal tea, and here is this dedicated lady cooking entire meals selflessly all the time. All glories to her."

"I can't believe how many books that person has written. They have a fulltime job, too. They've dedicated all of their leisure hours towards glorifying the Supreme Lord. They've travelled the world and done extensive research, using what they've found to further argue in favor of devotional service being the highest occupation for man. They've put their name to their work, and they've presented it to many respectable institutions. They don't shy away from the pressure, and they continue to write to this very day. Their guru must be so pleased with them. The Supreme Lord Himself must be dictating the words from within. All glories to them."

"I can't believe how many books that person has distributed. Selflessly, without any personal motivations, and without fear, they've hit the streets to give the gift of transcendental knowledge. In centuries past, finding real knowledge was very difficult. Famous personalities would build libraries instead of churches to help further expand the intellect of the populace. Still, even in those libraries filled with thousands of books, one would not find transcendental wisdom. This is only available today to the masses due to the work of a sincere follower of the Supreme Lord in the devotional tradition. But even that effort wouldn't have been enough. There needed to be an army of book distributors, ready to bring the most valuable knowledge to the people. I have trouble sending food back at a restaurant, not wanting to offend the waiter. Here this person is rejected constantly, by so many people. They have to work so hard just to get a single person to buy a book. They do this all for their guru, and so to me they are the best servant. I feel tiny in their presence. All glories to them."

In these scenarios, one person is praising another for the devotional service they offer to the Supreme Lord or one of His representatives. It is said that when one ascends to the higher stages of bhakti-yoga, they feel more and more humbled. They appreciate everyone else's service more and more. This stands in stark contrast to material life, where more success means more competition, which means more envy of others. Rather than be happy that a competitor has entered the arena to sell the same product I've been selling, I try my best to knock them down. Their success is my loss, and vice versa.

Such is not the case in devotional service, where more competitors to the field only means more success for the people at large in changing their consciousness for the better. The world is a better place when more people are compassionate, austere, clean and honest. These four qualities are an afterthought in bhakti-yoga; they come very easily to one who always chants the holy names: Hare Krishna Hare Krishna, Krishna Krishna, Hare Hare, Hare Rama Hare Rama, Rama Rama, Hare Hare.

It is only natural to try to judge offerings, to assess which are better than others. It is a good way to gauge one's own progress. If someone else is doing so much, it serves as impetus to offer some more. In Janakpur a long time ago, a queen offered her daughters to the Supreme Lord in His incarnation of Shri Rama. It would be very difficult to try to surpass such an offering, so the humble souls instead appreciate what a wonderful soul Sunayana was.

Here she praises God for knowing the people, and she asks that He love her daughters very much. The eldest, Sita, married Rama, and Sita's younger sister married Lakshmana, one of Rama's younger brothers. The queen's brother-in-law had two daughters also, who married Rama's two other younger brothers. While these daughters would be considered cousins normally, to Sita they were like sisters as well. This is how things work in small communities following ancient traditions; the cousins, aunts and uncles spend so much time around each other that there are no divisions made as to which child belongs to which parent. Every child within the family is a brother or sister.

So Sunayana essentially offered four daughters to God; this was her service at the time. And these daughters would make the sons happy in so many ways. The mother affectionately embraced them again and again as they were leaving. The mother made the offering and then had to watch as her precious children left her, likely to never return.

The devotee can't compete with Sunayana, or let alone with so many others, but the appreciation itself is worthwhile. The sentiment is what counts most to the Supreme Lord, so whatever genuine offering one can make, even if small the effect is the same as if the offering were of something much greater. The best sacrifice for the modern age is the chanting of the holy names, and so anyone has the chance to please the all-knowing Shri Rama.

Essay - Dear To Everyone

In the Bhagavad-gita, it is said that one who works in devotion, being a pure soul, remains dear to everyone and everyone is dear to them. The Sanskrit word to reference the "everyone" is bhuta, which means living entities. The soul working in devotion maintains control over the mind and the senses, and so they are not entangled by their work. They maintain compassion for all living entities as well, not just human beings. From this verse from the Janaki Mangala, we get a real life example to give proof to the claim made by Shri Krishna in the Gita.

"One who works in devotion, who is a pure soul, and who controls his mind and senses, is dear to everyone, and everyone is dear to him. Though always working, such a man is never entangled." (Lord Krishna, Bhagavad-gita, 5.7)

Here the beloved Sita Devi, the daughter of King Janaka, is preparing to leave the kingdom she has called home for many years. She is moving away permanently, never to return. The people knew this day was approaching. As a good king, Janaka paid attention to the rules of propriety. It was protocol to get the daughter married when she reached an appropriate age. With Sita the task was difficult due to her extraordinary nature and the amazing way in which she was found. There was no horoscope available for Janaka to match. Her character was so splendid that no prince in the world seemed a good fit.

The father decided on a contest of strength, and Shri Rama from Ayodhya won it. He was the ideal match, even before stepping up to Lord Shiva's famous bow. Thus the people were thrilled that Sita got the right husband. Still, sadness was imminent, and here began the sorrowful departure of their beloved Sita, who was ready to go to Rama's home in Ayodhya.

Sita was dear to the people of the town because of her nature. She loved everyone, as they were all protected by her father Janaka. She was dear to the women as well. They looked at her as their precious daughter, even though she already had a mother in Queen Sunayana. Sita was gentle in behavior, respectful in association, and virtuous in mind. She loved every single person, and so everyone loved her as well.

When she was about to leave, the horses, the cows, the deer and the birds all became restless. The horses had seen her often, as they were employed in pulling the royal chariots. The cows provided milk to the community, and they were protected by the royal family. The deer also loved Sita very much, as she was originally from the forest-like environment. Janaka had found her one day while ploughing a field. Nature was Sita's original home, and the inhabitants of that nature all held affection for her. The birds had witnessed her sweet speech and her charming childhood play. In calling out to one another, they would describe her wonderful activities, which culminated for them in the marriage ceremony to never be forgotten.

Rama, the new husband, saw all of this. He heard the request of Sita's mother made moments prior. The mother asked Rama to always remember them, to accept Sita as a kind offering. One of the many other names for Rama is Bhagavan. This Sanskrit word means "one who is most fortunate." That name befits Him based on His marriage to Sita alone, for He received a companion for life who was dear to everyone in the town she called home. She would be very dear to Rama as well.

From this verse from the Janaki Mangala, we also get a good way to judge whether someone is indeed dear to everyone or not. We also know whether they are at the height of saintliness. Sita wasn't kind only to the human beings. The animals were so much respected as well. Just as the family pets are sad to see the owners leave for a day of work, the many animals in Janakpur were restless when they saw Sita about to leave them for good. This means that she treated them all as affectionate family members, which gives further indication of her saintly character.

Sita works only in devotion, since her mind is always tied to Shri Rama's interests. Along the same lines, anyone who works for the satisfaction of Sita and Rama becomes dear to everyone. As they hold the beloved Janaki so dear, they are also benevolent to the creatures that are under the protection of her husband, who is the Supreme Lord, the source of all men, and all living entities in fact.

VERSE 169

परे निसानहि घाउ राउ अवधहिं चले।
सुर गन बरषहिं सुमन सगुन पावहिं भले।।169।।

pare nisānahi ghā'u rā'u avadhahiṁ cale |
sura gana baraṣahiṁ sumana saguna pāvahiṁ bhale ||169||

"To the beating of drums, it was announced that the king was returning to Ayodhya. The many demigods rained down flowers, the aura was good, and everything looked beautiful." (169)

Essay - Calming Worries

As nothing in life tends to remain fixed, there is uncertainty, which ironically enough is constant. That brings worry, which then leaves the concerned hoping for signs from above that things will be okay. In this scene from the Janaki Mangala, all parties involved are very sad at having to part. But for those being left behind, the sorrow is greater, and so any indications to show that things will be alright are welcome. The demigods in the sky provide just that, the needed omens to calm everyone's fears.

Imagine this scenario. It's a cold winter's night. You come home from a hard day's work. You went to the gym after your day was over at the office to get in a good workout. Now you're at home, ready to take a shower to freshen up. There's only one problem: no hot water. "Oh no," you think. "What do I do now? Everyone is away on vacation, so if I don't do something about this, no one will. Taking a shower is one thing, but soon the whole house will reach the freezing point."

You go downstairs to the basement and try to manually start the oil burner. It kicks on, runs for about thirty seconds, and then shuts off again. "Well, I'm going to have to call someone," you say to yourself. The problem is that it is late at night. The oil delivery company is closed for the day. They won't be able to come until the morning at the earliest. Then you will have to keep your fingers crossed that the filling of the oil tank will solve the problem. There could be a burner issue instead. That requires a call to another company. In the meantime, you have to make it through the cold night. So worried are you that you naturally look to the heavens for help.

"O Lord, I can't believe how cold it is. Why is this happening to me? I'm not the right person to handle these responsibilities. Can you give me a sign that things will be alright? I worry too much as it is, but anything you can do to allay my fears will be greatly appreciated."

While such situations occur regularly, in Janakpur a long time ago the sorrow was over losing the association of a beloved princess. She, her sister, and their cousins had just gotten married at the same time to the four sons of King Dasharatha of Ayodhya. The good host, King Janaka, got the guests to stay as long as he possibly could. Everyone was so happy in each other's association, in having a new family, but alas there were other responsibilities to tend to. King Dasharatha and his sons had to go home eventually and here the sound of drums indicates that the time for their departure has arrived.

In such instances, the pain of separation is typically stronger for the party being left. They are seeing their guests leave, so they will naturally feel an emptiness afterwards. Here the signs from above provide some comfort. Things will be okay, as the scene was beautiful and the omens all auspicious. The residents of the celestial region dropped flowers on the departing guests. This was quite common already, as Rama was in the group. He is the Supreme Lord in an incarnation specific to a time and circumstance. In the spiritual world, it is said that all speech is song and all movement dance. And wherever the Lord goes, beautiful sounds play in the background and flowers are laid out.

The same applies to His descents in the material world, the realm we presently inhabit. The flowers are dropped whenever something good is about to happen or whenever there is cause for celebration. Though this was a bittersweet moment, it was worth celebrating, since it marked the union of two wonderful families. It was the conclusion to the timeless pastime of Shri Rama's marriage to Sita, Janaka's eldest daughter. Though the townspeople were losing a beloved princess, they had gained a family to keep in their hearts for all of time. The auspicious omens of that moment told them that it was indeed proper for Sita to go to Ayodhya with Rama. And more importantly, it was auspicious for everyone to remember that beloved couple, who is still honored to this day.

VERSE 170

जनक जानकिहि भेटि सिखाइ सिखावन।
सहित सचिव गुर बंधु चले पहुँचावन।।170।।

janaka jānakihi bheṭi sikhā'i sikhāvana |
sahita saciva gura bandhu cale pahumcāvana ||170||

"Janaka embraced Janaki and instructed her on everything that needed to be instructed. Going to his ministers, guru, and relatives, he brought them to the farewell procession." (170)

Essay - Bhakta-Vatsala

Janaka held affection for her when he first found her on that famous day in the field. He was looking to please God by holding a sacrifice. To that end, he had the field ploughed. To his surprise, God rewarded him with a brand new baby daughter. The Brahman-realized king momentarily fell from his position in dispassion by harboring so much paternal affection for this precious gem. But in fact he was actually rising to the platform of bhakti-yoga, where one is protected directly by the Supreme Lord.

Since He offers that protection, the Supreme Lord is described as bhakta-vatsala. Vatsala is the affection offered in the mood of devotional service known as vatsalya-rasa. Awe and reverence aren't the only options for souls looking to connect with God. In the more intimate dealings, one can become God's friend. They can become His lover, and they can also become His parent.

In the role of the parent, the affection offered is unique. The good parent always thinks about their child and how they will protect them. Instead of looking to take, they seek any opportunity to give. Even when the child is grown up and ready to enter the real world, the good parent never stops giving. They offer help in guiding the child through school and work. They offer care even when the child has children of their own. Whatever the situation, the mood of paternal affection remains.

In this scene from the Janaki Mangala, Janaka has his last opportunity for offering direct affection to his daughter Sita. She is married now, set to leave for her husband's kingdom. He offers her good instruction, all done with love. He is Sita's protector, though she is so powerful that she doesn't require one. Just as one can become the father or mother of the Supreme Lord, the same opportunity is there for the Lord's eternal consort.

"The Supreme Personality of Godhead is known as bhakta-vatsala. He is never described as jnani-vatsala or yogi-vatsala. He is always described as bhakta-vatsala because He is more inclined toward His devotees than toward other transcendentalists." (Shrila Prabhupada, Shrimad Bhagavatam, 3.24.29 Purport)

Janaka was the protector of Sita while she was raised in his kingdom of Janakpur, and throughout his life Janaka was protected by the bhakta-vatsala, the Supreme Lord. In the Vedic scriptures God is not described to be the protector of the theoretician. He is not the supreme benefactor of the mental speculator. Nor does He explicitly protect the yogi, the kind who meditates. He is specifically affectionate towards the devoted souls, and His protection is offered with intelligence, even if it seems otherwise.

As Sita's protector, Janaka provided a good home for her. He kept her safe and showed her the proper example to follow. Janaka's protection was seen by the eyes, but what was more subtle was the protection offered by God Himself. He arranged to have Sita enter Janaka's family. Through her presence, Janaka gained Rama as a son-in-law. Rama is the bhakta-vatsala in person. He gives a manifest version of the protection offered by God.

He cared for Janaka by maintaining the king's vow. For Sita's marriage, Janaka had decided on a contest. Upon seeing Rama, however, Janaka wanted Sita to get married to Him right away. That would have broken the rules of the contest, and so Rama protected everything by winning the contest Himself. He looked over Janaka's fortunes, the same way that Janaka oversaw Sita's protection from childhood until marriage.

The same affectionate hand is not offered to the yogi or the jnani because there is a vital desire inherently lacking in those pursuits. The jnani is after knowledge first, and the yogi after control of the senses. In bhakti, or devotion, one doesn't have to be knowledgeable. One doesn't even have to be very renounced. In bhakti, due to the efforts of the bhakta-vatsala, there is success under any circumstance. Whether one is literate or not, whether they can concentrate for hours on end or not, since they have devotion they can always love God. He specifically shows them the ways that are best suited for them.

That bhakta-vatsala gives protection to any soul in the Kali-yuga in the form of the holy names. One need only regularly chant, "Hare Krishna Hare Krishna, Krishna Krishna, Hare Hare, Hare Rama Hare Rama, Rama Rama, Hare Hare," with firm faith, conviction, and a desire to please the Lord, and the direct affection is guaranteed to come.

VERSE 171

प्रेम पुलकि कहि राय फिरिय अब राजन।
करत परस्पर बिनय सकल गुन भाजन॥171॥

prema pulaki kahi rāya phiriya aba rājana |
karata paraspara binaya sakala guna bhājana ||171||

"With love and excitement, Janaka said to Dasharatha, 'Please come back now.' The kings then exchanged requests, with their words full of goodness." (171)

Essay - It's a Tie

It is not uncommon for a husband and a wife to argue. After all, they spend so much time in each other's company. They know each other's faults, and strong points as well. More importantly, they likely have a close relationship, so they do not feel shy in voicing their opinions. They are not too concerned with what the other person may think of them, since the relationship is as close as one can get.

Imagine a situation where the couple argues over which person has the better father. The husband begins.

"The glories of my father cannot be counted. He raised three boys with the help of his beautiful and faithful wife. He worked all day, tirelessly, without complaining once. He was kind to us, but firm as well. He instilled discipline in us, and more importantly he taught us to respect others. He was kind to all guests that came to the home, and you would be hard pressed to find anyone who doesn't like him. He is terrific in all respects. I can't think of any other father like him."

Hearing this, the wife feels compelled to respond. She has a terrific father too, she believes.

"Well, my father is the kindest person on earth. He never watches television. He never drinks. He never smokes. He's always spending time with his children, helping them with whatever they need. His wife never has to yell at him because he never does anything wrong. On the weekends, he volunteers at various charitable organizations. He is well known throughout the community for his generosity. He never once laid a hand on any of us children growing up, but he still made sure we weren't spoiled. He naturally loves everyone, even strangers. He has no problem pulling over to the side of the road to help a stranded motorist. He'll do this even if he has somewhere he needs to be. He doesn't get angry when others insult him. I think he is the best father in the world."

A similar situation, which was more difficult to reconcile, existed in Janakpur a long time ago. Two fathers were meeting for perhaps the final time, as one was the guest and the other the host. The guest was returning home with his four sons, who had just been married through the host's arrangement. The host was the donor and the guest the receiver.

The guest was a defender of righteousness on earth. He had been called upon many times in the past to deal with the miscreant class. "Wouldn't it be great if everyone got along? Wouldn't it be great if there was no war? Why can't everyone live in peace?" These are yearnings of man since the beginning of time. Yet we see conflict nevertheless, as not everyone wants to play by the rules. Some have no problem cheating, stealing, and using violence. In such cases, the easy way to maintain peace is to give in. "Go ahead, come in my house and take everything. Go ahead, plunder the wealth of society. Go ahead, kill whomever you want."

The innocent people are not safe unless they have defenders. The guest in this situation, King Dasharatha, was the greatest defender of the innocent. Therefore he was highly exalted, respected throughout the world. The host had his own set of good qualities. He was dispassionate. This meant that he never played favorites while administering justice. He didn't change the laws on a whim to suit a campaign donor or to avert a drop in his poll numbers. Even if someone didn't like what he did, he stayed with his decisions since they were in accordance with righteous principles passed on since the beginning of time.

"This supreme science was thus received through the chain of disciplic succession, and the saintly kings understood it in that way. But in course of time the succession was broken, and therefore the science as it is appears to be lost." (Lord Krishna, Bhagavad-gita, 4.2)

The host, King Janaka, carried out his responsibilities, despite being known as an expert transcendentalist. Here we see that he also felt thrills from time to time. He was not above emotion. He didn't force himself to act like a robot. He had love and affection for his daughter Sita, and that naturally extended to Sita's new father-in-law, King Dasharatha.

In this scene Janaka is kindly requesting Dasharatha to stay. "Don't go home yet. This is your home as well. You can stay here as long as you like." This is the proper etiquette when dealing with a departing guest. Janaka was more than following etiquette here. As a pious king himself, he had so much respect for Dasharatha. The King of Ayodhya felt likewise about Janaka. Thus they exchanged many requests with each other, in pure goodness.

In the household of Sita and Rama, a hypothetical debate over who has the better father cannot be settled. It would end in a draw, as the goodness found in each father is without limit. It is no wonder then that Sita and Rama are adored by superior authorities on all matters of life, like Shri Hanuman.

VERSE 172

कहेउ जनक कर जोरि कीन्ह मोहि आपन।
रघुकुल तिलक सदा तुम उथपन थापन।।172।।

> kahe'u janaka kara jori kīnha mohi āpana |
> raghukula tilaka sadā tuma uthapana thāpana ||172||

"With folded hands Janaka said, 'Please take me as your own. You are the tilaka of the Raghu family, and you always take care of the destitute.'" (172)

Essay - A Great Maintainer

When turning to spiritual matters, there are many levels of understanding. There is the concept of an original person, the entity from whom everything emanates. Then there is the personality from whom this specific universe comes. Then there are also the presiding deities within the creation. Once everything is made, someone is put in charge of destroying at the appropriate time. That is the nature of the material; nothing is fixed. What goes up, must come down. That which is born must eventually die. The time in between calls for maintenance, and the personality in charge of maintaining is Lord Vishnu.

Brahma is the creator and Shiva the destroyer. Interestingly enough, Vishnu is also the origin of everything. His role as maintainer in the material creation is in an expansion form. There are different Vishnus, though they represent the same personality. As a guna-avatara, or incarnation to manage a mode of material nature, Vishnu maintains the material creation. Yet He is never material, so He is also the maintainer of the surrendered souls, who have no attachment to the material energy.

What does it mean to be free of attachment? We can think of it like going to work every day and not being stressed out over the results. If our job is in maintenance, we will meet so many difficult situations. A customer may have done something ill-advised and caused great damage to their machine. If we arrive at their home to fix it, it may take a long time to get the job done. The longer it takes, the more frustrated the customer gets. Their harsh words won't change the situation; the job is the job.

In other situations the job is easier. It is a routine fix, something over which the customer does not get angry. Whether there is good treatment or not, as a repairman I don't let anything affect my job. I get my work done. I am not attached to the outcome, for what can I really do? I can try my best and then deal with the outcome.

A person who is not attached to the material energy carries the same attitude into everything they do that is not directly related to serving the Personality of Godhead. He is above the material nature, as He is the opposite of temporary. He remains fixed in His position for all of time. Indeed, the human brain is incapable of truly understanding what that means. There is always a beginning to a beginning and an end to an end. The Supreme Lord is the beginning of all beginnings, and beyond any end. He has always been the Supreme Lord and will always continue to be in the future.

As He is above the material nature, He is superior to it as well. Therefore He can maintain anyone. He indirectly maintains through the forces of nature, but that maintenance is not very pleasing. The rain pours down water in the Spring to make sure the flowers blossom. That same rain can bring pain to someone else who is relying on good weather. The direct maintenance, however, is always beneficial. Sometimes it is offered through a proxy, such as the king.

"The Blessed Lord said: I instructed this imperishable science of yoga to the sun-god, Vivasvan, and Vivasvan instructed it to Manu, the father of mankind, and Manu in turn instructed it to Ikshvaku." (Bhagavad-gita, 4.1)

In the ancient time periods, the maintenance was carried out by the saintly kings. In this scene from the Janaki Mangala, two of those kings are saying goodbye to one another. King Janaka, an ideal ruler in his own right, kindly requests King Dasharatha to consider him to be his own. Dasharatha ruled the earth following the principles laid down at the beginning of creation by the Supreme Lord. Here Janaka describes Dasharatha as the tilaka, or sacred mark, of the Raghu family. Dasharatha's line descended from the famous King Ikshvaku, and this line also had the famous King Raghu in it.

Janaka says that Dasharatha picks up those who need to be lifted, and so he asks that Dasharatha consider him in this light. This is a very nice attitude to have, since by the chain of disciplic succession Dasharatha's work is actually God's. When the government agent collects taxes to be deposited into the treasury, he is doing the work of the head of the government. The head is ultimately responsible. In the same way, when Dasharatha maintains the surrendered souls, it is actually the Supreme Lord who is ultimately responsible.

In all his modesty, Janaka here hides the fact that he was a great maintainer as well, an equal representative of the Supreme Lord. He had the good fortune of receiving the eternal consort of the Supreme Lord as his daughter. Dasharatha was so blessed that he received God in a lila-avatara as a son. Dasharatha's son Rama and Janaka's daughter Sita wed in a grand ceremony in Janaka's kingdom, and here the groom's party is all set to return home. Both kings maintained their children very well, and Dasharatha is asked to extend his care to all in Janaka's family.

The devoted souls, who follow the teachings of God passed on in the Bhagavad-gita, are always ready to rescue the downtrodden, for they know that God's mercy is without limit. The power in the holy name itself can deliver countless souls with a single utterance. Therefore in the modern era, where the saintly kings are no longer to be found, the maintenance of the greatest maintainer flows through the chanting of the holy names by His devotees: Hare Krishna Hare Krishna, Krishna Krishna, Hare Hare, Hare Rama Hare Rama, Rama Rama, Hare Hare.

VERSE 173

बिलग न मानब मोर जो बोलि पठायउँ।
प्रभु प्रसाद जसु जानि सकल सुख पायउँ।।173।।

bilaga na mānaba mora jo boli paṭhāya'um̐ |
prabhu prasāda jasu jāni sakala sukha pāya'um̐ ||173||

"' Please do not take it ill of me that I sent for you. I know that I received all happiness by the glory of your grace, O lord.'" (173)

Essay - Calling Each Other Prabhu

Such is the nature of fraternal organizations that the members address each other with notable terms. They are part of a unique club, so they honor each other's preferred status by an identifiable form of address. "Brother" is the most commonly used term, and "sister" is the corresponding one for organizations of ladies. In devotional circles, one would be surprised to note that the English translation for the term of choice is "lord." This is the word used in this verse from the Janaki Mangala, and it is offered by one king to another.

"Hello Prabhu; Prabhu, can I offer you any more prasadam; Prabhu, please accept my obeisances; Nice to see you again, Prabhu." You can hear such statements quite often in devotional societies. If someone new to the scene doesn't know what the word "Prabhu" means, they may think it refers to someone who is very dear. "They say Prabhu to every other guy, so it must be a nice way to address them. It also comes in handy if they don't know the other person's name. They can just say Prabhu and not get into trouble. It sounds like a nice word, so it must mean someone who is very dear."

Indeed, if a word is always used in a specific context, others will start to identify that word with that particular context. But "prabhu" is a Sanskrit word that means "lord." It is used quite often in Vedic literature, as it is synonymous with the Supreme Personality of Godhead. Other corresponding terms are bhagavan, ishvara, and natha.

Those who are trying to serve the Supreme Lord with body, mind, and speech address each other as "prabhu" in order to remain humble. They won't address their teachers in this way, for their acknowledged superior position earns them a distinct title. But all others are made to feel superior with the word that means "lord." This helps to maintain the devotional attitude within the servant. "My objective is to think of everyone else as superior to me. Even if others are not practicing devotional service so much, I know that if they do take it up seriously, they will do a much better job at it than me. Plus, I have so much I can learn from them. I am only a pretender, for I harbor material ambitions on the inside. These are so difficult to renounce, and so I need to stay in the association of other prabhus. Also, I've noticed that if I spend some time chanting the holy names and reading important books, my ego gets puffed up. Then I start to think of myself as prabhu instead of dasa, which I really am. Therefore I look forward to any opportunity to address another as prabhu."

From the behavior of King Janaka referenced above, we see one of the benefits to associating with someone whom we would address as "prabhu." King Dasharatha is about to return home to Ayodhya. Janaka had originally called for him. Janaka was hosting a marriage ceremony for his daughter Sita, and Dasharatha's son Rama was the chosen groom. Dasharatha was a powerful and respected king, so he was not under obligation to listen to anyone. Janaka kindly asked him to visit his town to consent to the marriage ceremony for Shri Rama and then take part in the festivities.

"Thereupon, after inviting my father-in-law, the elderly King Dasharatha, to Mithila and receiving his approval, my father gave me away to Rama, the knower of the self." (Sita Devi speaking to Anasuya, Valmiki Ramayana, Ayodhya Kand, 118.52)

Dasharatha was more than happy to accept, and he felt so much love for Janaka and his family. Therefore Janaka didn't need to ask pardon for sending for Dasharatha. Here he does so anyway, and he explains why. He says that by Dasharatha's mercy [prasada], all happiness came to him. Through the good king's efforts, Rama was raised to be a righteous, courageous, and attentive prince. Through the king's good will, Rama was allowed to marry Sita, which eased Janaka's mind. The king of Mithila always worried about who would protect his beautiful daughter. He drew up a difficult contest precisely to find someone who would be strong enough to defend her against rogues and thieves. Rama was a godsend, and so through His victory in the contest, the honor got passed up the chain to the immediately preceding link, King Dasharatha.

This exchange between two kings reveals so many important truths. By doing good work, past generations are honored. By receiving the mercy of a pure soul, one gets all happiness in life. The disciple who kindly questions the spiritual master about the most important topics feels the same sort of happiness, for the guru gives them the ability to always worship. Janaka and Dasharatha were both kings, but

Janaka genuinely felt himself inferior. From that position he was fit to offer all respects, and the King of Ayodhya was more than happy to receive such kind words. Based on their behavior it is no wonder that the Supreme Lord and His eternal consort appeared in their families. It is also not surprising that those kings are still remembered to this day, for they displayed exemplary behavior.

VERSE 174

पुनि बसिष्ठ आदिक मुनि बंदि महीपति।
गहि कौसिक के पाइ कीन्ह बिनती अति॥174॥

puni basiṣṭha ādika muni bandi mahīpati |
gahi kausika ke pā'i kīnha binatī ati ||174||

"Then the king offered prayers to Vashishtha and the other munis. Approaching Vishvamitra's lotus feet, he offered many prayers." (174)

Essay - Bringing God Into My Life

A fully joyful man is known to do strange things. From his ecstasy he throws caution to the wind and starts to give thanks to anyone and everyone. Even if he is in a supposedly superior position, he feels so humbled by his good fortune that he offers respects to so many others. This verse from the Janaki Mangala is an instance of such a mannerism, except that the actor is following protocol at the same time. Though he is described as mahipati here, which means "protector of the earth," he remains humble before others who are known as the godly figures of this earth.

Consider this scene. A man is out of work for a long time. He has not been able to find a job. More than just struggling to pay for his monthly expenses, he feels down as a person. He feels as if he is not valuable to society. Then one day through good fortune he is able to land a job. His brother knows someone who is in charge at a company. They are able to get this unemployed person employment. The newly hired man feels so happy to finally have gotten a job. He is humbled by the process, and feeling very thankful he offers all respects to both his brother and his new boss.

Consider another scene. A man holds his first child in his arms for the first time. After having been married for a few years, his wife finally got pregnant. Both husband and wife were eager to start a family, and they knew the struggles that lay ahead. Nevertheless, the first moment of holding his child made the husband overjoyed. Knowing that he was now in charge of protecting this innocent person instilled a stronger sense of responsibility in him. He is also very appreciative of his wife, who had been in labor for a long time. He offers her so much respect, love and attention. He is so thankful for her presence in his life.

Life is full of similar situations, but nothing can compare to having God enter your life. The term "God" is rather vague, as one can even mistake a basic auspicious occurrence with God's direct intervention. With King Janaka, there was no vagueness. The Supreme Lord in a visible form appeared in his life. First came the Lord's eternal consort, Sita Devi. She entered Janaka's life mysteriously from a field. Janaka then gladly took on the role of father. Through arranging for her marriage, Janaka received Shri Rama as a son-in-law. Rama is Narayana, or the source of men. He is Krishna, or the all-attractive Supreme Personality of Godhead. He is Vishnu, who is all-pervading and opulently adorned, served by many goddesses of fortune simultaneously. He is Janardana, or the maintainer of all living entities. He is the source of the material and spiritual worlds. Everything emanates from Him.

"I am the source of all spiritual and material worlds. Everything emanates from Me. The wise who know this perfectly engage in My devotional service and worship Me with all their hearts." (Lord Krishna, Bhagavad-gita, 10.8)

In the scene referenced above, Rama is about to return home to Ayodhya. He is taking Sita with Him, for they are married now. Though Janaka is a powerful king, here he offers respectful obeisances to Vashishtha, who is the family priest in Ayodhya. He gives respects by offering prayers to the other munis, or sages, who are there. He then makes a special approach to the lotus feet of Vishvamitra. It was this forest-dwelling sage who was most responsible for Rama entering Janaka's life. Rama and His younger brother Lakshmana were serving Vishvamitra in the forest when they were led by the sage to Janaka's city. If not for the sage's mercy, Rama would not have appeared at the contest of the bow and won Sita's hand in marriage.

Simply by his words and his behavior Vishvamitra earned the respect of someone who protected the earth. The sage did not demand that others worship him. He did not tell others that he was their guru. He did not force Janaka to make obeisances. The wise king, who was so thankful to have the greatest gift in the world, Shri Rama in his life, knew who was responsible for his fortune. He was never puffed up by his stature, for he knew that all good things come through the mercy of the devoted souls, who are rare to this world and yet still carry a far-reaching influence.

All objects in the material world are perishable. Brahman, or truth, is the only thing that remains. Narayana is the source of Brahman, so He is ultimately responsible for giving life to anything. In the darkness of ignorance, the conditioned living entity forgets the presence of Narayana. It is the humble sage who kindly awakens the bewildered soul, reminding them of both God's presence and the eternal relationship as servant to Him. Through this kindness, the demigods of this earth automatically become worshipable, as shown by Janaka. With every utterance of the holy names, Hare Krishna Hare Krishna, Krishna Krishna, Hare Hare, Hare Rama Hare Rama, Rama Rama, Hare Hare, the magnitude of their mercy increases. By keeping love for Sita and Rama in his heart, Janaka offered the highest respect to Vishvamitra and the other sages associated with the Lord.

VERSE 175

भाइन्ह सहित बहोरि बिनय रघुबीरहिं।
गदगद कंठ नयन जल उर धरि धीरहिं॥175॥

bhā'inha sahita bahori binaya raghubīrahiṁ |
gadagada kaṇṭha nayana jala ura dhari dhīrahiṁ ||175||

"Then to Rama and His brothers Janaka requested many times. With tears in his eyes and a throat choked up, he tried to keep his heart calm." (175)

Essay - Keeping The Heart Calm

It's a common scene. A famous athlete has decided to hang it up. The decision wasn't easy. Once he ruled the sport. He was the leading scorer, the most valuable player, and accustomed to hoisting the championship trophy. Writers were in competition with one another to be the first to tag him as the "greatest of all-time." But that same time went to work on his skills. Eventually, his abilities diminished to the point that he was no longer valuable enough to keep on a team.

A press conference is scheduled where the player is expected to announce their retirement. They step up to the microphone, offer a few pleasantries, and then explain why it is they no longer will compete in the sport that has been their life since a very young age. Though they try, at one point they begin to shed tears. "I promised so and so I wouldn't do this," they say, as they fight back the tears and the choked throat. But the moment is too intense for them to hold back. They think of all the sacrifices others made for them. They think of all that they will miss. Though they never cry otherwise, at that moment they cannot hold back.

Indeed, others feel similarly helpless in situations specific to their lives. When they least expect it, as if they have no control over their body, they begin to shed tears. King Janaka faced that a long time ago, except his loss of control was rooted in love for the person each one of us has loved deep inside for the longest time. The individual can be identified best by the spirit soul residing within the body. Though that is the last thing with which we choose to identify, it is the only force that remains steady. We have difficulty realizing it is there until it finally leaves, at the time of death.

All of the individual's emotions are rooted in the soul's natural love for God. Hatred, envy, anger and the like are the inverse of the loving propensity. Like an upside down mirror, they still belong to the same source as the converse emotions of affection, kindness, and attachment. When pure love for God reawakens, there is ecstasy. That emotion is so strong that it is impossible to control. It rushes in like a tidal wave, especially when one is in the presence of the loveable object, the Supreme Personality of Godhead.

Here Janaka is bidding adieu to Shri Rama and His three younger brothers. All four were just married through Janaka's arrangement. Thus they are leaving home and taking with them the precious daughters dear to the community of Janakpur. In this verse from the Janaki Mangala it is said that Janaka is constantly requesting Rama. His throat is choked up and tears fill his eyes, and he tries to keep his heart steady. If you don't have control over your emotions, how will you speak? If you're overcome with intense affection, it will be difficult for the words to come out.

Janaka steadied himself enough to make his heartfelt plea to Rama, asking that He always remember them. Unlike the individual living entity, God is without flaw. He never falls down. He never fails to deliver on something needed for the devotee. Since His presence within the consciousness is the most important boon anyone could ask for, it is granted immediately upon request. Especially when someone as pious and respected as Janaka asks, the gift remains manifest all the time, never to be hidden away through a temporary fall into the material ocean of attachment, aversion, greed, selfishness and envy.

Just as Janaka fought his emotions to make his kind request to the Supreme Lord standing in front of him, the devoted souls who always chant the holy names have a difficult time keeping their emotions in check. Just hearing the name "Rama" brings to mind the dearest son of King Dasharatha. When they hear the name again, they remember how happy He made Janaka by winning the contest of the bow. They have trouble keeping the tears from coming when they remember Rama's dearest wife Sita, who is the beloved daughter of Janaka.

When they hear the name "Krishna" they think of the darling of Vrindavana, who roamed this earth as the affectionate son of mother Yashoda and Nanda Maharaja. They get choked up thinking about how He transformed a humble fruit vendor's products into jewels when they made a kind offering to Him. The name brings to mind the famous lecture on all matters of life that Krishna gave on the battlefield to the distressed warrior Arjuna. The name reminds them of the shelter Krishna provides through lifting giant mountains like Govardhana.

As the name brings so much joy, it is no wonder that the heart has a difficult time remaining calm in the presence of the Supreme Lord, who is non-different from His names. So many names are there to keep the devoted soul always in ecstasy, and so these souls never tire of reciting those names. Janaka was able to make his requests, and Rama immediately granted them. In the same way, Rama immediately comes to the souls who chant His names in a pure way.

VERSE 176

कृपा सिंधु सुख सिंधु सुजान सिरोमनि।
तात समय सुधि करबि छोह छाड़ब जनि।।१७६।।

kṛpā sindhu sukha sindhu sujāna siromani |
tāta samaya sudhi karabi choha chāraba jani ||176||

" ' O ocean of mercy, O ocean of happiness, O crest-jewel of great souls, from time to time please remember us, dear son, and don't let go of Your love.' " (176)

Essay - Rama Navami

Shri Rama, the person honored on the occasion of Rama Navami, is the crest-jewel of all great men. Sujana refers to great souls, those who are wiser than most. Their wisdom is directly tied to their vision. They see the spirit within all creatures. This vision is stronger than x-ray. The doctor in the examination room can see the hairline fracture of a bone, but no image will give an indication of the presence of the soul. For that, knowledge and training are required.

"The humble sage, by virtue of true knowledge, sees with equal vision a learned and gentle brahmana, a cow, an elephant, a dog and a dog-eater [outcaste]." (Lord Krishna, Bhagavad-gita, 5.18)

The wise soul sees with equal vision so many different creatures. The unintelligent cannot see this, for their vision is not sharpened. They make distinctions between man and woman. They offer affection to one type of animal and a butcher's knife to another. They are kind to their family members but apathetic towards their neighbors. Such a dichotomy in outlook is understandable given the lack of pure vision.

Spirit is equally present in all forms of life, and so one who can understand this is very valuable to others. They are truly a great soul; they show their greatness in their behavior and also the wisdom they offer to others. Rama is the crest-jewel of such men since He always has the equal vision. Not only does He see everyone equally, He is the lone entity who witnesses everything. In His expansion as the Supersoul, He is the all-pervading witness, a neutral observer who is just standing by, waiting to offer guidance when asked.

"The Supersoul, the Supreme Personality of Godhead, seated beside the individual soul, is the witness of the individual soul's activities and is the source of consciousness. The Supersoul gives the jiva an opportunity to act freely, and He witnesses his activities." (Shrila Prabhupada, Bhagavad-gita, 8.4 Purport)

Rama's travels with the individual from body to body also make Him an ocean of mercy. No one else is so kind to us. No one else knows everything about us, from our faults to our good attributes. We keep secrets from one another because revealing too much information may leave us vulnerable. Others may keep vital information with them, to be used when a favor is needed. It may also be used if an argument ensues. The Supreme Lord sees everything, and He remembers all as well. And He is still kind enough to travel with us, to stay close by our side. When one is fortunate enough to realize the need for connecting with Him, they find that He gives them an endless flow of mercy. He allows them to glorify Him without end, which is the most enjoyable aspect of life. One only really comes to life when they are glorifying God.

Rama is also the ocean of happiness. Just study the countenances of His closest associates, like Sita, Lakshmana and Hanuman. In service to Rama, Hanuman is always blissful. The only time he finds unhappiness is if he feels inadequate in serving. Still, he never gets discouraged, for he knows he will be happy in service to Rama only. The same applies to Sita and Lakshmana, who follow Rama wherever He goes. They are only unhappy when physically separated from Him, when unable to serve Him directly.

In this scene from the Janaki Mangala, King Janaka rightly points out Rama's glorious nature. He addresses Rama as the ocean of mercy, the ocean of happiness, and the crest-jewel of all great souls. Janaka asks that Rama remember him from time to time. Rama is here set to return home to Ayodhya, having just married Sita, who is Janaka's daughter. Janaki is one of her names, referencing how dear she is to her father.

Janaka asks Rama to not let go of His love for them. This is a very nice request, and indeed it is impossible for Rama to ever forget those who are dear to Him. He doesn't forget the souls who always forget Him, so He surely always remembers those who choose to remain with Him in consciousness. On the occasion of Rama Navami, which celebrates the appearance of Shri Rama into this world, the devoted souls follow Janaka's lead and pray that the dear Lord remember them from time to time.

How does one tell that Rama hears their request? Indeed, the mere ability to recite His names, such as those found in the maha-mantra, indicates that the ocean of mercy is flowing nearby. By reciting, Hare Krishna Hare Krishna, Krishna Krishna, Hare Hare, Hare Rama Hare Rama, Rama Rama, Hare Hare, the person remembers Rama, who in turn always remembers them. Rama takes the vow to always give shelter to the surrendered souls, so it is not possible for Him to abandon the love He feels for great souls like Janaka. In a similar manner, those who love Rama never cease in celebrating Him, paying special attention on auspicious days like the one that marks His appearance into this world, the day the crest-jewel of the Raghu dynasty finally arrived, the day Sita's husband appeared in this earthly plane, and the day Shri Hanuman's life and soul first graced this realm with His transcendental form.

CHAND 22

जनि छोह छाड़ब बिनय सुनि रघुबीर बहु बिनती करी।
मिलि भेटि सहित सनेह फिरेउ बिदेह मन धीरज धरी।।
सो समौ कहत न बनत कछु सब भुवन भरि करुना रहे।
तब कीन्ह कोसलपति पयान निसान बाजे गहगहे।।22।।

jani choha chāṛaba binaya suni raghubīra bahu binatī karī |
mili bheṭi sahita saneha phire'u bideha mana dhīraja dharī ||
so samau kahata na banata kachu saba bhuvana bhari karuṇā rahe |
taba kīnha kosalapati payāna nisāna bāje gahagahe ||22||

"Hearing the request of 'don't give up Your love', Rama made many entreaties in return. After embracing each other with love, with a controlled mind Janaka returned." (Chand 22.1)

"Words cannot describe that environment. All the people were full of sadness. Then to the very jubilant sound of drums, Dasharatha, the ruler of Koshala, proceeded home." (Chand 22.2)

Essay - Giving Him A Problem

Imagine a celebrity, someone who is very famous. Perhaps they are on the radio every day, holding an audience of millions, who listen with rapt attention and are given to comment on every opinion offered. The person could also be someone who has done good things for others, perhaps someone in a position of power who was able to save a valuable community landmark. Or maybe the person in question is a famous recording artist whose songs have touched the lives of many.

Regardless the person, the treatment from the general public is more or less the same: adulation.

"Oh, thank you so much for what you do. I can't tell you how much you've changed my life. I wouldn't be where I am today if it weren't for you. You are so wonderful. Please keep doing what you are doing. There is no way to properly express my gratitude for your presence. You are simply a terrific person. If more people were like you, we wouldn't have so many problems in the world."

This kind of praise isn't hard to imagine, but what is more difficult to conceive of is being on the receiving end. How would you feel if random strangers came up to you and treated you this way? Sure, it would be nice, but what if you didn't consider yourself to be so special. "Hey, I'm just an ordinary guy. I'm not that amazing person you think I am. I put my pants on one leg at a time, just like every other guy. I cry, I laugh, I get sick, I have fears, just like all of you out there."

But in a quick meeting with an adoring fan, there is no time to explain. The celebrity in question gets overrun by the praise, and so they have to learn to accept it. They must find their own way to say "thanks" in return, to repay the debt of gratitude they owe. The more famous they become, the more great things they do, the bigger the problem is for them in returning appreciation.

This situation gives us a neat trick to use in giving a problem to the Supreme Personality of Godhead. He has done the most amazing things. By our estimation, this universe is quite complex. We can barely understand the cycle of the human birth and death, but there are so many other creatures as well. Then this planet is hard to understand, which has a constantly changing climate. Indeed, the fact that we think we can predict the climate means that there is some regularity to the workings of this planet. Patterns emerge from some intelligence, so through some design the earth exists in a state that can be studied.

But in fact the complexity is too great to know anything with certainty. Then there is the moon, which is also complex. Throw in the other planets and you have generations' worth of study to keep you busy. By the way, all that study doesn't give a definitive answer as to the origin. We get that only from authorized books like the Shrimad Bhagavatam. In works like that we find that this amazing universe constantly comes and goes, and this happens through the breathing of the Supreme Lord.

God invites endless praise through His breathing alone. He exhales to create the universes, and He inhales to take them back into His gigantic body. He does many other praiseworthy things as well. In Janakpur a long time ago, for instance, He lifted an extremely heavy bow to win the contest for the hand in marriage of Sita Devi, the king's daughter. There is no end to the glories of this achievement. No one else in the world could lift that bow. It was only Rama, who is the same Supreme Lord of tremendous breathing potency appearing in an apparently human form.

That is not an ordinary human form. As a simple test for the validity of this claim, we can try offering praise to that form. The deeds and words of that form are always tied to it. So by constantly praising the heroic feat of Rama's lifting of the bow to win Sita's hand, we see that the form of Rama is not ordinary. Rama has a difficult time repaying the praise directed His way, but He is the Supreme Lord, so it is a nice problem to present to Him.

In this scene from the Janaki Mangala, Rama returns kind entreaties to Janaka, Sita's father. The two embraced, and then Janaka regained his composure while returning to the rest of the guests, who were set to depart. A fallible human being has a tough time repaying kind words offered to them. At best, they can continue to do whatever it is that makes them appreciated. As the human birth is destined for destruction, so too is the work of any great man.

Not so with Rama, who though leaving the immediate vicinity, stays around forever through the accounts of His deeds. He remains in the sound vibration of His names as well. And so the ability to constantly chant mantras like "Hare Krishna Hare Krishna, Krishna Krishna, Hare Hare, Hare Rama Hare Rama, Rama Rama, Hare Hare", gives a chance at offering repayment. Even with this chanting, the devoted souls continue to offer praise to Rama, who then assumes more debt as a result. This is the kind gift the devoted souls happily offer to the Supreme Lord, who welcomes the problem of repaying kindness to such sweet individuals.

Essay - The Show Must Go On

As they say in show business, "the show must go on." When bad things happen, if there is sadness, there is no point in dwelling on it for too long. What good will that do, anyway? You've got your life still, so you must act to maintain it. You must tend to your responsibilities or others will be harmed. In this scene from the Janaki Mangala, the lord of Koshala, King Dasharatha, is set to return to his kingdom. It is sad for the people being left behind, but on the other side there will be a jubilant celebration.

Imagine this scene. You've had a rough day. You heard some bad news at the wrong time. You didn't have time to digest it all. The thing is, you have a concert to attend scheduled for this particular day. Your friend bought the tickets many months back. You didn't foresee any problems. But that's how life goes sometimes. The worst things happen at the worst possible times.

Since your friend spent so much money on the tickets, you decide to go to the concert anyway. You're intent on not having a good time. You're going to sit in your seat and just observe. But when the headline band comes out on stage, others around you start to get excited. Then the lead singer tries his best to pump everyone up.

"Alright, this is a hands up kind of gig. You're not gonna just sit around. Everybody up. We need you to make some noise. You there, in the back. On your feet. Mr. Sourpuss back there, you need to get up. Everyone else around you is up and clapping; you have to join them."

Embarrassed by the attention now upon you, you decide to get up. And eventually, after a few songs, you start to have a good time. You forget your troubles. You remember that you actually like this band, that there was a reason you wanted to attend this concert in the first place.

In the verse referenced above, we see that the people of Janakpur were extremely sad. Everyone was in bad spirits, as their beloved Sita and Rama were set to return home. Such are the ways of the world that no person's physical association is fixed. At some point in time the Supreme Lord appears and gives pleasure to the residents of that area. Then He leaves and goes somewhere else, leaving the same people very sad.

In this instance, the event that brings sadness to the people of Janakpur will bring happiness to the people of Koshala. Therefore the sound of the drums is very jubilant as Dasharatha sets to embark. There is actually nothing to be sad about, as a wonderful pastime has just concluded. Everyone will remember how Rama lifted the bow to win the contest. They will remember how Rama and Sita looked perfect for one another. They will remember how the two fathers, kings of their respective lands, were equal in good qualities and affection for one another. They will remember how Sita accepted her marriage vows and how she never breaks her word. They will remember how Janaka arranged for the marriages of Rama's three younger brothers as well, being swept away by the happiness of the occasion.

Goswami Tulsidas says that words cannot describe that moment when Dasharatha and family were ready to leave - tremendous sadness combined with eager anticipation. The memory of that event would stay with the people, just as the memory of Rama and family remained with the people of Ayodhya. They hadn't seen their beloved prince in a long time. Now He was set to return home with a new wife, the most beautiful woman in the world at that. The royal family would expand, which meant that the store of love found within the heart would have to expand as well. Each citizen would find affection in a reservoir thought to be empty to offer to Sita and the other beloved princesses coming to the city. Rightfully, the grand return would be accompanied by very loud drums, letting everyone know that the lord of the land had returned triumphantly and happily.

VERSE 177

पंथ मिले भृगुनाथ हाथ फरसा लिए।
डाटहिं आँखि देखाइ कोप दारुन किए।।177।।

pantha mile bhṛgunātha hātha pharasā li'e |
ḍāṭahiṁ āṁkhi dekhā'i kopa dāruna ki'e ||177||

"On the way they met Parashurama. Holding a weapon in his hand, he yelled at them and showed his angry eyes." (177)

Essay - Challenge Accepted

God is one. This is not a new revelation emerging from the suddenly popular spiritual teacher. This is not the product of the mind which has contemplated matters beyond this lifetime. It is a truth that exists eternally, waiting to be heard and accepted by the living entity, who is godlike but not God Himself. It is a truth necessary to be understood by the devoted sentimentalist, who considers their religious path to be the only one worth adopting. It is a truth that must be accepted, even in the face of contradicting evidence, such as with the case of the meeting of Lord Rama and Parashurama. One is the son of King Dasharatha and the other the offspring of Jamadagni, but both are incarnations of the Supreme Lord. And at the time of their meeting, the original Lord remains safely in His own abode.

How is this possible? If God is one, is He not a singular entity? How can He be more than one person? And who is superior, Rama or Parashurama? Rama is also known as Ramachandra, for He has a moonlike face and acts like the moon to the water-lilies that are the members of the Ikshvaku dynasty. Parashurama is the wielder of the axe, a raging mad fighter turned ascetic. He destroyed the warrior race twenty-one times over as revenge for offenses against him and his family. Rama is Vishnu Himself, but then so is Parashurama. So how could they possibly meet?

The meeting took place when Rama and His party were returning home to Ayodhya. Rama is the incarnation of Vishnu who is famous for having defeated the evil king of Lanka, Ravana. He is famous for many other things as well, including the lifting of the bow of Lord Shiva. That feat took place in the kingdom of Videha, in front of a host of other princes who were vying for the hand of Sita Devi, the daughter of King Janaka. That bow initially belonged to Devarata, and it was passed along in the family until it reached King Janaka, also known as Shiradhvaja. The contest was to see who could lift the bow. No one could except Ramachandra, and so then He married Sita. On the way home from the marriage ceremony, His group ran into Parashurama.

The priests in the royal party offered obeisances, but that did little to pacify the famous fighter's anger. He made a proposition to Rama directly. String this other bow that was in his possession, and from there the two could engage in conflict. Dasharatha, Rama's father, responded first, trying to defuse the situation. Parashurama ignored him and continued to address Ramachandra directly. Parashurama gave more information on the history of the bow which Rama just broke. He also spoke of this new bow that was brought into the equation. A long time back Vishnu and Shiva engaged in a conflict, being asked by the celestials to see who had superior prowess. Vishnu won the conflict by nullifying the strength of Shiva's bow. Lord Shiva then passed his bow on to Devarata. The bow Vishnu used in the conflict was passed on to Jamadagni's family. And so now Parashurama had that bow and requested that Rama draw an arrow to it. Rama had already strung Shiva's bow, so now it was time to do the same with Vishnu's.

Rama accepted the first part of the challenge. He put an arrow to the bow without a problem. He would not engage in conflict, however. He crushed Parashurama's pride by accurately pointing out that the arrow had to destroy something now that it was drawn. Parashurama could lose either the regions he had won through asceticism or his ability to travel at the speed of the mind. Knowing that the sage Kashyapa had previously told him that the regions of the earth were not a suitable habitation for him, Parashurama opted for the former. His pride humbled, he realized that Rama was indeed Vishnu Himself. He then left the scene.

So through the meeting of two avataras, or incarnations, of the Supreme Lord, the supremacy of the Supreme Lord was established, namely in His incarnation of Ramachandra. Seems like circular logic, an unnecessary adventure that only serves to further confuse the less intelligent. But in fact, through curbing the pride of the angry Parashurama, Rama's glory was further established, which allows one's faith in Rama to increase all the more. A similar thing occurred during Shri Krishna's advent, when He and Arjuna went to visit Vishnu Himself.

These contradictory episodes are only possible with God, who is above all the dualities we encounter on a daily basis. He is both here and not here. As Parashurama, He is both a kshatriya and a brahmana. As Ramachandra, He is both a pacifist and a courageous fighter. He is both respectful and disrespectful. He was initially respectful to Jamadagni's son, but through stringing the bow He crushed the pride of the fiery-tempered wielder of the axe.

Just as He can exist in His eternal abode in the Vaikuntha planets and here on earth in two incarnations simultaneously, know that He can be with every single living entity at the same time. The deity in the home of one devotee is just as representative of God as the deity in another home. He can hear an unlimited number of prayers offered simultaneously, and He can rescue anyone, regardless of their background, their country of origin, their native language, or their level of intelligence. He always hears the prayers of the devotees, and just like in stringing both the bow of Shiva and the bow of Vishnu, He can accomplish the seemingly impossible feat of lifting even the most sinful person in the world into the heights of transcendental bliss and ecstasy that are known only to devotional service.

Essay - Different Versions

You've heard of the "telephone game?" In some regions it goes by a different name, but the rules are pretty much the same. You start with a point of fact. It can be something very simple, like say that I had the flu last year. I then whisper that fact into the ear of another person. They have one responsibility: relay that fact to one other person. They don't have to do anything else. The chain continues until you reach a person who is many times removed from me. Then you ask them what was the fact that they learned, and it is almost never the same. They might think that I had a much more serious illness or that I am dead altogether.

As Vedic literature has accounts of talking monkeys, flying monkeys, sages drinking entire oceans, women giving birth to one hundred children, half-men/half-lion appearing out of pillars, and one man destroying an entire society many times over, it is natural to assign "myth" status to these works. The thinking goes like this:

"There was some original event that happened, and then the tale got passed on. Each person in the link wanted to outdo the predecessor in terms of poetic ability. If it was a boring event, no one will be interested in hearing about that. So they decided to exaggerate a little. They bent the truth, and then with each person in the chain following suit, you ended up with the descriptions that were not believable. It's like the telephone game but spanning hundreds of years."

This viewpoint seems to be validated by the contradicting stories of the same event found in Vedic literature. For instance, in the famous Ramayana, the central character, Lord Rama, breaks the bow of Lord Shiva to marry the daughter of King Janaka. On His way back home, Rama encounters Parashurama, an angry warrior turned sage, who is upset that Rama broke the bow of Shiva. He challenges Rama to string another bow, to which Rama happily accepts. Rama then crushes the pride of Parashurama. This is the sequence of events described above in the verse from the Janaki Mangala, which is a wonderful poem authored by the saint Tulsidas, who lived in India during medieval times.

In a more famous work by the same Tulsidas, the meeting with Parashurama takes place earlier. It occurs while everyone is still in Janaka's kingdom. There is some back and forth between Parashurama and Lakshmana, Rama's younger brother. That dialogue is missing in the original telling of the Ramayana. The telling of Rama's life with the meeting with Parashurama occurring earlier is found in other works of Vedic literature as well. So how do we reconcile these differences? Tulsidas himself has authored two different versions. Did he make one of them up? Was he a chain in the telephone game and then got the actual telling wrong?

"Never was there a time when I did not exist, nor you, nor all these kings; nor in the future shall any of us cease to be." (Lord Krishna, Bhagavad-gita, 2.12)

The nature of the material world sheds some light on the issue. This isn't our first go around in a body. We have lived before. Never was there a time that I did not exist. That is a factual statement. It is told by Shri Krishna to Arjuna on the battlefield of Kurukshetra. Krishna can utter the statement and have it be accurate. So can Arjuna, so can I, and so can you. We may not have existed with the same height and hair color. We may not have even been in the same species. But we still existed. The distant past is really no different than the immediate past. I existed five minutes ago. I know this for a fact. Just extrapolate out and take it as fact that you existed at any point in the past.

This eternal existence is made possible by the properties of the soul. The soul is spirit, which is immutable, unchangeable and primeval. It is not slain when the body is slain. Since I am spirit soul, I will exist perpetually into the future. There are changes, though. These occur to the things which are not spirit, i.e. matter. So the natural conclusion is that the universe goes through cycles of creation and destruction, just as the bodies of the individual living entities do. With cycles in the creation, you get repeat births and deaths. Within these cycles, the Supreme Lord Himself appears and disappears, maintaining His nature, which is changeless.

"Unintelligent men, who know Me not, think that I have assumed this form and personality. Due to their small knowledge, they do not know My higher nature, which is changeless and supreme." (Lord Krishna, Bg. 7.24)

So in some cycles of the creation, Parashurama meets Rama earlier, and in some cycles the meeting takes place later. In some cycles, there is an argument with Lakshmana, and in some cycles there isn't. In either case, the meetings are factual. The descriptions found in Vedic literature are also accurate; though they seemingly contradict. Something that takes place in a different era, and maybe in a different universe of planets, is still relevant to our understanding. And so wise saints like Tulsidas, who are fully aware of the nature of the material and spiritual worlds, have no problem passing on different accounts in different works.

The proof is in the pudding, as they say, and so the authenticity of a Vedic work which seems to contradict a previous work in minor details can be determined by the presence of God Himself. Is His name prominent? Are His activities in accord with His stature as the Supreme Personality of Godhead? Is the message the same, that devotional service is the highest engagement for humankind? So whether Parashurama was pacified in Janakpur or along the route back home to Ayodhya, the glory of Rama still shines. He is the superior incarnation of the Supreme Lord, and in either telling His victory is prominent, leaving no room for doubt that He is indeed Vishnu Himself, the chief of the gods.

VERSE 178

राम कीन्ह परितोष रोष रिस परिहरि।
चले सौंप सारंग सुफल लोचन करि।।178।।

rāma kīnha paritoṣa roṣa risa parihari |
cale saumpa sāraṅga suphala locana kari ||178||

"Rama pacified the anger of the sage and took his wrath away. Giving away the Sharanga bow, He left, providing the best fruit for the eyes." (178)

Essay - Dazzling Everyone

Having working eyes is extremely beneficial. If you lose your hearing, generally you can still be productive if your eyes are working. If you lose your sight, you will have a more difficult time managing, as others will need to help you out in many instances. The eyes are the gateway to the external world, allowing you to see objects, make identifications, and then act accordingly. So many things thus give pleasure to the eyes, and those things equate to fruits. The fruit is the resultant object of work, and the work of getting a human body endowed with eyes has many fruits in the form of pleasing visions. A best fruit, according to Vaishnava saints devoted in full consciousness, is the sight of a victorious Supreme Personality of Godhead when facing an apparently challenging situation. This suphala, or best fruit, is witnessed by only a rare few, but the descriptions of it are kindly passed on for future generations to relish.

Isn't God challenged every day? Do not the transgressions of the rules of propriety attack the long established rules and regulations passed on by the Supreme Lord? If such challenges take place all the time, why are the constant victories absent? Actually, the challenges always fail. Whosoever thinks themselves to be God must eventually bow down to the undefeated champion known as death. Death is synonymous with time, kalah in Sanskrit, as time is what goes to work on any gain. I look forward to the Christmas presents my parents will give me this year, but eventually the holiday season will pass and the objects of excitement will lose their value. This is time at work.

The challenger to God loses to time every single day. Otherwise they would have no reason to fear. They would have no need to proclaim themselves the best, either. If they knew their prominence would remain forever, they would be at complete peace. They would be atmarama, or self-satisfied. Unfortunately for them, the only person who is always atmarama is the Supreme Lord, who once appeared on earth as Ramachandra, the dark-complexioned eldest son of King Dasharatha. His moon-like face made Him adored by all in His family.

With His activities, Rama gave the fruit to the eyes. This fruit is for every kind of eyes, even the animals. Yet only the devoted souls relish the taste of the fruit. They recognize it for what it is, and so the Supreme Lord makes it available exclusively for them. He intentionally seeks the greatest challenges, situations which put fear into the devoted souls. These souls worry that He might not be able to accomplish the task. He could be ridiculed afterwards for having failed, which increases the worry.

One such situation occurred when Rama and His family were returning to Ayodhya from Janakpur. Rama had just married Sita Devi, the daughter of King Janaka. He earned her hand by lifting and stringing a bow that originally belonged to Lord Shiva. Rama was so strong that the bow broke when He bent it with string. This raised the ire of Parashurama, who intercepted the group on their path back home.

Parashurama is also God; an incarnation of the same Vishnu who appeared as Rama. So in this instance Vishnu created a challenge for Vishnu to solve. This can only mean that the purpose was to give the best fruit to the eyes. Parashurama is in a different visible manifestation; he also has a different mood. He is always angry. He carried around his axe like the sheriff in town eager to put away the criminals. Parashurama did not like that Shiva's bow was broken, so he challenged Rama to string Vishnu's bow. He offered it to Rama, and Rama then strung it so quickly that everyone was amazed. Then Rama said that the arrow now could not go to waste, and it would destroy either Parashurama's ascetic merit or the regions in the heavenly realm that he conquered. Parashurama opted for the latter.

Parashurama's pride was hurt, and in the process his anger subsided. Thus Rama did an amazing thing. He withstood a challenge from a person who had previously destroyed the warrior race on earth many times over. Rama then handed the bow over to Varuna, the demigod in charge of the oceans. That bow is called the Sharanga, and it is always associated with Vishnu. It has its own history, being passed on in a chain of famous personalities.

"All the sages said: Dear Dhruva, O son of King Uttanapada, may the Supreme Personality of Godhead known as Sharngadhanva, who relieves the distresses of His devotees, kill all your threatening enemies. The holy name of the Lord is as powerful as the Lord Himself. Therefore, simply by chanting and hearing the holy name of the Lord, many men can be fully protected from fierce death without difficulty. Thus a devotee is saved." (Shrimad Bhagavatam, 4.10.30)

Goswami Tulsidas allows any person to taste this fruit for the eyes, even if they weren't there in the first place. This makes the saints of the Vedic tradition so kind; kinder than anyone we know. Others can provide different fruits for the eyes, but none of these are the best. The vision of a victorious Rama remains forever, even into future lifetimes. Time can never act against these visions. Time works at the beck and call of Rama, who says as much in the Bhagavad-gita.

"Among the Daitya demons I am the devoted Prahlada; among subduers I am time; among the beasts I am the lion, and among birds I am Garuda, the feathered carrier of Vishnu." (Lord Krishna, Bhagavad-gita, 10.30)

Rama is the same Krishna, the speaker of the Gita. He is time, which is His impersonal manifestation. As time cannot act against the best fruit of the eyes that is the vision of a victorious God, it means that the impersonal is always subordinate to the personal. The wise take shelter of the personal, which can handle the awesome bow known as Sharanga and then renounce it within a second, not needing any weapon to carry out its work.

RETURINING TO AYODHYA

VERSE 179

रघुबर भुज बल देखि उछाह बरातिन्ह।
मुदित राउ लखि सनमुख बिधि सब भाँतिन्ह॥179॥

raghubara bhuja bala dekhi uchāha barātinha |
mudita rā'u lakhi sanamukha bidhi saba bhāṁtinha ||179||

"Seeing the strength of Rama's arms, the barata party became so excited. The king was so happy that the Lord allowed this to occur in his presence." (179)

Essay - Defusing A Tense Situation

Pick your favorite difficult situation. Something where you don't see any option for things getting better, a situation where you're in a lot of trouble and you can't envision a way out. Know that in the worst of these moments, the Supreme Lord has the strength to rescue you and everyone else affected. This fact should be obvious, but within the moment it is difficult to see clearly. A party happily returning from a marriage ceremony for four couples suddenly faced a tense situation. They relied on the strength of the arms of the Supreme Lord, and thus they felt so excited afterwards.

You're on a boat. It's a quiet Sunday afternoon. Everything seems to be going well. You're relaxing, for a change. No deadlines to worry over. No contemplating the projects that are due in the upcoming week. No screaming kids running around the house making a mess. Just you, your wife, and a few friends floating on the lake. Suddenly you notice a leak in the boat. Water is entering fast. No one knows what to do. Do you have to abandon the ship? Is there a way to plug the hole? Then one of your friends rides to the rescue, very calmly. He figures out how to stop the leak. Now everyone feels so relieved. The last thing they wanted to do was jump in the water and have to swim back to shore.

This is one example of an emergency situation, but the one faced by the barata party returning to Ayodhya was much more serious. It could perhaps be likened to a situation where a bomb is about to go off. The clock is ticking and the expert squad is called in to defuse it. With Parashurama, the extent of the damage could have been much worse. An incarnation of Vishnu himself, he previously had destroyed the entire warrior class twenty-one times over. He was known for his fiery temper, and his weapon of choice was the axe.

When he intercepted the barata party, he was again angry. Rama, the chief of the Raghu dynasty, had just lifted, strung, and broken Lord Shiva's bow in the assembly of King Janaka. That bow had a famous history, and now Parashurama wanted to see if Rama could string the corresponding bow belonging to Vishnu. Rama was not scared. He was not worried. Previously, as an adolescent, he had faced a similar challenge while serving the guru Vishvamitra. Rama and His younger brother Lakshmana lived with the sage for some time, acting as bodyguards in effect. One time the hermitage was attacked by the Rakshasa named Maricha. Maricha previously had carried out many similar attacks, and so he thought this one would be successful as well. He thought wrong.

"Then I, resembling a cloud and having molten-golden earrings, made my way into Vishvamitra's ashrama, for I was very proud of my strength due to the boon given to me by Lord Brahma. As soon as I entered, Rama quickly noticed me and raised His weapon. Though He saw me, Rama strung His bow without any fear." (Maricha speaking to Ravana, Valmiki Ramayana, Aranya Kand, 38.16-17)

Maricha was impressed by the fact that Rama strung His bow so effortlessly as the attack was going down. Rama did not flinch. He did not hesitate. The same occurred when He was challenged by Parashurama. Rama easily strung the bow and then curbed the pride of the fiery-tempered wielder of the axe. The barata party was so excited to see this. It was like a bomb had been defused. Rama's father, King Dasharatha, thanked God that this scene was able to occur in front of his eyes.

We may not think we are in as much trouble, but the repetition of birth and death is itself an emergency situation, especially for the human being. The animal can't make any strides in this area. They are more or less stuck with waiting it out. They don't have the intelligence to understand God. More importantly, they don't have any way to take shelter of Him. The human being can. They can get the same protection from the same very powerful arm, extended by the same chief of the Raghu dynasty.

That strength is passed on in full in the name itself. The name of Rama, chanted with faith, devotion and full dependence, can fix the emergency situation of the impending rebirth, which is guaranteed for the soul who is not conscious of God at the time of death. The rescue from the name of Rama brings the same excitement, which stays day after day through the constant chanting of those names: Hare Krishna Hare Krishna, Krishna Krishna, Hare Hare, Hare Rama Hare Rama, Rama Rama, Hare Hare.

The change will surprise us. No longer will we invest our hopes for a better life in practices that are meant to only bring temporary results. No longer will we feel the melancholy from lacking a direction in life, a purpose to our actions. Instead, we will thank the good Lord for transforming us and allowing us to get a slight glimpse into His immense potency, which can defuse any tense situation, large or small.

VERSE 180

एहि बिधि ब्याहि सकल सुत जग जसु छायउ।
मग लोगन्हि सुख देत अवधपति आयउ।।180।।

> ehi bidhi byāhi sakala suta jaga jasu chāya'u |
> maga loganhi sukha deta avadhapati āya'u ||180||

"In this way all four sons were married, and their fame spread throughout the world. Giving happiness to the people along the way, the lord of Ayodhya came home." (180)

Essay - A Good Father

Say that you're expecting your first child with your wife. You prepared for this. You knew that you were ready to start a family. But as the time of the birth approaches, you ask yourself some questions. "Will I be a good father? How should I act? Am I cut out to give protection to someone so young and innocent? In fact, what makes a good father? How does he act?" The time and circumstance dictate the requirements, though love is what guides properly in all circumstances. The lord of Ayodhya a long time ago had a tremendous responsibility, which he fulfilled to the satisfaction of everyone.

"Just be there for them. That's the majority of the parenting role. If you're not there, you can't guide. You can't protect if you're always away. Just be there for your kids, and they will figure out that you are the authority figure. They won't expect that much of you anyway. Just having you around is enough." King Dasharatha was around for his four sons. They came to him after a long time. It is not uncommon in modern times to marry at an advanced age. Dasharatha did not have this problem. He had three wives, which was not out of the ordinary during the more pure age known as Treta, the second of the four time periods of creation. With each successive period, dedication to virtue declines within society. Dasharatha loved and protected his three wives.

It was the son who was late in arriving. The king needed one to continue the family line. He was in a most famous family, one that traced its origin to the sun-god, Vivasvan. Finally, after performing a sacrifice for the purpose, Dasharatha received four beautiful sons through his three wives. He was there for those sons. He guided them. He protected them. He put them in the custody of the royal priest at the appropriate time.

The marriage of his eldest son Rama took place through Vishvamitra's direction. Vishvamitra was one of the priest-like men who was trusted by Dasharatha to guide his sons. Vishvamitra took care of Rama and His younger brother Lakshmana for a period. Though Dasharatha didn't arrange for the marriage of Rama to Sita, he gave his consent. He also arrived for the ceremony, bringing along Rama's two other brothers. The kind father of Sita, Janaka, was so swept away by the moment that he offered to have Dasharatha's three other sons get married as well. So the king of

Ayodhya went to Janaka's city to agree to one marriage, and he returned home with all four of his sons married.

In the above referenced verse from the Janaki Mangala, it is said that the fame of those four marriages spread throughout the world. This can refer to the husbands and wives themselves and also to Dasharatha. Honor ascends. It cannot be passed on to future generations, because those generations have nothing to do with the act that warranted the honor in the first place. If you do something good, the praise extends upwards, in the direction of the parents. Through Rama's marriage to Sita, the honor ascended to the father Dasharatha. The marriages of the three other brothers further increased the fame of the good father.

It is also said here that Dasharatha gave happiness to the people along the way back home. Think of it like the parade celebrating a notable personality. They travel on a car through the city streets, with so many well-wishers looking on and waving. They line up early just to get a brief look at the person in question. This is sort of how it was when Dasharatha and his sons returned home to Ayodhya. The people caught a glimpse of the triumphant party, who were led by the good father.

That father's primary qualification was his love for the eldest son Rama, who is God. And so in all situations, whether one wants to be a good father, mother, brother, sister, friend, etc. - if they have love for God then things will work themselves out. To have love for God is not very difficult; it lies deep within us. It is a part of us that no one or thing can take away. It is aroused through devotional service, bhakti-yoga, which is best practiced today through the chanting of the holy names: Hare Krishna Hare Krishna, Krishna Krishna, Hare Hare, Hare Rama Hare Rama, Rama Rama, Hare Hare.

CELEBRATIONS IN AYODHYA

VERSE 181

होहिं सुमंगल सगुन सुमन सुर बरषहिं।
नगर कोलाहल भयउ नारि नर हरषहिं।।181।।

hohiṁ sumaṅgala saguna sumana sura baraṣahiṁ |
nagara kolāhala bhaya'u nāri nara haraṣahiṁ ||181||

"With the great auspiciousness and the good aura, the demigods rained down flowers. The city was filled with sounds of rejoicing, and the men and women were very happy." (181)

Essay - A Hero's Welcome

The aura was perfect for the return of Dasharatha and his four sons. All the omens were good. There was nothing negative looming. Not too long prior, the omens were mixed. There were ominous signs that troubled the king and his party. There were auspicious signs which cancelled those out. The guru pointed out the auspiciousness, and his prediction was validated when Rama averted the potential disaster of an angry Parashurama. But now the aura was all-auspicious, fitting for the triumphant return home.

Perhaps you have a difficult time believing in God. Even if you do accept that He exists, you're not really sure what He looks like. Is there only one manifestation? Can't He have more than one appearance? Therefore your idea is vague. Still, if someone were to tell you that God was planning on visiting your home, what would you do? Most likely you would straighten up. Time to throw out that pizza box that's been sitting on the kitchen table for the past few days. Time to organize all the junk mail that you have yet to sort through. Time to fix up the living room and make sure there are clean towels in the bathrooms.

Actually, you would do these things for any important guest. But God is the most important person to ever come to your home. Therefore you have to go the extra mile. You'll decorate further. You'll put flowers everywhere. You'll make every room smell pleasant. You'll set aside a path for the Supreme Lord to walk through as He enters. You'll have a nice seat awaiting Him. You'll make sure that the best food and drink will be on hand, in large amounts. God creates the oceans without blinking an eye, so He can easily drink up that same volume of liquid. He consumes the clarified butter poured into official sacrifices in His honor. He accepts the foodstuffs kindly prepared and set in front of His many temple deities around the world. He accepts these things simultaneously, all the while staying one.

"The Lord is situated in everyone's heart as the Supersoul. Does that mean that He has become divided? No. Actually, He is one. The example is given of the sun: the sun, at the meridian, is situated in his place. But if one goes for five thousand miles in all directions and asks, 'Where is the sun?' everyone will say that it is shining on his head. In the Vedic literature this example is given to show that although He is undivided, He is situated as if divided." (Shrila Prabhupada, Bhagavad-gita, 13.17 Purport)

Though He rests within everyone's heart as the Supersoul, He is one. He is never divided. He can expand, for sure, but this doesn't mean that His original form loses anything. He is Ramachandra, the eldest son of Dasharatha, but this doesn't mean that while He's on earth as Rama He is suddenly no longer Krishna. And when He lifts Govardhana Hill in Vrindavana, it doesn't mean that He is no longer Rama.

In the same way, though He is the Supersoul residing in my heart, He is also within yours. It is the same person. Therefore He sees more than anyone else. Take all the newspaper reporters in the world, combine their eyesight, memory, and ability to craft stories describing what they've seen and you get some idea of how amazing God is in just His role as the Supersoul.

Since He is so amazing, you must have an amazing welcome ready for Him. For an idea of how that welcome should appear, look no further than Ayodhya during the time of Rama's return. Here Goswami Tulsidas says that all the qualities were good, saguna. There was great auspiciousness, sumangala. And the demigods rained down flowers. So the omens were good, the aura was good, and the physical appearance was good as well.

The sound of rejoicing filled the city, and the men and women were very happy. That in itself is the best welcome. If you arrive somewhere and the hosts are not happy to see you, how will you feel? "Oh alright, you can come in, if you have to. Don't expect any food, because we're almost out. Don't sit on the couch; you'll mess it up. Rather, sit on the floor. And don't think of eating anywhere near the furniture. Stand over in that corner and eat whatever food you can find in here."

This isn't so nice a welcome. The opposite reception makes you feel so good. And so the excitement of the men and women made the welcome all the more special. They had plenty to be excited about. Rama and Lakshmana, two of Dasharatha's four sons, were finally returning home. They had left to protect the sage Vishvamitra from the attacks of evil night-rangers. Now they were returning home safe and sound, married as well. The other two sons also came home with brides, and so the proud father had plenty to rejoice over.

One of Rama's many names is Raghuvira, which means the hero of the Raghu dynasty. He is brave, righteous, and always concerned with the welfare of those who are under His protection. And so the hero got the perfect welcome in Ayodhya, where everyone spontaneously rejoiced at His triumphant return. He protected Vishvamitra, won the contest in Janakpur, married the beautiful Sita, and now finally came back.

Essay - Always An Auspicious Time

This verse from the Janaki Mangala says that the time of Shri Rama's return to Ayodhya saw auspiciousness everywhere. All the omens were good. This means that it wasn't snowing. It could be the first day of Spring, the beginning of baseball season in America, but this doesn't mean that the weather will automatically cooperate. It could also be very warm on an autumn day. The setting isn't always ideal, and in life not all moments are auspicious. But here everything is just right, and it is not surprising considering that Rama is the Supreme Lord Himself.

In fact, there can never be an inauspicious moment for Rama. The term does not apply to Him. Inauspicious means something that is not conducive to meeting the objective at hand. If your job is to put a roof on a housing structure on a particular day, rain is inauspicious for you. The rain will get in the way of doing your job. For the farmer, the opposite is true; the rain is auspicious. Therefore good and bad are relative. The same occurrence, rain in this case, can help one person and hurt another.

When the discussion turns to the spiritual, auspicious and inauspicious relate to the afterlife. "Is God going to be happy with what I'm doing? Will I go to hell if I do this?" Then if I do something nice, like open up a hospital for sick children, I wonder how much benefit is set to come my way. "Boy, I better make it into heaven now. This is a really good thing I'm doing." If we refrain from eating meat, someone may ask us, "So, if you eat something that has meat in it, are you going to hell?" Similarly, if we perform a specific ritual in the home, someone may ask, "By doing this, are you guaranteed a spot in heaven?"

"From the highest planet in the material world down to the lowest, all are places of misery wherein repeated birth and death take place. But one who attains to My abode, O son of Kunti, never takes birth again." (Lord Krishna, Bhagavad-gita, 8.16)

In the Bhagavad-gita, Shri Rama, in His original form of Shri Krishna, explains that even this idea of heaven and hell is relative. The auspiciousness and inauspiciousness of spiritual life, where the objective is still on material enjoyment and the avoidance of material distress, are thus not absolute. There are many heavenly planets, and several hellish ones as well. Residence in any of these places, from the highest to the lowest, is not temporary since birth and death take place there.

Rama is aja, or unborn. He is also ajita, which means unconquerable. No one can say that God was born on a particular day. And no one can say that He has ever been conquered by time. Time has no influence on Him. In His home the concept of an appropriate time has no meaning. There is no such thing as an inappropriate place since nothing can ever harm Him.

Knowing this, why would the demigods rain down flowers as He returned to Ayodhya during His earthly pastimes? Why would there be auspicious omens everywhere, with the citizens celebrating His return home? The only conclusion is that the auspiciousness mentioned here is to give an indication to others that the Supreme Lord in a most wonderful form is within vicinity. He is never outside of any area, but we don't always notice His presence. In fact, we almost never notice it, though it is always within our heart, where He lives in His expansion as the Supersoul.

As the Supersoul is more difficult to notice, and as it is possible to have an inauspicious aura when the Supersoul is present, we get further justification for the truth that the personal manifestation, the incarnation or God Himself as Krishna, is superior in all respects. Whenever the personal form, in a visible manifestation, is there for the eyes to relish there is auspiciousness all around.

As there can never be an inauspicious setting for the Supreme Lord, the same holds true for devotion to Him. While we consult with the proper authorities for the proper date and time to hold an important function like a wedding, something like chanting the holy names can be done anywhere and at any time. There is never a loss. In fact, the greatest loss is giving up the chanting of the holy names in favor of something else, something which keeps one away in consciousness from the Supreme Lord.

"Tulsi emphatically says, 'O mind, hear what I am saying and always take it to heart, for this will benefit you. Remembering Shri Rama's holy name is the greatest profit, and forgetting Him is the worst loss.'" (Dohavali, 21)

The people of Ayodhya understood the greatest gain they received in the triumphant return of Rama, His brothers, and their father Dasharatha. The same mentality is held by Rama's staunchest supporters today, who take advantage of the valuable gift of devotion passed on to them by the highly merciful spiritual teachers of the Vaishnava tradition. Such fortunate souls never pass up an opportunity to chant, "Hare Krishna Hare Krishna, Krishna Krishna, Hare Hare, Hare Rama Hare Rama, Rama Rama, Hare Hare."

VERSE 182

घाट बाट पुर द्वार बजार बनावहिं।
बीथीं सींचि सुगंध सुमंगल गावहिं।।182।।

ghāṭa bāṭa pura dvāra bajāra banāvahiṁ |
bīthiṁ sīñci sugandha sumaṅgala gāvahiṁ ||182||

"In the gates of the city, the steps by the river, and the stores they made decorations for a welcome. Sprinkling so much fragrant water on the roads, they sang of the great auspiciousness." (182)

Essay - Everything Stops

When visiting important pilgrimage sites in India, the word "ghata" comes up quite often. There is the ghata named after this person and the ghata named after that person. "You must visit these," the tour guide will tell you. From the context used, it would seem that the ghata is a place of greater significance than what it actually is, steps leading to a body of water. The major rivers in India are considered sacred, like the Ganges, Yamuna and Sarayu. Bathing in them is considered very auspicious, as they are associated with the Supreme Personality of Godhead. Therefore the steps that lead towards these bodies of water become very important.

Stores are where commerce takes place. If you own a store, you likely earn a living through it. In America it is said that the majority of jobs get created through small businesses, such as the storefronts found on the busiest roads of the city. Nothing is guaranteed in such ventures. Just because you are profitable today doesn't mean that you will be tomorrow. If you become very profitable, you become a target for your enemies, who consist not only of rival businesses but politicians as well. Your employees have the freedom to leave your business and go work somewhere else. Therefore the store owners are always preoccupied.

The gates of the city give the first glimpse of your town to the foreign traveler. If they have never been to your town before, they will get the first impression from the gates. In modern times there are large signs on the roads leading in. "Welcome to such and such city," the sign will say. Then it might list some interesting facts, things for which the city is famous.

In Ayodhya a long time ago, everything stopped for the arrival of a beloved son. The steps leading to the river were now decorated. So were the stores and also the gates to the city. It was like a holiday, where everything stops and the people get a break in order to relax. Here the break was for rejoicing. No one told them it was a holiday. Everyone acted spontaneously. They were so happy that Rama was back. He was coming home with a new wife, the beautiful Sita Devi, the daughter of King Janaka. Also coming home were Rama's three younger brothers and their father, the king of the town.

The people sprinkled fragrant water on the roads and constantly sang of the auspiciousness. A clay field requires regular watering in order to stay loose and soft. Sort of like the maintenance of a clay tennis court, the dirt roads required careful attention in order to stay fit for travel by carts. The fragrant water used here provided for a nice atmosphere. Far from the congested and foul smelling city streets of today, Ayodhya on that day looked and felt wonderful, from home to home.

Everything stopped because of the nature of Rama. The people loved Him so much. He had every good quality imaginable. He was kind. He was forgiving. He knew the truth. He was self-realized. He understood the difference between matter and spirit. He did not view one citizen as an enemy and another as a friend. He looked at everyone as a well-wisher, and in fact that's what they were. He never ran from responsibility. No matter how difficult the task was, Rama would take it up when asked. He was not worried about losing anything. If he had to lose the whole world to protect His citizens, He would. And He would not be any sadder as a result.

These are some of the qualities of God. He is the ultimate well-wishing friend. He is the supreme enjoyer and also the proprietor of all the worlds. It is in the makeup of the soul to serve. This means that we feel best when we act for someone else's enjoyment. In therapist speak, it is considered bad to depend on someone else for your happiness. "You'll never be happy that way because you can't control how someone else feels." It may be the case that the recipient's reaction is out of our control, but there is no denying that service is what lights up the otherwise disillusioned embodied soul stuck in a seemingly endless cycle of happiness and misery, which are neatly packaged inside of the two events of birth and death.

"And whoever, at the time of death, quits his body, remembering Me alone, at once attains My nature. Of this there is no doubt." (Lord Krishna, Bhagavad-gita, 8.5)

If you're going to act for someone else's enjoyment, might as well make it God's. He is the supreme enjoyer. This means that He is the person who will appreciate your efforts the most. He will reward you accordingly. Not necessarily with a new car or a large balance of money, He'll give you an even better gift: devotion. With that reward you can drop everything and prepare for a grand celebration in His honor at any time. With that gift you can be blissful even in a tense situation. With that reward you can concentrate on His lotus feet that traversed the fragrantly watered streets of Ayodhya. And most importantly, with devotion you can remember Him at the time of death, the time when what you think matters most.

VERSE 183

चौकैं पूरैं चारु कलस ध्वज साजहिं।
बिबिधि प्रकार गहागह बाजन बाजहिं।।183।।

caunkaiṁ pūraiṁ cāru kalasa dhvaja sājahiṁ |
bibidhi prakāra gahāgaha bājana bājahiṁ ||183||

"They drew patterns using colored rice flour, laid down four kalashas, and hoisted flags, decorating everything nicely. In the street many kinds of jubilant music played." (183)

Essay - A Part Of Me To Stay

The Supreme Lord is part of me. He exists within me in His plenary expansion of the Supersoul, also known as the Paramatma. As such, I am never actually separated from Him. In ignorance of this fact, I have been roaming through different bodies in lifetime after lifetime. The properties apply to every other conditioned living entity also. Since He is actually part of us, serving God is not very difficult. In the above referenced verse from the Janaki Mangala we see that basic items such as rice flour and flags suffice for perfect worship.

When I forget that God is part of me, I look for success without Him. I strive for material opulence. This is very difficult. One store location isn't enough for the businessman. They must expand. Relatively high employment rates for a nation aren't sufficient. If the total output of goods and services doesn't grow from one quarter to the next, there is a panic over the economy.

As such, there must be progress. Instead of living simply and growing one's own food on the land that they have claim to, the citizen must travel very far each day to earn a living. Instead of being content with a simple lifestyle that provides enough basic necessities, the individual must constantly buy new things. "Out with the old and in with the new." And of course there is never enough. Even with such accumulation peace remains absent, and without peace there cannot be happiness.

"One who is not in transcendental consciousness can have neither a controlled mind nor steady intelligence, without which there is no possibility of peace. And how can there be any happiness without peace?" (Lord Krishna, Bhagavad-gita, 2.66)

In the devotional consciousness, there is peace no matter the situation. Whether one is living on a farm or in a penthouse apartment, they remember that God is part of them. Therefore they act for His interest first. They can have many cars or just one. They can have a lot of money or very little. They are not dependent on the objects. Satisfied in the relationship to the Supreme, they are known as atmarama.

To see how this works, we can study the behavior of the residents of Ayodhya a long time ago. They wanted to celebrate. They were so happy that their beloved son, Shri Rama, was returning home a married man. Rama's father was the king.

Dasharatha got all four of his sons married at the same time, so there was so much to rejoice over in the city.

The people did not require much. They used basic items like pots, flags and flour, and there was no deficiency in the celebration. The devotion is what made the atmosphere. They had pure and spontaneous love for Rama, who is the Supreme Lord in an incarnation specific to a time and place. Rama is the very same Vishnu who resides in the heart as the Supersoul. He is the very same Krishna who roams the sacred land of Vrindavana, sweetly playing His flute and giving pleasure to the cows and the senses. He is the same Brahman, which is the impersonal effulgence of God that lacks definition. Rama is the definition behind the generic term of "God," which is a vague concept.

These residents didn't necessarily know that Rama was God. They didn't have to. They knew that their lives depended on Him, and more specifically, their devotion to Him. Rama was part of their lives, the central figure in fact. Knowing this, the people had success in the things that mattered the most to them. Their success was seen not in their external wealth but rather in their display of affection.

And so that same affection can be shown by anyone, for the same Rama stays with every single person as the Supersoul. It is the etiquette when visiting temples of Vishnu, or God, to bring an offering upon entering. Something simple like a flower or a fruit is sufficient. It is the thought which counts. The neophyte thinks that God only resides in the temple, but the actual fact is that God is everywhere. This means that He can be worshiped everywhere.

Through the simple chanting of the holy names, "Hare Krishna Hare Krishna, Krishna Krishna, Hare Hare, Hare Rama Hare Rama, Rama Rama, Hare Hare," one can worship God. This chanting can be done by any person, even one who doesn't know the difference between spirit and matter. This mantra can be chanted for one second or for multiple hours consecutively. It can be recited by both the rich and the poor and the lucky and the unlucky.

One doesn't have to travel very far to chant these names, either. The people of Ayodhya simply had to go out into the streets, where they played jubilant music. Rama was pleased by their welcome, and the citizens remained dear to Him forever. It is no wonder that the Almighty chose such a place to appear and call home for many years during the Treta Yuga.

VERSE 184

बंदनवार बितान पताका घर घर।

रोपे सफल सपल्लव मंगल तरुबर।।१८४।।

bandanavāra bitāna patākā ghara ghara |
rope saphala sapallava maṅgala tarubara ||184||

"In home to home they set up altar areas and hoisted flags. They planted trees bearing fruits, blossoms, and other auspicious signs." (184)

Essay - Pious Trees

Trees are good for us. This only makes sense. Aside from being integral to a beautiful backdrop, providing the proper setting for a nature scene, they provide shade to the weary traveler. They give the comfort of shade on a hot summer's afternoon. They give a resting place for the bookworm who enjoys being outdoors. And in the scientific analysis, they provide the vital oxygen that is necessary for breathing in the human species. Still, there are grades of trees, with some considered pious and others impious. The scene referenced above speaks of pious trees.

Sin gets you further away from your true identity of spirit soul, which is part and parcel of God and thus servant of Him for all of eternity. Sin isn't so difficult to understand. There are sins in just about every category of activity. If you put the wrong type of gasoline in your automobile, you're committing a sin. The reason is that the mistake will lead to a negative reaction, something particularly unwanted. Putting the right type of gasoline in the car is piety; it yields a desired result. Piety is auspicious and sin inauspicious.

In terms of trees, a sinful one does not yield fruits. Every living entity survives off other living entities. This is nature's way. There is something called the food chain which basically explains the same concept. The human being is the lone species that has discretion. It has a choice in its diet. Just because it has dominion over other creatures doesn't mean it has license to kill without limits. Just as the human being does not normally kill other human beings and a few selected animals like cats and dogs, when in a state of sobriety it does not kill any other animals for food.

This leaves the vegetables. But even then there is some sin involved, as the vegetables are cut away, made lifeless, when the time is right for consumption. The only kind of diet that is totally free of violence is one based on fruits. The fruits fall from the trees at the appropriate time. Shri Ramachandra, the Supreme Personality of Godhead in His incarnation form famous for ridding the world of the evil Rakshasa named Ravana, once remarked that for the mature human being there is no other fear than death. He compared it to the ripened fruit, which has no other fate than to fall.

"Just as the ripened fruit has no other fear than falling, the man who has taken birth has no other fear than death." (Lord Rama, Valmiki Ramayana, Ayodhya Kand, 105.17)

The fruit's fateful descent, its inevitable fall from the tree, does not involve violence. By approaching the tree, one who picks up such fruits and eats them can survive. Indeed, a person could survive just remaining near such a tree. Therefore the fruit-bearing trees are considered pious in the Vedas. They are better than the non-fruit-bearing ones, which are thus considered sinful. The fruit-bearing tree is also found in the heavenly realm. There you can ask for anything from the trees and receive it immediately. Thus these trees are known as desire trees [kama-taru, sura-taru, kalpa-vriksha].

In this verse from the Janaki Mangala, we read that the residents of Ayodhya planted trees that bore fruits, blossoms and other auspicious signs. They did this as a welcome for the Supreme Lord, who was returning to their town after having been away for a while. In home to home they set up altars and flags as well. Home is where the heart is, and so when there is worship in the home, the heart is properly situated. It remains connected to God, even though it may be far away from a formal devotional atmosphere. It may be many miles away from others practicing devotion, but the heart can stay just as connected with God through the altar in the home.

In the same way that the pious trees are those which produce fruits, there can also be pious books. Those works which yield the fruit of devotion to God, bhakti, are the most pious. Every page, which likely originates from a tree, is filled with descriptions that bring the heart closer to the eternal occupation of devotional service. Conversely, the mundane literature keeps one away from God. Those works keep the mind unfortunately situated in maya, or illusion. And so one cannot survive on such works; they need to constantly shift their attention.

The pious works stand alone in greatness. They become the main source of sustenance for the devoted soul and they also pass the test of time, bringing future generations so much joy. The mango is the king of fruits, making the mango tree the most pious on earth. Devotion to Rama is the king of all fruits given in literature, and so those works which describe Him have a value that cannot be measured.

CHAND 23

मंगल बिटप मंजुल बिपुल दधि दूब अच्छत रोचना।
भरि थार आरति सजहिं सब सारंग सावक लोचना।।
मन मुदित कौसल्या सुमित्रा सकल भूपति-भामिनी।
सजि साजु परिछन चलीं रामहि मत्त कुंजर गामिनी।।23।।

maṅgala biṭapa mañjula bipula dadhi dūba acchata rocanā |
bhari thāra ārati sajahiṁ saba sāraṅga sāvaka locanā ||
mana mudita kausalyā sumitrā sakala bhūpati-bhāminī |
saji sāju parichana calīṁ rāmahi matta kuñjara gāminī ||23||

"Planting auspicious trees, decorating with rice flour, filling the thalis with yogurt and grass for the arati, the lovely ladies looked beautiful with their fawn-like eyes." (Chand 23.1)

"Kausalya, Sumitra and all of the beautiful women of the court were happy in the mind. Decorating themselves and preparing everything, they rushed towards Rama, walking like mad elephants." (Chand 23.2)

Essay - A Happy Reception

In the chand sections of his Janaki Mangala, Goswami Tulsidas sums up some of the preceding verses. Here we get a review of how Shri Rama's return home with His new wife Sita was celebrated in Ayodhya, the dhama that is home to both the Raghu dynasty and all of Rama's votaries. If the Lord's devotees don't live there physically, they at least remain there in spirit.

And what do they remember when contemplating that lovely place? So many important moments in Rama's life took place there. One of them was His return home from having gone on a lengthy journey with the sage Vishvamitra. Rama's younger brother Lakshmana also went along. The two left home unmarried, but returned home with beautiful brides, who happened to be sisters. Rama's father, the family priest, and Rama's two other younger brothers, who were now married too, also returned home.

When the four princes returned the residents of Ayodhya held something like a wedding reception. In the modern age, it is not surprising to find close family members spread apart geographically. One person lives in one country and another person lives across the ocean. Even when the family members live in close proximity, it is not a guarantee for frequent visits. If someone lives nearby, you think, "Oh, I can see them anytime." Saying this repeatedly, enough time passes that the visits become rare.

As everyone is spread out and busy with their daily lives, for the occasion of a marriage it is not likely that all the important people can attend. The event might not fit into their schedule. Perhaps they don't want to travel so far to witness a ceremony they have no real interest in. Perhaps there is an ongoing squabble with the person hosting the event.

Whatever the reason, a good way to satisfy the needs of many is to have multiple ceremonies. Have a ceremony in one place and a second one later on in a different place. This gives more people a chance to celebrate with you. All of the people of Ayodhya could not attend Rama's wedding in Janakpur. They didn't even know that He was there, for the Lord left their midst on a critical mission. He was asked to protect the peaceful sages residing in the forest from the attacks of wicked night-rangers. As police may be called to duty at any time and any place, so Rama and Lakshmana were expected to go anywhere they were needed.

As Rama is the Supreme Personality of Godhead in an incarnation form, He doesn't require much to be satisfied. The gesture is what counts most, not the quantity or the extravagance. If a person from today were to time travel to Ayodhya during Rama's time, they may mistakenly think that the people were poor. The people lived in simple dwellings, did not have electricity, and lived off the land. But based on the offerings made, we see that the people were anything but poor.

They planted pious trees all around. A pious tree is one that bears fruits. Conversely, a sinful tree is more or less for decoration. It does not provide nourishment. If you plant a pious tree, someone many years down the road can benefit from your work. If a banana falls from the tree and gives them food, you played a hand in feeding them.

Thalis were filled and made ready for an arati, or a ceremonial offering of a lamp. Everyone was decorated nicely, and this was the case in each home. Tulsidas tells us that the women in the homes arranged everything. They were housewives, working women and independent at the same time. No one told them to worship Rama. This kind of worship is spontaneous, and it is most appreciated. These women wanted nothing from Rama; rather they wanted only to give.

And these were the most beautiful women, having eyes like a fawn. We know that the people of Ayodhya had shri, or beauty. Rama brought back shri personified in Sita Devi, the daughter of King Janaka. Sita is Lakshmi, who has many other names, with Shri being one of them. Where there is God, there is the goddess of fortune. Where there is Lakshmi Devi, there is opulence. And so it was fitting that the reception in Ayodhya was lacking nothing.

Essay - Up To You

Is God mean? Is He perpetually angry? Does He insist that we submit to His will? Is He just waiting to punish us for our transgressions? When we finally come around, do we have to pay homage to Him every day? Are we supposed to cower in terror every time we're in His presence? This verse from the Janaki Mangala gives us an idea of what it's like when the individual consciousness is dovetailed with the supreme consciousness. There is spontaneous devotion, and the only fear is over missing wonderful moments due to the quick passage of time.

Here Goswami Tulsidas describes the women of the court in Ayodhya. There is Kausalya. She is the eldest queen to King Dasharatha. Her son is Rama, the Supreme Lord Vishnu in an incarnation form. That God incarnates as a human being should not surprise us. He expands to create this amazing universe. Though the living entity seemingly emerges from the womb of the mother, the wise person knows that the seed from the father is required first. And prior to that, some other force is necessary. The father cannot simply combine any aspect of his body with a mother's womb and get a child.

The entire creation thus sprung from someone else. The material chunk, if you will, is known as the mahat-tattva in Sanskrit. This total material substance is also Brahman, which we typically equate with the spiritual energy. The spiritual side of Brahman enters the mahat-tattva to give us the universe that we barely perceive with our eyes. Our planet is very small in comparison to all that is manifest. We can barely see what's going on across the street, let alone what is taking place across the globe.

"The total material substance, called Brahman, is the source of birth, and it is that Brahman that I impregnate, making possible the births of all living beings, O son of Bharata." (Lord Krishna, Bhagavad-gita, 14.3)

If you took all that is possible to be seen, you get the full combination of Brahman and matter. God expands to accomplish this: both the material and spiritual energies come from Him. The living entities are separated expansions of His and the divine incarnations are the personal expansions. Shri Rama is different from other living entities in that He does not have to enter into the mahat-tattva and go through the typical cycle of birth and death. He simply appears, and His form is always transcendental. There is no difference between body and spirit for Him.

Kausalya plays the role of Rama's mother. Then there is Queen Sumitra, who is also married to Dasharatha. From her womb appear the brothers Lakshmana and Shatrughna. The third queen is Kaikeyi, and she is the youngest. She gives birth to Bharata, making four beautiful sons for Dasharatha. Rama is Vishnu Himself and the other three are partial expansions of Vishnu. Rama is the eldest and their leader, and in this scene all four brothers are returning home as newly married men.

Tulsidas says that all the women in the court were happy in the mind. And why wouldn't they be? Their sons were returning home. Rama was especially missed, as He had been away for a while. The women all dressed up for the occasion. Rama was greeted by the ladies as would a king on his ascension to the throne.

It is said that when the women went towards welcoming Rama and His brothers, they all walked like mad elephants. This seems like a strange comparison to make, but in Vedic literature a statement like this appears quite often. "Gaja gamini" means the walk of an elephant, and when applied to a woman it is a way to describe the beautiful way in which they walk. In this situation the women were compared to mad elephants, indicating that their beautiful walk was of a brisker pace.

They were not compelled to attend this ceremony. They did not do so out of fear. They were not worried about incurring God's wrath. Instead, they worried that they would miss the chance to celebrate one of the great moments in His life on earth. They feared that time would get the best of them. For this reason they hurried, thinking of Rama the whole time.

In the devotional consciousness, the minutes sometimes do seem like hours, especially when there is separation. In separation one's fondness for God increases. During this time thoughts develop as to how one will please and serve Him when His association comes again. And so in this very lifetime the same thoughts can come to us if there is a desire to regain His association. This is the meaning to life, to love God and want to serve Him. There is no reason to fear Him, as in Ayodhya Rama could do nothing to stop the kind offerings of the queens, who were His mothers. In devotional service one can act as a friend, a parent, an admirer, or even a lover of God. There needn't be any fear, as simply from the sound of the holy names the proper view of the Supreme Lord comes to the mind: Hare Krishna Hare Krishna, Krishna Krishna, Hare Hare, Hare Rama Hare Rama, Rama Rama, Hare Hare.

VERSE 185

बधुन सहित सुत चारिउ मातु निहारहिं।
बारहिं बार आरती मुदित उतारहिं।।185।।

badhuna sahita suta cāri'u mātu nihārahiṁ |
bārahiṁ bāra āratī mudita utārahiṁ ||185||

"Staring again and again at their four sons and their wives, the mothers waved the arati lamps." (185)

Essay - Daughters-In-Law

We all know of the "mother-in-law" problem. They are our mother, but not really. We are not biologically related to them. In adulthood, or close to it, we get a brand new authority figure enter our lives. They have motherly affection for our spouse. They've shown this affection for a long time. They know that after the marriage of the son or daughter they should let go a little, but can any single event ever stop us from loving our offspring? This means that the mother-in-law is sure to give us trouble, for she wants to ensure that her child is still okay, even after moving in with their spouse. This presents somewhat of a problem for us, for we can't push back fully, for otherwise our spouse will get upset. This scene from the Janaki Mangala gives us a mother-in-law's perspective. She too has a lot to worry over, but here she is more than pleased with the new member of the family.

Indeed, in this situation there are multiple mothers and multiple daughters-in-law. Rama, Bharata, Lakshmana and Shatrughna were the four sons of King Dasharatha of Ayodhya. There were three mothers to these four brothers. Kausalya gave birth to Rama, Kaikeyi to Bharata, and Sumitra to Lakshmana and Shatrughna. But there was no rivalry amongst either the brothers or the mothers. No one thought that this mother is not my birth mother and this mother is. No one thought that this child is really my son and this child isn't.

That's a nice situation to be in, having three loving mothers. It means the family extends, and with a large family you have a large support system. In the Vedic tradition, the marriages are arranged, which means that when the wives come home after marriage, it is their first time in that area. Here the mothers are meeting the wives of the four brothers for the first time. The brothers got married away from home, in Janakpur. The mothers were in Ayodhya, and from the verse above we get their initial reaction.

They kept looking at the daughters-in-law. The new wives were very beautiful, and perfect in behavior. Imagine moving in with your husband and seeing that he has three mothers around to protect him. This would be a daunting situation for anyone, but Sita and her relatives acted as if they were coming home again. It was Sita's marriage to Rama that set everything in motion. From there, Sita's father arranged to have Rama's three brothers get married at the same time.

Just as each mother in Ayodhya considered Rama to be their son, they considered Sita to be their daughter. "In-law" had no significance here. Sita's nature is such that anyone with a sober mind will have affection for her. She has no bad qualities. She is virtuous in every way. It would make sense that she is a perfect match for Rama, of whom even enemies have difficulty speaking ill.

"I have not seen any person in this world, be they an enemy or one punished for heinous sins, speak ill of Rama, even in His absence." (Lakshmana speaking to Kausalya, Valmiki Ramayana, Ayodhya Kand, 21.5)

If you love God, you get the perfect son, if you so desire. This was the case for the wives of Dasharatha. Rama is the Supreme Lord in a special incarnation appearing in the Treta Yuga, or second time period of creation. His three younger brothers are partial incarnations of God, so all the elders in Ayodhya were uniquely blessed.

If you love God, you get the perfect daughter-in-law, if you so desire. Your "cup runneth over" with love. Though you previously thought you couldn't love anyone any more than you did God, you make more room for His wife. In bhakti-yoga, or devotional service, you make even more room for those dear to Rama, like Hanuman. Then you make further room for those who are dear to Hanuman, like Goswami Tulsidas.

Then you increase your love for those who support the devotees of Hanuman, who facilitate the spreading of the glories of Shri Rama and those who work for His interest. In this way the love always increases in devotional service; the opposite of how it is in material affairs. If I love my wife, I may not love another's wife. If I love my husband, I have less affection to give someone else. And love in devotional service never breaks; the mothers in Ayodhya kept their love for their daughters-in-law. In the not too distant future, they would have to live without Sita, but they maintained a strong affection for the blameless wife of the prince of Ayodhya. Anyone who does so gets supremely benefitted.

VERSE 186

करहिं निछावरि छिनु छिनु मंगल मुद भरीं।
दूलह दुलहिनिन्ह देखि प्रेम पयनिधि परीं॥186॥

karahiṁ nichāvari chinu chinu maṅgala muda bharīṁ |
dūlaha dulahininha dekhi prema payanidhi parīṁ ||186||

"Again and again they happily threw money as gifts to celebrate the auspiciousness. Looking at the brides and grooms, they drowned in an ocean of love." (186)

Essay - I Can't Help Myself

From this verse, we see another difference between bhakti-yoga and any other system for self-improvement. Whether that system be readily acknowledged as secular or religious in nature, the resultant consciousness is what matters when giving an assessment. Is there love for God? Is there a reward sought? Is that reward of the personal variety? Here there is so much love that the people feel helpless. There is nothing that can be done to escape from the ocean of bhakti, which brings eternally refreshing waters and an auspiciousness never before seen.

"If bhakti-yoga brings so much love, and if it is so spontaneous at the highest levels, why the need to talk about it? Why not let others develop that attachment on their own? Why analyze things?"

Everyone is looking for self-improvement. Even those not following a diet or reading a book by an acknowledged expert in a field look for happiness. If everyone had the answers to everything, there would be no lamentation. There would be no sadness at the passing of another. Everyone would go to sleep on time, wake up on time, and eat on time. There would never be any problems at home or the office. Every piece of technology would work as advertised. There would never be a need to upgrade anything since everyone would be satisfied with what they had.

But we know that these conditions do not exist. To put my body back into shape, I follow a diet routine coupled with exercise. To improve my financial situation, I get further educated. Perhaps I switch jobs as well. To improve my home life, I look for a spouse. In old age, I look for ways to pass the time in peace. In this way I am always searching.

"O best among the Bharatas [Arjuna], four kinds of pious men render devotional service unto Me - the distressed, the desirer of wealth, the inquisitive, and he who is searching for knowledge of the Absolute." (Lord Krishna, Bhagavad-gita, 7.16)

Religious life isn't necessarily different. In the Bhagavad-gita, Lord Krishna says that four kinds of people initially approach Him. Some are looking for wealth and some for the alleviation of distress. Some are inquisitive and others are looking for further knowledge after knowing Him a little bit. These are the four kinds that approach Krishna, the Supreme Personality of Godhead. Then there are other religious paths such as jnana, karma, and yoga. These are knowledge, work and meditation respectively. In each case there is a personal desire. Even if there is a basic understanding of the Supreme Lord, that information doesn't get top priority. The focus is on the individual's happiness first. How will I improve myself? How will I feel better? How will I become enlightened?

Bhakti-yoga holds a unique spot because in the matured condition there is no personal desire. Those in this stage of bhakti don't even know that they are practicing anything. They know only love for God. They think of His welfare first. They worry not over their personal fortunes. Whether they are rich or poor, of solid health or ill, with family or all alone - these are not important to them. "Is God happy? Am I spending time with Him? Is He pleased with my work? Is He enjoying the fruits to my efforts? He is my well-wisher, so does He have good reason to wish me well?"

"The sages, knowing Me as the ultimate purpose of all sacrifices and austerities, the Supreme Lord of all planets and demigods and the benefactor and well-wisher of all living entities, attain peace from the pangs of material miseries." (Lord Krishna, Bg. 5.29)

In Ayodhya a long time ago, queens in the kingdom happily celebrated the auspicious occasion of the four royal princes' return home as married men. As part of the welcoming ceremony, the mothers to these princes repeatedly threw money and offered gifts. They did this very happily. This was the first time they were seeing the wives of their sons, so they kept looking at both.

While looking again and again, the mothers drowned in an ocean of love. The love here is transcendental since the objects of affection are the Supreme Lord and His direct expansions. The wives are goddesses of fortune. So by looking at them, the mothers were essentially worshiping them. They did not worship as a mere ritual. They had not done something bad the previous day and then now worshiped in order to be absolved of sin. They were not afraid of punishment in the afterlife.

The love of the mothers was so strong that they were bound by it. This is bhakti-yoga. The rasa of bhakti is like an ocean made up of nectar that gives immortality. For this reason when describing bhakti-yoga Shrila Rupa Gosvami names his book Bhakti-rasamrita-sindhu. This ocean is very inviting. All are welcome to jump in and take advantage. There is only one requirement: love. Have love for God. Love Him so much that you don't care what others think. Love Him so much that no one can take that love away from you. Love Him so much that no matter where you end up, either in this life or the next, you will never abandon Him. The queens in Ayodhya felt this way, and so their behavior teaches us so much.

VERSE 187

देत पावड़े अरघ चलीं लै सादर।
उमगि चलेउ आनंद भुवन भुइँ बादर।।187।।

deta pāvaṛe aragha calīṁ lai sādara |
umagi cale'u ānanda bhuvana bhu'iṁ bādara ||187||

"Laying out the carpet and offering water, they respectfully took them across. Walking with excitement, there was full joy and bliss from the earth to the sky."
(187)

Essay - From The Earth To The Sky

The French author Jules Verne wrote a book whose title in English translates to "From The Earth to the Moon." It was written long before the space programs launched rockets into outer space. Who wouldn't be enamored with the other world? Who wouldn't want to see what's out there beyond the horizon? While this verse from the Janaki Mangala doesn't specifically give us hints on how to accomplish space travel, it does provide a mechanism for spreading joy and bliss into the sky. That joy starts on the earth, and it comes from a special interaction.

The event referenced here is a kind of wedding reception. The wedding already happened somewhere else. It took place in Tirahuta, and the wedded couples are now in Ayodhya. The reception in Ayodhya is just as important, for it is where the couples will live. As part of that welcome, a carpet gets laid out. As the couples walk across, the ladies of the court respectfully sprinkle water. As the sons and their new wives walk across, everyone feels tremendous joy and bliss, which then extend into the sky.

This latter part is not possible with an ordinary wedding. In times past there was no way to extend a celebration beyond the local area, as today's forms of communication were not yet invented. Today we could post pictures from the event online and have others see them from across the globe. Thus they could share in the joy. We could record the event and then show it again later on, to a different audience. We could also tell others about it after the fact, essentially recreating the moment with our words.

But in none of these mechanisms does the joy automatically spread into the sky at the precise moment things are occurring. The marriage here was for Sita and Rama. Rama is the prince of Ayodhya, and He has three younger brothers. Their marriages took place at the same time. So four couples are walking across the welcome carpet. The eyes of the queens are fixed on four handsome grooms and four beautiful brides.

Rama is God. He is the full embodiment of bliss, knowledge and eternality. He appears differently depending on the situation. Others may not know Him fully, but He is always above the darkness of the material existence. The words used to praise

Him are uttama, or above darkness. Since He is the purusha, or person, above the mode of ignorance, one of His many names is Purushottama. The land where He resides in His form of Jagannatha, which means "Lord of the universe," is known as Purushottama-kshetra.

This event is a celebration of Rama's marriage to Sita, and so everyone from above is watching. And if we analyze further, we see that the joy and bliss spring from devotion. People are practicing devotion to Sita and Rama and feeling wonderful in the process. Their joy automatically shoots into the sky and soars to the heavenly region and beyond.

This is instructive for those looking for a meaning to life. In ordinary work, not everyone else will notice. We can try to go to the moon, but we cannot stay there. Even if we achieve residence in a heavenly realm through our pious deeds, we can't remain in the higher planets forever. Devotional service does not suffer from the same defect. Not only do we derive joy from devotion during this lifetime, but our happiness extends all the way to the upper regions. The Supreme Lord and His associates take notice. And at the time of death, we get to soar through the sky and beyond the material covering, happily reaching the supreme abode, the param dhama, the place where the Supreme Lord resides with His eternal associates.

VERSE 188

नारि उहारु उघारि दुलहिनिन्ह देखहिं।
नैन लाहु लहि जनम सफल करि लेखहिं।।188।।

nāri uhāru ughāri dulahininha dekhahiṁ |
naina lāhu lahi janama saphala kari lekhahiṁ ||188||

"When the women opened up the veils to see the brides, they realized the meaning to their eyes, making their births successful." (188)

Essay - Janma Saphala

How do we make this life successful? We are destined to die, and previously we lived elsewhere. This is the basic definition of reincarnation, and even within this lifetime we see that there is past and present, with a singular animating force within the local body that transcends the different periods of time. We have this one life right now, so what is our true purpose? How do we make this journey successful? Goswami Tulsidas says that it's as easy as removing a veil. This was literally true for several queens many thousands of years ago, and it is figuratively true for all others. When the veil of ignorance gets removed and one sees with the eyes of shastra, they get the sweetest vision on which to contemplate. A single glance in the proper mood fulfills the human birth, making it saphala, or fruitful.

Who are we? What are we made of? Each aspect of the body contains so many atoms. We could say that we're a collection of chemicals. Those chemicals get grouped into five distinct elements: earth, water, fire, air and ether. These elements constitute all the bodies we see around us. Some living creatures have more fire than water, and some have more air than fire. Therefore not all creatures are the same; there are different species.

"Earth, water, fire, air, ether, mind, intelligence and false ego - altogether these eight comprise My separated material energies." (Lord Krishna, Bhagavad-gita, 7.4)

The gross elements are those we can see, and beyond the vision are the three subtle elements: mind, intelligence and ego. Intelligence is finer than the mind, and the ego is finer than the intelligence. Finer than the finest is the spirit soul. This soul is who we are. We are not anything else. The ego can change. When we identify with the gross elements that temporarily surround the soul, our ego is false. When we identify as spirit soul, part and parcel of the Supreme Spirit, our ego is no longer false.

Even when our ego is real once again, we still have these elements around us. With this covering of the body we get the senses. We can see, smell, taste, touch and hear. So what are we supposed to do with these abilities? Should we eat anything and everything? Should we eat as much as we want? Should we smell nice perfumes only? Should we see beautiful people of the opposite sex? Should we hear our praises and shun those who criticize us?

There are generally two choices. One is to enjoy as much as possible. This is bhoga. The opposite is tyaga, or renunciation. When I've enjoyed too much or when I don't like what I've tried to enjoy, I decide to shut off the senses.

"I just won't eat anything. I'm sick of getting fat. I'll close my eyes so I don't have to see the tragedies around us. I'll never touch anyone ever again, for they only cause me trouble."

The superior choice is dovetailing the senses and the sense-acquiring objects with service to God. When this is done, we get the true meaning to the senses. In the above referenced verse, Goswami Tulsidas makes one of his favorite comparisons. He says that in devotional service, one realizes the meaning to having eyes. Not surprisingly, the incident that elicits this comparison relates to seeing the Supreme Lord's closest associates in a loving mood.

Here there are three queens in Ayodhya looking at the four new brides who have come to their new home. These brides are from Janakpur, and they recently got married to the four sons of the king of Ayodhya. The queens, the mothers to the four sons, felt so happy when they gazed upon their new daughters-in-law. They removed the veils on the wives, for typically the married women wore veils. As part of the welcoming ceremony, the mothers were allowed to look behind the veils. They got to see the faces of the beautiful brides. In so doing, they received meaning to their eyes.

Their lives became successful because of their emotions from such an interaction. They had pure love for these women, who are goddesses of fortune. Sita Devi, the wife of the eldest prince Rama, is the goddess of fortune herself. Rama's three younger brothers are partial expansions of the Supreme Lord, so their wives are also goddesses of fortune.

We are born into the darkness of ignorance. As proof of this fact, we automatically identify with the temporary body, which is nothing more than a collection of the five gross and three subtle elements of material nature. The veil gets removed through the instructions of those who follow in the mood of the queens of Ayodhya. One who loves God can teach others how to love Him. They give the knowledge necessary to derive the true meaning to the Vedic literature, the most comprehensive of all works describing the science of self-realization.

When internally purified, the living entity can see with the eyes of shastra. They can see the influence of the Divine everywhere. With their eyes now opened, they are free to love God all the time. Thus they make their life successful. They understand that all of their senses are meant to be used in service to God, and through such a path all the senses take on their true meaning. The living entity itself, who is a spirit soul at the core, realizes their actual position: servant of God, meant to always be in love.

VERSE 189

भवन आनि सनमानि सकल मंगल किए।
बसन कनक मनि धेनु दान बिप्रन्ह दिए॥189॥

bhavana āni sanamāni sakala maṅgala ki'e |
basana kanaka mani dhenu dāna bipranha di'e ||189||

"Upon arriving at the residence, they performed all the auspicious rituals with all due honor. They gave away clothes, gold, jewels and cows to the brahmanas." (189)

Essay - With All Due Honor

Humility is required for donating generously. One must realize that what they earn is not totally of their own making. They are not solely responsible for their good fortune. This knowledge makes it easier to part with possessions for the sake of another. Humility is also required to accept charity. Who wants to be dependent on others? Who wants to be labeled a parasite, someone feeding off others? In this verse from the Janaki Mangala, we get an example of each: giving in charity and accepting it. There is humility on both sides, and the offerings are done in the proper way.

Who is actually rich? Who has real wealth? Consider one person who has plenty of food to eat. They don't own a giant estate. They may not even have air conditioning to keep them cool in the hot summer months. They get exercise by walking on the local fields. They are generally at peace. They don't worry so much.

Now consider another person. They are very wealthy. Their high-rise apartment would fetch top dollar on the open market. They hob nob with the elite in society. When they fly anywhere, it's in first class. And yet their health is not so good. To maintain the lavish lifestyle, they have to work long hours. In the fever of earning money, they forget to eat. They have plenty of food available, but they don't eat on time. Since they are constantly stressed, they've developed a bad habit of relying on drugs to get them through the day. They need a pill to deal with anxiety, a pill to keep them awake during the day, and a pill to help them sleep at night.

From these two scenarios, we see that money alone doesn't make a person rich with assets. Generally, if a person can eat, sleep, mate and defend without issue, they are not poor. Especially in the category of eating, if everything is done sufficiently, poverty is absent. From this rule we see that the gifts mentioned in the verse quoted above allowed the recipients to live just fine. The recipients didn't otherwise work for a living. They relied on charity to maintain their livelihood.

The charity they received was clothes, gold, cows and jewels. The cows would have been enough. If you have a small plot of land and maintain a few cows, you don't have to worry about eating. You have a solution to the food problem. And actually, for one who owns such land, receiving more cows increases their wealth. They don't need a huge retirement fund. They don't need a lavish apartment that is difficult to maintain. More cows equals more food, which equals less poverty.

Fortunately, the recipients were not too proud to accept this charity. They weren't beggars in the ordinary sense. They were not lazy. They were more than capable of earning a living in the traditional way, but they sacrificed that for focusing on spiritual life. And not only for themselves, their efforts would help the rest of society as well. In a sense, they were owed the charity they received, even though they would never think like that.

The donations came as a way to celebrate an auspicious occasion. Four princesses were entering their new home, newly married to the four sons of King Dasharatha of Ayodhya. The queens of the court happily escorted them into the residence, paying them all honor with performing auspicious rites. Part of the ceremony was distributing gifts to the vipras, the priests who were very wise. In the name of the four daughters-in-law, charity was given to worthy recipients.

If the vipras were too proud to accept charity, how would the royal family have celebrated properly? They were not attached to their possessions. They didn't want to throw them away, though. What sense would that make? They didn't want to give them to people who were not deserving of them.

And if the royal family were too proud to give away gifts, how would the vipras survive? Who would teach the society about the difference between matter and spirit? Who would sing the glories of the Supreme Lord and His eternal consort? Who would inform others of the divine natures of Shri Rama and Sita Devi, the beloved couple who resided in Ayodhya, God and His energy appearing in apparently human form? Who would provide wise counsel to the royal order? Who would act as the brains of society?

From this verse we see the importance of maintaining the genuine priestly order. We see that in Vedic culture, auspicious occasions are celebrated not with enjoyment of wine and women, but rather with giving generously in charity to the valuable intelligentsia of society. Shri Rama is God Himself, and so it makes sense that those celebrating Him on earth would behave properly. It makes sense that they would help to maintain those who are so dear to Rama, the legitimate brahmanas of the community. And in accepting those gifts, the vipras maintained their devotion to Rama, whose limitless glories fill the pages of Vedic literature.

VERSE 190

जाचक कीन्ह निहाल असीसहिं जहँ तहँ।
पूजे देव पितर सब राम उदय कहँ॥190॥

jācaka kīnha nihāla asīsahiṁ jahaṁ tahaṁ |
pūje deva pitara saba rāma udaya kahaṁ ||190||

"They gave the beggars whatever they asked for and more, who gave their blessings here and there. Then they did puja to the devas and the forefathers for Rama's good fortune." (190)

Essay - Nothing Left

Sharanagati is full surrender to the Divine. Full surrender means full dependence. When there is full dependence, there cannot be anything left to hold on to. Other objects may be there, and to outsiders it may appear that there are remaining attachments, but in the mind of the surrendered soul there is only their beloved Supreme Personality of Godhead. He is their only hope for salvation. He is their only reason for living, for in service to Him they derive the most happiness. They know this both in theory and in practice.

Imagine this scene. You're taking a big exam today. This is important; it will determine where you end up next year. If you perform well, you'll have your pick of school. You won't be at the mercy of admission committees. They will all want you, for from your grades and exam performance it will be impossible to deny you. So you've studied a lot for this exam. But you're still very worried. You see that your friends are worried too. Classmates are assembled on this Saturday morning, all as nervous as you. Normally this day of the week is reserved for rest, for unwinding by watching hours of television. But not today. Everyone has their "game face" on.

As you head towards the examination room, you notice that there is a line, and it is not moving quickly. After a while you figure out the cause of the delay: there is a security check prior to entry. Each person has to remove their mobile telephones. This shouldn't be causing a problem, you think. There were explicit instructions given beforehand that smartphones and such devices were not allowed in the examination room. Yet everyone seems to have them on their person. The phones aren't the only thing. Some have papers stashed in their jacket pockets. Others have little notes scribbled on various parts of their body. Some are wearing headphones. Some actually brought their books with them.

"Everyone, may I have your attention please," announces the security person at the front of the line. "The items listed on this sign right here are not allowed in the examination room. If you'll please put them away right now, this line will move much more quickly. The time for studying is over. You have to rely on your brains now. There is no other way." Thus the students surrender to the moment. They no longer have support from the outside. They are forced to rely on only themselves to pass the examination.

The experience is similar for the devoted souls in sharanagati. They intentionally weaken themselves, leaving no objects of distraction. In full dependence, the bliss they experience from devotional service is much higher. They feel true love in this dependence, as they are completely vulnerable. Without vulnerability there cannot be a full interaction of love.

The symptoms of this vulnerability are shown in the verse quoted above. Here the family in Ayodhya is not holding anything back. They already gave away so many gifts to the worthy members of society, the priests. Now they are giving the beggars of the town whatever they want. In return the beggars are giving their blessings. The royal family had plenty to give away, and more importantly they were not worried since they had love for Rama, the Supreme Lord in His incarnation form which roamed the earth during the Treta Yuga, the second time period of creation.

As if giving away gifts was not enough, the family members sacrificed even more. They held a puja, or worship ceremony, for the devas, or demigods. You have a demigod in charge of practically every aspect of material life. They wanted all the devas to bless Rama. They also did a puja for the forefathers, those appearing previously in their family.

It should be noted that none of these acts were necessary. Rama does not need anyone's blessings. He does not require help from any demigod, human being, animal, or plant. He is fully self-sufficient; He is the only person who can claim so. Yet the offerings indicate full surrender on the part of the family members in Ayodhya. They were celebrating the marriage of Rama to Sita, and also the marriages of Rama's younger brothers to Sita's relatives from Janakpur.

In full surrender, they had no concern for Rama's strengths. They did not remember how He had already defeated wicked night-rangers in the forest. They were not remembering how Tataka and Subahu were driven away from Vishvamitra's ashrama. Instead they were worried about Rama. They wanted life to be perfect for Him. They wanted Him to have every comfort. They were not concerned with their own welfare. If giving away gifts and holding pujas would help Rama, His brothers and their wives, then they would repeat such acts day after day.

This concern for Rama equates to the achievement of life's mission. Such concern is real love, and since it is tied to the Supreme Lord, it lasts forever. It transcends the bounds of birth and death. All that has happened in the past is of no concern to the person who has the brightest future ahead of them, one where they worship God in full surrender, leaving all attachments behind.

VERSE 191

नेगचार करि दीनह सबहि पहिरावनि।
समधी सकल सुआसिनि गुरतिय पावनि।।191।।

negacāra kari dīnaha sabahi pahirāvani |
samadhī sakala su'āsini guratiya pāvani ||191||

"They gave gifts of clothes to all who were entitled. All the guests, the female attendants, and the wives of the gurus received gifts." (191)

Essay - Gift Dilemma

Here the gift-giving at a famous marriage reception continues. There is no consumption of alcoholic beverages. There is no first dance for the married couple. The guests get the top priority, and they are not going to leave empty-handed. The Supreme Lord is making sure of that. The wives in His royal family are making sure everyone who deserves to get a gift gets one. No one is shut out, and so in the spiritual world the reciprocation of love continues, without end to the exchanges.

Imagine this scenario. Someone's invited you to their wedding. You don't mind going. They're a good friend. Amidst all the other planning you have to do, there is the gift. You ask yourself a series of questions:

"How much should I give? Well, how much did they give me for my wedding? I am travelling quite a ways for theirs. I've heard that if you have to spend for travel, you can give a smaller gift. What about the people who can't attend? I've heard that if you're invited, you're compelled to get a gift. If you can't make it then you have to give something at least. Then I've heard the stories of people basing their gift on their assessment of the wedding hall. If it's a nice place, you're supposed to give more. You're supposed to figure out how much the couple paid per person, and then match that in your cash donation. I've heard of people going to the wedding reception with a blank check in their pocket. Upon surveying the situation, they then fill in an appropriate amount. I must say, this is all too much for me to handle."

In Ayodhya a long time ago, the wedding reception was for the king's four sons. The royal family had wealth, so they didn't require anything. Still, everyone in the town celebrated to the best of their ability. There were no misers, including the hosts. And so everyone went away with gifts. In the traditional way, the women were the managers of finance in the homes. When a gift needed to be given, they would pick something and give it away.

Here the three wives of King Dasharatha are continuing to give away gifts. They gave clothes to all who were entitled. Anyone who came up to them received something nice. Who doesn't appreciate a nice shirt? What woman wouldn't want a beautiful sari to wear to the next important function? These were simpler times, so clothes as a gift were well appreciated.

In the royal court, there were female attendants and wives to the gurus. They received gifts as well. One may wonder how the royal family could afford to make such donations. Rama is the Supreme Lord in an incarnation form. He is the husband of the goddess of fortune, Lakshmi Devi. On earth He wed Lakshmi in her most beautiful form of Sita. This wedding took place in Janakpur, the land of Sita's father Janaka.

Here Ayodhya welcomes Sita and Rama. Rama's three younger brothers were married simultaneously, so the festivities are for four marriages. Where there is the goddess of fortune, there is an endless supply of wealth, jewels, clothes, gold and cows. There is no shortage if Lakshmi Devi is in a favorable mood. When she is with her husband, she profusely distributes charity to those dear to Him. The special qualification of the residents of Ayodhya is that they were all dear to Rama. He loved every one of them, and so it is not surprising that everyone received gifts to their heart's content.

Bhakti-yoga is unique in that the service continues regardless of what gifts are or aren't received. Whether one gets a lot or very little from the Supreme Lord, they continue in their devotion. The greatest gift in life is to have a best friend to whom kind words can be offered day after day. That best friend can only be God, since He lives forever in His transcendental form. His land of Ayodhya also remains forever manifest, including the good work of His closest associates.

The gift dilemma for the devotee is how to offer more and more service, and God's dilemma is how to repay that life dedicated to service to Him. This is a good problem for each to have, and they take turns in topping one another. One second the devotee does something amazing and the next Rama replies with an amazing act of His own. The sparring continues, with everyone winning. This happens only in spiritual life, entry to which is very easy in this age. One can open the door to transcendental bliss through just the chanting of the holy names: Hare Krishna Hare Krishna, Krishna Krishna, Hare Hare, Hare Rama Hare Rama, Rama Rama, Hare Hare.

VERSE 192

जोरीं चारि निहारि असीसत निकसहिं।
मनहुँ कुमुद बिधु-उदय मुदित मन बिकसहिं।।192।।

jorīṁ cāri nihāri asīsata nikasahiṁ |
manahuṁ kumuda bidhu-udaya mudita mana bikasahiṁ ||192||

"Looking at the four pairs, they gave their blessings as they departed. Like the white lily blooming at the rising of the moon, happiness grew in their hearts." (192)

Essay - Happiness Is Rising

Who is God? Where does He live? What does He want from us? Is it better to ask things of Him or offer something to Him? If it's the latter, what could He possibly want from us? Where do we make these offerings? The above referenced verse from the Janaki Mangala gives an example of offerings made to Him and the resultant effect. The reciprocation is tremendous, delivering a reward far superior to anything that could be asked for directly.

What are things that we could ask for? Well, perhaps we're not feeling so well. Last night I ate something that isn't sitting well with me. Now my stomach hurts. I'm in so much pain that I can't do anything. I can't even sleep. It feels like I need to throw up, but I can't. Therefore I don't have any relief. As a last resort I pray to God.

"O Lord, please help me out. I know I'm suffering the reaction to some past mistake. I did something wrong for sure. I have too many sins to count. I swear to be good from now on. Just make this pain go away. I can't live like this."

And what happens when the pain does go away? Naturally, we soon forget about the whole ordeal. We don't remember the promises we made under duress. We carry on as usual. "As usual" means continuing in a life of material sense gratification, where the only time we remember the good Lord is when we again want something. Thus happiness does not increase. It comes for a brief moment, and then goes away. It is like the sun that peaks out from the clouds only to get hidden again.

Imagine another situation. You come home from work one day and happily greet your children. You are so happy to see them that you give them candy bars. You picked these up on your way home since they asked you for them. Your wife had advised against it, but you couldn't help yourself. Your children are so happy to receive these gifts. The problem is the next time they aren't as happy. They want more. The candy bars are not enough. Pretty soon you regret ever having given them the gift in the first place.

The senses of the living entity act in this way. Satisfying them only makes them want more in the future. And to reach the same satisfaction requires more the second time around. By following the desires that constantly flow in, like a rushing river, happiness remains elusive.

"A person who is not disturbed by the incessant flow of desires - that enter like rivers into the ocean which is ever being filled but is always still - can alone achieve peace, and not the man who strives to satisfy such desires." (Lord Krishna, Bhagavad-gita, 2.70)

As they say during the Christmas season, it is better to give than it is to receive. When applying this principle to the relationship to God, the previous situation turns around completely. Whereas asking for things doesn't lead to permanent happiness, and makes one even more upset with the Supreme Lord in the chance that the desired object doesn't come to fruition, giving to God brings happiness that only increases.

In the above referenced verse from the Janaki Mangala, happiness is on the rise. It comes from offering blessings to four newlywed couples. The women in the royal court generously gave these blessings. The recipients didn't require them, but they accepted them anyway. The head of the newlywed couples was Shri Rama, the Supreme Lord in a famous incarnation form. Rama can grant anything to anyone. As soon as someone wants something, He can ask His eternal consort, Lakshmi Devi, to give it to them. God never runs out. The pie that is the spiritual world is infinite. Taking away one part does not diminish the whole. To us this is inconceivable, or achintya.

The women here felt happy because offering blessings to God is totally natural. The reaction is automatic as well; hence the comparison to the kumuda flower. That flower is the white water-lily; it opens up at the rise of the moon. It opens more and more as the moon heads towards its peak in the sky. In the same way, the more one offers blessings to God, the more happiness they feel in the heart.

The comparison is not entirely accurate, though, as the happiness in devotional service never reaches an end. The space in the heart only increases to make more room for happiness. It is no wonder, then, that the devoted souls continue to offer blessings to God, hoping for only the best for Him. In the heightened state of devotion, they care not for their own welfare, which is automatically maintained by Rama, His wife Sita, and Rama's three younger brothers and their consorts, who happily returned to Ayodhya and were blessed by all the people who loved them so very much.

CHAND 24

बिकसहिं कुमुद जिमि देखि बिधु भइ अवध सुख सोभामई।
एहि जुगुति राम बिबाह गावहिं सकल कबि कीरति नई।।
उपबीत ब्याह उछाह जे सिय राम मंगल गावहीं।
तुलसी सकल कल्यान ते नर नारि अनुदिन पावहीं।।24।।

bikasahiṁ kumuda jimi dekhi bidhu bha'i avadha sukha sobhāma'ī |
ehi juguti rāma bibāha gāvahiṁ sakala kabi kīrati na'ī ||
upabīta byāha uchāha je siya rāma maṅgala gāvahīṁ |
tulasī sakala kalyāna te nara nāri anudina pāvahīṁ ||24||

"As the kumuda flower blooms at the sight of the moonrise, like that Ayodhya alighted in happiness. All the poets sing of the glories of Rama's wedding." (Chand 24.1)

"Those who sing of the auspicious occasion of the initiation and the wedding of Sita and Rama with excitement get countless auspicious blessings day after day, says Tulsi." (Chand 24.2)

Essay - Unifying All Poets

This one poet wants to write about love. They've been scorned too many times in the past. They've had many unpleasant experiences in the romance department. This other poet wants to write about nature. They particularly enjoy the spring season. The flowers in bloom, the honeybees buzzing about, the gradual departure of the cold winter chill - these things are ripe to be described in verse. With as many topics as there are for discussion, in those directions the various poets will turn. One topic, however, can unify all. In the above referenced verse from the Janaki Mangala, the kavis, the poets of sharp intellect, unify in praise of the wedding of Sita and Rama.

Poetry may not appear to be so valuable today, but its influence is still present, though one has to look a little harder to see it. As the noted playwright and poet Shakespeare quipped, brevity is the soul of wit. The less amount of words you can use to convey your message, the more powerful the message will be. Consider the song versus the book. If I can put my thoughts into a melodious song, it will be easy for others to repeat it. With a few lines, so many others will parrot my sentiments, even without knowing fully what the words mean.

Meanwhile, the same sentiments described at length in a paper or book are not as easily consumed by the public. For starters there is the time factor. Listening to a song requires much less time than reading a book. You can listen to the same song many times in the same amount of time it takes to read the book just once.

So the power of poetry is still alive and well in the form of the song. In times past, poetry was also put into song, and the words became more meaningful due to the limited communications channels. In ancient times, there was no television or radio. There weren't newspapers, either. If you wanted to describe something important, you needed to put your words into poetry and then hopefully be able to sing the resultant verses.

The kavis thus became very important. In the Vedic tradition, the kavi can be likened to a bard. It is said that the famous Homer had memorized his lengthy works like the Illiad and the Odyssey. He would recite them from memory when called upon. Similarly, Vyasadeva and Valmiki Muni could also recite their lengthy works without using reference tools. Hardly anything in history compares to the Mahabharata in length and substance, and Vyasadeva had the entire thing memorized.

The verse quoted above comes from a very short work known as the Janaki Mangala. It is authored by a kavi whose name is Tulsidas, which means "servant of the tulasi plant." The tulasi plant is a goddess, and she is very dear to the Supreme Lord Vishnu. Vishnu is the personal form of God, a clearer picture to give definition to the abstract concept of a supreme controller. Janaki refers to the daughter of King Janaka. Her name is also Sita, and she is the eternal consort of Vishnu's incarnation of Rama, the prince of Ayodhya.

Thus the kavi who is a servant of Tulasi Devi, who is dear to Vishnu, authored a poem turned into song for glorifying the Supreme Lord in His incarnation of Rama, particularly focusing on the marriage of Rama to Sita. From this verse we can gather that Tulsidas did not do anything new by authoring his poem. At the time of Rama's wedding, so many kavis sung of the glorious event. They all united on the one subject matter. And they described the event very happily, for everyone in the town was happy.

The happiness of the people was like the blooming of the white water-lily at the ascent of the moon in the night sky. This means that the people of Ayodhya were spontaneously happy; no one had to tell them to react in a certain way. They were not afraid of the royal family. They would not get punished if they did not react appropriately. Rather, no one could stop them from being happy. Even if Rama were to tell them to stop celebrating, they wouldn't. He was their bright moon, Ramachandra, and they were the water-lilies connected to Him. This relationship represents real yoga, the connection of the individual soul to the Supreme Lord.

Just as the spontaneous happiness of the people was a sign of perfect yoga, so too the singing of the kavis in celebration of Rama's wedding gave an indication that they were not separated from God in interests. Poetry covering any other subject is limiting. It is not yoga since the connection to the Divine is not direct. There is a connection to God's separated energy, known as the material nature. Sita Devi is the pleasure potency energy, and in the marriage to Rama the pleasure energy and the energetic unite. The energy that are the poets always sing of that wonderful occasion, showing that only in yoga is there eternal happiness full of activity.

Essay - Show It Again

The glories of the marriage of Sita and Rama know no end. Hearing about it is not enough. Each word used to describe that sacred event opens up so many avenues for study and discussion. Rama is the Supreme Lord in an incarnation form and Sita His eternal consort, so this infinite expansion makes sense. The material world is like the branches coming from the inverted tree whose root is the spiritual sky, the imperishable abode of God in His personal form.

"That supreme abode is called unmanifested and infallible, and it is the supreme destination. When one goes there, he never comes back. That is My supreme abode." (Lord Krishna, Bhagavad-gita, 8.21)

The spiritual realm is described as unmanifest in the Bhagavad-gita, the definitive word on Vedanta, the end of all knowledge. Unmanifest to us means unseen. It's like the air. We know that it's there, but we can't see it. We have to perceive the effect it has on manifest objects in order to detect its presence. Since we cannot see the spiritual sky, we think that the "unmanifest" description means that there is a lack of variety there.

But that is actually not the case. The inverted tree that expands to create the material world is compared to a reflection of a tree seen in water. The reflection is not the real object. If you go to reach for the branches within the water, all you'll get is water; you won't get the branches. Similarly, the material world is temporary and always changing; so what you see is not completely real. The real thing is in the original object, which is the spiritual world.

Proof that there is tangible form in the spiritual world comes from events like those described in the verse above from the Janaki Mangala. Here we have glorification of a sacred thread investiture and a wedding. These are not ordinary events. The author, Goswami Tulsidas, says that one who sings of these events with great attention and excitement gets auspiciousness coming to them day after day.

The same events in the material world don't have the same properties. Take this situation for example. You and your husband recently got married. It was a grand occasion. All your friends, close family, and even distant relatives attended. There were so many photographers there that a passerby would have thought a royal family from England was getting married.

After the ceremony, you and your husband moved in together. As is common for newlyweds in their new home, you invite so many guests to come over and visit. One day your good friends from childhood arrive. Due to a scheduling conflict, they couldn't attend your wedding. When they come over, you play the video recording from your wedding. They enjoy the presentation very much, and they lament the fact that they couldn't have attended.

Now imagine that a week later you invite them over to your home again. You decide to show them the same wedding video. Will they like this? Would you want to sit through the entire thing again? Maybe in the odd circumstance you'll both get a kick out of seeing everything again, but once you reach a third or fourth viewing in so short a timespan, you get little enjoyment. There are diminishing returns; everyone will want to watch anything else.

With the marriage of Sita and Rama, the same event can be relived day after day. Goswami Tulsidas gives his blessing that you'll get all auspiciousness, kalyana, by singing of the event with excitement. A very similar verse appears in the Ramacharitamanasa from the same author. In that book, the verse says that one gets auspiciousness from hearing about the wedding of Sita and Rama. Singing creates hearing, and so the two verses have essentially the same meaning.

And why is there kalyana from repeated singing? There is complexity to the event. You don't have only Sita and Rama. You have Janaka, Sita's father. From hearing his name one time, your mind can go into contemplation of his great qualities. You can ponder how he was a detached yogi, expert in mysticism. You can then appreciate how he loved Sita instantly when he found her as a baby one day in the ground. If you get bored with that direction, you can remember how he is considered one of the twelve mahajanas, or great-souls, who are authorities on devotional service to God. Sita appeared as the daughter to such a mahajana, which only further increased his greatness.

Tulsidas mentions Rama's upabita, or investiture of the sacred thread, along with the wedding to Sita. In the Janaki Mangala, we don't get any descriptions of Rama being given a sacred thread by any teacher. The sacred thread comes at the time of initiation, and it marks the second birth, the one into Vedic culture, given by the guru, or spiritual master. We do get descriptions of Rama and His younger brother following the guru Vishvamitra into the forest and protecting him from the attacks of wicked night-rangers. This is the upabita that Tulsidas refers to, as it is the training of Rama and Lakshmana by a celebrated sage of the Vedic tradition. Thus one can contemplate on the exact meaning to initiation and the sacred thread. It is more than just a rite of passage. It is more than just a ceremonial function reserved for the higher classes. Upabita actually means something; it relates to specific training.

Rama does not require such training, but He undergoes it anyway to set the proper example. The tests He passed cannot be imitated by anyone, and neither can His marriage. This earth has never seen such a spectacle. Thankfully there needn't be competition in this area. One can delight in the marriage of Sita and Rama as if it were for their two best friends, for God is the supreme well-wisher. His eternal consort favors those who are dear to Rama, and so by being happy for the beloved couple's happiness, one is guaranteed to get auspiciousness day after day, as the author promises.

Essay - Training Exercise

The upavita is the sacred thread, which is worn around the shoulder. It has special significance, though commonly today one receives it as part of a ceremonial function. Sort of like the bar mitzvah or confirmation, those sons born into high class families go through a ceremony where they receive the upavita. From this verse from the Janaki Mangala, we see that the sacred thread is more than just an ornament. It means something, and who better than God to explain that meaning.

The upavita goes to the twice-born. What does it mean to be born twice? The first birth is obvious; it occurs from the womb of the mother. Everyone has this birth. To be alive means to have taken the first birth. The second birth is actually more important; it signals entry into spiritual understanding. Think of it like being admitted to school, except the education is the highest there is. The instruction deals with the difference between matter and spirit, the true position of the soul, which is the identifying agent within all creatures.

"This knowledge is the king of education, the most secret of all secrets. It is the purest knowledge, and because it gives direct perception of the self by realization, it is the perfection of religion. It is everlasting, and it is joyfully performed." (Lord Krishna, Bhagavad-gita, 9.2)

The second birth comes from the guru, or spiritual master. Shri Ramachandra, the Supreme Personality of Godhead appearing on earth in a beautiful incarnation form many thousands of years ago, was of the royal order. Therefore His "second birth" related to learning the military arts. He was not expected to be a brahmana, which means one who knows Brahman, which is the non-differentiated spiritual energy. I am Brahman and so are you. In fact, so is the cat, the dog, the elephant, and the cow. Anything we consider to be life is Brahman, or spirit, in its true identity.

Goswami Tulsidas says that one who sings with excitement of the upavita of Shri Ramachandra gets all auspiciousness every day. The verse quoted above sums up what has been detailed in the work known as the Janaki Mangala. Interestingly, there is no previous mention of a sacred thread being given to Rama. There is no mention of an official ceremony where Rama, the eldest son of the king of Ayodhya, gets a sacred thread from a guru.

Upavita is a compound Sanskrit word. Upa means "to bring closer" and vita can refer to "trained." Combining the two, we get a definition of "bringing one closer in order to train them." This is the more applicable meaning to the upavita mentioned here by Tulsidas. The great poet does describe how Rama and His younger brother Lakshmana received training in the military arts from the brahmana Vishvamitra.

So the sacred thread is more than just a decoration. It is more than just an indication of entry into instruction. The person getting the sacred thread must do something in order to earn it. As Rama is God, it makes sense that He was asked to do something extraordinary to earn His stripes. God does not require this training. He doesn't need anyone to teach Him anything. Yet in order to give the proper lesson to future generations, He humbly served Vishvamitra and did whatever the sage asked.

And what was asked of Rama? The sages in the forest of Dandaka were being harassed by evil night-rangers. These were ogre-like creatures who had no morals and could change their shapes at will. Using black magic, they could appear in one second and then vanish the next. They didn't fight fairly. Rama and His younger brother Lakshmana were asked to defend against such attackers.

Rama's training was successful, and through Vishvamitra's blessings He eventually went to Janakpur, where He wed Sita. One of her other names is Janaki, and so we get the main subject of the work of Tulsidas. The training required for ordinary souls, who are not God, is not as difficult. We do not need to slay wicked night-rangers all by ourselves. We wouldn't be able to accomplish such a task anyway, as our abilities are paltry in comparison to Rama's.

To earn the vital second birth, one simply needs love for Rama. With love for the Supreme Lord, there is love for the guru, who is the spiritual master representing Rama's interests on earth. If one doesn't yet have love for Rama, if they don't know who He is or are not certain of His divinity, faith in the guru is enough. Following their instructions, inquiring submissively and humbly serving their interests, one can pass the tests necessary to enter the second and more important life.

The guru is most pleased by the disciple who always chants the holy names: Hare Krishna Hare Krishna, Krishna Krishna, Hare Hare, Hare Rama Hare Rama, Rama Rama, Hare Hare. This chanting is identical with singing the glories of the upavita of Rama and His marriage to Sita. It is identical with love for God, which is the pinnacle achievement in life. This chanting pleases the bona fide spiritual master, and it opens the door to eternal spiritual life.

Essay - Doing The Work For Us

"We're supposed to think about God. We're supposed to remember Him at all times. If we're having trouble remembering, then make a plan to remember throughout the day; in essence remembering to remember. They say to chant the holy names: Hare Krishna Hare Krishna, Krishna Krishna, Hare Hare, Hare Rama Hare Rama, Rama Rama, Hare Hare. Repeat this mantra all the time, and all good things will come. But I can't do this. I need more. I can't see how the enjoyment will come that is necessary to continue on."

The saints of the Vedic tradition indeed do make such recommendations. They believe so strongly in them that they'll dedicate their whole lives to repeating the same message. Rather than stay bound to home and family, remaining safe from the scrutiny of the public, they abandon everything to facilitate extended travel. By moving about, they are better able to spread the message of divine love, which they say is awakened through the remembrance mentioned above. Some saints go one step further: they hand us information to help us in our remembrance.

We can take the example of the above quoted verse from the Janaki Mangala. Here Goswami Tulsidas says that singing of the glories of the sacred thread investiture of Shri Rama and His marriage to Sita will bring auspiciousness day after day. The singing should be done with attention, with some sort of interest. Since it will bring auspiciousness daily, obviously the singing should take place repeatedly.

This recommendation doesn't come out of left field. We shouldn't dismiss it outright, thinking it impossible to do. If there is a God, why not remember Him? If He is so great, what is the harm in remembering Him day after day? We claim that the difficulty is that we can't see Him. Sure, His influence is everywhere. Not a blade of grass moves without His sanction. There cannot be life without His glance. In the Vedas it is said that at the beginning of the creation, according to our present timeline anyways, there was only a chunk of matter. Granted, it was a large chunk, but it had the properties of matter nonetheless. It was lacking consciousness. It was just awaiting change. Most importantly, it required the instigation of a spiritual force in order to do anything. That force came from God, who injected a portion of His potency into the material chunk, thereby giving birth to the life that presently surrounds us.

"The total material substance, called Brahman, is the source of birth, and it is that Brahman that I impregnate, making possible the births of all living beings, O son of Bharata." (Lord Krishna, Bhagavad-gita, 14.3)

We don't remember being there at the beginning of the creation, so it's hard to keep that event in our mind. So unless we see a personality who is God then we can't really remember Him so well. But hearing is just as effective in spiritual matters; hence the recommendation for chanting. Chanting is kirtanam and hearing is shravanam. Together, they make the two most potent methods of bhakti-yoga, or devotional service. Yoga is the mission for the living entity. Yoga is complete concentration; it transcends laziness, fatigue, chaos, despair, hopelessness, and all other negative conditions. It is a firm link to the Divine, and it is best maintained through bhakti, or divine love. Indeed, bhakti-yoga is the culminating stage of all other yoga practices.

Tulsidas recommends that we always sing of the glorious event of Rama's marriage to Sita. But there are so many marriages that take place. Why not remember a marriage of a famous king from recent times? Why not watch our own wedding video over and over again? To help us in accepting his recommendation, Tulsidas provides information into the natures of Sita and Rama. Sita is the energy of God. She is the pleasure potency, and she acts only for God's pleasure. Rama is God Himself, non-different from the original Personality of Godhead. Some may call Him Krishna, Vishnu, or by some other name, but the personality addressed is the same in each case.

Rama is God and Sita is His wife. Tulsidas gives information of how their marriage took place. His Janaki Mangala poem is dedicated to that blessed event that occurred many thousands of years ago. The Janaki Mangala also describes the training Rama received from the guru Vishvamitra. Rama is God, so He doesn't need anyone's help. Yet He is so kind that He pretends to need instruction from respected personalities. In this case, Rama and His younger brother Lakshmana took training in the military arts, conducted with the bow and arrow during the time period in question. The spiritual teachers could also instruct disciples in how to run businesses, govern a kingdom, and see the spiritual equality in all beings. Vishvamitra's guidance was important because of his love for Rama. If the spiritual guide has love for God, then he is worth approaching.

We have trouble remembering God. We would rather worry over the future of the economy of the nation. We would rather plan our upcoming week. We would rather spend hours zoning out, forgetting our troubles. But as Tulsidas says, remembering brings auspiciousness. There is no loss on our part, though we think there is. We think we will miss out on fun, but bhakti-yoga is the only actually fun activity. It increases the happiness of the participant, making more room in the heart for the love that overflows. That love first appears through hearing, and to make sure the love continues to grow, the benevolent saints of the Vedic tradition give us plenty to hear.

Essay - Sharing With The World

If you are fortunate enough to come across the king of education, raja-vidya, that is Vedanta and understand it perfectly, knowing full well that everything emanates from the Supreme Personality of Godhead, you should share this wisdom with others. This is to save both them and yourself. Your speech will show how much you know. Not so much facts and figures, but your true understanding - that will be revealed. And the message will be so powerful that others will be enlightened in the process. Goswami Tulsidas, not requiring self-purification due to his constant engagement in devotional service, here gives a benefit to all of humanity, sharing the secret to life with so many, both contemporaries and those yet to take birth.

Let's pretend that you agree to this assignment that I give to you. You are to be liked. That is it. I'll pick a specific sphere of influence, and you do the rest. It doesn't have to be in an entire society; only in a limited area, like your place of work or school. How will you go about accomplishing the task? One option is to give gifts to people. Find out what each person wants and then go out and buy it. This will win you some friends in the interim, but it is an expensive option. What if someone wants a car? What if someone wants to go away on a vacation? How are you going to pay for this? Moreover, why will you want to when all you're getting is their approval? And that approval will only be based on something you give to them; it has nothing to do with who you are as a person.

"The mode of passion is born of unlimited desires and longings, O son of Kunti, and because of this one is bound to material fruitive activities." (Lord Krishna, Bhagavad-gita, 14.7)

Material desire is such that it will never be satisfied. If you're craving pizza today, once you eat it you won't all of a sudden stop craving pizza. In the future, you will want to eat it more; it will take more indulgence to reach the same level of temporary satisfaction. And so by giving gifts to others, they may like you for only a short period of time.

Another option is to do favors for them. Ask each person what they want accomplished and then go out and do it. Again, this is an expensive road to travel, as you will have a difficult time doing so much for so many. They may not appreciate you after a while, also, for they will want something else done. Since you came through before, you are expected to do so again. If for some reason you don't, then you're not liked, more so than if you hadn't done anything for them to begin with.

The easiest way to complete the assignment is to remain silent. Just don't say anything. Smile when you see the other person. Listen to them attentively. Whatever opinion they volunteer, agree with. Don't pass judgment. Be supportive. In this way you will be liked quickly. What can anyone say about you? You have no opinions and you rarely speak. They have nothing to criticize.

In this way your silence buys the confidence of others. But what if you know that they aren't meeting life's true mission? What if you know that their constant intoxication is a sign of defeat against the illusory forces of maya? What if you know that their abilities in so many different areas would really be useful once they were directed towards devotional service, which is an endless occupation?

The benevolent saints take the risk of spreading the glories of the Supreme Lord. They speak out when necessary. They assert the superiority of the devotional path, bhakti-yoga. They know this choice will make them unpopular with many, but since they've realized for themselves that devotion is the best way to go in life, they are undeterred. Here Goswami Tulsidas tells everyone how to find auspiciousness day after day. And this auspiciousness is for everyone, regardless of their present circumstances. Whether they are from India or not, whether they even believe in God or not, in following his formula they are guaranteed to be benefitted.

That auspiciousness comes from regularly singing about the auspicious events of a training period and a wedding. The training, upavita, was for Rama and Lakshmana, two brothers who roamed this earth a long time ago. The wedding was for the same Rama to the daughter of King Janaka, Sita Devi. Tulsidas himself took great delight in singing of these two wonderful incidents. He easily could have kept the information to himself. He could have remained silent in the presence of others, for that would have made him very popular. He could have sung to himself in a small room in a house, and thus not be phased by the constant comings and goings of the living entities, who must die after taking birth.

Tulsidas shared his wisdom with many others. He wrote his own song of the events so that the message would travel more quickly and to more areas. That writing transcends time, as it is available to this day. Thus the message continues to travel. The revelations of a genuine saint withstand the test of time. Guided from within by God Himself, they find the best way to share the message with as many as possible. They give others a hint on how to accomplish the same. "Glorify God. Be happy in His service, and give others the same gift." All of that is accomplished today through the chanting of the holy names: Hare Krishna Hare Krishna, Krishna Krishna, Hare Hare, Hare Rama Hare Rama, Rama Rama, Hare Hare. Works like the Janaki Mangala give us the meaning to these names.

Essay - Not Ready To Say Goodbye

The Janaki Mangala is a short collection of verses that tells a story. Though a story, it is a summary, as the details from that one event alone would fill volumes. The original telling comes from the Ramayana of Valmiki, which was authored in Sanskrit. Since then it has been retold countless times, even by one of the main participants herself, Sita Devi. In the original Ramayana she offers her own summary to the wife of a sage. That sage's wife already knew the story, but she wanted to hear it again. The same sentiment is shared by Tulsidas here, who blesses those who sing and hear of this tale over and over again.

"I have heard, O Sita, that your hand in marriage was won by the renowned Raghava on the occasion of the self-choice ceremony [svayamvara]. O Maithili, I wish to hear that story in detail. Therefore please narrate to me the entire sequence of events as you experienced them." (Anasuya speaking to Sita Devi, Valmiki Ramayana, Ayodhya Kand, 118.24-25)

Perhaps the following has happened to us on more than one occasion. We pick up a book that interests us. We heard about it on television, where the author was interviewed during a promotional tour for the release of the book. We liked them when they were in the public eye, and so since they now have a book out we're interested in reading it.

It ends up being more than just a basic memoirs that give notes on events in chronological order. Instead, it is like a compelling story, a page-turner if you will. It is difficult to put down. We get emotionally invested in the outcome, where we are attached to the loveable characters and disgusted by the loathsome ones.

As we're cruising through the book, something dawns on us.

"Hey, if I finish this book too quickly, what am I going to read later on? There's only so much of this left. I will feel empty afterwards. I will feel alone. I don't know what to do. Maybe I should read more slowly. I will ration my reading; this way I'll get to stay in the story longer."

If we feel this way about an ordinary book with ordinary characters, imagine the attachment that comes from hearing about the Supreme Personality of Godhead. He is the most loveable character. He has beauty, wealth, strength, fame, wisdom and renunciation to the highest degree. Above that, He is the most merciful person. He is an ocean of mercy, and that ocean flows to those who love Him and are dedicated to spreading His glories throughout the universe.

Those wonderful qualities belong to His closest associates as well. So we wouldn't blame someone for wanting to ration their hearing of the story of the wedding of Sita and Rama. Rama is God Himself and Sita is His eternal consort.

The Supreme Lord can most certainly appear in the manifest world whenever He so chooses. Just because we can't see Him now doesn't mean that He doesn't exist. Indeed, even when He appears in an incarnation form like He did with Rama, He remains hidden from the eyes of the foolish and less intelligent.

"I am never manifest to the foolish and unintelligent. For them I am covered by My eternal creative potency [yoga-maya]; and so the deluded world knows Me not, who am unborn and infallible." (Lord Krishna, Bhagavad-gita, 7.25)

The highly fortunate see Him in all His glory. They record His activities and then pass on that information to others. There are people who didn't witness the events firsthand. With the marriage of Sita to Rama, only the people in Janakpur directly saw what happened. The celestials from the sky also watched, but all others were shut out. Then there were the festivities in Ayodhya, Rama's home. The people of Ayodhya warmly welcomed Sita to their home, who arrived there accompanied by Rama and His three younger brothers and their new brides.

From that story you hear of wonderful characters like Janaka. There was no other king like him, and in qualities he could only be matched by Dasharatha from Ayodhya. Thus it was fitting that Janaka's daughter married Dasharatha's son. Then you have the guru Vishvamitra, who kindly led Rama to Janakpur to take part in the contest of the bow. You have the devoted younger brother Lakshmana, who is always there to support Rama. You have the loving mothers in Ayodhya, who achieved the fruit of an existence by having motherly affection for Sita.

The verse above is the last one from the Janaki Mangala. Does this mean that the story is over? Does it mean that one has to return to a life devoid of God's association? To ease the worried mind, Tulsidas says that anyone who sings of these glorious events, Rama's marriage and His training in the forest with Vishvamitra, gets auspiciousness day after day. This means that you can hear the story over and over again and not get bored. It is an exercise worth trying. The boon is made possible through the Supreme Lord Himself, who is an infallible and inexhaustible being. His name alone carries that potency, and so one can also repeatedly chant the maha-mantra and never have to say goodbye to their beloved Lord of their life-breath: Hare Krishna Hare Krishna, Krishna Krishna, Hare Hare, Hare Rama Hare Rama, Rama Rama, Hare Hare.

ABOUT THE AUTHOR

The author, Sonal Pathak, can be contacted via email at info@krishnasmercy.org.